Lecture Notes in Artificial Intelligence 13263

Subseries of Lecture Notes in Computer Science

Series Editors

Randy Goebel
University of Alberta, Edmonton, Canada
Wolfgang Wahlster
DFKI, Berlin, Germany
Zhi-Hua Zhou
Nanjing University, Nanjing, China

Founding Editor

Jörg Siekmann
DFKI and Saarland University, Saarbrücken, Germany

More information about this subseries at https://link.springer.com/bookseries/1244

Martin Michalowski · Syed Sibte Raza Abidi ·
Samina Abidi (Eds.)

Artificial Intelligence in Medicine

20th International Conference
on Artificial Intelligence in Medicine, AIME 2022
Halifax, NS, Canada, June 14–17, 2022
Proceedings

 Springer

Editors
Martin Michalowski (iD)
University of Minnesota
Minneapolis, MN, USA

Syed Sibte Raza Abidi (iD)
Dalhousie University
Halifax, NS, Canada

Samina Abidi (iD)
Dalhousie University
Halifax, NS, Canada

ISSN 0302-9743 ISSN 1611-3349 (electronic)
Lecture Notes in Artificial Intelligence
ISBN 978-3-031-09341-8 ISBN 978-3-031-09342-5 (eBook)
https://doi.org/10.1007/978-3-031-09342-5

LNCS Sublibrary: SL7 – Artificial Intelligence

This Springer imprint is published by the registered company Springer Nature Switzerland AG
The registered company address is: Gewerbestrasse 11, 6330 Cham, Switzerland

Preface

The European Society for Artificial Intelligence in Medicine (AIME) was established in 1986 following a very successful workshop held in Pavia, Italy, the year before. The principal aims of AIME are to foster fundamental and applied research in the application of artificial intelligence (AI) techniques to medical care and medical research, and to provide a forum at biennial conferences for discussing any progress made. Thus, the main activity of the society until recently has been the organization of a series of biennial conferences, held in Marseilles, France (1987), London, UK (1989), Maastricht, The Netherlands (1991), Munich, Germany (1993), Pavia, Italy (1995), Grenoble, France (1997), Aalborg, Denmark (1999), Cascais, Portugal (2001), Protaras, Cyprus (2003), Aberdeen, UK (2005), Amsterdam, The Netherlands (2007), Verona, Italy (2009), Bled, Slovenia (2011), Murcia, Spain (2013), Pavia, Italy (2015), Vienna, Austria (2017), and Poznan, Poland (2019).

AIME made a decision at its board meeting in 2019 to make the AIME conference truly international and host it in North America for the first time in 2020. However, due to the global coronavirus pandemic, the decision was made to forgo an in-person meeting for the 2020 conference (the 18th iteration), which was to be held in Minneapolis, USA, for a virtual one. The continued pandemic in 2021 forced the organizers of the 19th AIME conference, originally planned to be hosted in Porto, Portugal, to go virtual as well. Therefore, the 20th International Conference on Artificial Intelligence in Medicine (AIME 2022) represents the first in-person AIME conference to be held outside of Europe. This volume contains the proceedings of AIME 2022, hosted by Dalhousie University in Halifax, Canada, during June 14–17, 2022.

The AIME 2022 goals were to present and consolidate the international state of the art of AI in biomedical research from the perspectives of theory, methodology, systems, and applications. The conference included two invited keynotes, full, short, and demonstration papers, tutorials, a workshop, and a doctoral consortium. In the conference announcement, authors were invited to submit original contributions regarding the development of theory, methods, systems, and applications for solving problems in the biomedical field, including AI approaches in biomedical informatics, molecular medicine, and health-care organizational aspects.

Authors of papers addressing theory were requested to describe the properties of novel AI models potentially useful for solving biomedical problems. Authors of papers addressing theory and methods were asked to describe the development or the extension of AI methods, to address the assumptions and limitations of the proposed techniques, and to discuss their novelty with respect to the state of the art. Authors of papers addressing systems and applications were asked to describe the development, implementation, or evaluation of new AI-inspired tools and systems in the biomedical field. They were asked to link their work to underlying theory, and either analyze the potential benefits to solve biomedical problems or present empirical evidence of benefits in clinical practice. All authors were asked to highlight the value their work created for the patient, provider, and institution through its clinical relevance.

AIME 2022 received 113 submissions across all types of paper categories. Submissions came from authors in 29 countries, including submissions from Europe, North and South America, Asia, Australia, and Africa. All papers were carefully peer-reviewed by experts from the Program Committee, with the support of additional reviewers, and by members of the Senior Program Committee. Each submission was reviewed in most cases by three reviewers, and all papers by at least two reviewers. The reviewers judged the overall quality of the submitted papers, together with their relevance to the AIME conference, originality, impact, technical correctness, methodology, scholarship, and quality of presentation. In addition, the reviewers provided detailed written comments on each paper and stated their confidence in the subject area. One Senior Program Committee member was assigned to each paper and they wrote a meta-review and provided a recommendation to the scientific chair.

A small committee consisting of the AIME 2022 scientific chair, Dr. Wojtek Michalowski (University of Ottawa), and ourselves as conference co-chairs, Dr. Martin Michalowski (University of Minnesota) and Dr. Syed Sibte Raza Abidi (Dalhousie University), made the final decisions regarding the AIME 2022 scientific program, with input from the application demonstration chair Dr. William Van Woensel (Dalhousie University) for the demonstration papers. This process began with virtual meetings starting in March 2022. As a result, 16 long papers (an acceptance rate of 15%), 11 short papers, 12 posters, and 7 demonstration papers were accepted. Each long paper was presented in a 20-minute oral presentation during the conference. Each short paper was presented in an 8-minute presentation, and the posters and demonstration papers were presented during dedicated sessions on the main conference days. The papers were organized according to their topics in the following main themes: (1) Knowledge-based Systems; (2) Machine Learning; (3) Medical Image Processing; (4) Predictive Modeling; and (5) Natural Language Processing. The 2021 Rising Star Award winner (Dr. Arianna Dagliati) gave an invited talk describing her research in temporal data mining. Prizes were awarded for best student paper, best bioinformatics paper, and a new John Fox memorial award for the best paper in the fields of Computer Interpretable Guidelines, Soundness and Safety in Critical Systems, or Explainability.

AIME 2022 had the privilege of hosting two invited keynote speakers: Dr. David L. Buckeridge, Professor in the School of Population and Global Health at McGill University, giving the keynote entitled "Translating AI into Practice in Healthcare – Opportunities, Challenges, and Possible Solutions," and Dr. Bo Wang, Assistant Professor in the Department of Laboratory Medicine and Pathobiology and Department of Computer Science at the University of Toronto and CIFAR AI Chair at the Vector Institute, describing "Opportunities and challenges of artificial intelligence for organ transplantation."

The doctoral consortium received nine PhD proposals that were peer reviewed. AIME 2022 provided an opportunity for six of these PhD students to present their research goals, proposed methods, and preliminary results. A scientific panel consisting of experienced researchers in the field provided constructive feedback to the students in an informal atmosphere. The doctoral consortium was chaired by Arianna Dagliati (University of Pavia).

Two workshops were initially accepted for AIME 2022, with acceptance decisions made by the conference co-chairs and the workshop chair Dr. Jose M. Juarez (University of Murcia). However, due to unforeseen circumstances only one workshop took place during AIME 2022. This workshop focused on the challenges and problems of applying AI in nursing and provided a platform for discussions about the recent advances, cutting edge AI methods, and charting a path forward for nursing AI. The workshop was chaired by nursing faculty from universities in Canada, USA, and Europe, with submissions presented by experts in AI and nursing from around the globe. The work from this workshop will be extended and presented in a special journal issue devoted to the topic.

In addition to the workshop, four interactive half-day tutorials were presented prior to the AIME 2022 main conference. The accepted tutorials were selected by the tutorial chair Dr. Enea Parimbelli (University of Pavia) along with the conference co-chairs, and they included (1) Using Machine Learning on mHealth-based Data Sources, (2) End-user Development of Mobile AI-based Clinical Apps using Punya, (3) Machine learning for complex medical temporal sequences, and (4) Data Science for Starters: How to Train and be Trained.

We would like to thank everyone who contributed to AIME 2022. First of all, we would like to thank the authors of the papers submitted and the members of the Program Committee together with the additional reviewers. Thank you to the Senior Program Committee for writing meta-reviews and to members of the Senior Advisory Committee for providing guidance during conference organization. Thanks are also due to the invited speakers, as well as to the organizers of the tutorials, the workshop, and the doctoral consortium panel. Many thanks go to the local Organizing Committee who helped plan this conference and all of the events surrounding it. The free EasyChair conference system (http://www.easychair.org/) was an important tool supporting us in the management of submissions, reviews, selection of accepted papers, and preparation of the overall material for the final proceedings. We would like to thank Springer and the Artificial Intelligence Journal (AIJ) for sponsoring the conference. Finally, we thank the Springer team for helping us in the final preparation of this LNAI book.

May 2022   Martin Michalowski
                                                                     Syed Sibte Raza Abidi

Organization

General Chairs

Martin Michalowski   University of Minnesota, USA
Syed Sibte Raza Abidi   Dalhousie University, Canada

Program Committee Chairs

Wojtek Michalowski   University of Ottawa, Canada
   (Scientific Program)
Arianna Dagliati   University of Pavia, Italy
   (Doctoral Consortium)
Enea Parimbelli   University of Pavia, Italy
   (Tutorial Program)
William Van Woensel   Dalhousie University, Canada
   (Demonstration)
Jose M. Juarez (Workshop)   University of Murcia, Spain

Local Organizing Committee

Syed Sibte Raza Abidi   Faculty of Computer Science, Dalhousie University,
   (Local Organization   Canada
   Chair)
Samina Abidi (Local   Faculty of Medicine, Dalhousie University, Canada
   Organization Chair)
Karthik Tennankore   Faculty of Medicine, Dalhousie University, Canada
Jason Quinn   Faculty of Medicine, Dalhousie University, Canada
Osama Loubani   Faculty of Medicine, Dalhousie University, Canada
Sean Christie   Faculty of Medicine, Dalhousie University, Canada
Calvino Cheng   Faculty of Medicine, Dalhousie University, Canada
Jaber Rad   Faculty of Computer Science, Dalhousie University,
     Canada
Ali Daowd   Faculty of Computer Science, Dalhousie University,
     Canada
Nelofar Kureshi   Faculty of Computer Science, Dalhousie University,
     Canada
Anne Publicover   Faculty of Computer Science, Dalhousie University,
     Canada
Margie Publicover   Faculty of Computer Science, Dalhousie University,
     Canada

Senior Program Committee

Riccardo Bellazzi	Università di Pavia, Italy
Carlo Combi	Università degli Studi di Verona, Italy
Michel Dojat	Inserm, France
Adela Grando	Arizona State University, USA
Milos Hauskrecht	University of Pittsburgh, USA
Pedro Henriques Abreu	University of Coimbra, Portugal
John Holmes	University of Pennsylvania, USA
Jose M. Juarez	University of Murcia, Spain
Elpida Keravnou-Papailiou	University of Cyprus, Cyprus
Nada Lavrač	Jozef Stefan Institute, Slovenia
Xiaohui Liu	Brunel University London, UK
Peter Lucas	University of Twente, The Netherlands
Mar Marcos	Universitat Jaume I, Spain
Stefania Montani	University of Piemonte Orientale, Italy
Robert Moskovitch	Ben-Gurion University, Israel
Barbara Oliboni	University of Verona, Italy
Enea Parimbelli	University of Pavia, Italy
Pedro Pereira Rodrigues	University of Porto, Portugal
Silvana Quaglini	University of Pavia, Italy
David Riaño	Universitat Rovira i Virgili, Spain
Lucia Sacchi	University of Pavia, Italy
Stefan Schulz	Medical University of Graz, Austria
Yuval Shahar	Ben-Gurion University, Israel
Gregor Stiglic	University of Maribor, Slovenia
Stephen Swift	Brunel University London, UK
Allan Tucker	Brunel University London, UK
Blaz Zupan	University of Ljubljana, Slovenia

Program Committee

Samina Abidi	Dalhousie Univeristy, Canada
Rute Almeida	Universidade do Porto, Portugal
Amparo Alonso-Betanzos	University of A Coruña, Spain
Josè Luis Ambite	University of Southern California, USA
Nariman Ammar	University of Tennessee Health Science Center, USA
Josè P. Amorim	FCTUC, Portugal
Pavel Andreev	University of Ottawa, Canada
Ognjen Arandjelovic	University of St Andrews, UK
Mahir Arzoky	Brunel University London, UK
Naveen Ashish	InferLink Corporation, USA
Luís Azevedo	University of Porto, Portugal
Pedro Barahona	Universidade NOVA de Lisboa, Portugal
Simone Bianco	IBM, USA

Miriam Santos   University of Coimbra, Portugal
Abeed Sarker   Emory University, USA
Isabel Sassoon   Brunel University London, UK
Michael Ignaz Schumacher   University of Applied Sciences Western Switzerland
                              (HES-SO), Switzerland
Floriano Scioscia   Polytechnic University of Bari, Italy
Arash Shaban-Nejad   University of Tennessee Health Science Center, USA
Erez Shalom   Ben-Gurion University, Israel
Yuan Shang   University of Arizona, USA
Karthik Srinivasan   University of Kansas, USA
Darmoni Stefan   University of Rouen, France
Manuel Striani   University of Piemonte Orientale, Italy
César Teixeira   University of Coimbra, Portugal
Annette Ten Teije   Vrije Universiteit Amsterdam, The Netherlands
Paolo Terenziani   Università del Piemonte Orientale, Italy
Samson Tu   Stanford University, USA
Frank Van Harmelen   Vrije Universiteit Amsterdam, The Netherlands
Alfredo Vellido   Universitat Politècnica de Catalunya, Spain
Francesca Vitali   University of Arizona, USA
Dimitrios Vogiatzis   The American College of Greece and NCSR
                              "Demokritos", Greece
Dongwen Wang   Arizona State University, USA
Jens Weber   University of Victoria, Canada
Szymon Wilk   Poznan University of Technology, Poland
Antje Wulff   TU Braunschweig and Hannover Medical School,
                              Germany
Leila Yousefi   Brunel University London, UK
Pierre Zweigenbaum   Université Paris-Saclay, France

Application Demonstration Reviewers

Szymon Wilk   Poznan University of Technology, Poland
Annette ten Teije   Vrije Universiteit Amsterdam, The Netherlands
Samina Abidi   Dalhousie Univeristy, Canada
Alessio Bottrighi   Università del Piemonte Orientale, Italy
Floriano Scioscia   Polytechnic University of Bari, Italy
Giuseppe Loseto   Polytechnic University of Bari, Italy
Evan Patton   Massachusetts Institute of Technology, USA
Shruthi Chari   Rensselaer Polytechnic Institute, USA
Sabbir Rashid   Rensselaer Polytechnic Institute, USA

Translating AI into Practice in Healthcare – Opportunities, Challenges, and Solutions (Invited Talk)

David L. Buckeridge[1,2]

[1] McGill University, Montreal, Canada
[2] McGill University Health Centre, Montreal, Canada
david.buckeridge@mcgill.ca
http://mchi.mcgill.ca

Abstract. The potential for Artificial Intelligence (AI) in healthcare has been evident for decades and the opportunity has grown with increasing volumes of data and advances in machine learning. Despite this potential, the translation of AI-based innovations into healthcare practice has been limited by challenges along the development and implementation pipeline. For example, barriers to data access, technology debt in clinical practice, and limited AI expertise in healthcare systems pose challenges to translation. Potential solutions exist for many challenges and health systems should align solutions to create environments that support the translation of effective AI-based innovations to healthcare settings.

Keywords: Artificial intelligence · Healthcare · Implementation

1 Opportunities

Researchers and clinicians have long recognized the potential for artificial intelligence (AI) to support decision-making in healthcare [1]. Decades of research have advanced our understanding of the ability of AI to support decisions by clinicians (e.g., diagnosis, therapy), healthcare administrators (e.g., scheduling, resource demand prediction), and patients (e.g., chronic disease management). Given the increasing volumes of data and advances in machine learning, technology leaders have argued that AI will transform the practice of medicine [2].

2 Challenges

Despite the potential, empirical assessments have found little evidence of AI-enabled applications impacting healthcare [3]. This gap, between the potential of AI and the reality in clinical care, is the result of challenges that innovators face in developing, evaluating, and deploying AI-based healthcare products and services. At the development stage, assembling and coordinating the necessary clinical and AI expertise can be challenging. Another challenge at this stage is access to data from multiple settings sufficient for developing robust models capable of generating unbiased output from real data. In terms of evaluation, quantifying the effectiveness and cost-effectiveness of AI has proved to be challenging, with generally few, poor-quality evaluations available [4]. Finally, deployment and scaling of AI is often challenged by the technology debt in clinical practice settings and the limited expertise and resources available for managing and maintaining AI within healthcare systems.

3 Solutions

Fortunately, there is considerable activity to overcome the challenges encountered in translating AI into clinical practice. Many academic health centers, often with private-sector partners, have established centers for clinical innovation. These centers bring together expertise in healthcare, AI, and management with the goal of designing high-impact products and services that have the potential to scale. Solutions to data access are also being developed, including data governance frameworks that span clinical practice and research, federated approaches to model building, and advances in synthetic data generation. Evaluation remains challenging, but adoption of guidelines for evaluation studies [5] and networks for pragmatic trials and real-world evidence offer promise. Deployment and scaling of AI will be supported by broader digital transformation to modernize healthcare settings with a focus on interoperability [6]. Finally, training and establishment of data science units within healthcare systems [7], ideally jointly across operations and research can also support deployment and management of AI in healthcare.

References

1. Musen, M.A., Middleton, B., Greenes, R.A.: Biomedical informatics. Comput. Appl. Heal. Care Biomed. 795–840 (2021)
2. Bajwa, J., Munir, U., Nori, A., Williams, B.: Artificial intelligence in healthcare: transforming the practice of medicine. Futur. Heal. J. **8**, e188–e194 (2021)
3. Yin, J., Ngiam, K.Y., Teo, H.H.: Role of artificial intelligence applications in real-life clinical practice. Syst. Rev. J. Med. Int. Res. **23**, e25759 (2021)
4. Voets, M.M., Veltman, J., Slump, C.H., Siesling, S., Koffijberg, H.: Systematic review of health economic evaluations focused on artificial intelligence in healthcare: the tortoise and the cheetah. Value Health **25**, 340–349 (2022)
5. Luo, W., et al.: Guidelines for developing and reporting machine learning predictive models in biomedical research: a multidisciplinary view. J. Med. Int. Res.**18**, e323 (2016)
6. Ricciardi, W., et al.: How to govern the digital transformation of health services. Eur. J. Public Heal. **29**, 7–12 (2019)
7. Desai, M., et al.: Establishing a data science unit in an academic medical center: an illustrative model. Acad. Med. **97**, 69–75 (2022)

Contents

Medical Image Processing

Predictive Modeling

Tutorials

Knowledge-Based Systems

Explainable Decision Support Using Task Network Models in Notation3: Computerizing Lipid Management Clinical Guidelines as Interactive Task Networks

William Van Woensel[1]([⊠]) [iD], Samina Abidi[1] [iD], Karthik Tennankore[2,3] [iD], George Worthen[2] [iD], and Syed Sibte Raza Abidi[1] [iD]

[1] Dalhousie University, Halifax, NS B3H 4R2, Canada
`william.van.woensel@dal.ca`
[2] Dalhousie University, Nova Scotia Health, Halifax, NS, Canada
[3] Kidney Research Institute Nova Scotia (KRINS), Halifax, NS, Canada

Abstract. Knowledge-driven Clinical Decision Support (CDS) involves the computerization of paper-based clinical guidelines to issue evidence-based recommendations at points-of-care. The computerization of such guidelines in terms of a Task Network Model (TNM) conveniently models them as intuitive workflow models, which can be executed against patient health profiles. We present the GLEAN model that encodes an extensible Finite State Machine (FSM) executional semantics for modular TNM. Extensibility is provided in terms of a high-level formalism for defining execution semantics of custom TNM constructs. GLEAN is implemented using the Notation3 Semantic Web language, which provides powerful features for decisional criteria and queries, and offers integration with the HL7 FHIR standard. We explain CIG workflows as visual, intuitive workflow diagrams that are guided by a concrete patient profile at runtime. As a use case, we computerized guidelines on lipid management for Chronic Kidney Disease (CKD), a challenging problem for many Primary Care Providers (PCPs). To educate PCP on lipid management for CKD, we leverage GLEAN's easy modularization of CIG and CIG explanations as visual runtime workflows.

Keywords: Clinical Decision Support · Lipid Management · Computer Interpretable Guidelines · Semantic Web · Notation3

1 Introduction

A Clinical Practice Guideline (CPG) aims to standardize and improve care by recommending evidence-based diagnosis, prognosis, and treatment options for a particular illness; CPGs are manually compiled by committees of experts, based on evidence synthesized mostly from (large-scale) clinical trials [1]. Knowledge-driven Clinical Decision Support (CDS) involves the computerization of paper-based CPGs into Computer-Interpretable Guidelines (CIG). In doing so, CDS can issue recommendations for a given patient profile in line with the latest clinical evidence.

M. Michalowski et al. (Eds.): AIME 2022, LNAI 13263, pp. 3–13, 2022.
https://doi.org/10.1007/978-3-031-09342-5_1

Task Network Models (TNM) are a type of CIG representation model focusing on workflow-oriented guidelines, i.e., with decisional criteria determining which sequences of diagnosis and treatment tasks to be performed, based on the patient's profile. By computerizing such guidelines using TNM, software can *execute* the guideline workflow given a runtime patient profile [2]. A variety of task-network CIG models have been developed over the years, including Asbru [3], PROforma [4], GLIF3 [5], and the CPG Ontology [6]. The execution semantics, or computational model, of TNM, are mostly described in terms of a Finite State Machine (FSM): a clinical task is assigned one of a finite number of states (e.g., inactive, active, completed), with a task moving between states via *transitions* that depend on decisional criteria, passage of time, the state of related tasks, etc. A CIG FSM can be constructed based on the states and transitions of its constituent tasks. However, CIG literature rather informally describes the FSM, i.e., transitions that move clinical tasks from one state to another. Moreover, while the underlying FSMs tend to be similar, most TNM languages define their own expression language to represent decisional criteria and query TNM. These factors make it difficult for other parties to reproduce and extend the work.

As a resource for building Explainable Clinical Decision Support, we present our work on the minimal, executable GuideLine Execution and Abstraction in N3 (GLEAN) model, based on the CIG literature on the TNM paradigm. In contrast to the state of the art, we present execution semantics in terms of an FSM with explicitly defined states and transition rules. Moreover, we provide a high-level formalism to define new state transition rules, which allows others to extend GLEAN with semantics for new or customized TNM constructs. The GLEAN ontology can be found online [7]. The FSM is implemented using the Notation3 (N3) Semantic Web (SW) language [8], leveraging its support for Scoped Negation As Failure (SNAF), powerful built-ins, and quoted graphs. Further, N3 is a superset of RDF, the core SW language, meaning that one can (a) use expressive SW formalisms, such SPARQL or N3 itself, to represent decisional criteria and querying TNM; and (b) integrate with Electronic Health Records (EHR) through the HL7 FHIR [9] standard, with its RDF notation. In general, this project highlights the usefulness of N3 for health informatics [10–13]. A GLEAN CIG can be explained as a visual, interactive workflow guided by a patient profile at runtime, and can be executed on any standards-compliant N3 reasoner (eye [14] and jen3 [15]).

As a use case, we computerize lipid management guidelines [16] for Chronic Kidney Disease (CKD), which is known to be a challenging problem for Primary Care Providers (PCPs). To guide and educate PCPs towards evidence-informed lipid management, we utilized GLEAN to computerize the guideline workflows as TNM CIG, leveraging the resulting workflow visualization and modularization of complex guidelines.

2   GLEAN Ontology

Figure 1 shows the core classes and relations in the GLEAN ontology that encode a core set of TNM constructs based on the CIG literature [3–5]. The full ontology can be found online [7]. We informally summarize these constructs below:

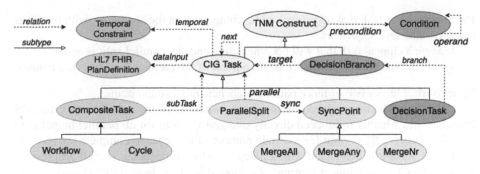

Fig. 1. Core classes in the GLEAN ontology.

TNM Construct: Any type of TNM construct, including *Tasks* and *DecisionBranches*. *precondition*: any construct can have a *Condition* as pre-condition; the workflow will not proceed until the precondition is met.

Condition: Conditions can be conjunctive or disjunctive and involve comparisons or logical operations (any N3 built-in [8]). See online documentation [7] for details.

Task: Any clinical task pertaining to diagnosis, prognosis, treatment, or other purpose.
   next: the next task is only active once the prior task is completed (i.e., a sequential relation; we elaborate on task states, such as *active* and *completed*, below).
   temporal: a range of temporal constraints can be associated with TNM constructs; we formally define these constraints in our prior work [17].
   dataInput: clinical tasks can be associated with a FHIR *PlanDefinition* resource, which specifies the activity to acquire a data element; this includes taxonomical concepts identifying the element, and constraints that must be satisfied by the data. This allows generating a UI to validate and submit an annotated EHR record [13].

DecisionTask: A clinical task involving a decision to be made. This introduces a branching point in the workflow, with branches being alternative task sequences.
   branch: a branch originating from this decision task. One or several can be followed at runtime, depending on their associated condition.

DecisionBranch: A decisional branch that will be followed at runtime if its decisional criteria (in terms of the associated condition) are met.
   target: this task becomes active if the branch's precondition is met. (If the task is part of a sequential relation, the branch will actually involve a task sequence.)

CompositeTask: A task that consists of a set of sub-tasks, which allows modularizing a comprehensive guideline to reduce complexity (also called a subguideline [5]). The CIG *Workflow* itself is a type of *CompositeTask*, as are *Cycles* (not elaborated here).
   subTask: a task that is part of this composite task. The status of the composite task is propagated to its subtasks (e.g., *active*), and vice-versa (e.g., *completed*).

ParallelSplit: A task that introduces a branching point in the workflow, with branches being parallel task sequences.

branch: a clinical task that will become active once its parallel split is active.

syncPoint: indicates the synchronization point of the parallel branches (see below).

SyncPoint: Merges two or more parallel branches into a single point.

Subclasses are distinguished by their *wait condition* re the completion of parallel branches: i.e., whether to proceed directly (*mergeAny*), wait for all parallel branches to complete (*mergeAll*), or wait for a certain number of branches to complete (*mergeNr*).

Each CIG task is associated with a lifecycle, which reflects the overall progression through the CIG workflow at runtime. We show this lifecycle as an FSM below (state transitions are unlabeled to avoid cluttering the figure):

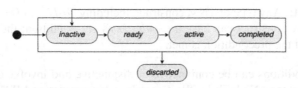

Fig. 2. CIG task lifecycle as an FSM.

Informally, a CIG task travels from *inactive* to *ready* when it is next in line for execution; moves from *ready* to *active* once its pre-condition is met; and finally moves to the *completed* state upon completion. When a task is part of a non-followed decisional branch, it is moved to the *discarded* state. More concretely, transitions between states are governed by the utilized TNM constructs and user input: e.g., given a sequential relation between t_1 and t_2, task t_2 will move to the *ready* state once t_1 is *completed*; or, a user can explicitly indicate whether a task is *completed* or *discarded*. GLEAN formalizes state transitions for each TNM construct: together with Fig. 2, this constitutes a complete picture of an FSM (we provide all transition rules online [7]).

We define a high-level formalism for writing state transition rules in N3. In a nutshell, N3 encodes information in terms of subject-predicate-object (s/p/o) statements that together form a graph; curly braces indicate a quoted graph, which can be used as an s/p/o; a question mark (?) indicates a variable. For more details on the N3 syntax (including a Backus-Naur Form) and semantics, we refer to the W3C Community Group report [8]. We illustrate our high-level state transition formalism below (placeholders between angular brackets, omitting namespaces):

```
{
    { <condition statements> } rdf:type state:Guard .
    ?construct state:in <prior-state>
} state:transit { ?construct state:in <new-state> } .
```

Code 1. High-level formalism for state transitions.

This is a single statement, with *state:transit* as predicate and quoted graphs as subject and object: the subject stipulates the condition for the state-transition to occur; the object indicates the new task state. The state-transition condition is met if (a) all conditions in the quoted graph with type *state:Guard* (guard condition), and (b) the TNM construct (*?construct* variable) is currently in the *<prior-state>*. Then, the TNM construct will be moved to *<new-state>*. Below, we show a transition rule for sequential relations:

```
{ { ?e1 :next ?e2 . ?e1 state:in :Completed } rdf:type state:Guard .
  ?e2 state:in :Inactive
} state:transit { ?e2 state:in :Ready } ;
  state:reason :readyNextOfCompletedEntity . # reason for the transition
```

Code 2. State transition rule for sequential relations.

The guard condition (*state:Guard*) stipulates that $?e_2$ is part of a sequential relation (*next*), where the prior construct *?e1* is in the *completed* state. In that case, and if $?e_2$ is in the *inactive* state, it will be moved to the *ready* state. Below, we show a more complex transition rule for subtasks of compound tasks:

```
{ { ?composite a :CompositeTask ; state:in :Active ; :subTask ?sub .
    <> log:notIncludes { ?prev :next ?sub }
  } a state:Guard .
  ?sub state:in :Inactive
} state:transit { ?sub state:in :Ready } ;
  state:reason :readySubTasksOfActiveCompositeTask .
```

Code 3. State transition rule for sub-tasks of compound tasks.

The guard condition (*state:Guard*) references a *CompositeTask* (*?composite*) in the *active* state, which has a subtask (*?sub*) that does not rely on a prior task, i.e., the dataset does not include (*log:notIncludes*) a sequential relation targeting *?sub* (this is an example of Scoped Negation as Failure (SNAF) in N3). If the *subTask* does rely on a prior task, the sequential relation would govern the state transition (see Code 2). If the guard condition is met, and *?sub* is *inactive*, it will be moved to the *ready* state.

To implement this state-transition formalism, we translate the transition rules to Linear Logic implications [18]. Indeed, classic or intuitionistic logic is not fully suitable for our purpose: after deriving the conclusion from *inactive => active*, the premise should no longer hold, as a task can only be in one state at a time. Linear logic solves this problem by consuming the premise after deriving the conclusion; stable truths can be indicated where such a reaction should not exist [11]. A custom N3 rule performs introspection on state transition rules and generates corresponding Linear Logic implications [7], which are supported by both the eye [14] and jen3 [15] N3 reasoners.

3 Computerizing and Executing Lipid Management CPG

Effective management of abnormal lipids (or dyslipidemia) by PCP is challenging, especially with regards to the prescription of lipid-lowering drugs (most commonly statins) and in cases of multi-morbidity (e.g., CKD and diabetes). Our intent is to (a) computerize the KDIGO guidelines for lipid management in CKD [16], and (b) incorporate the resulting CIG within a point-of-care CDS system for PCP use. Using only the core TNM constructs from the GLEAN ontology (Fig. 1), we manually modeled the complex CPG in terms of modular sub-guidelines—including evaluate lipid profile, follow-up lipid profile, and dyslipidemia treatment. The resultant visual workflow (see below) was validated by a team of 6 domain experts, including 3 nephrologists and 3 pharmacists, with 2 supervising physicians compiling and integrating the feedback. To execute the guideline, we pass the modular CIG to a standards-compliant N3 reasoner (e.g., eye [14], jen3 [15]) loaded with the GLEAN ontology. After passing patient data to the reasoner at runtime, we capture the corresponding state transitions.

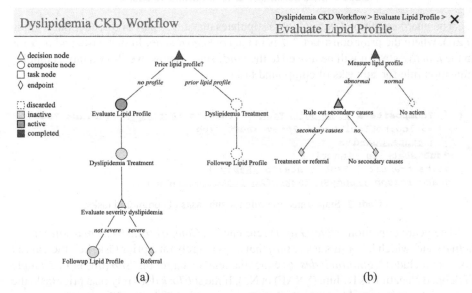

(a)   (b)

Fig. 3. (A) Main lipid management guideline; (B) Evaluate Lipid Profile.

We visualize the execution of the GLEAN CIG as an interactive workflow diagram: at runtime, PCP can traverse the workflow by entering patient health data; outcomes of the decision logic will be directly reflected in the workflow. This visualization is useful as an educational tool, e.g., for PCP to learn about effective lipid management; future work involves a UI that facilitates quick data entry with short narrative explanations. Figure 3 shows parts of the lipid management CPG at increasing granularity (see online [7] for the full CIG). In the main guideline (A), *"Prior lipid profile"* visualizes a *DecisionTask* with two *DecisionBranches* (Fig. 1), targeting the *Evaluate Lipid Profile* and *Dyslipidemia Treatment* sub-guidelines (*Workflow* instances), respectively. Depending on their *Condition*, one of the branches will be followed: if the patient's lipid profile was previously assessed (*prior lipid profile*), the workflow proceeds directly to *Dyslipidemia Treatment*; otherwise (*no profile*), *Evaluate Lipid Profile* will be activated. This decision logic is encoded in N3 using HL7 FHIR (see below). This visualization of the CIG execution illustrates the type (e.g., decision; Fig. 1) and current state (e.g., inactive, active) of tasks. Double-clicking a sub-guideline (circle) will open a new window (Fig. 3B);

clicking a task that requires health data input opens a form (Fig. 4B), generated from its FHIR *PlanDefinition* (this is described elsewhere [13]). Alternatively, patient health data can be directly retrieved from a connected EHR.

Regarding the lipid evaluation sub-guideline (Fig. 3B), a sequence of *DecisionTasks* and *DecisionBranches* check whether, after measuring the lipid profile, an abnormal lipid profile is found; if so, secondary causes should be ruled out.

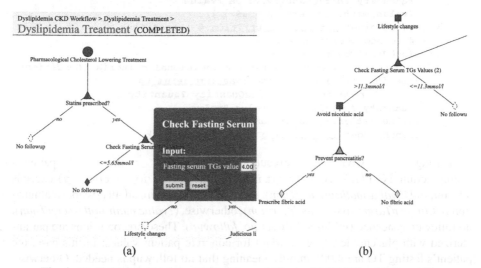

Fig. 4. Dyslipidemia Treatment: (A) TG <= 5.65 mmol/l (B) TG > 11.3 mmol/l.

After the lipid evaluation is completed (see above), the *Dyslipidemia Treatment* sub-guideline will be activated (Fig. 4). We consider the following case: a PCP evaluates a 55-year-old female patient with diabetes and an estimated glomerular filtration rate of 35 ml/min/1.73 m^2. As part of cholesterol lowering treatment (details not shown), she was initiated on a statin. Subsequently, the patient's fasting serum triglycerides (TG) are measured (*Check Fasting Serum TG Values*; name obscured). We show the (simplified) encoding of this *DecisionTask* and its branches below (N3 syntax):

```
:fasting_serum_tgs_values a wf:DecisionTask ;
  rdfs:label "Check Fasting Serum TGs Values" ;
  cig:dataInput :fasting_serum_tgs_report ; #HL7 FHIR PlanDefinition
  wf:decisionBranch [ # first DecisionBranch
    wf:blockUntilCondition true ;
    wf:precondition [ cond:premise { # decisional criteria (Condition)
        ?obs fhir:Observation.code :fasting_serum_tg ;
            fhir:Observation.valueQuantity ?quantity .
        ?quantity fhir:Quantity.value ?value .
        ?value math:greaterThan 5.65 } ] ;
    wf:branchTarget :assess_malnutrition # target task
  ] , [ # second DecisionBranch
    wf:blockUntilCondition true ;
    wf:precondition [ cond:premise { # decisional criteria (Condition)
        ?obs fhir:Observation.code :fasting_serum_tg ;
            fhir:Observation.valueQuantity ?quantity .
        ?quantity fhir:Quantity.value ?value .
        ?value math:notGreaterThan 5.65 } ] ;
    wf:branchTarget :no_followup ] . # target task
```

During CIG execution, if the patient's fasting serum TG (*fhir:Observation.code:fasting_serum_tg*) exceeds 5.65 mmol/l (*?value math:greaterThan*), the PCP should inquire about possible malnutrition (*wf:branchTarget:assess_malnutrition*); otherwise, (*?value math:notGreaterThan*), no followup is needed (*wf:branchTarget:no_followup*). These preconditions are parameterized with placeholders (e.g., *?value*) for concrete patient values; in this case, the patient's fasting TG are 4.00 mmol/L, meaning that no followup is needed. Otherwise, as shown in Fig. 4B, lifestyle changes would be indicated that depend on occurrence of malnutrition. In the rare case that fasting TG lies above 11.3 mmol/l, the PCP is advised to avoid nicotinic acid, and talk to the patient about alternatively prescribing fibric acid to prevent pancreatitis due to severe hypertriglyceridemia, or to remain on a statin to reduce cardiovascular risk.

4 Related Work

CIG representation models can be categorized into Document Models, Decision Trees and Probabilistic Models, and Task Network Models (TNM) [2]. This paper focuses on TNM as they encode a workflow that can be executed against a patient profile.

To the best of our knowledge, PROforma [4] presents the most complete definition of execution semantics for TNM. Sutton et al. define operational semantics for PROforma in terms of an abstract machine, whose state is described by 4 variables, including *properties* and *changes*. Task states include dormant, in-progress, discarded, and completed; which are comparable to our inactive, active, discarded and completed states. A user can apply operations to change task states (e.g., *confirmTask*, *commitCandidate*). The *runEngine* operation propagates state transitions to other tasks: if a task's associated initialize, start, discard, or completion conditions are met, as per the current *properties* table, the task is moved to corresponding new state, as captured in *changes* table. After all applicable transitions are performed, the transitions captured in the *changes* table are applied to the *properties* table. At that point, the *runEngine* operation is re-executed until no more changes are made, thus following a fixpoint-style algorithm. Compared to us, these task conditions encapsulate state transition rules but they are not elaborated. In our case, a reasoner executes a set of formal state transition rules, and can internally use e.g., a fixpoint-style or logical programming algorithm.

GLIF3 [5] encodes a guideline at 3 levels of increasing detail: a high-level conceptual flowchart; a computable, logical specification, and an implementable specification. A custom expression language (GELLO) is utilized to query patient data and decisional criteria. To facilitate integration with EHR, the GLIF3 ontology includes a Clinical Information Model (CIM; based on HL7 RIM). One can specify task and decisional details in terms of sub-guidelines to reduce complexity. The object-oriented nature of the GLIF3 model aims to support extensibility; similarly, constructs from the GLEAN ontology can be subclassed, and new state transition rules written, to introduce new constructs. In contrast to us, GLIF3 explicitly supports multiple entry points into a workflow. A GLIF3 frame-based ontology and validation constraints are available.

Alternatively, guidelines can be viewed in terms of *patient states* as opposed to *task states*. GLIF3 defines a *Patient_State_Step* outfitted with a label that characterizes the current patient state [5]. Hong et al. [11] introduce weighted transition logic, based on linear logic, to explicitly model state changes from clinical actions: e.g., when taking Paracetamol, a patient's initial state (e.g., body temperature 40 °C) is consumed and the reduced temperature (e.g., 37 °C) is inferred [18], with an associated duration, cost, comfort and belief. The resultant state transition graph enables finding pathways towards a desired target state. Currently, our interest lies on driving workflow execution given health input data and clinician choices; we revisit this in future work.

5 Conclusion

We presented the GLEAN model that encodes a formal Finite State Machine (FSM) execution semantics for clinical guidelines modeled as Task Network Models (TNM). A pivotal aspect of GLEAN is its extensibility: we supply a high-level formalism for adapting our core minimal FSM with state transitions for new TNM constructs. E.g., future work involves transition rules for more nuanced decision models such as argument [19] and utility theory [5]—if needed, new N3 built-ins can be developed. Compared with the works discussed in Sect. 4, our work offers an explicit and extensible FSM execution semantics. Using GLEAN, we were able to fully computerize the lipid management guidelines for CKD, offering modularization and intuitive runtime visualization. The resultant visual workflow was validated by a team of clinicians.

Future work involves mechanisms to validate and verify GLEAN FSMs: validation in terms of ontology or shape constraints [20] (e.g., decision tasks requiring at least 2 branches), and verification in terms of decidability of the FSM. We aim to integrate our prior work on temporal constraints [17], using custom N3 built-ins (e.g., *withinPeriodOf*). We plan to view TNM in terms of patient-states as well; this allows comparing patient outcomes with guideline intentions [3]. To facilitate health data input and provide shorter narrative explanations, we will develop a wizard-style UI as a complement to the current workflow visualization. Currently, CIG are manually computerized using the GLEAN ontology, which is in line with the state of the art; studying their automated extraction using NLP methods is future work. We aim to perform a formal evaluation of our CDS prototype with PCPs to study its usability, usefulness, and educational value; and will test its integration within the PCP clinical workflow.

References

1. Brush, J.E., Radford, M.J., Krumholz, H.M.: Integrating clinical practice guidelines into the routine of everyday practice. Crit. Pathways Cardiol. J. Evid.-Based Med. **4**, 161–167 (2005)
2. Peleg, M.: Computer-interpretable clinical guidelines: a methodological review. J. Biomed. Inform. **46**, 744–763 (2013)
3. Shahar, Y., Miksch, S., Johnson, P.: The Asgaard project: a task-specific framework for the application and critiquing of time-oriented clinical guidelines. Artif. Intell. Med. **14**, 29–51 (1998)
4. Sutton, D.R., Fox, J.: The syntax and semantics of the PROforma guideline modeling language. J. Am. Med. Inform. Assoc. **10**, 433–443 (2003). https://doi.org/10.1197/jamia. M1264
5. Boxwala, A.A., Peleg, M., Tu, S., Ogunyemi, O., Zeng, Q., Wang, D.: GLIF3: a representation format for sharable computer-interpretable clinical practice guidelines. J Biomed Inf. **37**, 147–161 (2004)
6. Jafarpour, B., Abidi, S.S.R., Abidi, S.R.: Exploiting semantic web technologies to develop OWL-based clinical practice guideline execution engines. IEEE J. Biomed. Heal. Inf. **20**, 388–398 (2016)
7. Van Woensel, W.: GLEAN. https://github.com/william-vw/glean
8. Arndt, D., Van Woensel, W., Tomaszuk, D.: Notation3: draft community group report. https:// w3c.github.io/N3/spec/. Accessed 08 Jan 2022
9. HL7 International: HL7 Fast Health Interop Resources (FHIR). https://www.hl7.org/ind ex.cfm
10. Arndt, D., Van Woensel, W.: Towards supporting multiple semantics of named graphs using N3 rules. In: 13th RuleML+RR 2019 Doctoral Consortium and Rule Challenge, CEUR-WS.org (2019)
11. Sun, H., Arndt, D., De Roo, J., Mannens, E.: Predicting future state for adaptive clinical pathway management. J. Biomed. Inform. **117**, 103750 (2021)
12. Arndt, D., et al.: Ontology reasoning using rules in an eHealth context. In: Bassiliades, N., Gottlob, G., Sadri, F., Paschke, A., Roman, D. (eds.) RuleML 2015. LNCS, vol. 9202, pp. 465–472. Springer, Cham (2015). https://doi.org/10.1007/978-3-319-21542-6_31
13. Van Woensel, W., Abidi, S.R., Abidi, S.S.R.: Towards model-driven semantic interfaces for electronic health records on multiple platforms using notation3. In: 4th International Workshop on Semantic Web Meets Health Data Management (SWH 2021), New York (2021)
14. De Roo, J.: Euler Yet another proof Engine – EYE. https://josd.github.io/eye/
15. Van Woensel, W.: JEN3. https://github.com/william-vw/jen3
16. KDIGO: clinical practice guideline for lipid management in chronic kidney disease. https:// kdigo.org/wp-content/uploads/2017/02/KDIGO-2013-Lipids-Guideline-English.pdf
17. Van Woensel, W., Abidi, S.S.R., Abidi, S.R.: Decision support for comorbid conditions via execution-time integration of clinical guidelines using transaction-based semantics and temporal planning. Artif. Intell. Med. **118**, 102127 (2021)
18. Girard, J.-Y.: Linear logic: its syntax and semantics. In: Girard, J.-Y., Lafont, Y., Regnier, L. (eds.) Advances in Linear Logic, pp. 1–42 (1995)

19. Kogan, A., Peleg, M., Tu, S.W., Allon, R., Khaitov, N., Hochberg, I.: Towards a goal-oriented methodology for clinical-guideline-based management recommendations for patients with multimorbidity: GoCom and its preliminary evaluation. J. Biomed. Inform. **112**, 103587 (2020). https://doi.org/10.1016/j.jbi.2020.103587
20. Knublauch, H., Kontokostas, D.: Shapes Constraint Language (SHACL). W3C Recommendation, 20 July 2017. https://www.w3.org/TR/shacl/

Towards an AI Planning-Based Pipeline for the Management of Multimorbid Patients

Malvika Rao[1(✉)], Martin Michalowski[2], Szymon Wilk[3], Wojtek Michalowski[1], Amanda Coles[4], and Marc Carrier[5]

[1] University of Ottawa, Ottawa, ON, Canada
`mrao@uottawa.ca`
[2] University of Minnesota, Minneapolis, MN, USA
[3] Poznan University of Technology, Poznan, Poland
[4] King's College London, London, UK
[5] The Ottawa Hospital, Ottawa, ON, Canada

Abstract. Treatment of patients with multimorbidity is one of the greatest challenges for clinical decision support. While evidence-based management of specific diseases is supported by clinical practice guidelines, concurrent application of multiple guidelines requires checking for possible adverse interactions between interventions and mitigating them, before a management plan is constructed. In earlier work, we developed an approach that casts the problem of multimorbidity management as an AI planning problem. In this paper we build on this earlier work and make progress towards creating a pipeline that inputs disease and patient-specific information and outputs a management plan. We describe research focused on selected aspects of pipeline development and illustrate these aspects with a clinical case implemented using the PDDL planning language and the OPTIC planner.

Keywords: Multimorbidity · AI planning · End-to-end pipeline

1 Introduction

Clinical practice guidelines (CPGs) and their computer interpretable versions (CIGs) address a single disease whereas patients often suffer from multimorbidity, which is particularly prevalent in older adults [2]. The management of a multimorbid patient requires simultaneous use of multiple CPGs that may recommend disease-specific but overall conflicting treatments resulting in adverse interactions. Thus, the identification and mitigation of adverse interactions and the construction of a management plan, free of these interactions, are crucial components of a clinical decision support [12]. We refer to the identification and mitigation of adverse interactions and the creation of a interaction-free management plan as the *multimorbidity problem*.

© The Author(s), under exclusive license to Springer Nature Switzerland AG 2022
M. Michalowski et al. (Eds.): AIME 2022, LNAI 13263, pp. 14–23, 2022.
https://doi.org/10.1007/978-3-031-09342-5_2

In [11] we introduced MitPlan 1.0, that applied AI planning to address the multimorbidity problem. We subsequently expanded our work into MitPlan 2.0 [10], an extended framework that brings our approach fully into the AI planning paradigm by considering the identification and mitigation of adverse interactions and the creation of a management plan as a single planning problem. This expansion is accomplished using a novel representation that unifies all information pertinent to adverse interactions, enabling the planner to produce the optimal solution (management plan) if one exists. Following typical conventions in solving planning problems, we use the Planning Domain Definition Language (PDDL) to model the problem and a domain independent planner (OPTIC [3]) to solve it.

Our long term goal is to create a pipeline that builds on MitPlan 2.0 and inputs information stored in CIGs, in external sources such as adverse interaction repositories, and in drug ontologies, and provides clinical decision support by generating a management plan with explanations for applied mitigations. Creating such a pipeline requires research on three components: *representation* of clinical information and knowledge that can be reasoned over, *computation* to infer a management plan for complex patient cases, and *explainability* of the inferences made in generating the management plan to help the physician in the treatment of the patient.

In this paper we describe advancements in the representation and computation components of a pipeline. We introduce a new formal representation of revision operators (ROs) – constructs that describe and address adverse interactions – to facilitate the automated translation of input data to PDDL and the detection of adverse interactions. We assume CIGs are given in the form of *actionable graphs* (AGs) that are conceptually based on task-network models [15]. More specifically, AGs are directed graphs with nodes capturing clinical contexts, decisions, actions, and goals, and arcs capturing scheduling constraints between nodes (also allowing for parallel and alternative nodes – see [11] for details).

The computational model is the representation in PDDL of the multimorbidity problem, and we refer to it as *refined computational model* because of the improvements we made to handle complex clinical scenarios and to increase computational efficiency. We describe an automated process that translates AGs and ROs into the refined computational model. This model is then input into the inference engine (in our case the OPTIC planner) to create an internal plan that is subsequently translated into a management plan (with possible explanations). The formalization of ROs and automated translation of AGs facilitate interfacing with external knowledge stored in ontologies and knowledge repositories so this knowledge can be automatically processed and added to the refined computational model.

Illustrative Example: To clinically ground and motivate our contributions, we use a simple clinical case as a running example throughout this paper. The case is of a 70 year old male diagnosed with chronic kidney disease (CKD) and hypertension (HTN), and at high risk of developing cardiovascular disease (CVD). Recently this patient has experienced an irregular heartbeat and has been diagnosed with atrial fibrillation (AFib). The patient's prescribed medication includes an erythropoietin stimulating agent (ESA), a calcium channel blocker (CCB), and low dose aspirin.

2   Related Work

The multimorbidity problem is an active area of research and several computational approaches have been developed to address it. These approaches are complimentary to the MitPlan 2.0 pipeline in their aim to support the breadth of multimorbidity problem features. Fernandez-Olivares *et al.* [5] describe a temporally-focused multi-agent AI planning approach. In their approach, each agent derives a possible management plan, while patient preferences along with other metrics are used to select the plan that is most suited to the patient. However, their approach does not support some of the clinical complexities such as multiple revisions needed to address adverse interactions. The GLARE-SSCPM system [13] supports physicians to detect and manage adverse interactions as well as merge multiple CIGs. It uses reasoning techniques to address temporal constraints and goals to interactively construct management plan. However there is no optimization involved in generating this plan.

The GoCom [9] system takes a goal-driven approach, where CIG actions are associated with clinical goals and interacting goals are identified and mitigated. Unlike our approach, a physician decides which management plan to select among a number of alternative solutions. Jafarpour *et al.* [8] present a dynamic approach that takes into consideration the evolving nature of a management planning and reconciles different CIGs at execution time. In contrast, MitPlan 2.0 is a static approach designed to be used during a specific patient physician encounter where a treatment time horizon is established. Alaboud and Coles [1] address the problem of managing patients' medication regimes using AI planning to model the continuously changing nature of the multimorbidity problem. However, they focus on medication dosing and do not consider broader mitigation aspects of the problem. Van Woensel *et al.* [14] present a framework where CIGs and evolving patient data are integrated, and adverse interactions mitigated, at execution time according to policies based on clinical knowledge. Their approach supports temporal constraints and employs a local search algorithm to find an optimal task schedule. However, they focus on optimization of an objective function related to temporal constraints and they do not consider other patient or encounter-specific metrics.

3   The MiPlan 2.0 Pipeline

In MitPlan 2.0 we leveraged the shared characteristics between the multimorbidity problem and AI planning. In the multimorbidity problem one starts with

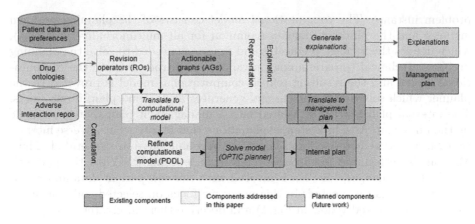

Fig. 1. MitPlan 2.0 pipeline (Color figure online)

the current health condition of a patient and the need to establish a management plan. A management plan is a sequence of *clinical actions* (such as administration of medications, tests, etc.) that achieves the *clinical goals* (such as improving health status, addressing a specific complaint, etc.), subject to clinical constraints (such as time, resources, etc.), is free of adverse interactions, and is optimal with respect to selected metrics (such as cost of medication, likelihood of adherence to medication, etc.). Analogously, in AI planning one starts at the initial state of a problem and looks for a sequence of *planning actions* from initial to *goal state*, subject to preconditions and effects, such that the identified sequence is optimal with respect to defined metrics.

Clinical actions are activities related to patient treatment as defined in the guidelines and represented in the corresponding AGs as action and decision nodes. These actions are mapped to components of the PDDL planning task as planning objects that are used by planning actions during the process of achieving the goal state. Hence, planning actions operate on planning objects and represent manipulations needed to find a management plan. Relationships between nodes in the AG are captured using predicates and functions. A clinical goal is a node in the AG that, when reached, signifies that the management for the given disease (or part thereof) has been completed and the desired effect has been achieved. The clinical goal is a terminal node in the AG when management planning is to be exhaustive, or it is a node placed somewhere between the context node (root of AG) and a terminal node when a predefined management planning horizon is provided. A *planning goal* is a specification of the goal state to achieve an optimal plan. In our formulation, the planning goal is a conjunction of the goal nodes from all AGs specific to the patient's multimorbid condition.

Information about adverse interactions and ways to mitigate them coming from the guidelines and secondary knowledge sources is encoded in ROs. The MitPlan 2.0 pipeline (see Fig. 1) takes CIGs represented as AGs, and ROs as input. Next, ROs and AGs are automatically translated into the PDDL planning problem instance. The computational model consists of the planning problem instance and the planning domain (common for all multimorbidity problems), which defines the actions, predicates and functions needed to solve the planning problem. Technical (programming) advances are introduced into the computational model and the resulting refined computational model is provided to the planner which solves the problem and generates an internal plan, if one exists. The internal plan is then translated into a management plan that is readable by the physician. As a final step, explanations that clarify what adverse interactions, if any, were identified and how they were mitigated are generated. Thus, MitPlan is customized for a patient/physician encounter. When the patient's health status changes, MitPlan is invoked with the new patient data and a new management plan is created. In this paper we focus on selected components of the pipeline (colored yellow in Fig. 1) and describe them in greater detail.

3.1   Revision Operators

In this work, we propose a new formal representation of ROs. Each RO mitigates a single clinical adverse interaction and consists of triggering conditions and mitigating actions. Triggering conditions comprise the set of clinical actions and contexts (nodes in AGs) that result in an adverse interaction. Mitigating actions refer to the clinical actions required to mitigate the adverse interaction. Specifically, an RO takes the form of a logical rule: *premise* → *conclusion*, where the premise defines the triggering conditions for an adverse interaction and the conclusion (*add*, *replace*) revises parts of an AG by introducing new mitigating actions, or replacing existing clinical actions with new mitigating actions, respectively. For simplicity, MitPlan 2.0 implements the removal of clinical actions as their replacement with a "do nothing" or *no-op* action. Clinical and mitigating actions are associated with metrics such as (but not limited to) *execution cost* (exec), *preference cost* (pref), and the *time duration* (duration) of the action. A predefined default value is assigned if no value is specified for these metrics. A clinical goal does not represent an action. Rather, it just signals that planning should be stopped at this point, and is therefore not associated with any metrics. The planning horizon (and thus the location of a goal node) is decided by the physician for a specific encounter, and clinical goals are not modified by ROs.

Due to space limitations, we describe only the *replace* operation. The reserved keyword *replace* is followed by the set of clinical actions that must be replaced and then by the set of mitigating actions that replace them. We use the special terms (*or*, *and*, *then*) to indicate when the set of mitigating actions are alternatives to one another, must be carried out in parallel, or must be carried out in sequence, respectively. Specific examples are described below.

In MitPlan 2.0, the objective function minimizes a weighted sum of user-identified metrics, where the weights are chosen to reflect the metrics' relative importance, and both metrics and weights are tailored to a specific clinical context. Patient preferences are captured by alternative actions with different preference costs, such that an alternative action preferred by a patient is set to be less costly. Information about patient preferences is acquired and either added directly to the AG by associating alternative actions with preference costs, or included as part of ROs where newly introduced actions are associated with costs reflective of those preferences.

By default, we assign an execution cost to each planning object in the computational model, and the objective function minimizes overall cost (including preference cost). Clinical actions introduced by ROs to mitigate adverse interactions have a higher execution cost than the clinical actions they revise. As a result the planner always attempts to select the original clinical actions. If a feasible plan does not exist because of adverse interactions, more costly actions specified in the ROs are selected. If several actions are equally suitable to mitigate an adverse interaction, the planner selects those actions that minimize the value of the objective function (alternatively there might exist multiple optimal solutions).

Illustrative Example (Cont.): We show how the ROs are represented in the clinical case introduced in Sect. 1. This case involves adverse interactions which are mitigated with a set of three ROs (RO_1, RO_2, RO_3), described next. For illustrative purposes we use a default execution cost of 100.

– RO_1 : (AFib, CCB, BB) → {*replace*(BB, no-op[exec: 100])}
  For a patient diagnosed with AFib, the simultaneous clinical actions of prescribing CCB and BB (beta blocker) medications represent an adverse interaction (triggering condition). The clinical action of prescribing BB is removed (mitigating action).
– RO_2 : (CKD, PCB) → {*replace*(PCB, SCB[exec: 100])}
  A patient diagnosed with AFib might be prescribed a potassium channel blocker (PCB) for anti-arrhythmic therapy. The triggering condition specifies that PCB prescribed to a patient diagnosed with CKD represents an adverse interaction. The clinical action of prescribing PCB is replaced with the mitigating action of prescribing a sodium channel blocker (SCB) medication.
– RO_3 : (AFib, low-dose-aspirin) → {*replace*(low-dose-aspirin, warfarin[exec: 100; pref: 20] *or* DOAC[exec: 100; pref: 5])}
  For a patient diagnosed with AFib, prescribing low dose aspirin (for CVD prevention) represents an adverse interaction (triggering condition). The clinical action of prescribing low dose aspirin is replaced with the mitigating action of prescribing an anticoagulant such as warfarin or a direct oral anticoagulant (DOAC). According to this RO, the patient's preference is to be prescribed DOAC rather than warfarin as seen in the preference cost of the action associated with prescribing DOAC being lower than that of the action prescribing warfarin.

Multi-action Revisions: Building further on the illustrative example, we implement multi-action revisions, that is, a situation where the conclusion component of an RO consists of a sequence of mitigating actions rather than a single action. Treating CKD and HTN requires lifestyle management as part of the patient's treatment and lifestyle management may vary from patient to patient, as illustrated below.

- RO_4 : (CKD, HTN, lifestyle-management) $\rightarrow$ {*replace*(lifestyle-management, DASH-diet[exec: 100] *then* sodium-intake-restriction[exec: 100])}
  The triggering condition indicates that, for a patient diagnosed with CKD and HTN, and told to manage their lifestyle in a non-specific way, their generic lifestyle management is replaced by two mitigating actions described in the conclusion of RO_4 – the DASH diet followed by restricting sodium intake.

Temporal Constraints: In the illustrative example, a patient's CVD risk is managed with a DOAC as anticoagulation therapy. Considering that CKD patients are predisposed to oral lesions and tooth decay, it is determined that the patient needs to undergo a dental procedure that is associated with a high risk of periprocedural bleeding. The patient's anticoagulation medication (DOAC) needs to be stopped 2 days prior to the procedure and restarted 1 day after the procedure. This requirement is represented using a sequence of actions in the conclusion of the revision operator RO_5.

- RO_5 : (CKD, AFib, DOAC, dental-procedure) $\rightarrow$ {*replace*((DOAC, no-op[exec: 100; duration: 4 days] *then* DOAC[exec:10; duration: lifetime])}

3.2   Translation to Computational Model

MitPlan 2.0 creates the computational model (*Translate to computational model* in Fig. 1) with a Python module using the NetworkX library to manipulate the AGs extended with the ROs, patient data and preferences. The manipulated AGs are automatically translated into a unified representation within the PDDL planning problem instance for a given patient encounter [4]. This unified problem representation enables the planner to optimize over all the information available, including contingencies introduced by ROs and patient preferences, and it is constructed in two steps: (1) the AG is expanded to include all mitigating actions recommended by applicable ROs as well as alternative actions required for representing patient preferences, and (2) the triggering condition of each RO is encoded as a binary vector identifying the set of clinical actions and contexts that define an adverse interaction.

Illustrative Example (Cont.): During translation, the unified internal problem representation for the clinical case involving the first three ROs is constructed as follows. No-op actions are introduced to the AG for AFib, with a higher cost than that of BB medication, as alternative actions to those representing BB medication, to model the removal of BB medication as per RO_1. In addition, the AG for AFib is expanded to include an action for SCB, as per RO_2. As per RO_3, the AG for CKD is expanded to include two alternative actions – an action for prescribing a DOAC and an action for prescribing warfarin, with a lower preference cost associated with DOAC than warfarin to represent the patient's preference for the former over the latter. Finally, the triggering conditions for RO_1, RO_2, and RO_3 are encoded as binary vectors.

0.023: (makedecisionnode d afibtype cardio) [0.010]
0.034: (makedecisionnode d3 bpcontrol2 p1) [0.010]
0.034: (makedecisionnode d2 ferritin metabolicabnormality) [0.010]
0.034: (takeactionnode d cardio improve) [0.010]
0.045: (makedecisionnode d2 metabolicabnormality p5) [0.010]
0.045: (makedecisionnode d improve recur) [0.010]
0.045: (executeparallelstartnode d3 p1) [0.010]
0.056: **(makedecisionnode d recur newscb)** [0.010]
0.056: (executeparallelstartnode d2 p5) [0.010]
0.056: (takeparallelactionnorevisions d3 p1 pace12wks pace12wks_end) [0.010]
0.056: (takeparallelactionnorevisions d3 p1 pdiuret12wks pdi12wks_end) [0.010]
0.067: **(takeactionnode d newscb g)** [0.010]

.

.

.

0.149: (checkgoal d g) [0.001]
0.149: (checkgoal d2 g2) [0.001]
0.149: (checkgoalnorevisionops d3 g3) [0.001]

Fig. 2. Part of the internal plan for the illustrative example

3.3 Refined Computational Model

A recent review of the literature on multimorbid disease management identified a set of key features that characterize a multimorbid problem [12]. Implementing some of these features, such as delaying a treatment to avoid an overlap or capturing a temporal relationship between AGs, required improving the representation of the planning problem. As a result, we were able to implement more complex mitigations, consider AGs with a large number of nodes, and deal with sequences of parallel clinical actions including nested parallel actions. We handled the processing of parallel actions, and incorporated temporal constraints by using durative actions in PDDL to associate a time duration with an action. We were also able to handle situations where the conclusion component of an RO involves a set of mitigating actions.

All these additions resulted in a significant increase in the planner's search space and consequently growth in its runtime. In order to address this issue we revised the problem representation to reduce the planning search space. For example, we introduced preconditions in planning actions to direct the planner's search away from taking certain actions, where those actions might lead to an interaction or prevent reaching the goal. We also modelled certain planning actions as PDDL+ [7] events which execute instantly when their preconditions hold. This reduced the number of possible choices the planner considered and sped up search. Incorporating these changes and solving the refined computational model required the use of the versions PDDL 2.1 [6], PDDL+, and the OPTIC planner which supports it.

Illustrative Example (Cont.): As a result of the additions and refinements described above, we were able to generate an internal plan within reasonable processing time. Figure 2 shows such a plan for the illustrative example introduced earlier. In this plan we have highlighted (in bold) an action of prescribing SCB (labeled as *newscb*) that replaces an action of prescribing PCB as defined by RO_2.

4   Conclusion and Future Work

In this paper, we presented selected improvements that move us closer to completing the MitPlan 2.0 pipeline. We formalized the representation of the ROs to facilitate their creation using external repositories. We described how the AGs, ROs, patient data and patient preferences are automatically translated into a computational model expressed in PDDL. We showed how the computational model was refined in order to reduce the search space and support complex multimorbidity problems. All of these advancements enable MitPlan 2.0 to solve larger and more complex clinical cases and therefore position our work closer to prospective evaluation.

Our future work will focus on generating explanations for specific mitigations, moving towards creating ROs from drug ontologies and adverse reaction repositories, and enriching the semantic representation of clinical actions to support reasoning at the level of medication classes and specific medications within them. An interesting question raised by this research is the notion of clinical case complexity. The number of AGs, their size and structure, the number and types of interactions, the constraints on the problem, and the size of the search space seem to be factors that contribute to the complexity of a clinical case, but their interplay is uncertain. Therefore, our future research will also explore the notion of clinical case complexity and what factors impact solvability of the multimorbidity problem.

Acknowledgements. We thank Jean-Luc Blais-Amyot and Maxime Côté-Gagné for their programming work on the automated translation component. We thank the reviewers for their helpful feedback. This research was supported by funding from the Telfer Health Transformation Exchange and the Natural Sciences and Engineering Research Council of Canada.

References

1. Alaboud, F.K., Coles, A.: Personalized medication and activity planning in PDDL+. In: Proceedings of 29nd International Conference on Automated Planning and Scheduling (ICAPS), pp. 492–500 (2019)
2. Barnett, K., Mercer, S., Norbury, M., Watt, G., Wyke, S., Guthrie, B.: Epidemiology of multimorbidity and implications for health care, research, and medical education: a cross-sectional study. Lancet **380**, 37–43 (2012)
3. Benton, J., Coles, A.J., Coles, A.: Temporal planning with preferences and time-dependent continuous costs. In: Proceedings of 22nd International Conference on Automated Planning and Scheduling (ICAPS), vol. 22, pp. 2–10. AAAI Publications (2012)

4. Blais-Amyot, J.L., Cote-Gagne, M.: MitPlan generation of PDDL based on CPGS. Honours Project report, University of Ottawa (2021)
5. Fernandez-Olivares, J., Onaindia, E., Castillo, L., Jordan, J., Cozar, J.: Personalized conciliation of clinical guidelines for comorbid patients through multi-agent planning. Artif. Intell. Med. **96**, 167–186 (2019)
6. Fox, M., Long, D.: PDDL2.1: an extension to PDDL for expressing temporal planning domains. J. Artif. Intell. Res. **20**, 61–124 (2003). https://doi.org/10.1613/jair.1129
7. Fox, M., Long, D.: Modelling mixed discrete-continuous domains for planning. J. Artif. Intell. Res. **27**, 235–297 (2006)
8. Jafarpour, B., Raza, S., Van Woensel, W., Sibte, S., Abidi, R.: Execution-time integration of clinical practice guidelines to provide decision support for comorbid conditions. Artif. Intell. Med. **94**, 117–137 (2019)
9. Kogan, A., Peleg, M., Tu, S.W., Allon, R., Khaitov, N., Hochberg, I.: Towards a goal-oriented methodology for clinical-guideline-based management recommendations for patients with multimorbidity: GoCom and its preliminary evaluation. J. Biomed. Inf. **112**, 103587 (2020)
10. Michalowski, M., Rao, M., Wilk, S., Michalowski, W., Carrier, M.: MitPlan 2.0: enhanced support for multi-morbid patient management using planning. In: Tucker, A., Henriques Abreu, P., Cardoso, J., Pereira Rodrigues, P., Riaño, D. (eds.) AIME 2021. LNCS (LNAI), vol. 12721, pp. 276–286. Springer, Cham (2021). https://doi.org/10.1007/978-3-030-77211-6_31
11. Michalowski, M., Wilk, S., Michalowski, W., Carrier, M.: A planning approach to mitigating concurrently applied clinical practice guidelines. Artif. Intell. Med. **112** (2021)
12. O'Sullivan, D., et al.: Towards a framework for comparing functionalities of multimorbidity clinical decision support: a literature-based feature set and benchmark cases. To appear in AMIA 2021 (2021)
13. Piovesan, L., Terenziani, P., Molino, G.: GLARE-SSCPM: an intelligent system to support the treatment of comorbid patients. IEEE Intell. Syst. **33**(6), 37–46 (2018)
14. Van Woensel, W., Abidi, S., Abidi, S.: Decision support for comorbid conditions via execution-time integration of clinical guidelines using transaction-based semantics and temporal planning. Artif. Intell. Med. **118**, 102127 (2021)
15. Wilk, S., Michalowski, M., Michalowski, W., Rosu, D., Carrier, M., Kezadri-Hamiaz, M.: Comprehensive mitigation framework for concurrent application of multiple clinical practice guidelines. J. Biomed. Inform. **66**, 52–71 (2017)

A Knowledge Graph Completion Method Applied to Literature-Based Discovery for Predicting Missing Links Targeting Cancer Drug Repurposing

Ali Daowd[1(✉)], Samina Abidi[2], and Syed Sibte Raza Abidi[1]

[1] NICHE Research Group, Faculty of Computer Science, Dalhousie University, Halifax, Canada
ali.daowd@dal.ca
[2] Medical Informatics, Department of Community Health and Epidemiology,
Dalhousie University, Halifax, Canada
ssrabidi@dal.ca

Abstract. Cancer literature contains a rich body of implicit knowledge which can play an important role in drug repurposing. However, classical knowledge retrieval techniques used in Literature Based Discovery (LBD) suffer from the problem of incomplete knowledge extraction resulting in a large number of knowledge entities being missed. Recently, knowledge graphs (KGs) have been used to represent literature-derived knowledge and support knowledge discovery by representing relations between concepts. Knowledge Graph Completion (KGC) has been proposed as a method to augment knowledge represented as a KG by predicting potential missing relations between concepts in a KG. We posit that KGC methods can be applied to LBD with the goal of augmenting KGs and finding implicit knowledge by reasoning over the KG. In this paper, we present KGC methods (such as FocusE-TransE) to predict missing relations between head and tail entities, rather than the standard head or tail prediction task. Our focus is the generation of a cancer-focused drug repurposing KG, via LBD, replicating recent cancer drug repurposing discoveries. We utilized a time-slicing approach to construct incomplete KGs using semantic triples extracted from cancer literature. Next we apply our KGC methods to augment the base KG, and apply discovery patterns on the augmented KG to generate drug-gene-disease semantic paths that replicate recent cancer drug repurposing discoveries. Further, we assessed the LBD output by comparing drug-disease associations reported in the literature. Our work presents a scalable knowledge discovery framework combining KGC, LBD, and associations measures to discover meaningful implicit knowledge from the literature.

Keywords: Knowledge graph · Knowledge graph completion · Literature based discovery · Drug repurposing · Cancer

1 Introduction

The published biomedical literature contains a significant volume of implicit knowledge that if discovered can contribute to incidental findings about complex issues such as

M. Michalowski et al. (Eds.): AIME 2022, LNAI 13263, pp. 24–34, 2022.
https://doi.org/10.1007/978-3-031-09342-5_3

gene-disease associations, cancer pathogenesis, and new indications for existing drugs (i.e., drug repurposing). Given the cost and extensive research required to develop new drugs, the use of computational approaches such as genetic network analysis, semantic inference, and deep neural networks, have emerged as an alternative to reduce the effort needed to explore new therapeutic purposes of existing drugs [1]. Recent research has shown that literature-derived Knowledge Graphs (KG) represent an efficient and cost-effective strategy to investigate drug repurposing [2, 3]. Literature-derived knowledge is extracted using knowledge retrieval tools in the form of semantic triples (*subject-relation-object*). However, current knowledge retrieval tools are not capable of extracting complete knowledge from the literature, resulting in incomplete and sparse literature-derived KGs [4]. Knowledge incompleteness is an indication of poor KG quality, which in turn can negatively impact the drug discovery process. Recently, Knowledge Graph Completion (KGC) has been proposed as a novel method to solve the problem of KG incompleteness and sparsity [5]. KGC methods improve the quality of KGs by predicting missing knowledge entities and relations in a KG. We posit that KGC methods can complement literature-based discovery (LBD) when applied in a targeted manner by predicting missing semantic relations between KG entities, thereby augmenting the knowledge within a KG for knowledge discovery.

In this paper, we propose a medical literature based knowledge discovery approach for cancer drug repurposing by addressing the universal problem of KG incompleteness. We present KGC methods based on representation learning to first augment incomplete literature-derived KGs, and next to use the augmented KGs to identify new indications for existing drugs (i.e. drug repurposing). We apply KGC methods to (a) learn low-dimensional embeddings of KG entities and relations, and (b) augment the baseline KGs by using the trained embeddings to predict plausible relations between previously unlinked entities, as opposed to head or tail entity prediction which has been the standard in most KGC studies. Specifically, using a time-slicing approach we aim to generate knowledge in the form of *drug-gene-disease* semantic associations from literature prior to a certain date - i.e., when these associations were not discovered in the literature yet. Next, we evaluate the generated associations by comparing *drug-disease* associations reported in the current literature. Experimental results show that our KGC methods can predict plausible semantic relations between KG entities, thus augmenting incomplete KGs with new knowledge to facilitate the discovery of new knowledge. The contributions of our work are as follows: (i) we address the problem of incomplete knowledge in literature-derived KGs using novel KGC methods; (ii) we combine KGC methods, KG augmentation, and literature-based discovery approaches to replicate biomedical discoveries reported in the literature for cancer drug repurposing; (iii) we simulate knowledge discovery experiments using a time-slicing approach to evaluate our methods.

2   Background and Related Work

A KG is a multi-relational directed graph containing heterogeneous knowledge from various sources. Formally, KGs consists of a collection of head-relation-tail (h, r, t) triples which are represented as nodes and edges. Biomedical KGs are constructed from manually curated databases or by employing text mining methods to extract knowledge from textual sources, such as published literature. Regardless of the knowledge source, biomedical KGs suffer from a universal problem of incompleteness [5]. KGs created from manually curated databases contain well-established knowledge but updating these KGs with latest published literature is a challenge due to the time and effort needed in manual curation. On the other hand, text mining methods can extract explicit knowledge with high precision, however, these methods suffer from low recall rates which result in missing many already established associations between biomedical entities reported in the literature [4].

Various KGC methods, such as rule-based reasoning, probabilistic graph models, and representation learning, have been proposed to solve the KG incompleteness problem by augmenting KGs with new relational facts [5]. KGC methods based on probabilistic graph models and rule-based reasoning suffer from poor scalability and are not suitable for current large-scale KGs [5]. KGC methods based on representation learning have gained attention in recent years. Representation learning based KGC methods rely on knowledge graph embedding models to learn low-dimensional representations while preserving the structural information and graph properties [5, 6]. Consequently, the learned graph embeddings can be used for two prediction tasks: (1) relation prediction, and (2) entity prediction. In the former, the task is to predict missing relations between existing entities in a KG (*head, ?, tail*), while in the latter task aims to predict missing head or tail entities: (*head, relation, ?*) or (*?, relation, tail*). Generally, KGC methods can be classified into 3 classes based on the underlying KG embedding model: tensor decomposition, geometric, and deep-learning [6]. Recently, numeric-aware models emerged to leverage numeric edges in KGs [7]. These models are considered as extensions of existing models, and present an add-on layer for the graph embedding architectures that considers numeric weights associated with edges. Weighted edges in KGs may signify importance, uncertainty, or strength of relations between the head and tail entity. The premise of numeric-aware models is that edges with high numeric values should have greater impact on the model training [7].

A typical KGC method based on representation learning operates as follows: (1) entity and relation embeddings are initialized randomly, (2) negative samples are generated from the KG triples by corrupting the head, tail or relation of a positive triple with a randomly selected entity from the graph, (3) Algorithm iterates over positive and negative samples to update initialized embeddings by optimizing a loss function that maximizes scores for positive triples and minimizes scores for the negative ones.

Over the past years, a number of studies applied representation learning methods to complete biomedical KGs to prioritize gene-disease associations [8], identify drug-drug interactions [9], and predict potential drug side effects [10]. More recently, representation learning based KGC have been applied on large biological KGs for drug repurposing. However, most approaches characterize drug repurposing discovery as a task of predicting missing head or tail entities. In that sense, KGC methods are not used for KG augmentation and no reasoning over KGs is performed for knowledge discovery, rather the graph embeddings generated by KGC methods are primarily used to predict nearest head or tail entities for a given partial triple. For example, [3] applied KGC methods on a literature-derived KG to discover new drugs for Parkinson's disease. The authors framed drug discovery as a task of predicting head entities: (?, TREAT, Parkinson's

Disease). Another study applied KGC methods, combined with a literature-based discovery approach, on a KG derived from COVID-19 literature to predict new therapeutic applications of existing drugs for COVID-19 – i.e., (*?, TREATS, COVID-19*) [2]. To our knowledge, the only study that performed relation prediction on a biomedical KG is [11]. However, the KG used in their work is based on a curated knowledge base, and relation prediction was performed as a benchmark to compare different KG embeddings, rather than knowledge augmentation.

To summarize, majority of published works in this area frame KG based knowledge discovery as entity prediction tasks. We posit that applying KGC methods to predict relations between unlinked entities in the KG, and then reasoning over augmented KGs via a discovery pattern based approach, particularly for drug repurposing offers the advantage of inferring new relations between a *drug* and a *disease* via shared genetic associations, and validating the discovery pattern generated from augmented KGs by cross-referencing discovered associations against manually curated databases.

3   Methods

We present our knowledge discovery framework for cancer drug repurposing by leveraging (i) literature-derived KGs constructed from semantic triples extracted from cancer-related literature; (ii) KGC methods to augment incomplete literature-derived knowledge, and (iii) a discovery pattern based approach to replicate *drug-gene-cancer* discoveries reported in the literature. Our approach differs from existing works, as we frame KGC as a relation prediction task, as opposed to predicting head or tail entities for a given partial triple. Consequently, we utilize predicted relations to augment baseline KGs with new associations between existing entities in baseline KGs.

3.1   Extraction of Literature-Derived Knowledge

Our primary source of knowledge to construct literature-derived KGs is PubMed. We searched PubMed using a combination of cancer-related MeSH terms and title/abstract keywords to retrieve manuscript IDs (PMID) for cancer related articles. Our literature search strategy included MeSH terms such as neoplasm, carcinogenesis, cell proliferation, and apoptosis. For title/abstract keywords, we utilized terms pertaining to the hallmarks of cancer, such as glycolysis, angiogenesis, inflammation, DNA repair, cell migration, and cell growth. We used a combination of 22 MeSH terms and 30 title/abstract keywords, and restricted our search to articles published between 1960–2021 to retrieve 6,798,300 PubMed abstracts related to cancer.

We extract literature-based knowledge from the retrieved abstracts by leveraging the Semantic Medline Database (SemMedDB); a repository of semantic triples extracted from PubMed abstracts using the SemRep knowledge extraction tool [4]. SemRep combines syntactic and semantic methods and leverages structured biomedical knowledge contained in the Unified Medical Language System (UMLS) [4]. Extracted semantic triples are in the form of *subject-relation-object* triples. We extracted 23,998,*065 subject-relation-object* triples from SemMedDB.

Extracted semantic triples are filtered and processed to create a baseline knowledge-base from which we build the literature-derived KGs. Given that we are interested in drug-gene-disease patterns, we focused on semantic triples belonging to the following semantic groups: Drugs and Chemicals, Gene or Genome, Physiology, and Disease or Syndrome. We filtered out triples where the subject or object are identical or represent generic biomedical concepts, such as *cells*, *proteins*, and *genes*. We retained triples with 13 semantic relations that were deemed useful for drug repurposing - e.g., INHIBITS, CAUSES, TREATS, PREVENTS, and STIMULATES.

Literature-derived knowledge is inherently noisy and may include many non-meaningful triples. To identify meaningful associations that occur more than expected by random chance, we assigned them weights using Normalized Pointwise Mutual Information (NPMI). NPMI is commonly used in LBD to identify concepts that occur together with greater probability than chance alone. Computed weights range from -1 to $+1$, with -1 indicating that concept pairs do not occur together, and $+1$ indicating that concepts always occur together. Triples with high NPMI weights constitute concepts with highly specific associations relevant for knowledge discovery. The filtration and processing resulted in a knowledge base consisting of 106,579 unique concepts, 13 semantic relations, and 2,583,245 triples.

3.2 Knowledge Graph Construction via Time-Slicing

Time-slicing is a technique used in LBD to split the literature-derived knowledge into training and evaluation sets using publication dates as cut-offs [12]. We are using time-slicing because to develop and validate our KGC approach we need to construct multiple KGs using literature published prior to a specific date—these KGs will be incomplete with respect to the current literature because with a progressive update of the literature new knowledge is added which in turn augments the KG developed. By applying our KGC approach to the KG with potentially missing associations we will be augmenting the KG with newer associations—the augmented KG will be compared with the KG developed using current knowledge to validate the performance of our KGC approach in terms of discovery of associations noted in the newer KG.

To prepare time-sliced KGs, we surveyed cancer-related PubMed articles published within the last 15 years to identify publications that discovered novel drug repurposing associations that can be characterized as a chain of *drug-gene-disease* associations. Our intent is to replicate discoveries reported in the literature using time-sliced KGs constructed from literature-derived knowledge prior to the specified date of discovery. Table 1 outlines 4 PubMed publications identified through our survey, which are considered to have discovered novel drug-cancer associations via an intermediate gene. We specifically use the publication dates of these 4 articles as cut-off dates for time-slicing. Since the publication dates in Table 1 are from different time periods, we construct 4 time-sliced KGs—one for each publication. For example, to replicate the discovery made by Capper et al., we set the time-slicing cut-off date as 2016 for KG construction, while post-cut-off knowledge is used for evaluation. This ensures that direct associations between drug and cancer concepts are eliminated from time-sliced KGs. Given the incomplete nature of literature-derived knowledge, we note that drug-gene associations were notably missing from time-sliced KGs as the drugs were novel at the time of discovery, whereby fewer than 100 articles reported such associations.

Table 1. Identified *drug-gene-cancer* associations reported in the literature

Publication (publication date)	Drug-Gene-Cancer Associations
Capper et al. (2016) [13]	Abiraterone – CYP17A1 – Breast Cancer
Kühnle et al. (2009) [14]	Tariquidar –ABCB1– Breast Cancer
Schmidt et al. (2015) [15]	BGJ398 –FGFR– Gastric Cancer
Bar-Zeev et al. (2018) [16]	Elacridar –ABCB1–Gastric Cancer

3.3 Representation Learning via KG Embeddings

Representation learning based KGC involves training KG embedding models to learn low-dimensional vector representations of KG entities and relations. We use the numeric-aware FocusE-TransE model, which is an extension of the TransE model with an add-on layer (FocusE) designed for numeric-enriched triples [7]. FocusE-TransE describes a triple as a translation between the head (h) and tail (t) entities through the relation (r) in a continuous embedding space. The goal is to make the sum of h and r embeddings as close as possible to the t embedding. Plausibility of relations is measured by employing a distance based scoring function δ such as L1 or L2 norm. The FocusE layer modifies distance based scores by leveraging the numeric values associated with r to maximize the margin between scores assigned to true triples and those assigned to negative triples. Thus, the FocusE layer increases the loss of the model and forces it to focus on triples with high numeric edge values. We use FocusE-TransE due to its ability to consider numeric edges and its good prediction performance [7].

FocusE-TransE is implemented and deployed using the AmpliGraph library [17]. A total of 4 models, for each time-sliced KG, were trained to learn low-dimensional embeddings for entities and relations. Model hyperparameters were tuned using a grid-search strategy: embedding dimensions (k) {200, 400, 600}, learning rate (lr) {0.01, 0.001, 0.0001}, and regularization coefficient (λ) {0.01, 0.001, 0.0001}. Additionally, the FocusE layer adds structural influence (β) parameter to modulate the influence of edge weights on training. Models were trained for a maximum of 2000 epochs with the option of early stopping.

3.4 Knowledge Graph Augmentation

Representation learning based KGC entails using trained KG embeddings to predict new knowledge entities and relations. As such, we augment the incomplete time-sliced KGs with new knowledge by predicting relations between previously unlinked entities. To do so, we first identify entity pairs which are not linked via a semantic relationship in the

KG, but have some notion of association reported in the literature. We identify such associations by leveraging the MEDLINE co-occurrences (MRCOC) dataset; which is a large network of Medical Subject Heading (MeSH) descriptors that occur together in PubMed articles. MeSH descriptors are manually assigned to PubMed articles based on human interpretation of the contents of the article. MeSH descriptors provide a concept-level implicit summary of a given article, and are suitable resource for knowledge augmentation. We mapped descriptors in MRCOC to UMLS, and extracted a subset of *drug-gene* and *gene-disease* concepts that exist in the KG as entities, but are not linked via a semantic relation. For example, *Abiraterone* (drug) and *CYP17A1* (gene) are co-occurring entities in MRCOC but are not linked via a semantic relationship in the time-sliced KGs. Extracted concept pairs are then used as input for trained embeddings to predict plausible semantic relations. Given a partial triple (*Abiraterone, ?, CYP17A1*), the trained model iteratively fills the missing relation with all known relations in the KG, and applies a scoring function to predict plausible semantic relation. The output of the relation prediction is a set of completed semantic triples which are used to augment time-sliced KGs. Table 2 outlines four distinct time-sliced KGs constructed from semantic triples extracted from PubMed literature up to the specified cut-off dates, and augmented with additional triples using KGC. We note that KG augmentation involved a targeted set of concepts to eliminate noise while keeping the size of the KG manageable for knowledge discovery.

Table 2. Time-sliced KGs before and after augmentation

Time-slice KG (cut-off dates)	Unique entities	Unique relations	Triples before augmentation	Triples after augmentation
KG – 1 (2016)	12,306	13	113,363	114,127
KG – 2 (2009)	10,582	13	92,818	93,294
KG – 3 (2015)	12,295	13	113,176	114,257
KG – 4 (2018)	13,832	13	113,479	114,109

3.5 Knowledge Discovery from the KG

We apply relation- and closed-based discovery approaches by traversing augmented KGs to generate semantic patterns consisting of logical chains of three concepts, then cross-validate them with *drug-gene-cancer* associations reported in post-cut-off literature (Table 1). Relation-based discovery leverages semantic relations between concepts to identify causal mechanistic associations. This approach filters implausible associations, such as *drug*-CAUSES-*gene*, while retaining plausible ones, for example: *drug*-INHIBITS-*gene*. The relation-based discovery process begins with a pre-defined source concept, and traverses the KG using logical patterns of semantic relations. We focus on the following pattern of semantic relations: *source*-[inhibits, stimulates, interacts_with]-*intermediate*-[causes, predisposes, associated_with]-*target*. In closed-based discovery, the *source* and *target* concepts are pre-defined, and the goal is to identify *intermediate* concepts which may expound the association between the source and target. To facilitate the discovery process, we represent augmented KGs on a Neo4j graph database and leverage its query language, Cypher, to encode graph relation- and closed-based discovery procedures.

4 Results

4.1 Evaluation of Relation Prediction

We evaluate the performance of KGC methods by using subsets of semantic triples from corresponding post-cut-off KG as the evaluation set. We select semantic triples with NPMI values in top 80th percentile, as it indicates the performance in predicting relations between highly specific and rare concepts. Approximately 80% of semantic triples in the evaluation set consisted of drug-gene and gene-cancer associations. We masked the relations between head and tail entities in the evaluation set to create partial triples, e.g. (*Luteolin, ?, NFE2L2*), to evaluate our method's predictive performance by comparing *top k* predicted relations to unmasked relations in the evaluation set. We utilize the Hits@K metric which reflects the accuracy of relation prediction by computing the proportion of correctly predicted relations at k, where $k = 1$ [17].

Evaluation results for relation prediction are outlined in Table 3. We achieve an av-erage Hits@1 $= 0.62$ on a total of 8,193 evaluation triples. Given that literature-derived KGs are arguably complex and contain considerable amount of noise, our evaluation results suggest that KGC methods can learn reasonable representations of relations between entities in literature-derived KGs. Our results indicate that the FocusE-TransE model can reliably predict plausible semantic relations between highly specific relatively rare concepts, which is useful for knowledge discovery.

Table 3. Evaluation of relation prediction task

Time-sliced KG	Hits@1	# of evaluation triples
KG – 1	0.63	1,146
KG – 2	0.65	4,951
KG – 3	0.61	1,124
KG – 4	0.58	972

4.2 Literature-Based Knowledge Discovery Output

We report the output of relation- and closed-based discovery from the baseline and augmented KGs in Table 4. Overall, the average number of semantic patterns generated by closed discovery is significantly lower compared to relation-based discovery due to its strict KG traversal conditions. With respect to KG augmentation, we clearly observe that patterns from augmented KGs outnumber patterns generated from baseline KGs; this demonstrates that targeted relation prediction via KGC is an effective approach to improve quality of literature-derived KGs. Upon cross-validation of semantic patterns with knowledge from the post-cut-off literature set (Table 1), our methods replicated 4 *drug-gene-cancer* associations reported in the literature. Since many drug-gene associations were missing from baseline KGs, discoveries reported in the literature could only be replicated using augmented KGs. Mean ranks of discovery patterns, based on NPMI, are higher for closed discovery as the *source* and *target* nodes are pre-defined prior to discovery. The associations discovered by our methods are as follows:

1. Abiraterone - INHIBITS - CYP17A1 - PREDISPOSES - Breast Cancer
2. Tariquidar - INHIBITS - ABCB1- ASSOCIATED_WITH - Breast Cancer
3. BGJ398 - INTERACTS_WITH – FGFR - PREDISPOSES - Gastric Cancer
4. Elacridar - INHIBITS - ABCB1 - ASSOCIATED_WITH - Gastric Cancer

The results demonstrate that KGC methods, combined with LBD, can generate plausible explanations for associations between drugs and cancers. For example, discovered association #1 provides mechanistic associations between Abiraterone and Breast Cancer as proposed by Capper et al. [13]. Similarly, association #3 replicates the finding that BGJ398 can be used to target stomach cancer due to its interaction with FGFR [15]. The results show that our methods are not only capable of predicting plausible semantic relations, but can also discover meaningful future knowledge.

Table 4. LBD output for augmented and baseline KGs

Discovery approach	Knowledge graph	Average # of semantic patterns	Semantic patterns reported in literature	Mean rank of discovery patterns
Closed based discovery	Augmented KG	37	4	21.4
	Baseline KG	12	0	–
Relation based discovery	Augmented KG	774	4	104.3
	Baseline KG	268	0	–

5   Conclusion and Future Work

We proposed a novel knowledge discovery framework for drug-repurposing by combining KGC methods and LBD. The novelty of our work is in framing KGC as a task of relation prediction as opposed to entity prediction. Additionally, we leverage MeSH descriptors as the primary knowledge resource for KGC to (a) capture implicit knowledge for a given PubMed article; and (b) counter limitations of traditional knowledge extraction methods. The contribution of our work is a scalable framework for knowledge discovery using augmented literature-derived KGs. While our focus is drug repurposing, we posit that our methods can be extended to other applications, such as discovering novel biomarkers for diseases and explaining molecular mechanisms in cancer biology. Our work has several limitations; firstly, using UMLS as the primary terminological resource results in a varied set of hierarchical concepts referring to closely related entities. We plan to utilize UMLS hierarchy to map broad concepts to more specific descendants. Secondly, NPMI metrics do not consider the semantics for a given triple. In a previous study, we demonstrated that semantic-based methods can significantly improve knowledge discovery [18]. We plan to leverage distributional semantics in the future to assign edge weights based on semantic relatedness to provide more accurate representation based learning.

References

1. Pushpakom, S., et al.: Drug repurposing: progress, challenges and recommendations. Nat. Rev. Drug Disc. **18**, 41–58 (2019)
2. Zhang, R., Hristovski, D., Schutte, D., Kastrin, A., Fiszman, M., Kilicoglu, H.: Drug repurposing for COVID-19 via knowledge graph completion. J. Biomed. Inform. **115**, 103696 (2021)
3. Zhang, X., Che, C.: Drug repurposing for Parkinson's disease by integrating knowledge graph completion model and knowledge fusion of medical literature. Future Internet **13**, 14 (2021)
4. Kilicoglu, H., Rosemblat, G., Fiszman, M., Shin, D.: Broad-coverage biomedical relation extraction with SemRep. BMC Bioinform. **21**, 1–28 (2020). https://doi.org/10.1186/s12859-020-3517-7
5. Chen, Z., Wang, Y., Zhao, B., Cheng, J., Zhao, X., Duan, Z.: Knowledge graph completion: a review. IEEE Access **8**, 192435–192456 (2020)
6. Rossi, A., Barbosa, D., Firmani, D., Matinata, A., Merialdo, P.: Knowledge graph embedding for link prediction: a comparative analysis. ACM Trans. Knowl. Disc. Data (TKDD) **15**, 1–49 (2021)
7. Pai, S., Costabello, L.: Learning embeddings from knowledge graphs with numeric edge attributes. arXiv preprint https://arxiv.org/abs/2105.08683 (2021)
8. Choi, W., Lee, H.: Identifying disease-gene associations using a convolutional neural network-based model by embedding a biological knowledge graph with entity descriptions. PLoS ONE **16**, e0258626 (2021)
9. Bougiatiotis, K., Aisopos, F., Nentidis, A., Krithara, A., Paliouras, G.: Drug-drug interaction prediction on a biomedical literature knowledge graph. In: Michalowski, M., Moskovitch, R. (eds.) Artificial Intelligence in Medicine, vol. 12299, pp. 122–132. Springer, Cham (2020). https://doi.org/10.1007/978-3-030-59137-3_12
10. Nováček, V., Mohamed, S.K.: Predicting polypharmacy side-effects using knowledge graph embeddings. AMIA Summits Transl. Sci. Proc. **2020**, 449 (2020)
11. Chang, D., Balažević, I., Allen, C., Chawla, D., Brandt, C., Taylor, R.A.: Benchmark and best practices for biomedical knowledge graph embeddings. In: Proceedings of the Conference. Association for Computational Linguistics. Meeting, vol. 2020, p. 167 (2020)
12. Henry, S., McInnes, B.T.: Literature based discovery: models, methods, and trends. J. Biomed. Inform. **74**, 20–32 (2017)
13. Capper, C.P., Larios, J.M., Sikora, M.J., Johnson, M.D., Rae, J.M.: The CYP17A1 inhibitor abiraterone exhibits estrogen receptor agonist activity in breast cancer. Breast Cancer Res. Treat. **157**(1), 23–30 (2016). https://doi.org/10.1007/s10549-016-3774-3

14. Kühnle, M., et al.: Potent and selective inhibitors of breast cancer resistance protein (ABCG2) derived from the p-glycoprotein (ABCB1) modulator tariquidar. J. Med. Chem. **52**, 1190–1197 (2009)
15. Schmidt, K., et al.: Targeting fibroblast growth factor receptor (FGFR) with BGJ398 in a gastric cancer model. Anticancer Res. **35**, 6655–6665 (2015)
16. Bar-Zeev, M., Kelmansky, D., Assaraf, Y.G., Livney, Y.D.: B-Casein micelles for oral delivery of SN-38 and elacridar to overcome BCRP-mediated multidrug resistance in gastric cancer. Eur. J. Pharm. Biopharm. **133**, 240–249 (2018)
17. Costabello, L., Pai, S., Van, C.L., McGrath, R., McCarthy, N., Tabacof, P.: AmpliGraph: a library for representation learning on knowledge graphs (2019)
18. Daowd, A., Barrett, M., Abidi, S., Abidi, S.S.R.: A framework to build a causal knowledge graph for chronic diseases and cancers by discovering semantic associations from biomedical literature. In: 2021 IEEE 9th International Conference on Healthcare Informatics (ICHI), pp. 13–22. IEEE (2021)

An Ontology to Support Automatic Drug Dose Titration

David Riaño[1]([✉]) [ID], José-Ramon Alonso[2], Špela Pečnik[3],
and Aida Kamišalić[3] [ID]

[1] Universitat Rovira i Virgili, Av. Paisos Catalans 26, 43883 Tarragona, Spain
david.riano@urv.cat
[2] Hospital Clinic de Barcelona, C/Villaroel 171, 08036 Barcelona, Spain
[3] Faculty of Electrical Engineering and Computer Science, University of Maribor,
Koroska cesta 46, Maribor 2000, Slovenia

Abstract. Drug dose titration (DT) is the clinical process of progressively adjusting the dose of a medication for the maximum benefit of the patient. Several DT clinical models exist based on the elementary concepts of null, initial, and maximal doses, as well as, dose increments and decrements. These values depend on the target disease, the drug considered, and some parameters such as the patient's age, gender, weight, and race. This paper describes the formalization of this knowledge as an ontology, and its use to detect chronic hypertension patient treatment deviations from standard DT models with regard to drug replacement (step-1 treatment) and drug supplementation (step-2 treatment).

Keywords: Drug prescription · Drug dose titration · Decision-support system · Biomedical ontologies and terminologies · Biomedical knowledge acquisition and representation · Knowledge-based reasoning in biomedicine

1 Introduction

Drugs are essential to clinical practice. Drug prescription is a health-care professional action commonly assigned to physicians. In the last years, multiple studies and publications reported on the risks of wrong drug prescriptions. Medication errors cause 7000 to 9000 deaths per year [27] and affects approximately 1.3 million people each year in the United States [31]. They are a major public health burden estimated in the European Union at an annual cost of 21.8 billion Euros [13], while in the United States is estimated that looking after patients with errors associated to medication exceeds 40 billion Dollars per year [27]. Over 25% of medication errors reported in the UK during 2017 and 2018 were related to medication prescriptions, whereby 11.5% were due to the wrong dose, 7.3% to wrong medication, and 8% attributed to wrong frequency [4]. The WHO recommends the use of drug computer assisted systems in order to detect and correct wrong prescriptions before they may affect the patients [30].

M. Michalowski et al. (Eds.): AIME 2022, LNAI 13263, pp. 35–46, 2022.
https://doi.org/10.1007/978-3-031-09342-5_4

Drug prescription is a complex knowledge-based task that depends on multiple factors, such as the target disease (i.e., one same drug can be recommended for several diseases), the patient's demographic group (e.g., sex, age, race, weight, etc. may condition a prescription), the patient's comorbidity (i.e., some prescriptions must be adjusted depending on the patient's secondary diseases), the drug (i.e., some diseases can be confronted with alternative drugs), the dose and route (i.e., some drugs can come in different dosages and routes of administration), the frequency (e.g., od, bid, tid, qid stand for once, twice, three or four times per day), and the accompanying drugs (i.e., some clinical cases require a poly-pharmacy solution that may affect each single-drug prescription), among other possible affecting factors.

Only the one-drug prescription may entail multiple decision issues, which may be aggravated by the lack of published scientific evidence on the correct drug, dosage, or taking frequency. In these circumstances, physicians use to adopt a drug titration process (DT) consisting on progressively adjusting the dose of a medication for the maximum benefit without adverse effects [15]. Different studies are investigating DT regimens [3,12,14,17] as well as proposing patient specific drug regimen models [18,19,28]. Even though other dosing regimens are available, such as response-guided titration, still DT is the method being predominantly used and recommended [14,26]. It consists of prescribing an initial dose that is subsequently increased until the target issue is controlled (steady dose) or the maximum dose is reached. At this point, if the target issue is not under control, the two most frequent actions are replacing the current drug by an alternative drug or adding a second-line drug to the current drug. Both options require the activation of new DT procedures.

In [24,25], we proposed a formal language to represent DT procedures in order to help physicians in the pharmacological treatment of patients. This language was supported by a simple ontology about drugs that required additional extension in order to incorporate more sophisticated constrains about prescriptions within DT procedures. Here, we present a new version of the ontology for alternative and supplementary drug titration procedures. Please note that we left out of this study considerations on poly-pharmacy above two drugs and drug interactions, which will be presented in later studies.

In health-care, information about drugs tends to follow a disease-to-drug approach, in which the pathology is what marks the important information about the medicine. Our interest, however is more in the drug-to-disease direction, where drugs contain relevant information on their prescription for different diseases. In this second view, literature review shows that formalizing knowledge about drugs for computer use has been considered from, at least, five different perspectives:

1. The traditional approach, which is followed by codification systems such as ATC/DDD [32] or health-care ontologies such as SNOMED-CT [2] (see *Drug or medicament (substance) class*), which aim at providing a classification of drugs, a suggestion of daily dose recommendations for adults, or a set of constraints respect to other clinical concepts such as uses, measurements, sensitization, methods of administration, etc.

2. The chemical approach [8] such as the CheBI [10], the CO [6], or the CHEM-INF [11] ontologies, whose main objective is the molecular description and classification of drugs.
3. The legal approacch followed by ontologies such as DrOn [9], PDRO [5], OCRx [21], or [23], whose main concern is the formalization of health-care systems legal drug identification, referencing, and use.
4. The consulting approach such as the online service Drugs.com that provides a catalogue of drugs with general information but also information on side effects, pregnancy and breastfeeding considerations, drug interactions and dosages, in textual form.
5. The drug interaction checkers approach such as Epocrates [7], WebMD [29], or Medscape [16], which focus on the identification of drug interactions and possible solutions.

Most of these systems do not satisfy our need to formalize the necessary information about drugs which is required in a DT process. Drug.com is an exception, because in its dosage chapter, available for each medicine in the catalog, it provides information on initial doses, dose increments and maximum doses, which is essential for the definition of DT processes. Unfortunately, this information is in textual format.

In this work, we browsed Drug.com in order to manually detect DT knowledge units corresponding to standard null, initial, and maximum doses, as well as recommended drug increments and decrements for 44 drugs in the management of hypertension. These were, eight beta-blockers (BB), ten ACE-inhibitors (ACEi), six thiazide-like diuretics (TLD), one potassium-sparing diuretic (PSD), eight angiotensin-II receptor blockers (ARB), three alpha-blockers (AB), and eight calcium channel blockers (CCB). This process is described in Sect. 2.1. Then these DT knowledge units were introduced in the DT ontology that is described in Sect. 2.2. Finally, the ontology was tested on the implementation of all the clinical evidences contained in the 2019 guideline on hypertension published by the NICE [20], with regard to the introduction of alternative and supplementary drugs. Specifically the ontology was used to detect deviations of patient's clinical records from the guideline indications (see Sect. 3). The results are discussed in Sect. 4.

2   Methods

2.1   Identification of DT Knowledge Units

Focused on the disease of hypertension (HTN) and also on its management with beta-blockers, ACE-inhibitors, diuretics, angiotensin-II receptor blockers, alpha-blockers, and calcium channel blockers, we used Drugs.com to manually extract information which is relevant to the DT procedures. Specifically, we analyzed eight beta-blockers: Acebutolol, Atenolol, Bisoprolol, Metoprolol (tartrate), Metoprolol (succinate), Nadolol, Nebivolol, Propranolol; ten ACE-inhibitors: Benazepril, Captopril, Enalapril, Fosinopril, Lisinopril, Moexipril,

Perindopril, Quinapril, Ramipril, and Trandolapril; six thiazide-like diuretics: Chlorothiazide, Chlorthalidone, Hydrochlorothiazide, Indapamide, Metolazone (Zaroxolyn), and Metolazone (Mykrox); one potassium-sparing diuretic: spironalactone; eight angiotensin-II receptor blockers: Azilsartan (Edarbi), Candesartan (Atacand) Eprosartan, Irbesartan (Avapro), Losartan (Cozaar), Olmesartan (Benicar), Telmisartan (Micardis), and Valsartan (Diovan); three alpha-blockers: Doxazosin (Cardura), Prazosin (Minipress), and Terazosin, and eight calcium channel blockers: Amlodipine (Norvasc), Diltiazem (Cardizem, Tiazac, others), Felodipine, Isradipine, Nicardipine, Nifedipine (Procardia), Nisoldipine (Sular), and Verapamil (Calan SR, Verelan), which were suggested by the Mayo Clinic[1].

With regard to doses, we observed textual recommendations such as:

- "**Bisoprolol** Dosage (**Beta-blocker**): Usual **Adult** Dose for **Hypertension. Initial dose: 5 mg orally once a day.** Dose Titration: If desired response is not achieved, may **increase the dose to 10 mg**, then 20 mg if necessary. **Maximum dose: 20 mg per day**"
- "**Ramipril** Dosage (**ACE-Inhibitor**): Usual **Adult** Dose for **Hypertension. Initial dose: 2.5 mg orally once a day** for patients not taking a diuretic. **Maintenance dose: 2.5 to 20 mg/day** in one or two equally divided doses"
- "**Ramipril** Dosage (**ACE-Inhibitor**): Usual **Adult** Dose for **Congestive Heart Failure. Initial dose: 2.5 mg orally twice a day. Maintenance dose: 5 mg orally twice a day**"
- "**Hydrochlorothiazide** Dosage (**diuretic**): Usual **Adult Dose** for **Hypertension. Initial dose: 25 mg orally once daily. Maintenance dose: May increase to 50 mg orally daily**, as a single or 2 divided doses"
- "**Hydrochlorothiazide** Dosage (**diuretic**): Usual Pediatric Dose for **Hypertension. Less than 6 months:** Up to **3 mg/kg/day** orally in **2 divided doses. Less than 2 years: 1 to 2 mg/kg/day orally daily** as a single dose or in 2 divided doses. **Maximum dose 37.5 mg per day. 2 to 12 years: 1 to 2 mg/kg/day orally daily** as a single dose or in 2 divided doses. **Maximum dose: 100 mg per day**"

All these DT knowledge units were based on the concepts of patient group (e.g., adult, <6 months, etc.), disease (i.e., HTN), and drug type (i.e., beta-blocker, ACE-inhibitor, diuretic, etc.). Additionally, they brought information on the initial dose, maximum dose, and drug increments. Sometimes, drug increments did not appear explicitly. In such cases, increments were forced to be equal to the initial dose. The table in the Appendix provides a summary of all the DT knowledge units found. For instance, hydrochlorothiazidel is a diuretic for HTN, with four different administrations depending on the age of the patient. For adults, the initial dose is 12.5 mg bid, and can be increased to 25 mg bid with one increment of 12.5 mg bid. Note that, for younger patients, doses are

---

[1] https://www.mayoclinic.org/diseases-conditions/high-blood-pressure/diagnosis-treatment/drc-20373417.

expressed in mg/kg and the weight of the patient has to be known. Race is also a condition to consider for trandolapril. When several dose intensifications exists without an explanation on when to apply one or the other, the one less intensive was chosen. The manual process of DT knowledge extraction from Drugs.com was supervised by JRA (author), an experienced physician.

2.2   The DT-support Ontology

All the DT information found in Drugs.com concerning the drug management for HTN patients with BB, ACEi, TLD, PSD, ARB, AB, and CCB was manually extracted and formalized in a DT-support ontology (DTON). We were not aware of ontologies containing this sort of knowledge, therefore reuse was not possible. Extending some existing ontology with this new knowledge was considered but discarded due to the lack of flexibility of this option. Our final decision was to make DTON from scratch. Once completed, this OWL2 ontology was composed of 15 classes, 5 object properties, 12 data property, and 74 individuals. For this purpose, we adopted an incremental development approach in which the new knowledge conditions (e.g., dose constraints) found in the incorporation of new drugs could modify and/or extend the previous ontology structure, constraints, and individuals. At the moment, the FAIR principles (i.e., making the ontology findable, accessible, interoperable, and reusable) [22] were left for the future, although the ontology can be shared upon request to the author DR in its interoperable and reusable OWL2 representation.

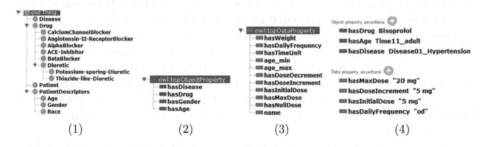

Fig. 1. DTON Basic Components: (1) Classes, (2) Object Properties, (3) Data Properties, and (4) **bisoprolol-adult-HTN** Individual.

Classes. The main classes in the DTON ontology are Drug, Disease, Patient, and PatientDescriptors (see Fig. 1(1)). There are six subclasses of Drug involved in this study (CalciumChannelBlocker, Angiotensin-II-ReceptorBlocker, AlphaBlocker, ACE-Inhibitor, BetaBlocker, and Diuretic). With Diuretic having two subclasses. The individuals of these subclasses are the ones enumerated in the appendix (8 BBs, 10 ACEi, 7 diuretics, 8 ARBs, 3 ABs, and 8 CCBs). The class Disease has two individuals (Disease01_Hypertension and Disease02_Chronic-Heart-Failure) representing hypertension and chronic heart failure, respectively.

The class Patient is used to represent the different lines in the table of the appendix. The individuals of this class contain patient descriptors such as the patient's age, gender, and race, that were represented with the namesake classes. For class Age, we defined the individuals corresponding to the 10 time intervals represented in Fig. 2, which were the ones required to represent the current knowledge about drugs. For instance, *child* individual corresponds to a 2–6 year patient. For the patient descriptor class Gender, two individuals were defined (Male, Female) representing male and female, respectively. For patient's descriptor class Race two individuals were defined (Black, noBlack), needed to represent the knowledge about the drug Trandolapril.

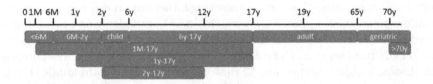

Fig. 2. DT time ranges.

Properties. The class Patient has four object properties (see Fig. 1(2)): has-Disease points to the patient's Disease (i.e., instance Disease01_Hypertension or Disease02_Chronic-Heart-Failure), hasDrug to the patient's drug (i.e., any individual of the class Drug), hasGender to the patient's gender (i.e., Male or Female individuals), and hasAge to the patient's age (i.e., one of the 10 time individuals of class Age). These are appreciated in the example shown in Fig. 1(4).

Patients also have seven data properties (see Fig. 1(3)): hasWeight (with the patient's weight in kg, which is required to compute doses expressed as mg/kg), hasDailyFrequency (with possible values od, bid, tid, and qid), hasNullDose, hasInitialDose, and hasMaxDose containing the corresponding null, initial, and maximum doses in the appendix (see an example in Fig. 1(4)). Properties has-DoseIncrement and hasDoseDecrement quantify the standard drug increments and decrements.

Properties age_min, age_max, and hasTimeUnit correspond to the class Age, and they are used to inform about the [min, max] numerical values of the age intervals in Fig. 2, and the units in which these intervals are expressed (Monthly or Yearly), respectively.

Individuals. The ontology counts with 70 individuals: 7 correspond to the class Patient, 2 to the class Disease, 44 to Drug subclasses, 13 to class Age, 2 to Gender, and 2 to class Race. In Fig. 1(4), we show one of these individuals, corresponding to the third DT knowledge unit (row 3) in the table of the appendix, with all the object and data properties instantiated to the corresponding values.

2.3   The DT-support Ontology Interface

In order to provide an easy management of the DT ontology, we implemented a Java user interface, based on the class `Ontology`. Once loaded, the ontology can be used to find the drug titration knowledge units with the method `drugTitration(drug, age, disease)`. See Fig. 3. Detailed information on the doses (null, initial, and maximum), dose variations (increments and decrements), and daily frequency (od, bid, tid, qid) can be obtained by means of the available drug titration getters.

```
Ontology ont = new Ontology("DTON.owl");
DrugTitration dt = ont.drugTitration("Bisoprolol", "adult", "Hypertension");
String nullDose  = dt.getNullDose();
String initDose  = dt.getInitDose();
String maxDose   = dt.getMaxDose();
String doseIncr  = dt.getDoseIncr();
String doseDect  = dt.getDoseDecr();
String dailyFreq = dt.getDailyFreq();
```

Fig. 3. DTON ontology Java interface.

3   Testing the Ontology

Hypertension (HTN) is a chronic condition that, according to the WHO, increased from 594 million in 1975 to 1.13 billion in 2015. HTN guidelines have evolved from specific management clinical algorithms in the 2000s s guidelines, to the fragmented units of knowledge in the 2020s s guidelines [20]. Among these knowledge units, we can found step-1 recommendations of a particular drug under certain conditions (e.g., "offer an ACEi or an ARB to adults starting step 1 antihypertensive treatment who [...] are aged under 55 but not of black African or African–Caribbean family origin") or alternative drugs (e.g., "if an ACEi is not tolerated, for example because of cough, offer an ARB"), but also step-2 s-line drugs to supplement the results obtained by first-line drugs (e.g., "if HTN is not controlled in adults taking step 1 treatment of an ACEi or ARB, offer the choice of one of the following drugs in addition to step 1 treatment: a CCB or a thiazide-like diuretic").

Nine of such type of statements were formalized by instantiating the generic models on alternative drug DT, and supplementary drug DT introduced in [25], which are summarized in the state transition diagram of Fig. 4. The table at the bottom of the figure shows the instantiation of the respective guideline statements "offer an ACEi to adults starting step 1 antihypertensive treatment who [...] are aged under 55 but not of black African or African–Caribbean family origin and, if the ACEi is not tolerated, offer an ARB" (alternative DT), and "offer an ARB to adults starting step 1 antihypertensive treatment who have type 2 diabetes and are of any age or family origin and, if HTN is not controlled, offer a CCB in addition to step 1 treatment" (supplementary treatment).

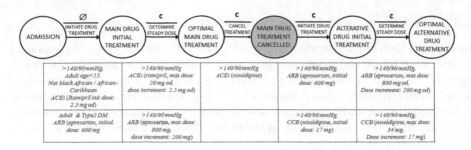

Fig. 4. Alternative and supplementary drug dose titration models.

The DTON ontology was integrated with the decision support system described in [24,25] for DT analysis, which was not originally based on a formal ontology. This system analyzes the short and long term pharmacological treatments of patients, and detects deviations from standard DT models, such as the models introducing alternative and supplementary drugs that require additional DTs. As reported in [24,25], we can use the system to detect deviations from the recommended initial dose, maximum doses exceeded, and wrong dose increments and decrements.

Table 1. HTN guideline statements tested and results (BA/CA: Black-African or Caribbean-African. DM: Diabetes mellitus. WID: wrong initial dose, MDE: maximum dose exceeded, WDI/D: wrong dose increments and decrements).

Statement	Condition	Action	N. pat	WID	MDE	WDI/D
1	Type-2 DM, ACEi not tolerated	-ACEi +ARB	123	21	5	10
2	<55, not BA/CA, ACEi not tolerated	-ACEi +ARB	156	12	81	84
3	≥55, no type-2 DM, CCB not tolerated	-CCB +TLD	203	44	10	20
4	BA/CA, no type-2 DM, CCB not tolerated	-CCB +TLD	164	32	10	13
5	ACEi/ARB does not control HTN	+CCB	262	60	40	19
6	ACEi/ARB does not control HTN	+TLD	314	55	36	20
7	CCB does not control HTN	+ACEi	185	37	9	5
8	CCB does not control HTN	+ARB	144	30	12	11
9	CCB does not control HTN	+TLD	219	39	30	10

For the test, the drugs in bold (see Appendix) were taken. The nine HTN clinical guideline [20] statements tested, concerning step-1 and step-2 treatment of HTN, are summarized in Table 1. For instance, statement 1 says that for type-2 diabetic patients receiving ACEi, which is not tolerated, ACEi is replaced by the alternative drug of the type ARB. Statement 8 says that for any HTN patient receiving a CCB drug, which is unable to control HTN, a supplementary drug of the type ARB should be incorporated to the treatment.

The DTON ontology was tested on a range of 123–262 patients, accounting for 758, 1007, 888, 719, 1620, 1934, 1088, 665, and 969 encounters, respectively. Relative to the number of encounters, wrong initial doses (WID) were more frequent in statements 3, 4, and 9 ($\geq 4.5\%$), the greatest maximum doses excesses (MDE) were detected for statements 2 (8%) and 9 (3.1%). Dose increment and decrement errors were proportionally more frequent for statement 2 (8.3%). In general, knowledge represented by statement 2 is the least fulfilled by the patients whose records were analyzed, with a total 17.6% of wrong DT decisions, and therefore the one requiring more attention in the management of HTN patients.

4   Discussion and Conclusions

Drug titration (DT) is a knowledge-intensive task performed by physicians, which is prone to medical errors, as it has been quantified at national and international levels. Artificial Intelligence offers interesting technologies to develop computer systems to support clinicians in this task, as the WHO recommends. Here, we introduced DTON, a formal ontology that gathers dose information about drugs and which is a key component of the DT decision support system described in [24, 25]. Once integrated, DTON was successfully applied to detect deviations from standard DT statements in the management of HTN patients. Extensions to further drugs, guidelines, and DT constraints [1] are possible, but they could imply minor modifications of the current ontology, according to the incremental knowledge engineering approach adopted. At the moment, only retrospective analysis of data has been tested. In the future, prospective use of the DT support system is planned. Other two main research lines will be continued: on the one hand, the extension of DT models to consider, e.g., drug interactions and adverse drug effects and, on the other hand, the application on multi-center databases for DT clinical quality assessment.

Acknowledgments. The authors acknowledge support from the Slovenian Research Agency (Research Core Funding No. P2-0057) and the Spanish Ministry of Science and Innovation (Funding Code PID2019-105789RB-I00).

Appendix. Summary of drug information in the ontology

Drug Type	Drug Name	Patient Group	Disease	Init dose	Max dose	Dose incr	Frequency
BB	Acebutolol	adult	HTN	200 mg	400 mg	200 mg[*]	bid
	Atenolol	adult	HTN	50 mg	100 mg	50 mg[*]	od
	Bisoprolol	**adult**	**HTN**	**5 mg**	**20 mg**	**5 mg**	**od**
	Metoprolol (tartrate)	adult	HTN	50 mg	90 mg	50 mg[*]	Bid
	Metoprolol (succinate)	adult	HTN	25 mg	450 mg	25 mg[*]	od
	Nadolol	adult	HTN	40 mg	320 mg	40 mg[*]	od
	Nebivolol	adult	HTN	5 mg	40 mg	5 mg[*]	od
	Propranolol	adult	HTN	40 mg	640 mg	40 mg[*]	od
		Child	HTN	0.04 mg/kg	8 mg/kg	0.04 mg/kg	Qid
		1y-17y	HTN	0.3 mg/kg	213 mg/day	1.3 mg/kg	Tid
ACEi	Benazepril	adult	HTN	10 mg	80 mg	10 mg[*]	od
		6y-17y	HTN	0.2 mg/kg	40 mg/day	0.2 mg/kg[*]	od
	Captopril	adult	HTN	25 mg	450 mg	25 mg	Tid
	Enalapril	adult	HTN	5 mg	40 mg	5 mg[*]	od
		1M-17y	HTN	0.08 mg/kg	0.58 mg/kg	0.08 mg/kg[*]	od
	Fosinopril	adult	HTN	10 mg	40 mg	10 mg[*]	od
	Lisinopril	adult	HTN	5 mg	80 mg	5 mg[*]	od
		Geriatric	HTN	2.5 mg	40 mg	2.5 mg	od
		6y-17y	HTN	0.07 mg/kg	0.61 mg/kg	0.07 mg/kg[*]	od
	Moexipril	adult	HTN	7.5 mg	60 mg	7.5 mg[*]	od
	Perindopril	adult	HTN	4 mg	16 mg	4 mg[*]	od
		>70y	HTN	4 mg	16 mg	4 mg	od
	Quinapril	adult	HTN	10 mg	80 mg	10 mg	od
	Ramipril	**adult**	**HTN**	**2.5 mg**	**20 mg**	**2.5 mg**[*]	**od**
	Trandolapril	adult non-black	HTN	1 mg	4 mg	1 mg[*]	od
		adult black	HTN	2 mg	4 mg	2 mg[*]	od
TLD	Chlorothiazide	adult	HTN	500 mg	1000 mg mg	500 mg[*]	od
		<6M	HTN	5 mg/kg	125 mg	5 mg/kg[*]	Bid
		6M-2y	HTN	5 mg/kg	125 mg	5 mg/kg[*]	Bid
		2y-12y	HTN	5 mg/kg	500 mg	5 mg/kg[*]	Bid
	Chlorthalidone	adult	HTN	25 mg	100 mg	50 mg	od
	Hydrochlorothiazide	**adult**	**HTN**	**12.5 mg**	**25 mg**	**12.5 mg**[*]	**bid**
		< 6M	**HTN**	**1.5 mg/kg**	**1.5 mg/kg**	**0 mg/kg**	**bid**
		6M-2y	**HTN**	**0.5 mg/kg**	**1 mg/kg**	**0.5 mg/kg**[*]	**bid**
		2y-12y	**HTN**	**0.5 mg/kg**	**50 mg**	**1.5 mg/kg**[*]	**bid**
	Indapamide	adult	HTN	1.25 mg	-	-	od
	Metolazone (Zaroxolyn)	adult	HTN	2.5 mg	-	-	od
	Metolazone (Mykrox)	adult	HTN	0.5 mg	-	-	od
PSD	Spironalactone	adult	HTN	50–100 mg	400 mg	50 mg	od
ARB	Azilsartan (Edarbi)	-	-	80 mg	80 mg	0 mg	od
	Candesartan (Atacand)	adult	HTN	16 mg	32 mg	8 mg	od
		1y-6y	HTN	0.2 mg/kg	-	-	od
		6y-17y <50kg	HTN	4–8 mg	-	-	od
		6y-17y >50kg	HTN	8–16 mg	-	-	od
	Eprosartan	**adult**	**HTN**	**600 mg**	**800 mg**	**200 mg**	**od**
	Irbesartan (Avapro)	adult	HTN	150 mg	300 mg	150 mg	od
	Losartan (Cozaar)	adult	HTN	50 mg	100 mg	50 mg	od
		>=6y	HTN	0.7 mg/kg	50 mg	-	od
	Olmesartan (Benicar)	adult	HTN	20 mg	40 mg	20 mg	od
		6y-16y 20–35kg	HTN	10 mg	20 mg	10 mg	od
		6y-16y >35kg	HTN	20 mg	40 mg	20 mg	od
	Telmisartan (Micardis)	adult	HTN	40 mg	-	-	od
	Valsartan (Diovan)	adult	HTN	80 mg	320 mg	80 mg	od
		6y-16y	HTN	1.3 mg/kg	40 mg	-	od
AB	Doxazosin (Cardura)	adult	HTN	1 mg	16 mg	Double	od
	Prazosin (Minipress)	adult	HTN	1 mg	10 mg	-	Bid
	Terazosin	adult	HTN	1 mg	20 mg	2 mg	od
CCB	Amlodipine (Norvasc)	adult	HTN	5 mg	10 mg	5 mg	od
		geriatric	HTN	2.5 mg	10 mg	2.5 mg	od
		6y-17y	HTN	-	5 mg	-	od
	Diltiazem (Extended Release Caps.)	adult	HTN	120 mg	540 mg	120 mg	od
	Felodipine	adult	HTN	5 mg	-	-	od
		geriatric	HTN	2.5 mg	-	-	od
		>1y	HTN	2.5 mg	10 mg	2.5 mg	od
	Isradipine (Immediate-release Caps.)	adult	HTN	2.5 mg	20 mg	2.5 mg	Bid
	Nicardipine (oral Immediate-release)	adult	HTN	20 mg	-	-	Tid
	Nifedipine (Procardia)	adult	HTN	10 mg	40 mg	10 mg	Tid
	Nisoldipine	**adult**	**HTN**	**17 mg**	**34 mg**	**17 mg**	**od**
	Verapamil (Calan SR)	adult	HTN	120 mg	480 m	120 mg	od

(*) If no explicit information is found about dose increments, they are made equal to initial dose.

Notation: (BB) beta-bocker, (ACEi) angiotensin converting enzyme inhibitor, (TLD) thiazide-like diuretic, (PSD) potassium-sparing diuretic, (ARB) angiotensin-II receptor blocker, (AB) alpha-blocker, and (CCB) calcium channel blocker.

References

1. Anselma, L., Terenziani, P., Montani, S., Bottrighi, A.: Towards a comprehensive treatment of repetitions, periodicity and temporal constraints in clinical guidelines. Artif. Intell. Med. **38**(2), 171–95 (2006). https://doi.org/10.1016/j.artmed.2006.03. 007
2. Bhattacharyya, S.B.: Introduction to SNOMED CT. Springer, Heidelberg (2015)
3. Carroll, R., Mudge, A., Suna, J., Denaro, C., Atherton, J.: Prescribing and up-titration in recently hospitalized heart failure patients attending a disease management program. Int. J. Cardiol. **216**, 121–27 (2016)
4. Connelly, D., Cotterell, M.: Medication errors: where do they happen? Pharm. J. Inforgraphic (2019)
5. Ethier, J.F., Goyer, F., Fabry, P., Barton, A.: The prescription of drug ontology 2.0 (PDRO): more than the sum of its parts. Int. J. Environ. Res. Public Health **18**, 12025 (2021). https://doi.org/10.3390/ijerph182212025
6. Feldman, H.J., Dumontier, M., Ling, S., Haider, N., Hogue, C.W.: CO: a chemical ontology for identification of functional groups and semantic comparison of small molecules. FEBS Lett. **579**(21), 4685–4691 (2005). https://doi.org/10.1016/j.febslet.2005.07.039
7. Fox, G.N., Kaleem, U., Music, E.: Epocrates essentials: is the expanded product an improvement? J. Fam. Pract. **54**(1), 57–63 (2005)
8. Gómez-Pérez, A., Martínez-Romero, M., Rodríguez-González, A., Vázquez, G., Vázquez-Naya, J.M.: Ontologies in medicinal chemistry: current status and future challenges. Curr. Top. Med. Chem. **13**(5), 576–590 (2013)
9. Hanna, J., Joseph, E., Brochhausen, M., Hogan, W.R.: Building a drug ontology based on RxNorm and other sources. J Biomed. Semant. **4**(1), 44 (2013). https://doi.org/10.1186/2041-1480-4-44
10. Hastings, J., de Matos, P., et al.: The ChEBI reference database and ontology for biologically relevant chemistry: enhancements for 2013. Nucleic Acids Res. **41**(Database issue), D456–D463 (2013). https://doi.org/10.1093/nar/gks1146
11. Hastings, J., Chepelev, L., et al.: The chemical information ontology: provenance and disambiguation for chemical data on the biological semantic web. PLoS One **6**(10), e25513 (2011). https://doi.org/10.1371/journal.pone.0025513
12. Hickey, A., Suna, J., et al.: Improving medication titration in heart failure by embedding a structured medication titration plan. Int. J. Cardiol. **224**, 99–106 (2016)
13. Health first Europe, declaration for patient safety working document (2017). https://healthfirsteurope.eu/wp-content/uploads/2017/12/PS-Declaration-Working-Document-004.pdf
14. Landry, M., Lafrenière, S., Patry, S., Potvin, S., Lemasson, M.: The clinical relevance of dose titration in electroconvulsive therapy: a systematic review of the literature. Psychiatry Res. **294**, 113497 (2020)
15. Maxwell, S.: Chapter 2: therapeutics and good prescribing: choosing a dosing regime. In Walker BR, et al. (eds.). Davidson's Principles and Practice of Medicine, p. 34. Elsevier Health Sciences (2013). ISBN 978-0-7020-5103-6
16. Multi-drug interaction checker (2021). http://reference.medscape.com/drug-interactionchecker
17. Michel, M.C., Staskin, D.: Understanding dose titration: overactive bladder treatment with fesoterodine as an example. Europ. Urology Suppls. **10**, 8–13 (2011)

18. Miftahurrohmah, B., Iriawan, N., Wulandari, C., Dharmawan, Y.S.: Individual control optimization of drug dosage using individual Bayesian pharmacokinetics model approach. Procedia Comput. Sci. **161**, 593–600 (2019)
19. Mirinejad, H., Gaweda, A.E., Brier, M.E., Zurada, J.M., Inanc, T.: Individualized drug dosing using RBF-Galerkin method: case of anemia management in chronic kidney disease. Comput. Methods Programs Biomed. **148**, 45–53 (2017)
20. NICE. Hypertension in adults: diagnosis and management (2019). www.nice.org.uk/guidance/ng136
21. Nikiema, J.N., Liang, M.Q., Després, P., Motulsky, A.: OCRx: canadian drug ontology. Stud. Health Technol. Inf. **281**, 367–371 (2021)
22. Poveda-Villalón, María, Espinoza-Arias, Paola, Garijo, Daniel, Corcho, Oscar: Coming to terms with fair ontologies. In: Keet, C. Maria., Dumontier, Michel (eds.) EKAW 2020. LNCS (LNAI), vol. 12387, pp. 255–270. Springer, Cham (2020). https://doi.org/10.1007/978-3-030-61244-3_18
23. Reyes-Peña, C., Vidal, M. T., Bravo, M., Motz, R.: Drug ontology for the public mexican health system. In CEUR Workshop Proceedings, pp. 58–69 (2020)
24. Riaño, David, Kamišalić, Aida: Modelling and assessment of one-drug dose titration. In: Tucker, Allan, Henriques Abreu, Pedro, Cardoso, Jaime, Pereira Rodrigues, Pedro, Riaño, David (eds.) AIME 2021. LNCS (LNAI), vol. 12721, pp. 459–468. Springer, Cham (2021). https://doi.org/10.1007/978-3-030-77211-6_55
25. Riaño, D., Alonso, J.R., Pečnik, S., Kamišalić, A.: Modelling and assessing one- and two-drug dose titrations. Submitted as selected invited paper to AIIM (2022)
26. Schuck, R.N., Pacanowski, M., Kim, S., et al.: Use of titration as a therapeutic individualization strategy: an analysis of food and drug administration-approved drugs. Clin. Transl. Sci. **12**(3), 236–39 (2019)
27. Tariq RA, Vashisht R, Sinha A, et al.: Medication dispensing errors and prevention. In: StatPearls. Treasure Island (FL): StatPearls Publishing (2022). https://www.ncbi.nlm.nih.gov/books/NBK519065/
28. Truda, G., Marais, P.: Evaluating warfarin dosing models on multiple datasets with a novel software framework and evolutionary optimisation. J. Biomed. Inf. **113**, 103634 (2019)
29. Drugs & medications browser (2021). https://www.webmd.com/drugs/2/index
30. Medication errors: technical series on safer primary care. geneva: world health organization (2016). Licence: CC BY-NC-SA 3.0 IGO
31. WHO launches global effort to halve medication-related errors in 5 years (2017). https://www.who.int/news/item/29-03-2017-who-launches-global-effort-to-halve-medication-related-errors-in-5-years
32. WHO collaborating centre for drug statistics methodology: guidelines for ATC classification and DDD assignment 2021. 24th Edition (2021). https://www.whocc.no/filearchive/publications/2021_guidelines_web.pdf

Ontological Representation of Causal Relations for a Deep Understanding of Associations Between Variables in Epidemiology

Thibaut Pressat Laffouilhère[1,2,3]([✉]), Julien Grosjean[1,4], Jean Pinson[5],
Stéfan J. Darmoni[1,4], Emilie Leveque[2], Emilie Lanoy[6], Jacques Bénichou[2,7],
and Lina F. Soualmia[3,4]

[1] CHU Rouen, Department of Biomedical Informatics, Rouen University Hospital, Rouen, France
{t.pressat,julien.grosjean,stefan.darmoni}@chu-rouen.fr
[2] CHU Rouen, Department of Biostatistics, Rouen University Hospital, Rouen, France
{emilie.leveque,jacques.benichou}@chu-rouen.fr
[3] Normandie Univ, UNIROUEN, LITIS-TIBS EA 4108, Rouen, France
lina.soualmia@chu-rouen.fr
[4] INSERM U1142 LIMICS, Sorbonne Université, Paris, France
[5] CHU Rouen, Department of Surgery, Rouen, France
jean.pinson@chu-rouen.fr
[6] Biostatistics and Epidemiology Unit, Gustave-Roussy, Villejuif, France
emilie.lanoy@wanadoo.fr
[7] INSERM U1018, CESP, Université Paris-Saclay, Paris, France

Abstract. Understanding statistical results is crucial in order to spread right conclusions. In observational studies, statistical results are often reported as associations without going further. However, each association comes from causal relations. Causal diagrams are visual representations enabling to understand causal mechanisms behind the association found. In the era of big data and growing number of variables, visual approaches become inefficient. Ontological representation of causality and reasoning could help to explain statistical results. OntoBioStat is a domain ontology related to covariate selection and bias for biostatistician users. It was designed using expert corpus from comprehensive literature review, and validated by three biostatisticians accustomed to causal diagrams. In this paper, we focused on the presentation of an OntoBioStat's feature able to infer explanations about statistical associations. The ontologization of the feature of interest resulted in 14 object properties, three classes and five Semantic Web Rule Language rules. Each rule allows to infer a different object-property that explains statistical association between two variables. Rules are based on *isCauseof* statements between different individuals. OntoBioStat feature performances were illustrated through a real-life retrospective observational study. From 28 instances and 48 object properties stated, a set of 1,939 object properties were inferred. OntoBioStat explained 65% of the 48 statistical associations found. In conclusion, OntoBioStat could help to explain a part of the significant statistical associations between two variables but cannot yet predict significant ones.

Keywords: Ontology · Epidemiology · Causality

M. Michalowski et al. (Eds.): AIME 2022, LNAI 13263, pp. 47–56, 2022.
https://doi.org/10.1007/978-3-031-09342-5_5

1 Introduction

The representation of causal relations between variables in epidemiology is crucial for estimating a true causal effect and also for explaining spurious associations between two variables. Several knowledge representations could be used such as the Sufficient Component Cause (SCC) model [1], Directed Acyclic Graphs (DAGs) [2], or Causal Diagrams (CDs) [3]. These latter enable researchers to represent variables as nodes, and causal relations as directed (→), bidirected (↔) or non-directed (–) edges. A unidirectional edge from a node X to a node Y means that X is one of the causes of Y. Two variables share an ancestor if they have a common cause (bidirectional edge). Two variables share a descendant if they have a common constant (not variable) effect (non-directional edge). CDs have been widely used to represent collider-bias or over-adjustment bias, both resulting in spurious associations [4, 5]. Interpreting statistical association in observational studies is an open discussion in the epidemiologists' community. Researchers might be discouraged to explain all the associations (spurious or not) found during the research process, because of the amount of growing variables and statistical tests. Moreover, young ones could misinterpret association in bivariate or multivariate analysis. CD or DAG that are actual standard for covariate selection have poor expressivity and hence limited knowledge representation.

In order to help researchers in (re)producing, understanding their statistical results and sharing hypothesis based on knowledge representation in biomedical research, ontologies could be used. Several ontologies in the domain of biology and statistics have been created such as Ontology of Biological and Clinical Statistics (OBCS) [6] mapped with Statistical Ontology (STATO) (http://stato-ontology.org) and Ontology of Biomedical Investigations (OBI) [7] or the Ontology of Clinical Research [8]. However, they do not cover the understanding of the association found between two variables. In this context, an ontology dedicated to the covariate selection and causal representations may be more useful. Statistical Learning Ontology can answer to "What are the variables correlated with…?" but the answer is based on statements only queried with SPARQL, and not by inferences [9]. Ontologies representing causal relation are numerous [10–12] but their design was not driven by the competency question cited above and their formalism not adapted to the sufficient, counterfactual and necessary cause representation.

We designed the OntoBioStat [13] ontology in order to assist biostatiscians users and researchers in many tasks such as causal diagram design, covariate selection, and for providing explanations for the statistical association between two variables. In this paper, we focus on the latter feature corresponding to the seventh and last competency question. Hence, only a subset of the ontology will be presented. The paper is organized as follows: first the structure of OntoBioStat is introduced, then the feature of interest, and finally a use case is provided to illustrate our work. The obtained results are discussed, and we give an outlook to further work.

2 Materials and Methods

2.1 The OntoBioStat Ontology and Feature Focus

OntoBioStat is a domain ontology related to covariate selection and bias for causal inference in observational studies intended for biostatistician users. The last version is publicly available at https://bioportal.bioontology.org/ontologies/OBS. OntoBioStat is expressed using the Ontology Web Language (OWL) standard [14] and was designed using Protégé 5.5 [15]. OntoBioStat is composed by: (i) 53 classes, such as 'Variable', 'Covariate' or 'Path_Modifier'; (ii) 33 object-properties, such as *isCauseof* or *Share_ancestor*; (iii) 11 data-properties; (iv) nine equivalent class axioms; (v) 28 instances; and (vi) 29 rules in Semantic Web Rule Language (SWRL). The reasoning process is supported by Pellet inference tool [16]. OntoBioStat provides a broad framework for knowledge representation needed in case of covariate selection for true causal estimation between two variables. Variables representation integrates 'Meta_Variable' subclasses such as 'Location' and 'Period'. Three types of causal relation are represented: (i) counterfactual probabilistic cause represented with object properties presented in this article (e.g. *isCauseof*); (ii) necessary causes with upper classes; and (iii) sufficient cause with object properties not described here (*Contraindication* and *Absolute_indication*). Object properties related to interaction (*isModifiedby*), missing data cause (*isCauseofNA*), and the explicit statement of no causal relation (*NotCauseof*) were defined but not developed here either.

The OntoBioStat feature was built using a corpus from comprehensive literature review. Articles about covariate selection or bias for statistical modelling using DAGs (or CDs) were included. The following query was processed in PubMed: [Directed Acyclic Graph OR Causal Diagram] with English language filter. The extracted terms related to this feature are definitions, representations, and synonyms of relations used in DAGs and CDs. The extracted corpus contains seven terms describing four relations between two variables: (i) direct effect/child/descendant is represented with a unidirectional/single headed arrow/arc/edge; (ii) common/share cause/ancestor/parent is represented with bidirectional/two-headed arrow; (iii) share descendant is represented with undirected/non-directional path (one or more succession of edges); and (iv) indirect effect (effect mediated by another variable) [3, 4, 17–21]. This corpus was validated manually by three biostatisticians (TPL, ELa, ELe) accustomed to the use of DAGs and observational studies. The feature's ontologization was driven by (i) corpus, (ii) tutorial for building DAG and CD published in peer review articles or books [22–24], (iii) theoretical cases from CD representation such as bidirected, non-directed, directed edges, and (iv) the seventh competency question: 'What type of relation exists between two variables?'. Indeed, OntoBioStat design was built in order to answer seven competency question about confounding and bias.

In this section we focus on 14 non-reflexive object-properties (Fig. 1), three classes, and five SWRL rules (rule (1), rule (2), rule (3), rule (4), and rule (5)).

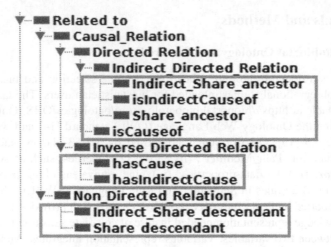

Fig. 1. OntoBioStat object properties representing variables relations. (Color figure online)

Related_to (X, Y) is a symmetric property that means that a significant statistical association between X and Y should exist. The *Inverse_Directed_Relation* properties are inferred thanks to inverse properties. Bidirectional edges (share ancestor) and non-directional edges (share descendant) in CDs were defined as symmetric properties. *isCauseof*, *hasCause*, and *isIndirectCauseof* are asymmetric object-properties. *Causal_Relation, Directed_Relation, Indirect_Directed_Relation, Inverse_Directed_Relation, Non_Directed_Relation* were created in order to group the eight initial properties represented in Fig. 1 (red framed) and in Fig. 2. For a better understanding, and because the inferred properties are numerous, only few of them are displayed in the Fig. 2. Indirect relations are causal relations between two variables when a third stands between them. Directed relations refer to CD representation with directed edges. Non directed relations refer to the undirected edge from CD.

Inferred_Variable(?y) ∧ Inferred_Variable(?x) ∧ *Inverse_Directed_Relation*(?y, ?x)
∧ *Inverse_Directed_Relation*(?z, ?y) → *isIndirectCauseof* (?x, ?z)   (1)

Covariate(?z) ∧ Inferred_Variable(?y) ∧ *isCauseof* (?z, ?x) ∧ *isCauseof* (?z, ?y) →
Share_ancestor(?x, ?y)   (2)

Path_Modifier(?z) ∧ Inferred_Variable(?x) ∧ Inferred_Variable(?y) ∧ *isCauseof* (?y,
?z) ∧ *isCauseof* (?x, ?z) → *Share_descendant*(?x, ?y)   (3)

Covariate(?y) ∧ *Share_ancestor*(?x, ?y) ∧ *Inverse_Directed_Relation*(?z, ?y) →
Indirect_Share_ancestor(?x, ?z)   (4)

Path_Modifier(?z) ∧ Inferred_Variable(?y) ∧ Inferred_Variable(?x) ∧ *Directed_Relation*

(?y, ?z) ∧ *Indirect_Directed_Relation*(?x, ?z) → *Indirect_Share_descendant*(?x, ?y)

∧ *hasDescendant*(?y, ?z) ∧ *hasDescendant*(?x, ?z)   (5)

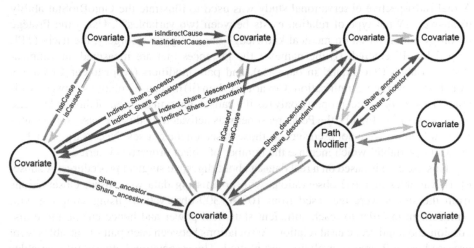

Fig. 2. Example of inferences based on *isCauseof* statements (in blue). Inverse properties (in green) and partial inferences are based on OntoBioStat SWRL rules (in red). (Color figure online)

Grouping the eight properties in upper object properties enables to reduce the number of SWRL rules. Indeed, SWRL rules do not allow the use of 'OR'. For example, *Share_ancestor* is defined by: *isCauseof* and *isCauseof* or *isCauseof* and *isIndirect-Causeof* or *isIndirectCauseof* and *isIndirectCauseof*. *Share_ancestor* is also summarized by *Inverse_Directed_Relation* and *Inverse_Directed_Relation* (rule 1). *Related_to* descendants are inferred based on *isCauseof* statements.

The class 'Covariate' *subClassof* 'Variable' has to be stated in order to infer the *Causal_Relation* descendants. Concerning the *Non_Directed_Relation* descendant, the class 'Path_Modifier' has to be stated instead of 'Covariate'. A path modifier is a variable that is constant and adjusted for or use in matching methods in order to estimate true causal effect between two variables [25]. The class 'Inferred_Variable' groups 'Covariate', 'Exposure', and 'Outcome'. These three classes are useful in order to answer different competency questions about confounding that are not developed here. 'Path_Modifier' is a "dead end". Hence, inferred edges may be pointed at it but cannot start from, it except in case of *Share_ancestor* or *hasCause* (Fig. 2).

In all the rules x, y, and z are different individuals in order to respect the non-reflexive object properties. Indeed, given four variables w, x, y, z: z *isCauseof* x and w, and the couple (x, w) *isCauseof* y. Without 'differentFrom' statements y *Indirect_Share_ancestor* with y. In the rule (1) x and y must be 'Inferred_Variable' because transitivity is interrupt by any 'Path_Modifier'. In the rule (4) y must be a 'Covariate' for the same reason. In the rule (5) *Directed_Relation* ($\rightarrow$, $\rightarrow$ $\rightarrow$, $\leftrightarrow$, $\leftrightarrow$ $\rightarrow$) and *Indirect_Directed_Relation* ($\rightarrow$ $\rightarrow$, $\leftrightarrow$, $\leftrightarrow$ $\rightarrow$) enable to infer two types of *Indirect_Share_descendant*. Indeed, two variables indirectly share a descendant if one of them is a direct cause of descendant, or if both are indirect cause of descendant (share ancestor included) (Fig. 2).

2.2 Use Case

A real retrospective observational study was used to illustrate the OntoBioStat ability to answer: "What type of relation exists between two variables?". Using the Protégé ontology editor, based on medical knowledge about digestive surgery, the users (TPL helped by JP) entered: (i) the name of the instances that are measured and unmeasured variables ('Covariate' in our case), and path modifiers (Adjustment_Covariate, Matched_Covariate, Stratification_Covariate); then (ii) the causal relations between variables (*isCauseof* object property only) as if a causal diagram or a causal directed acyclic graph was drawn. Finally, the Pellet reasoner was activated. In this use case, some OntoBioStat features were not used such as those based on the classes 'Necessary_Variable' or 'Meta_Variable' which increase the number of object properties inferred.

This use case is based on a real dataset about digestive surgical procedures. A subset of 16 variables and 102 observations with no missing data were used. Observations from the subset were increased from 102 to 300 observations using sampling with replacement in order to reach sufficient statistical power and hence enable more discussion about indirect causal relation. Associations between each pair of variables were assessed using Pearson correlation and plotted. The association between two variables was expressed as *p-value* (no estimate and no confidence interval). Significant *p-values* (<0.05) were explained with OntoBioStat inferences. The Protégé interface provides 'explain inference' feature that displays the reasoner steps for a given inference. Object properties are not mutually exclusives. For example, an association could be explained by *Share_ancestor* and *isCauseof*. Two multivariate models were computed in order to give examples of the class 'Path_Modifier' impact. The models results were expressed with estimate and *p-value* before and after adjustment. Statistical analyses were performed using R software and the corrplot package.

3 Results

An amount of 28 different instances of 'Covariate' and 48 *isCauseof* were entered, and then 1,939 object properties were inferred in less than five seconds (Fig. 3).

A total of 48 p-values were significant (Fig. 4) and 31 were explained by the following object properties: (i) ten *isCauseof* (e.g. **corticosteroid therapy** *isCauseof* **immunosuppression**); (ii) 12 *isIndirectCauseof* (e.g. **sex** *isIndirectCauseof* **ASA score** because **sex** *isCauseof* **arthritic disease**, **arthritic disease** *isCauseof* **organe failure at the beginning** *isCauseof* **ASA score**); (iii) ten *Share_ancestor* (e.g. **bmi** and **diabete** *Share_ancestor* **health behavior**); (iv) 11 *Indirect_Share_ancestor* (e.g. **surgical complication at 90 days** (Clavien-Dindo) *Indirect_Share_ancestor* with **post operative intensive care unit** because **Hinchey** *isCauseof* **organe failure at the beginning** and **surgical complication at 90 days** (Clavien-Dindo) and **organe failure at the beginning** *isCauseof* **post operative intensive care unit**). Two explanations (two different object properties) were given for 12 associations.

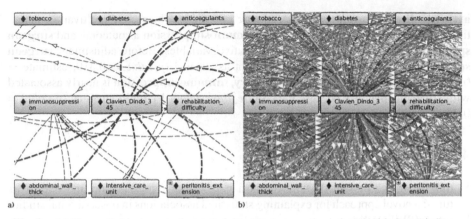

Fig. 3. a) isCauseof object properties stated, b) object properties inferred with OntoBioStat.

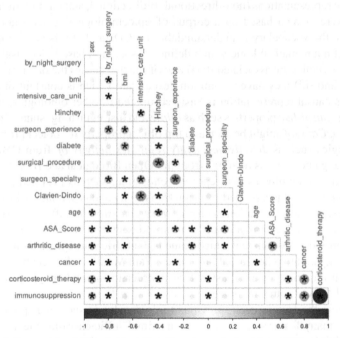

Fig. 4. Correlation matrix of 16 variables. Significant correlations (p < 0.05) are highlighted with a star symbol.

The first multivariate statistical model is a linear regression with **ASA score** as outcome and **sex** and **arthritic disease** as explicative variables. Before adjustment **sex** and **ASA score** are associated because **sex** *isIndirectCauseof* **ASA score** (*p-value* = 0.004, estimate = −0.25). After adjustment for **arthritic disease, sex** is no longer associated with **ASA score** because the path was intercepted by the 'Path_Modifier'

arthritic disease (*p-value* = 0.09, estimate = −0.14). The second multivariate statistical model is a logistic regression with **immunosuppression** as outcome and **surgeon specialty** and **by night surgery** as explicative variables. Before adjustment **surgeon specialty** and **immunosuppression** are not associated (*p-value* = 0.319, estimate = 0.72). After adjustment for **by night surgery, immunosuppression** is nearly associated with **surgeon specialty** because they *Share_descendant* **by night surgery** (*p-value* = 0.08, estimate = 1.36).

4   Discussion

In this paper, we presented OntoBioStat a new causal representation and one of its features: a novel approach for explaining statistical associations in observational studies based on SWRL rules.

Concerning causal representation, OntoBioStat succeeds in the implementation of the CDs edge representations (non-directional, bidirectional, and unidirectional). Object properties were created based on a corpus of epidemiological articles about CDs or DAGs, hence the vocabulary is understandable by CDs and DAGs users. Object properties respect mathematical logic which defines association based on causal reasoning. Indeed, two variables are associated if: (i) one of the two causes the other, (ii) they share an ancestor, and (iii) they have a common descendant which is constant in the sample studied. This causal representation is basic compared to other ontologies of causation representing *causal-like* properties such as *allow* and distinguishing 'states' from 'event' classes [10]. *isCauseof* might be seen as a top object property for object properties from other ontologies such as *directly negatively regulates activity of* from OBO Relation Ontology that gather various relations from the Open Biological and Biomedical Ontology [26]. Existing ontologies that represent causation, such as [27] and [10], inferred *explain* or *maycause* object properties using transitivity and is_a relation. However, they do not represent indirect relation such as *Share_ancestor* or sufficient cause such as *Contraindication,* and cannot infer any common descendant. The class 'Path_Modifier' integration provides a significant added value to OntoBioStat representation, and hence reasoning compared to other causal ontologies. Path Modifier class enables to deal with variables that are constant or adjusted for, in order to infer *Share_descendant* object property and 'block' some inferences.

Concerning the feature itself, previous tools developed such as R package dagitty [28] provide many features (path analysis, minimal sufficient adjustment sets) but not the explanation feature nor the complex causal representation.

Concerning statistical association explanations, unlike previous manual and visual approaches using DAG or CD representations, OntoBioStat provides automatic inferences. Indeed, visual approaches become inefficient with the growing number of variables. In our use case, OntoBioStat explained 64.5% of the associations, and 35.5% of the associations remained unexplained. These could be due to erroneous initial knowledge (wrong statements) and multiple statistical testing. Indeed, 136 statistical tests were computed hence near than five percent (n = 7) of these tests discovered an association by mistake. Moreover, a *p-value* < 0.05 does not necessarily mean that an association is clinically significant. Object properties inferred are numerous (n = 1,939) but not always useful for the biostatistician and redundant. Indeed, *isCauseof* statements produce the five following inferences because of hierarchy and inverse relations: *hasCause*, *Inverse_Directed_Relation*, *Directed_Relation*, *Causal_Relation*, and *Related_to*. These five are not always relevant but are needed for simpler SWRL rules and deliver superficial information. In a final interface, inferences would be provided without irrelevant information and focus by default on the eight object properties framed in red in Fig. 1.

In conclusion, despite this interesting 'explanation' feature, it is important to note that OntoBioStat cannot predict significant associations, neither their strength nor their sign. In order to improve OntoBioStat formalism, *isCauseof* object property will be mapped with other ontologies such as the OBO Relation Ontology. In a future use case, OntoBioStat domain will be extended from covariate selection and bias in observational study to knowledge mining using existing drug knowledge graph with thousands of relations [29].

References

1. Rothman, K.J., Greenland, S.: Causation and causal inference in epidemiology. Am. J. Public Health. **95**(S1), S144–S150 (2005)
2. Pearl, J.: Causality: Models, Reasoning, and Inference. Cambridge University Press, Cambridge, p. 384 (2000)
3. Greenland, S., Pearl, J., Robins, J.M.: Causal diagrams for epidemiologic research. Epidemiology **10**(1), 37–48 (1999)
4. Schisterman, E.F., Cole, S.R., Platt, R.W.: Overadjustment bias and unnecessary adjustment in epidemiologic studies. Epidemiology **20**(4), 488–495 (2009)
5. Westreich, D.: Berkson's Bias, selection Bias, and missing data. Epidemiology **23**(1), 159–164 (2012)
6. Zheng, J., Harris, M.R., Masci, A.M., Lin, Y., Hero, A., Smith, B., et al.: The Ontology of Biological and Clinical Statistics (OBCS) for standardized and reproducible statistical analysis. J. Biomed. Semant. **7**(1), 53 (2016)
7. Bandrowski, A., et al.: The ontology for biomedical investigations. PLoS ONE **11**(4), e0154556 (2016)
8. Sim, I., Tu, S.W., Carini, S., Lehmann, H.P., Pollock, B.H., Peleg, M., et al.: The Ontology of Clinical Research (OCRe): an informatics foundation for the science of clinical research. J. Biomed. Inform. **52**, 78–91 (2014)
9. Behnaz, A., Bandara, M., Rabhi, F.A., Peat, M.: A statistical learning ontology for managing analytics knowledge. In: Mehandjiev, N., Saadouni, B. (eds.) Enterprise Applications, Markets and Services in the Finance Industry: 9th International Workshop, FinanceCom 2018, Manchester, UK, June 22, 2018, Revised Papers, pp. 180–194. Springer International Publishing, Cham (2019). https://doi.org/10.1007/978-3-030-19037-8_12
10. Kahn, C.E.: Transitive closure of subsumption and causal relations in a large ontology of radiological diagnosis. J. Biomed. Inform. **61**, 27–33 (2016)
11. Galton, A.: States, processes and events, and the ontology of causal relations. Frontiers in artificial intelligence and applications. In: Formal Ontology in Information Systems. vol. 239, pp. 279–292 (2012)
12. Rovetto, R.J., Mizoguchi, R.: Causality and the ontology of disease. Appl. Ontology **10**, 79–105 (2015)
13. Pressat Laffouilhère, T., Grosjean, J., Bénichou, J., Darmoni, S.J., Soualmia, L.F.: Ontological models supporting covariates selection in observational studies. Stud. Health Technol. Inform. **27**(281), 1095–1096 (2021)

14. Bock, A., et al.: Smith, OWL 2 Web Ontology Language, W3C Recommendation (2009)
15. Musen, M.A.: The protégé project: a look back and a look forward. AI Matters. Assoc. Comput. Mach. Specif. Interest Group Artif. Intell. 1(4), 4–12 (2015)
16. Sirin, E., Parsia, B., Grau, B.C., Kalyanpur, A., Katz, Y.: Pellet: a practical OWL-DL reasoner. Web Semant. 5(2), 51–53 (2007)
17. Howards, P.P., Schisterman, E.F., Poole, C., Kaufman, J.S., Weinberg, C.R.: 'Toward a clearer definition of confounding' revisited with directed acyclic graphs. Am. J. Epidemiol. 176(6), 506–511 (2012)
18. VanderWeele, T.J., Robins, J.M.: Directed acyclic graphs, sufficient causes, and the properties of conditioning on a common effect. Am. J. Epidemiol. 166(9), 1096–1104 (2007)
19. VanderWeele, T.J., Robins, J.M.: Four types of effect modification: a classification based on directed acyclic graphs. Epidemiology 18(5), 561–568 (2007)
20. VanderWeele, T.J.: Mediation and mechanism. Eur J Epidemiol. 24(5), 217–224 (2009)
21. Shpitser, I., VanderWeele, T.J.: A complete graphical criterion for the adjustment formula in mediation analysis. Int. J. Biostat. 7(1), 16 (2011)
22. Digitale, J.C., Martin, J.N., Glymour, M.M.: Tutorial on directed acyclic graphs. J. Clin. Epidemiol. S0895–4356(21), 00240–00247 (2021)
23. VanderWeele, T.J., Staudt, N.: Causal diagrams for empirical legal research: a methodology for identifying causation, avoiding bias and interpreting results. Law Probab Risk 10(4), 329–354 (2011)
24. Shrier, I., Platt, R.W.: Reducing bias through directed acyclic graphs. BMC Med. Res. Methodol. 8, 70 (2008)
25. Grimes, D.A., Schulz, K.F.: Bias and causal associations in observational research. Lancet 359(9302), 248–252 (2002)
26. Smith, B., Ceusters, W., Klagges, B., Köhler, J., Kumar, A., Lomax, J., et al.: Relations in biomedical ontologies. Genome Biol. 6(5), R46 (2005)
27. Besnard, P., Cordier, M.-O., Moinard, Y.: Ontology-based inference for causal explanation. In: Zhang, Z., Siekmann, J. (eds.) KSEM 2007. LNCS (LNAI), vol. 4798, pp. 153–164. Springer, Heidelberg (2007). https://doi.org/10.1007/978-3-540-76719-0_18
28. Ankan, A.: Wortel, I.M.N., Textor, J.: Testing graphical causal models using the R package "dagitty". Curr. Protoc. 1, e45 (2021)
29. Lelong, R., et al.: Assisting data retrieval with a drug knowledge graph. Stud. Health Technol. Inform. 14(289), 260–263 (2022)

Explainable Clinical Decision Support: Towards Patient-Facing Explanations for Education and Long-Term Behavior Change

William Van Woensel[1]([⊠]) [iD], Floriano Scioscia[2] [iD], Giuseppe Loseto[3] [iD], Oshani Seneviratne[4] [iD], Evan Patton[5] [iD], Samina Abidi[1] [iD], and Lalana Kagal[5] [iD]

[1] Dalhousie University, Halifax, NS B3H 4R2, Canada
william.van.woensel@dal.ca
[2] Polytechnic University of Bari, 70125 Bari, BA, Italy
[3] LUM University "Giuseppe Degennaro", 70010 Casamassima, BA, Italy
[4] Rensselaer Polytechnic Institute, Troy, NY 12180, USA
[5] Massachusetts Institute of Technology, Cambridge, MA 02143, USA

Abstract. There is an increasing shift towards the self-management of long-term chronic illness by patients in a home setting, supported by personal health electronic equipment. Among others, self-management requires comprehensive education on the illness, i.e., understanding the effects of nutritional, fitness, and medication choices on personal health; and long-term health behavior change, i.e., modifying unhealthy lifestyles that contribute to chronic illness. Smart health recommendations, generated using AI-based Clinical Decision Support (CDS), can guide patients towards positive nutritional, fitness, and health behavioral choices. Moreover, we posit that *explaining* these recommendations to patients, using Explainable AI (XAI) techniques, will effect education and positive behavior change. We present our work towards an explanation framework for rule-based CDS, called EXPLAIN (EXPLanations of AI In N3), which aims to generate human-readable, patient-facing explanations.

Keywords: Explainable AI · Clinical Decision Support · Semantic Web

1 Introduction

To improve the quality of life of long-term chronic patients and reduce the pressure on healthcare systems, patients are being increasingly encouraged to self-manage their illness in a home setting [17]. Effective patient self-management is known to require comprehensive education on the illness, i.e., understanding the effects of nutritional, fitness, and drug choices on personal health [10]; and long-term health behavior change, i.e., modifying unhealthy lifestyles that possibly led to and are currently exacerbating chronic illness [16]. We hypothesize that *explaining* smart health recommendations, generated using Artificial Intelligence

© The Author(s), under exclusive license to Springer Nature Switzerland AG 2022
M. Michalowski et al. (Eds.): AIME 2022, LNAI 13263, pp. 57–62, 2022.
https://doi.org/10.1007/978-3-031-09342-5_6

(AI) methods, will (a) improve education, by outlining the underlying rationale in terms of environmental factors, health, and biological processes; and (b) effect long-term behavior change by explaining the risks and benefits of choices and presenting scientific evidence. Indeed, Social Cognitive Theory (SCT) [4] stipulates that health behavior will not be changed without sufficient motivation; among others, motivation is influenced by knowledge on the health risks and benefits of behaviors, which is in line with our approach as described above.

Explanations should be tailored to user characteristics and goals [11,13]: in our case, patients with differing levels of health literacy and cognitive ability, and goals including education and behavior change. Chari et al. [7] identified a range of explanation types from the literature, with different levels of complexity, granularity and system interactivity, and formalized them as the Explanation Ontology. Based on our target audience and their needs, we identify the following useful types of explanations from Chari et al. [7] : (i) *everyday*, explaining recommendations in line with user's knowledge; (ii) *contrastive*, explaining why this recommendation was chosen over another one; (iii) *contextual*, highlighting (modifiable) context factors leading to the recommendation; (iv) *case-based*, explaining what happened the last time the recommendation was (not) followed; (v) *scientific*, highlighting the underlying scientific evidence; and (vi) *trace-based*, outlining the sequence of reasoning steps that led to the recommendation. In general, producing these explanations will require rich knowledge of the patient health profile, including prior decisions, health parameters and environmental context. Personal Health Knowledge Graphs (PHKG), capture this data in the form of a Knowledge Graph (KG); allowing integration with other domain-specific KGs to perform reasoning tailored to the specific patient [12].

We present early work towards an explanation framework, called EXPLAIN (EXPLanations of AI In N3), which generates patient-facing explanations for health recommendations as issued by rule-based AI models. Using EXPLAIN, we implemented two custom explanations styles for trace-based explanation (see above): *narrative*, an everyday explanation that textually narrates the reasoning trace; and *visual*, using a visual layout with pictograms and links for navigating the trace. We aim to apply our work to improve education and behavior change in a self-management setting; here, we consider patients with Chronic Obstructive Pulmonary Disease (COPD), who are prone to acute exacerbations or "flare-ups" with severe symptoms such as choking and breathlessness that often result in hospitalization. The early recognition and treatment of flare-ups has been shown to reduce hospitalization risk. Based on the clinical literature, we compiled a rule-based AI model for (a) stratifying patients into yellow or red zones, based on their exacerbation risk; and (b) suggesting activities based on exertion levels and environmental factors. For a general overview of explainability in knowledge based systems, we refer to Chari et al. [6].

2   Methods

Clinical guidelines, compiled by committees of experts based on the latest medical literature, present evidence-based recommendations on how to diagnose, prognose, and treat illness. Such guidelines can be computerized to provide automated, knowledge-driven CDS, supporting health providers with clinical decision making [9] or patients with self-managing their illness [14]. We computerized clinical guidelines for smart health recommendations into a rule-based AI model serving as a CDS. Below is an example CDS rule in Notation3 (N3) [3]:

```
{?p :hasColoredPhlegm true}=>{?p :stratified :YellowZone }.
```
Listing 1.1. In case the patient (*?p*) has phlegm coloration (*hasColoredPhlegm*), the rule recommends they are stratified in the yellow zone (medium risk of flare-up).

We have developed an initial version of EXPLAIN as a declarative and extensible framework for patient-facing explanations. To implement the core framework logic, we utilize N3 [3], which offers (a) expressive features, such as Scoped Negation as Failure (SNAF), quoted graphs, and series of powerful built-ins; and (b) extensibility, allowing explanation plugins as declarative N3 rulesets. We implemented a bottom-up explanation generation process, producing (1) *Human-readable descriptions* of recommendations, starting with descriptions for individual terms, and building on these to describe the full recommendation, supporting predicates with placeholders (e.g., "has %s exertion") and functors (e.g., math operators); and (2) *High-level explanations* that explain the reasoning behind the recommendation, including *narrative* (an "everyday" explanation) and *visual* (using a visual, navigable layout) explanation styles.

To generate the high-level explanations in step (2), EXPLAIN requires access to the reasoning behind a rule-based recommendation. To that end, we rely on derivation proofs in the Proof Markup Language (PML) [5]. As an interlingua for sharing proofs, PML allows decoupling rule-based AI models from human-readable explanations: a PML-based explanation process, such as EXPLAIN, can thus support any rule-based model that outputs PML, and vice-versa. Currently, we extended *AndroJena* [1] with support for PML proofs [15]; state-of-the-art reasoners such as *eye* [8], which already have an extensive proof mechanism, could be outfitted with PML output as well. In PML, a *NodeSet* represents an intermediary inference or final recommendation, for which an *InferenceStep* provides a justification in terms of other *NodeSets*. The example *NodeSet* below captures a concrete recommendation based on Listing 1.1 from the rule-based CDS, together with the reasoning behind it (using N3):

```
:nodeSetA a pml:NodeSet, pml:hasConclusion [
    prov:value [
        rdf:subject copd:patientA; rdf:predicate copd:stratified;
        rdf:object copd:YellowZone ] ] ;
    prov:wasGeneratedBy [
        a pml:Derivation , pml:InferenceStep ;
        prov:qualifiedAssociation [
            prov:hadPlan :rule1; prov:agent <jena.apache.org> ];
        prov:qualifiedUsage [
            prov:hadRole pml:Antecedent; prov:entity :nsA1 ].
```
Listing 1.2. PML output for a reasoning process behind a recommendation.

The recommendation (*pml:hasConclusion*), which advises (*prov:value*) to stratify the patient into the yellow zone, is justified by a single *Inference Step* (*prov:wasGeneratedBy*). This step involved executing *:rule1* (Listing 1.1) (*prov:qualifiedAssociation, prov:hadPlan*), using an intermediary inference (*prov:qualifiedUsage*) from NodeSet *:nsA1* (*prov:entity*, not shown); this inference supports the rule's single antecedent (*pml:hadRole pml:Antecedent*).

Based on this PML, EXPLAIN generated both a *visual* and *narrative* explanation (Fig. 1); explaining the recommendation as placing the patient in the yellow zone, with a description of the implications, together with the underlying reasons (exertion, phlegm coloration and amount; any of these reasons would suffice). In *visual*, after tapping on the first reason, the underlying reasoning behind it is shown—i.e., a 7 (1-10) was entered for activity exertion[1].

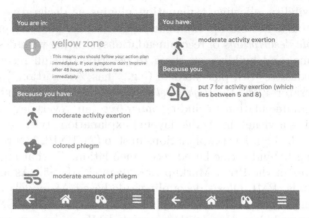

You are stratified into the yellow zone because you have moderate activity exertion, colored phlegm, and moderate amount of phlegm. This means you should follow your action plan immediately. If your symptoms don't improve after 48 hours, seek medical care immediately.
You have moderate activity exertion because you put 7 for activity exertion (which lies between 5 and 8).
You have moderate amount of phlegm because you put 7 for phlegm amount (which lies between 5 and 8).

Fig. 1. Visual and narrative explanation of stratification into yellow zone.

3   Conclusion

In this paper, we described our preliminary work on the EXPLAIN framework for human-readable, patient-facing explanations of rule-based AI models. To utilize the EXPLAIN framework, an application needs to provide PML proof dumps of rule-based recommendations (e.g., as generated by Jena, Eye). Currently, a major limitation involves our reliance on rule-based AI models, and support for only one explanation type (trace-based). An immediate goal involves extending EXPLAIN with more complex, interactive explanation types as described before;

---

[1] Future work involves describing the underlying scientific explanation as well.

and supporting data-driven AI models (e.g., neural networks). We will first evaluate the patient-facing explanations with health providers; our eventual goal is to perform an application-grounded evaluation with actual patients. Finally, to involve patients in the development of XAI solutions, we aim to incorporate explanation-as-a-service into Punya, an end-user development platform [2].

References

1. AndroJena. https://github.com/lencinhaus/androjena
2. Punya platform. http://punya.mit.edu/
3. Arndt, D., Van Woensel, W., Tomaszuk, D.: Notation3: draft community group report (2021). https://w3c.github.io/N3/spec/
4. Bandura, A.: Social cognitive theory of self-regulation. Organ. Behav. Hum. Decis. Process. **50**(2), 248–287 (1991)
5. Berners-Lee, T., McCusker, J., Del Rio, N.: Provenance Markup Language (PML 3.0). https://github.com/timrdf/pml
6. Chari, S., Gruen, D.M., Seneviratne, O., McGuinness, D.L.: Foundations of explainable knowledge-enabled systems. In: Knowledge Graphs for eXplainable Artificial Intelligence: Foundations, Applications and Challenges, Studies on the Semantic Web, vol. 47, pp. 23–48. IOS Press (2020). https://doi.org/10.3233/SSW200010
7. Chari, S., Seneviratne, O., Gruen, D.M., Foreman, M.A., Das, A.K., McGuinness, D.L.: Explanation ontology: a model of explanations for user-centered AI. In: Pan, J.Z., Tamma, V., d'Amato, C., Janowicz, K., Fu, B., Polleres, A., Seneviratne, O., Kagal, L. (eds.) ISWC 2020. LNCS, vol. 12507, pp. 228–243. Springer, Cham (2020). https://doi.org/10.1007/978-3-030-62466-8_15
8. De Roo, J.: Euler Yet another proof Engine - EYE. https://josd.github.io/eye/
9. Peleg, M.: Computer-interpretable clinical guidelines: a methodological review. J. Biomed. Inf. **46**(4), 744–763 (2013)
10. Rose-Davis, B., Van Woensel, W., Abidi, S.R., Stringer, E., Abidi, S.S.R.: Semantic knowledge modeling and evaluation of argument theory to develop dialogue based patient education systems for chronic disease self-management. Int. J. Med. Inf. **160**, 104693 (2022)
11. Sanneman, L., Shah, J.A.: A situation awareness-based framework for design and evaluation of explainable AI. In: Calvaresi, D., Najjar, A., Winikoff, M., Främling, K. (eds.) EXTRAAMAS 2020. LNCS (LNAI), vol. 12175, pp. 94–110. Springer, Cham (2020). https://doi.org/10.1007/978-3-030-51924-7_6
12. Shirai, S., Seneviratne, O., McGuinness, D.L.: Applying personal knowledge graphs to health. CoRR abs/2104.07587 (2021). https://arxiv.org/abs/2104.07587
13. van der Waa, J., Nieuwburg, E., Cremers, A., Neerincx, M.: Evaluating XAI: a comparison of rule-based and example-based explanations. Artif. Intell. **291**, 103404 (2021)
14. Patton, E., Van Woensel, W., Seneviratne, O., Loseto, G., Scioscia, F., Kagal, L. Development of AI-enabled apps by patients and domain experts using the punya platform: a case study for diabetes. In: 20th International Conference on Artificial Intelligence in Medicine (2022)
15. Van Woensel, W.: AndroJena + PML. https://github.com/william-vw/androjena_jre

16. Van Woensel, W., Baig, W.H., Abidi, S.S.R., Abidi, S.R.: A semantic web framework for behavioral user modeling and action planning for personalized behavior modification. In: 10th International Conference on Semantic Web Applications and Tools for Life Sciences. CEUR, Rome, Italy (2017)
17. World health organization: innovative care for chronic conditions. Technical report (2002). https://www.who.int/chp/knowledge/publications/icccglobalreport.pdf

Machine Learning

Assessing Knee Osteoarthritis Severity and Biomechanical Changes After Total Knee Arthroplasty Using Self-organizing Maps

Kathryn Young-Shand(✉) ⓘ, Patrice Roy ⓘ, Michael Dunbar ⓘ,
Syed Sibte Raza Abidi ⓘ, and Janie Wilson ⓘ

Dalhousie University, Halifax, NS, Canada
kathryn.young@dal.ca

Abstract. This study aimed to develop an unsupervised Self-Organizing Map (SOM) based framework to map variability in longitudinal Osteoarthritis (OA) gait biomechanics, and characterize progression pathways within the SOM. Three-dimensional knee kinematics and kinetics observations of asymptomatic (n = 236), moderate knee OA (n = 341), severe knee OA (pre Total Knee Arthroplasty (TKA); n = 145) and post-TKA (n = 201) gait were collected. Principal component analysis (PCA) was applied to frontal and sagittal knee angle and moment waveforms, resulting in an uncorrelated PC score dataset describing 95% of gait waveform variability. PC scores, spatiotemporal gait, and demographic features were applied to the SOM, followed by hierarchical clustering. Clusters were validated by examining inter-cluster differences by chi-squared, k-way ANOVA and Kruskal Wallis tests. OA clinical severity transitioned from mostly asymptomatic to mostly severe across the SOM's x-axis. Age and BMI increased, and gait speed decreased across the SOM. This coincided with worsening knee biomechanics, captured by reduced flexion angle magnitudes, reduced stance-phase flexion moment range, and reduced knee adduction moment mid-stance unloading. Three clusters within the SOM were characterized as 1) High Function Gait; 2) Low Function Gait; and 3) Moderate Function Gait. Knee biomechanics during OA gait can be characterized using SOMs to provide a multidimensional interpretation of gait biomechanics severity pathways. Longitudinal changes in individual SOM location can provide insight into OA progression pathways, with utility to support interventions targeting current or predicted individual functional needs.

Keywords: Cluster analysis · Self-organized maps · Phenotypes · Gait analysis

1 Introduction

Knee Osteoarthritis (OA) is a complex degenerative disease with marked heterogeneity, increasingly being characterized in terms of phenotypes [1–3]. Proposed phenotypes often include biomechanical or structural components deemed to emerge in both OA

Student paper submission.

© The Author(s), under exclusive license to Springer Nature Switzerland AG 2022
M. Michalowski et al. (Eds.): AIME 2022, LNAI 13263, pp. 65–75, 2022.
https://doi.org/10.1007/978-3-031-09342-5_7

disease initiation and manifestation processes [1–3]. OA variability in terms of phenotypes are thought to evolve over the course of the disease process, with end stage joint degradation converging along a common pathway for all patients [2]. To date, OA phenotypes investigation has lacked information on joint-level biomechanics. Further, they have only been derived from cross-sectional datasets, captured at various static time points within the OA progression pathway, defined using variable severity criteria [3–5]. These temporal snapshots have provided no insights into phenotypes that span the longitudinal OA disease progression process, thus limiting our ability to understand if phenotype-specific progression pathways exist. We argue that as we aim to propose phenotype-specific prevention and intervention strategies, a longitudinal view of OA progression before and after interventions such as Total Knee Arthroplasty (TKA) is required to identify phenotypes that impact personalized treatments.

A growing number of studies have applied epidemiological and Machine Learning (ML) based unsupervised clustering to OA populations to discover phenotypes that characterize biomechanically-related variability associated with symptoms, muscle strength, obesity, radiographic severity, cartilage wear, knee alignment, or spatiotemporal features. Specifically, Pinedo Villanueva et al. used hierarchical clustering to identify a high pain group after TKA, the most common end-stage treatment for severe OA [6]. Behrend et al. used hierarchical clustering to characterize three OA clusters based on self-reported joint scores [7]. Knoop et al. applied k-means to identify five clusters based on radiographic severity, muscle strength, BMI, and depression [5]. Incorporating objective functional measures, Elbaz et al. used k-means to report four clusters using spatiotemporal gait parameters [8]. Finally, Waarsing et al. used a model-based clustering approach to identify clusters by demographics, cartilage features, mechanical alignment, and self-reported symptoms, with clusters strongly characterized by joint-level structural degradation [4], indicative of variable functional loading [9]. Not yet characterized is how phenotypes span the OA disease progression process, variability that is important to informing personalized OA interventions.

This study aimed to quantify OA profiles using an unsupervised ML framework to cluster and visually map variability in demographic and knee joint kinematic and kinetics during gait using Self-Organizing Maps (SOM), and to gain novel insights on individual biomechanics spanning OA disease onset and progression. The proposed SOM was trained on longitudinal gait patterns from multiple participants to capture varying levels of knee OA severity: asymptomatic, moderate OA, severe OA prior to TKA (pre-TKA), and post-TKA. Mapped regions and clusters were hypothesized to demonstrate knee biomechanics variability associated with disease severity, and provide evidence of OA phenotypes traveling a multitude of progression pathways relevant to informing targeted treatment strategies.

2   Methods

2.1   Dataset and Feature Selection for Clustering

This is a secondary study using three-dimensional knee joint kinematic and kinetic gait laboratory data collected between 2001–2018 ($n = 945$ gait session/observations; $j = 502$ knees). Participants belonged to one of six OA clinical groups: i) asymptomatic adults with no musculoskeletal injury, disease, or recent surgeries; ii) moderate knee OA diagnosed clinically according to the American College of Rheumatology criteria and not deemed TKA candidates [10]; iii) severe knee OA, seen within one-month pre-TKA; iv) TKA recipient, seen one and/or two years post-TKA; v) TKA revision patient seen within one month pre-revision; vi) and one and/or two years post-revision. As part of the gait protocol, each participant walked along a five-meter walkway wearing comfortable walking shoes at a self-selected speed. Lower-limb external ground reaction forces and kinematics were captured using a force platform sampling at 2000 Hz, synchronized to an optoelectronic motion capture system sampling at 100 Hz. Knee joint angles and moments during gait were represented in the joint coordinate system [11]. Net resultant knee joint moments were calculated using inverse dynamics [12–14], and amplitude normalized to body mass. Gait waveforms were normalized to one complete gait cycle (0–100%). Principal Component Analysis (PCA) was applied to frontal and sagittal plane angle and moment waveforms, resulting in a PC score dataset and corresponding PC loading vectors describing the major modes of variability throughout the gait cycle [15]. Five flexion angle, adduction angle, flexion moment, and adduction moment PCs were retained capturing $\geq 95\%$ of the waveform variance explained.

Kinematic and kinetic gait PC scores (PCs 1–5 for each waveform; 20 gait features), participant age, sex, body mass index (BMI), gait speed, and percent of gait cycle in stance from each session comprised our initial study dataset ([945x25]; 25 features). Distance measures applied during clustering can be sensitive to magnitude and scale differences of input features, and outliers. The dataset was therefore standardized to z-scores (mean = 0, standard deviation = 1), and 13 outlier observations exceeding Tukey's outer fence (3*IQR) were removed ([932x25]). Feature relevance was assessed in terms of clinical group separation by ANOVA f statistic feature ranking using a Bonferroni correction, accepting observations at the 0.002 significance level ($\alpha/25$; $\alpha = 0.05$). Three weakly relevant features (p > 0.002) were removed (adduction angles PC3–4, flexion moment PC5). Consistent with prior studies [4, 5, 8], participant sex was not included in cluster analysis, as features of sex were expected to present in gait waveforms [16, 17]. The final dataset included 923 gait observations and 21 features ([923x21]; $j_{knees} = 495$; Table 1), divided into training (95% of data, [878x21]; $j_{knees} = 484$), and test sets (5% of data, [45x21], $j_{knees} = 45$) to maximize the training data size to achieve good a clustering output.

2.2 Self-Organizing Map (SOM) for Clustering

An unsupervised machine learning SOM [18] was applied to gain insights into the natural organization of OA gait biomechanics. SOMs are artificial neural networks that project high-dimensional data onto a connected (typically two-dimensional) network of nodes, thus providing an interactive visualization of the emergent clusters. SOMs are similarity graphs and cluster diagrams, where similar features in the input feature space remain spatially proximal in the lower-dimensional mapped space.

In our experiments the SOM was initialized with an 11x11 ($i = 121$ node) feature space with hexagonal nodes to achieve 5–10 observations per node [19]. Each node was defined by the equation, $m_i = [v_1, v_2, ..., v_{21}]$, where i denotes the index on the 121-node SOM, and v denotes vector weights for the 21 clustering features. The SOM methodology followed a recursive, stepwise learning process [18, 20]. The learning rate parameter decreased linearly to 0 over the learning process, with initial learning rates $l =$ 0.06:1 tested in this analysis. Here, training times $t = 1000{:}3000$ were tested, defined to approximate 10 times the number of mapped nodes ($121*10 = 1210$) [19]. SOMs were generated for each learning rate and training time condition. After evaluation, 10 best performing SOM models were retained—these SOMs minimized the Euclidean norm difference between each observation input vector and their assigned node vector, also termed quantization error, qe [20].

2.3 Hierarchical Clustering of the SOM and Statistical Analysis

Each of the 10 retained SOMs were applied to hierarchical (bottom-up) clustering to characterize phenotype regions within the SOM. Ward's minimum variance criteria was used [21], minimizing total within-cluster variance; the most used approach in the OA literature [3]. The quality of each cluster was determined using silhouette width, s, criterion [22], which measured how similar node i was to its own cluster (cohesion) compared to other clusters (separation) bound by ± 1 (-1 "misclassified" to 1 "well-clustered"). The cluster model with the greatest count of positive s coefficients among nodes was selected. The advantage of this selection approach is that it maximized for the number of nodes better represented by their own cluster over a neighboring one. Final clusters were validated by examining inter-cluster differences among features highly relevant during feature ranking, and those characterizing OA clinical severity [23, 24], symptoms [25], self-reported outcomes [26], and sex [16]. Chi-squared (sex), k-way ANOVA (PC scores, gait speed, percent stance, age, BMI), Kruskal Wallis tests (OA clinical classification) were used. Post-hoc tests used Tukey's HSD criterion for parametric features, and pair-wise Pearson's chi-squared tests for categorical (nominal) features. Bonferroni corrections adjusted for multiple comparisons accepting $p \le 0.002$.

3   Results

The trained SOM model is presented in Fig. 1. Each node represents a different combination of knee biomechanic and demographic features, with similar feature combinations mapping proximal to each other. After applying hierarchical clustering, a three cluster (k = 3) model was selected having the least number of negative nodes (5/121) by silhouette coefficient (model $s = 0.16$). The following provides an observation-based interpretation of each cluster.

Cluster 1: 'High Knee Function'. Contained the largest proportion of the training data's asymptomatic (86%, 193/225) and moderate OA (45%, 147/324) observations. Observations in this cluster were from younger participants (53.8 $\pm$ 9.9 years; cluster 1 < 2,3; p < 0.001), with the lowest BMIs (27.9 $\pm$ 4.7 kg/m^2; 1 < 3 < 2; p < 0.001), and fastest self-selected walking speeds (1.4 $\pm$ 0.2 m/s; 2 < 3 < 1; p < 0.001). This cluster also spent the least amount of their gait cycle in stance (63.4 $\pm$ 0.2%; 1 < 3 < 2; p < 0.001). In the sagittal plane, this cluster walked with greater overall knee flexion angle magnitudes throughout the gait cycle (PC1, 2 < 3 < 1, p < 0.001), with more flexion angle range of motion (PC4, $3 < 2 < 1$, $p < 0.001$) and more biphasic flexion/extension loading/un-loading moments during stance (PC2, $2,3 < 1$, $p < 0.001$). In the frontal plane, they had higher overall stance-phase adduction angle magnitudes (more varus, PC1, $2,3 < 1$, $p < 0.001$) and more dynamic frontal plane un-loading/loading range patterns of the knee adduction moment (first peak to mid-stance PC2, $2 < 3 < 1$, $p < 0.001$; mid-stance to second peak PC3, $2 < 3 < 1$, $p < 0.001$) (Fig. 2, Table 1).

Cluster 2: 'Poor Knee Function'. Differed the most from Cluster 1. It contained the greatest proportion of severe knee OA (78%, 108/138) and post-TKA (58%, 111/191) participants. This cluster had a greater ratio of female observations relative to the first cluster (56% vs. 39%, $p < 0.001$), with the greatest mean BMI (34.4 ± 6.2 kg/m^2), and slowest walking speeds (1.0 ± 0.2 m/s) among the clusters. Gait observations in this cluster spent a greater amount of the gait cycle in stance ($66.9 \pm 2.1\%$), walked with the greatest knee flexion moment loading magnitudes overall (PC1; $2 < 1,3$; $p < 0.001$), the least knee flexion angle magnitudes (PC1; $2 < 3 < 1$; $p < 0.001$), least knee extension at heal strike and late stance (PC3; $2 < 1,3$; $p < 0.001$), and lowest flexion (PC2; $2,3 < 1$; $p < 0.001$) and adduction moment (PC2-PC3; $2 < 3 < 1$; $p < 0.001$) loading/un-loading ranges during stance (Fig. 2, Table 1).

Cluster 3: 'Moderate Knee Function'. Was spatially between the first two clusters visually in the SOM. It contained the largest proportion of moderate OA (34%, 111/324), and the second greatest representation of post-TKA (26%, 49/191) observations. This cluster also had a higher ratio of female observations (58% vs. 39%, $p < 0.001$) than the first cluster, and mean BMIs (30.7 ± 4.6 kg/m^2), gait durations in stance ($64.7 \pm 1.5\%$), and walking speeds (1.2 ± 0.1 m/s) between the first two clusters. Features of knee kinematics and kinetics during gait in frontal and sagittal planes were between Clusters 1 and 2. The only exception to this being stance-phase flexion angle range, which was lower in this intermediate group than Clusters 1 and 2 (PC4, $3 < 2 < 1$, $p < 0.001$) (Fig. 2, Table 1).

From our cluster-level interpretation [27], the progression of knee biomechanics severity (i.e. worsening) and OA clinical severity could generally be represented from bottom left (mostly asymptomatic, Cluster 1) to top right (mostly pre or post-TKA, Cluster 2), across the x-axis of the SOM, with age and BMI increasing, and gait speed decreasing stepwise across clusters (Table 1, Fig. 1). Knee biomechanics during gait also worsened from bottom left to top right along the SOM (Figs. 2).

To demonstrate the utility of the SOM in characterizing OA phenotypes and progression pathways, the mapped SOM locations of six participants' gait observations have been illustrated in Fig. 1. These cases support a left-to-right progression pattern over time, but provide evidence of variable two-dimensional pathways during moderate OA progression (Fig. 1b, d) and during post-TKA recovery (Fig. 1e, f).

Table 1 Demographic and spaciotemporal features of clusters of training and test datasets.

	1: High knee function		2: Low knee function		3: Moderate knee function		p	Post hoc
Clinical Group (training, n=878)								
Asymptomatic (n/225, %)	193	86%	7	3%	25	11%		
Moderate (n/324, %)	147	45%	66	20%	111	34%		
Severe/Pre-TKA (n/138, %)	8	6%	108	78%	22	16%		
Post-TKA (n/191, %)	31	16%	111	58%	49	26%	<0.001	
Sex								
Female (n, %)	149	39%	162	56%	119	58%		
Male (n, %)	230	61%	130	45%	88	43%	<0.001	1 vs 2; 1 vs 3
Age (years, SD)	53.8	(9.9)	63.9	(8.7)	63.0	(8.0)	<0.001	1<2,3
BMI (kg/m^2, SD)	27.9	(4.7)	34.4	(6.2)	30.7	(4.6)	<0.001	1<3<2
Stance percent (%, SD)	63.4	(1.5)	66.9	(2.1)	64.7	(1.5)	<0.001	1<3<2
Speed (m/s, SD)	1.4	(0.2)	1.0	(0.2)	1.2	(0.1)	<0.001	2<3<1
Clinical group (test, n=45)								
Asymptomatic (n, %)	9	43%	0	0%	2	17%		
Moderate (n, %)	11	52%	2	17%	4	33%		
Severe/Pre-TKA (n, %)	0	0%	6	50%	1	8%		
Post-TKA (n, %)	1	5%	4	33%	5	42%	<0.001	

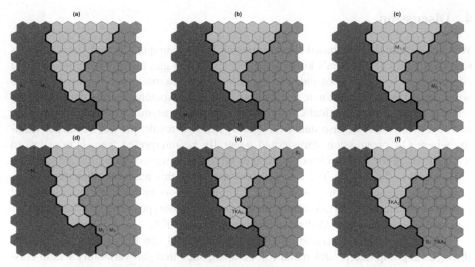

Fig. 1. Final SOM depicting cluster 1 (High Knee Function, blue), cluster 2 (Low Knee Function, red), and cluster 3 (Moderate Knee Function, yellow). Pathways of six patients are shown in (a)-(f), describing A (asymptomatic), M (moderate), S (severe OA/pre-TKA) and TKA (post-TKA) clinical classifications. Subscripts represent observation order for longitudinal context.

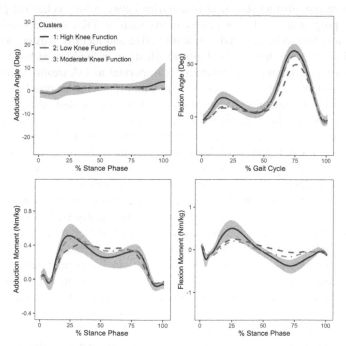

Fig. 2. Mean pre-TKA gait waveforms of cluster 1 (High Knee Function, blue solid), cluster 2 (Low Knee Function, red dashed), and cluster 3 (Moderate Knee Function, yellow dot-dashed). Grey denotes mean ± SD of the clinically classified asymptomatic group for reference (n = 236).

4   Discussion

We demonstrate that ML based clustering using SOMs can quantify and visually represent the quality of a person's knee biomechanics during gait along a multidimensional
continuum. Cluster analysis aided in the directional interpretation of gait mechanics
within the SOM, where we note that gait biomechanics worsened across the SOM, cor-
relating to changes in clinical OA severity in terms of asymptomatic, moderate OA,
and severe knee OA disease state descriptors [23]. Our results provide construct validity, where OA progression status could generally be interpreted from bottom left to
top right along the SOM, mirroring changes typically observed during OA progression
[23], and post-TKA [26]. The unsupervised nature of this analysis, objectively mapping demographic and gait observations without *a-priori* knowledge, provides novel
insights into heterogenous OA feature combinations (phenotypes), and how they progress
longitudinally during the OA disease process and post-TKA.

The three clusters described within the SOM model can be further characterized
through subgroup interpretation at the node-level, such that gait variability within clusters is not lost. Higher order cluster and node-level interpretation allows us to characterize a high volume (up to 121) of functional regions or phenotypes within the SOM.
This type of analysis may be advantageous for a disease such as OA. Although we
speak of distinct phenotypes [3], recent studies have demonstrated large degrees of overlap between clinically classified groups when attempting to separate them statistically
[28, 29]. Therefore, distinct statistical boundaries between biomechanical phenotypes
through OA progression and after interventions such as TKA may not exist. This is
the first OA and biomechanics study to characterize and identify clusters with respect
to this continuum, while having an ability to illustrate individuals at boundaries. The
acceptance of this continuum of variability is important as OA treatment and surgical
interventions propose approaches specific to patient biomechanics profiles.

OA variability is generally discussed cross-sectionally at static time points within
the OA disease process [4, 5, 8, 16, 17, 25, 26], with end-stage progression considered
to converge into a common journey [2]. Our SOM framework lends support that not all
pathways are common. Figure 1b–d illustrates this with three moderate OA individuals
who map to different SOM regions during their first gait observations, and progressed
along different pathways. Further, individuals b and c both demonstrated stable mapping during their first two gait observations, with a change in functional mapping at
observation three, giving a temporal granularity to their pathway. We have shown that
SOMs provide the novel utility to objectively illustrate and monitor individual OA jour-
neys longitudinally. This is an important outcome as monitoring these pathways would
provide new longitudinal understanding of variability in disease manifestation, with the
potential to predict patient trajectories or identify sudden declines in functional status
pre (Fig. 1c) or post-operatively (Fig. 1f). Our results can potentially inform optimal timing of non-invasive therapies targeting current and anticipated symptoms or functional
deficiencies, enabling more preventative and personalized care.

SOMs have shown a unique utility for assessing treatment effects of non-invasive
and surgical intervention strategies. For instance, post-TKA, the majority (58%) of gait
observations mapped to the most severe 'Low Knee Function' cluster. The remaining
16% and 26% of observations mapped to the higher functioning 'High Knee Function'

and 'Moderate Knee Function' clusters respectively. The concept of a biomechanical ceiling effect, such that post-TKA gait patterns statistically map to disease-state gait over asymptomatic gait is consistent with two recent studies [28, 29], highlighting deficiencies in TKA to restore normative function. It has also been demonstrated that gait improvements from arthroplasty are cluster specific [30], and that individuals with higher gait functioning pre-operatively experience the least functional and self-reported improvements post-TKA [26]. We therefore might expect TKA candidates mapping to 'High Knee Function' regions to experience less benefit from arthroplasty. Indeed, Knoop et al. used cluster analysis to identify subsets OA patients, characterizing a "minimal joint disease phenotype" using radiographic severity, muscle strength, BMI, and depression attributes [5]. This cohort of patients were less symptomatic and may not have needed specific interventions to manage their OA, possibly coinciding with some clinical OA individuals classified to our 'High Knee Function' group. Future models should explore training SOMs on clinically captured gait features, in combination self-reported OA outcomes. Anchoring regions where conservative therapeutics or surgical intervention occurred against self-reported and biomechanics improvements presents an opportunity to assess multi-modal treatment efficacy, and systemize intervention timing and selection by SOM regions. This may be particularly relevant for TKA wait list management, to objectively prioritize patients by region with the greatest need and improvement potential. Visually interpretable patient mapping may offer a novel, unbiased vehicle for individualized intervention decision making, prioritization, and monitoring, or developing interventions targeting deficiencies tailored to SOM regions, potentially yielding greater response success.

A limitation of our study was variability between explored SOM models, suggestive of weak model repeatability. The selected model also had a low mean silhouette width (0.16), i.e., clusters may not be interpretable as distinct groups. However, we believe this reflects natural biomechanical variability through knee OA progression and variability associated with pain, sex, and obesity. This study used secondary data, where we had limited access to complete longitudinal data in all individuals and other diverse attributes, restricting SOM region and pathway interpretation to being knee joint specific. Further, with observations over a 17-year period, evolving OA demographics, clinical approach or rehabilitation standards, the generated clusters may need to be calibrated to represent current OA and TKA populations.

This study was the first to propose a ML framework to characterize and cluster multi-dimensional knee kinetic, kinematic and demographic data for diverse patients along the OA disease continuum; up to 121 location-based OA progression phenotypes can be characterized. Three large clusters were identified, aiding in SOM directional interpretation that coincide with clinical OA severity from asymptomatic to end stage OA. A unique clinical aspect of this framework is the ability to objectively characterize multivariable OA progression pathways longitudinally, and measure the effect of interventions on knee joint kinematic and kinetic function. Next steps require anchoring mapped locations relative to patient-reported outcomes after intervention, to identify high/low risk intervention regions. Validated progression maps could provide individual trajectory models, aiding in intervention planning and outcome prediction, developing patient prioritization practices, or tailoring treatment to SOM regions targeting individual manifestations, which we believe may support improved treatment success.

References

1. Andriacchi, T.P., Favre, J., Erhart-Hledik, J.C., Chu, C.R.: A systems view of risk factors for knee osteoarthritis reveals insights into the pathogenesis of the disease. Ann. Biomed. Eng. **43**(2), 376–387 (2014). https://doi.org/10.1007/s10439-014-1117-2
2. Castaneda, S., Roman-Blas, J.A., Largo, R., Herrero-Beaumont, G.: Osteoarthritis: a progressive disease with changing phenotypes. Rheumatology **53**, 1–3 (2013)
3. Deveza, L.A., Melo, L., Yamato, T.P., Mills, K., Ravi, V., Hunter, D.J.: Knee osteoarthritis phenotypes and their relevance for outcomes: a systematic review. Osteoarthritis Cartilage, Osteoarthritis Res. Soc. **25**, 1926–1941 (2017)
4. Waarsing, J.H., Bierma-Zeinstra, S.M.A., Weinans, H.: Distinct subtypes of knee osteoarthritis: data from the osteoarthritis initiative. Rheumatology **54**, 1650–1658 (2015)
5. Knoop, J., et al.: Identification of phenotypes with different clinical outcomes in knee osteoarthritis: data from the osteoarthritis initiative. Arthritis Care Res. **63**, 1535–1542 (2011)
6. Pinedo-Villanueva, R., Khalid, S., Wylde, V., Gooberman-Hill, R., Soni, A., Judge, A.: Identifying individuals with chronic pain after knee replacement: a population-cohort, cluster-analysis of Oxford knee scores in 128,145 patients from the English national health service. BMC Musculoskelet. Disord. **19**, 354 (2018)
7. Behrend, H., Zdravkovic, V., Giesinger, J., Giesinger, K.: factors predicting the forgotten joint score after total knee Arthroplasty. J. Arthroplasty **31**, 1927–1932 (2016)
8. Elbaz, A., Mor, A., Segal, G., Debi, R., Shazar, N., Herman, A.: Novel classification of knee osteoarthritis severity based on spatiotemporal gait analysis. Osteoarthritis Cartilage/OARS Osteoarthritis Res. Soc. **22**, 457–463 (2014)
9. Andriacchi, T.P., Koo, S., Scanlan, S.F.: Gait mechanics influence healthy cartilage morphology and osteoarthritis of the knee. J. Bone Joint Surg. **91**, 95–101 (2009)
10. Altman, R., et al.: Development of criteria for the classification and reporting of osteoarthritis: classification of osteoarthritis of the knee. Arthritis Rheumatol. **29**, 1039–1049 (1986)
11. Grood, E.S., Suntay, W.J.: A joint coordinate system for the clinical description of three-dimensional motions: application to the knee. J. Biomech. Eng. **105**, 136–144 (1983)
12. Li, J., Wyss, U.P., Costigan, P.A., Deluzio, K.J.: An integrated procedure to assess knee-joint kinematics and kinetics during gait using an optoelectric system and standardized X-rays. J. Biomed. Eng. **15**, 392–400 (1993)
13. Deluzio, K.J., Wyss, U.P., Li, J., Costigan, P.A.: A procedure to validate three-dimensional motion assessment systems. J. Biomech. **26**, 753–759 (1993)
14. Costigan, P.A., Wyss, U.P., Deluzio, K.J., Li, J.: Semiautomatic three-dimensional knee motion assessment system. Med. Bio. Eng. Comput. **30**, 343–350 (1992)
15. Deluzio, K.J., Astephen, J.L.: Biomechanical features of gait waveform data associated with knee osteoarthritis. Gait Posture **25**, 86–93 (2007)
16. Wilson, J.L.A., Dunbar, M.J., Hubley-Kozey, C.L.: Knee joint biomechanics and neuromuscular control during gait before and after total knee arthroplasty are sex-specific. J. Arthroplasty **30**, 118–125 (2015)
17. Paterson, K.L., et al.: The influence of sex and obesity on gait biomechanics in people with severe knee osteoarthritis scheduled for arthroplasty. Clin. Biomech. **49**, 72–77 (2017)
18. Kohonen, T.: Self-organizing formation of topologically correct feature maps. Bio. Cybermetrics. **43**, 59–69 (1982)
19. Westerlund, M.L.: Classification of Kohonen Self-Organizing Maps, pp. 1–16. Soft Computing, Haskoli Islands (2005)
20. Kohonen, T.: The self-organizing map. Proc. IEEE. **78**, 1464–1480 (1990)
21. Ward, J.H.: Hierarchical grouping to optimize an objective function. J. Am. Stat. Assoc. **58**, 236–244 (1963)

22. Rousseeuw, P.J.: Silhouettes: a graphical aid to the interpretation and validation of cluster analysis. J. Comput. Appl. Math. **20**, 53–65 (1987)

23. Astephen, J.L., Deluzio, K.J., Caldwell, G.E., Dunbar, M.J.: Biomechanical changes at the hip, knee, and ankle joints during gait are associated with knee osteoarthritis severity. J. Orthop. Res. **26**, 332–341 (2008)

24. Astephen, J., Deluzio, K., Caldwell, G., Dunbar, M., Hubley-Kozey, C.: Gait and neuromuscular pattern changes are associated with differences in knee osteoarthritis severity levels. J. Biomech. **41**, 868–876 (2008)

25. Wilson, J., Stanish, W., Hubley-Kozey, C.: Asymptomatic and symptomatic individuals with the same radiographic evidence of knee osteoarthritis walk with different knee moments and muscle activity. J. Orthop. Res. **35**, 1661–1670 (2017)

26. Young-Shand, K.L., Dunbar, M.J., Wilson, J.L.A.: Individual gait features are associated with clinical improvement after total knee arthroplasty. J. Bone Joint Surg. Open Access **5**, e0038-e111 (2020)

27. Abidi, S.S.R., Roy, P.C., Shah, M.S., Jin, Y., Yan, S.: A data mining framework for glaucoma decision support based on optic nerve image analysis using machine learning methods. J. Healthcare Inf. Res. **2**(4), 370–401 (2018). https://doi.org/10.1007/s41666-018-0028-7

28. Biggs, P., Whatling, G., Wilson, C., Metcalfe, A., Holt, C.: Which osteoarthritic gait features recover following total knee replacement surgery? PLoS ONE **14**, e0203417 (2019)

29. Outerleys, J., Dunbar, M., Richardson, G., Hubley-Kozey, C., Wilson, J.: Quantifying achievable levels of improvement in knee joint biomechanics during gait after TKA relative to osteoarthritis severity. J. Appl. Biomech. **37**, 1–31 (2021)

30. Young-Shand, K., Roy, P., Abidi, S.R., Dunbar, M., Wilson, J.A.: Gait biomechanics phenotypes among total knee arthroplasty candidates by machine learning cluster analysis. J. Orthop. Res. (2022). https://doi.org/10.1007/s41666-018-0028-7

NeuralSympCheck: A Symptom Checking and Disease Diagnostic Neural Model with Logic Regularization

Aleksandr Nesterov[1]([✉]) [iD], Bulat Ibragimov[2] [iD], Dmitriy Umerenkov[1] [iD],
Artem Shelmanov[2,3] [iD], Galina Zubkova[1] [iD], and Vladimir Kokh[1] [iD]

[1] Sber AI Lab, Moscow, Russia
AINesterov@sberbank.ru
[2] AIRI, Moscow, Russia
[3] Skoltech, Moscow, Russia

Abstract. The symptom checking systems inquire users for their symptoms and perform a rapid and affordable medical assessment of their condition. The basic symptom checking systems based on Bayesian methods, decision trees, or information gain methods are easy to train and do not require significant computational resources. However, their drawbacks are low relevance of proposed symptoms and insufficient quality of diagnostics. The best results on these tasks are achieved by reinforcement learning models. Their weaknesses are the difficulty of developing and training such systems and limited applicability to cases with large and sparse decision spaces. We propose a new approach based on the supervised learning of neural models with logic regularization that combines the advantages of the different methods. Our experiments on real and synthetic data show that the proposed approach outperforms the best existing methods in the accuracy of diagnosis when the number of diagnoses and symptoms is large. The models and the code are freely available online (https://github.com/SympCheck/NeuralSymptomChecker).

Keywords: Neural networks · Symptom checker · Diagnostic model

1 Introduction

Health systems need to balance three critical qualities: accessibility, quality, and cost. These three qualities unfortunately often compete over a limited pool of resources, and improving one of these qualities leads to losses in others. This is known as the "iron triangle" of healthcare. Mobile networks, big data, and artificial intelligence are promising directions for improving quality and accessibility while decreasing costs. In [15], authors show that in 2012 35% of adult US citizens at least once used the internet for self-diagnosis. Self-diagnosis commonly starts with queries to search engines. While highly accessible and free, the quality of the results may be unsatisfactory, and results may be irrelevant, inaccurate, or even harmful.

M. Michalowski et al. (Eds.): AIME 2022, LNAI 13263, pp. 76–87, 2022.
https://doi.org/10.1007/978-3-031-09342-5_8

To increase the quality of self-diagnosis, several symptom-checker systems have been proposed [15,16]. Such systems present users with several additional questions about existing or potential symptoms and use this information to suggest possible diagnoses and recommend visiting a specialist physician. The disease diagnosing process can be modeled as a sequence of questions and answers: a physician asks a patient questions about his/her symptoms and uses the answers to identify the disease. While asking the questions, the physician pursues two goals. Firstly, the answer to each question must be the most informative in the current context. Secondly, after a series of questions and answers, a correct diagnosis should be identified.

This work presents a symptom checker based on a logic regularisation framework [1], which outperforms the state-of-the-art results achieved with methods based on reinforcement learning (RL). Unlike the RL systems, the proposed symptom checker is simple both in implementation and training. We split the system into symptom recommendation and diagnosis prediction submodels and implement the novel logic regularisation framework that allows us to train the submodels simultaneously with the standard backpropagation and to treat the symptom suggestion as a multi-label classification task. The latter, in turn, allows to deal with the problem of big and sparse symptom space by using the Asymmetric loss [13]. In contrast to RL-based systems, the diagnoses predicted with our system also do not depend on the order of presented symptoms. The contributions of the paper can be summarized as follows:

- We present a symptom checker that outperforms state-of-the-art systems based on reinforcement learning or knowledge graphs in the task of diagnosis prediction both on real world and synthetic datasets.
- Instead of the RL framework, we apply logic regularisation to train the symptom checker, showing that simpler models can achieve state-of-the-art results.
- Unlike the predictions of the RL-based diagnosis systems, the predictions of our system do not depend on the order of the revealed symptoms.
- Our system is easier to implement, train and requires less computational resources than state-of-the-art RL-based systems.
- Reframing the symptom recommendation problem as a multi-label classification task allows dealing with the big and sparse symptom space using the Asymmetric loss [13].

2   Related Work

Early works concerning automated symptom clarification and diagnostics were based on the naive Bayes classifier, decision trees, and other information-gain methods [8,9]. Due to simplicity and various drawbacks, such systems do not achieve high diagnostics quality. There are also attempts to use rule-based expert systems [3]. The performance of such systems depends on the quality of the rules and medical knowledge bases. Therefore, scaling and modifying them is very difficult.

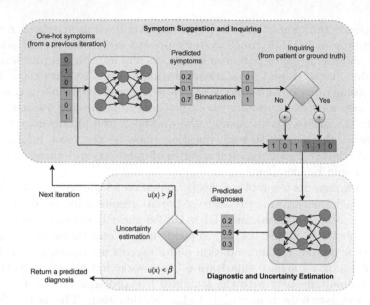

Fig. 1. The architecture of the symptom checker model

Several recent works [6,7,12,16,17] demonstrate effectiveness of RL-based methods for these tasks. In the RL framework, the symptom clarification and diagnosis prediction tasks are framed as a Markov decision process [16,17]. This leads to the unwanted quality of RL-based systems that the final diagnosis depends on the order in which the symptoms are revealed. Despite impressive results, the RL-based approach is plagued with several difficulties. Firstly, the possible symptoms and diagnoses are numbered from hundreds to a tenth of thousands, which leads to a huge decision space. Secondly, the number of symptoms present in each case is tiny compared to all possible symptoms, leading to a sparse decision space. To overcome this difficulties, in [7,16], the authors propose ensembling that helps to reduce the decision space for each individual ensemble component and improve the qualitative performance. Peng et al. [12] addresses the sparsity of decision space by proposing special reward estimation and regularisation techniques. To increase the diagnostic performance, other models use context (age, sex, location) [7] or information from knowledge graphs [20].

In [4,10], the authors note that the decision to stop the dialog made by an RL-agent can be sub-optimal because the agent is penalized for long conversations. To solve the problem, they use uncertainty estimation [11] of the diagnosis as a stopping criteria. The quality of diagnostics improves, because the agent makes more steps, and the diagnostics model receives more information.

Our logic regularisation framework is similar to RL-based methods as it both models the dialog between the physician and the patient and achieves high-quality results. At the same time, our system is easier to implement and train, and its predictions are independent of the order of revealed symptoms.

3 Symptom Checker Model

We propose a symptom checker model, NeuralSympCheck, consisting of two neural submodels: a network for suggesting symptoms that should be inquired from a patient and a model for performing actual diagnostics. The architecture of the model is presented in Fig. 1.

The symptom checker works iteratively. On each iteration, it receives a set of already known symptoms (as well as the information about the absence of some symptoms) and tries to guess the most probable symptom of a patient with the symptom suggestion submodel. The factual information about the presence of the corresponding symptom is inquired from a patient. Then known symptoms and the factual information about the presence/absence of the suggested symptom are used by the diagnostics submodel to predict the disease. We quantify the uncertainty of this prediction, and if it is intolerably high, we start a new iteration of symptom clarification, in which the symptom suggestion submodel receives extended information about symptoms. We note that despite splitting the whole model into two submodels during the inference, they are trained jointly end-to-end with a logic regularization mechanism: the diagnostics submodel learns how to correctly predict diseases with limited information, while the symptom suggestion submodel learns to suggest the most crucial evidence for diagnostics.

3.1 Symptom Suggestion and Diagnostics Submodels

The symptom suggestion submodel receives two vectors that encode information known so far about the symptoms. The first vector accumulates the information about present symptoms stored using one-hot encoding, while the second vector stores one-hot encoded information about known absent symptoms.

The architecture of the submodel is a feed-forward neural network, in which each linear layer is followed by batch normalization, a dropout layer, and a ReLU activation. The model's output is a probability distribution of possibly present symptoms obtained via the softmax function.

The most probable symptom is queried from the patient (during training, it is taken from the gold standard). Then, the actual information about the presence or absence of the symptom is added to the corresponding vectors.

The diagnostics submodel takes the extended available information about symptoms as input and predicts a patient's diagnosis. The symptoms are encoded in the same way as the input for the symptom suggestion submodel and the architecture is also the same. The output of the diagnostics model is a probability distribution of potential diseases obtained via the softmax function.

3.2 Training with Logic Regularization

During training, we perform the same iterative process of symptom suggestion and diagnosis prediction until the uncertainty of the latter is not low enough. The training of both submodels is performed end-to-end, so the gradient from the diagnostics submodel is propagated into the symptom suggestion submodel.

Since the diagnostics submodel takes as input discrete data encoded in one-hot vectors instead of differentiable softmax distributions, the straightforward stacking of these two submodels requires indifferentiable operations. To mitigate this problem and train submodels with the standard backpropagation algorithm, we use a simplified implementation of the Gumbel-softmax approximation [5] without stochastic sampling.

The overall training loss L is combined from two components: the symptom prediction loss L_s and the diagnosis prediction loss L_d: $L = \lambda L_s + L_d$, where $\lambda > 0$ is a hyperparameter. L_s is the Asymmetric loss [13] designed for multi-label classification to mitigate the data skewness towards particular classes:

$$L_s = \begin{cases} L_+ = (1 - p)^{\gamma_+} \log(p) \\ L_- = (p_m)^{\gamma_-} \log(1 - p_m), \end{cases} \tag{1}$$

where p is a symptom prediction probability, γ_+, γ_- are focusing hyperparameters, $p_m = max(p - m, 0)$, $m \geq 0$ is a margin hyperparameter. L_d is a simple cross-entropy loss commonly used for the standard multi-class classification.

The suggested approach to training these two submodels lies in the paradigm of analytic-synthetic logic regularization. In the analytical approach, a complex model is trained as a sequence of small independent architectures, which improves the interpretability of the solution. In contrast, the synthetic approach trains a single model on a significant target problem (end-to-end), which increases the solution's flexibility. In this paper, none of the approaches described can meet the essential requirements for symptom suggestion. Firstly, symptom suggestion cannot be viewed as task-independent of diagnosis prediction since the goal of this step is not to propose the most likely symptom but the symptom that would potentially reduce the uncertainty of the second submodel the most. Secondly, with the standard end-to-end learning, the information necessary for interpreting and identifying symptoms is lost.

The proposed architecture, in which the predictions of the first submodel are fed to the input of the second submodel and the gradients from the second submodel are propagated to the first submodel, is an attempt to encapsulate both approaches within a single architecture and take advantage of the benefits of each. Such an analytic-synthetic system benefits from two-way regularization: using an explicit symptom prediction subproblem to solve the diagnosis detection problem and using the end goal of the whole problem to regularize the symptom prediction solutions. Because the proposed architecture, in a sense, imitates the logic of decision-making by physicians in real life (additional cyclic tests until the diagnosis is certain), the proposed framework can be considered as one of the variants of logic regularization [14, 21].

3.3   Uncertainty Estimation of the Diagnostics Submodel

Following Lin et al. [10], we quantify the uncertainty of the diagnostics submodel and use it as a criterion for stopping "questioning" a patient about additional symptoms. This resembles conducting the diagnostics in real life, as a physician collects more evidence only until he is sure enough about the diagnosis. Furthermore, different diseases require a different amount of evidence to make a reliable conclusion, as some diseases are more ambiguous than others. Therefore, exhaustive questioning or asking a fixed considerable number of symptoms is impossible since we would like to make a reliable conclusion as soon as possible, saving time and effort of patients. This also helps speed up training and prevents overfitting, which eventually leads to better performance of the diagnostics submodel.

In this work, for quantifying uncertainty u of a diagnosis d for a case x, we rely on the entropy of the diagnostics submodel output distribution $p(d|x)$ obtained with softmax: $u(x) = E_{p(d|x)}[-\log p(d|x)]$.

We ask for more symptoms until uncertainty of a disease prediction becomes lower than a predefined threshold: $u(x) < \beta, \beta \in (0,1)$ or we exceed a predefined maximum number of attempts Q. The values Q and β are hyperparameters that are selected using a validation dataset.

4   Experiments

4.1   Data

Real World Data. The *MuZhi* dataset was created by Zhongyu et al. [17] from real dialogues on the Chinese healthcare internet portal[1]. This dataset encompasses 66 symptoms and four diseases. The dataset consists of 710 records containing the raw dialogue and normalized symptoms checked during the dialogue, either found or not. The symptoms from each record are tagged either as explicit or implicit. The explicit symptoms are the symptoms initially presented by the patient before the beginning of the dialogue. The presence or absence of implicit symptoms is discovered during the recorded dialogue.

The *Dxy* Dialogue Medical [19] dataset is based on dialogues from a popular Chinese medical forum[2]. It consists of 527 unique dialogues, five diseases, and 41 symptoms. The symptoms from each record are tagged either as explicit or implicit as in the MuZhi dataset.

Synthetic Data. The MuZhi and Dxy datasets are limited in the number of symptoms and diseases. To check the performance of our model in the case of significant symptom and diseases spaces, we used a synthetic dataset *SymCat* presented in [7] with modifications from [12]. This dataset is created from the similarly named symptom and disease database SymCat[3]. It contains information about 474 symptoms and 801 related diseases.

The dataset is built following the procedure: select a disease from the list; select the symptoms from aposteriori distribution using a Bernoulli experiment for each symptom; split the symptoms into implicit and explicit groups as in the MuZhi and Dxy datasets. As in previous works [4,12], to evaluate the system performance on different scales, we use three versions of the dataset with the varying number of diseases – 200, 300, and 400. We note that we did not find the

---

[1] https://muzhi.baidu.com/.

[2] https://dxy.com/.

[3] http://www.symcat.com/.

source code of the generating procedure used in [4, 12]. Therefore, although we reproduced the generation process according to their description, there might be minor deviations. Dataset statistics is presented in Table 3 in Appendix A.

4.2   Experimental Setup

Hyperparameters and Training Details. Model and training hyperparameters, including the number of hidden layers, dropout ratio, layer size, learning rate, number of epochs, scaling coefficient of the multi-label loss, and the uncertainty threshold are selected on the validation datasets using the Optuna package[4]. To reduce optimization search space, we use the same number of layers with the same size in both submodels. The selected values are presented in Table 4 in Appendix A. Training is performed using the corrected version of Adam with linear decay of the learning rate and warm-up. The focusing hyperparameters are fixed: $\gamma^+ = 1, \gamma^- = 4$. The maximum number of attempts $Q = 50$.

Evaluation Metrics. The quality of disease prediction is evaluated using the top-k accuracy metric Acc@k ($k \in 1, 2, 3$). For each example, if a true disease is present among the top k predictions in the output probability distribution of the model, it is considered as the correct answer of the model. In ablation studies, we also use weighted macro F1 to evaluate symptom prediction quality.

Baselines. We compare the proposed NeuralSympCheck model with several models from the previous work [2, 4, 12, 18–20] and with two simple baselines based on a feedforward neural network. These baselines have the same architecture as submodules: several fully-connected layers with batch normalization, ReLU activation, and dropout regularization. The first baseline performs multi-label disease classification using only the starting explicit symptoms (baseline ex). The second baseline uses both explicit and implicit symptoms (baseline ex&im), which is unrealistic and very strong assumption.

4.3   Results and Discussion

Table 1 presents the main experimental results on small datasets MuZhi and Dxy. On the MyZhi dataset, our NeuralSympCheck model achieves the new state-of-the-art, outperforming all the baselines and the models from the previous work. On the Dxy dataset, our model outperforms the first baseline and most of the systems from the previous work, only falling behind the recently proposed RL-based systems presented in [2, 4, 19]. We attribute this to the fact that Dxy is smaller, contains less number of symptoms, and has a smaller average number of implicit symptoms that can be clarified for the final diagnosis.

As we can see from Table 2, on the more extensive synthetic datasets based on SymCat, NeuralSympCheck also achieves state-of-the-art results, outperforming

---

[4] https://optuna.org.

Table 1. Diagnostics Acc@1 (%) on the *MuZhi* and *Dxy* datasets

Model	MuZhi	Dxy
Baseline ex	61.3	66.4
Baseline ex&im	65.8	77.3
Peng at al. [12]	71.8	75.7
Xu at al. [19]	73.0	74.0
Xia at al. [18]	73.0	76.9
Zhao at al. [20]	69.7	74.0
He at al. [4]	72.6	**81.1**
Guan at al. [2]	65.5	80.8
Our best results	**74.5**	75.7

Table 2. Results (%) on the test part of the *SymCat* datasets

Model	200 diseases			300 diseases			400 diseases		
	Acc@1	Acc@3	Acc@5	Acc@1	Acc@3	Acc@5	Acc@1	Acc@3	Acc@5
Baseline ex	46.7	70.6	81.1	41.1	63.0	73.4	36.3	57.0	67.8
Baseline ex&im	82.6	96.7	99.1	78.4	94.0	98.0	74.4	92.0	97.0
Peng at al. [12]	54.8	73.6	79.5	47.5	65.1	71.8	43.8	60.8	68.9
He at al. [4]	55.6	80.7	89.3	48.2	73.8	84.2	44.6	69.2	79.5
Our best results	**63.2**	**89.3**	**96.7**	**54.8**	**81.2**	**91.1**	**49.8**	**76.6**	**87.9**

all previous models and the first baseline. The best results are achieved for each number of possible diagnoses. Our model does not reach the performance of the second unrealistic baseline trained on both explicit and implicit symptoms. This may happen because NeuralSympCheck overcomes the uncertainty threshold early and stops clarifying additional symptoms. We note that our solution outperforms models from the previous work with a significant margin. We attribute this remarkable achievement to using a conceptually novel model architecture that is better adapted to the big and sparse symptom space.

4.4 Ablation Studies

The goal of the first ablation study is to evaluate the effect of the symptom prediction loss (Table 5 in Appendix B). We train our model using only the first diagnosis prediction loss with a fixed number of clarification iterations. This helps to improve Acc@1 of the diagnostics model. However, this results in a substantial reduction of symptom-suggestion model F1 compared to training with both losses. We conclude that training only with the diagnosis classification loss facilitates the symptom suggestion submodel to exceedingly adjust its predictions in the direction of best coherence with the predicted diagnosis.

In the second ablation study, we evaluate the effect of uncertainty estimation. Table 5 in Appendix B shows that models using uncertainty estimation achieve the best results in terms of the Acc@1 metric for diagnosis prediction. However, the F1 metric for symptom prediction is significantly lower. The obtained results can be explained by the fact that models using uncertainty estimation conduct fewer symptom clarification iterations that are only necessary to achieve model confidence in the correct diagnosis.

We also test the hypothesis that additional symptoms help to reduce the uncertainty of the diagnosis submodel predictions. Figure 2 in Appendix B shows that, indeed, regardless of the dataset, the more iterations of symptom refinement are performed, the less uncertain the diagnostics submodel predictions are.

5   Conclusion

We presented a novel model for symptom and diagnosis prediction based on supervised learning. It outperforms recently proposed RL-based counterparts and mitigates some of their limitations, such as the complexity of learning, the fundamental flaws of the Markov process, and the complexity of applying RL-based methods in practice. By leveraging asymmetric loss, we overcome the problem of large and sparse symptoms space. We propose an approach that allows training the symptom suggestion and the diagnosis prediction models in an end-to-end fashion with standard backpropagation. We are the first to use logic regularization for the considered task, which effectively helps to predict relevant symptoms for diagnostics. Finally, uncertainty estimation of diagnosis prediction is used as a stopping criterion for asking about new symptoms. Our NeuralSympCheck model achieves the new state of the art on datasets with large symptom and diagnosis spaces.

We want to emphasize the practical significance of this work because the presented model is relatively easy to implement, stable in training, and not demanding on computational resources. This makes it possible to apply the proposed model in real-world medical systems, which is our future work direction.

Acknowledgements. We are grateful to anonymous reviewers for their valuable feedback. The work was supported by the RSF grant 20-71-10135.

A   Dataset Statistics and Hyperparameters

Table 3. Dataset statistics

	MuZhi	Dxy	SymCat 200	SymCat 300	SymCat 400
Total dialogues	710	527	1,110,000	1,110,000	1,110,000
Training dialogues	568	423	1,000,000	1,000,000	1,000,000
Validation dialogues	-	-	100,000	100,000	100,000
Testing dialogues	142	123	10,000	10,000	10,000
Unique diagnoses	4	5	200	300	400
Unique symptoms	66	41	326	350	367
Average number of explicit symptoms	2.4	3.1	1.9	2.0	2.0
Average number of implicit symptoms	2.4	1.2	1.9	2.0	2.0

Table 4. Hyperparameters of the models that showed the best results on validation datasets

Hyperparams	MuZhi	Dxy	SymCat 200	SymCat 300	SymCat 400
Size of the first layer	6,000	10,000	8,000	8,000	8,000
Size of the second layer	3000	-	-	-	-
Dropout probability	0.4	0.5	0.5	0.5	0.5
Multilabel loss coefficient	1.6	0.6	1	1	1
Minimum uncertainty value, β	0.5	0.3	0.3	0.4	0.4
Number of epochs	35	5	5	10	10
Learning rate	5e−5	1e−3	1e−3	1e−2	1e−2

B   Additional Experimental Results

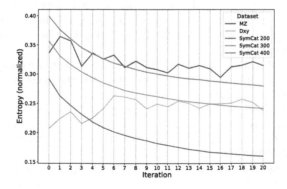

Fig. 2. Change of entropy value depending on iteration of symptom inquiring

Table 5. Ablation studies results (% Acc@1 by diagnosis/F1 weighted by symptoms)

	MuZhi	Dxy	SymCat 200	SymCat 300	SymCat 400
Only diagnosis loss	67.2/32.7	71.9/24.0	70.7/23.7	64.1/24.5	57.6/24.4
Two losses, without entropy	70.3/10.2	69.0/32.8	59.6/35.0	53.8/33.2	47.7/32.3
With entropy	68.3/28.4	69.1/19.2	63.2/20.7	54.8/15.8	49.8/14.5

References

1. Asai, A., Hajishirzi, H.: Logic-guided data augmentation and regularization for consistent question answering. In: Proceedings of the 58th Annual Meeting of the Association for Computational Linguistics, pp. 5642–5650 (2020). https://doi.org/10.18653/v1/2020.acl-main.499
2. Guan, H., Baral, C.: A Bayesian approach for medical inquiry and disease inference in automated differential diagnosis. arXiv preprint arXiv:2110.08393 (2021)
3. Hayashi, Y.: A neural expert system with automated extraction of fuzzy if-then rules and its application to medical diagnosis. In: Advances in Neural Information Processing Systems, pp. 578–584 (1991)
4. He, W., Mao, X., Ma, C., Hernández-Lobato, J.M., Chen, T.: BSODA: a bipartite scalable framework for online disease diagnosis. In: Proceedings of ACM Web Conference (WWW-2022) (2022)
5. Jang, E., Gu, S., Poole, B.: Categorical reparameterization with gumbel-softmax. In: Proceedings of ICLR (2017)
6. Janisch, J., Pevný, T., Lisý, V.: Classification with costly features as a sequential decision-making problem. Mach. Learn. **109**(8), 1587–1615 (2020). https://doi.org/10.1007/s10994-020-05874-8
7. Kao, H.C., Tang, K.F., Chang, E.: Context-aware symptom checking for disease diagnosis using hierarchical reinforcement learning. In: Proceedings of the AAAI Conference on Artificial Intelligence, vol. 32 (2018)
8. Kohavi, R., et al.: Scaling up the accuracy of naive-bayes classifiers: a decision-tree hybrid. In: Proceedings of KDD, vol. 96, pp. 202–207 (1996)
9. Kononenko, I.: Machine learning for medical diagnosis: history, state of the art and perspective. Artif. Intell. Med. **23**(1), 89–109 (2001). https://doi.org/10.1016/S0933-3657(01)00077-X
10. Lin, J., Chen, Z., Liang, X., Wang, K., Lin, L.: Towards causality-aware inferring: a sequential discriminative approach for medical diagnosis. arXiv preprint arXiv:2003.06534v4 (2022)
11. McAllister, R., Kahn, G., Clune, J., Levine, S.: Robustness to out-of-distribution inputs via task-aware generative uncertainty. In: 2019 International Conference on Robotics and Automation (ICRA). pp. 2083–2089. IEEE (2019). https://doi.org/10.1109/ICRA.2019.8793552
12. Peng, Y.S., Tang, K.F., Lin, H.T., Chang, E.: Refuel: exploring sparse features in deep reinforcement learning for fast disease diagnosis. Adv. Neural Inf. Process. Syst. **31**, 7322–7331 (2018)
13. Ridnik, T., et al.: Asymmetric loss for multi-label classification. In: Proceedings of the IEEE/CVF International Conference on Computer Vision, pp. 82–91 (2021). https://doi.org/10.1109/ICCV48922.2021.00015
14. Riegel, R., et al.: Logical neural networks. arXiv preprint arXiv:2006.13155 (2020)

15. Semigran, H.L., Linder, J.A., Gidengil, C., Mehrotra, A.: Evaluation of symptom checkers for self diagnosis and triage: audit study. BMJ, **351** (2015). https://doi.org/10.1136/bmj.h3480
16. Tang, K.F., Kao, H.C., Chou, C.N., Chang, E.Y.: Inquire and diagnose: neural symptom checking ensemble using deep reinforcement learning. In: NIPS Workshop on Deep Reinforcement Learning (2016)
17. Wei, Z., et al.: Task-oriented dialogue system for automatic diagnosis. In: Proceedings of the 56th Annual Meeting of the Association for Computational Linguistics (Volume 2: Short Papers), pp. 201–207 (2018). https://doi.org/10.18653/v1/P18-2033
18. Xia, Y., Zhou, J., Shi, Z., Lu, C., Huang, H.: Generative adversarial regularized mutual information policy gradient framework for automatic diagnosis. In: Proceedings of the AAAI Conference on Artificial Intelligence, vol. 34, pp. 1062–1069 (2020). https://doi.org/10.1609/aaai.v34i01.5456
19. Xu, L., Zhou, Q., Gong, K., Liang, X., Tang, J., Lin, L.: End-to-end knowledge-routed relational dialogue system for automatic diagnosis. In: Proceedings of the AAAI Conference on Artificial Intelligence, vol. 33, pp. 7346–7353 (2019). https://doi.org/10.1609/aaai.v33i01.33017346
20. Zhao, X., Chen, L., Chen, H.: A weighted heterogeneous graph-based dialog system. IEEE Trans. Neural Networks Learn. Syst. pp. 1–6 (2021). https://doi.org/10.1109/TNNLS.2021.3124640
21. Zhou, Y., et al.: Clinical temporal relation extraction with probabilistic soft logic regularization and global inference. In: Proceedings of the AAAI Conference on Artificial Intelligence, vol. 35, pp. 14647–14655 (2021). https://doi.org/10.1109/TNNLS.2021.3124640

Extracting Surrogate Decision Trees from Black-Box Models to Explain the Temporal Importance of Clinical Features in Predicting Kidney Graft Survival

Jaber Rad[1] , Karthik K. Tennankore[2] , Amanda Vinson[2] ,
and Syed Sibte Raza Abidi[1(✉)]

[1] NICHE Research Group, Faculty of Computer Science, Dalhousie University, Halifax, Canada
{jaber.rad,ssrabidi}@dal.ca
[2] Department of Nephrology, Faculty of Medicine, Dalhousie University, Halifax, Canada
{KarthikK.Tennankore,Amanda.Vinson}@nshealth.ca

Abstract. Prognostic modelling using machine learning techniques has been used to predict the risk of kidney graft failure after transplantation. Despite the clinically suitable prediction performance of the models, their decision logic cannot be interpreted by physicians, hindering clinical adoption. eXplainable Artificial Intelligence (XAI) is an emerging research discipline to investigate methods for explaining machine learning models which are regarded as 'black-box' models. In this paper, we present a novel XAI approach to study the influence of time on information gain of donor and recipient factors in kidney graft survival prediction. We trained the most accurate models regardless of their transparency level on subsequent non-overlapping temporal cohorts and extracted faithful decision trees from the models as global surrogate explanations. Comparative exploration of the decision trees reveals insightful information about how the information gain of the input features changes over time.

Keywords: Explainable AI · Surrogate modelling · Kidney transplantation

1 Introduction

Machine Learning (ML) methods are well suited for prognostic modelling, in particular to perform survival analysis of outcomes following organ transplantation [1]. Specific to kidney transplantation, ML methods have been utilized for identifying clinical attributes of donors and recipients to predict kidney organ survival. Although the resultant ML models show high prediction accuracy, they suffer from low clinical uptake as their decision logic is not apparent to physicians and as such, they are regarded as 'black-box' models. For kidney transplant survival analysis, physicians need to know which donor and recipient features contribute most to graft loss and which features have a higher relative influence on graft loss at different time points. eXplainable Artificial Intelligence (XAI) is an emerging research theme that aims to explain the underlying decision logic and feature importance within black-box ML models, thus making them interpretable and transparent to users [2].

In this paper, we present a model-agnostic XAI approach that is applied to explain the temporal importance of clinical features related to kidney transplant, using a large cohort of elderly kidney transplant recipient survivors (i.e. those free of early graft loss or death) over 10 years provided by the Scientific Registry of Transplant Recipients (SRTR). Our approach is to initially learn a black-box ML model, with high prediction accuracy, using complex ML algorithms, and then render the trained ML model into a simplified interpretable *surrogate model* that can explain the input-output mapping of the black-box ML model. In our work, we trained ML models predicting transplant survival/failure for different temporal cohorts, and next applied our XAI-based surrogate modelling approach to generate decision trees that explain attribute importance over time. The explanations are useful to match kidney transplant donors and recipients to achieve prolonged transplant survival. The results have been validated by kidney transplant specialists who also provided the clinical relevance of the explanations.

2 Related Work

In a recent survey, Díez-Sanmartín [1] reviewed ML methods used in the last four years for end-stage kidney disease, noting that studies analyzing the survival of kidney recipients are majorly based on uninterpretable methods (e.g. neural network and ensemble methods). A few studies have proposed XAI approaches to explain the prediction models. Lauritsen [3] introduced an XAI early warning score (xAI-EWS) and applied it to generate visual explanations of the predictions in an acute kidney injury (AKI) case using temporal convolutional network (TCN) as the ML model and a deep Taylor decomposition (DTD) method as the explainer. da Cruz et al. [4] applied LIME, Shapley values and global surrogates to recursively eliminate less relevant features to predict AKI in cardiac surgery patients. Li et al. [5] developed an XGBoost model to predict prognosis of IgAN patients and used the SHAP method to interpret the results. Feature importance analysis based on Gini impurity metric has been used in recent studies in nephrology to rank the features based on their clinical relevance [6, 7]. We note that previous studies of ML methods applied to kidney transplant do not engage specialists to interpret and validate clinical feature information in prediction models. Furthermore, we note that current perturbation-based feature importance measures do not reveal useful information. On the contrary, the proposed surrogate approximation approach allows the illustration of ML models' decision process in a traceable way highlighting the relationships among features [8]. To the best of our knowledge, this is the first study that utilizes surrogate modelling to investigate the influence of time on the relative importance of clinical predictors on graft loss following kidney transplantation.

3 Our XAI Approach: Surrogate Decision Tree Generation

Our XAI approach is to apply global post-hoc model-agnostic explainability techniques that do not look inside the black-box ML model, rather rely on the input and output of the ML model to provide explanations of the model's decision logic. The rationale for using this approach is: (a) we do not intend the explanation to be tied to the internal architecture of the model, rather to its input-output mapping. In this way, our XAI approach can be applied to interpret the workings of any ML method; and (b) we do not want to disturb or alter the architecture of the ML models in an attempt to explain its working—any post-training changes to the ML model are likely to introduce bias.

We use the *surrogate modelling* approach that distills a complex black-box model (referred to as teacher) into a simplified interpretable surrogate model (referred to as student) [2]. For representing surrogate models, we chose decision trees over rule-sets as user studies show that there is difficulty in comprehending the conditional structure of rulesets [8]; decision trees offer simplicity, close approximation and visual explanation of the influence of features towards their nonparametric structural representation.

We intend to examine the changes in temporal importance of clinical features toward kidney transplant survival over a 10-year period. As such, we generated one cohort per year (nonoverlapping) and trained survival prediction models for each cohort using different ML methods; the best performing model for each cohort was taken as the teacher to approximate a surrogate model—using TREPAN [9], a global model-agnostic tree induction algorithm—to explain the temporal importance of features. Figure 1 provides an overview of the approach, with details to follow in later sections.

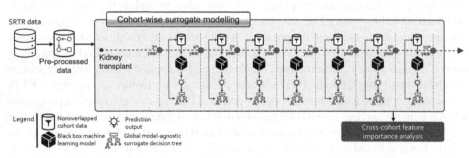

Fig. 1. Our XAI approach to investigate the temporal importance of features in kidney transplant

4 Methodology and Methods

4.1 Data Preparation

This study used data from the Scientific Registry of Transplant Recipients (SRTR). The SRTR data system includes data on all donors, wait-listed candidates, and transplant recipients in the US, submitted by the members of the Organ Procurement and Transplantation Network (OPTN). The Health Resources and Services Administration

(HRSA), U.S. Department of Health and Human Services provides oversight to the activities of the OPTN and SRTR contractors.

We used a dataset of kidney transplants between 2000 and 2014, comprising pre-transplant clinical features about both donors and recipients. Our focus is investigating outcomes in survivors, i.e. those who have survived for a period of time after transplantation but remain at high risk of subsequent graft loss. This information may be most valuable for elderly recipients who would be expected to experience a higher risk of both death and graft loss compared to younger recipients. Therefore, for the purposes of this analysis, we chose a subset of elderly (>65) recipients of deceased donor kidney transplants (with complete data) who were alive and without graft failure, 3 years following transplantation. The outcome was events of failure either due to graft loss or death with a functioning graft. Thus, survival depends on the time-to-event period of interest. The data is right-censored—i.e. cases not labelled as failed during the period cannot be considered survived reliably due to the incompleteness of recorded information about adverse events. Censored patients are dealt with as

$$D(i, M, N) = \begin{cases} failed & IF\,(M * 365 \leq d_i < N * 365\ AND\ s_i = failed) \\ survived & IF\,(d_i \geq N * 365\ AND\ s_i = failed)\ OR\ (d_i \geq 8 * 365\ AND\ s_i \neq failed) \\ removed & ELSE \end{cases}$$

where $D(i, M, N)$ denotes the decision made for patient i for the period between M and N years after transplant (cohort of analysis), d_i is the number of days the patient survived and s_i is the graft status. We note that a patient is considered survived in a cohort if failure was recorded in one of the proceeding cohorts or if no failure was recorded for more than 8 years [7]. This not only estimated the number of *truly* survived patients but also helped address the class imbalance problem of having significantly more survived cases than graft failures. The patients were then partitioned into seven non-overlapping temporal cohorts each spanning one year, starting from the third year. Figure 2 shows the outcome distribution in each cohort (See [7] for more details about the data).

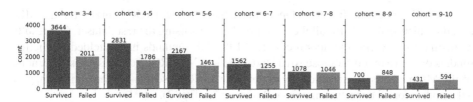

Fig. 2. Outcome distribution in each temporal cohort

4.2 Step1: Learning Graft Survival Prediction Models

As per the initial step of our XAI approach, we developed transplant survival prediction models for each temporal cohort. We used Artificial Neural Network (ANN), Random Forest (RF), and eXtreme Gradient Boosting (XGBoost) algorithms—the rationale for selecting these ML algorithms is that they were mostly used in prior transplant studies and thus offer a potential performance comparison with prior studies [1, 10]. We also developed soft voting classifiers (Vclf) on tuned ANN, RF and XGBoost to improve the prediction performance. Training of the ML models in each temporal cohort is done on 80% of the data using grid search cross-validation, and the trained models were evaluated on the unseen 20% test set. Python language and Scikit-learn package were used to develop and evaluate the prediction performance of the ML models.

4.3 Step 2: Surrogate Model Development

We used TREPAN [9], a global model-agnostic tree induction algorithm that by looking at the teacher ML model, recursively derives a surrogate CART decision tree. We generated surrogate models for all the ML models for each cohort. TREPAN has the advantage over conventional inductive learning algorithms in that it does not rely on the original instances to decide the best splits for each node of the tree, rather it generates new samples based on the distribution of the original instances and constraints (i.e., conditions that filter the range of accepted values for the features in that particular node). Also, a feature can appear multiple times in the extracted tree. TREPAN algorithm allows for setting maximum tree size (number of nodes) as the stopping criterion for tree extraction. We used an implementation of the TREPAN algorithm from generalizedtrees Python library [11] to build and visualize the surrogate models. The performance of the surrogate trees was measured in terms of fidelity—i.e. the percentage of input data on which the prediction by the surrogate tree agrees with that by the teacher model. It is noted that built-in tree visualization features of ensemble methods (e.g. plot_tree in XGBoost) which visualize single trees from a forest cannot be used in this study as they provide local explanations while we aim to extract global trees.

5 Experimental Results

5.1 Graft Survival Prediction Performance of ML Models (the Teachers)

Figure 3 illustrates the Receiver Operating Characteristic (ROC) curves for the ML-based prediction models for all the 7 temporal cohorts using the test dataset. Our results show that for any given temporal cohort, all the ML methods have yielded prediction models that have relatively close Area Under the ROC (AUROC) curve scores—i.e. none of the ML methods are significantly better. The AUROC scores for the entire range of ML models for all cohorts range from 0.62 to 0.73 (Fig. 3).

5.2 Performance of the Surrogate Models (Student): Fidelity and Prediction

We developed surrogate decision trees for all the ML models for each cohort. For each cohort we select the surrogate model with the highest fidelity with its teacher (i.e. ML model) and use it to explain the working of the ML model. Fidelity of the surrogate models is measured without pruning the trees thus allowing exploration of the full trees. Figure 4 illustrates the fidelity of the derived surrogate models (with unconditional depth) to their teachers in each cohort. The fidelity scores range from 73% to 98%, confirming that in each cohort there is a surrogate model that resembles its black-box teacher.

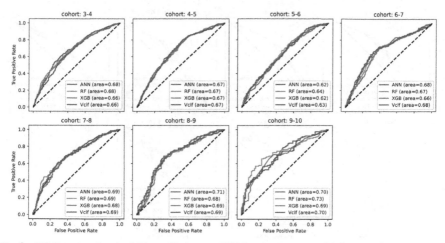

Fig. 3. ROC curves for the ML prediction models for the 7 temporal cohorts using the test set.

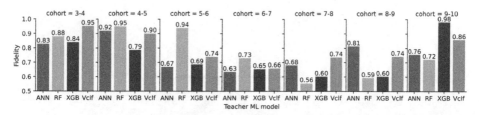

Fig. 4. Fidelity of the decision trees to their black-box models in each temporal cohort.

Next, we measured the prediction accuracy of all the generated surrogate models for a specific cohort using ROC curves. Figure 5 shows our results which indicate that within a cohort, the prediction accuracy of the generated surrogate models is quite close (note that in each cohort we used multiple ML models to generate prediction models). This result shows that our approach is generating surrogate models that are quite similar to their teachers—since the ML models had quite close prediction accuracy (see Fig. 3), their surrogate models are exhibiting the same prediction accuracy trend (Fig. 5).

To illustrate the nature of the surrogate model (represented as a decision tree), in Fig. 6. we present a section of a surrogate tree for cohort 7–8 which is pruned to a maximum size of ten nodes for visualization purposes.

5.3 Selecting the Surrogate Model for Explainability

To explain changes in feature importance over time, we selected the best representative ML model and its surrogate tree for each temporal cohort using the weighted average criterion—the weights are intuitively derived to indicate significance of the measures.

$$R_{surrogate} = ((AUROC_{teacher} * 3) + (Fidelity_{surrogate} * 2) + AUROC_{surrogate})/6,$$

where $R_{surrogate}$ is the representativeness score, $AUROC_{teacher}$ is AUROC score of the teacher ML model, $Fidelity_{surrogate}$ is the fidelity score of the surrogate model, and

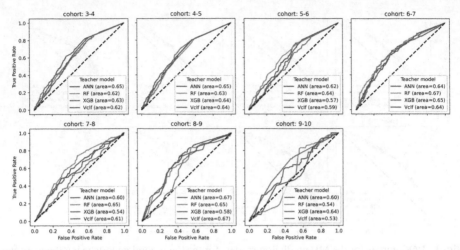

Fig. 5. ROC curves for the surrogate decision trees for the 7 temporal cohorts using the test set.

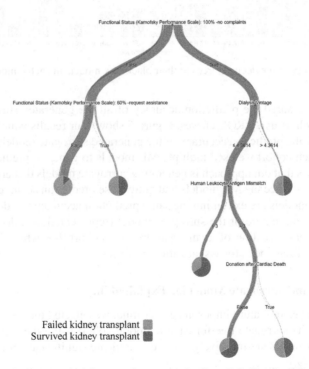

Fig. 6. A pruned surrogate decision tree for temporal cohort 7–8 (Teacher ML model: Vclf).

$AUROC_{surrogate}$ is AUROC score of the surrogate model on the ground truth. The tree with the highest $R_{surrogate}$ score was selected for the cross-cohort feature importance analysis. Table 1 shows the black-box ML models and their corresponding surrogate decision trees for each cohort selected.

Table 1. ML model and their surrogate decision trees selected for explainability

	Yearly Cohort						
	3–4	4–5	5–6	6–7	7–8	8–9	9–10
Chosen tree (highest $R_{surrogate}$ score)	S_{Vclf} *	S_{RF}	S_{RF}	S_{RF}	S_{Vclf}	S_{ANN}	S_{XGB}
AUROC of the teacher ML model	0.66	0.67	0.64	0.67	0.69	0.71	0.69
Fidelity of the surrogate to its teacher	0.95	0.95	0.94	0.73	0.74	0.81	0.98
AUROC of the surrogate tree	0.62	0.63	0.64	0.67	0.61	0.67	0.64

* S_x: Surrogate decision tree extracted from the teacher ML model x.

5.4 Expert's Interpretation of Temporal Changes to Feature Importance

We use *information gain* to denote the influence of time on a feature's contribution to transplant survival. Table 2 shows the top 10 features across each temporal cohort. An interpretation of the results—i.e. influence of changes in the importance of key transplant attributes over time as provided by kidney transplant experts is given below.

Table 2. Influence of time on the information gain of clinical features on graft survival. *Feature ranking* denotes the depth of the feature in the decision tree—the closer the feature to the root of the decision tree, the higher its importance in graft survival. *Freq* denotes the number of appearances of the feature in the tree. Attributes are color-coded to make it easy to follow their importance over time (see [7] for more details about the features).

Feature ranking	Cohort 3-4 Feature name	Freq.	Cohort 4-5 Feature name	Freq.	Cohort 5-6 Feature name	Freq.	Cohort 6-7 Feature name	Freq.	Cohort 7-8 Feature name	Freq.	Cohort 8-9 Feature name	Freq.	Cohort 9-10 Feature name	Freq.
1	vintage	471	vintage	173	functstat_30% - severely disabled	1	functstat_100% - no complaints	1	functstat_100% - no complaints	1	functstat_100% -no complaints	1	vintage	5
2	functstat_30% - severely disabled	6	functstat_30% - severely disabled	2	vintage	205	functstat_70% - unable to do normal activity	1	functstat_60% - req assistance	1	functstat_80% - some sx	1	functstat_100 % -no complaints	2
3	dwt	70	dwt	27	rwt2	88	hlamm	44	functstat_80% - some sx	1	functstat_90% - minor sx	1	-	-
4	rcmv_Pos	15	rdm2_No DM	16	rcvd_Yes	11	functstat_90% - minor sx	17	functstat_90% - minor sx	1	functstat_70% - unable to do normal activity	1	-	-
5	rht100	22	rbmisimp_>34.99	2	dht100	3	vintage	199	functstat_70% - unable to do normal activity	1	rwt2	69	-	-
6	rhtn_Yes	1	functstat_90% - minor sx	22	dwt	19	rcvd_Yes	1	dcd_Yes	12	dbmisimp_<=18.49	1	-	-
7	rbmisimp_>34.99	1	rwt2	18	rsex_Male	22	functstat_80% - some sx	9	hlamm	29	vintage	59	-	-
8	dbmisimp_>34.99	2	rcmv_Pos	5	rcad_No CAD	6	rsex_Male	16	vintage	61	esrddxsimp_Other	1	-	-
9	dbmisimp_>24.99-29.99	1	rsex_Male	19	cit	14	esrddxsimp_PCKD	1	dbmisimp_>34.99	1	dcd_Yes	9	-	-
10	dcd_Yes	3	ragetx	3	rracesimp_White	1	pkpragroup	49	rht100	35	rracesimp_Black	2	-	-

This study focused on elderly recipients surviving the early period following transplantation. Much insight can be derived from the relative importance of baseline clinical features (at the time of transplantation) on outcomes in each period of observation. As noted in Table 2, functional status continues to have a major influence on outcomes despite only being captured at baseline. In keeping with the literature, functional impairment has been identified as an important factor influencing short-term and long-term outcomes following transplantation [12, 13]. This expands the potential importance of functional status, defined by the Karnofsky Performance Scale (KPS) in elderly kidney transplant survivors. Similarly, while dialysis vintage would be expected to be ameliorated after transplantation, our analysis suggests that a long pre-transplant dialysis exposure may continue to play an important role in outcomes for elderly transplant survivors [14]. Again, pre-transplant dialysis vintage is an established predictor of post-transplant outcomes, but our study would suggest that its relative importance wanes over time, potentially due to the restoration of normal physiology resulting from transplantation. In addition to understanding the influences of pre-transplant variables on outcomes informed by this analysis, our findings suggest focuses for future study. For example, functional impairment is not routinely captured longitudinally after transplantation but considering the importance of even baseline functional status, the results suggest that longitudinal capture should be prioritized.

Some survival analyses that compare the relative importance of characteristics (for example low versus high functional status) utilize factors measured at one point to provide a single measure of risk, provided certain assumptions are not violated. While this approach is valuable, both clinicians and providers may be faced with how best to make a clinical decision on a patient at a point in time beyond the date of their transplant. The ML based analysis discussed in this study emphasizes that the relative importance of some features changes over time, contingent on whether a patient has survived up to that point. Therefore, a prudent extension of this work would be to rederive clinical risk prediction models, using those factors that most contribute to all-cause graft survival, as determined by the extraction of surrogate decision trees and ranking of the relative influence of variables over time. We believe this may provide a given patient with a more global impression of their probability of survival, based on the totality of only those factors identified as being most important. Patients wish to know such information irrespective of how far out they are from the date of their transplantation, and providers may make care decisions or use novel treatments or supports for patients identified as being vulnerable to graft failure based on their characteristics.

6   Concluding Remarks

In this paper, we present a ML model-agnostic XAI method to predict the importance of clinical features in kidney allografts, based on evaluating pre-transplant donor-recipient features. Our approach for generating surrogate models provides a transparent mechanism to open the ML black box without losing prediction accuracy and introducing any biases to the base ML models. Our results indicate that the surrogate models closely mimic the performance of the ML models.

The research questions and experiments were conducted using real-life kidney transplant data and in collaboration with kidney transplant specialists who provided a clinical interpretation of the cross-cohort temporal analysis of the features, identifying interesting feature importance patterns that we plan to study to understand temporal functional impairment as a precursor to graft survival prediction. Cross-cohort analysis has given insights into longitudinal factors that influence patient and graft survival.

This approach would have even more value in the setting of a longitudinal analysis where similar factors are repeated annually. For example, comorbid conditions, functional status and age would be expected to change over time. Therefore, using this feature importance identification method may be even more helpful in identifying those at highest risk of graft loss, where this additional information is available.

A challenge regarding surrogate modelling is that a high-fidelity explanation can be misleading since it may not capture causality between features and teacher ML model predictions. To achieve highly trustable explanations, we plan to investigate neural-symbolic explainability methods to increase the comprehensibility of the surrogate explanations by incorporating domain knowledge graphs and ontologies.

Acknowledgments. The data reported here have been supplied by the Hennepin Healthcare Research Institute (HHRI) as the contractor for the Scientific Registry of Transplant Recipients (SRTR). The interpretation and reporting of these data are the responsibility of the authors and in no way should be seen as an official policy of or interpretation by the SRTR or the U.S. Government.

References

1. Díez-Sanmartín, C., Sarasa-Cabezuelo, A., Andrés Belmonte, A.: The impact of artificial intelligence and big data on end-stage kidney disease treatments. Expert Syst. Appl. **180**, 115076 (2021)
2. Barredo Arrieta, A., et al.: Explainable Artificial Intelligence (XAI): concepts, taxonomies, opportunities and challenges toward responsible AI. Inf. Fusion **58**, 82–115 (2020)
3. Lauritsen, S.M., et al.: Explainable artificial intelligence model to predict acute critical illness from electronic health records. Nat. Commun. **11**, 1–11 (2020)
4. da Cruz, H.F., et al.: Using interpretability approaches to update "black-box" clinical prediction models: an external validation study in nephrology. Artif. Intell. Med. **111**, 101982 (2021)
5. Li, Y., Chen, T., Chen, T., Li, X., Zeng, C., Liu, Z., Xie, G.: An interpretable machine learning survival model for predicting long-term kidney outcomes in IgA nephropathy. In: AMIA Annual Symposium Proceedings, vol. 2020, p. 737 (2020)
6. Moreno-Sanchez, P.A.: Features importance to improve interpretability of chronic kidney disease early diagnosis. In: Proceedings - 2020 IEEE International Conference on Big Data, Big Data 2020, pp. 3786–3792 (2020)
7. Naqvi, S.A.A., Tennankore, K., Vinson, A., Roy, P.C., Abidi, S.S.R.: Predicting kidney graft survival using machine learning methods: prediction model development and feature significance analysis study. J. Med. Internet Res. **23**, e26843 (2021)
8. Guidotti, R., Monreale, A., Ruggieri, S., Turini, F., Giannotti, F., Pedreschi, D.: A survey of methods for explaining black box models. ACM Comput. Surv. **51**, 1–42 (2018)
9. Craven, M.W., Shavlik, J.W.: Extracting tree-structured representations of trained networks. Neural Inf. Process. Syst. **8**, 24–30 (1995)
10. Moreno-Sanchez, P.A.: Development and evaluation of an explainable prediction model for chronic kidney disease patients based on ensemble trees (2021). https://arxiv.org/abs/2105.10368

11. Sverchkov, Y.: Generalizedtrees. https://github.com/Craven-Biostat-Lab/generalizedtrees. Accessed 04 Nov 2021
12. Yoo, J., Park, C.G., Ryan, C.: Impact of physical function on 1-year kidney transplant outcomes. West J. Nurs. Res. **42**, 50–56 (2020)
13. Chu, N.M., Chen, X., Bae, S., Brennan, D.C., Segev, D.L., McAdams-Demarco, M.A.: Changes in functional status among kidney transplant recipients: data from the scientific registry of transplant recipients. Transplantation **105**, 2104–2111 (2021)
14. Haller, M.C., Kammer, M., Oberbauer, R.: Dialysis vintage and outcomes in renal transplantation. Nephrol. Dial. Transplant. **34**, 555–560 (2019)

Recurrence and Self-attention vs the Transformer for Time-Series Classification: A Comparative Study

Alexander Katrompas[1], Theodoros Ntakouris[2], and Vangelis Metsis[1(✉)]

[1] Texas State University, San Marcos, TX 78666, USA
{amk181,vmetsis}@txstate.edu
[2] University of Patras, Patras, Greece
ntakouris@ceid.upatras.gr

Abstract. Recently the transformer has established itself as the state-of-the-art in text processing and has demonstrated impressive results in image processing, leading to the decline in the use of recurrence in neural network models. As established in the seminal paper, Attention Is All You Need, recurrence can be removed in favor of a simpler model using only self-attention. While transformers have shown themselves to be robust in a variety of text and image processing tasks, these tasks all have one thing in common; they are inherently non-temporal. Although transformers are also finding success in modeling time-series data, they also have their limitations as compared to recurrent models. We explore a class of problems involving classification and prediction from time-series data and show that recurrence combined with self-attention can meet or exceed the transformer architecture performance. This particular class of problem, temporal classification, and prediction of labels through time from time-series data is of particular importance to medical data sets which are often time-series based (Source code: https://github.com/imics-lab/recurrence-with-self-attention).

1 Introduction

The transformer architecture has shown superior performance to recurrent networks (RNN) and convolutional (CNN) networks, particularly in the areas of text translation and processing [13], as well as recently in image classification [17]. Self-attention only models, based on the transformer, are also showing promise in time-series classification [16]. While the majority of these non-temporal data (i.e. image and text) have some form of order, they are not inherently temporal nor continuous in nature. Text data and images are processed by transformers as discrete data tokens or patches where the value of one token does not necessarily affect the value of a neighboring token. While order and position matter in text prediction, the strength of the relationships between tokens is at least semi-independent of proximity and requires positional encoding for modeling. [13]. This applies to images as well [15].

M. Michalowski et al. (Eds.): AIME 2022, LNAI 13263, pp. 99–109, 2022.
https://doi.org/10.1007/978-3-031-09342-5_10

Conversely, time-series data are typically continuous, and proximity is important to the current time-step and the current classification/prediction [9]. This study will show it is this difference in time-series data characteristics which make recurrence combined with self-attention important to temporal classification/prediction.

Previous work has shown that time-series classification can benefit from the addition of self-attention to recurrent neural networks [6]. The main contribution of this paper is to demonstrate that in the case of temporal classification/prediction, neither self-attention nor recurrence is all you need, but rather it is recurrence combined with self-attention which provides the most robust modeling for this class of problems. The goal of this work is to compare and contrast self-attention alone, i.e. the transformer, against combined recurrence and attention to achieve the optimal time-series modeling. This is verified through a series of experiments on nine different publicly available data sets, empirical observations, and theoretical evidence.

2   Background

2.1   Recurrent Neural Networks

Recurrent networks are particularly adept at maintaining temporal information through the recurrence mechanism, which feeds the current recurrent layer's output back to input layer, thereby including each current output to the subsequent input and forming a temporal chain of causality by maintaining an internal state (i.e. "memory"). This architecture allows the RNN to more effectively model time-series data than most other networks [4]. The term "recurrent neural network" is used broadly to refer to a collection of specific network architectures. Of interest in this study is the LSTM which has proven itself as one of the most robust of the RNN architectures [4,10].

While RNNs have proven themselves in a variety of tasks, especially temporal modeling, they have some drawbacks including computational complexity and the heavier weighting of nearer time-steps [5,7,13]. The latter characteristic is of interest to this study. A RNN's "memory" has a time-dependent feature, which is both a shortcoming and a benefit. RNNs tend to weigh the most recent information more heavily than long past information, analogous to a weighted moving average. This is a benefit in modeling time-series data where more recent information should be weighed heavier [10]. However, it is also a shortcoming in two regards: 1) long past information is "forgotten" even when it is useful, and 2) within any particular sequence we may not always wish a weighting strictly based on proximity in time.

2.2   Self-attention

Attention mechanisms, originally created for text prediction, allow the network to "attend" to portions of a sequence out of order, stressing the importance of one token or another within a sequence, thereby creating a better representation of the sequence [4, 13]. There are several types of attention mechanisms, all of which work similarly within a neural network to create a "relationship within a relationship"; the latter relationship being the neural network input/output and the former being some relation between the sequence tokens which are more (or less) important to the neural network prediction. Attention can be generally described as a weight or "context vector" of importance within a sequence [2, 7, 8].

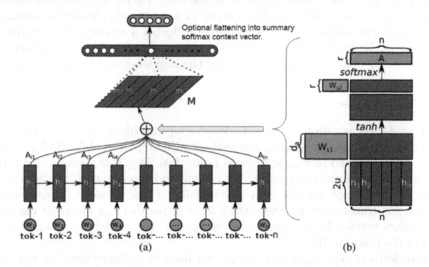

Fig. 1. Attention-based LSTM model (a) [7] with a self-attention layer (b).

Self-attention (see Fig. 1) is an attention mechanism directly relating different positions of a sequence in order to compute a better representation of that sequence. Self-attention differs from other attention mechanisms in that rather than calculating an entire summarized context vector based on input/output prediction, self-attention is directly calculating sequence-portion importance relative to other sequence-portions [4, 7, 13, 17].

2.3   LSTM with Self-attention

When combined with LSTM architectures, attention operates by capturing all LSTM output within a sequence and training a separate layer to "attend" to some parts of the LSTM output more than others [7]. For an input sequence $x = (x_1, x_2, ..., x_T)$ the LSTM layer produces the hidden vector sequence $h = (h_1, h_2, ..., h_T)$ and output $y = (y_1, y_2, ..., y_T)$ of the same length, by iterating the following equations from $t = 1$ to T.

$$h_t = \mathcal{H}(W_{xh}x_t + W_{hh}h_{t-1} + b_h) \tag{1}$$

$$y_t = W_{hy}h_t + b_y \tag{2}$$

where the W terms denote weight matrices, the b terms denote bias vectors, and $\mathcal{H}$ is the hidden layer function. In this fashion, self-attention learns to weigh portions of a sequence for relative feature importance [15].

The attention used in this study is multiplicative self-attention and uses the following attention mechanism:

$$h_t = tanh(W_x x_t + W_h h_{t-1} + b_h) \tag{3}$$

$$e_t = \sigma(h_t^T W_a h_{t-1} + b_t), a_t = softmax(e_t) \tag{4}$$

where h_t is the hidden node output from the LSTM layer in a two-dimensional matrix. e_t is the sigmoid activation output of the attention two-layer network, where W_a is the attention network weights, producing a corresponding matrix of the attention network activations. a_t is the softmax activation of e_t producing a context vector "alignment score" weighing the importance of the sequences [6].

2.4   Transformer

The transformer is a deep learning model which primarily uses the self-attention mechanism for modeling and eliminates the RNN component. Like RNNs, transformers are designed to handle ordered input data (e.g. text, images) for tasks such as translation, summarization, prediction, and classification. Unlike RNNs, transformers do not process data sequentially at the encoder (input) stage. Instead, the transformer processes the tokens in parallel and identifies the context of each token relative to other tokens, which then confers meaning to each word in the sentence [13].

Transformers typically adopt an encoder-decoder architecture. The function of the encoder layers is to generate encodings that contain information about which parts of the inputs are relevant to each other. Each decoder layer does the opposite, taking all the encodings and using their incorporated contextual information to generate an ordered output sequence. To achieve this, each encoder and decoder layer makes use of a self-attention mechanism [13]. One or more fully connected layers can be attached at the end of the encoder part of the transformer to create a sequence classification architecture.

Because transformers do not process data in order at the encoder (input) layer, they do not understand order on their own (which RNNs understand by design). To solve this, transformers use positional encoding to maintain order in output (discussed further in Sects. 3.1) [13].

2.5   Temporal Classification and Prediction

Text and image processing require ordered information and relative position matters, however, strict sequential ordering and proximity do not matter (or at least matter less) [2,13]. Conversely, time-series data are highly dependent on absolute order, proximity, and absolute position [9]. Further, while text and image data are typically processed in discrete "chunks" such as words or patches, time-series data are typically processed as a series of continuous signal measurements in which the strongest relationships to any given time-step are with the immediately preceding time-steps.

Given the characteristics of text/image data versus time-series it can immediately be seen why the transformer has enjoyed such success with text and image processing. Not only is recurrence not needed, but it can also be argued it is counter productive to use an architecture based on continuous temporal flow for such tasks. By that same logic, it is also fair to question the transformer's suitability for true time-series data and temporal classification, even considering recent promising advances [16]. To do so we first identify an important and common class of temporal classification and pattern matching problem which is highly time-dependent.

The time-series problem in question is the classification or prediction of a temporal "event" (i.e. label) through time. For example, given a continuous ECG signal can we identify heart abnormalities, or given accelerometer readings from a smart device can we detect activities of daily life (ADLs), and can we do so with superior results to both RNNs alone and the transformer. Such tasks require pattern matching and modeling data which have three very specific characteristics. 1) *Sequential nature*: The data to be modeled is true time-series data, continuous and in-order, sampled at reasonably regular rates. 2) *Natural order*: The data to be modeled are natural and not artificially staged into fixed, discrete, disparate labels. 3) *Temporal label classification from time-series data*: The classification labels are occurrences through time from time-series data and not single-point, discrete classifications.

3 Models

3.1 Time-Series Transformer

Architecture: The time-series transformer used in this study is built directly from the transformer described in [13] with a modified output for time-series classification, and eliminating positional encoding as it is not needed (see Sect. 3.1). The self-attention mechanism is identical to [13], as is the encoder architecture, including layer normalization and feed-forward components. Since decoding is not needed, the decoder is replaced with dense layers, leading to the final dense layer for output. Figure 2a illustrates this architecture.

Positional Encoding: In the traditional encoder-decoder transformer relative and/or absolute positional encoding is needed to preserve order within sequences and in output [12,13], and to signify the absolute position of each token in the sequence, as the same token can appear in different positions of a sequence for different samples. However, in time series where each token is a single time-step, i.e. a signal measurement appearing as a scalar real number or a vector (in the case of multiple channels), positional encoding does not add any information. The same real number may never appear again in the dataset or it may appear multiple times within the same sequence. Thus adding a positional encoding to time-series data only adds another feature to be learned from the training data, which does not add any benefit to the prediction performance. This is verified in practice, as in all our experiments attempting positional encoding, accuracy declined between 1% and 4% regardless of hyper-parameter tuning.

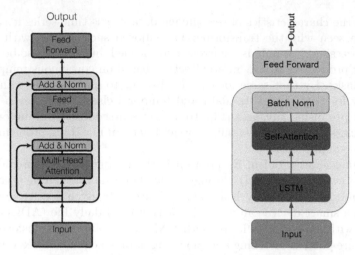

(a) Time-series transformer architecture.   (b) LSTM with self-attention architecture.

Fig. 2. Overview of neural network architectures evaluated in this study.

3.2 LSTM with Self-attention

Architecture: The basis for an LSTM plus self-attention model is that we wish to model sequences in order through time (the LSTM component) while also attending to portions of a sequence which may be more or less relevant (self-attention), thereby making a better representation of each sequence. In this way, we are modeling ordered temporal sequences which are better representations of themselves through the attention mechanism, while at the same time allowing the LSTM memory to remember and model time-series dependencies. Figure 2b illustrates the overall LSTM/self-attention architecture.

Figure 3 illustrates the conceptual flow of data "weight" through both a LSTM model (top) and a LSTM plus attention model (bottom). Darker shading indicates a stronger relationship to LSTM memory and/or attention. As data flows through an LSTM more recent data is "weighted" heavier than past data. The top flow (LSTM alone) illustrates that data is weighted smoothly both intra-sequence and inter-sequence.

The lower flow of Fig. 3 shows LSTM plus self-attention with each sequence modeled according to self-attention. Within a sequence, we can see some time-steps as more or less important to the sequence overall. As stated in [13], through self-attention we can *"form a better overall representation of the sequence."*

Sequence Length: Deep learning architectures require the continuous time series to be broken down into fixed-length sequences for training. Sequence length is a hyper-parameter which can be tuned on a per-model basis. Model accuracy is sensitive to sequence length selection which makes both intuitive and theoretical sense. When modeling time-series data with a self-attention component we are attending more or less to portions of a sequence. Therefore if we make the

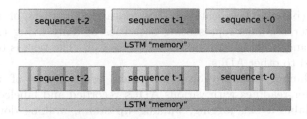

Fig. 3. Conceptual data flow through LSTM (top) versus LSTM plus self-attention (bottom). Darker shading indicates higher importance.

sequence very long then the model essentially degrades to attention only due to the LSTM's decreased ability to model time-steps too far in the past. In the reverse case, imagine the sequence length being simply 1 or 2 time-steps. In that case, there is not enough information for self-attention to intelligently attend to portions of sequence, and the model degrades to LSTM-only. Therefore, as sequence length is lengthened or shortened, more or less emphasis is placed on the self-attention mechanism versus the LSTM. For this study sequence length was selected through grid search.

4   Experiments

Set-Up: In each experiment, hyper-parameters were selected through grid-search and are noted in the referenced code. Sequence lengths, being of particular note, were selected as follows: SmartFall: 50, MobiAct: 200, Australian National Weather Observations: 5, Air Quality: 4, mHealth: 200, ECG: 100.

Data Sets: Data sets were chosen with the following rationale: (i) Satisfying the criteria of Sect. 2.5. (ii) Verification and comparison to similar LSTM-only studies with ADLs and time-series data [6,14]. (iii) ADL data sets, and ECG sets, representing medical data. (iv) Sufficiently different classification tasks which bear little to no resemblance to each other, other than the fact they satisfy the criteria of Sect. 2.5. (v) A mix of temporal classification (SmartFall, MobiAct, mHealth, EEG) and temporal prediction (Australian BOM, CO prediction). (vi) A mix of data sizes from 100s to 100,000s of instances. (vii) Both binary classification/predication and multi-label classification.

   The data sets used are the following:

- *mHealth* (multi-label classification): Human behavior recording, analysis, and classification based on multi-modal body sensing [3].
- *ECG Heartbeat Categorization* (multi-label classification): Two collections of heartbeat signals derived from two datasets in heartbeat classification, the MIT-BIH Arrhythmia Dataset[1] and The PTB Diagnostic ECG Database[2].

---

[1] https://www.physionet.org/content/mitdb/1.0.0/.

[2] https://www.deepdyve.com/lp/de-gruyter/nutzung-der-ekg-signaldatenbank-cardiodat-der-ptb-ber-das-internet-uemKpjIFzM.

- *SmartFall* (binary classification): The data set consists of raw (x, y, z) accelerometer readings representing activities of daily living (ADLs), such as walking and running with falls interspersed [6]. The task is to label a fall as compared to other ADLs.
- *MobiAct* (binary classification): The data set consists of raw (x, y, z) accelerometer readings with various ADLs recorded and labeled [6,14]. The task is to label a fall, jogging, walking up stairs, walking down stairs, as compared to other ADLs.
- *Australian BOM National Weather Observations* (binary prediction): Observations of a number of weather elements each day in various Australian cities for years 2008 to 2017. The task is to predict rain/no-rain tomorrow [1].
- *Air Quality Time-Series data UCI* (binary prediction): Hourly averaged responses from an array of 5 metal oxide chemical sensors embedded in an air quality device [11]. The task is to predict if CO levels will rise/fall tomorrow.

The larger data sets were split into train, validation, and test 60/20/20. The smaller sets are split into train and test 80/20. For the data sets with validation sets, each model was run ten times and test set averages were calculated and recorded. In the case of smaller sets without validation sets, each model was run with 5-fold cross-validation and test set averages were calculated and recorded.

4.1   Results

All binary classification/prediction task results are presented in Table 1. The macro-averaged results for all classes of mHealth and EEG data set are shown in Tables 2 and 3. The detailed per-class results can be found in Appendix A. LSTM only results have been conducted on the same and similar data sets in other work [6,14]. In all cases and without exception, LSTM plus self-attention outperformed stand-alone LSTM models. Therefore, results for stand-alone LSTM are omitted for brevity since they do not alter the results of this study. Further, as shown in detail in this study, LSTM plus self-attention was generally superior to self-attention alone (i.e. the transformer).

Accuracy of the LSTM plus self-attention model showed an increase in validation accuracy over the transformer between 1.2% (MobiAct jog detection) and 14.4% (CO prediction). Precision increased from 1.4% (MobiAct jog detection) to 324.5% (SmartFall fall detection). Recall ranged from a decrease of 3.7% (MobiAct stairs up detection) to an increase of 8.7% (SmartFall fall detection). F1 increased from 0.7% (MobiAct jog detection) to 53.7% (SmartFall fall detection). Further, in all cases except one (Mobi-Act Jog), the LSTM plus self-attention architecture ROC-AUC and PR-AUC showed significant improvement over the transformer architecture.

For the mHealth data set, the LSTM/Attn model proved superior for all but one category, with overall accuracy being .85 versus .82 and a weighted average .87 versus .82. In the case of EEG classification, both models achieve extremely high accuracy, 0.99, however, the detailed per category results still show a very slight advantage to the LSTM/Attn model.

Table 1. Results comparing performance metrics of LSTM+self-attention against the Transformer for each *binary classification* dataset. Acc = Accuracy, Prec = Precision, Rec = Recall, F1 = F1-score, ROC=Area under ROC curve, PR = Area under Precision-Recall curve. SF = SmartFall, MA-[F/J/Up/Dn] = MobiAct [Fall/Jog/StairsUp/StairsDown], Rain = Australian BOM, CO = Carbon Monoxide.

	SF		MA-F		MA-J		MA-Up		MA-Dn		Rain		CO	
	tran	lstm	tran	lstm	tran	lstm	tran	lstm	tran	lstm	tran	lstm	tran	lstm
Acc	.886	**.961**	.900	**.937**	.957	**.968**	.894	**.936**	.900	**.916**	.848	**.923**	.659	**.754**
Prec	.196	**.832**	.622	**.767**	.976	**.990**	.868	**.972**	.891	**.956**	.486	**.827**	.422	**.698**
Rec	.782	**.869**	.913	**.953**	.977	**.975**	.967	**.932**	**.964**	.790	**.847**	.927	.651	**.715**
F1	.313	**.850**	.740	**.850**	.976	**.983**	.914	**.952**	.926	**.941**	.601	**.837**	.512	**.706**
ROC	.593	**.906**	.802	**.878**	**.872**	.868	.906	**.919**	**.906**	.888	.722	**.890**	.628	**.747**
PR	.542	**.862**	.811	**.887**	.987	.987	.960	**.961**	**.966**	.957	.699	**.858**	.659	**.771**

Table 2. Averaged results of mHealth data set (13 classes). Acc: Accuracy, Prec: Precision, Rec: Recall, F1: F1-score, MacrAvg: Macro Average, WAvg: Weighted Avg.

	LSTM w/Attn			Transformer			Support
	Prec	Rec	F1	Prec	Rec	F1	
MacrAvg	**0.76**	**0.83**	**0.78**	0.71	0.68	0.67	202k
WAvg	**0.87**	**0.85**	**0.85**	0.82	0.82	0.82	
Acc	**0.85**			0.82			

Table 3. Averaged results of ECG Classification data set (5 classes).

	LSTM w/Attn			Transformer			Support
	Prec	Rec	F1	Prec	Rec	F1	
MacrAvg	0.93	**0.99**	0.95	0.93	0.97	0.95	21.9k
WAvg	0.99	0.99	0.99	0.99	0.99	0.99	
Acc	0.99			0.99			

5 Conclusion

The LSTM plus self-attention model outperformed and proved superior to the time-series transformer in temporal classification and prediction. In particular, we believe this work shows that a combination of overall temporal modeling (the RNN component) along with fine-grained sequence modeling (self-attention) addresses this specific class of problem with state-of-the-art results. We believe this is notable since this particular class of problem, natural time-series data and temporal classification/prediction, is common and of particular importance to tasks such as medical data analysis and prediction, ADL classification, process control, natural event prediction, financial and economic modeling, and many other similar high-value tasks. This work shows recurrence is not only valuable but that it is a particularly and specifically valuable partner to self-attention, demonstrating that for this particular class of problem, attention may not be all you need.

References

1. Australian Bureau of Meteorology (BOM): Australia, rain tomorrow. Australian BOM National Weather Observations
2. Bahdanau, D., Cho, K., Bengio, Y.: Neural machine translation by jointly learning to align and translate. arXiv **1409**, September 2014
3. Banos, O., et al.: Design, implementation and validation of a novel open framework for agile development of mobile health applications. Biomed. Eng. OnLine **14**(2), S6 (2015)
4. Cheng, J., Dong, L., Lapata, M.: Long short-term memory-networks for machine reading. In: Proceedings of the 2016 Conference on Empirical Methods in Natural Language Processing, pp. 551–561, January 2016
5. Hochreiter, S., Schmidhuber, J.: Long short-term memory. Neural Comput. **9**(8), 1735–1780 (1997). https://doi.org/10.1162/neco.1997.9.8.1735
6. Katrompas, A., Metsis, V.: Enhancing LSTM models with self-attention and stateful training. In: Arai, K. (ed.) IntelliSys 2021. LNNS, vol. 294, pp. 217–235. Springer, Cham (2022). https://doi.org/10.1007/978-3-030-82193-7_14
7. Lin, Z., et al.: A structured self-attentive sentence embedding, March 2017
8. Luong, M.T., Pham, H., Manning, C.: Effective approaches to attention-based neural machine translation, August 2015
9. Qin, Y., Song, D., Cheng, H., Cheng, W., Jiang, G., Cottrell, G.: A dual-stage attention-based recurrent neural network for time series prediction, April 2017
10. Rahman, L., Mohammed, N., Al Azad, A.K.: A new LSTM model by introducing biological cell state. In: 2016 3rd International Conference on Electrical Engineering and Information Communication Technology (ICEEICT), pp. 1–6 (2016)
11. De Vito, S.: Air quality data set. https://archive.ics.uci.edu/ml/datasets/Air+quality
12. Shaw, P., Uszkoreit, J., Vaswani, A.: Self-attention with relative position representations, pp. 464–468, January 2018
13. Vaswani, A., et al.: Attention is all you need. In: 31st Conference on Neural Information Processing Systems (NIPS 2017), June 2017
14. Vavoulas, G., Chatzaki, C., Malliotakis, T., Pediaditis, M., Tsiknakis, M.: The MobiAct dataset: recognition of activities of daily living using smartphones. In: Proceedings of the International Conference on Information and Communication Technologies for Ageing Well and e-Health, pp. 143–151. SciTePress (2016)
15. Wang, J., Yang, Y., Mao, J., Huang, Z., Huang, C., Xu, W.: CNN-RNN: a unified framework for multi-label image classification. In: 2016 IEEE Conference on Computer Vision and Pattern Recognition, April 2016
16. Wu, N., Green, B., Ben, X., O'Banion, S.: Deep transformer models for time series forecasting: the influenza prevalence case (2020)
17. Zhao, H., Jia, J., Koltun, V.: Exploring self-attention for image recognition, pp. 10073–10082, June 2020

A   Appendix: Detailed Classification Report Results

(See Tables 4 and 5).

Table 4. Experimental results mHealth data set. Cat: Category, Acc: Accuracy, Prec: Precision, Rec: Recall, F1: F1-score, MacAvg: Macro Average, WAvg: Weighted Avg

LSTM w/Attn					Transformer				
Cat	Prec	Rec	F1	Sup	Cat	Prec	Rec	F1	Support
Null	**0.94**	0.86	**0.89**	135,542	Null	0.88	**0.88**	0.88	135,542
Standing	0.60	0.98	0.74	6,144	Standing	**0.71**	0.98	**0.82**	6,144
Sitting	**0.72**	1.00	**0.84**	6,144	Sitting	0.71	0.89	0.79	6,144
Laying	0.92	0.98	0.95	6,144	Laying	0.92	0.98	0.95	6,144
Walking	**0.50**	**0.91**	**0.65**	6,144	Walking	0.47	0.44	0.45	6,144
Stairs-Up	**0.71**	0.48	0.57	6,144	Stairs-Up	0.64	**0.76**	**0.69**	6,144
Bends	0.89	**0.90**	**0.90**	5,274	Bends	0.89	0.65	0.75	5,274
Arm elev	**0.79**	0.57	**0.66**	4,864	Arm elev	0.70	0.57	0.63	4,864
Knee bend	0.66	0.49	0.56	5120	Knee bend	0.83	0.54	0.66	5,120
Cycling	0.51	0.79	0.62	6144	Cycling	**0.75**	**0.81**	**0.78**	6,144
Jogging	**0.88**	**0.89**	**0.89**	6144	Jogging	0.71	0.39	0.51	6,144
Running	**0.83**	1.00	**0.91**	6144	Running	0.55	0.9	0.68	6,144
Jumping	1.00	**0.95**	**0.97**	2,048	Jumping	0.46	0.05	0.09	2,048
MacAvg	**0.76**	**0.83**	**0.78**	202,000	MacAvg	0.71	0.68	0.67	202,000
WAvg	**0.87**	**0.85**	**0.85**	202k	WAvg	0.82	0.82	0.82	202k
Acc	**0.85**	202,000			Acc	0.82	202,000		

Table 5. Experimental results ECG Classification data set. Cat: Category, Acc: Accuracy, Prec: Precision, Rec: Recall, F1: F1-score, MacAvg: Macro Average, W. Avg: Weighted Average, 0: Non-Ectopic, 1: Superventrical Ectopic, 2: Ventricular Ectopic, 3: Fusion, 4: Unknown

LSTM w/Attn					Transformer				
Cat	Prec	Rec	F1	Sup	Cat	Prec	Rec	F1-score	Support
Cat	Prec	Rec	F1	Support	Cat	Prec	Rec	F1	Support
0	1.00	0.99	1.00	18,118	0	1.00	0.99	1.00	18,118
1	0.82	**1.00**	**0.90**	556	1	0.82	0.87	0.84	556
2	1.00	0.97	0.98	1,448	2	0.95	0.99	0.97	1,448
3	0.81	**1.00**	0.90	162	3	**0.87**	0.99	**0.93**	162
4	1.00	0.99	1.00	1,616	4	1.00	0.99	1.00	1,616
MacAvg	0.93	**0.99**	0.95	21.9k	MacAvg	0.93	0.97	0.95	21900
WAvg	0.99	0.99	0.99	21.9k	WAvg	0.99	0.99	0.99	21.9k
Acc	0.99	21.9k			Acc	0.99	21.9k		

Integrating Graph Convolutional Networks (GCNNs) and Long Short-Term Memory (LSTM) for Efficient Diagnosis of Autism

Kashaf Masood$^{(\boxtimes)}$ and Rasha Kashef

Ryerson University, Toronto, ON M5B 2K3, Canada
{kashaf.masood,rkashef}@ryerson.ca

Abstract. Artificial intelligence (AI) has a wide range of practices in biotechnology, specifically for automated diagnosis of behavioural disorders, including autism spectrum disorder (ASD). With the rise and severity of this disorder, machine learning and deep learning methods have proven to provide efficient and less invasive diagnosis for individuals with ASD. Although various deep learning techniques have been employed to achieve a more robust diagnosis for ASD, hybrid graph convolutional neural networks (GCNNs) for ASD diagnosis are not addressed prominently in the literature; GCNNs have received significant adoption in image processing. This paper proposes and evaluates a hybrid deep learning model that combines the power of GCNNs and long short-term memory (LSTM) for ASD diagnosis. The proposed GCNN-LSTM model provides an efficient diagnosis for ASD by identifying the brain functionality between anterior and posterior areas of the brain. The proposed GCNN-LSTM model and other baseline classifiers are trained and tested on various ASD-related fMRI brain images from the Autism Brain Imaging Data Exchange (ABIDE) database. Experimental results show that the proposed model achieved an accuracy of up to 75%, AUC up to 80%, Precision up to 82%, Recall of up to 85%, and F1-score of up to 83%, thus outperforming the baseline classifiers.

Keywords: Autism spectrum disorder · Graph Convolutional Neural Networks (GCNNs) · Long Short-Term Memory (LSTM)

1 Introduction

Autism spectrum disorder (ASD) is a neurodevelopmental disorder that affects how a person behaves during social communication and interaction [1]. Due to the severity of the social impairment caused by ASD, it can cause lifelong struggle for people with this disorder. With the increasing rate of diagnosis for ASD, it is crucial to focus on effective and non-invasive diagnosis for patients [2]. Currently, ASD is mainly diagnosed through the autism diagnostic observation schedule (ADOS) testing and clinical opinion [2]. However, this approach is time-consuming and invasive for the patient. Researchers have proposed various machine learning alternatives which are applied to MRI images for effective diagnosis [2]. Ideally, when designing a machine learning algorithm to

© The Author(s), under exclusive license to Springer Nature Switzerland AG 2022
M. Michalowski et al. (Eds.): AIME 2022, LNAI 13263, pp. 110–121, 2022.
https://doi.org/10.1007/978-3-031-09342-5_11

diagnose ASD, specific considerations must be made to increase performance. Firstly, there must be a strong scientific understanding of ASD and ASD diagnosis before an effective computational algorithm can be achieved [4]. Additionally, the datasets used in the studies should be large and encompass most sub-populations for accurate and unbiased results [5]. In recent research, it is observed that there exist gaps in the behavioural science aspect of the algorithm, which hinders effective decision-making through machine learning [3]. Additionally, datasets are lacking in sub-categorical data. Existing AI-based methods for ASD diagnosis are limited in their performance, specifically accuracy and computational time. Using the advances in Convolutional Neural Networks (CNNs), various classification problems have been addressed [5–8]. However, limited research has been conducted on ASD diagnosis systems using graphs as inputs, focusing on graph convolutional neural networks (GCNNs) [9] as the primary machine learning model. GCNNs have shown promising performance in binary classification problems [8]. GCNNs reduce over-fitting effects on graph structures and address the problem of blown up and vanishing gradients using their re-normalization. In addition, the Long Short-Term Memory (LSTM) [10] is known for its capability to learn temporal features and solve the long-term dependency problem. Thus, in this paper, we combine the power of both GCNNs and LSTM to propose a hybrid model (GCNN-LSTM) that focuses on introducing LSTMs in Graph Convolutional Neural Networks (GCNNs) to create a more robust and accurate Autism classifier. This work analyzes the effectiveness of adding LSTMs when diagnosing Autism using the Autism Brain Imaging Data Exchange (ABIDE) database. We also compared the performance to multiple baselines, including GCNN, LSTM, SVM, KNN, XGBoost, Random Forest, and Decision Trees.

2 Related Work and Background

Various research has been undergone in ASD prediction and diagnosis using machine learning and deep learning techniques. This section will focus on different learning types, including machine learning and deep learning models.

2.1 Machine Learning Models

Plitt et al. [11] focused on testing the robustness of resting-state fMRI image datasets on supervised learning algorithms, including L-SVMs, compared to the use of behavioural scores as the primary datasets. They found that the accuracy on fMRI datasets was high; however, the behavioural scores yielded better results. Yamagata et al. [12] used the ABIDE database; however, the goal of their study was to determine whether a person had the endophenotype of ASD rather than ASD itself. They used sparse logistic regression (SLR) as their predictive model and leave-one-pair-out cross-validation (LOPOCV) to evaluate the classifiers' performance. Their research found a specific brain functional connectivity related to ASD. Chen et al. [13] created their classification models using random forest, particle swarm optimization, and SVM. They concluded that the random forest classifier outperformed the other two classifiers. Zhou and Doug [14] implemented both functional and structural MRI images in their study that implemented graph theory for classifying and analyzing functional connectivity in autistic individuals. They found that, for children, there exists less functional connectivity in the cingulum and cortex and recorded four distinct features that distinguish an ASD participant. Wang et al. [15] employed autoencoders and SVM-Recursive Feature Elimination (RFE) to determine the features in fMRI images related to ASD. Authors in [16] determined the best feature that provided insight on ASD classification using functional connectivity and improved the accuracy for large datasets. Stevens et al. [17] used hierarchical clustering and the Gaussian mixture model to create an unsupervised machine learning algorithm as applied to large samples of data to determine phenotypes of Autism. [18] proposed an unsupervised learning method known as single-cell interpretation via multi-kernel learning (SIMLR) with data clustering. Brain networks were implemented to better understand brain connectivity's relationship with ASD [18]. [19] used attention-based semi-supervised dictionary learning (ASSDL) to perform ASD classification. The use of reinforcement learning models for automated diagnosis of ASD is limited in the literature. Dong et al. [20] used a combination of reinforcement and deep learning on EEG data to perform ASD classification. They fed EEG data into a CNN model, then optimized by reconstructing the model using the reinforcement Q-learning model. Rane et al. [21] used a LASSO model on rs-fMRI images for ASD diagnosis. Sen et al. [22] introduced a machine learning method that uses 3D sMRI and 4D rs-fMRI to classify ASD using structural texture and functional connectivity components in datasets. Table 1 summarizes the recent state-of-the-art research work on ASD diagnosis and related works using machine learning-based models.

2.2 Deep Learning Models

Heinsfeld et al. [6] and Guo et al. [23] used deep neural networks (DNNs). In [6], they focused their research on distinguishing different functional connectivity patterns in ASD individuals. In [23], they integrated stacking spare encoders (SAE) for feature learning purposes which yielded better performance than DNNs [12]. Thomas et al. [24] and Shahamat and Abadeh [7] applied deep-learning techniques using 3D-CNNs. In [24], they focused on exploring transformations on brain imaging which would allow for a more comprehensive training of datasets. On the other hand, authors in [7] implemented genetic algorithm-based brain masking (GABM) which first trained the fMRI images using 3D-CNNs and then used a genetic algorithm to extract distinct features from images. They found that using the GABM algorithm achieved better performance. In [25], they created various hybrid models that used the 3D-CNNs along with LSTMs and 1D convolutions. They also included RNNs among their models. They found that all three models have the best performance compared to baselines. Ismail et al. [5] applied a CAD system on the cerebral cortex and cerebral white matter of the MRI images for feature fusion. Aghdam et al. [26] used deep belief networks (DBNs) to create an ASD diagnosis tool using both s-MRI and fMRI. They used automated anatomical labelling (AAL) for feature characterization. They found that using different image types resulted in better performance and that there is a change in gray matter in ASD individuals. Li et al. [27] used deep transfer learning neural networks (DTL-NN), which integrate sparse autoencoders. Compared to the SVM and other deep learning networks tested on the same datasets, their model outperformed the baselines. Anirudh and Thiagarajan [8] used graph-structured data for their Graph-CNN model integrated with bootstrapping to decrease sensitivity. They focused on regions of interest in the fMRI images; their proposed model outperformed other baselines. Roy et al. [33] proposed a hybrid deep learning model that integrated 1D convolutions and deep gated recurrent units (GRU). The model was used to classify abnormality in time series EEG data. Table 2 summarizes the ASD diagnosis research using deep learning models.

Table 1. ASD diagnosis systems using machine learning

Paper [Ref]	Prediction model	Dataset/modality	Goal of study
[11]	L-SVM, L2LR	ABIDE/rs-fMRI	To compare the fMRI functional connectivity to behavioural scores to provide an ASD diagnosis
[12]	SLR	ABIDE/rs-fMRI and MRI scanned	To identify siblings with ASD phenotype using machine learning
[21]	LASSO	ABIDE/rs-fMRI	To use the LASSO model on rs-fMRI images for ASD diagnosis
[27]	Random forest	ABIDE/rs-fMRI	To implement a random forest classifier and functional connectivity patterns to diagnose ASD
[14]	Random tree	ABIDE/rs-fMRI	To use machine learning combined with graph theory to improve the ASD classification process
[15]	SVM-RFE	ABIDE/rs-fMRI	To improve performance of ASD classification using SVM-RFE learning on rs-fMRI images
[16]	SVM-RFE	ABIDE/rs-fMRI	To determine the features that provide insight on ASD classification using functional connectivity

(continued)

Table 1. (*continued*)

Paper [Ref]	Prediction model	Dataset/modality	Goal of study
[17]	Clustering, Gaussian mixture	Skills assessment data	To use clustering and Gaussian mixture to determine ASD phenotypes with treatment response
[18]	SIMLR	ABIDE/rs-fMRI	To understand the relationship between MRI regions of interest for ASD diagnosis
[22]	Unsupervised CNN, Autoencoders	ABIDE/3D sMRI 4D rs-fMRI	To introduce a method that uses 3D sMRI and 4D rs-fMRI to classify ASD using structural texture and functional connectivity components
[19]	ASSDL dictionary	ABIDE/rs-fMRI	To use unlabeled data and a semi-supervised dictionary to diagnose ASD
[20]	Q-learning, CNN	rs-EEG	To develop a CNN model reconstructed based on the Q-learning model

Table 2. ASD diagnosis systems using deep learning

Paper [Ref]	Prediction model	Dataset/modality	Goal of study
[6]	DNN	ABIDE I/rs-fMRI	To use deep learning for ASD diagnosis when integrating large datasets with only brain activation data
[24]	3D-CNN	ABIDE/rs-fMRI	To explore transformations that will retain spatial brain imaging information using temporal data and train a more holistic dataset using 3DCNN

(*continued*)

Table 2. (*continued*)

Paper [Ref]	Prediction model	Dataset/modality	Goal of study
[16]	CNN	ABIDE/rs-fMRI	To introduce a new deep learning framework to diagnose ASD
[5]	A shape-based CAD system	ABIDE/rs-fMRI	To propose a shape-based CAD system that uses MRI images as data and feature fusion for better performance
[7]	3D-CNN, genetic based brain masking	ADNI, ABIDE/rs-fMRI	To implement 3D-CNN for binary ASD classification using MRI scans
[26]	DBN	ABIDE I & ABIDE II/rs-fMRI and sMRI	To use DBN for the aggregation of ASD MRI, white matter, and grey matter data for automated classification of ASD through automatic anatomical labelling
[8]	G-CNN + bootstrap ping	ABIDE/rs-fMRI	To propose a model using a graph-based approach combined with bootstrapping for better connection exploration
[23]	DNN with SAE	ABIDE/rs-fMRI	To implement a DNN with feature selection and functional connectivity analysis of the whole brain to binary classify ASD
[25]	3D-CNN + LSTM + 1D convolution	ABIDE I (NYU and UM sites)/rs-fMRI/fMRI	To implement 3D convolutional LSTMs and 3D-CNNs to create a high performing algorithm that classifies ASD when using rs-fMRI images

3   The Proposed Hybrid GCNN-LSTM Model

The purpose of GCNN is to learn spatial features, as GCNNs integrate graph input into convolutional networks and can be viewed as both a spectral and spatial method [9, 28]. The LSTM learns temporal features and solves the long-term dependency problem [28]. Due to the spectral and spatial characteristics of the resting-state functional MRI images in Autism diagnosis and the need for temporal feature handling, the proposed hybrid model, GCNN-LSTM, combines Graph Convolutional Networks (GCNNs) and Long Short-Term Memory (LSTMs). The GCNN adopted in our proposed model focused on reducing the effects of over-fitting on the graph structures and addressing the problem of blown up and vanishing gradients using their re-normalization. In the GCNN-LSTM model, the LSTMs are particularly integrated to solve the vanishing gradient and long-term dependency problems in recurrent neural networks (RNNs) using constant error carousels (CECs) and memory blocks. These carousels allow the error signals to be recognized using gates. The memory blocks are created by connecting input and output gates to the CEC to create a more complex architecture with input and output weights connected to the network during training. Various gates are integrated, including forget, output, and input gates. In this paper, we combine the power of both GCNN and LSTM to propose a hybrid model (GCNN-LSTM) as discussed next. The GCNNs model includes one input and output layer and multiple hidden layers, depending on the model's depth. There exist two units of LSTM connected to the output of the GCNN layers. Both input and hidden layers in the GCNN-LSTM model comprise graph convolution layers. The input to the GCNN-LSTM input layer is a graph with shape [871, 2000], which is generated from ASD population graph structures obtained from the fMRI images using the conversion techniques in [28]. The output of the GCNN-LSTM model (size [871, 2]) is then sent to the classification layer for the diagnosis stage. The Architecture for the GCNN-LSTM model is shown in Fig. 1.

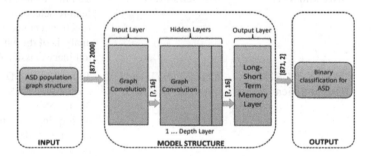

Fig. 1. Architecture for proposed GCNN-LSTM hybrid model.

4   Experimental Results

4.1   Datasets

The dataset used to test the performance of the proposed hybrid algorithm and comparison models is obtained from the Autism Brain Image Data Exchange (ABIDE) data-base.

The database consists of resting-state functional MRI images (fMRI) from 573 control individuals and 539 images from individuals who have ASD. In the GCNN-LSTM hybrid model, a total of 871 fMRI images were used for testing and training, with 403 individuals having ASD and 468 non-ASD individuals. 70% of the total dataset was used during training of the model, while 30% was used to test the model. The Configurable Pipeline for the Analysis of Connectomes (CPAC) performed functional preprocessing on the fMRI images.

4.2 Validation Measures

Accuracy, the area under the curve (AUC), precision, recall, and F1-score [29–33] are the validation measures applied to the proposed and baseline models. These validation measures were used to assess the performance of the proposed hybrid model to determine its effectiveness in classifying ASD. Various values are used for these calculations, the most relevant being the number of true positives (TP), the number of true negatives (TN), the number of false positives (FP), and the number of false negatives (FN) calculated during the duration of the test. Accuracy determines whether the classifiers correctly categorize data using the initial constraints [29].

$$Accuracy = \frac{|TP + TN|}{|TP + TN + FP + FN|} \quad (1)$$

By computing the area under the ROC curve, a scalar measure is produced that can be compared to other AUC metrics to better assess the performance of a classifier [30]. The greater the value of the area under the curve, the better performance of the classifier. The precision determines the ratio of predicted ASD positive classifications that are truly positive cases, while recall determines the ratio of true positive ASD classifications that were accurately predicted positive [31].

$$Precision = \frac{TP}{(TP + FN)} \quad (2)$$

$$Recall = \frac{TP}{(TP + FP)} \quad (3)$$

The F1-score combines the precision and recall metrics to create a new method of evaluating a classifier. The F1-score can be calculated without the negative cases, which is useful when this value is unknown or too large [32].

$$F1\text{-Score} = \frac{TP}{TP + \frac{1}{2}(FP + FN)} \quad (4)$$

4.3 Performance Evaluation

We evaluated the performance of the GCNN-LSTM model compared to the state-of-the-art models, including GCNN, LSTM, SVM, KNN, XGBoost, Random Forest, and Decision Trees. Due to the randomization of the baselines during training and testing, we have run the baselines for 10 trials. To randomize the GCNN-LSTM and GCNN models, the initial seed values were changed 10 times to create 10 randomized trial data for each model. The average performance of each model was computed by averaging the 10 trials. As observed in Fig. 2, the GCNN-LSTM model achieved the best performance compared to the adopted baseline models using the hybrid learning graph convolution and recurrent neural networks. The percentage of improvement in each validation metric, including Accuracy, AUC, Precision, Recall, and F1-Score, is reported in Table 3. The GCNN-LSTM achieved an improvement of up to 41%, 60%, 58%, 66%, and 60% in the Accuracy, AUC, Precision, Recall, and F1-Score metrics, respectively. As observed in Table 4, the GCNN-LSTM model has an overhead of only 8% and 5% additional time compared to the individual GCNN and LSTM models, while still maintaining high quality of diagnosis as reported in Table 3.

Table 3. % of improvement in performance using the hybrid model

	Accuracy	AUC	Precision	Recall	F1 score
GCNN	11%	9%	21%	12%	17%
LSTM	37%	29%	37%	70%	53%
SVM	15%	12%	26%	63%	44%
KNN	27%	25%	35%	66%	50%
XGBoost	25%	33%	38%	46%	42%
Random forest	37%	31%	42%	55%	48%
Decision tree	41%	60%	58%	63%	60%

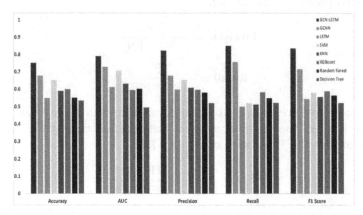

Fig. 2. Performance metrics for the baseline models and the proposed models

Table 4. The computational time of the hybrid model compared to baseline models

Model	Time (s)
GCNN-LSTM	2.3617
GCNN	2.1721
LSTM	2.2343
SVM	8.9093
KNN	1.8708
XGBoost	3.9915
Random forest	3.8670
Decision tree	4.1607

5   Conclusion and Future Work

This paper proposed a novel hybrid GCNN-LSTM deep learning classifier for ASD diagnosis. We used fMRI datasets from the ABIDE database for training and testing the algorithm. Overall, through analysis of the results, the proposed hybrid model outperforms baseline classifiers introduced in the study, specifically GCNN, LSTM, SVM, KNN, XGBoost, Random Forest, and Decision Trees. Future research should investigate hybrid GCNN combinations with other deep learning models to study which hybrid model performs optimally. Other future works involve training and testing different datasets to diagnose other behavioural disorders, including Alzheimer's disease.

References

1. Barlow, D.H., et al.: Abnormal psychology: an integrative approach, 8th edn. Nelson Education Ltd., Toronto, Ontario (2018)
2. Pagnozzi, A.M., et al.: A systematic review of structural MRI biomarkers in autism spectrum disorder: a machine learning perspective. Int. J. Dev. Neurosci. **71**, 68–82 (2018)
3. Bone, D., et al.: Applying machine learning to facilitate autism diagnostics: pitfalls and promises. J. Autism Dev. Disord. **45**(5), 1121–1136 (2015)
4. Hyde, K.K., et al.: Applications of supervised machine learning in autism spectrum disorder research: a review. Rev. J. Autism Dev. Disord. **6**(2), 128–146 (2019)
5. Ismail, M., et al.: A new deep-learning approach for early detection of shape variations in autism using structural MRI. In: 2017 IEEE International Conference on Image Processing, pp. 1057–1061 (2017)
6. Heinsfeld, A.S., et al.: Identification of autism spectrum disorder using deep learning and the ABIDE dataset. NeuroImage Clin. **17**, 16–23 (2018)
7. Shahamat, H., Abadeh, M.S.: Brain MRI analysis using a deep learning-based evolutionary approach. Neural Netw. **126**, 218–234 (2020)
8. Anirudh, R., Thiagarajan, J.J.: Bootstrapping graph convolutional neural networks for autism spectrum disorder classification. In: ICASSP, pp. 3197–3201 (2019)
9. Liu, Z., Zhou, J.: Introduction to graph neural networks. Synth. Lect. Artif. Intell. Mach. Learn. **14**(2), 1–127 (2020)

10. Chen, J., Xu, X., Wu, Y., Zheng, H.: GC-LSTM: graph convolution embedded LSTM for dynamic link prediction. arXiv preprint arXiv:1812.04206 (2019)
11. Plitt, M., et al.: Functional connectivity classification of autism identifies highly predictive brain features but falls short of biomarker standards. NeuroImage Clin. **7**, 359–366 (2015)
12. Yamagata, B., et al.: Machine learning approach to identify a resting-state functional connectivity pattern serving as an endophenotype of autism spectrum disorder. Brain Imaging Behav. **13**(6), 1689–1698 (2018). https://doi.org/10.1007/s11682-018-9973-2
13. Chen, C.P., et al.: Diagnostic classification of intrinsic functional connectivity high-lights somatosensory, default mode, and visual regions in autism. NeuroImage Clin. **8**, 238–245 (2015)
14. Zhou, Y., Yu, F., Duong, T.: Multiparametric MRI characterization and prediction in autism spectrum disorder using graph theory and machine learning. PLoS ONE **9**(6), e90405 (2014)
15. Wang, C., Xiao, Z., Wu, J.: Functional connectivity-based classification of autism and control using SVM-RFECV on rs-fMRI data. Phys. Med. **65**, 99–105 (2019)
16. Wang, C., Xiao, Z., Wang, B., Wu, J.: Identification of autism based on SVM-RFE and stacked sparse auto-encoder. IEEE Access **7**, 118030–118036 (2019)
17. Stevens, E., et al.: Identification and analysis of behavioral phenotypes in autism spectrum disorder via unsupervised machine learning. Int. J. Med. Inform. **129**, 29–36 (2019)
18. Soussia, M., Rekik, I.: Unsupervised manifold learning using high-order morphological brain networks derived from T1-w MRI for autism diagnosis. Front. Neuroinformatic **12**, 70 (2018)
19. Yang, M., et al.: Attention based semi-supervised dictionary learning for diagnosis of autism spectrum disorders. In: 2019 IEEE International Conference on Multimedia & Expo Workshops (ICMEW) (2019)
20. Dong, H., et al.: Subject sensitive EEG discrimination with fast reconstructable CNN driven by reinforcement learning: a case study of ASD. Neurocomputing **449**, 136–145 (2021)
21. Rane, S., et al.: Developing predictive imaging biomarkers using whole-brain classifiers: application to the ABIDE I dataset. Res. Ideas Outcomes **3**, e12733 (2017)
22. Sen, B., Borle, N.C., Greiner, R., Brown, M.R.: A general prediction model for the detection of ADHD and Autism using structural and functional MRI. PLoS ONE **13**(4), e0194856 (2018)
23. Guo, X., et al.: Diagnosing autism spectrum disorder from brain resting-state functional connectivity patterns using a deep neural network with a novel feature selection method. Front. Neurosci. **11**, 460 (2017)
24. Thomas, R.M., et al.: Classifying autism spectrum disorder using the temporal statistics of resting-state functional MRI data with 3D convolutional neural networks. Front. Psychiatry **11**, 440 (2020)
25. El-Gazzar, A., Quaak, M., Cerliani, L., Bloem, P., van Wingen, G., Mani Thomas, R.: A hybrid 3DCNN and 3DC-LSTM based model for 4D spatio-temporal fMRI data: an ABIDE autism classification. In: Zhou, L., et al. (eds.) OR 2.0/MLCN -2019. LNCS, vol. 11796, pp. 95–102. Springer, Cham (2019). https://doi.org/10.1007/978-3-030-32695-1_11
26. Akhavan Aghdam, M., Sharifi, A., Pedram, M.M.: Combination of rs-fMRI and sMRI Data to Discriminate Autism Spectrum Disorders in Young Children Using Deep Belief Network. J. Digit. Imaging **31**(6), 895–903 (2018). https://doi.org/10.1007/s10278-018-0093-8
27. Li, H., Parikh, N.A., He, L.: A novel transfer learning approach to enhance deep neural network classification of brain functional connectomes. Front. Neurosci. **12**, 491 (2018)
28. Parisot, S., et al.: Disease prediction using graph convolutional networks: application to autism spectrum disorder and Alzheimer's disease. Med. Image Anal. **48**, 117–130 (2018)
29. Vajar, P., Emmanuel, A.L., Ghasemieh, A., Bahrami, P., Kashef, R.: The internet of medical things (IoMT): a vision on learning, privacy, and computing. In: 2021 International Conference on Electrical, Computer, Communications and Mechatronics Engineering (ICECCME), pp. 1–7. IEEE (2021)

30. Kashef, R.: ECNN: enhanced convolutional neural network for efficient diagnosis of autism spectrum disorder. Cogn. Syst. Res. **71**, 41–49 (2022)
31. Sewani, H., Kashef, R.: An autoencoder-based deep learning classifier for efficient diagnosis of autism. Children **7**(10), 182 (2020)
32. Shirazi, Z.A., de Souza, C.P., Kashef, R., Rodrigues, F.F.: Deep learning in the healthcare industry: theory and applications. In: Computational Intelligence and Soft Computing Applications in Healthcare Management Science, pp. 220–245 (2020)
33. Roy, S., Kiral-Kornek, I., Harrer, S.: ChronoNet: a deep recurrent neural network for abnormal EEG identification. In: Riaño, D., Wilk, S., ten Teije, A. (eds.) AIME 2019. LNCS (LNAI), vol. 11526, pp. 47–56. Springer, Cham (2019). https://doi.org/10.1007/978-3-030-21642-9_8

Hierarchical Deep Multi-task Learning for Classification of Patient Diagnoses

Salim Malakouti[✉][iD] and Milos Hauskrecht[iD]

Computer Science Department, University of Pittsburgh, Pittsburgh, USA
salimm@cs.pitt.edu

Abstract. Recent years have witnessed an increased interest in the biomedical research community in developing machine learning models and methods that can automatically assign diagnostic codes (ICD) to patient stays based on the information in their Electronic Health Records (EHR). However, despite the recent advances, accurate automatic classification of diagnostic codes continues to face challenges, especially for low-prior diagnostic codes. To alleviate the problem, we propose to leverage information in the diagnostic hierarchy and better utilize the dependencies among diseases in this hierarchy. We develop a new hierarchical deep multi-task learning method that learns classification models for multiple diagnostic codes at the different levels of abstraction in the disease hierarchy while allowing the transfer of information from high-level nodes, more general diagnoses codes to the low-level ones, more specific diagnostic codes. After that, we refine the initial hierarchical model by utilizing the relations and information that can discriminate better between competing diseases. Our empirical results show that our new method and its refinement outperform baseline machine learning architectures that do not leverage the hierarchical structure of target diagnoses tasks or disease-disease relationships.

Keywords: Hierarchical multi-task learning · Patient diagnoses classification · International classification diseases

1 Introduction

The widespread adoption of electronic health records (EHRs) has introduced the opportunity to process and extract valuable knowledge from massive data warehouses of real-time and diverse clinical data recorded during patient's hospitalizations. One interesting problem is the automatic assignment of diagnostic codes to patients' hospital stays. If the problem is solved successfully, it can help to improve a number of hospital workflows related to both clinical decision-making and administration of healthcare systems. First, diagnostic codes such as the International Classification of Diseases (ICD) are commonly used for hospital reimbursement. The codes are currently assigned to patients by a human annotator (a trained nosologist) after discharge. An effective solution can help

© The Author(s), under exclusive license to Springer Nature Switzerland AG 2022
M. Michalowski et al. (Eds.): AIME 2022, LNAI 13263, pp. 122–132, 2022.
https://doi.org/10.1007/978-3-031-09342-5_12

to speed up the annotation process and alleviate its cost. Second, an automated diagnostic system could help physicians by providing a concise, automated, and easily accessible summary of patients' conditions and problems not only at the time of discharge but also during the patient's hospital stay. Hence, it can act as a decision support tool that can recommend and bring to the attention of physicians possible patient diagnoses that have not yet been considered. Therefore, recent years have witnessed an increased interest in developing machine learning methods that can automatically assign diagnoses to patient stays based on the information in their electronic health records (EHR) [18–20]. However, despite recent advancements, multiple challenges making the solutions more practical remain to be solved.

The problem of assigning diagnostic codes to a patient covers is a multi-label or multi-task problem that covers many different diseases. These are organized in various hierarchies or lattice structures, abstracting individual low-level diagnoses into subcategories. This hierarchical structure plays a significant role in the human diagnostic process. Briefly, clinicians are likely able to recognize or reject a high-level diagnostic category much earlier and with a higher certainty than more specific diseases that reside on the lower levels of the hierarchy. Moreover, when the EHR info is incomplete, and information is missing making decisions about some low-level diagnoses may not be feasible. Hence structuring the diagnostic process in a top-down manner based on a hierarchy often helps the clinician to make rapid progress in pursuing feasible diagnoses and arrive at diagnostic conclusions even while additional information is required for a final decision on the most reasonable lower-level assignment. The objective of our work is to bring and leverage the available disease hierarchies into the automatic diagnostic and model learning process. Our conjecture is that machine learning solutions that utilize hierarchies lead to better and more accurate models, and that they can also learn from smaller amounts of available data. The ability to learn models from smaller datasets is important since many low-level diagnoses are rare; that is, they come with a low class prior.

One possible direction for modeling diagnostic code dependencies is multi-task learning. Multi-task learning methods (MTL) have been effective in learning improved machine learning models by facilitating the transfer of knowledge between a set of related target tasks. However, the methods may also fail or are less effective when relations among tasks vary a great deal and when negative transfer in between the tasks may occur [22, 26]. As a result, classic MTL approaches alone may not be sufficient when facing a large number of diagnostic tasks organized in a complex hierarchical structure that can involve task asymmetry and various degrees of task heterogeneity. Therefore, hierarchical multi-task learning methods (HMTL) that can handle hierarchical relations have been proposed to solve an array of problems in natural language processing [23], computer vision [4], speech recognition [9], and even applied to clinical diagnosis problems. However, the limitation of the past hierarchical modeling work for supporting medical diagnoses tasks was somewhat limited and failed to integrate modern deep learning methods to learn more generalizable representations of patients' EHR data sequences. In addition, these methods could not effectively leverage asymmetries and heterogeneity of parent-child relations in existing hierarchies. Our objective in this work is to develop and test new deep learning models and methods across a broad range of diseases organized in the ICD-9 disease hierarchy that leads to improved diagnostic classification models.

We propose a new hierarchical deep learning method that leverages the hierarchical structure of patient diagnoses to facilitate the transfer of information in a top-down fashion, from higher-level diagnostic codes with stronger classification models to lower-level ones. After that, we further refine the initial hierarchical model with a new disease interaction layer. Motivated by the field of differential diagnoses, the interaction layer learns to capture additional patterns from patients' EHR data to better discriminate among competing diagnoses and to fine-tune the predictions of the hierarchical layer. Finally, we compare the performance of our proposed method with baseline algorithms using the MIMIC-III dataset and the ICD-9 diagnosis hierarchy.

2   Related Work

In the following, we briefly review models used for EHR data analysis, solutions for assigning patients instances to diagnoses, and methods for leveraging hierarchies of prediction tasks.

EHR Data Analysis and Automated Diagnoses: Most recent work on EHR clinical data analysis and modeling has utilized modern deep learning architectures to learn a low-dimensional representation of patient data based on various NLP model architectures and sequence summaries. These include models based on autoencoders [19], word2vec embeddings and CBOWs summaries [25], recurrent neural networks [2,12,20], and various transformer and BERT architectures [13,21]. These new architectures often lead to improvement of predictive performance over classic featurization methods on a variety of clinical prediction and classification tasks.

One popular application of the above methods was the problem of automatic assignment of diagnoses to patients' EHR sequences [18–20]. Briefly, Miotto et al. [19] used a denoising autoencoder to generate a low-dimensional representation of the patient state and applied it to multiple clinical classification problems, including patient diagnosis. On the other hand, Rajkomar et al. [20], and Lipton et al. [14] used Recurrent Neural Network (RNN) architecture to predict patient discharge diagnoses from a set of clinical variables and sequences of their observations. The diagnostic task was cast as a multi-label classification problem. Finally, Malakouti and Hauskrecht [18] used unsupervised low-dimensional summaries based on SVD to predict patient discharge diagnoses by leveraging a broad range of clinical data (labs, medications, procedures, etc.). The lower-dimensional features were then used to learn independently trained classification models to classify a broad range of patient diagnoses.

While the ML models for supporting the assignment of diagnoses to patients' EHRs have been quite popular, only a limited number of works have tried to leverage and improve the performance of these diagnostic models with the help of disease hierarchies available in ICD-9 and ICD-10 codes. One methodology specifically designed to work with the disease hierarchy was Hierarchical Adaptive MTL (HA-MTL) [17] that relied on an iterative algorithm to learn improved SVM classification models for individual diseases via top-down, and bottom-up sharing of predictive information across the hierarchy [17]. Their results showed that sharing of the predictive information may indeed lead to improved classification models, with top-down sharing accounting for the majority of the improvement. However, we note that the design of these hierarchical methods was somewhat limited and did not use modern EHR sequence embedding methods.

Hierarchical Multi-task Learning: Multi-task learning (MTL) methods have been proposed to exploit task relationships, their commonalities, and differences to learn improved classification models by allowing transfer of knowledge between the target tasks [27]. In recent years, deep multi-task learning approaches have also shown promising results [3]. Unfortunately, the main shortcoming of early MTL methods is that they relied heavily on the relatedness of target tasks; hence negative transfer could happen when tasks are not sufficiently similar [22]. Various methods have been proposed to prevent negative transfer that leverage underlying task clusters [6,16], task-task relatedness [1,8,15], or facilitate an asymmetric transfer of knowledge [10,11]. However, neither of these approaches is sufficient to prevent negative transfer when a large number of heterogeneous tasks with various levels of similarities are available. To address these shortcomings, hierarchical multi-task learning methods (HMTL) were introduced [5,17,28]. Hierarchical deep MTL methods have also been proposed that leverage the hierarchical structure of a set of carefully selected NLP tasks by allowing inductive transfer of features between task-specific RNN blocks [23]. In computer vision, HD-MTL was proposed, which first learned a visual tree for a large set of atomic object classes and then leveraged the inter-class relatedness in the visual tree to jointly learn more representative deep CNNs and a more discriminative tree classifier for the target tasks [4]. However, to the extent of our knowledge, this work will be the first attempt to propose a deep HMTL method that leverages the diagnoses hierarchy to promote a top-down transfer of features from parents to children while modeling the interactions between closely related tasks at the same level of the hierarchy (siblings). Additionally, our proposed method is the first attempt to also incorporate disease-disease interactions of sibling diagnoses to learn improved diagnostic classifiers.

3 Methodology

Let D be the number of target diagnostic tasks of varying difficulty organized in a hierarchical structure H. Our goal is to learn classification models for each of these tasks by taking advantage of task relations reflected in H.

The patients' EHRs are formed by complex sequences of observations, physiological events, treatments, and procedures. To facilitate the learning of classification models, the EHR sequences are often replaced with a compact vector-based representation that attempts to summarize the information in EHRs relevant to the specific prediction tasks. This transformed representation is also referred to as embedding. In the following, we first describe the basic architecture for transforming the data in EHRs to a lower-dimensional embedding. After that, we propose a refinement of this architecture by incorporating a hierarchical multi-task learning layer that facilitates sharing of embeddings among related tasks. Finally, we add a new model layer that incorporates disease-disease interactions to learn additional task-specific features that aim to further refine the different diagnostic models.

3.1   EHR Data Pre-processing and Initial EHR Transformation

We have adopted a three-step process to generate initial patient representations from a wide range of patient clinical data (Fig. 1). In Step 1, binary events representing lab results, medications, vital signs, and procedures are generated from the patient's raw medical records. In Step 2, the events are divided into T segments of equal length (24 h window size). The events in each time segment are then represented by normalized Bag-of-Words (BoW) vectors. Finally, the normalized BoW vectors for each segment are then transformed using a supervised feed-forward layer (Fig. 2: Embedding Layer). The weights of the feed-forward layer are learned from available data, and its output defines the initial EHR embedding vector v_t where $t \in \{1, 2, .., T\}$. Please note there is one embedding vector v_t per segment of time per patient.

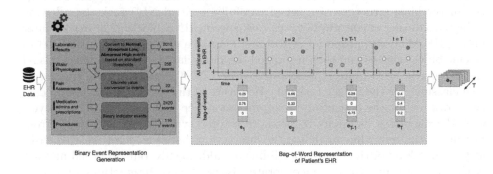

Fig. 1. Preprocessing steps to learn lower-dimensional representation of EHR

3.2   Hierarchical Multitask Learning Layer

Multi-task learning aims to train target tasks simultaneously and, hence, learn improved classification models by facilitating the transfer of knowledge between related tasks. In deep multi-task learning methods, this similarity is often achieved through either a set of common latent feature layers shared by all or groups of related tasks or through imposed similarities between a set of task-specific constrained feature layers. However, traditional methods may fail to efficiently leverage task relationships when facing a large number of heterogeneous tasks with various levels of similarities. There, hierarchical MTL methods aim to leverage underlying task hierarchies to efficiently direct sharing of information between target tasks.

Our proposed layer learns a separate set of task-specific neural network blocks for each target task in any arbitrary hierarchy while facilitating the inductive transfer of features in a top-down fashion by sharing hidden states of parent tasks with its children (see Fig. 2). Additionally, following Sanh et al. [23] we use shortcuts (blue arrows) so that each target task can have access to the original EHR feature embeddings. This dual input mechanism enables each target task to either learn new features from the shared EHR embeddings, adopt features from more general categorical parent tasks p (black arrows), or combine these two sets of features in order to learn improved classification models. This is analogous to clinicians distinguishing specific diagnoses types by examining additional information that helps identify them from the other members of a group of diseases with similar symptoms. Task-specific blocks in this work are modeled using a bi-directional LSTM encoder architecture. The encoders take as input the concatenated vector of original EHR embeddings (v_t vectors) and the hidden states of their parent task p at each timestamp t (h_t^p). Next, a max-pooling layer ($max([h_1^m, h_2^m, ..., h_T^m])$) for each target task was adopted to combine task-specific LSTM hidden states at all timestamps. Finally, a feed-forward layer with a sigmoid activation function was adopted to learn the final classification scores for each target task.

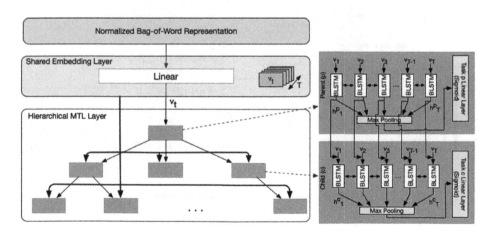

Fig. 2. The proposed HLSTM network architecture.

3.3   Disease-Disease Interaction Layer

Differential diagnoses in medicine refer to distinguishing a particular patient's disease from a set of competing diagnoses with similar features through systematic methods of acquiring and examining additional data. Similarly, a comprehensive machine learning solution should capture such disease-disease interactions to classify patients' diagnoses accurately. Therefore, we propose a fine-tuning step that is trained separately as a second step and learns to capture additional patterns from patients' EHR data to improve the initial predictions by the hierarchical layer. The interaction layer, defines the final prediction probability for the target task m as $\hat{f}^m = sigmoid(f^m + \Delta f^m)$ where f^m is the initial score based on the hierarchical model and Δf^m determines the change to the scores based on the disease-disease interactions with its siblings. Motivated by the field of differential diagnoses, a task-specific feature attention-based learning block is adopted to learn additional features (Fig. 3). First, a single linear layer is used to learn a low-dimensional task-specific feature vector v_t^m from the original EHR embeddings v_t for each target task m. This is followed by a scaled dot-product attention layer similar to the multi-head attention mechanism proposed in "Attention is All You Need" [24] that uses v_t^m vectors and the initial classification scores S^m from task m's siblings to learn a set of importance weights α_t^m for each timestamp t. Finally, a final feature vector is obtained as $v^m = \sum_t^T \alpha_t^m v_t^m$. Please note that this task-specific architecture uses the initial predictions of siblings and the original EHR embeddings to capture new information from the most important window segments during a patient's hospitalization to fine-tune the initial predictions.

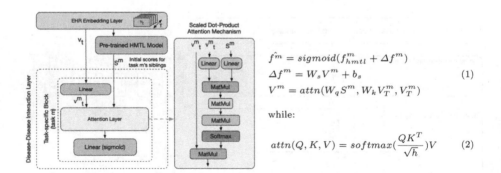

$$f^{\hat{}m} = sigmoid(f_{hmtl}^m + \Delta f^m)$$
$$\Delta f^m = W_s V^m + b_s \qquad (1)$$
$$V^m = attn(W_q S^m, W_k V_T^m, V_T^m)$$

while:

$$attn(Q, K, V) = softmax(\frac{QK^T}{\sqrt{h}})V \qquad (2)$$

Fig. 3. Task specific interaction layer

4   Experiments

Data Description: The experiments in this section are conducted using the MIMIC-III dataset [7], an open-access EHR dataset collected over a 12-year time span. Only patients included in the MetaVision subset, including 22,046 visits, were included since the coding terminology used for patients' clinical data has a higher coherency. Finally, ICD-9 discharge diagnostic codes were used to create diagnostic labels. Since medical diseases are only recorded using the lower level leaf diagnostic codes, binary labels for the diagnostic categories were created by applying a logical OR operation between all its children. Finally, we consider only diagnoses and diagnostic categories that satisfy a minimum cut-off threshold ($N_{min} = 100$) on the number of patients with that diagnosis (D = 1228) to ensure sufficient positive sample sizes.

Implementation Details: The proposed HLSTM architecture was implemented with a linear embedding layer of dimension 256 and the task specific bi-LSTM used a hidden state of size 32. For evaluation, we adopted the weighted area under the receiver operating curve (AUROC) and the area under the precision-recall curve (AUPRC), which is suggested to be more suitable when using the average of the metrics across multiple imbalanced target tasks with varying skewedness [20]. Finally, a random split of (70%/30%) the data was generated to create train and test sets.

Overall Performance: In this section, we compare the overall performance of our proposed method with baselines including: (1) multi-label LSTM architecture which included a bidirectional LSTM layer, followed by a max-pooling layer and a linear layer with sigmoid activation function to classify all target tasks (multi-label lstm), (2) and MTL lstm implementation that adopted a shared feature embedding layer as the common feature layer while using task-specific lstm blocks that share information through the shared embedding layer. All baselines utilize the same EHR feature learning method as HMTL and use mean binary cross-entropy loss for training.

Our empirical results show that our HMTL method results in strong improvements across all tasks, while the interaction layer also introduces slight improvements over the HMTL layer. These improvements are consistent among both categorical and low-level leaves (low-prior and imbalanced), showing that the proposed method was able to transfer information top-down in an effective manner (Table 1).

Table 1. Comparison of overall performance of proposed method with baselines (average AUROC and AUPRC)

Method name	All nodes		Category nodes		Leaf nodes	
	AUROC	AUPRC	AUROC	AUPRC	AUROC	AUPRC
Multi-label lstm	0.76	0.74	0.752	0.735	0.766	0.742
MTL lstm	0.69	0.674	0.724	0.70	0.675	0.653
HMTL	0.805	0.799	0.801	0.796	0.808	0.80
HMTL + Interaction layer	0.817	0.803	0.806	0.801	0.815	0.806

Task Level Analysis: While the overall results show strong improvements across all diagnoses and diagnostic categories ($M = 1228$), it's still valuable to evaluate the performance of the model across individual tasks. Figure 4 shows improvements in the individual target diagnostic tasks with respect to both weighted AUROC and weighted AUPRC metrics. In general, our proposed method resulted in considerable improvement ($\Delta > 0.05$) of nearly 50% of target tasks while preventing negative transfer with more 91% of classifiers performing at least as good as the baseline models ($\Delta \geq 0$). In fact, only a handful of very rare diagnoses (2% of $0.004 \geq prior < 0.01$ group) demonstrated considerably lower performance that the baseline models ($\Delta < -0.05$). While a perfect MTL method is expected to only result in positive improvements, this has proven difficult in practice, especially when facing a large number of target tasks [26]. We conjecture that the negative improvements are mainly due to the imperfect hierarchy designs caused by residual categories that include diagnoses not closely aligned with other diseases. This motivates research and development of future HMTL methods that simultaneously learn to improve the existing hierarchies for machine learning tasks.

Fig. 4. Performance improvements of individual tasks compared to the baseline multi-label LSTM models

5   Conclusion

We propose a new hierarchical deep learning method that leverages the hierarchical structure of patient diagnoses to allow the transfer of information in a top-down fashion, from higher-level diagnostic codes with stronger classification models to lower-level ones. After that, we refine the initial hierarchical model with a new disease interaction layer, utilizing the task relationships and new patient information to learn classifiers that can better discriminate between competing diagnoses. Our results show that our proposed method strongly outperforms baselines across all target tasks, resulting in positive transfer in nearly 50% and preventing negative transfer in 92% of the target diagnoses.

References

1. Ben-David, S., Schuller, R.: Exploiting task relatedness for multiple task learning. In: Schölkopf, B., Warmuth, M.K. (eds.) COLT-Kernel 2003. LNCS (LNAI), vol. 2777, pp. 567–580. Springer, Heidelberg (2003). https://doi.org/10.1007/978-3-540-45167-9_41
2. Choi, E., et al.: Mime: multilevel medical embedding of electronic health records for predictive healthcare. arXiv preprint arXiv:1810.09593 (2018)
3. Crawshaw, M.: Multi-task learning with deep neural networks: a survey. arXiv preprint arXiv:2009.09796 (2020)
4. Fan, J., et al.: HD-MTL: hierarchical deep multi-task learning for large-scale visual recognition. IEEE Trans. Image Process. **26**(4), 1923–1938 (2017)
5. Han, L., Zhang, Y.: Learning tree structure in multi-task learning. In: Proceedings of the 21th ACM SIGKDD International Conference on Knowledge Discovery and Data Mining, pp. 397–406. ACM (2015)
6. Jacob, L., Vert, J.P., Bach, F.R.: Clustered multi-task learning: a convex formulation. In: Advances in Neural Information Processing Systems, pp. 745–752 (2009)
7. Johnson, A.E., et al.: MIMIC-III, a freely accessible critical care database. Sci. Data **3**, 160035 (2016)
8. Kang, Z., Grauman, K., Sha, F.: Learning with whom to share in multi-task feature learning. In: ICML, vol. 2, p. 4 (2011)
9. Krishna, K., Toshniwal, S., Livescu, K.: Hierarchical multitask learning for CTC-based speech recognition. arXiv preprint arXiv:1807.06234 (2018)
10. Lee, G., Yang, E., Hwang, S.: Asymmetric multi-task learning based on task relatedness and loss. In: International Conference on Machine Learning (2016)
11. Lee, H.B., Yang, E., Hwang, S.J.: Deep asymmetric multi-task feature learning. In: International Conference on Machine Learning, pp. 2956–2964. PMLR (2018)
12. Lee, J.M., Hauskrecht, M.: Modeling multivariate clinical event time-series with recurrent temporal mechanisms. Artif. Intell. Med. **112** (2021)
13. Li, Y., et al.: BEHRT: transformer for electronic health records. Sci. Rep. **10**(1), 1–12 (2020)
14. Lipton, Z.C., Kale, D.C., Elkan, C., Wetzel, R.: Learning to diagnose with LSTM recurrent neural networks. arXiv preprint (2015)
15. Long, M., Cao, Y., Wang, J., Jordan, M.I.: Learning transferable features with deep adaptation networks. arXiv preprint arXiv:1502.02791 (2015)
16. Lu, Y., Kumar, A., Zhai, S., Cheng, Y., Javidi, T., Feris, R.: Fully-adaptive feature sharing in multi-task networks with applications in person attribute classification. In: IEEE Conference on Computer Vision and Pattern Recognition (2017)
17. Malakouti, S., Hauskrecht, M.: Hierarchical adaptive multi-task learning framework for patient diagnoses and diagnostic category classification. In: 2019 IEEE International Conference on Bioinformatics and Biomedicine (BIBM). IEEE (2019)
18. Malakouti, S., Hauskrecht, M.: Predicting patient's diagnoses and diagnostic categories from clinical-events in EHR data. In: Riaño, D., Wilk, S., ten Teije, A. (eds.) AIME 2019. LNCS (LNAI), vol. 11526, pp. 125–130. Springer, Cham (2019). https://doi.org/10.1007/978-3-030-21642-9_17
19. Miotto, R., Li, L., Kidd, B.A., Dudley, J.T.: Deep patient: an unsupervised representation to predict the future of patients from the electronic health records. Sci. Rep. **6**, 26094 (2016)
20. Rajkomar, A., et al.: Scalable and accurate deep learning with electronic health records. NPJ Digit. Med. **1**(1), 1–10 (2018)

21. Rasmy, L., Xiang, Y., Xie, Z., Tao, C., Zhi, D.: Med-BERT: pretrained contextu-alized embeddings on large-scale structured electronic health records for disease prediction. NPJ Digit. Med. **4**(1), 1–13 (2021)
22. Rosenstein, M.T., Marx, Z., Kaelbling, L.P., Dietterich, T.G.: To transfer or not to transfer. In: NIPS 2005 Workshop on Transfer Learning, vol. 898, pp. 1–4 (2005)
23. Sanh, V., Wolf, T., Ruder, S.: A hierarchical multi-task approach for learning embeddings from semantic tasks. In: Proceedings of the AAAI Conference on Arti-ficial Intelligence, vol. 33, pp. 6949–6956 (2019)
24. Vaswani, A., et al.: Attention is all you need. In: Advances in Neural Information Processing Systems, pp. 5998–6008 (2017)
25. Zhang, J., Kowsari, K., Harrison, J.H., Lobo, J.M., Barnes, L.E.: Patient2Vec: a personalized interpretable deep representation of the longitudinal electronic health record. IEEE Access **6**, 65333–65346 (2018)
26. Zhang, W., Deng, L., Zhang, L., Wu, D.: Overcoming negative transfer: a survey. arXiv preprint arXiv:2009.00909 (2020)
27. Zhang, Y., Yang, Q.: A survey on multi-task learning. arXiv preprint arXiv:1707.08114 (2017)
28. Zweig, A., Weinshall, D.: Hierarchical regularization cascade for joint learning. In: International Conference on Machine Learning, pp. 37–45 (2013)

TTS-GAN: A Transformer-Based Time-Series Generative Adversarial Network

Xiaomin Li, Vangelis Metsis[✉], Huangyingrui Wang,
and Anne Hee Hiong Ngu

Texas State University, San Marcos, TX 78666, USA
{x_l30,vmetsis,h_w91,angu}@txstate.edu

Abstract. Signal measurements appearing in the form of time series are one of the most common types of data used in medical machine learning applications. However, such datasets are often small, making the training of deep neural network architectures ineffective. For time-series, the suite of data augmentation tricks we can use to expand the size of the dataset is limited by the need to maintain the basic properties of the signal. Data generated by a Generative Adversarial Network (GAN) can be utilized as another data augmentation tool. RNN-based GANs suffer from the fact that they cannot effectively model long sequences of data points with irregular temporal relations. To tackle these problems, we introduce TTS-GAN, a transformer-based GAN which can successfully generate realistic synthetic time-series data sequences of arbitrary length, similar to the real ones. Both the generator and discriminator networks of the GAN model are built using a pure transformer encoder architecture. We use visualizations and dimensionality reduction techniques to demonstrate the similarity of real and generated time-series data. We also compare the quality of our generated data with the best existing alternative, which is an RNN-based time-series GAN.

TTS-GAN source code: github.com/imics-lab/tts-gan

Keywords: Generative Adversarial Network · Transformer · Time-series analysis · Medical signal

1 Introduction

Data shortage is often an issue when analyzing physiology based time-series signals with deep learning models. Unlike images and text data used in computer vision (CV) and natural language processing (NLP) tasks, which are abundant on the web, such signals are collected as sensor measurements resulting from physical or biological process. Especially when such processes involve human subjects, data collection, annotation, and interpretation is a costly endeavour. Furthermore, differences in the various collection configurations make it harder for data collected in different settings to be merged together to form larger

M. Michalowski et al. (Eds.): AIME 2022, LNAI 13263, pp. 133–143, 2022.
https://doi.org/10.1007/978-3-031-09342-5_13

datasets. Deep learning models require large amounts of data to train success-fully. Training deep learning models with a high number of trainable parameters on small datasets results in over-fitting and low generalization capabilities. As a compromise researchers are forced to train shallower deep learning models that are not capable of capturing the full complexity of the problem at hand. This is a common situation encountered in medical and health-related machine learning research.

Generative Adversarial Networks (GANs), first introduced in 2014 [1], have been gaining traction in the deep learning research field. They have successfully generated and manipulated data in CV and NLP domains, such as high-quality image generation [2], style transfer [3], text-to-image synthesis [4], etc. There has also been a movement towards using GANs for time series and sequential data generation, and forecasting. The review paper [5] gives a thorough summary of GAN implementations on time series data.

A GAN is a generative model consisting of a generator and discriminator, typically two neural network (NN) models. The generator takes as input ran-dom vectors of specified dimensions and generates output vectors of the same dimension that are similar to the real training data. The discriminator is a binary classifier used to distinguish the real data and generated data. The generator and discriminator are updated by back-propagation alternately, playing a zero-sum game against each other and until they reach an equilibrium.

The transformer architecture, which relies on multiple self-attention lay-ers [6], has recently become a prevalent deep learning model architecture. It has been shown to surpass many other popular neural network architectures, such as CNN over images and RNN over sequential data [7,8], and it has even displayed properties of a universal computation engine [9]. Some works have already tried to utilize the transformer model in GAN model architecture design with the goal to either improve the quality of synthetic data or to create a more efficient train-ing process [10,11] for image and text generation tasks. In work [10], the author, for the first time, built a pure transformer-based GAN model and verified its performance on multiple image synthesis tasks.

Previous efforts for creating a time-series GAN have mainly relied on Recur-rent Neural Network (RNN)-based architectures [12–14]. Since the transformer was first invented to handle very long sequential data and does not suffer from a vanishing gradient problem, theoretically, a transformer GAN model should per-form better than other RNN-based models on time-series data. In this work, we follow a process similar to the one Jiang et al. [10] followed for image generation, adapted for time-series data.

Since time-series data are not easily interpretable by humans, we use PCA [15] and t-SNE [16] to map the multi-dimensional output sequence vec-tors into two dimensions to visually observe the similarity in the distribution of the synthetic data and real data instances. For a more quantitative comparison, we also measure several well-known signal properties and compare the similar-ity of the transformer-generated as well as RNN-generated sequences with real sequences of the same class.

Our contributions can be summarized as follows:

- We create a pure transformer-based GAN model to generate synthetic time-series data.
- We propose several heuristics to more effectively train a transformer-based GAN model on time-series data.
- We qualitatively and quantitatively compare the quality of the generated sequences against real ones and against sequences generated by other state-of-the-art time-series GAN algorithms.

The rest of the paper is organized as follows. Section 2 discusses the background and most popular applications of GANs and transformer models. In Sect. 3, we provide the details of our TTS-GAN model architecture and how we process time-series data to feed this model. In Sect. 4, we visually and quantitatively verify the fidelity of the synthetic data. Section 5 summarizes our work and concludes this paper.

2 Background

2.1 Generative Adversarial Networks (GANs)

GANs consist of two models, a generator and a discriminator. These two models are typically implemented by neural networks, but they can be implemented with any form of differentiable system that maps data from one space to the other. The generator tries to capture the distribution of true examples for new data example generation. The discriminator is usually a binary classifier, discriminating generated examples from the true examples as accurately as possible. The optimization of GANs is a minimax optimization problem, in which the goal is to reach Nash equilibrium [17] of the generator and discriminator. Then, the generator can be thought to have captured the real distribution of true examples.

GANs have had many applications in different areas, but mostly in CV and NLP. For example, it can generate examples for image datasets [18], front view faces [19], text-to-image translation [4], etc. While these successes have drawn much attention, GAN applications have diversified across disciplines such as time-series data generation. The work [5] gives a thorough summary of the GAN implementations in this field. The applicability of GANs to this type of data can solve many issues that current dataset holders face. For example, GANs can augment smaller datasets by generating new, previously unseen data. GANs can replace the artifacts with information representative of clean data. And it can also be used to denoise signals. GANs can also ensure an extra layer of data protection by generating deferentially private datasets containing no risk of linkage from source to generated datasets.

2.2 Transformer

The transformer is the state-of-the-art neural network architecture. Unlike recurrent neural networks, which consume a sequence token by token, in a transformer network, the entire sequence is fed into layers of transformer modules. The representation of a token at a layer is then computed by attending to the latent representations of all the other tokens in the preceding layer. Many works in the NLP field have proved its performance [6,8].

Given its strong representation capabilities, researchers have also applied transformers to computer vision tasks. In a variety of visual benchmarks, transformer models perform similar to or better than other types of networks, such as convolutional and recurrent networks. The work in [7] builds a model named ViT, which applies a pure transformer directly to sequences of image patches. The work in [10] builds a pure transformer GAN model to generate synthetic images, where the discriminator designing idea is from the ViT model. The multidimension time-series data we are dealing with has similarities from both texts and images, meaning a sequence contains both temporal and spatial information. Each timestep in a sequence is like a pixel on one image. The whole sequence contains an event or multiple events happening, which is similar to a sentence in NLP tasks.

In this work, we adapt the ideas used in [7] and [10] for images, and view a time-series sequence as a $C \times H \times W$ tuple, where C is the number of channels of the time-series data, H corresponds to the height of the image, but for time-series that value is set to 1, and W corresponds to the width of the image, which for times-series is the number of timesteps in the sequence. We divide the tuple into multiple patches on the W axis and provide positional encoding to each patch. To our best knowledge, it is the first work to implement such an idea to process time-series data and apply it to a transformer GAN model.

3   Methodology

3.1   Transformer Time-Series GAN Model Architecture

The TTS-GAN model architecture is shown in Fig. 1. It contains two main components, a generator, and a discriminator. Both of them are built based on the transformer encoder architecture [6]. An encoder is a composition of two compound blocks. A multi-head self-attention module constructs the first block and the second block is a feed-forward MLP with GELU activation function. The normalization layer is applied before both of the two blocks and the dropout layer is added after each block. Both blocks employ residual connections.

The generator first takes in a 1D vector with N uniformly distributed random numbers values within the range (0,1), i.e. $N_i \sim U(0,1)$. N represents the latent dimension of the synthetic signals, which is a hyperparameter that can be tuned. The vector is then mapped to a sequence with the same length of the real signals and M embedding dimensions. M is also a hyperparameter that can be changed and not necessarily equal to real signal dimensions. Next, the sequence is divided into multiple patches, and a positional encoding value is added to each patch. Those patches are then input to the transformer encoder blocks. Then the encoder blocks outputs are passed through a Conv2D layer to

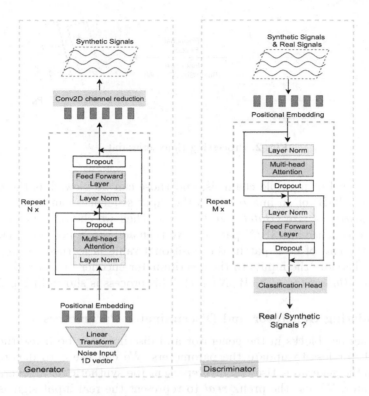

Fig. 1. TTS-GAN model architecture

reduce the synthetic data dimensions. The Conv2D layer is set to have a kernel size $(1,1)$, which won't change the width and height of the synthetic data. The filter size is set to the same dimension size as the real data sequences. Therefore, a synthetic data sequence after the generator transformer encoder layers with a data shape $(hiddendimensions, 1, timesteps)$ will be mapped to $(realdatadimensions, 1, timesteps)$. In this way, a random noise vector is transformed into a sequence with the same shape as the real signals.

The discriminator architecture is similar to the ViT model [7], which is a binary classifier to distinguish whether the input sequence is a real signal or synthetic one. In the ViT model, an image is divided evenly into multiple patches with the same width and height. However, in TTS-GAN, we view any input sequences like an image with a height of 1. The timesteps of the inputs are image widths. Therefore, to add positional encoding on time series inputs, we only need to divide the width evenly into multiple pieces and keep the height of each piece unchanged. This process is explained in detail in Sect. 3.2.

3.2   Processing Time-Series Data Like an Image

We view a time-series data sequence like an image with a height equal to 1. The number of timesteps is the width of an image, W. A time-series sequence can have

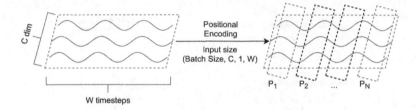

Fig. 2. Processing time-series data

a single channel or multiple channels, and those can be viewed as the number of channels (RGB) of an image, C. So the input sequences can be represented with the matrix of size $(BatchSize, C, 1, W)$. Then we choose a patch size N to divide a sequence into W/N patches. We then add a soft positional encoding value by the end of each patch, the positional value is learned during model training. Therefore the inputs to the discriminator encoder blocks will have the data shape $(BatchSize, C, 1, (W/N) + 1)$. This process is shown in Fig. 2.

3.3   Updating Generator and Discriminator Parameters

The transformer blocks in the generator and discriminator both use the Mean Squared Error loss to update the parameters. We can use z to denote input vectors to the generator. Use $G(z)$ to represent the synthetic data generated by the generator. We use the prefix *real* to represent the real input signals. $D(x)$ is the classification output of the discriminator. x can be the real signals or synthetic signals. *real_label* is set to 1 and *fake_label* is set to 0. To stabilize the GAN model training, some heuristics can be used when setting label values. For example, we can use soft labels that *real_label* is a float number close to 1 and *fake_label* is a float number close to 0. Sometimes, we can also flip the values of the *real_label* and the *fake_label*. The usefulness of these strategies has been so fat been tested only on a case-by-case basics. The discriminator loss can be represented as:

$$d\_real\_loss = MSELoss(D(real), real\_label)$$
$$d\_fake\_loss = MSELoss(D(G(z)), fake\_label)$$
$$d\_loss = d\_real\_loss + d\_fake\_loss$$

The discriminator loss is the sum of real data loss and fake data (synthetic data) losses. The generator loss can be represented as:

$$g\_loss = MSELoss(D(G(z)), real\_label)$$

4   Experiments

4.1   Datasets

We evaluate the TTS-GAN model on three datasets. Simulated sinusoidal waves, UniMiB human activity recognition (HAR) dataset [20] and the PTB Diagnostic

ECG Database [21,22]. A few raw data samples for each dataset are shown in Fig. 3a.

The **sinusoidal waves** are simulated with random frequencies A and phases B values between [0, 0.1]. The sequence length is 24 and the number of dimensions is 5. For each dimension $i \in \{1, ..., 5\}$, the sequence can be represented with the formula $x_i(t) = sin(At + B)$, where $A \in (0, 0.1)$ and $B \in (0, 0.1)$. A total number of 10000 simulated sinusoidal waves are used to train the GAN model.

For the **UniMiB datase** [20], we select 2 categories (Jumping and Running) samples from 24 subjects' recordings to train GAN models. The two classes have 600 and 1572 samples respectively. Every sample has 150 timesteps and three accelerator values at each timestep. All of the recordings are channel-wisely normalized to a mean of 0 and a variance of 1.

The **PTB Diagnostic ECG dataset** [21,22] contains human heartbeat signals in two categories, normal and abnormal with 4046 and 10506 samples respectively. Each sequence represents a heart beat sampled 125 Hz. The original length of each sequence is 188, padded with zeros at the end to create fixed-length sequences. We only use the timesteps 5 to 55 of each sample, which is the part of the sequence containing the most useful information of the heatbeat.

4.2   Evaluation

We evaluate TTS-GAN using qualitative visualizations and quantitative metrics, and compare it with Time-GAN [13], which is the best current alternative.

Raw Data Visualization: Figure 3b shows samples of synthetic data generated by TTS-GAN. Comparing them to the real data in Fig. 3a, we can observe that the synthetic data present visually similar signal patterns to the real data.

Visualizations with PCA and t-SNE: To further illustrate the similarity between the real data and synthetic data, we plot visualization example graphs of data point distributions mapped to two dimensions using PCA and t-SNE in Fig. 4. In these plots, red dots denote original data, and blue dots denote synthetic data generated by TTS-GAN. Again, we notice a similar distribution pattern between real and synthetic data.

Similarity Scores: To quantitatively compare the similarity of the real and generated sequences, we defined two similarity scores, average cosine similarity (avg_cos_sim) and average Jensen-Shannon distance (avg_jen_dis). The detailed definition of these similarity metrics is given in Appendix B. We first extract 7 well-known signal features from each signal channel C, to form a $7 \times C$ dimensional feature vector for each sequence. The avg_cos_sim measures the average cosine similarity among all real signals and synthetic signals of the same class. Values closer to 1 indicate high similarity between two feature vectors. The Jensen-Shannon distance is a method of measuring the similarity between two probability-like distributions. We consider each extracted feature to be a normally distributed array of values and compute the Jensen-Shannon distance for corresponding features between real and synthetic feature vectors. The

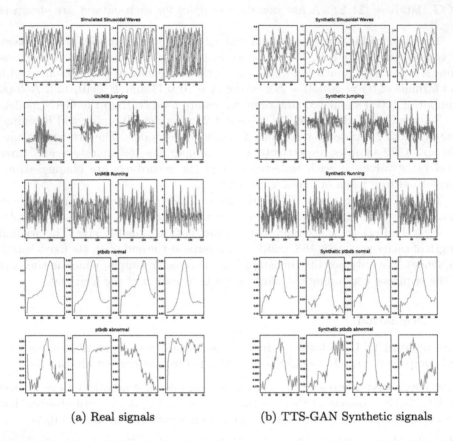

(a) Real signals   (b) TTS-GAN Synthetic signals

Fig. 3. A visual comparison of real data and their corresponding synthetic data generated by TTS-GAN.

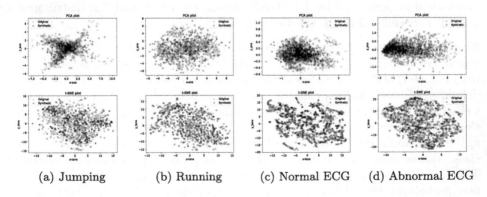

(a) Jumping   (b) Running   (c) Normal ECG   (d) Abnormal ECG

Fig. 4. The PCA and t-SNE test for real and synthetic data generated by TTS-GAN.

Table 1. The similarity scores between real data and synthetic data of 5 different datasets. avg_cos_sim, the bigger the better. avg_jen_dis, the smaller the better. Bold texts identify better results.

Model name	Similarity Score	Sinusoidal	Jumping	Running	Normal	Abnormal
TTS-GAN	avg_cos_sim	**0.9936**	**0.9982**	0.9988	0.9855	**0.9768**
	avg_jen_dis	**0.0980**	**0.0870**	0.0497	**0.1861**	**0.2911**
Time-GAN	avg_cos_sim	0.9935	0.9980	**0.9989**	**0.9878**	0.9719
	avg_jen_dis	0.1226	0.0924	**0.0470**	0.1883	0.3354

avg_jen_dis is the average of all feature vector distances. A value closer to zero means a pair of signals have a small distance from each other and thus share similar distributions. As it can be observed from the experimental results shown in Table 1, synthetic samples show a high average cosine similarity and low Jensen-Shannon distance for different signal classes. In addition, TTS-GAN wins against Time-GAN in 7 out of 10 cases.

5   Conclusions

In this work, we build a transformer-based GAN model (TTS-GAN) that is able to generate multi-dimensional time-series data of various lengths. A visual comparison of the raw signal patterns as well as data point distributions mapped in two dimensions show the similarity of the original data and the synthetic data. Two similarity scores are also used to quantitatively further verify the fidelity of the synthetic data. Overall, the experimental results demonstrate the viability of TTS-GAN as a generator of realistic time-series, when trained on real samples.

References

1. Goodfellow, I., et al.: Generative adversarial nets. In: Advances in Neural Information Processing Systems, vol. 27 (2014)
2. Ledig, C., et al.: Photo-realistic single image super-resolution using a generative adversarial network. In: Proceedings of the IEEE Conference on Computer Vision and Pattern Recognition, pp. 4681–4690 (2017)
3. Bousmalis, K., Silberman, N., Dohan, D., Erhan, D., Krishnan, D.: Unsupervised pixel-level domain adaptation with generative adversarial networks. In: Proceedings of the IEEE Conference on Computer Vision and Pattern Recognition, pp. 3722–3731 (2017)
4. Zhang, H., et al.: StackGAN: text to photo-realistic image synthesis with stacked generative adversarial networks. In: Proceedings of the IEEE International Conference on Computer Vision, pp. 5907–5915 (2017)
5. Brophy, E., Wang, Z., She, Q., Ward, T.: Generative adversarial networks in time series: a survey and taxonomy. arXiv preprint arXiv:2107.11098 (2021)
6. Vaswani, A., et al.: Attention is all you need. In: Advances in Neural Information Processing Systems, pp. 5998–6008 (2017)

7. Dosovitskiy, A., et al.: An image is worth 16×16 words: transformers for image recognition at scale. arXiv preprint arXiv:2010.11929 (2020)
8. Devlin, J., Chang, M.-W., Lee, K., Toutanova, K.: BERT: pre-training of deep bidirectional transformers for language understanding. arXiv preprint arXiv:1810.04805 (2018)
9. Lu, K., Grover, A., Abbeel, P., Mordatch, I.: Pretrained transformers as universal computation engines. arXiv preprint arXiv:2103.05247 (2021)
10. Jiang, Y., Chang, S., Wang, Z.: TransGAN: two pure transformers can make one strong GAN, and that can scale up. In: Thirty-Fifth Conference on Neural Information Processing Systems (2021)
11. Diao, S., Shen, X., Shum, K., Song, Y., Zhang, T.: TILGAN: transformer-based implicit latent GAN for diverse and coherent text generation. In: Findings of the Association for Computational Linguistics: ACL-IJCNLP 2021, pp. 4844–4858 (2021)
12. Esteban, C., Hyland, S.L., Rätsch, G.: Real-valued (medical) time series generation with recurrent conditional GANs. arXiv preprint arXiv:1706.02633 (2017)
13. Yoon, J., Jarrett, D., Van der Schaar, M.: Time-series generative adversarial networks (2019)
14. Ni, H., Szpruch, L., Wiese, M., Liao, S., Xiao, B.: Conditional Sig-Wasserstein GANs for time series generation. arXiv preprint arXiv:2006.05421 (2020)
15. Wold, S., Esbensen, K., Geladi, P.: Principal component analysis. Chemom. Intell. Lab. Syst. **2**(1–3), 37–52 (1987)
16. Van der Maaten, L., Hinton, G.: Visualizing data using t-SNE. J. Mach. Learn. Res. **9**(11) (2008)
17. Ratliff, L.J., Burden, S.A., Sastry, S.S.: Characterization and computation of local NASH equilibria in continuous games. In: 2013 51st Annual Allerton Conference on Communication, Control, and Computing (Allerton), pp. 917–924. IEEE (2013)
18. Goodfellow, I., et al.: Generative adversarial networks. Commun. ACM **63**(11), 139–144 (2020)
19. Huang, R., Zhang, S., Li, T., He, R.: Beyond face rotation: global and local perception GAN for photorealistic and identity preserving frontal view synthesis. In: Proceedings of the IEEE International Conference on Computer Vision, pp. 2439–2448 (2017)
20. Micucci, D., Mobilio, M., Napoletano, P.: UniMiB shar: a dataset for human activity recognition using acceleration data from smartphones. Appl. Sci. **7**(10), 1101 (2017)
21. Bousseljot, R., Kreiseler, D., Schnabel, A.: Nutzung der EKG-Signaldatenbank CARDIODAT der PTB über das internet (1995)
22. Goldberger, A.L., et al.: PhysioBank, PhysioToolkit, and PhysioNet: components of a new research resource for complex physiologic signals. Circulation **101**(23), e215–e220 (2000)
23. Mao, X., Li, Q., Xie, H., Lau, R.Y., Wang, Z., Paul Smolley, S.: Least squares generative adversarial networks. In: Proceedings of the IEEE International Conference on Computer Vision, pp. 2794–2802 (2017)

A   Appendix 1: Training Details

We conduct all experiments on an Intel server with a 3.40 GHz CPU, 377 GB RAM memory and 2 Nvidia 1080 GPUs. For all datasets, the synthetic data are generated by a generator that takes random vectors of size $(100, 1)$ as inputs. The transformer blocks in the generator and discriminator are both repeated three times. We adopt a learning rate of $1e - 4$ for the generator and $3e - 4$ for the discriminator. We follow the setting of LSGAN [23] and use loss function described in Sect. 3.3 to update model parameters. An Adam optimizer with $\beta_1 = 0.9$ and $\beta_2 = 0.999$, and a batch size of 32 for both generator and discriminator, are used for all experiments.

B   Appendix 2: Similarity Scores

Feature Extraction. We extract several meaningful features from each input data sequence. They are the median, mean, standard deviation, variance, root mean square, maximum, and minimum values of each input sequence. Suppose we compute m features from all channels of each sequence and get a feature vector with the format $f = <feature_1, feature_2, ..., feature_m>$.

Average Cosine Similarity. For each pair of real signal feature vector f_a and synthetic signal feature vector f_b, the vector has the size m, we can compute its cosine similarity as:

$$cos\_sim_{ab} = \frac{f_a \cdot f_b}{\|f_a\| \, \|f_b\|} = \frac{\sum_{i=1}^m f_{ai} f_{bi}}{\sqrt{\sum_{i=1}^m f_{ai}^2} \sqrt{\sum_{i=1}^m f_{bi}^2}}$$

The average cosine similarity score is the average of each cosine similarity between pairs of feature vectors corresponding to real and synthetic signals of the same class. The average cosine similarity is computed as follows, where n the total number of signals:

$$avg\_cos\_sim = \frac{1}{n} \sum_{i=1}^n cos\_sim_i$$

Average Jensen-Shannon Distance. The average jensen-shannon distance is the average of jensen-shannon distance between each feature from real signals and synthetic signals. For each pair of real signal feature f_{i_real} and synthetic signal feature f_{i_syn}, we can compute its jensen-shannon distance as:

$$jen\_sim_i = \sqrt{\frac{D(f_{i\_real}\|m) + D(f_{i\_syn}\|m)}{2}}$$

where m is the pointwise mean of f_{i_real} and f_{i_syn} and D is the Kullback-Leibler divergence. The average jensens-shannon distance is computed as:

$$avg\_jen\_dis = \sum_{i=1}^m jen\_sim_i$$

Instrumented Timed Up and Go Test Using Inertial Sensors from Consumer Wearable Devices

Miguel Matey-Sanz(✉)📵, Alberto González-Pérez📵, Sven Casteleyn📵,
and Carlos Granell📵

Institute of New Imaging Technologies, Universitat Jaume I, Castellón, Spain
{matey,alberto.gonzalez,sven.casteleyn,carlos.granell}@uji.es

Abstract. Precision medicine pursues the ambitious goal of providing
personalized interventions targeted at individual patients. Within this
vision, digital health and mental health, where fine-grained monitoring
of patients form the basis for so-called ecological momentary assessments
and interventions, play a central role as complementary technology-
based and data-driven instruments to traditional psychological treatments. Mobile devices are hereby key enablers: consumer smartphones
and wearables are ubiquitously present and used in daily life, while they
come with the necessary embedded physiological, inertial and movement
sensors to potentially recognise user's activities and behaviors. In this
article, we explore whether real-time detection of fine-grained activities
- relevant in the context of wellbeing - is feasible, applying machine
learning techniques and based on sensor data collected from a consumer
smartwatch device. We present the system architecture, whereby data
collection is performed in the wearable device, real-time data processing
and inference is delegated to the paired smartphone, and model training
is performed offline. Finally, we demonstrate its use by instrumenting
the well-known Timed Up and Go (TUG) test, typically used to assess
the risk of fall in elderly people. Experiments show that consumer smartwatches can be used to automate the assessment of TUG tests and obtain
satisfactory results, comparable with the classical manually performed
version of the test.

Keywords: Timed Up and Go · Smartwatch · Mobile sensing

1 Introduction

In healthcare, a variety of well-known physical fitness tests are being applied
to assess the physical abilities or decline of healthy subjects, people in physical recovery, elderly, or individuals with specific physical, cognitive or mental
disabilities. Such tests rely on monitoring and measuring several parameters,
such as balance, flexibility, strength, coordination, endurance, speed, dexterity,
etc., and are traditionally administered by a trained professional who observes
the subject and (manually) records the various required criteria (e.g., performed

repetitions, timings). Examples of such tests include the Fullerton Functional Fitness Test [17], the Groningen Fitness Test [11], or the Timed Up and Go (TUG) test [2], among others.

Technological developments in sensor-based measuring equipment, and particularly the increasingly widespread availability of sensor-packed smartphone and wearables (e.g. smartwatches), provide promising opportunities to move from expert-administered to automated technology-assisted self-administered tests. Specifically, through the systematic ecological capturing of inertial and movement sensor measurements, researchers aim to develop a clinically valid alternative to conduct fitness tests. In this article, we focus on the automation of the TUG test using a consumer smartwatch paired with a smartphone app.

The TUG test is a widely used test to assess balance and mobility in elderly subjects [2] or individuals with pathologies such as Parkinson's disease [16], and is often used to measure the risk of falling [1]. The test consists of measuring how long it takes for a subject to stand up from a chair, walk 3 m, turn around, walk back to the chair and sit down. In most TUG automation studies, the total time required to complete the test is calculated, ignoring the time spent on each of the individual sub-phases. While capturing the total time is sufficient in some use cases, a finer control to detect and segment each of the contained sub-phases can reveal specific subject's weaknesses (e.g., sitting down, walking) and indicate specific problems (e.g., deteriorating upper leg muscle strength, motor skill problems), or reveal subtle changes in the patient's performance when exposed to prolonged monitoring. Therefore, some studies have focused on automatic detection and segmentation of all sub-phases using inertial measurement units (IMU) in sensing devices. This required either specialised sensor equipment or specific sensing environment setups (e.g., multiple sensors scattered over the body [18], sensors on the back [3] or on the abdomen [8]). Such sophistication poses a barrier to switch from lab experimentation to a real-world setting.

Early TUG automation studies using smartphones still required unnatural and error-prone setups, requiring the subject to wear the smartphone on specific body parts (e.g., on the trunk [21], the chest [5] or the back [12]). More recently, some studies explored the use of a smartphone placed more naturally (e.g. pants pocket or similar), to automate the TUG test [20]. While such approaches open the door for automated detection of actions in mobile-based Ecological Momentary Assessment (EMA) [19] using commercially available mobile devices, the specific location where the smartphone has to be worn still hinders ubiquitous use (e.g. users not carrying smartphone at home, women keeping it in their purse, using a neck pouch). Despite potential advantages (i.e. always worn, more suitable natural wearing location, additional sensors), the use of smartwatches for TUG test automation is, to the best of our knowledge, not yet explored.

In this article, we present and describe a system capable of automating the TUG test using a consumer WearOS-based wrist-worn smartwatch, which collects accelerometer and gyroscope sensor data, and a paired smartphone capable of measuring and segmenting the TUG test sub-phases in real time, using sliding window feature extraction based on an offline-trained machine learning model. The system is experimentally evaluated, showing favorable results.

2 Related Work

The automation of the TUG test assessment is widely present in the literature. For Parkinson disease (PD), Salarian et al. [18] proposed the iTUG (i.e., instrumented TUG) to automatically detect, separate and analyse test subcomponents (e.g., step cadence, arm-swing velocity, turning duration) using IMUs, showing that extracted metrics proved significantly different between PD and control subjects. The main drawback was the excessive number of sensing units. Kleiner et al. [9] successfully used a single BTS G-Sensor placed in the lumbar region to quantify the duration of the TUG test. von Coelln et al. [6] used a Dynaport MT unit on the lumbar region in subjects at risk of developing PD. Their results associated several metrics extracted from the test to the risk of developing PD.

As regards TUG automation for predicting the risk of falls, Zakaria et al. [22] used a 3D accelerometer and three 1D gyroscopes in the lumbar region, demonstrating significant differences between the parameters extracted from each phase of the TUG test for high and low risk participants. Using the DYSKIMOT sensing unit in the lumbar region, Buisseret et al. [4] showed that raw data obtained from running the TUG test improved the accuracy of fall risk prediction.

Moving from specialised devices to mainstream smartphones, Mellone et al. [15] compared a smartphone's 3D accelerometer with a specialized TUG test measuring unit. The results showed similar and satisfactory results for both devices, but the smartphone required additional pre-processing due to sampling rate variability issues. Likewise, Meigal et al. [14] reconstructed users' trajectories using the IMU of a smartphone placed on the back of the head, using the TUG test as a use case, and found comparable accuracy as with much more expensive systems (e.g., motion capture systems). Given the increasing number of studies, Coni et al. [7] studied the usefulness of TUG test instrumentation compared with standard clinical methods, and concluded that additional features describing the state of the patient could be obtained.

Another stream of research focuses on the viability of smartphones for automating TUG tests. Chan et al. [5] validated a smartphone app designed to measure TUG test performance. Similarly, Madhushri et al. [12] showed a smartphone app to automate and quantify well-known mobility tests, including the TUG test. Furthermore, Tchelet et al. [21] developed a smartphone app to be used on various parts of the trunk (i.e., sternum, abdomen and waist), providing gait biomarkers extracted from the TUG test execution.

All previous studies required the smartphone to be put in unusual places, namely on the chest, trunk or lumbar region. In contrast, Silva et al. [20] and Lein et al. [10] used the smartphone placed in the pants pockets to carry out the TUG test with satisfactory results. Today, wearable devices such as smartwatches provide similar sensing capabilities compared to smartphones, and have the advantage of additional sensors (e.g. heart rate), always being worn, always worn in the same position (wrist), which is further more differential (due to arm movements). This makes them ideal candidates and less intrusive devices for TUG test automation. Nevertheless, to the best of our knowledge, no other studies explored consumer smartwatches for TUG test automation.

3   System Overview

We developed a system to instrument the TUG test (i.e., automatically obtain its results) using a consumer WearOS smartwatch as a sensing device and a paired Android smartphone as the computing device responsible for data processing, inference and obtaining the test results. These results correspond to the total duration of the test and the duration of each sub-phase (i.e., stand up, first walk, first turn, second walk, second turn and sit down).

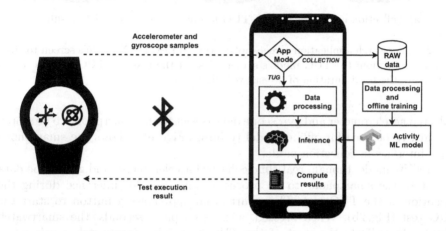

Fig. 1. Overall system architecture

Figure 1 shows the architecture of the designed system. The smartwatch device runs an application to allow the user to start the data collection process (for ML model training) or to start the execution of the TUG test. When instructed, the smartwatch starts the data collection process and sends the collected data on a regular basis to the paired smartphone device through Bluetooth. In COLLECTION mode, the smartphone stores the incoming data into a file to offline-train the model later. In TUG mode, the smartphone device processes the incoming data in real time, and infers the current activity that the user is performing. Once the smartphone detects that the user has finished the test (i.e., the user sat down), it prompts the smartwatch to stop the data collection process, computes the test results, and sends the total time of the test to the smartwatch to provide feedback to the user. Next, we describe the three parts of the system: the smartwatch, the machine learning model for activity inference and smartphone apps. All code and data (i.e., apps source code, data processing, code for training, trained model and experiment results) are publicly available [13].

3.1   Smartwatch Application

The smartwatch app is tasked with collecting 3D accelerometer and gyroscope samples, either in COLLECTION mode or TUG mode. In the former mode,

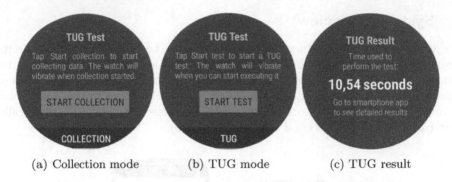

(a) Collection mode   (b) TUG mode   (c) TUG result

Fig. 2. Smartwatch application screenshots: (a) COLLECTION mode's screen to start the data collection; (b) TUG mode's screen to start the test; (c) TUG mode's screen that shows the total duration of a test execution.

collected accelerometer and gyroscope data is sent to the smartphone to be stored in a file, to be used for offline model training. Figure 2a shows the smartphone app's interface in collection mode.

In TUG mode, though, real-time collected accelerometer and gyroscope data is sent to the smartphone to be processed and used for inference during the execution of the TUG test. The smartwatch app shows a button to start the TUG test (Fig. 2b). When pressed, after a couple a seconds, the smartwatch vibrates to indicate the start of the TUG test. The smartwatch continues to collect data until the test execution ends, either automatically detected by the smartphone or because the user manually stops the test from the smartwatch. After the test is completed, the smartwatch app displays the total duration of the test execution (Fig. 2c), prompting the user to open the smartphone app to see the total time and the duration of each sub-phase (Fig. 3b).

In both modes, the smartwatch app collects data from the accelerometer and gyroscope at a sample rate 100 Hz and sends it to the smartphone in batches of 50 samples by default, although both parameters are configurable.

3.2   Activity Inference Model

The main objective of the activity inference model is to recognize five human activities (i.e., sit, stand up, walk, turn and sit down) given an input feature array. The machine learning model used is an MLP (Multilayer Perceptron) built using the Python Keras API[1]. The model is composed by one input and one hidden layer with 256 neurons each, and batch normalization before the non-linear ReLU activation layer. The output layer is composed by 5 neurons with a SoftMax activation function, which outputs the probability of the input features to belong to any of the five objective activities.

Regarding the training phase, the model has been offline trained using data from 60 TUG test runs by a single subject (male, age 24), collected with a

---

[1] https://keras.io.

TicWatch Pro 3 GPS equipped with a STMicroelectronics LSM6DSO IMU sensor. The 3D accelerometer and gyroscope collected samples were first temporally aligned to match each accelerometer sample to its closest gyroscope sample. Then, a 50-sample sliding window with 50% overlap was used to group the samples for feature extraction. Once a raw sample window was ready, it was normalized within a range of $[-1, 1]$ to preserve its nature (i.e., positive and negative values), using as maximum and minimum values the value range reported by the sensor (smartwatch) manufacturer. After the normalization, 47 features were extracted from the temporal domain, including: seven features (mean, median, maximum, minimum, STD, RMS, and range) for each axis from accelerometer and gyroscope samples; pitch and roll from accelerometer samples; and rotational angle for each axis from gyrsoscope samples. After feature extraction, 4308 instances were available, of which 70% were used for model training (80%) and tuning (20%), and 30% for testing.

Lastly, the trained Keras model is converted to the TensorFlow Lite[2] format, ready to be executed in mobile devices. Then, the model is uploaded to Firebase Custom ML[3], from where it is downloaded and used by the smartphone app.

All software package versions used are specified in [13].

3.3 Smartphone Application

In COLLECTION mode, the smartphone app is only responsible for storing incoming data into a file for use for the model offline training. In TUG mode, the smartphone app is responsible for processing the data collected by the smartwatch, feeding the processed data into a machine learning model to infer the activity the user is performing. When the test is complete, it analyses the inferred data and computes the TUG test results. Only the total duration of the TUG test is sent to the smartwatch (Sect. 3.1), but the smartphone app displays how long each sub-phase took for all the executed tests (Fig. 3). Unlike the smartwatch app, the smartphone app performs three core functions: data processing, model inference, and processing of results.

First, when it comes to data processing, the smartphone app recreates the same data processing steps as those of the activity inference model for offline training (Sect. 3.2), i.e., temporally aligning samples, normalization, and sliding window feature extraction.

Second, the TensorFlow Lite model - offline trained to recognize the five activities performed during the TUG test (sit, stand up, walk, turn and sit down) - is downloaded during app initialization from Firebase Custom ML. Note that this model is interchangeable. After each model inference, the resulting inferred activity is stored and combined with previous inferences to determine the phase of the test. When the last activity (sit down) of the TUG test is recognised, it signals the end of the test and, consequently, the smartphone app automatically notifies the smartwatch to stop collecting data.

---

[2] https://www.tensorflow.org/lite.
[3] https://firebase.google.com/docs/ml-kit/use-custom-models.

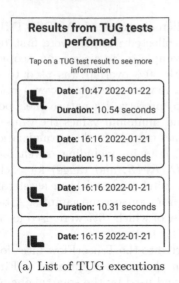

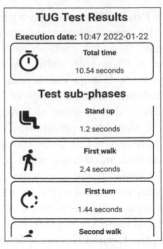

(a) List of TUG executions   (b) Results of TUG execution

Fig. 3. Smartphone app screenshots: (a) Overview of all TUG test executed, showing total execution time; (b) Sub-phase inferred time of a single TUG test.

Finally, processing the test results implies that all the activities estimated during the test run are analysed once the test is complete. Each activity estimate is analysed considering preceding and subsequent estimates to determine the boundaries between activities. These boundaries allow to calculate the duration of the test and each of the sub-phases. The results are stored in the smartphone app and the total duration of the test is sent to the smartwatch to provide feedback to the user (Sect. 3.1).

4   Evaluation

An experiment for evaluation purposes was performed using a TicWatch Pro 3 GPS smartwatch running WearOS 2.33 and a paired Honor 9 smartphone running Android 9. Five healthy individuals (3 male, 2 females; age range [26–45], average 33.31, median 30) performed the TUG test using our system in the same environment until 10 successful runs were achieved. A run is considered successful when the system is able to determine the duration of the test and each of its sub-phases, regardless of whether the system was able to automatically detect the end of the test or the subject had to finish it manually. While performing the experiment, they were also video-recorded to manually compute the duration of the test and each of its sub-phases. These manual results were then compared with those obtained automatically by the system.

The root mean square error (RMSE) in Table 1 shows that the system presents low errors for standing up and the first walk sub-phases (375 ms and 387 ms), with the exception of Subject 04, and for the sitting down sub-phase

(322 ms) where subject 5 performed significantly better. Higher errors (564 ms and 707 ms) are observed in the second walk and second turn sub-phases, which can be explained due to the subjects usually performing these phases in a continuous manner (i.e., start second turn while still executing second walk). Regarding the total duration of the test, the RMSE from the results of all subjects is 568 ms.

Table 2 shows the mean of differences and the agreement limits (CI95%) of the Bland-Altman analysis for the total duration of the TUG runs and each of the sub-phases. The analysis shows very good mean results for all sub-phases except for the second turn, where the system has a bias of 0.54 s. The total duration is also biased 0.44 s, which means that the system tends to overestimate the duration of the executions. These results are significantly better than others reported in the literature –around 1 s [9,21]–, and in line with other studies such as [3], but without the need to use specialised sensing devices placed in particular body locations. In [3,21], the evaluation was performed by a small population of healthy individuals ($n = 11$ and $n = 4$, respectively) as in the present study, while in [9] a larger group ($n = 30$) of PD subjects was used.

An important part of the system is the automatic completion of the test execution. For Subjects 01 and 03 the system was only able to automatically detect the end of the test in 50% of the executions, while for Subjects 02 and 04 the success ratio reached up to 90%, and 100% for Subject 05. Table 1 explains this behaviour, since subjects with a higher RMSE value for the sitting down sub-phase had a lower success ratio in completing the automatic test run, while subjects with lower RMSE values had a higher success ratio.

We also evaluated the system in terms of failed test executions. In some test runs, the system could not estimate the time for each of the sub-phases. The number of failed executions were 2, 4, 2, 3 and 5 for subjects 01, 02, 03, 04 and 05. These errors were mainly caused by the misrecognition of both turn sub-phases due to its smooth transitions with the next activities.

We acknowledge some limitations and room for future improvement in our study. First, model training could be extended with data from multiple subjects from different age ranges (i.e., different movement patterns) to improve robustness. Second, the use of a single smartwatch device could be extended with various devices to assess the impact of device heterogeneity. Third, only a small amount of healthy, relatively young subjects participated in the experiment; we consider this an initial step to a broader evaluation with a more heterogeneous population (e.g. elderly, people with Parkinson's disease, etc.). Despite this limitations, we consider our system a successful proof-of-concept, and an initial step towards larger, more generalized experimentation.

4.1 Clinical Relevance

The satisfactory results of the TUG test automation with mainstream mobile devices suggest that similar systems could be scaled to clinical practices enabling self-assessments, both for the TUG test but also beyond, in health to automatically detect activities in indoor/outdoor environments, in cases where sudden changes in patient's activities could signal early prevalence for health conditions.

Table 1. RMSE of total times (milliseconds) calculated by the system and by visual inspection of recorded videos, both by individual subject and aggregate.

	Total	Stand up	First walk	First turn	Second walk	Second turn	Sit down
Subject 01	611	237	350	578	293	549	348
Subject 02	533	217	219	561	516	698	305
Subject 03	760	173	276	255	589	534	499
Subject 04	406	654	679	294	875	946	224
Subject 05	460	277	206	137	353	726	73
All subjects	568	375	387	405	564	707	322

Table 2. Bland-Altman agreement between system and manual results.

	Mean of differences (seconds)	Agreement Limits (CI95%)
Total duration	0.44	$[-0.26, 1.1]$
Stand up	0.11	$[-0.56, 0.78]$
First walk	-0.0003	$[-0.76, 0.76]$
First turn	0.041	$[-0.75, 0.83]$
Second walk	-0.25	$[-1.2, 0.74]$
Second turn	0.54	$[-0.37, 1.4]$
Sit down	0.0094	$[-0.62, 0.64]$

5   Conclusion

This work demonstrated that smartwatch devices and online model inference on smartphones can be successfully used to automate the execution of the well-known TUG test, paving the way for less intrusive, mobile-based EMA methods for prolonged monitoring for both clinical and wellness practices. Looking at the future, improving the accuracy of the inference model in the turn and sit down phases would definitely make our system more robust and exportable to real-world settings.

Acknowledgments. Miguel Matey-Sanz and Alberto González-Pérez are funded by the Spanish Ministry of Universities [grants FPU19/05352 and FPU17/03832]. This study was supported by grant PID2020-120250RB-100 (SyMptOMS-ET) funded by MCIN/AEI/10.13039/501100011033.

References

1. Barry, E., Galvin, R., Keogh, C., Horgan, F., Fahey, T.: Is the timed up and go test a useful predictor of risk of falls in community dwelling older adults: a systematic review and meta-analysis. BMC Geriatr. **14**(1), 1–14 (2014)

2. Berg, K.O., Maki, B.E., Williams, J.I., Holliday, P.J., Wood-Dauphinee, S.L.: Clinical and laboratory measures of postural balance in an elderly population. Arch. Phys. Med. Rehabil. **73**(11), 1073–1080 (1992)
3. Beyea, J., McGibbon, C.A., Sexton, A., Noble, J., O'Connell, C.: Convergent validity of a wearable sensor system for measuring sub-task performance during the timed up-and-go test. Sensors **17**(4), 934 (2017)
4. Buisseret, F., et al.: Timed up and go and six-minute walking tests with wearable inertial sensor: one step further for the prediction of the risk of fall in elderly nursing home people. Sensors **20**(11), 3207 (2020)
5. Chan, M.H., et al.: A validation study of a smartphone application for functional mobility assessment of the elderly. Hong Kong Physiother. J. **35**, 1–4 (2016)
6. von Coelln, R., et al.: Quantitative mobility metrics from a wearable sensor predict incident parkinsonism in older adults. Parkinsonism Relat. Disord. **65**, 190–196 (2019)
7. Coni, A., et al.: Comparison of standard clinical and instrumented physical performance tests in discriminating functional status of high-functioning people aged 61–70 years old. Sensors **19**(3), 449 (2019)
8. Ishikawa, M., et al.: Gait analysis in a component timed-up-and-go test using a smartphone application. J. Neurol. Sci. **398**, 45–49 (2019)
9. Kleiner, A.F.R., et al.: Timed up and go evaluation with wearable devices: validation in Parkinson's disease. J. Bodyw. Mov. Ther. **22**(2), 390–395 (2018)
10. Lein, D.H., Willig, J.H., Smith, C.R., Curtis, J.R., Westfall, A.O., Hurt, C.P.: Assessing a novel way to measure three common rehabilitation outcome measures using a custom mobile phone application. Gait Posture **73**, 246–250 (2019)
11. Lemmink, K.A., Han, K., de Greef, M.H., Rispens, P., Stevens, M.: Reliability of the Groningen fitness test for the elderly. J. Aging Phys. Act. **9**(2), 194–212 (2001)
12. Madhushri, P., Dzhagaryan, A.A., Jovanov, E., Milenkovic, A.: A smartphone application suite for assessing mobility. In: 38th Annual International Conference of the IEEE Engineering in Medicine and Biology Society, pp. 3117–3120. IEEE (2016)
13. Matey-Sanz, M.: Code and data resources for "Instrumented Timed Up and Go test using inertial sensors from consumer wearable devices", January 2022. https://doi.org/10.5281/zenodo.5928744
14. Meigal, A., Reginya, S., Gerasimova-Meigal, L., Prokhorov, K., Moschevikin, A.: Analysis of human gait based on smartphone inertial measurement unit: a feasibility study. In: 22nd Conference of Open Innovations Association, pp. 151–158. IEEE (2018)
15. Mellone, S., Tacconi, C., Chiari, L.: Validity of a smartphone-based instrumented timed up and go. Gait Posture **36**(1), 163–165 (2012)
16. Morris, S., Morris, M.E., Iansek, R.: Reliability of measurements obtained with the timed "up & go" test in people with Parkinson disease. Phys. Ther. **81**(2), 810–818 (2001)
17. Różańska-Kirschke, A., Kocur, P., Wilk, M., Dylewicz, P.: The Fullerton fitness test as an index of fitness in the elderly. Med. Rehabil. **10**(2), 9–16 (2006)
18. Salarian, A., et al.: iTUG, a sensitive and reliable measure of mobility. IEEE Trans. Neural Syst. Rehabil. Eng. **18**(3), 303–310 (2010)
19. Shiffman, S., Stone, A.A., Hufford, M.R.: Ecological momentary assessment. Annu. Rev. Clin. Psychol. **4**, 1–32 (2008)
20. Silva, J., Sousa, I.: Instrumented timed up and go: fall risk assessment based on inertial wearable sensors. In: IEEE International Symposium on Medical Measurements and Applications (MeMeA), pp. 1–6. IEEE (2016)

21. Tchelet, K., Stark-Inbar, A., Yekutieli, Z.: Pilot study of the EncephaLog smartphone application for gait analysis. Sensors **19**(23), 5179 (2019)
22. Zakaria, N.A., Kuwae, Y., Tamura, T., Minato, K., Kanaya, S.: Quantitative analysis of fall risk using tug test. Comput. Methods Biomech. Biomed. Eng. **18**(4), 426–437 (2015)

Learning to Adapt Dynamic Clinical Event Sequences with Residual Mixture of Experts

Jeong Min Lee[✉][iD] and Milos Hauskrecht[iD]

Department of Computer Science, University of Pittsburgh, Pittsburgh, PA, USA
{jlee,milos}@cs.pitt.edu

Abstract. Clinical event sequences in Electronic Health Records (EHRs) record detailed information about the patient condition and patient care as they occur in time. Recent years have witnessed increased interest of machine learning community in developing machine learning models solving different types of problems defined upon information in EHRs. More recently, neural sequential models, such as RNN and LSTM, became popular and widely applied models for representing patient sequence data and for predicting future events or outcomes based on such data. However, a single neural sequential model may not properly represent complex dynamics of all patients and the differences in their behaviors. In this work, we aim to alleviate this limitation by refining a one-fits-all model using a Mixture-of-Experts (MoE) architecture. The architecture consists of multiple (expert) RNN models covering patient sub-populations and refining the predictions of the base model. That is, instead of training expert RNN models from scratch we define them on the residual signal that attempts to model the differences from the population-wide model. The heterogeneity of various patient sequences is modeled through multiple experts that consist of RNN. Particularly, instead of directly training MoE from scratch, we augment MoE based on the prediction signal from pretrained base GRU model. With this way, the mixture of experts can provide flexible adaptation to the (limited) predictive power of the single base RNN model. We experiment with the newly proposed model on real-world EHRs data and the multivariate clinical event prediction task. We implement RNN using Gated Recurrent Units (GRU). We show 4.1% gain on AUPRC statistics compared to a single RNN prediction.

1 Introduction

Clinical event sequences in Electronic Health Records (EHRs) record detailed information about the patient condition and patient care as they occur in time. In recent years, we have witnessed increased interest of machine learning community in developing machine learning models and solutions to different types of problems defined upon information in EHRs. Examples of the problems are automatic patient diagnosis [25, 26], mortality prediction [33], detection of patient management errors [9, 10], length of stay predictions [27], or sepsis prediction [11]. Interestingly, the overwhelming majority of the proposed solutions in recent years are based on applications of modern autoregressive models based on Recurrent neural networks (RNN), such as LSTM or GRU, and their variants. However, the problem with many of these works is that they aim to learn one autoregressive model to fit all patients and their records. This may limit the ability of the models to represent well the dynamics of heterogeneous patient subpopulations their trends, and outcomes.

The goal of this paper is to study ways of enhancing the one-fits-all RNN model solution with additional RNN models to better fit the differences in patient behaviors and patient subpopulations. We study this solution in the context of multivariate event prediction problem where our goal is to predict, as accurately as possible, the future occurrence of a wide range of events recorded in EHRs. Such a prediction task can be used for defining general predictive patient state representation that can be used, for example, to define similarity among patients or for predicting patient outcomes.

To represent different patient subpopulations and their behaviors we explore and experiment with the mixture of experts architecture [14]. However, instead of training multiple RNN models from scratch, we first train the all-population model and train the mixture on the residual signals, such that the models augment the output of the all population model. Hence we name our model Residual Mixture of Experts (R-MoE). The rationale for such a design is that residual subpopulation models may be much simpler and hence easier to learn. Moreover, this design simplifies the subpopulation model switching, that is, more subpopulation models can be used to make predictions for the same patient at different times.

R-MoE aims to provide flexible adaptation to the (limited) predictive power of the population model. We demonstrate the effectiveness of R-MoE on the multivariate clinical sequence prediction task for real-world patient data from MIMIC-3 Database [15]. The experiments with R-MoE model show 4.1% gain on AUPRC compared to a single GRU-based prediction. For the reproducibility, the code, trained models, and data processing scripts are available on this link: https://github.com/leej35/residual-moe.

2   Related Work

Subpopulation and Adaptive Models. The goal of the adaptive models is to address the drift of distribution in data. In clinical and biomedical research areas, this is a particularly important issue due to the heterogeneity of overall patient population and its subpopulations. For instance, when a model that is trained on the overall patient population is used for a target patient that belongs to a certain subpopulation, there is no guarantee that the model would perform well.

One traditional approach used to address the problem is to divide (cluster) the patients into subgroups using a small set of patients' characteristics (features) and train many different subpopulation models for these groups. The subpopulation model for the target patient is chosen by matching the corresponding group features [12,13]. Another related approach is to flexibly identify the subpopulation group that closely matches the target patient through similarity measures and build the subpopulation model for the target patient from this patient group [7,32]. An alternative way is to adapt the parameters of the population models to fit the target patient. In the NLP area, non-parametric memory components are used to build adaptive models that sequentially update the model's parameters [8,17]. In the clinical domain, simpler residual models that learn the difference (residuals) between the predictions made by population models and the desired outcomes are learned for continuous-valued clinical time series and achieve better forecasting performance [24].

Neural Clinical Sequence Models. Neural-based models have become more popular in recent years for modeling clinical sequence data. Especially, they have advantages such as flexibility in modeling latent structures and capability in learning complex patient state dynamics. More specifically, word embedding methods (e.g., CBOW, Skip-gram) are used to obtain compact representation of clinical concepts [3,6] and predictive patient state representations [5]. For autoregressive clinical sequence modeling, neural temporal models (e.g., RNN, GRU) and attention mechanism are used to learn patient state dynamics [18,22], predict future states progression [20], and predict clinical variables such as diagnosis codes [25,26], readmission of chronic diseases [28], medication prescriptions [1], ICU mortality risk [33], disease progression of diabetes and mental health [30], and multivariate future clinical event occurrences [19,21,23].

3 Methodology

3.1 Neural Event Sequence Prediction

In this work, our goal is to predict the occurrences and non-occurrences of future clinical (target) events $\boldsymbol{y}'_{t+1}$ for a patient given the patient's past clinical event occurrences $\boldsymbol{H}_t$. Specifically, we assume that the patient's clinical event history is in a sequence of multivariate input event vectors $\boldsymbol{H}_t = \{\boldsymbol{y}_1, \ldots, \boldsymbol{y}_t\}$ where each vector $\boldsymbol{y}_i$ is a binary $\{0, 1\}$ vector, one dimension per an event type. The input vectors are of dimension $|E|$ where E are different event types in clinical sequences. The target vector is of dimension $|E'|$, where $E' \subset E$ are events we are interested in predicting. We aim to build a predictive model δ that can predict $\hat{\boldsymbol{y}}'_{t+1}$ at any time t given the history $\boldsymbol{H}_t$.

One way to build δ is to use neural sequence models such as RNN and LSTM. In this work, we use Gated Recurrent Units (GRU) [2] to build a base prediction model δ_{base} with input embedding matrix $\boldsymbol{W}_{emb} \in \mathbb{R}^{|E| \times \epsilon}$, output projection matrix $\boldsymbol{W}_o \in \mathbb{R}^{d \times |E'|}$, bias vector $\boldsymbol{b}_o \in \mathbb{R}^{|E'|}$, and a sigmoid (logit) activation function σ. At any time step t, we update hidden state $\boldsymbol{h}_t$ and predict target events in next time step $\hat{\boldsymbol{y}}'_{t+1}$:

$$\boldsymbol{v}_t = \boldsymbol{W}_{emb} \cdot \boldsymbol{y}_t \qquad \boldsymbol{h}_t = \mathrm{GRU}(\boldsymbol{h}_{t-1}, \boldsymbol{v}_t) \qquad \hat{\boldsymbol{y}}'_{t+1} = \sigma(\boldsymbol{W}_o \cdot \boldsymbol{h}_t + \boldsymbol{b}_o)$$

All parameters of δ_{base} ($\boldsymbol{W}_{emb}, \boldsymbol{W}_o, \boldsymbol{b}_o$ and GRU) are learned through stochastic gradient descent (SGD) algorithm with the binary cross entropy loss function.

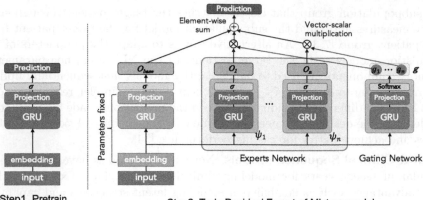

Fig. 1. Architecture of R-MoE model. First we train base model δ_{base}. Then, we fix parameters of δ_{base} and train parameters of Mixture-of-Experts consists of Experts network and Gating network with the combined prediction of δ_{base} and the MoE. With this way, MoE can learn to adapt the residual of δ_{base}.

This GRU-based neural sequence model has a number of benefits for modeling complex high-dimensional clinical event time-series: First, we can obtain a compact real-valued representation of high-dimensional binary input vector y through low-dimensional embedding with W_{emb}. Second, we can model complex dynamics of patient state sequences through GRU which can model nonlinearities of the sequences. Third, complex input-output associations of the patient state sequences can be learned through a flexible SGD-based end-to-end learning framework.

Nonetheless, the neural approach cannot address one important peculiarity of the patient state sequence: the heterogeneity of patient sequences across patient populations. Typically, clinical event sequences in EHRs are generated from a pool of diverse patients where each patient has different types of clinical complications, medication regimes, or observed sequence dynamics. While the average behavior of clinical event sequences can be captured well by a single neural sequence model, the model may fail to represent the detailed dynamics of heterogeneous clinical event sequences for individual patients.

3.2   Residual Mixture-of-Experts

In this work, we address the heterogeneity issue of the neural sequence model by specializing it with a novel learning mechanism based on Mixture-of-Experts (MoE) architecture. The dynamics of heterogeneous patient state sequences can be modeled through a number of experts; each consists of GRU which is capable of modeling non-linearities and temporal dependencies. Particularly, in this work, instead of simply replacing the GRU model δ_{base} with MoE, we *augment* δ_{base} with MoE. The key idea is to specialize the Mixture-of-Experts to learn the residual that δ_{base} cannot capture. As shown in Fig. 1, the proposed model R-MoE consists of δ_{base} module and Mixture-of-Experts module.

The Mixture-of-Experts module consists of n experts $\psi_1, \ldots, \psi_n$ and a gating network G which outputs a n-dimensional vector $\boldsymbol{g}$. The output $\boldsymbol{o}_{moe}$ of the MoE module can be written as follows:

$$\boldsymbol{o}_{moe} = \sum_{i=1}^{n} \boldsymbol{g}_{[i]}(\boldsymbol{v}_t) \cdot \psi_i(\boldsymbol{v}_t) \tag{1}$$

Each expert ψ_i consists of GRU with its hidden state dimension d', output projection matrix $\boldsymbol{W}_o^i \in \mathbb{R}^{d' \times |E'|}$, and a bias vector $\boldsymbol{b}_o^i \in \mathbb{R}^{|E'|}$. Given an input in low-dimensional representation $\boldsymbol{v}_t$, an expert ψ_i outputs $\boldsymbol{o}^i$:

$$\boldsymbol{h}_t^i = \text{GRU}^i(\boldsymbol{h}_{t-1}^i, \boldsymbol{v}_t) \qquad \boldsymbol{o}^i = \sigma(\boldsymbol{W}_o^i \cdot \boldsymbol{h}_t^i + \boldsymbol{b}_o^i) \qquad i \in 1, \ldots, n$$

The gating network G have the same input and a similar architecture, except that its output $\boldsymbol{g}$'s dimension is n and it is through *Softmax* function. $\boldsymbol{g}_{[i]}$ in Eq. 1 represents i value in the vector $\boldsymbol{g}$.

$$\boldsymbol{h}_t^g = \text{GRU}^g(\boldsymbol{h}_{t-1}^g, \boldsymbol{v}_t) \qquad \boldsymbol{g} = Softmax(\boldsymbol{W}_o^g \cdot \boldsymbol{h}_t^g + \boldsymbol{b}_o^g)$$

The final prediction $\hat{\boldsymbol{y}}_{t+1}'$ is generated by summing outputs of the two modules $\boldsymbol{o}_{base} = \delta_{base}(\boldsymbol{H}_t)$ and $\boldsymbol{o}_{moe}$:

$$\hat{\boldsymbol{y}}_{t+1}' = \boldsymbol{o}_{base} + \boldsymbol{o}_{moe} \tag{2}$$

To properly specialize the Mixture-of-Experts on the residual, we train the two modules as follows: First, we train δ_{base} module, and parameters of δ_{base} are fixed after the train. Then, we train R-MoE module with the binary cross entropy loss computed with the final prediction in Eq. 2. With this way, R-MoE can learn to adapt the residual, which the base GRU cannot properly model. R-MoE provides flexible adaptation to the (limited) predictive power of the base GRU model.

4 Experimental Evaluation

In this section, we evaluate the performance of R-MoE model on the real-world EHRs data in MIMIC-3 Database [15] and compare it with alternative baselines.

4.1 Experiment Setup

Clinical Sequence Generation. From MIMIC-3 database, we extract 5137 patients using the following criteria: (1) length of stay of the admission is between 48 and 480 h, (2) patient's age at admission is between 18 and 99, and (3) clinical records are stored in Meta Vision system, one of the systems used to create MIMIC-3. We split all patients into train and test sets using 80:20 split ratio. From the extracted records, we generate multivariate clinical event time series with a sliding-window method. We segment all patient event time series with a time-window $W = 24$. All events that occurred in a time-window are aggregated into a binary vector $\boldsymbol{y}_i \in \{0, 1\}^{|E|}$ where i denotes a time-step of the window and E is a set of event types. At any point of time t, a sequence of vectors created from previous time-windows $\boldsymbol{y}_1, \ldots, \boldsymbol{y}_{t-1}$ defines an (input) sequence. A vector representing target events in the next time-window defines the prediction target $\boldsymbol{y}_t'$. In our work, a set of target events E' that we are interested in predicting is a subset of input event E.

Feature Extraction. For our study, we use clinical events in medication administration, lab results, procedures, and physiological results categories in MIMIC-3 database. For the first three categories, we remove events that were observed in less than 500 different patients. For physiological events, we select 16 important event types with the help of a critical care physician. Lab test results and physiological measurements with continuous values are discretized to high, normal, and low values based on normal ranges compiled by clinical experts. In terms of prediction target events E', we only consider and represent events corresponding to occurrences of such events, and we do not predict their normal or abnormal values. This process results in 65 medications, 44 procedures, 155 lab tests, and 84 physiological events as prediction targets for the total target vector size of 348. The input vectors are of size 449.

Baseline Models. We compare R-MoE with multiple baseline models that are able to predict events for multivariate clinical event time-series given their previous history. The baselines are:

- **Base GRU model (GRU):** GRU-based event time-series modeling described in Sect. 3.1. ($\lambda = 1e-05$)
- **REverse-Time AttenTioN (RETAIN):** RETAIN is a representative work on using attention mechanism to summarize clinical event sequences, proposed by Choi et al. [4]. It uses two attention mechanisms to comprehend the history of GRU-based hidden states in reverse-time order. For multi-label output, we use a sigmoid function at the output layer. ($\lambda = 1e-05$)
- **Logistic regression based on Convolutional Neural Network (CNN):** This model uses CNN to build predictive features summarizing the event history of patients. Following Nguyen et al. [29], we implement this CNN-based model with a 1-dimensional convolution kernel followed by ReLU activation and max-pooling operation. To give more flexibility to the convolution operation, we use multiple kernels with different sizes (2, 4, 8) and features from these kernels are merged at a fully-connected (FC) layer. ($\lambda = 1e-05$)
- **Logistic Regression based on the Full history (LR):** This model aggregates all event occurrences from the complete past event sequence and represents them as a binary vector. The vector is then projected to the prediction with an FC layer followed by an element-wise sigmoid function.

Model Parameters. We use embedding dimension $\epsilon = 64$, hidden state dimension $d = 512$ for base GRU model and RETAIN. Hidden states dimension d' for each GRU in R-MoE is determined by the internal cross-validation set (range: 32, 64, 128, 256, 512). The number of experts for R-MoE is also determined by internal cross-validation set (range: 1, 5, 10, 20, 50, 100). For the SGD optimizer, we use Adam [16]. For learning rate of GRU, RETAIN, CNN, and LR we use 0.005 and for R-MoE we use 0.0005. To prevent over-fitting, we use L2 weight decay regularization during the training of all models and weight λ is determined by the internal cross-validation set. Range of λ for GRU, RETAIN, CNN, and LR is set as (1e−04, 1e−05, 1e−06, 1e−07). For R-MoE, after observing it requires a much larger λ, we set the range of λ for R-MoE as (0.75, 1.0, 1.25, 1.5). We also use early stopping to prevent over-fitting. That is, we stop the training when the internal validation set's loss does not improve during the last K epochs ($K = 5$).

Evaluation Metric. We use the area under the precision-recall curve (AUPRC) as the evaluation metric. AUPRC is known for presenting a more accurate assessment of the performance of models for a highly imbalanced dataset [31].

4.2 Results

Table 1 summarizes the performance of R-MoE and baseline models. The results show that R-MoE clearly outperforms all baseline models. More specifically, compared to GRU, the best-performing baseline model, our model shows 4.1% improvement. Compared to averaged AUPRC of all baseline models, our model shows 8.4% gain.

Table 1. Prediction results of all models averaged across all event types

	LR	CNN	RETAIN	GRU	R-MoE
AUPRC	27.9266	28.4364	30.0276	30.4383	31.6883

To more understand the effectiveness of R-MoE, we look into the performance gain of our model at the individual event type level. Especially we analyze the performance gain along with the individual event type's occurrence ratio, which is computed based on how many times each type of event occurred among all possible segmented time-windows across all test set patient admissions. As shown in Fig. 2, we observe more performance gains are among the events that less occurred. More detailed event-specific prediction results of GRU and R-MoE models and corresponding performance gains (+%) are presented in Appendix.

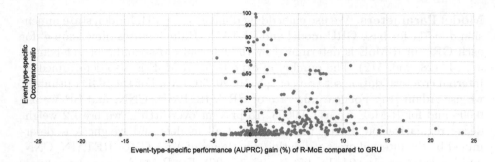

Fig. 2. Event-type-specific AUPRC performance gain of R-MoE compared to base GRU model (δ_{base}) and event-specific occurrence ratio. Each point represents each target event type among E'. Occurrence ratio is how much times each event occurred among all segmented time-windows across all test set patient data.

Model Capacity and Performance of R-MoE. To further understand the performance of R-MoE regarding the various model capacities, we analyze the effect of different numbers of experts and different dimensions of hidden states on the prediction performance. Note that as written in Sect. 4.1 the best hyper-parameter is searched through internal cross-validation (number of experts = 50 and hidden states dimension $d' = 64$). Then, for this analysis, we fix one parameter at its best and show how the performance of R-MoE in another parameter by varying model capacity. Regarding the number of experts, a critical performance boost has occurred with a very small number of experts. As shown in Fig. 3, with simply five experts, we observe 2.83% AUPRC gain compared to the baseline GRU model. With more experts, the performance is slowly increasing, but it slightly decreases after 50. Regarding different hidden states dimensions of GRU (d') in R-MoE, we observe changing it does not affect much of the difference in predictive performance as shown in Fig. 4.

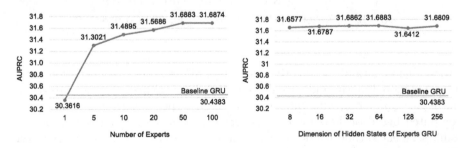

Fig. 3. Prediction performance of R-MoE on different number of experts. Hidden states dimension is fixed at 64.

Fig. 4. Prediction performance of R-MoE on different hidden states dimensions. Number of experts is fixed at 50.

Table 2. Prediction results of Mixture of Experts in Eq. 1 model (MoE) and the proposed Residual MoE model (R-MoE), differing number of experts with fixed hidden states dimension = 64.

Number of experts	1	5	10	20	50	100
MoE (ablation)	28.5138	28.0106	28.4324	29.5318	30.0813	30.8548
R-MoE	30.3616	31.3021	31.4895	31.5686	31.6883	31.6874
% difference	6.48	11.75	10.75	6.89	5.34	2.69

Ablation Study. To see the benefit of the residual learning framework in our model, we conduct an ablation study by training a simple mixture of experts (MoE) model described in Eq. 1 and comparing it with our model (R-MoE). As shown in Table 2, the residual learning framework shows its effectiveness obviously through the large margins in the evaluation metric. On average, over different model sizes, the residual learning brings 7.3% gain in AUPRC. Notably, the simple MoE model barely outperforms the base GRU model when it has maximum experts (100).

5   Conclusion

In this work, we have developed a novel learning method that can enhance the performance of predictive models of multivariate clinical event sequences, which are generated from a pool of heterogeneous patients. We address the heterogeneity issue by introducing the Residual Mixture-of-Experts model. We demonstrate the enhanced performance of the proposed model through experiments on electronic health records for intensive care unit patients.

Appendix: Event-Specific Prediction Results (AURPC)

Event Type	GRU	R-MoE Gain +%	Event Type	GRU	R-MoE Gain +%	Event Type	GRU	R-MoE Gain +%	Event Type	GRU	R-MoE Gain +%	Event Type	GRU	R-MoE Gain +%	Event Type	GRU	R-MoE Gain +%
[PHY]Heart Rhythm-A Paced	20.5	25.3	[LAB]Intubated	59.5	64.1	7.6	[LAB]Ayobvir	62.2	65.0	4.4	[LAB]Urine]Potassium	7.6	7.7	1.5	[LAB]Cholesterol, HDL	0.7	0.7	0.4	[LAB]Mupirocin (Prevacid)	13.5	13.3	-0.9

References

1. Bajor, J.M., Lasko, T.A.: Predicting medications from diagnostic codes with recurrent neural networks. In: ICLR (2017)
2. Cho, K., et al.: Learning phrase representations using RNN encoder-decoder for statistical machine translation. arXiv:1406.1078 (2014)
3. Choi, E., et al.: Medical concept representation learning from electronic health records and its application on heart failure prediction. arXiv:1602.03686 (2016)
4. Choi, E., et al.: RETAIN: an interpretable predictive model for healthcare using reverse time attention mechanism. In: Advances in NeurIPS (2016)
5. Choi, E., et al.: Using recurrent neural network models for early detection of heart failure onset. J. AMIA **24**(2), 361–370 (2017)
6. Choi, Y., et al.: Learning low-dimensional representations of medical concepts. AMIA Summits Transl. Sci. Proc. **2016**, 41 (2016)
7. Fojo, A.T., et al.: A precision medicine approach for psychiatric disease based on repeated symptom scores. J. Psychiatr. Res. **95**, 147–155 (2017)
8. Grave, E., et al.: Unbounded cache model for online language modeling with open vocabulary. In: Advances in NeurIPS, pp. 6042–6052 (2017)
9. Hauskrecht, M., Batal, I., Valko, M., Visweswaran, S., Cooper, G.F., Clermont, G.: Outlier detection for patient monitoring and alerting. J. Biomed. Inform. **46**(1), 47–55 (2013)
10. Hauskrecht, M., et al.: Outlier-based detection of unusual patient-management actions: an ICU study. J. Biomed. Inform. **64**, 211–221 (2016)
11. Henry, K.E., Hager, D.N., Pronovost, P.J., Saria, S.: A targeted real-time early warning score (trewscore) for septic shock. Sci. Transl. Med. (2015)
12. Huang, Z., et al.: Medical inpatient journey modeling and clustering: a Bayesian hidden Markov model based approach. In: AMIA, vol. 2015 (2015)
13. Huang, Z., et al.: Similarity measure between patient traces for clinical pathway analysis: problem, method, and applications. IEEE J-BHI **18**, 4–14 (2013)
14. Jacobs, R.A., Jordan, M.I., Nowlan, S.J., Hinton, G.E.: Adaptive mixtures of local experts. Neural Comput. **3**(1), 79–87 (1991)
15. Johnson, A.E., et al.: MIMIC-III, a freely accessible critical care database. Sci. Data **3**, 160035 (2016)
16. Kingma, D.P., Ba, J.: A method for stochastic optimization. arXiv:1412.6980 (2014)
17. Krause, B., et al.: Dynamic evaluation of neural sequence models. In: International Conference on Machine Learning, pp. 2766–2775 (2018)
18. Lee, J.M., Hauskrecht, M.: Recent context-aware LSTM for clinical event time-series prediction. In: Riaño, D., Wilk, S., ten Teije, A. (eds.) AIME 2019. LNCS (LNAI), vol. 11526, pp. 13–23. Springer, Cham (2019). https://doi.org/10.1007/978-3-030-21642-9_3
19. Lee, J.M., Hauskrecht, M.: Clinical event time-series modeling with periodic events. In: The 33rd International FLAIRS Conference (2020)
20. Lee, J.M., Hauskrecht, M.: Multi-scale temporal memory for clinical event time-series prediction. In: Michalowski, M., Moskovitch, R. (eds.) AIME 2020. LNCS (LNAI), vol. 12299, pp. 313–324. Springer, Cham (2020). https://doi.org/10.1007/978-3-030-59137-3_28
21. Lee, J.M., Hauskrecht, M.: Modeling multivariate clinical event time-series with recurrent temporal mechanisms. Artif. Intell. Med. (2021)

22. Lee, J.M., Hauskrecht, M.: Neural clinical event sequence prediction through personalized online adaptive learning. In: Tucker, A., Henriques Abreu, P., Cardoso, J., Pereira Rodrigues, P., Riaño, D. (eds.) AIME 2021. LNCS (LNAI), vol. 12721, pp. 175–186. Springer, Cham (2021). https://doi.org/10.1007/978-3-030-77211-6_20
23. Liu, S., Hauskrecht, M.: Nonparametric regressive point processes based on conditional Gaussian processes. In: Advances in NeurIPS (2019)
24. Liu, Z., Hauskrecht, M.: Learning adaptive forecasting models from irregularly sampled multivariate clinical data. In: The 30th AAAI Conference (2016)
25. Malakouti, S., Hauskrecht, M.: Hierarchical adaptive multi-task learning framework for patient diagnoses and diagnostic category classification. In: IEEE BIBM (2019)
26. Malakouti, S., Hauskrecht, M.: Predicting patient's diagnoses and diagnostic categories from clinical-events in EHR data. In: Riaño, D., Wilk, S., ten Teije, A. (eds.) AIME 2019. LNCS (LNAI), vol. 11526, pp. 125–130. Springer, Cham (2019). https://doi.org/10.1007/978-3-030-21642-9_17
27. Miotto, R., Li, L., Kidd, B.A., Dudley, J.T.: Deep patient: an unsupervised representation to predict the future of patients from the electronic health records. Sci. Rep. 6, 26094 (2016)
28. Nguyen, P., Tran, T., Venkatesh, S.: Finding algebraic structure of care in time: a deep learning approach. arXiv abs/1711.07980 (2017)
29. Nguyen, P., et al.: Deepr: a convolutional net for medical records. IEEE J. Biomed. Health Inform. 21(1), 22–30 (2016)
30. Pham, T., et al.: Predicting healthcare trajectories from medical records: a deep learning approach. J. Biomed. Inform. 69, 218–229 (2017)
31. Saito, T., Rehmsmeier, M.: The precision-recall plot is more informative than ROC plot when evaluating binary classifiers on imbalanced datasets. PloS One (2015)
32. Visweswaran, S., Cooper, G.F.: Instance-specific Bayesian model averaging for classification. In: Advances in NeurIPS (2005)
33. Yu, K., et al.: Monitoring ICU mortality risk with a long short-term memory recurrent neural network. In: Pacific Symposium on Biocomputing. World Scientific (2020)

Improving Prediction Models' Propriety in Intensive-Care Unit, by Enforcing an Advance Notice Period

Tomer Hermelin[1] , Pierre Singer[2] , and Nadav Rappoport[1] [(✉)]

[1] Department of Software and Information Systems Engineering, Faculty of Engineering,
Ben-Gurion University of the Negev, Be'er Sheva, Israel
hermelit@post.bgu.ac.il, nadavrap@bgu.ac.il
[2] Rabin Medical Center, Petah Tikva, Israel
psinger@clalit.org.il

Abstract. Intensive-Care-Units (ICUs) are time-critical, and sufficient reaction time is crucial. Previous studies of systems for alerting life-threatening events in the ICU, suffer from "immediate" events bias. In this research, we present a new approach for outcome prediction in ICU admissions, which takes into consideration the constraint of an advance notice of a predicted outcome. We showcase the approach over mortality and sepsis-3 predictions and compare it to existing approaches. We've created a set of Neural Network models that implement and evaluate the existing and the suggested approaches using the MIMIC-III data. We show that the performance is affected significantly when enforcing a notice period for mortality prediction, but not affected for sepsis-3 prediction. Further, we examine whether models need to be trained for a specific notice period, or whether the approach could be incorporated at the evaluation level. We found that adding notice enforcement post-model training, has no significant performance loss compared to incorporating the notice period during training, within the bounds of the trained lookahead. The concept of adding Alert-Interval could be applied to other clinical scenarios, where having advance notice is essential.

Keywords: Intensive care units · Deep learning · Forecasting · Electronic health records

1 Introduction

An intensive care unit (ICU) is a special department of a hospital or health care facility that provides intensive treatment care. Patients admitted to the ICU usually have severe or even life-threatening illnesses and injuries, and therefore are at high risk of mortality. The admitted patients are provided with constant care and close supervision. The goal of the ICU admission is to nurse the patients to a vigorous and stable condition, so they can be released from the ICU and continue to receive the care needed in a step-down unit or at home. However, not all admissions end up successfully. Statistics show that around 11.5% of patients admitted to the ICU die during admission [1]. Close monitoring and

© The Author(s), under exclusive license to Springer Nature Switzerland AG 2022
M. Michalowski et al. (Eds.): AIME 2022, LNAI 13263, pp. 167–177, 2022.
https://doi.org/10.1007/978-3-031-09342-5_16

the adoption of Electronic Medical Records (EMR) has made patient data in the ICUs frequently sampled and abundant for leveraging Data-Science solutions. At these ICUs, where response time is critical, leveraging this data to provide risk alerts for patients' future events (like death, sepsis onset, cardiac arrest, organ failure, etc.) can improve the care given in the ICU and reduce the death rate.

1.1 Background

Predicting mortality and sepsis onset during ICU admissions are reviewed in Fu et al. and in Islam et al. [2, 3]. Prediction models in this clinical scenario can be categorized into two main groups based on their approach: Cut-Off and Intervallic (see Fig. 1 for illustration). A Cut-Off model is a model which uses information from the first X hours to predict the outcome (for example, died or discharged) of the ICU admission (or in some cases, outcome after some period, like patient's status after 24 h from admission or 30 days from release). In this type of model, there is a single prediction per ICU admission. Common values for X are 24 h and 48 h [4–7]. In contrast, an Intervallic model is a model which provides multiple predictions during the ICU admission. Each prediction refers to a prediction-window (a slice of time from the patient's admission), where the prediction is based on the patient's data up to the prediction-window, and it predicts whether the patient will have an event within the prediction-window's time. A common setting for a prediction window is 1, 6, and 24 h [8–13]. Some models use multiple Prediction-Window sizes, evaluating the forecasting ability of different "horizons" [14].

There are additional variations of these two types of models, which are less common/applicative, that we don't implement for comparison in this model, like "Rolling Cut-Off" models, which is a hybrid of the two methods. In "Rolling Cut-Off" there is a sliding prediction point, similar to intervallic models, but the prediction is with regards to the rest of the admission [15].

Each type of model has drawbacks. Cut-Off models are not scoped in time, making it hard to focus the efforts when read alerts are needed most. Therefore, it may not be useful as a real-time alert system. Additionally, it leverages only the available data up to the Cut-Off point, regardless of the patient's admission duration and when a prediction is made. In contrast, the Intervallic approach does provide a scoped prediction (for a specific prediction-window) and leverages the data up to the required prediction point. However, by definition, such models have a prediction window that is immediately following the time of prediction. This introduces a disadvantage that characterizes twofold: (i) Applicative-wise: this does not ensure a minimum advance notice period for intervention. (ii) Performance evaluation-wise: it can be easier for prediction models to predict events that will occur close to the prediction time over events occurring farther from prediction time. Clinical events are often gradual and progressive events. Predictions that occur adjacent to the predicted event can rely on signals that indicate that event in a "straight-forward" manner. Therefore, it can be considered as a type of data leaking. These disadvantages are relevant to the Cut-Off approach as well, however, with less significance.

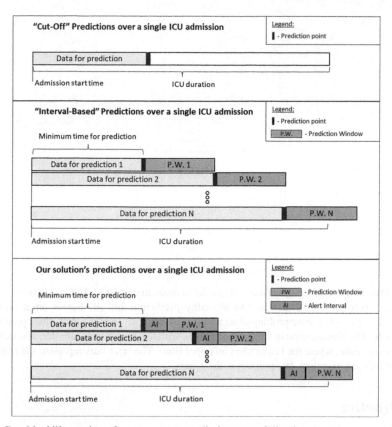

Fig. 1. Graphical illustration of two common prediction types following the new proposed Notice approach. In Cut-Off, each admission is assigned a single prediction at a pre-defined time, and the prediction is typically about the admission outcome. In Intervallic, each admission is assigned multiple predictions, depending on the length of admission and the prediction's window-size. In the Notice approach, there are also multiple predictions per admission. However, the prediction window is distanced from the prediction time.

One way to demonstrate the effect of the distance of the event from the prediction point on the performance's evaluation is by breaking the ROC AUC performance of a "Cut-Off's" model by the time of the event (Fig. 2). We can see that when predicting whether mortality will occur any time during the entire admission, using the data from the first 24 h of admission, the ROC AUC drops as the admissions get longer. However, for sepsis prediction, such a drop is mild.

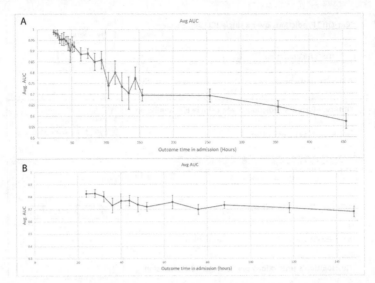

Fig. 2. Prediction performance of a cut-off model as measured by ROC AUC per admission length bin, using 10-fold cross-validation. (A) Mortality prediction and (B) Sepsis onset prediction. Performance drops for more prolonged admissions in mortality, while sepsis onset prediction is more stable. The bins increase in width to avoid bins with low numbers of samples. The ticks mark the bin's start time, where the last bin has no upper limit. The error bars represent the confidence intervals for each averaged data point over the x-axis.

2 Objective

Our objective in this paper is to propose a new approach for outcome prediction, and to demonstrate it applicability for mortality and sepsis onset prediction during ICU admissions. The new approach is designed to consider a minimal advance notice for alerting, while maintaining the prediction scoped like the Intervallic approach. We do so by adding an alert-Interval between the prediction time and the prediction window. We call this new type of models "Notice models".

2.1 Notation and Problem Formalizing

Formally, we want to be able to generate a predictor F, where given:

- $X_{i,j} \in \mathbb{R}^d$ – Single ICU admission data point, limited to events in time-window $[i, j]$, where $0 < i < j$
- $Y_{i,j} \in \mathbb{R}^d$ – Label indicating whether outcome occurred within time-window $[i, j]$
- ST $\in \mathbb{R}_+$ – Start-time for first admission prediction
- PS $\in \mathbb{R}_+$ – Prediction Step / interval between each two prediction points
- PWS $\in \mathbb{R}_+$ – Prediction Window Size
- AI $\in \mathbb{R}_+$ – Alert Interval. Minimal notice time for the prediction

Then for a given ICU admission, our target function is:

$$\forall t \in \{ST + iPS, i \in [0, \infty)\}, F\left(X_{t-LB,t}, AI, PWS\right) = Y_{t+AI, t+AI+PWS}$$

where:

- ICU admission has not concluded until time $t + AI$
- LB is the lookback (or observation window), chosen for the model. It is addressed as a hyperparameter to tune.

3 Materials and Methods

3.1 Evaluation

We evaluated our models using Area Under the Receiver Operating Characteristics (AUC). The drawback of evaluating AUC in Intervallic/notice models is that longer admissions are counted more times than shorter admissions, as these admissions appear in more prediction-windows. Such evaluation metric treats every observation of prediction event evenly. However, longer admissions have more prediction windows and therefore account for a bigger portion of the performance's estimation. There is also sense in evaluating the model in a way that gives each admission the same weight, independently of its duration. Therefore, we used Weighted AUC (WAUC) as an additional evaluation metric, where every sample (prediction) is weighted inversed proportionally to the number of samples (prediction windows) of its admission. The weights of all predictions that belong to the same admission sum up to 1. The difference between AUC and WAUC is exemplified in Appendix A.

3.2 Clinical Data and Cohort Definitions

In this study we've used the MIMIC-III (Medical Information Mart for Intensive Care III) dataset from the Beth Israel Deaconess Medical Center (BIDMC), Boston, Massachusetts. The MIMIC-III database contains, clinical data, from 53,423 adult ICU stays from 38,597 adult patients [1].

We've removed all admissions of patients that are under the age 18, or admissions shorter than the time of the first prediction-window. As a result, we excluded 8,656 admissions, resulting in the remaining 44,767. For sepsis-3 outcome prediction, we've also filtered 21,208 admissions of patients' that had first sepsis occurred prior to their first admission prediction window (see below), resulting in 23,559 admissions. For both outcomes, the split to train-validation-test was done at a patient level. The train set consisted of 80% of the patients, validation 10% of the patients and test was 10% of the patients.

For sepsis-3 labels, we followed the approach described at Goldstein et al. for identifying ICU acquired sepsis [16]. To avoid interpreting ongoing cases as several instances, we've kept only the first case of sepsis of each patient and added a constrain that there was no additional antibiotics administration in the 24 h preceding the antibiotics administration of the diagnosed case.

3.3 Data Preprocessing

The dataset is constructed so that each prediction-point and its associated data and prediction-window is an independent entry. The prediction-point is defined as the time during the admission when a prediction is taking place. The prediction-window is defined as the time span for which the prediction gives the prediction about. The prediction-window's label (i.e., case or control) is determined by whether the predicted outcome's time is within that time window.

The data used for prediction include age, sex, admission type, an indicator for whether the patient had a recorded previous ICU admission in the database. laboratory test results, vital signs, diagnosis, procedures, and medications. Only data available prior to the prediction-point and during the defined lookback window by the configuration was used. In Notice models, we drop out the data accumulated between the prediction-point and the prediction-window (the Alert-Interval timeframe) (Fig. 1).

Numerical features were transformed to count of measures, minimal value, maximal value, average value, variance of the values, first value, last value, and warning/Flag count for abnormal measurements. For categorical features (like oxygen delivery device), we've only taken the count/existence-indicator of measure.

In our case, missing data is missing not at random, as missing data is often a result of caregivers' decisions. When handling missing values and normalizing, we wanted to make sure the information of not having a value for a certain feature doesn't get lost. We've chosen the following approach for normalizing each feature:

$$x_{norm} = \begin{cases} \frac{x_{orig} - Min(\{x \in X_{train}\})}{Max(\{x \in X_{trian}\}) - Min(\{x \in X_{train}\})} + C, & if \ X_{orig} \neq NaN \\ 0, & otherwise \end{cases}$$

where X_{train} is a set of all original values of the feature in the train set, and C is set to 0.1. This ensures different values between missing and non-missing values.

3.4 Model Development

We've trained a fully connected Deep Neural Networks model for every configuration examined. Each model type has its own hyperparameters tuned, using the validation set, where best configuration was chosen according to the ROC AUC metric. A few rounds of tuning were performed, where in each round for each parameter in Table 1, few values around its best value from the previous round were examined. Then the models were evaluated on the test set for both AUC and WAUC.

For simplicity, we focus here on a small set of configurations. However, other configurations can be easily adapted, changing the alert-interval, prediction-window size, etc. For each predicted outcome, we've implemented the three models, Cut-Off, Intervallic, and Notice. We've created the Intervallic and Notice configurations as a pair so that the prediction horizon for the models is the same. However, an Alert-Interval is added for the Notice model, making the Notice configuration a more challenging task, as the events close to the prediction point are excluded.

For each configuration, we've tuned hyper-parameters independently to maximize its potential. The hyper-parameters include conventional Deep-Learning hyper-parameters and the lookback size the model used to compute the features for each prediction entry. The show-cased configurations are detailed in Table 1.

Table 1. Experiment specifications. ST-Start time; PS-Prediction Step; PWS-Prediction window size; AI-Alert interval. NN-Dims- a triplet for the number of neurons in each fully connected layer. For all layers in all configurations, the chosen dropout rate is 0.25.

Configuration	Specifications	Hyperparameters (NN-Dims; Weight-Decay; Lookback)
Mortality cut-off	$ST = 24h, PS = PWS = Inf, AI = 0$	{1200,600,250}; 0.0005; 24h
Mortality intervallic	$ST = 24h, PS = PWS = 18, AI = 0$	{1000,500,200};0.00075; 24h
Mortality notice	$ST = 24h, PS = PWS = 12, AI = 6$	{900,400,200}; 0.0005; 24h
Sepsis cut-off	$ST = 24h, PS = PWS = Inf, AI = 0$	{800,400,150}; 0.00075; 24h
Sepsis intervallic	$ST = 24h, PS = PWS = 18, AI = 0$	{900,400,150}; 0.0005; 24h
Sepsis notice	$ST = 24h, PS = PWS = 12, AI = 6$	{600,300,100}; 0.0005; 36h

4 Results

Table 2 details the results of each model configuration that was trained and evaluated with 10 different random model initializations. Results are presented as mean AUC and mean WAUC with 95% confidence interval. In Table 3, we detail the results of the Intervallic configurations models evaluated on their paired counterpart Notice configuration test sets.

Table 2. Experiment results

Configuration	Mean AUC	AUC CI	Mean WAUC	WAUC CI
Mortality cut-off	0.869	0.0026	0.869	0.0026
Mortality intervallic	0.891	0.0015	0.933	0.002
Mortality notice	0.866	0.0017	0.91	0.0021
Sepsis cut-off	0.783	0.0046	0.783	0.0046
Sepsis intervallic	0.76	0.0034	0.739	0.0068
Sepsis notice	0.76	0.0065	0.722	0.0093

Table 3. Intervallic models' results on Notice test set

Configuration	Test set	Mean AUC	AUC CI	Mean WAUC	WAUC CI
Mortality intervallic	Notice	0.864	0.0016	0.906	0.003
Sepsis intervallic	Notice	0.758	0.0048	0.727	0.0087

When examining the results in Table 2, we can observe that the WAUC scores are higher than their AUC counterparts for mortality prediction while lesser for sepsis onset prediction. When comparing performance across different configurations, the ranking could change, depending on the used metric, AUC or WAUC. For mortality prediction, the Cut-Off model outscores the Notice model with respect to AUC, but the Notice outperforms with a higher WAUC.

For mortality prediction, the Intervallic model outperforms the Notice model, when evaluating each model with their configuration's test set. We've expected this behavior, as the prediction-horizons for both tasks are the same, but the Notice model is not evaluated using close events, which are 'easier' to predict, as illustrated in Fig. 2A. When evaluating the Intervallic models on its paired Notices test set, which incorporates alert interval (the size of the injected alert-interval to the Intervallic test set is equivalent to the parallel Notice model), the Intervallic's model results dropped close to the Notice ones.

For sepsis onset prediction, the Intervallic and Notice models performed quite similarly according to the AUC metric, while there is a slight gap in favor of the Intervallic in the WAUC. Once again, when evaluating the Intervallic models on an adjusted test set, the Intervallic's model results dropped close to the Notice ones.

5 Discussion

We suggest a more adequate approach for evaluating alert systems in the clinical setting, incorporating a constraint for ahead notice into the model's evaluation. This type of evaluation may be more adequate for such alert systems, as alerting for an event which is going to happen within a short time period, may not be helpful for the staff, as they may know about it already, or they may not be able to do anything to change it. The concept of creating an alert system with a prediction model is not limited to mortality or sepsis onset prediction but can be used for other clinical and even non-clinical settings.

Mortality prediction demonstrated a scenario where "immediate" signals give a strong indication for the upcoming outcome and when enforcing an advance notice, the results changed significantly. In sepsis onset prediction, the "immediate" signals didn't affect the prediction much. We see this sits well with the observation illustrated in Fig. 2. The slope of the mortality prediction is steep and the slope for sepsis is relatively stable, with almost similar performance for faraway events as close ones.

Comparing variant solutions and different architectures could result in having the Intervallic and Notice approaches rank models differently (due to different performance gaps between Intervallic and Notice in each solution), changing the selected "best" model, depending on which approach you take. In our future work, we plan to examine comparisons where this is the case. Additionally, we argue there is still work in incorporating this concept into an applicable system in ICUs. Having a confident short-notice prediction is also valuable and should be considered when planning a holistic solution. It was shown that alert systems integrated into the ICU have much lower AUC than expected [17]. We scope out from this paper the topic of generating a production alert-system from the models.

The fact that the Intervallic performs like the Notice model on the Notice test set (rather than having the Notice outperform the Intervallic on the Notice), shows there is no gain from "focusing" on this specific subset of events in the prediction-window. This means that the alert-interval could be defined independently from the model development process, configurable in size after the model is trained. Although one can argue that for mortality prediction there was a statistically significant gain, we believe this gain is not sufficient and that the fact the models were tuned independently could also contribute to differences in performance.

While the Cut-Off model doesn't have Alert-Interval, it generally predicts further events than the Notice model. On the other hand, the bound that the Notice model provides on the predicted event is much tighter and more informative than the Cut-Off model. These are aspects way against each other, thus it's hard to rank the tasks' difficultness.

6 Conclusions

There are currently two main types of approaches for predicting outcomes in ICU admissions, Cut-Off and Intervallic. The Intervallic is the more applicative one. In our new Notice approach, we suggest further improving the applicability of the Intervallic approach, in scenarios that benefit a heads-up on the predicted event of at least a pre-defined time. This is done by adding an Alert-Interval constraint over the model's data. Empirical experiments show that adding this constraint could affect model performance significantly in some outcome predictions, resulting in better model evaluation (and better model selection, when comparing several models). Adding the alert-interval could be done at inference time alone (and not necessarily during training). This allows the alert-interval to be configured post training and to be applied on already existing, trained models. The concept of adding Alert-Interval could be applied to other clinical scenarios, where having advance notice is important. We also saw that there are scenarios where there is a significant difference between measuring this task with WAUC rather than with AUC.

Appendix A

We demonstrate here the difference between the Area Under the Curve (AUC) and Weighted AUC (WAUC) metrics used in the paper, using a simplified example. We define a negative window as period of time when the outcome of interest was not observed (e.g., the patient didn't die during this window) and a positive window as a time-window when the outcome of interest was observed. Our example composed of 3 admitted patients and two potential models with the following attributes:

- Patient-0 has a single positive prediction-window (to enable ROC AUC calculation).
- Patient-1 has 4 negative prediction-windows.
- Patient-2 has 20 negative prediction-windows
- Both models are correct on Patient-0's prediction.
- Model-1 is mistaken in 2 prediction-windows of patient-1 (50% mistake rate) and correct in the rest of the prediction-windows.
- Model-2 is mistaken in 2 of the prediction-windows for patient-2 (10% mistake rate) and correct in the rest of the prediction-windows.
- When calculating the AUC or WAUC, the models' mistaken prediction-windows are given the highest prediction-score and the rest of the prediction-windows are given prediction-scores in a correct order according to their labels.

In such a case, the standard AUC metric will be indifferent regarding which model to choose (both AUC scores are 0.92), as number of mistaken prediction-windows are similar to both models and it doesn't matter for which admission the mistakes were made. However, when weighting each admission equally (looking on the quality of prediction per admission), model-2 outperformed model-1 as its achieves an WAUC of 0.95 while model-1 gets only 0.75 (Fig. 3).

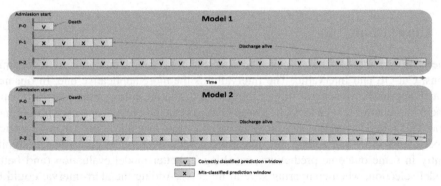

Fig. 3. Illustration of the given example. The two models predict for the same patients and the same set of prediction windows (yellow rectangles). Correct classifications are marked with green 'v's and misclassifications with red 'x's. (Color figure online)

References

1. Johnson, A.E.W., et al.: MIMIC-III, a freely accessible critical care database. Sci. Data. **3**, 160035 (2016). https://doi.org/10.1038/sdata.2016.35
2. Fu, L.-H., et al.: Development and validation of early warning score system: a systematic literature review. J. Biomed. Inform. **105**, 103410 (2020). https://doi.org/10.1016/j.jbi.2020.103410
3. Islam, M., Nasrin, T., Walther, B.A., Wu, C.-C., Yang, H.-C., Li, Y.-C.: Prediction of sepsis patients using machine learning approach: a meta-analysis. Comput. Methods Program. Biomed. **170**, 1–9 (2019). https://doi.org/10.1016/j.cmpb.2018.12.027

4. Ge, W., Huh, J.-W., Park, Y.R., Lee, J.-H., Kim, Y.-H., Turchin, A.: An interpretable ICU mortality prediction model based on logistic regression and recurrent neural networks with LSTM units. In: AMIA Annual Symposium Proceedings, vol. 2018, pp. 460–469 (2018)
5. Awad, A., Bader-El-Den, M., McNicholas, J., Briggs, J.: Early hospital mortality prediction of intensive care unit patients using an ensemble learning approach. Int. J. Med. Inform. **108**, 185–195 (2017). https://doi.org/10.1016/j.ijmedinf.2017.10.002
6. Zhu, Y., Fan, X., Wu, J., Liu, X., Shi, J., Wang, C.: Predicting ICU mortality by supervised bidirectional LSTM networks, 12 (2018)
7. Barton, C., et al.: Evaluation of a machine learning algorithm for up to 48-hour advance prediction of sepsis using six vital signs. Comput. Biol. Med. **109**, 79–84 (2019). https://doi.org/10.1016/j.compbiomed.2019.04.027
8. Yu, K., Zhang, M., Cui, T., Hauskrecht, M.: Monitoring ICU mortality risk with a long short-term memory recurrent neural network. In: Pacific Symposium Biocomputing, vol. 25, pp. 103–114 (2020)
9. Desautels, T., et al.: Prediction of sepsis in the intensive care unit with minimal electronic health record data: a machine learning approach. JMIR Med. Inform. **4**, e28 (2016). https://doi.org/10.2196/medinform.5909
10. Johnson, A.E.W., Mark, R.G.: Real-time mortality prediction in the Intensive Care Unit. In: AMIA Annual Symposium Proceedings, vol. 2017, pp. 994–1003 (2018)
11. An Interpretable Machine Learning Model for Accurate Prediction of Sepsis in the ICU. - Abstract - Europe PMC. https://europepmc.org/article/PMC/5851825. Accessed 03 Sep 2020
12. Mao, Q., et al.: Multicentre validation of a sepsis prediction algorithm using only vital sign data in the emergency department, general ward and ICU. BMJ Open **8**, e017833 (2018). https://doi.org/10.1136/bmjopen-2017-017833
13. Shashikumar, S.P., Li, Q., Clifford, G.D., Nemati, S.: Multiscale network representation of physiological time series for early prediction of sepsis. Physiol. Meas. **38**, 2235–2248 (2017). https://doi.org/10.1088/1361-6579/aa9772
14. Goldstein, B.A., Pencina, M.J., Montez-Rath, M.E., Winkelmayer, W.C.: Predicting mortality over different time horizons: which data elements are needed? J. Am. Med. Inform. Assoc. **24**, 176–181 (2017). https://doi.org/10.1093/jamia/ocw057
15. van Wyk, F., Khojandi, A., Mohammed, A., Begoli, E., Davis, R.L., Kamaleswaran, R.: A minimal set of physiomarkers in continuous high frequency data streams predict adult sepsis onset earlier. Int. J. Med. Inform. **122**, 55–62 (2019). https://doi.org/10.1016/j.ijmedinf.2018.12.002
16. Schvetz, M., Fuchs, L., Novack, V., Moskovitch, R.: Outcomes prediction in longitudinal data: study designs evaluation, use case in ICU acquired sepsis. J. Biomed. Inform. **117**, 103734 (2021). https://doi.org/10.1016/j.jbi.2021.103734
17. Wong, A., et al.: External validation of a widely implemented proprietary sepsis prediction model in hospitalized patients. JAMA Intern. Med. **181**, 1065–1070 (2021). https://doi.org/10.1001/jamainternmed.2021.2626

DP-CTGAN: Differentially Private Medical Data Generation Using CTGANs

Mei Ling Fang[1,2], Devendra Singh Dhami[2,3(✉)], and Kristian Kersting[2,3]

[1] Merck KGaA, Darmstadt, Germany
julie.fang@merckgroup.com
[2] Technical University of Darmstadt, Darmstadt, Germany
{devendra.dhami,kersting}@cs.tu-darmstadt.de
[3] Hessian Center for AI (hessian.AI), Darmstadt, Germany

Abstract. Generative Adversarial Networks (GANs) are an important tool to generate synthetic medical data, in order to combat the limited and difficult access to the real data sets and accelerate the innovation in the healthcare domain. Despite their promising capability, they are vulnerable to various privacy attacks that might reveal information of individuals from the training data. Preserving privacy while keeping the quality of the generated data still remains a challenging problem. We propose DP-CTGAN, which incorporates differential privacy into a conditional tabular generative model. Our experiments demonstrate that our model outperforms existing state-of-the-art models under the same privacy budget on several benchmark data sets. In addition, we combine our method with federated learning, enabling a more secure way of synthetic data generation without the need of uploading locally collected data to a central repository.

Keywords: Generative adversarial networks · Medical data generation · Differential privacy · Federated learning

1 Introduction

Machine learning has taken giant strides in recent years and has found wide applications affecting everyday life ranging from traffic accident prevention [25], spam filtering and phishing attacks detection [23] to several health care related tasks such as cancerous tumor detection [15], Parkinson's detection [8], drug-drug interaction prediction and discovery [7], and mortality prediction [5]. Since most clinical models are built on confidential patient records, data sharing is exceptionally rare. Protecting patient privacy is an essential obligation for researchers, but this also creates a bottleneck for fast, open, and accessible machine learning. Synthetic medical data that protects patients confidentiality could pave a way for machine learning to be extensively applied in high impact medical problems

---

M. L. Fang and D. S. Dhami—Equal contribution.

M. Michalowski et al. (Eds.): AIME 2022, LNAI 13263, pp. 178–188, 2022.
https://doi.org/10.1007/978-3-031-09342-5_17

and enable researchers to design a new generation of reproducible clinical decision support models, along with standardized performance benchmarks for new methods. Due to these issues, generation of synthetic data sets has been studied extensively [4,24] and this area of research has received a significant push [11,19] after the introduction of generative adversarial networks (GANs) [13] but most of the research has focused on image data and the issue of privacy in GAN based models has not been extensively addressed.

Furthermore, the majority of existing research efforts in generating synthetic data focus on the performance of the synthetic data and ignore potential data leakage from the published model, which might suffer from adversarial attacks. Linkage attacks can be launched by linking a target record to a single or group of records in a sensitive medical data set without direct identifiers. Membership inference attacks can be instantiated against deep generative models to identify whether a specific data record was used for training. Sensitive attributes of an individual such as income or disease history can be inferred.

To remedy this drawback, in this work, we go beyond the image data and propose DP-CTGAN, which incorporates differential privacy (DP) [9] into a conditional tabular generative adversarial network, CTGAN [31] to generate medical data[1]. We achieve DP by clipping the training gradient thereby bounding the gradient norms and injecting carefully calibrated noise. This enables DP-CTGAN to generate "secure" synthetic data, which can be shared freely among researchers without privacy issues. We also acclimatize our model to federated learning, a decentralized form of machine learning [17], and introduce federated DP-CTGAN (FDP-CTGAN). This enables a more secure way of generating synthetic data without the need of uploading locally collected data to a central repository. We differ from the state-of-the-art GAN models such as PATE-GAN [16] and DPGAN [30] as we make use of a conditional generator and are thereby able to capture different distributions present in the data.

Overall, we make the following important contributions: (1) We introduce a differentially private CTGAN capable of generating secure tabular medical data. (2) We adapt our model to the federated learning setting thereby providing a more secure way of medical data generation. (3) We outperform several state-of-the-art generative algorithms on several benchmark data sets thereby empirically proving the effectiveness of our proposed models.

The rest of the paper is organized as follows: after briefly reviewing the related work, we present our proposed DP-CTGAN and FDP-CTGAN models. We then present our extensive empirical results in several different real data sets before concluding by outlining future research directions.

2   Related Work

In the past decade, synthetic data are generated using statistical approach [3,27]. Recently, generative models using GANs and its variations have been

---

[1] We consider only tabular medical data set generation.

widely adopted due to its outstanding performance, flexibility and usability in generating tabular data, such as medical records. TableGAN [21] uses deep convolutional GAN [22] with an auxiliary classifier to produce statistically similar tabular data while preserving privacy. CorGAN [26] builds on pretrained denoising autoencoders [28] and 1-dimensional convolutional GANs, which captures important inter-correlation between features. HA-GAN [6] took a different approach and uses symbolic knowledge representation derived from human experts as a constraint in training Wasserstein GANs [14].

CTGAN [31] built upon Wasserstein GAN with gradient penalty in the PacGAN [18] framework and introduced several innovative preprocessing steps. Motivated by the success of this mechanism, in our work, we extend the current framework of CTGAN by incorporating the differential privacy, in the hope of making the synthetic data generation more robust, secure semantic-rich and real-world usable. As for the state-of-the-art, DPGAN [30] and PATE-GAN [16] are among the most successful endeavors that incorporate differential privacy in synthetic data generation. The former injects noise to gradients during training, while the latter builds GANs on top the Private Aggregation of Teacher Ensembles framework [20] which provides a tighter privacy bound. A detailed discussion on other privacy preserving GAN architecture can be found in [10].

3   DP-CTGAN

We now introduce our proposed model, DP-CTGAN (see Fig. 1). Before describing the architecture, it is important to justify the choice of using a CTGAN. The unique properties of tabular data pose difficulties for GANs to learn the tabular data distribution. These properties include correlated features, mixed data types such as discrete or continuous features, difficulty in learning from highly sparse vectors and potential mode collapse due to high class imbalance. To mitigate these issues, we choose CTGAN as the underlying generative model.

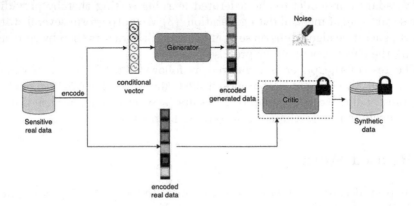

Fig. 1. DP-CTGAN. Sensitive training data is fed into a conditional generator to generate samples which can evenly cover all possible discrete values. At the same time, random perturbation is added to the critic to enforce privacy protection.

In DP-CTGAN, we employ the privacy accountant [1] to track the privacy loss and incorporate the differential private framework within a CTGAN model to capture correlated feature patterns as well as the complicated distributions. For preprocessing, mode-specific normalization is used for continuous columns so that the representation of the data learns the complicated distributions. Conditional generator tackles the imbalanced categorical columns and enables more efficient and even data generation. At the same time, fully-connected networks in generator and critic (or discriminator) are deployed to capture all possible correlations between columns. One of the intuitive approaches is to add noises in both the generator $\mathcal{G}$ and the critic $\mathcal{C}$. However, due to the minimax game of GAN's formulation, such an approach will increase the difficulties for convergence and privacy loss estimation, which lead to performance degradation of the models. We follow the rationale of [32] and opt to add random perturbation only in training $\mathcal{C}$. Since only the critic has access to the real data, it will be sufficient to control the privacy loss in training $\mathcal{C}$. In addition, the architecture of the critic in CTGAN is simpler than the generator, which utilizes batch normalization and residual layer to increase the performance. Thus, the critic has a relatively smaller number of parameters, which makes it easier to tightly estimate the privacy loss. We present DP-CTGAN training in Algorithm 1.

Algorithm 1. Train DP-CTGAN

Input: Training data $\mathcal{D}_{train}$, conditional generator parameters Φ_G, critic parameters Φ_C, batch size m, step size s, gradient clipping bound $\mathcal{C}$, noise scale σ, privacy budget (ϵ_0, δ_0)
Output: parameters Φ_G of a differentially private generator $\mathcal{G}$
1: **procedure** TRAIN
2:    **while** $\epsilon \leq \epsilon_0$ **do**
3:       **for** $1 \leq j \leq m$ **do**
4:          $N_d \leftarrow$ number of discrete columns from $\mathcal{D}_{train}$
5:          $d_i \leftarrow$ one hot discrete vector $\triangleright\ 1 \leq i \leq N_d$
6:          create masks $\{m_1, \ldots, m_{i^*}, \ldots, m_{N_d}\}_j$
7:          create conditional vectors $cond_j$ from masks
8:          $z_j \sim \mathcal{MVN}(0, I)$ $\triangleright$ sample from multi-variable normal dist.
9:          $\hat{r}_j \leftarrow$ Generator $(z_j, cond_j)$ $\triangleright$ generate synthetic data
10:         $r_j \sim$ Uniform $(\mathcal{D}_{train}|cond_j)$ $\triangleright$ get real data
11:         **for** $1 \leq k \leq s$ **do**
12:            sample $cond_k^j$, fake data $\hat{r}_k^j$, and real data r_k^j
13:            $\mathcal{L}_\mathcal{C} \leftarrow \frac{1}{s} \sum_{k=1}^{s} (\text{Critic}(\hat{r}_k^j, cond_k^j) - \text{Critic}(r_k^j, cond_k^j)) + \mathcal{L}_{\mathcal{GP}}$
14:            $\xi \sim \mathcal{N}(0, (\sigma\mathcal{C})^2 \mathcal{I})$ $\triangleright$ generate noise
15:            $\Phi_C \leftarrow \Phi_C - 0.0002 \times \text{Adam}(\nabla_{\Phi_c}(\mathcal{L}_\mathcal{C} + 10\mathcal{L}_{\mathcal{GP}} + \xi))$
16:         $\mathcal{L}_\mathcal{G} \leftarrow \frac{1}{m} \sum_{j=1}^{m} \text{CrossEntropy}(\hat{d}_{i^*,j}, m_{i^*}) - \frac{1}{m/s} \sum_{k=1}^{m/s} \text{Critic}(\hat{r}_k^s, cond_k^s)$
17:         $\Phi_G \leftarrow \Phi_G - 0.0002 \times \text{Adam}(\nabla_{\Phi_G} \mathcal{L}_\mathcal{G})$
18:         $\epsilon \leftarrow$ query $\mathcal{A}$ with δ_0 $\triangleright$ compute cumulative privacy loss
19:    **return** Φ_G

We start with defining the differential privacy budget (ϵ_0, δ_0). The number of discrete columns in the underlying data N_d is identified and a 1-hot vector for each of the discrete columns [**lines 4–5**] is created. Then masks that provide information about the required discrete variables are created [**line 6**] and conditional vectors are sampled from these masks [**line 7**]. These conditional vectors force the generator to generate samples from the required discrete variables. To model the continuous variables, we sample from a multi-variate normal distribution [**line 8**]. Then synthetic data is created, while real data is sampled from an uniform distribution with specified constraints [**lines 9–10**]. Note that the generator is conditional in nature and can be interpreted as the conditional distribution of rows given that particular value at that particular column. A critic is then used to access the conditional distribution of generated data with respect to real data along with gradient penalty to avoid mode collapse [**line 13**].

To incorporate privacy, we sample noises from the normal distribution. The training gradients of the critic are then clipped along with the injection of sampled noise thereby bounding the gradient norms [**lines 14–15**] ensuring the sensitivity is bounded. The generator is then used to create synthetic samples [**lines 16–17**]. Finally, after each iteration, we use a privacy accountant $\mathcal{A}$ to track the cumulative privacy loss [**line 18**]. This process iterates until reaching the privacy budget or convergence.

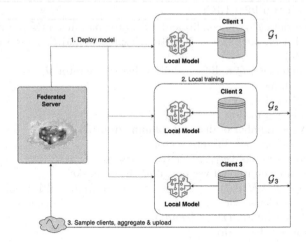

Fig. 2. Architecture of proposed **Federated DP-CTGAN**.

3.1   Federated DP-CTGAN

Traditionally, in federated learning, data is collected from different edge devices such as smartphones, censors or laptops, which will then be uploaded to a centralized server to train a machine learning model. However, such a model has access to the aggregated user-sensitive data, which makes it easier for attackers to break into the centralized server and steal the critical data.

We adapt our model to federated learning by incorporating the client sided differential privacy preserving federated optimization proposed by [12]. Each client has its own data set. After all clients have finished training, a set of clients are sampled randomly and their parameters are aggregated to approximate the true distribution parameters. This preserves the data privacy of the client even if the model is published. We present the overview of the federated DP-CTGAN (FDP-CTGAN) framework in Fig. 2. In each training round, the federated server deploys an initial model to each client. Local data set in the local client will be utilized for training the model. After the training is completed, the learned parameters of the generator will be aggregated with random mechanism and distributed back to the server.

Algorithm 2. Train FDP-CTGAN

Input: Training data $\mathcal{D}_{train}$, conditional generator parameters Φ_G, critic parameters Φ_C, batch size m, step size s, gradient clipping bound $\mathcal{C}$, noise scale σ, privacy budget (ϵ_0, δ_0), the set of clients (data owners) N

Output: parameters Φ_G of a differentially private generator $\mathcal{G}$

1: **procedure** TRAIN
2:     initialize generator parameters Φ_G and critic parameters Φ_C
3:     **for each** $n \in N$ **do**
4:         train n using algorithm 1
5:         store parameters Φ_{G_n} and Φ_{C_n}
6:     $\Phi_G \leftarrow$ sample and aggregate a batch of stored parameters
7:     **return** Φ_G

The algorithm for FDP-CTGAN is presented in Algorithm 2 and the steps are:

1. The federated server initializes a DP-CTGAN model and sends it to all clients.
2. In each round of generator training, generator is updated after the training process of the critic is completed.
3. After all clients participate in the training, aggregate the learned parameters from a pool of randomly sampled clients and distribute the parameters back to the server.

We make use of the privacy accountant $\mathcal{A}$ as in Algorithm 1 in order to keep track of the privacy loss of FDP-CTGAN. In this federated setting, the central server averages randomly selected client models after each communication round, in order to hide each client's contribution in the learning process and thus achieves the differential privacy on the client side.

4   Experiments

In this section, we first present the details of our experiment setup and then report the results of the data quality as well as compare with different state-of-the-art models. We aim to answer the following research questions: **Q1:** Can we effectively incorporate differential privacy in conditional tabular generative models? **Q2:** Does an extension to the federated learning setting beneficial for privacy-preservation?

4.1 Baselines and Datasets

We compare our models with various state-of-the-art methods. **1. CTGAN** [31]: is used as a non-differentially private baseline. **2. PATE-GAN** [16]): uses the Private Aggregation of Teacher Ensembles (PATE) framework to obtain high quality private synthetic data. **3. DPGAN** [30]: applies a combination of designed noise and clipping of weights, and uses the Wasserstein distance as an approximation of distance between real and generated probability distributions.

To evaluate the performance, we use 9 real data sets mostly (8/9) from medical domain. Out of all, 3 data sets adult, breast and seizure are from UCI repository [2], while cardio and cervical are from Kaggle. We also choose 4 real medical data sets specified in [6]: adni, mimic, nephrotic and ppmi.

4.2 Experimental Setup

We split the data set to train $\mathcal{D}_{train}$ and test $\mathcal{D}_{test}$ sets. First, we train the generative model using $\mathcal{D}_{train}$ and produce a synthetic data set $\mathcal{D}_{syn}$. We set $|\mathcal{D}_{train}| = |\mathcal{D}_{syn}|$. Then, we train various classifiers with $\mathcal{D}_{train}$ and $\mathcal{D}_{syn}$ respectively. We then evaluate each model's performance using $\mathcal{D}_{test}$ and average the result. The generative model is trained for 300 epochs with a batch size of 500. The differential privacy parameters used are given in Table 1.

Table 1. Differential privacy configurations for our proposed methods

	adni	adult	breast	cardio	cervical	mimic	nephrotic	ppmi	seizure
clip_coef	0.1	0.1	0.1	0.1	0.1	0.1	0.1	0.1	0.15
σ (noise scale)	3	1	4	1	8	2	3	2	1
ϵ	2.5	3	4	2	2	1	2.5	3	4.7
δ	1e−5	1e−5	1e−5	1e−5	1e−5	1e−5	1e−5	1e−5	1e−5

4.3 Evaluation Metrics

Given that synthetic data aims to replace the real data, where the distribution of synthetic data should approximate the real one as possible, it is however difficult to empirically compare the distribution of generative models [29]. In our evaluation, we address this problem by training predictive binary machine learning models on $\mathcal{D}_{syn}$ and test it on $\mathcal{D}_{test}$, so that we can compare the efficacy of classification tasks using AUROC and AUCPR. We aggregate the metrics of multiple prediction models to evaluate the synthetic data generators. By comparing the performance, we see how well the generative model capture the characteristic of the real data. Figure 3 illustrates the evaluation framework.

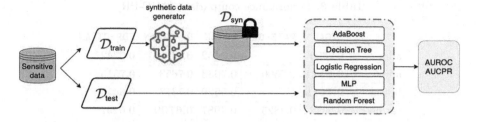

Fig. 3. Evaluation framework on synthetic data sets

4.4 Experimental Results

We are now ready to answer the posed research questions. We make our code publicly available: https://github.com/juliecious/CTGAN/tree/DP.

Q1. Incorporating DP in CTGAN: Tables 2 and 3 present the results of using DP-CTGAN to generate differentially private synthetic data. We can observe that in majority of the data sets, the performance decreases when compared to vanilla CTGAN with no privacy-preservation as expected. When compared to other privacy preserving GAN models, DP-CTGAN easily outperforms, thus answering **Q1**: Incorporating privacy in CTGAN leads to higher quality synthetic data compared to state-of-the-art GAN methods and is an effective alternative.

Table 2. Performance comparison (AUC-ROC)

	CTGAN	PATE-GAN	DPGAN	DP-CTGAN	FDP-CTGAN
adni	0.5052	-	0.5565	**0.5593**	0.5453
adult	**0.6739**	0.5008	0.5189	05097	0.5044
breast	**0.6820**	-	0.3740	0.6601	0.4694
cardio	0.4958	0.4648	0.4876	**0.6827**	0.5298
cervical	**0.6412**	0.4920	0.4617	0.5084	0.4956
mimic	**0.6992**	0.5871	0.5284	0.6312	0.5101
nephrotic	0.7188	-	-	**0.7292**	0.6354
ppmi	**0.6251**	0.4605	0.4784	05240	0.4712
seizure	0.4912	0.4869	0.4902	0.5000	**0.5187**

Q2. Adapting DP-CTGAN to federated setting: The results of extending DP-CTGAN to the federated setting is also shown in Tables 2 and 3. It can be concluded from the performance that FDP-CTGAN achieves a very similar performance to the DP-CTGAN and also outperforms the baselines in most cases. This answers **Q2**: adapting DP-GAN to the federated setting is certainly beneficial.

Table 3. Performance comparison (AUC-PR)

	CTGAN	PATE-GAN	DPGAN	DP-CTGAN	FDP-CTGAN
adni	0.2603	-	0.2452	**0.2946**	0.2742
adult	**0.8511**	0.7500	0.7633	0.7653	0.7515
breast	**0.7619**	-	0.5520	0.7377	0.6416
cardio	0.5072	0.4825	0.4987	**0.6709**	0.5297
cervical	**0.1714**	0.1343	0.0776	0.1325	0.1207
mimic	**0.4210**	0.3692	0.3421	0.3833	0.3474
nephrotic	0.9081	-	-	**0.9330**	0.8729
ppmi	**0.4889**	0.3478	0.3453	0.3984	0.3692
seizure	0.4017	0.2000	0.1992	**0.4086**	0.3602

5   Conclusion

We proposed a differentially private framework for synthetic medical data generation using CTGANs. The model aimed to capture the complicated distribution of the columns and reproduce an approximate synthesized version. We empirically show that our model can learn better distribution and thus outperform the state-of-the-art models in all scenarios. Furthermore, we attempt to find a flexible yet secure way to learn the distribution of locally stored data under the federated learning framework with calibrated randomized mechanism. Deriving theoretical justification on the privacy-preserving performance of DP-CTGAN and improving the performance of FDP-CTGAN with tighter privacy bound is an important future direction. Furthermore, applying our proposed methods on large-scale medical data sets is an interesting future avenue.

Acknowledgements. The authors thank the anonymous reviewers for their valuable feedback. This work was supported by the ICT-48 Network of AI Research Excellence Center "TAILOR" (EU Horizon 2020, GA No 952215) and the Nexplore Collaboration Lab "AI in Construction" (AICO). It benefited from "safeFBDC - Financial Big Data Cluster" (FKZ:01MK21002K), funded by the BMWK as part of the GAIA-X initiative, and the HMWK cluster projects "The Third Wave of AI" and "The Adaptive Mind".

References

1. Abadi, M., et al.: Deep learning with differential privacy. In: CCS (2016)
2. Asuncion, A., Newman, D.: UCI machine learning repository (2007)
3. Aviñó, L., Ruffini, M., Gavaldà, R.: Generating synthetic but plausible healthcare record datasets. arXiv preprint arXiv:1807.01514 (2018)
4. Buczak, A.L., Babin, S., Moniz, L.: Data-driven approach for creating synthetic electronic medical records. BMC Med. Inform. Decis. Making **10**, 1–28 (2010)
5. Deprez, P., Shevchenko, P.V., Wüthrich, M.V.: Machine learning techniques for mortality modeling. Eur. Actuar. J. **7**(2), 337–352 (2017). https://doi.org/10.1007/s13385-017-0152-4

6. Dhami, D.S., Das, M., Natarajan, S.: Beyond simple images: human knowledge-guided GANs for clinical data generation. In: KR (2021)
7. Dhami, D.S., Kunapuli, G., Das, M., Page, D., Natarajan, S.: Drug-drug interaction discovery: kernel learning from heterogeneous similarities. Smart Health 9, 88–100 (2018)
8. Dhami, D.S., Soni, A., Page, D., Natarajan, S.: Identifying Parkinson's patients: a functional gradient boosting approach. In: ten Teije, A., Popow, C., Holmes, J.H., Sacchi, L. (eds.) AIME 2017. LNCS (LNAI), vol. 10259, pp. 332–337. Springer, Cham (2017). https://doi.org/10.1007/978-3-319-59758-4_39
9. Dwork, C., Roth, A., et al.: The algorithmic foundations of differential privacy. Found. Trends Theor. Comput. Sci. 9(3–4), 211–407 (2014)
10. Fan, L.: A survey of differentially private generative adversarial networks. In: The AAAI Workshop on Privacy-Preserving Artificial Intelligence (2020)
11. Frid-Adar, M., Klang, E., Amitai, M., Goldberger, J., Greenspan, H.: Synthetic data augmentation using GAN for improved liver lesion classification. In: ISBI (2018)
12. Geyer, R.C., Klein, T., Nabi, M.: Differentially private federated learning: a client level perspective. arXiv preprint arXiv:1712.07557 (2017)
13. Goodfellow, I., et al.: Generative adversarial nets. In: NeurIPS (2014)
14. Gulrajani, I., Ahmed, F., Arjovsky, M., Dumoulin, V., Courville, A.: Improved training of Wasserstein GANs. In: NeurIPS (2017)
15. Havaei, M., et al.: Brain tumor segmentation with deep neural networks. Med. Image Anal. 35, 18–31 (2017)
16. Jordon, J., Yoon, J., Van Der Schaar, M.: PATE-GAN: generating synthetic data with differential privacy guarantees. In: ICLR (2018)
17. Konečný, J., McMahan, H.B., Yu, F.X., Richtárik, P., Suresh, A.T., Bacon, D.: Federated learning: strategies for improving communication efficiency. arXiv preprint arXiv:1610.05492 (2016)
18. Lin, Z., Khetan, A., Fanti, G., Oh, S.: PACGAN: the power of two samples in generative adversarial networks. In: NeurIPS (2018)
19. Mahmood, F., Chen, R., Durr, N.J.: Unsupervised reverse domain adaptation for synthetic medical images via adversarial training. IEEE T-MI 37, 2572–2581 (2018)
20. Papernot, N., Abadi, M., Erlingsson, U., Goodfellow, I., Talwar, K.: Semi-supervised knowledge transfer for deep learning from private training data. In: ICLR (2017)
21. Park, N., Mohammadi, M., Gorde, K., Jajodia, S., Park, H., Kim, Y.: Data synthesis based on generative adversarial networks. VLDB Endow. (2018)
22. Radford, A., Metz, L., Chintala, S.: Unsupervised representation learning with deep convolutional generative adversarial networks. In: ICLR (2016)
23. Salihovic, I., Serdarevic, H., Kevric, J.: The role of feature selection in machine learning for detection of spam and phishing attacks. In: Avdaković, S. (ed.) IAT 2018. LNNS, vol. 60, pp. 476–483. Springer, Cham (2019). https://doi.org/10.1007/978-3-030-02577-9_47
24. Shamsuddin, R., Maweu, B.M., Li, M., Prabhakaran, B.: Virtual patient model: an approach for generating synthetic healthcare time series data. In: ICHI (2018)
25. Tango, F., Botta, M.: Real-time detection system of driver distraction using machine learning. IEEE Trans. Intell. Transp. Syst. 14, 894–905 (2013)
26. Torfi, A., Fox, E.A.: CorGAN: correlation-capturing convolutional generative adversarial networks for generating synthetic healthcare records. In: FLAIRS (2020)

27. Tucker, A., Wang, Z., Rotalinti, Y., Myles, P.: Generating high-fidelity synthetic patient data for assessing machine learning healthcare software. NPJ Digit. Med. **3**, 1–13 (2020)
28. Vincent, P., Larochelle, H., Lajoie, I., Bengio, Y., Manzagol, P.A., Bottou, L.: Stacked denoising autoencoders: learning useful representations in a deep network with a local denoising criterion. JMLR (2010)
29. Walonoski, J., et al.: Synthea: an approach, method, and software mechanism for generating synthetic patients and the synthetic electronic health care record. JAMIA **25**, 230–238 (2018)
30. Xie, L., Lin, K., Wang, S., Wang, F., Zhou, J.: Differentially private generative adversarial network. arXiv preprint arXiv:1802.06739 (2018)
31. Xu, L., Skoularidou, M., Cuesta-Infante, A., Veeramachaneni, K.: Modeling tabular data using conditional GAN. In: NeurIPS (2019)
32. Zhang, X., Ji, S., Wang, T.: Differentially private releasing via deep generative model (technical report). arXiv preprint arXiv:1801.01594 (2018)

EpidRLearn: Learning Intervention Strategies for Epidemics with Reinforcement Learning

Maria Bampa[1(✉)], Tobias Fasth[1,2], Sindri Magnusson[1],
and Panagiotis Papapetrou[1]

[1] Department of Computer and Systems Sciences, Stockholm University,
Stockholm, Sweden
{maria.bampa,sindri.magnusson,panagiotis}@dsv.su.se,
tobias.fasth@folkhalsomyndigheten.se
[2] The Public Health Agency of Sweden, Solna, Sweden

Abstract. Epidemics of infectious diseases can pose a serious threat to public health and the global economy. Despite scientific advances, containment and mitigation of infectious diseases remain a challenging task. In this paper, we investigate the potential of reinforcement learning as a decision making tool for epidemic control by constructing a deep Reinforcement Learning simulator, called `EpidRLearn`, composed of a contact-based, age-structured extension of the SEIR compartmental model, referred to as `C-SEIR`. We evaluate `EpidRLearn` by comparing the learned policies to two deterministic policy baselines. We further assess our reward function by integrating an alternative reward into our deep RL model. The experimental evaluation indicates that deep reinforcement learning has the potential of learning useful policies under complex epidemiological models and large state spaces for the mitigation of infectious diseases, with a focus on COVID-19.

Keywords: Reinforcement learning · Mitigation policies · COVID-19

1 Introduction

The recent outbreak of the COVID-19 pandemic underlines the potentially catastrophic consequences of an epidemic outbreak not only for public health but also for the global economy and society as a whole. Moreover, identifying the most appropriate sequence of mitigation policies is a challenge [13], with the vast majority of the countries worldwide rapidly adopting mitigation measures to limit the impact of an ongoing pandemic. When making such decisions and studying the effect of prevention strategies on the population dynamics, officials usually rely on epidemiological models that predict and project the course of the epidemic. A classic example of such an epidemiological model is SEIR (see, e.g., Allen et al. [1]); the response to an emerging virus has been highly relying on such models for many decades, rendering them an effective tool for modeling, forecasting, and studying dynamics [4]. In the context of COVID-19, several

M. Michalowski et al. (Eds.): AIME 2022, LNAI 13263, pp. 189–199, 2022.
https://doi.org/10.1007/978-3-031-09342-5_18

studies have tried to assess the pandemic patterns using classic compartmental models while considering Non-Pharmaceutical Interventions (NPIs) [15].

Some other studies adopted extended versions of typical compartmental models to estimate epidemiological parameters and extrapolate the disease dynamics in the context of social distancing [3,10]. However, when results are dependent on heterogeneous individuals' characteristics, these compartmental models are inadequate as they fail to capture such characteristics. On the other hand, the development of prevention strategies that fulfill various criteria remains challenging and can lead to a complex sequential decision-making problem. A solution would be to use agent-based models that explicitly track the current epidemic state of individuals while dynamically introducing restrictions and modeling the effect of government restrictions on the spread of the epidemic. Modern Reinforcement Learning (RL) algorithms are well-suited for the problem of optimizing government response to epidemics. RL problems are closed-loop problems, where the learning system's actions influence its later inputs; the agents in RL learn what to do and map situations to actions to maximize a numerical reward signal [14].

Related Work. A wide body of research focused on creating optimal NPI mitigation policies with RL in the context of influenza and, more recently COVID-19 [6–8,12], while a few other works also included vaccination policies [17]. In the context of COVID-19, Ohi et al. [12] developed a virtual environment that mimics the simple SEIR to account for the lack of randomness inherent in the epidemiological equations. The reward is based on a random number generated by the healthy population and on the percentage of active cases, while their actions are introduced as three levels of contact restrictions of the population. Moreover, Libin et al. [8] constructed an age-structured model and tried to optimize the opening and closing of schools in between regions in the United Kingdom in the context of influenza. Nonetheless, creating optimal mitigation policies in the context of an epidemic is not a trivial task and entails sufficient reasoning on the chosen epidemic models and the underlying optimization components. Providing policy-makers with reasons to trust these AI-based decision-making models requires: (1) an epidemic model that captures the disease dynamics while having the flexibility to fit real epidemic data, (2) an action space that can be generalized or specific enough according to the stakeholders' needs, and (3) a justification of the optimization component (reward function) that actively influences the decisions of the RL agent. Hence, there is a need for a general-purpose RL-based epidemic model that addresses the above requirements.

Contributions. (1) We present and employ an extended SEIR compartmental model, called C-SEIR, a six-compartment, age-structured, contact-reduction based model that additionally considers groups of people that are infected but unreported, and recovered with PCR-negative and positive tests; in that way, C-SEIR models a more realistic COVID-19 case; (2) We introduce EpidRLearn, a general-purpose deep RL simulator that models an epidemic, using C-SEIR, and entails a set of actions based on various population contact reduction levels. It further employs a reward function that captures the trade-off between the increase of infections and the ramifications of contact reduction measures on the population; (3) We provide an extensive evaluation of the strategies proposed by EpidRLearn and investigate the agent's proposed actions by considering baseline policies and epidemic data, and an assessment of the reward function by incorporating in our model an alternative reward function from a recent benchmark.

2   EpidRLearn: Intervention Strategies for Epidemics with Reinforcement Learning

We define the RL problem by elaborating on its four components: environment, observations, actions, and reward.

The C-SEIR Environment. The RL environment of EpidRLearn is based on C-SEIR, the contact-based, age-structured SEIR compartmental model proposed in this paper. Our model extends the structure of the earlier SEIR models (susceptible (S), exposed (E), infected (I), and recovered (R), see, e.g., [8,12]) by (i) dividing compartment I into I^r (reported cases) and I^u (unreported cases), and (ii) dividing the R compartment into R^+ (PCR-positive population) and R^- (PCR-negative population). C-SEIR is defined as a system of Ordinary Differential Equations per age group $G_i \in [1, q]$:

$$\frac{dS_i}{dt} = -\beta_i S_i \sum_{j \in [1,g]} C_{ij} P_{ij} (\alpha I_j^u + I_j^r)/N_j$$

$$\frac{dE_i}{dt} = \beta_i S_i \sum_{j \in [1,g]} C_{ij} P_{ij} (\alpha I_j^u + I_j^r)/N_j - \mu E_i$$

$$\frac{dI^u{}_i}{dt} = \mu \eta E_i - \gamma I^u{}_i$$

$$\frac{dI^r{}_i}{dt} = \mu (1 - \eta) E_i - \gamma I^r{}_i \tag{1}$$

$$\frac{dR_i^+}{dt} = \gamma I_i^r + \gamma I_i^u - \psi R_i^+$$

$$\frac{dR_i^-}{dt} = \psi R_i^+.$$

C-SEIR is designed to simulate the spread of COVID-19 within and between a set of q population age groups $\mathbb{G} = \{G_1, \ldots, G_q\}$. A feature of C-SEIR is the usage of a $q \times q$ contact matrix C and a $q \times q$ contact reduction scalar matrix P. Each C_{ij} corresponds to the average contact frequency of an individual in age group G_i with an individual in age group G_j, while each P_{ij} is the contact reduction scalar value applied to C_{ij}. The risk of an individual in G_i getting infected by an individual in G_j is based on the transmission risk β_i, with

$$\beta_i = C_{ij} P_{ij} * (\alpha I^u{}_j + I^r{}_j)/N_j , \tag{2}$$

where α is an infectivity reduction scalar. The main role of P is to capture how the populations' contact patterns have changed throughout the pandemic. More concretely, for each day $t \in \{0, .., 365\}$ in the simulation the contact matrix is scaled by $P_{ij} \in [0, 1]$. A scalar of 0 implies no contacts between individuals in the corresponding age groups, while a scalar of 1 implies pre-pandemic contacts.

After getting exposed, the population stays in E for $\mu^{-1} = 5.1$ days (exposed rate) [9] on average before moving to either compartment I^r or I^u. Parameter η in compartments I^r or I^u defines the share of unreported cases. In these compartments, the population is infectious for $\gamma^{-1} = 5$ days (recovery rate) [16] and can during that time transmit the virus to the S population. The infected population moves to the R^+ compartment where it remains for an additional $\psi^{-1} = 5$ days (recovery rate). The population in the infected compartments (I^r, I^u) and the first recovered compartment (R^+) is assumed to be PCR-positive, i.e., the total time of PCR-positivity is ten days [5].

To demonstrate the utility of C-SEIR in our empirical evaluation (Sect. 4), we instantiate it to support three age groups ($q = 3$), i.e., G_1: 0–19, G_2: 20–69, and G_3: 70+ years old; but without loss of generality, our formulation holds for any number of age groups q and any configuration of age ranges. As a result, C becomes a 3×3 matrix, the configuration of which is based on an earlier epidemic study [11] and adapted to the Swedish demographics. In order to account for randomness in C-SEIR and the predictions, we transform the system of Ordinary Differential Equations (ODEs) into Stochastic Differential Equations (SDEs) by adding a Wiener process to each transition in the ODEs, hence adding stochastic noise [2]. The SDEs are evaluated at discrete time steps using the Euler-Maruyama approximation method [2].

Observations. The environment is observed after the agent has taken some action (at each time point t, i.e., each week). These observations S are passed to the agent serving as estimable information that can define the next action to be taken. This results in a total of $6 \times q$ parameters, one for each of the six compartments and one for each of the q age groups.

Actions. In order to reduce the spread of the epidemic, we need to limit the frequency of contacts between population groups. We hence define a set of actions $\mathcal{A}$ that impose population movement reductions. For simplicity and without loss of generality, we let the set of actions $\mathcal{A}$ correspond to four population movement reduction levels, i.e., $\mathcal{A} = \{A_0, A_1, A_2, A_3\}$, with A_0 describing a freely moving population with no imposed restrictions (Level 0), A_1 a movement reduction by 25% (Level 1), A_2 a movement reduction by 50% (Level 2), A_3 a movement reduction by 75% (Level 3). We note that the chosen action space is an estimation of the level of contact reductions in the population. While alternative (and additional) actions can be defined, an extensive definition of policies is not the main goal of this paper. Using any set of actions $\mathcal{A}$, we calibrate the movement of the population by modifying the contact reduction scalar P. As this scalar matrix can change per time unit t, we denote its configuration at time t as $P^{(t)}$. Before the start of an infectious disease, $P^{(0)}$ is an all-ones (i.e., unit) matrix, since the population still moves freely (following C). As the epidemic evolves and mitigation policies are imposed by $\mathcal{A}$, P is adjusted accordingly to reflect the movement reduction rate. At each time point t, the initial contact matrix

C is scaled by P^t yielding a modified contact matrix $C^t = P^t \cdot C$ that alters the population contact pattern. Without loss of generality, for our experimental setup, we assume the following configuration for P^t given action $a \in \mathcal{A}$:

$$P^t(a) = \begin{cases} P^{(0)}, & \text{if } a = A_0 \text{ (Level 0)} \\ 0.75 \times P^{(0)}, & \text{if } a = A_1 \text{ (Level 1)} \\ 0.50 \times P^{(0)}, & \text{if } a = A_2 \text{ (Level 2)} \\ 0.25 \times P^{(0)}, & \text{if } a = A_3 \text{ (Level 3)} \end{cases} \qquad (3)$$

Reward. Our reward function considers the trade-off between keeping the population contacts as unrestricted as possible while maintaining the infectious population low. The rationale is that we want to minimize the number of infected people while focusing on the populations' well-being; imposing interventions in the form of contact reductions in the population can have a negative impact on socioeconomic factors. The reward function is, hence, defined as follows:

$$r(s,a) = W_1 \times \texttt{FreeToMove}(s,a) + W_2 \times \texttt{InfectionState}(s,a). \qquad (4)$$

The fraction of healthy population at state s is $H(s) = \frac{S+E+R^-}{\texttt{TotalPopulation}}$. Then the first component of the reward can be defined as a function of $H(s)$ and each action $a \in \mathcal{A}$. Following our earlier instantiation of $\mathcal{A}$, the first component of the reward, denoted as $\texttt{FreeToMove}(\cdot)$, is defined as

$$\texttt{FreeToMove}(s,a) = \begin{cases} H(s), & \text{if } a = A_0 \\ 0.75 \times H(s), & \text{if } a = A_1 \\ 0.5 \times H(s), & \text{if } a = A_2 \\ 0.25 \times H(s), & \text{if } a = A_3 \end{cases} \qquad (5)$$

The second component of the reward, denoted as $\texttt{InfectionState}(\cdot)$, reflects the degree to which the infection decreases after an action is taken, i.e.,

$$\texttt{InfectionState}(s, s', a) = \sum_{i=1}^{q} \texttt{IS}_i(s, s', a), \qquad (6)$$

$\texttt{IS}_i(s, s', a)$ is the infection rate indicator for population group i, such that

$$\texttt{IS}_i(s, s', a) = \begin{cases} +0.5, & \text{if } I_i(s') < I_i(s) \ \& \ a = A_0 \\ -0.5, & \text{if } I_i(s') \geq I_i(s) \ \& \ a = A_0 \\ +0.5, & \text{if } I_i(s') > I_i(s) \ \& \ a \in \{A_1, A_2, A_3\} \\ -0.5, & \text{if } I_i(s') \leq I_i(s) \ \& \ a \in \{A_1, A_2, A_3\} \end{cases} \qquad (7)$$

Training EpidRLearn. We employ the Proximal Policy Optimization (PPO) algorithm to train our agent on data during the Spring/Summer period (period 1) and evaluate the policies using data from Autumn/Winter (period 2). The agent is trained for 10000 episodes with $\gamma = 0.99$, and at the end of each episode the environment is reset to an initial state. The policy is evaluated over 10 runs. The network consists of 1 hidden layer of 128 units with the Tahn activation function. Training is episodic (25 simulated weeks per episode). The benchmark policies are also considered during Autumn/Winter, starting after week 25. The reader may refer to the supplementary material and source code found in the Github repository[1] for additional information on model parameters and verification.

3   Model Instantiation

Fitting C-SEIR to Real Data. We demonstrate the steps for calibrating the C-SEIR parameters by fitting it to real-world data. We choose a region in Sweden as our COVID-19 use-case since Sweden is one of the few countries that followed a set of nonrestrictive recommendations. Considering an epidemic of two waves, the model fitting is divided into two periods, period 1 (Feb. 27, 2020 - Aug. 23, 2020) and period 2 (Aug. 24, 2020 - Dec. 31, 2020), with transmission risks β_{p1} and β_{p2}, respectively. We also estimate the contact reduction scalar P, i.e., the daily relative contact change compared to before the pandemic.

In Fig. 4 (left sub-figure), we show the C-SEIR model projection in conjunction with the reported case data indicating that we can closely match the epidemic trends. The same figure also depicts the daily number of observed and fitted infected over period 1 and period 2. Note that our model reports the number of currently infected (prevalence) while the use-case data reports the number of newly infected people per day (incidence). Therefore, we define the incidence of reported cases for each age-group i from C-SEIR as follows:

$$\text{IncidenceInfected}_i = E_i/\mu \times (1 - \eta) \qquad (8)$$

Baseline Policies. To empirically evaluate the convergence of EpidRLearn to an optimal policy we need to devise baseline policies. The baseline policies will serve as an approximation to the actual policies followed by Sweden and will allow us to compare the policy created by EpidRLearn to the approximate true ones. The baseline policies are created by 'enforcing' the agent to choose specific actions on pre-defined steps/weeks of the episode.

Policy I (Sweden ECDC). The first policy corresponds to the mitigation measures announced by the authorities of Sweden as reported by ECDC[2]. The mitigation measures listed in ECDC entail a list of interventions followed by the Swedish authorities, among other countries. For a fair model comparison, we need to map these interventions to the corresponding EpidRLearn actions in Eq. 3. In that way, the mapping of the baseline policies to the ECDC response data is an abstraction of the actual policies followed by Sweden.

---

[1] https://github.com/mariabampaai/epidrlearn.
[2] https://www.ecdc.europa.eu/en/publications-data/download-data-response-measures-covid-19.

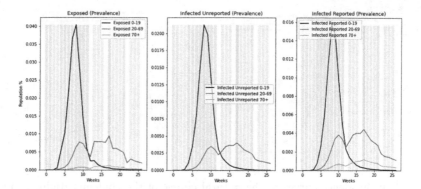

Fig. 1. The recommended optimal policy proposed by `EpidRLearn`. Red bars indicate Level 3, blue bars Level 2, green bars Level 1, and white bars Level 0 restrictions. (Color figure online)

Specifically, the Swedish policy, denoted as π_{SE}, is defined as follows:

$$\pi_{SE} = \begin{cases} a = A_0, & \text{if } w_i < 6 \\ a = A_1, & \text{if } 6 \leq w_i \leq 22 \\ a = A_2, & \text{if } w_i > 22 \end{cases} \qquad (9)$$

with w_i denoting the ith week from the onset of the pandemic. In other words, we presume that Sweden placed first a series of soft restrictions on the 6th week of the pandemic (Level 1 restrictions, A_1), which were further strengthened after the 22nd week (Level 2 restrictions, i.e., A_2).

Policy II (Use-case Fitted). In addition, our intuition is that it is not only the policies of a governmental authority that affect the development of a pandemic but also the degree to which people comply with those policies and recommendations. Motivated by this, our second baseline policy corresponds to the fitted output obtained for the contact reduction scalar P_{ij} as derived in Sect. 3, i.e., the scalar that captures how the population's contact patterns have changed throughout the pandemic. This fitted output reflects the actual compliance to the chosen policy (in our case the one defined by the Swedish authorities). After the curve fitting step, P_{ij} depicts the reductions in C_{ij} (the contact matrix) as seen in the observed data. Hence when the fitted scalar P is applied to C_{ij} it reduces the contact pattern of the various groups as seen in the real COVID-19 data. This, we presume, abstractly depicts the interventions taken by the Swedish government in the form of contact restrictions. As the fitted P_{ij} already measures all the interventions, we enforce the RL agent to only take Level 0 actions (i.e., A_0), hence defining the policy as follows: $\pi_{SE-F} = A_0$, if $w_i \geq 0$.

4   Empirical Evaluation

Optimal Policy Estimation and Reward Convergence. Figure 1 depicts the resulting policy for period 2. From right to left, we see the Prevalence of

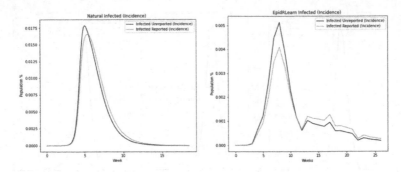

Fig. 2. Left: incidence curves of the natural course of the epidemic Right: incidence curves of the recommended policy. Whole population, reported and unreported cases.

Exposed, Infected Unreported, and Infected Reported per age group; each picture portrays the actions as colored bars (red for Level 3, blue for Level 2, green for Level 1, and white for Level 0 restrictions). We notice that in the first approximately 10 weeks, the policy primarily recommends Level 3 restrictions, potentially to minimize and slow down the peak of the infected population. Following that, the learned policy oscillates between actions within levels 0–3, and when the infection rate of age groups 20–69 and 70+ ascends, chooses one week of Level 2–3 restrictions. As the infectious population reduces, the agent mainly chooses actions of Level 0 to 1, mainly utilizing Level 1 restrictions.

We additionally compared the learned policy to the infection peak of the left sub-figure of Fig. 2 (the natural course of the epidemic as the sum over all age groups) and the baseline policies. The right sub-figure of Fig. 2 depicts the incidence curves of the learned policy over all age groups. We observe that EpidRLearn manages to reduce the incidence peak by at least a half compared to the epidemic's natural course. The reduction in the peak is expected as the agent enforces various levels of contact reductions.

Assessment of Optimal Policies. We demonstrate that EpidRLearn has learned something useful by comparing the incidence peaks and reward distributions with the baseline policies. Our results in Fig. 3 indicate that the RL agent identifies a mitigation policy that optimizes the defined reward by reducing the pandemic's peak, "flattening the curve" compared to the two baseline policies. More concretely, Fig. 3 compares the EpidRLearn policy to the baseline policies (Sweden and Sweden Fitted) for period 2. Comparing the incidence curves resulting from EpidRLearn policy to the Swedish baselines, we notice that the EpidRLearn policy reduces and shifts the incidence peak, i.e., "flatten the curve".

However, the reward of the fitted Swedish policy (in yellow color) is considerably higher; potentially due to the design of this baseline, since the contact reduction scalar already measures all the interventions for the fitted use-case, the RL agent chooses only actions of Level 0 (i.e., A_0) directing the reward to higher values. More importantly, we should emphasize that the provided policies are 'theoretically' optimal and coupled with the hypothetical use-case scenario studied here. In order to draw realistic conclusions for particular use-cases, e.g., Sweden, one would need to have access to the real and complete epidemiological data of each use-case, consider the possibility of new variants and re-calibrate C-SEIR to depict the previously mentioned. However, we can safely conclude that EpidRLearn can function as a strong assisting tool for the public health authorities to provide recommendations that reduce the epidemic spread by considering both the severity of the pandemic as well as other factors related to the general well-being of the population.

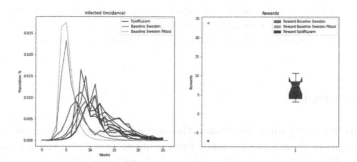

Fig. 3. Left: comparison of EpidRLearn and baselines, for each case reported is the sum of incidence infected (reported and unreported), Right: rewards for EpidRLearn over 10 simulated runs and baselines.

Assessment of Reward Function. We finally provide an evaluation of the reward function by incorporating in our model an alternative function from Libin et al. [8], as we believe their environment implementation is closer to that of EpidRLearn; on the other hand the model that was proposed by [12] is based on a more granular level of SEIR and a virtual representation of the population, rendering the combination of their set-up and reward less suitable for our work. We compare the incidence curves in Fig. 4 (right) and notice that EpidRLearn reduces and shifts the epidemic peak compared to the alternative reward function. This demonstrates the flexibility of EpidRLearn's reward component and the adjustability of EpidRLearn to incorporate in the model the stakeholders' requirements in the form of a reward function. For additional information on empirical verification, sensitivity analysis, and experiments, the reader may refer to the supplementary material in the provided GitHub repository.

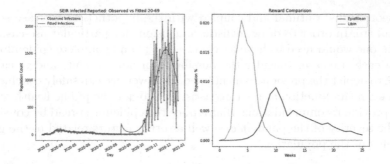

Fig. 4. Left:Fitting `C-SEIR` on the Swedish use-case data for age group 20–69. y-axis incidence of reported cases. Right: Comparison of the incidence infected (sum of reported and unreported) of the alternative to EpidRLearn reward. y-axis population %.

5   Conclusions

Finding an optimal policy to reduce the spread of an epidemic can be a challenging task in the space of unlimited interventions and potential socio-economic constraints. We demonstrated the potential of epidemic mitigation control using deep RL for COVID-19. The policy learned by `EpidRLearn` limits epidemic spread while taking into account the ramifications of continuous contact restrictions. Future work includes the study of a more granular epidemiological model, the consideration of mobility data, and contact restrictions between regions.

Acknowledgements. This work was supported by the Vinnova grant on "AI-supported design of more effective intervention strategies" and the Digital Futures EXTREMUM project.

References

1. Allen, E.J., Allen, L.J., Arciniega, A., Greenwood, P.E.: Construction of equivalent stochastic differential equation models. Stoch. Anal. Appl. **26**(2), 274–297 (2008)
2. Allen, L.J.: A primer on stochastic epidemic models: formulation, numerical simulation, and analysis. Infect. Dis. Modell. **2**(2), 128–142 (2017)
3. Cao, J., Jiang, X., Zhao, B., et al.: Mathematical modeling and epidemic prediction of COVID-19 and its significance to epidemic prevention and control measures. J. Biomed. Res. Innov. **1**(1), 1–19 (2020)
4. Cobey, S.: Modeling infectious disease dynamics. Science **368**(6492), 713–714 (2020)
5. Hu, Z., et al.: Clinical characteristics of 24 asymptomatic infections with COVID-19 screened among close contacts in Nanjing, China. Sci. China Life Sci. **63**(5), 706–711 (2020)
6. Khalilpourazari, S., Doulabi, H.H.: Designing a hybrid reinforcement learning based algorithm with application in prediction of the COVID-19 pandemic in Quebec. Ann. Oper. Res. **312**(2), 1261–1305 (2021)

7. Kwak, G.H., Ling, L., Hui, P.: Deep reinforcement learning approaches for global public health strategies for COVID-19 pandemic. Plos One **16**(5), 1–15 (2021)

8. Libin, P., et al.: Deep reinforcement learning for large-scale epidemic control. Technical report (2020)

9. Linton, N.M., et al.: Incubation period and other epidemiological characteristics of 2019 novel coronavirus infections with right truncation: a statistical analysis of publicly available case data. J. Clin. Med. **9**(2), 538 (2020)

10. Liu, Z., Magal, P., Seydi, O., Webb, G.: A model to predict COVID-19 epidemics with applications to south Korea, Italy, and Spain. medRxiv (2020)

11. Mossong, J., et al.: Social contacts and mixing patterns relevant to the spread of infectious diseases. PLoS Med. **5**(3), e74 (2008)

12. Ohi, A.Q., Mridha, M., Monowar, M.M., Hamid, M.A.: Exploring optimal control of epidemic spread using reinforcement learning. Sci. Rep. **10**(1), 1–19 (2020)

13. Richard, Q., Alizon, S., Choisy, M., Sofonea, M.T., Djidjou-Demasse, R.: Age-structured non-pharmaceutical interventions for optimal control of COVID-19 epidemic. PLOS Comput. Biol. **17**(3), 1–25 (2021)

14. Sutton, R.S., Barto, A.G.: Reinforcement Learning: An Introduction. MIT Press, Cambridge (2018)

15. Wang, C., et al.: Evolving epidemiology and impact of non-pharmaceutical interventions on the outbreak of coronavirus disease 2019 in Wuhan, China. MedRxiv (2020)

16. Wölfel, R., et al.: Virological assessment of hospitalized patients with COVID-2019. Nature **581**(7809), 465–469 (2020)

17. Yaesoubi, R., Cohen, T.: Dynamic health policies for controlling the spread of emerging infections: influenza as an example. PLoS One **6**(9), e24043 (2011)

Discovering Instantaneous Granger Causalities in Non-stationary Categorical Time Series Data

Noor Jamaludeen[1]([✉]), Vishnu Unnikrishnan[1], André Brechmann[2], and Myra Spiliopoulou[1]

[1] Knowledge Management and Discovery Lab,
Otto-von-Guericke University Magdeburg, Magdeburg, Germany
{noor.jamaludeen,vishnu.unnikrishnan,myra}@ovgu.de
[2] Combinatorial NeuroImaging, Leibniz Institute for Neurobiology,
Magdeburg, Germany
brechmann@lin-magdeburg.de

Abstract. Instantaneous Granger causality has been used in economy and physiological systems as a measure for quantifying directed effects from prior and contemporary observations to observations in the future. However, standard approaches are mostly unable to capture the instantaneous and the Granger causality together in non-stationary categorical time series where the exact order in which past observations occur has no influence on the causality. In this paper, we propose a novel machine learning-based instantaneous Granger causality (IGC) method that summarizes the past of the *cause time series* ignoring the temporal order of past observations within a window, and quantifies the dependency between these summaries and the *effect time series* at each time point independently. Furthermore, our approach allows monitoring the evolution of IGC over time. We apply our method on behavioral data collected from 76 participants in an auditory category learning experiment. The learning process can be seen as an evolution in the 'decision policies' across trials, where the current policy is derived from prior stimuli and (accumulated feedback to) prior responses of the participant. The dependency of the current response on the prior exposure to the stimuli and the subsequent responses makes IGC a useful tool in analyzing how the stimulus features contribute to the decision policy: we demonstrate that the instantaneous Granger causalities between stimulus features and responses can distinguish learners from non-learners at early phases of the experiment. Our evaluation shows that our new method outperforms the typically used approach 'Instantaneous Transfer Entropy' (ITE).

Keywords: Instantaneous granger causality · Non-stationary categorical time series · Auditory category learning

1 Introduction

Instantaneous Granger causality (IGC) is a statistical analysis to investigate whether the future of a time series X, in addition to the current and the past

M. Michalowski et al. (Eds.): AIME 2022, LNAI 13263, pp. 200–209, 2022.
https://doi.org/10.1007/978-3-031-09342-5_19

improve the predictions of the future of another time series Y [8]. Incorporating instantaneous effects to the Granger Causality (GC) plays an essential role in revealing dependencies in physiological systems [6], neurological systems [4], economy [9] and cognitive learning processes because humans and animals learn cumulatively where they use prior knowledge to solve subsequent learning tasks [14]. Category learning is a typical learning task: humans learn a category by identifying the relevant features on which the category is structured and ignoring the irrelevant ones [2]. Analysing the instantaneous Granger causalities (IGCs) between the relevant and irrelevant features of stimuli and their responses is a promising approach to capture the dynamics of learning by trial and error [7]. However, modeling human behaviour is challenging, because response series to the stimuli may change due to the evolution of the learning process, i.e. the data generating process is non-stationary. Subsequently, the effect of prior stimuli and of the responses to them on the responses to subsequent stimuli varies during the learning experience. Furthermore, humans memorize what events/stimuli they have encountered, but they do not necessarily remember the ordering of these encounters. This is problematic for conventional IGC, which relies on the exact order of past observations.

In this paper, we introduce a machine learning-based method that discovers IGC in non-stationary categorical time series which is able to deal with the aforementioned issues. We propose a method that creates summaries of prior stimuli and responses to them within a window, and captures the *dynamic* dependencies between the prior stimuli/responses and the subsequent ones through fitting multiple independent models that operate on the created summaries. Finally, since humans may change the features to which they pay attention, we propose a method that instantiates these IGCs at each time point and monitors the dynamics of the learning process.

This work is structured as follows: in Sect. 2 we discuss related work. We provide a detailed description of our method in Sect. 3. We evaluate it and discuss the results in Sect. 4, and we conclude on our findings in Sect. 5.

2 Related Work

Human behaviour is investigated in many disciplines. Neuroscience studies [10,19] show that different neural systems and pathways mediate rule-based category learning. Cognitive models [16] and reinforcement learning [12] are used to predict human response to a stimulus, while Gaussian mixture modeling are used to capture the dynamics of learning behaviour [1].

GC modeling has been already employed on FMRI data to model the dynamic interactions among brain regions [15]. Multivariate auto-regressive models were extended by including zero-lag interactions [5,11] to accommodate for instantaneous effects when discovering GC in numeric-valued time series. However, in category learning tasks, the features and the responses to stimuli are categorical. Hence, the discovery of directional interactions between features and participant responses demands I/GC methods that can process categorical time series.

Transfer entropy $\mathcal{T}E$ [18], mixture transition distribution-based [20], and graphical models [3] extract GC from categorical time series with non-linear dependencies but assume stationarity. Arguably, time series on (human) learning are not stationary, since responses to stimuli change as participants learn.

Xie et al. introduce a co-integration test and error correction to extract GC from non-stationary time series [22]. Rodrigues et al. detect short periods of IGC in stationary and non-stationary time series [17]. Ji et al. infer IGCs in nonlinear, non-stationary, bivariate time series with a new online measure by means of quantized kernel least mean square [13]. However, these methods are for numerical time series. Hence, there are to date no methods for the discovery of IGC in the non-stationary categorical time series found in learning experiments. Our approach deals with this challenge.

3   Methodology

We aim to discover Instantaneous Granger Causalities (IGC): if the past summary of time series X^i increases the probability of observing the values of time series X^j, we conclude that $X^i \xrightarrow[\text{IGC}]{} X^j$. We name X^i the *cause time series* and X^j the *effect time series*. We introduce first the summarization task for categorical time series and then our solution to the non-stationarity problem.

Summarizing Categorical Time Series for IGC. We observe time series of independent entities, e.g. experiment participants. Each entity generates a high-dimensional time series, where all dimensions are categorical. We stress that the effect and cause time series are different features of one entity's high-dimensional time series, and *not* time series of different entities.

Let u be an entity and $\mathcal{X}_u = \{X_u^1, X_u^2, \dots, X_u^D\}$ be the D-dimensional categorical time series of length N for this entity. For simplicity, we skip the index u hereafter. The time series of dimension i has the form $X_u^i \equiv X^i = (x_1^i, x_2^i, \dots, x_N^i), \forall i = 1 \dots D$. Each observation x_t^i in X^i at the time point t takes a value in C^i, a set of possible categories.

To model the relationship between two time series X^j and X^i, we derive a joint summary of the two time series for a fixed *memory*, i.e. number of remembered past observations. We define:

$$summary(j, i, t) = \{|x_k^i = a \wedge x_k^j = b|_{k=t-memory}^{t-1}, \forall a \in C^i, \forall b \in C^j\} \quad (1)$$

i.e. we count how often within *memory* we saw the combination a for X^i and b for X^j, for all $a \in C^i$ and $b \in C^j$. An example of this computation is given in Fig. 1(a).

We concatenate this summary to x_t^i as $\mathbf{s}_t^{ji} = (x_t^i, summary(j, i, t))$ and then generalize over all observations in X^i into the vector $\mathbf{S}^{ji} = (\mathbf{s}_1^{ji}, \mathbf{s}_2^{ji}, \dots, \mathbf{s}_N^{ji})$.

Deriving IGC from the Summaries. Our approach for IGC discovery is based on model learning and model comparison: for a time series X^j and for each time point t, we estimate the probability of observing x_t^j twice, once by training

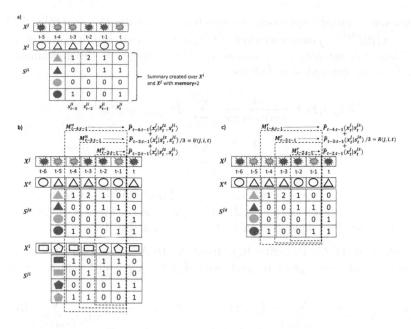

Fig. 1. (a): Summary S^{ji} of time series X^i (values as triangles and circles) and X^j (values are: blue, yellow) for a memory horizon $memory = 2$. (b) and (c): workflow for estimating the $IGC_{X^i \rightarrow X^j}$, with $min = 2$ and $max = 4$. In (b) three $M^u_{(.)}$ machine learning models trained on all time series including the cause time series X^i to estimate the $P_{(.)}(x^j_t | s^{jz}_t, s^{ji}_t)$. In (c) three $M^r_{(.)}$ machine learning models trained on all time series by excluding the cause time series X^i to estimate the $P_{(.)}(x^j_t | s^{jz}_t)$. (Color figure online)

a model on the past data of all time series data and once by excluding the candidate cause time series X^i and its summary towards X^j. Then, we compare the two estimated probabilities of observing x^j_t. If the probability estimated by considering X^i is significantly higher than the probability estimated by excluding it, then $X^i \xrightarrow{IGC} X^j$.

Let $\mathbf{S}^{j,1:D}_t$ denote the vector of all $\mathbf{s}^{jl}_t$ for $l = 1, \ldots D$ and $l \neq j$, and $\mathbf{S}^{j,1:D,\neg i}_t$ denote the vector that contains all $\mathbf{s}^{jl}_t$ except $\mathbf{s}^{ji}_t$. We estimate the probability of observing x^j_t given $\mathbf{S}^{j,1:D}_t$ by training a machine learning model $M^u_{t-p:t-1}$ over the set of past observations and their summaries $\{(\mathbf{S}^{j,1:D}_k, x^j_k), k = t-p \ldots t-1\}$ within a window of size p. We denote this probability as $P_{t-p:t-1}(x^j_t | \mathbf{S}^{j,1:D}_t)$. Similarly, we estimate $P_{t-p:t-1}(x^j_t | \mathbf{S}^{j,1:D,\neg i}_t)$, i.e. by excluding X^i from the data by training a model $M^r_{t-p:t-1}$. These probabilities can be estimated with any machine learning model such as support vector machine, logistic regression and naive Bayes classifier.

Resolving the Non-stationarity Challenge. To handle the non-stationarity in the data, we should determine how many lags/time points to consider.

We propose a greedy approach, in which we estimate $P_{t-p:t-1}(x_t^j|\mathbf{S}_t^{j,1:D})$ and $P_{t-p:t-1}(x_t^j|\mathbf{S}_t^{j,1:D,\neg i})$ over a window of varying size, between min and max number of lags, i.e. we vary $p \in [min, max]$. The averages of these estimates over $[min, max]$ are computed as follows:

$$U(j,i,t) \triangleq \frac{1}{max - min} \sum_{p=min}^{max} \widehat{P}_{t-p:t-1}(x_t^j|\mathbf{S}_t^{j,1:D}) \tag{2}$$

$$R(j,i,t) \triangleq \frac{1}{max - min} \sum_{p=min}^{max} \widehat{P}_{t-p:t-1}(x_t^j|\mathbf{S}_t^{j,1:D,\neg i}) \tag{3}$$

where $U(j,i,t)$ is the average of the estimated probabilities at time point t over the whole set of time series (cf. Eq. 2) and $R(j,i,t)$ is the average of the estimated probabilities at time point t when excluding X^i (cf. Eq. 3).

Discovery of IGC. To define IGC from X^i to X^j across all time points, we first estimate the average of $U(j,i,t)$ and $R(j,i,t)$ over all $t \in [min + 1, N]$ as:

$$\bar{U}(j,i) = \frac{1}{N - min} \sum_{t=min+1}^{N} U(j,i,t), \qquad \bar{R}(j,i) = \frac{1}{N - min} \sum_{t=min+1}^{N} R(j,i,t),$$

then IGC from X^i to X^j can be computed as follows:

$$IGC_{X^i \to X^j} = \bar{U}(j,i) - \bar{R}(j,i) \tag{4}$$

Finally, if $\bar{U}(j,i,t)$ is significantly greater than $\bar{R}(j,i,t)$, we conclude that $X^i \xrightarrow[IGC]{} X^j$.

Time-Variant IGC. The assumption that IGC from the beginning to the end of the time series does not change may not hold in all applications. Therefore, we quantify IGC at each time point t to monitor the IGC dynamics over time using the two quantities, $U(j,i,t)$ and $R(j,i,t)$ as follows:

$$IGC'_{X^i \to X^j}(t) = \begin{cases} U(j,i,t) - R(j,i,t) & \text{if } U(j,i,t) \text{ is significantly greater than } R(j,i,t) \\ 0 & \text{otherwise} \end{cases} \tag{5}$$

where $IGC'_{X^i \to X^j}(t)$ is the locally quantified IGC from X_i to X_j at time point t. If $IGC'_{X^i \to X^j}(t) > 0$, we conclude that $X^i \xrightarrow[IGC]{} X^j$ at time point t. All statistical tests are performed using Welch's t-test.

4   Results and Discussion

Dataset. We evaluate our method on behavioural data of a rule-based category learning experiment in the auditory domain [21]. This experiment used tones differing in five binary features, 'Duration' (Du), 'Direction' (Di), 'Loudness' (L), 'Speed' (S), and 'Frequency range' (F). Sound duration (short/long) and direction of pitch change (up/down) determined the category to be learned. 76 participants were assigned randomly to one of four target configurations formed as follows: short/up, short/down, long/up and long/down. The experiment consisted of 240 trials. At each trial, a complete single tone was played. In 25% of the trials, the tone belonged to the target configuration, and for the remaining 75%, tones were evenly distributed among the other three configurations. The participant labeled each tone as a target or non-target, then received feedback on whether the response was correct or not. After the experiment, the participants described the characteristic of the target tone. Based on this description, the experimenter determined whether a participant has learned the target category (learner) or not (non-learner) (14 out of 76).

We compare the results obtained by our proposed method to the transfer entropy with considering the instantaneous effects. Transfer entropy from X^i to X^j by considering the instantaneous effects of process X^i is computed as follows:

$$ITE_{X^i \rightarrow X^j} = H(X^j | X^{j-}) - H(X^j | X^{j-} \oplus X^i)$$

Since the participant responds only after the stimulus, there are instantaneous effects between stimuli and participant responses. Therefore, we compute the IGCs from each stimulus feature to the response (Res). Participants who learn the correct category, are expected to manifest significant IGCs from the relevant features ('Di' and 'Du') to 'Res'. We choose the significance level to be $\alpha = 0.05$ and the logistic regression model to estimate the probabilities of the responses. To tune the hyperparameters, min, max, and $memory$, we experiment with several values $min \in \{20, 30, 40\}$, $max \in \{50, 100, 150\}$, and $memory \in \{3, 7, 11\}$. We find that $min = 20$, $max = 50$, and $memory = 7$, yield the best separation between learners and non-learners using our IGC discovery method.

Our method succeeds in identifying 57 learners with significant $IGC_{Di \rightarrow Res}$ and 60 learners with significant $IGC_{Du \rightarrow Res}$, where 55 out of 62 learners exhibit the two causalities together as significant. Compared to ITE, that identifies only 28 and 16 learners with significant $ITE_{Di \rightarrow Res}$ and $ITE_{Du \rightarrow Res}$, respectively as shown in Table 1(a). Some participants fail to learn the correct category because they follow a single-feature policy where they attend to only one of the two relevant features. According to ITE, the majority of learners (18+6) follow exclusively one of the relevant features, compared to (2+5) learners retrieved by our method as shown in Table 1(b).

We next compare the overall performance of our method and the ITE to a hit rate-based classifier that labels participants with hit rate > 0.75 as learners and otherwise as non-learners. Since the four categories are uniformly distributed over all trials, a participant, who labels all stimuli as non-targets/targets, achieves a hit rate of 0.75. Despite the high sensitivity (95%) and specificity (85%) scored by the hit rate-based classifier, as reported in Table 2, our method achieves relatively high sensitivity (89%) and a better specificity (100%).

Additionally, our method models the dynamics in learning behaviour as participants transit across learning phases, and provides an explanation of why a participant did not learn or performed poorly. Figure 2 illustrates how the differences in $IGC's$ among learners (cf. Fig. 2(a)) and non-learners (cf. Fig. 2(b))

Table 1. (a) Number of participants with significant IGCs and *ITEs* per feature. (b) Number of participants, with single-feature policy, who exhibit significant IGCs and *ITEs* for exclusively one stimulus feature.

a) #participants		$Di \to Res$	$Du \to Res$	$L \to Res$	$S \to Res$	$F \to Res$
Learners(62)	IGC	57	60	0	0	0
	ITE	28	16	1	1	2
Non-learners(14)	IGC	7	2	0	0	1
	ITE	4	1	1	0	0
b) #participants		$Di \to Res$	$Du \to Res$	$L \to Res$	$S \to Res$	$F \to Res$
Learners(62)	IGC	2	5	0	0	0
	ITE	18	6	1	0	0
Non-learners(14)	IGC	7	2	0	0	1
	ITE	4	1	1	0	0

Table 2. Sensitivity & specificity of IGC, *ITE*, and hit rate-based classifier. The best performance is indicated in bold.

Metric	IGC	*ITE*	Hit rate-based classifier
Sensitivity (%)	89	15	**95**
Specificity (%)	**100**	**100**	85

are salient. We find four participants who performed poorly (hit rates < 0.76), although they successfully described the target category after the experiment. Three of them have significant IGC for only one of the two relevant features and one participant has these IGCs insignificant as shown in Fig. 2(c).

We exclude *ITE* from further comparisons due to its poor performance and inability to monitor the dynamics of IGCs over time. Detecting non-learners as early as possible and intervening to facilitate their learning is of high importance. Therefore, we investigate how early our method can distinguish learners from non-learners in comparison to the hit rate-based classifier. We assume that a participant has learned when s/he has consistently followed the correct decision policy, namely when s/he has expressed significant $IGC's$ from the relevant features to the response over several consecutive trials. Thus, we develop an **IGC**-based **L**earning **D**etection strategy (IGC-LD) that monitors the average

Table 3. A comparison between the performance of IGC-LD over a window of 25 consecutive trials and the hit rate-based classifier. The best performance per trial is indicated in bold.

(%) of identified learners before trial	75	100	150	200
IGC-LD	**56**	**76**	**87**	**98**
Hit rate-based classifier	48	61	68	74

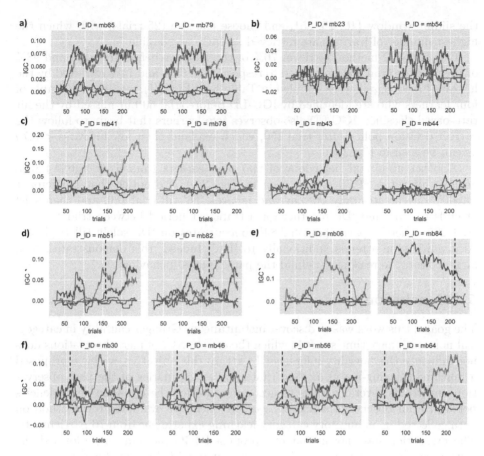

Fig. 2. (——)$IGC'_{Di\to Res}$, (——)$IGC'_{Du\to Res}$, (——)$IGC'_{S\to Res}$, (——)$IGC'_{L\to Res}$, and (——)$IGC'_{F\to Res}$. These graphs show the moving average of the IGC' over a window of 20 time points (trials). A comparison in the $IGC's$ between two learners in (a) and two non-learners in (b). (c) A group of participants (learners) reported the correct category after the experiment with hit rates < 0.76. (d) An example of two slow learners, with hit rates < 0.79, follow the correct decision policy after trial 150. The dotted black line indicates the trial at which the correct category learning has approximately taken place. (e) An example of two non-learners with hit rates > 0.75. Participant 'mb06' exhibits significant $IGC'_{Di\to Res}$ and $IGC'_{Du\to Res}$ between trial 181 and 205. Participant 'mb84' exhibits significant $IGC'_{Di\to Res}$ and $IGC'_{Du\to Res}$ after trial 210. (f) Four learners are identified by the IGC-LD before trial 60 and missed by the hit rate-based classifier.

value of the $IGC's$ of the relevant features to the response over a sliding window. Once this average becomes significantly greater than zero, we report that the participant has learned the correct category. This strategy enables us even to capture transient periods of realizing the correct category. We use the one sample t-test for the significance testing ($\alpha = 0.05$). We experiment with several sizes of the sliding window {10, 25, 35}, and choose the size (25 trials) with which the highest number of learners are retrieved as early as possible.

Our IGC-LD method retrieves 76% of the learners before trial 100 and 98% of them before trial 200, compared to respectively, 61% and 74% retrieved by the hit rate-based classifier, as detailed in Table 3. In Fig. 2(f), we see an example of four learners who are identified by IGC-LD before trial 60 but missed by the hit rate-based classifier. IGC-LD also observes two learners that begin to follow the correct decision policy after trial 150, which explains their low hit rates < 0.79 as can be seen in Fig. 2(d).

Another abnormal behaviour of two non-learners ('mb06' & 'mb84') who achieve hit rates >0.79 can be seen in Fig. 2(e). We notice that participant 'mb06' concentrates only on 'Du' and ignores 'Di' till trial 180, and then s/he attends to 'Du' and 'Di' together for a transient period between trial 181 and trial 205, whereas participant 'mb84' concentrates on 'Di' solely till trial 210. Afterward, s/he attends additionally to 'Du'. Indeed, this demonstrates, to a large extent, the reasoning behind the participants' behavior.

5   Conclusion

The goal of this work was to discover instantaneous Granger causality in categorical non-stationary time series in which the exact order of past observations does not influence the causality inference. To attain this objective, we have proposed a machine learning-based method that creates summaries of the past observation and trains several models to accommodate for the dynamic dependencies between prior observations and subsequent ones. We evaluated our method on data collected in an auditory category learning experiment from 76 participants. The evaluation has shown that our proposed IGC method outperformed the instantaneous transfer entropy. In addition, it provided reasonable explanations for ambiguous learning behaviour in some participants. Moreover, we presented a strategy that exploits our IGC method for early detection of when learning may have happened. The IGC-based early detection demonstrated a superior performance compared to the hit rate-based classifier. Our future plan is to improve the computational complexity of our method due to fitting several models.

References

1. Abolfazli, A., Brechmann, A., Wolff, S., Spiliopoulou, M.: Machine learning identifies the dynamics and influencing factors in an auditory category learning experiment. Sci. Rep. **10**, 1–12 (2020)
2. Ashby, F.G., Maddox, W.T.: Human category learning 2.0. Ann. New York Acad. Sci. **1224**, 147 (2011)
3. Eichler, M.: Graphical modelling of multivariate time series. Probab. Theory Relat. Fields **153**, 1–36 (2010)
4. Erla, S., Faes, L., Nollo, G., Arfeller, C., Braun, C., Papadelis, C.: Multivariate EEG spectral analysis elicits the functional link between motor and visual cortex during integrative sensorimotor tasks. Biomed. Signal Process. Control - BIOMED SIGNAL PROCESS CONTROL **7**, 221–227 (2012)

5. Faes, L., Erla, S., Porta, A., Nollo, G.: A framework for assessing frequency domain causality in physiological time series with instantaneous effects. Philos. Trans. Ser. A Math. Phys. Eng. Sci. **371**, 20110618 (2013)
6. Faes, L., Nollo, G., Porta, A.: Information domain approach to the investigation of cardio-vascular, cardio-pulmonary, and vasculo-pulmonary causal couplings. Front. Physiol. **2**, 80 (2011)
7. Goldstone, R.L., Lippa, Y., Shiffrin, R.M.: Altering object representations through category learning. Cognition **78**(1), 27–43 (2001)
8. Granger, C.: Investigating causal relations by econometric models and cross-spectral methods. Econometrica **37**, 424–38 (1969)
9. Gross, C.: Explaining the (non-) causality between energy and economic growth in the us-a multivariate sectoral analysis. Energy Econ. **34**, 489–499 (2012)
10. Helie, S., Shamloo, F., Zhang, H., Ell, S.: The impact of training methodology and representation on rule-based categorization: an fMRI study. Cogn. Affect. Behav. Neurosci. **21**, 717–735 (2021)
11. Hyvarinen, A., Zhang, K., Shimizu, S., Hoyer, P.: Estimation of a structural vector autoregression model using non-gaussianity. J. Mach. Learn. Res. **11**, 1709–1731 (2010)
12. Jarvers, C., et al.: Reversal learning in humans and gerbils: dynamic control network facilitates learning. Front. Neurosci. **10**, 535 (2016)
13. Ji, H., Chen, B., Yuan, Z., Zheng, N., Keil, A., Príncipe, J.C.: Online nonlinear granger causality detection by quantized kernel least mean square. In: Loo, C.K., Yap, K.S., Wong, K.W., Teoh, A., Huang, K. (eds.) ICONIP 2014. LNCS, vol. 8835, pp. 68–75. Springer, Cham (2014). https://doi.org/10.1007/978-3-319-12640-1_9
14. Lee, J.: Cumulative Learning, pp. 887–893. Springer, Boston (2012)
15. Lopez Paniagua, D., Seger, C.: Interactions within and between corticostriatal loops during component processes of category learning. J. Cogn. Neurosci. **23**, 3068–83 (2011)
16. Prezenski, S., Brechmann, A., Wolff, S., Russwinkel, N.: A cognitive modeling approach to strategy formation in dynamic decision making. Front. Psychol. **8**, 1335 (2017)
17. Rodrigues, J., Andrade, A.: Instantaneous granger causality with the Hilbert-Huang transform. ISRN Signal Process. **2013**, 1–9 (2013)
18. Schreiber, T.: Measuring information transfer. Phys. Rev. Lett. **85**, 461–464 (2000)
19. Seger, C., Mller, E.: Category learning in the brain. Ann. Rev. Neurosci. **33**, 203–219 (2010)
20. Tank, A., Fox, E., Shojaie, A.: Granger causality networks for categorical time series, June 2017
21. Wolff, S., Brechmann, A.: Carrot and stick 2.0: the benefits of natural and motivational prosody in computer-assisted learning. Comput. Hum. Behav. **43**, 76–84 (2015)
22. Xie, T., Wang, J.G., Xie, Z.T., Yao, Y., Liu, J.: Root cause diagnosis with error correction model based granger causality, pp. 1236–1241, May 2019

Comparison of Classification with Reject Option Approaches on MIMIC-IV Dataset

Gerta Salillari[1,2] and Nadav Rappoport[1]

[1] Ben-Gurion University of Negev, 84105 Be'er Sheva, Israel
salillari.1721455@studenti.uniroma1.it, nadavrap@bgu.ac.il
[2] Sapienza University, 00185 Rome, Italy

Abstract. This work compares two machine learning approaches that use the reject option method, i.e., the possibility to abstain from outputting a prediction in case the model is not confident about it, thus rejecting the sample.

We demonstrated the usability of such a model for predicting patients' mortality risk in ICU while maintaining an adequate level of accepted samples, using data from the MIMIC-IV database.

Two strategies have been compared: a single-model classifier, trained to directly predict the mortality rate of a patient in ICU and rejecting the sample if the confidence of the model is below a certain threshold, and a double-model boosted classifier which considers training a preceding model for determining whether a sample is predictable, i.e. a model classifies if the sample is going to be correctly predicted, and, only if it is, a second model outputs a mortality prediction, otherwise the sample is rejected since its prediction will likely be random.

The hypothesis is that the second strategy could give better results than the first one, considering a trade-off between the error rate and the amount of rejected samples.

We found that the two models are confident about two different classes: the Classifier-only Model is more confident to include in its predictions and to classify ICU staying instances in which the patient deceases, whereas the Boosted Reject Option Model considers those cases more difficult to predict, thus rejects them.

Keywords: Artificial intelligence · Machine learning · Prediction models · Electronic Health Records · EHR

1 Introduction

1.1 Statement of the Problem

The limited capacity of Intensive Care Units (ICUs) is a challenge for the doctors, who must make life-critical decisions about which patient to dismiss and which one to keep in ICU based on their health conditions and their risk of death. These decisions must be made with significant time constraints and limited resources.

Time constraints, limited resources, emotional burden all add to the stress the doctors are subject to, and they all factor into a very delicate decision-making process.

M. Michalowski et al. (Eds.): AIME 2022, LNAI 13263, pp. 210–219, 2022.
https://doi.org/10.1007/978-3-031-09342-5_20

A patient which is in ICU will likely need many exams and laboratory tests, which then the doctors will need to analyse. There exists an inherent trade-off in the selection and timing of lab tests between considerations of the expected utility in clinical decision-making of a given test at a specific time, and the associated cost or risk it poses to the patient [1].

1.2 Related Work

Mortality prediction algorithms have extensively been studied in the past [2–4]; however, they have been forced to predict a mortality risk for every instance even if their confidence in making such predictions for a particular instance was low.

The reject option is therefore used to give these algorithms the possibility to abstain from deciding when their confidence is low. Particular attention has been given to its cost-based mechanism: meaningful work has been done by Geifman and El-Yaniv [5, 6], Barlett and Wegkamp [7] focused on the optimisation of a particular loss function in the context of the cost minimisation for the reject option, as also did Yuan and Wegkamp [8]. Interestingly, Hanczar and Dougherty [9] explored a different application, fixing the accuracy of the classifier and thereby choosing a desired risk of error.

In this work, we rely on known models and approaches, like XGBoost and the reject option, but offer an innovative way of combining them. Rather than focusing on the cost functions or the risk assessment or minimisation, the focus is that of building a boosted classification model, where doubt expressed by the model via the reject option is shifted from the ICU patient mortality instance classification to the classification of the predictability of the instance itself. XGBoost implicitly tries to improve the output by considering misclassified instances. One of the limits of the classical approach is that instances that are potentially highly likely to be misclassified are not rejected by XGBoost, rather they are being classified regardless. In our approach, instead, XGBoost is allowed to reject a sample without enforcing a classification when it's likely to be random, in which case the decision would be delegated to the medical staff.

2 Material and Methods

2.1 Data

The Medical Information Mart for Intensive Care (MIMIC) data has been used to train and test the machine learning models. MIMIC-IV [11], the latest version of MIMIC provides medical data regarding over 60,000 patients admitted to ICUs.

2.2 Prediction Models

To accurately predict the mortality rate of patients in ICU while maintaining an adequate level of accepted instances, two strategies have been compared:

1. Train a machine learning model - the Classifier Model - that directly predicts the mortality of the patient. If the confidence of the predicted class of a sample is higher than a specified threshold, the prediction will be accepted, otherwise, the model will abstain from producing an output.

2. Train a chain of two models: first, train a model to predict the mortality of the patient (the Classifier Model, as above). Then, train a second model - the Acceptance Model - to predict the errors of the Classifier Model, to assess if the sample is predictable or not. The prediction of a new sample involves two steps. First, using the Acceptance Model, predict whether the sample is predictable or not. If yes, use the Classifier Model to predict the mortality; if the sample is not predictable, reject the sample. This strategy considers that the Acceptance Model is the one that has the reject option.

The hypothesis is that the second strategy, called the Boosted Reject Option, could give better results than the first one, considering a trade-off between the accuracy and the amount of rejected sample.

These models are trained with labelled data so they can predict instances where the label is missing. In a production environment, these models can be used to predict the mortality rate of ICU patients once they have been trained with labelled data. In the second approach, the sample is rejected using the Acceptance Model, given some threshold (score) of acceptance, and only if it is rejected, then the Classifier Model predicts the class.

2.3 Data Selection and Preprocessing

The goal of the decision-support system is to predict the mortality rate of a patient during the first hours of an ICU stay to support the practitioner, thus, to model at best real scenarios, only data from the first 24 h of each staying has been considered.

A restricted subset of features has been used, including demographic characteristics, such as age, gender, ethnicity etc., and mainly laboratory exams and reports. Data without a timestamp has been excluded as it was not possible to determine when it had been added to the dataset.

To reduce overfitting, the 50 most frequent laboratory exams have been considered; these account for ~77% of the total number of performed laboratory exams.

The subsampled dataset consists of 3,800,428 laboratory exams and 76,540 patient information recorded respectively, resulting in a total of 53,150 distinct patients and 74,331 ICU staying instances, each with 160 features.

Categorical values with an underlying semantic order, e.g., substance traces in exam results such as small, moderate, or large, have been transformed into numerical values. Unordered categorical data have been one-hot encoded or transformed into binary values whenever possible. Missing or erroneous laboratory exams data have been filtered out. Laboratory exams' reference ranges have been normalised following a MIN-MAX scaling so that results values within the reference ranges are scaled between 0 and 1, whilst results outside of the reference ranges are scaled to negative or above 1 if they are below or above the reference range respectively.

Time series data, like the same laboratory exam carried out several times within the first 24 h, have been flattened to the minimum, maximum, and median for each recorded laboratory exam value to preserve the most informative values.

Missing values for any given laboratory exam have been imputed using the median.

2.4 Preliminary Data Analysis

The number of ICU stays during which the patient survived was much higher than the number of ICU stays during which the patient died, resulting in an unbalanced distribution of the two categories with a deceased: survived ratio of 0.1227.

The laboratory exams carried out during the first 24 h of each ICU stay followed a gaussian distribution, with the number of exams ranging from 1 to more than 45, with an average of 27 exams per ICU stay.

To remove any type of pre-existing ordering, the data has been randomly shuffled. It has subsequently been divided into training, validation, and test set, corresponding respectively to 55%, 15% and 30% of the total dataset. Due to the highly unbalanced nature of the dataset, the data have been stratified to ensure a good representation of the classes' distribution. The prediction models (classifiers) in both strategies use the same training and validation set; the rejector model whilst using the union of the training and validation sets, splits it differently since it has a different target. The same test set has been held out for all models and strategies.

Model Selection. Different algorithms have been tested, among which Support Vector Machine (SVM), Random Forest, and XGBoost. Preliminary tests showed that XGBoost outperformed the other models in terms of accuracy and the consumed computational resources, thus it has been used for both models.

Optimization. The models' best hyperparameters have been optimized using grid search cross-validation approach, which evaluated the models at every position in the resulting grid of a defined search space.

Furthermore, given the high imbalance of the dataset, the positive instances have been weighted by a factor of 1 over death rate in the Classifier Model, and 1 over wrong predictions rate for the Acceptance Model.

3 Results

3.1 Strategy 1: Model Classifier

Overview. This is a single-model strategy whose direct goal is to predict the mortality of an ICU stay instance. An ICU stay instance predicted to survive is classified as CLASS 0 and on the contrary CLASS 1. If the confidence of the prediction is above a certain threshold the sample is accepted, otherwise, the model rejects the sample by abstaining from outputting a result (Fig. 1).

How low this threshold should be is ethically difficult to establish, thus, for research purposes, all possible thresholds have been explored. The model of this strategy is called Classifier.

Target and Results. The Log Loss score has been used to optimise the performance of the model, but particular consideration has been given to precision and recall as well: a high precision means that the instances the model can predict very well might be all

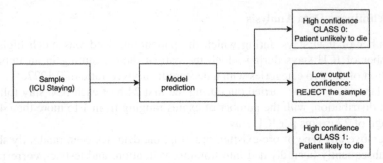

Fig. 1. Strategy 1: single classifier representation.

instances in which the patient survived during that ICU stay; although this is an important result, a bigger impact could be achieved by accurately predicting the ICU stays in which the patient died, thus the recall. Five-fold cross-validation has been used, and to evaluate and compare the performance of the models, additional metrics have been considered, such as Precision, Recall, Accuracy, and F1 score. The Classifier Model achieved a ROC AUC of 0.86 (Fig. 2).

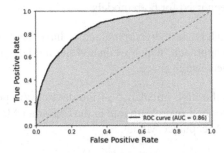

Fig. 2. Area under the receiver operating characteristic – classifier model.

Threshold Reject Option. In a first version of the reject option threshold system, the domain of the threshold varies in the region of the output confidence [0%–100%]: 0% corresponds to an absence of the rejections, thus acceptance and classification of all samples, and 100% corresponds to the model rejecting all instances and no classification being made.

This system, which considers a symmetric threshold among the two classes, leads to potentially counterintuitive results when the confidence distributions of the two classes are not distributed evenly across the confidence range (Fig. 3(a)).

Hence, a second version of the system has been studied: a quantile-based system, where the threshold is computed as the confidence that rejects a specific quantile of the ICU staying instances. In this second threshold system, the rejection is symmetric in terms of the fraction of rejected samples in each class (Fig. 3(b)).

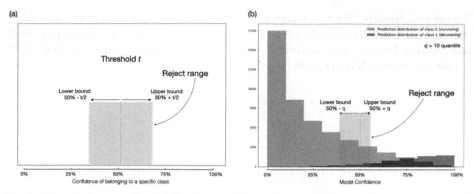

Fig. 3. Threshold system for the classifier model. (a) The threshold value is symmetric around 50%. (b) Quantile threshold system for the classifier model.

3.2 Strategy 2: Boosted Reject Option

Overview. The Boosted Reject Option is a double-model strategy. To train this model, firstly, the Classifier model classifies samples into two classes, as described above, but without the possibility to reject any instance. A new target label is created based on the output of the Classifier model, where the new classes are Class A (True Positives and True Negatives), and Class B (False Positives and False Negatives). Then a second model, the Acceptance Model, is trained to classify the ICU stay instances into the new classes A and B.

To make a new prediction, the new sample is first fed to the Acceptance Model. If the instance is classified to belong to the True Positives or True Negatives class (Class A), then the sample will be categorized by the Classifier Model as being an ICU staying instance where the patient is likely to survive (Class 0) or not (Class 1). Otherwise, Class B instances will be rejected.

The goal of the Acceptance Model is to identify instances that are correctly predictable by the Classifier Model and only if they are, the Classifier Model can output a prediction. If the Acceptance Model is not confident enough that the Classifier Model can correctly predict an instance, it rejects the sample (Fig. 4).

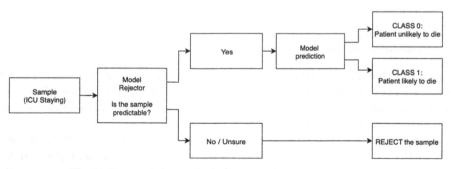

Fig. 4. Strategy 2: boosted reject option classifier representation.

Target and Results. For the Acceptance Model, the Log Loss score has been used to optimise the performance of the model, as well as the Five-fold cross-validation method, and additional metrics such as Accuracy, Precision, Recall and F1 score. The ROC AUC for the Acceptance Model is 0.86 (Fig. 5).

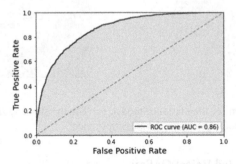

Fig. 5. Area under the receiver operating characteristic – acceptance model.

Threshold Reject Option. The threshold system domain ranges from 0% rejection, i.e., acceptance and further classification of all samples, to 100%, where the model rejects all instances thus no samples are accepted, and no classification is made (Fig. 6).

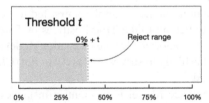

Fig. 6. Threshold system for the acceptance model.

3.3   Comparison of Two Strategies

We present below the results of the comparison between the two strategies. As can be seen from Fig. 7(a), as the models start rejecting samples, the error rate decreases. However, the Boosted Reject Option Model outperforms the Classifier-only Model since, for the same percentage of accepted samples, its error rate is lower.

As the percentage of accepted samples decreases, the mortality rate of the Classifier-only Model increases, while the mortality rate of the Boosted Reject Option Model decreases (Fig. 7(b)). The two models are confident about two different classes: the Classifier-only Model is more confident to include in its predictions and to classify ICU

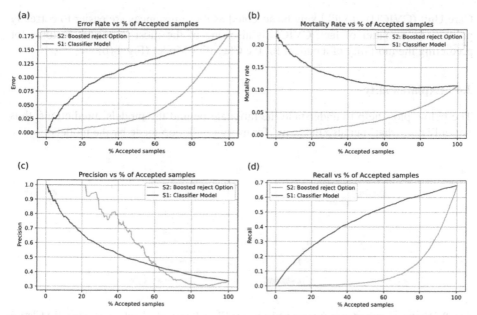

Fig. 7. Strategies comparison: (a) error rate vs. percentage of accepted samples, (b) mortality rate vs. percentage of accepted samples, (c) precision vs. percentage of accepted samples, (d) recall vs. percentage of accepted samples.

staying instances in which the patient deceases, whereas the Boosted Reject Option Model considers those cases more difficult to predict, thus rejects them.

With respect to precision, for more than 60% of accepted samples, the Boosted Reject Option Model outperforms the Classifier-only Model (Fig. 7(c)). However, in terms of Recall, the Classifier-only Model has a better performance than the Boosted Reject Option Model across all the sample acceptance percentage spectrum (Fig. 7(d)).

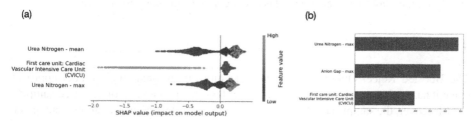

Fig. 8. Feature importance: (a) top 3 most important features for the acceptance model and their impact; (b) top 3 most important features for the classifier model.

As expected, there is a partial overlap of the most important features for the Classifier Model and the Acceptance Model. For what concerns the Acceptance Model (Fig. 8(a)), these are features with a clear distribution separation between the two classes (sample to be accepted or rejected): e.g., if an ICU stay first care unit is Cardiac Vascular Intensive

Care Unit (CVICU), it will likely be accepted as these instances are easier to correctly predict. As a matter of fact, CVICU is also one of the most important features for predicting the mortality of a patient for the Classifier Model (Fig. 8(b)).

3.4 Explainability

The below plots help to understand the rationale behind the models' predictions, thus not only the 'what' but also the 'why' for every prediction made by the models.

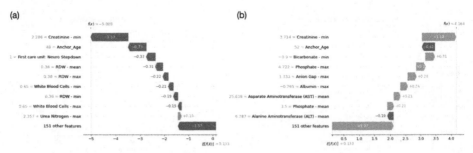

Fig. 9. Features' importance for two patients: (a) Class 0 patient - likely to survive, (b) Class 1 patient - unlikely to survive.

Figure 9(a) is an example of a patient likely to survive the staying and the main features that are responsible for this prediction. The maximum value recorded for the laboratory exam Urea Nitrogen is abnormal, which negatively impacts the patient's likelihood to survive. However, the sum of all the other features accounts for the patient to be classified as likely to survive since they positively contribute to their surviving prediction. On the contrary, Fig. 9(b) is an example of a patient predicted to decease. Although the age of the patient and their Alanine Aminotransferase mean values positively contribute to their likelihood of surviving, the rest of the features, have a heavier weight on the classifier decision to classify the stay as unlikely to survive.

4   Discussion

The Boosted Reject Option outperforms the more traditional single-model approach since it has higher precision and accuracy for the same percentage of accepted samples.

Moreover, the samples the Boosted Reject Option is less confident about, and rejects are cases in which the patients are less likely to survive, thus delegating the patients' conditions evaluation to medical experts.

The reject option might be associated with the cost of withholding the output, and the cost of making a wrong prediction. However, the rejection cost heavily depends on the value associated with a False Negative, i.e., a patient wrongly classified as not at death risk. This is ethically difficult to establish and outside of this work's scope.

Future developments of this work might consider a higher number of features. Limiting the analysis to the first 24 h of an ICU staying is an artificial limit imposed for the goal of this work; nevertheless, there is value in the laboratory exam repetition over time, hence integrating into the Boosted Reject Option Model a temporal analysis could bring to surface further information. In addition, instance-based learning methods or Ensemble Methods such as Staking could be explored, since, in academic literature, it has been shown that it could improve the models' performance [10]. However, they suffer from the above-mentioned limitation that the prediction would be enforced.

References

1. Cheng, L.F., Prasad, N., Engelhardt, B.E.: An optimal policy for patient laboratory tests in intensive care units. In: BIOCOMPUTING 2019: Proceedings of the Pacific Symposium, pp. 320–331 (2019)
2. Pirracchio, R., Petersen, M.L., Carone, M., Rigon, M.R., Chevret, S., van der Laan, M.J.: Mortality prediction in intensive care units with the Super ICU Learner Algorithm (SICULA): a population-based study. Lancet Respir. Med. **3**(1), 42–52 (2015)
3. Wong, L.S.S., Young, J.D.: A comparison of ICU mortality prediction using the APACHE II scoring system and artificial neural networks. Anaesthesia **54**(11), 1048–1054 (1999)
4. Alves, T., Laender, A., Veloso, A., Ziviani, N.: Dynamic prediction of ICU mortality risk using domain adaptation. In: 2018 IEEE International Conference on Big Data (Big Data), pp. 1328–1336. IEEE (2018)
5. Geifman, Y., El-Yaniv, R.: SelectiveNet: a deep neural network with an integrated reject option. In: Proceedings of the 36th International Conference on Machine Learning (2019)
6. Geifman, Y., El-Yaniv, R.: Selective classification for deep neural networks. In: Advances in Neural Information Processing Systems 30 (2017)
7. Barlett, P.L., Wegkamp, M.: Classification with a reject option using a hinge loss. J. Mach. Learn. Res. **9**, 1823–1840 (2008)
8. Yuan, M., Wegkamp, M.: Classification methods with reject option based on convex risk minimization. J. Mach. Learn. Res. **11**, 111–130 (2010)
9. Hanczar, B., Dougherty, E.R.: Classification with reject option in gene expression data. Bioinformatics **24**(17), 1889–1895 (2008)
10. Joshi, N., Srivastava, S.: Improving classification accuracy using ensemble learning technique (using different decision trees). Int. J. Comput. Sci. Mob. Comput. **3**(5), 727–732 (2014)
11. Physionet Homepage: https://physionet.org/content/mimiciv/0.4/

Predicting Waiting Time and Quality of Kidney Offers for Kidney Transplant Candidates

Jonathan Jalbert[1]([⊠]), Héloïse Cardinal[2], Andrea Lodi[3,4], Jean-Noël Weller[3], and Hugo-Maxime Tocco[3]

[1] Polytechnique Montréal, Montréal, Canada
jonathan.jalbert@polymtl.ca
[2] CHUM Research Centre, Montréal, Canada
[3] CERC, Polytechnique Montréal, Montréal, Canada
[4] Jacobs Technion-Cornell Institute, Cornell Tech and Technion - IIT, New York, USA

Abstract. In Canada, more than 3,500 patients are currently waiting for a kidney transplantation from a deceased donor. When a patient is registered on the transplant waiting list, both the expected waiting time before the first offer and its expected quality are unknown. This information is nonetheless crucial for transplant candidates in order to better manage their renal replacement therapy options, including accepting deceased donors with expanded criteria or identifying a living donor if expected waiting time is deemed too long. In this paper, we describe a novel method to estimate the arrival of future kidney offers and their quality for kidney transplant candidates. The method is based on the construction of a pseudo history of offers (occurrences and quality) for the current candidate using the past data of kidney donors and transplant candidates. The pseudo history is modeled with a marked Poisson process. The expected waiting time before the first offer and its expected quality for a given candidate can then be estimated. By providing such reliable quantitative estimates of time to and quality of future offers personalized to the transplant candidate, the proposed approach has the potential to guide and empower transplant candidates in managing their health condition.

Keywords: Kidney transplantation · Clinical decision support tool · marked Poisson process

1 Introduction

Renal transplantation improves both longevity and quality of life when compared to dialysis [1,2]. Currently, 60% of kidney transplantations in Canada originate from deceased donors [3]. Given the shortage of organ donors and the rising incidence of end-stage kidney disease (ESKD) [3], over 3, 500 patients in Canada

© The Author(s), under exclusive license to Springer Nature Switzerland AG 2022
M. Michalowski et al. (Eds.): AIME 2022, LNAI 13263, pp. 220–229, 2022.
https://doi.org/10.1007/978-3-031-09342-5_21

are currently waiting for a kidney transplantation from a deceased donor and this number is constantly growing [3]. Waiting time to kidney transplantation varies markedly by region [4,5] with reported median waiting times of 0.5 to 4.5 years in the United States [5], while national Canadian data is not readily available.

In addition to lower quality of life when compared to transplantation [1], longer waiting time on dialysis before transplantation is associated with poorer graft and recipient survival after transplantation [6]. Hence, providing information to transplant candidates with regards to the waiting time to the first and future offers and on the expected quality of these offers is crucial in helping transplant candidates make informed decisions on the various therapeutic options that exist to manage their ESKD. Recent studies have shown that kidney transplant candidates commonly have a limited understanding of the likely outcomes while on the waiting list and are demanding individualized information from their health care providers [7,8]. For them, having access to this information, even when negative outcomes were discussed, was felt as empowering and relieving [7,8]. In particular, the uncertainty around when a deceased donor kidney will become available reportedly leads to feelings of insecurity and doubt [8].

In Canada, the allocation of deceased donor kidneys is managed by provincial organ donation organizations (ODOs) for all kidney transplant candidates who are registered on their centralized waiting list. Although the allocation score varies by province, all Canadian ODOs' scores are based on elements of justice and utility according to a national consensus [9]. The most important factors that increase a candidate's probability of receiving an offer are longer time spent on dialysis, blood group types A or AB, and the absence of very high levels of pre-formed antibodies to non-self HLA. When the transplant physician and the transplant candidate decide to accept the offer, the main factors that are considered are the risks of infectious/cancer transmission (usually low or null if the offer is actually discussed with the candidate), and the quality of the offer, as some donors have features (e.g., older age, hypertension, diabetes) that are associated with shorter duration of kidney graft function [10].

The goal of the present paper consists in developing a method to better inform transplant candidates of the time they are expected to wait until they have a first deceased donor kidney offer and the frequency of future offers. The tool allows the candidate-physician team to estimate the waiting time between the next offers and the quality of those offers for a specific transplant candidate. It can also estimate the waiting time for an offer that is at least above a certain quality threshold. The first objective consists in constructing a pseudo history of offers to that candidate using the past data of deceased donor kidneys and kidney transplant candidates on the ODO waiting list. It is assumed that the arrival and quality of future kidney offers will be similar to those of past offers within the observation period. The second objective consists in modeling the pseudo history of offers with a marked Poisson process (MPP). The MPP is tailored for the specific candidate's characteristics and it is assumed that the process is the same for the future offers. The last objective consists in exploiting the model for estimating the time to first offer, the waiting time between the offers, the average quality of the future offers and the waiting time for an offer of better quality than a fixed pre-determined threshold. The remainder of this paper is as follows. Section 2 describes the past data on kidney donors, candidates and transplants. The proposed methodology to fulfill the objectives is described in Sect. 3. The method is illustrated and validated for a patient in Sect. 4. Section 5 contains the discussion and avenue for future work.

2   Data

We used the dataset from Transplant Quebec, the ODO managing and allocating deceased donors for the province of Quebec (Canada). Data on all deceased donor kidney offers that occurred between March 29th, 2012 and December 13th, 2017 and that led to at least one kidney transplant in Quebec were retrieved ($n = 1534$). After excluding offers that went to medical emergency cases ($n = 7$), the national hypersensitized registry ($n = 76$), pediatric candidates ($n = 24$), combined kidney and liver/pancreas ($n = 31$), we included 1385 deceased donor kidney offers that were managed using the allocation score for the general waiting list. Among the 848 donors included, mean age was 51 years (standard deviation, SD, 17), 44% were female, and 95% were Caucasian. Mean candidates' age was 52 years (SD 14), with 38% females. Candidates' race was unavailable. In the province of Quebec, the allocation score of a candidate for transplantation is a function of the candidate's age, time on the waiting list, the candidate's panel reactive antibodies, the HLA DR match with the donor, and the age difference between the candidate and the donor [11].

The quality of the offers is measured with the Kidney Donor Risk Index (KDRI), a score that has been derived from a kidney graft survival analysis of the US Scientific Registry of Transplant Recipients [10]. The KDRI is associated with the relative risk of post-transplant kidney graft failure and it can be converted in Kaplan-Meier based probabilities of kidney graft survival at various time points after transplantation [12]. Lower KDRI values indicate a longer expected longevity of the allograft after the transplant. We used the 10-variable KDRI equation, which includes the following independent variables: donor age, height, weight, ethnicity, history of hypertension, diabetes, cause of death, terminal serum creatinine, hepatitis C status and whether the donor is neurologically deceased or deceased after cardiocirculatory arrest.

3   Method

3.1   Constructing the Pseudo History for a Patient

A pseudo history of offers for a specific candidate is constructed using the past data of deceased kidney donors and kidney transplant candidates on the ODO waiting list. The offers that the specific candidate would have received, had he/she been present on the waiting list at the time of each past offer, are retrieved from the data from 2 years previous to the day when predictions need to be made. This can be at any time point starting from the day of waiting list registration, but for the purpose of this paper, we will assume that this is the day of waiting list registration. The Transplant Quebec allocation score is calculated for all ABO-compatible kidneys that could have been offered to the specific candidate had he/she been present on the waiting list at the time of the offers in the 2 years previous to waiting list registration. Note that the allocation score that the candidate would have obtained for these prior offers is calculated using the candidate's characteristics present on the day of wait list registration. Then, the allocation score obtained by the specific candidate for each past offer is compared to the score of the actual recipient of the second kidney that was placed. Offers where the specific candidate's scores were lower than those of the actual recipients of the second kidneys transplanted were filtered out from the pseudo history, as they would have never gone to the specific candidate. The pseudo history of the specific candidate is obtained by retrieving the time of the offers in the past 2 years and the quality of these offers estimated by the KDRI.

These calculations assume that the candidate will remain alive during his/her waiting time and will not be permanently withdrawn from the waiting list. Also, the longer the candidate waits on dialysis, the more points are given to his/her allocation score calculated at the time of an offer. Hence, in our work, a candidate's waiting time is updated annually for score calculation and a complete pseudo history is constructed for they first-year score. Another complete history can be constructed with the second-year allocation score, and so on.

3.2   Modeling the Kidney Pseudo Offers with a Marked Poisson Process

Let $X_0 = 0$ be the date on which the candidate is registered on the waiting list for kidney transplantation. For a given allocation score, let the sequence $X_1, X_2, \ldots$ be the time of offers. Let this sequence be modeled with a Poisson process of intensity $\lambda > 0$ [13]. Therefore, the waiting times between the offers $T_1, T_2, \ldots$, where $T_1 = X_1 - X_0$, $T_2 = X_2 - X_1$, etc., are independent and identically distributed according to the exponential distribution of mean $1/\lambda$.

The assumption of independence of waiting times in the Poisson process seems reasonable in the case of deceased donor kidney offer arrivals. Indeed, under normal circumstances, the death of the donor should not depend on the death of another donor. The assumption that waiting times between offers are distributed according to the exponential distribution will have to be verified with the data.

The offer arrival is modeled on a year-to-year basis. After a year, the candidate's allocation score is updated and the rate of the arrivals can be affected. Instead of using a more complex non-homogeneous Poisson process [13], we preferred to divide the period in homogeneous time slices where a homogeneous Poisson process is appropriate.

Due to the memoryless property of the exponential distribution, the waiting time T before the next offer from any point of origin is distributed as the exponential distribution of rate λ. Therefore, the probability that the next offer occurs before $t > 0$ is

$$\mathbb{P}(T \leq t) = 1 - e^{\lambda t}$$

and the expected time before the next offer is $\frac{1}{\lambda}$.

The quality of offers $Y_1, Y_2, \ldots$ are measured by the KDRI and are assumed to be independent, identically distributed from the cumulative distribution function F and independent from the arrival Poisson process. The sequence $(X_1, Y_1), (X_2, Y_2), \ldots$ is referred to as a marked Poisson process [13].

Suppose we are interested in offers of a quality higher than u. Let α denote the marginal probability that the offer quality is greater than u, i.e. $\mathbb{P}(Y \geq u) = \alpha$. Then, the offers exceeding the quality y arrive according to the Poisson process of intensity $\alpha\lambda$. Therefore, the probability that the next offer exceeding quality y occurs before $t > 0$ is

$$\mathbb{P}(T \leq t) = 1 - e^{\alpha\lambda t}$$

and the expected time before it occurs is $\frac{1}{\alpha\lambda}$.

3.3   Parameters Estimation and Inference

Let $t_1, \ldots, t_n$ be the *observed* waiting times of the candidate's pseudo history between the offers. The intensity of the Poisson process modeling the arrival of offers is estimated by

$$\hat{\lambda} = \frac{n}{\sum_{i=1}^{n} t_i}.$$

Let $y_1, \ldots, y_n$ be the *observed* qualities corresponding to the candidate's pseudo offers. For modeling the underlying distribution F, two options are possible. The first one consists in estimating F with the empirical distribution function. This approach has the advantage of not making any assumption on the quality distribution F, but the estimation is imprecise when the number of pseudo offers n is small. The second option is to assume a parametric distribution for F and to estimate the parameters with the quality of the pseudo offers. Since the number of pseudo offers is generally limited, the second option is used in this paper. The quality of the offers being a positive variable, the Log-normal distribution, the Gamma distribution and the Weibull distribution can notably be used to model the KDRI. For a given candidate, these distributions can be fitted to the pseudo offer KDRI and the distribution with the best fit can be retained.

4   Results

To illustrate the method, we focus on Candidate 3605, who was randomly selected from the database. No precise date or information that could lead to patient identification is provided in this work.

4.1   Pseudo History and Model Fit

Suppose the candidate is registered on the waiting list at time $x_0 = 0$. The pseudo offers that this candidate would have had, based on the history and on his/her first-year score, are given in Table 1. The corresponding waiting times between offers are 72, 246, 246 and 32 days.

Table 1. Pseudo offers computed for Candidate 3605 with their first-year score. The arrival of the offer is calculated in days from the moment the candidate is registered on the waiting list ($x_0 = 0$).

Time of the offer (days)	Quality (KDRI)
72	1.8628
318	2.0331
564	0.8386
596	2.5362

The estimated intensity of offers arrival is $\hat{\lambda} = 0.0067$, which can be expressed in *offer per day*. The kidney quality is modeled with the Weibull distribution of parameters $(3.5251, 2.0272)$, fitted by maximum likelihood. The Weibull distribution provides the best fit according to the Bayesian information criterion (BIC, [14]) among the considered distributions, as shown in Table 2.

Table 2. BIC values for distributions adjusted to KDRI values. A high BIC indicates a better fit.

Distribution	BIC
Weibull	−31.0414
Gamma	−34.1511
Log-normal	−35.9725

4.2   First Offer

With the model fit to the candidate's pseudo-history of offers, estimations of the waiting time and offer quality can be provided. As soon as Candidate 3605 is registered on the waiting list, the candidate can be informed that the expected waiting time before his/her first offer is 149 days and that the expected quality of the offer is 1.8246. Also, after 446 days of waiting, there is a 95% probability that the candidate will receive a first offer.

4.3   Next Best Offer

After receiving a first offer of quality 1.8628 after a 72-day wait, the patient may wonder how long he/she can expect to wait before receiving a new offer of higher quality than the first one. Using the fitted Weibull distribution, the probability that the next offer exceeds 1.8628 is $\hat{\alpha} = 0.4760$. Then, the offers of quality higher than 1.8628 arrive with an intensity of 0.0032 offers per day. The expected waiting time before a better offer is therefore 313 days. The probability that the candidate will receive a better offer in the next 938 days is 95%.

4.4   Model Validation

The fit of the statistical model to the data is difficult to assess with only 4 pseudo offers. To facilitate the statistical model evaluation, the candidate's pseudo offers calculated with the scores for the third year on the waiting list can be used. Based on the history, the candidate would have had 33 offers with this score. Figure 1 illustrates the fit of the exponential distribution to model these waiting times. It can be seen that the exponential distribution fits the waiting times very well. The Poisson process used for the arrival of offers seems therefore appropriate.

Figure 2 shows the Weibull distribution fitted to the quality of the 33 pseudo offers. Again, it can be seen that the quality of the offers is modeled very well by this distribution.

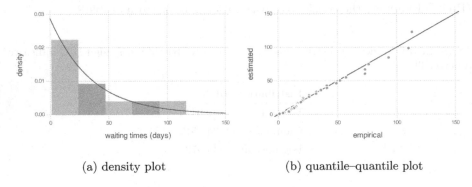

(a) density plot   (b) quantile–quantile plot

Fig. 1. Diagnostic plots to check the fit of the Poisson process to offer arrivals; (a) density of the exponential distribution fitted to the waiting times and (b) quantiles of the exponential distribution fitted to waiting times empirical quantiles.

5   Discussion

A method has been proposed in the present paper as a tool to better inform kidney transplant candidates and kidney transplant physicians as to the expected waiting time to the first and future offers and to the quality of future offers. These estimates of waiting time and offer quality are personalized, as they take into

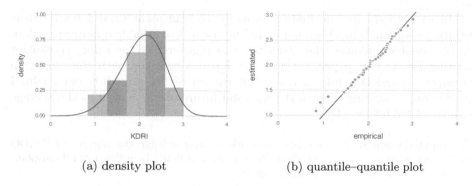

(a) density plot   (b) quantile–quantile plot

Fig. 2. Diagnostic plots to check the fit of Weibull distribution to quality of offers; (a) density of the Weibull distribution fitted to the offer KDRI and (b) quantiles of the Weibull distribution fitted to the KDRI empirical quantiles.

account the donor and candidate characteristics that are used in the ODO's allocation score. This information is crucial to empower transplant candidates to make informed choices about their therapeutic options for ESKD. Transplant candidates often feel insecurity and have doubts about whether and when an organ will become available and are demanding personalized information from their health care providers [7].

Our approach provides relevant and easily interpretable information to transplant physicians and candidates, as well as an estimate of the uncertainty around the estimates. For instance, in the example presented above, Candidate 3605 can plan work, family and leisure activities with the expectation of being on dialysis for approximately 149 days. The candidate can also observe that to get a better offer than the first one, if the KDRI is indeed 1.8 when the offer comes, it would take 2.5 years. Such long waiting time would be unacceptable for most candidates, and hence the candidate could tend to accept the offer. Our approach was developed to provide predictions in the province of Quebec, but could be adapted to other ODOs with different allocation scores. It can also provide a personalized estimate of time to next offer at any time point if the candidate is actively registered on the waiting list.

There are limitations to our study. Our approach does not explicitly account for the continuous change in allocation score as the candidate spends time on the waiting list and assumes that candidates remain alive and are not permanently removed from the waiting list. For simplicity, we chose to model the arrival of offers with a homogeneous Poisson process independently for each of the candidate's waiting years. In future studies, we will consider a non-homogeneous Poisson process to model the arrival of offers with a non-constant allocation score. The sample size of our study cohort was limited, which can affect the confidence of provided estimates. Last, our approach will need to be externally validated using retrospective data from another Canadian ODO.

In conclusion, the information provided to transplant candidates by their health professionals has been hampered by the lack of reliable quantitative data on the possible outcomes when candidates are registered on the kidney transplant waiting list. In this paper, we have developed a new approach that will help transplant physicians inform transplant candidates by providing personalized predictions of waiting time to the first and future offers, as well as the average quality of the future offers.

Acknowledgments. The authors would like to acknowledge the support of IVADO and thank Sylvain Lavigne, Marie-Josée Simard and Louis Beaulieu from Transplant Québec for their collaboration and support.

References

1. Laupacis, A., et al.: A study of the quality of life and cost-utility of renal transplantation. Kidney Int. **50**, 235–242 (1996)
2. Wolfe, R.A., et al.: Comparison of mortality in all patients on dialysis, patients on dialysis awaiting transplantation, and recipients of a first cadaveric transplant. N. Engl. J. Med. **341**(23), 1725–30 (1999)
3. Canadian Institute for Health Information. End Stage Kidney Disease and Kidney Transplants, 2010–2019-Data tables. https://www.cihi.ca/en/access-data-reports/results?query=wait+list+kidney+transplantation&Search+Submit=. Accessed 28 Jan 2022
4. King, K.L., et al.: Major variation across local transplant centers in probability of kidney transplant for wait-listed patients. J. Am. Soc. Nephrol. **31**(12), 2900–2911 (2020)
5. Davis, A.E., et al.: The extent and predictors of waiting time geographic disparity in kidney transplantation in the United States. Transplantation **97**(10), 1049–1057 (2014)
6. Meier-Kriesche, H.U., et al.: Effect of waiting time on renal transplant outcome. Kidney Int. **58**(3), 1311–1317 (2000)
7. Hart, A., Bruin, M., Chu, S., Matas, A., Partin, M.R., Israni, A.K.: Decision support needs of kidney transplant candidates regarding the deceased donor waiting list: a qualitative study and conceptual framework. Clin. Transplant **33**, e13530 (2019)
8. Burns, T., Fernandez, R., Stephens, M.: The experiences of adults who are on dialysis and waiting for a renal transplant from a deceased donor: a systematic review. JBI Database Syst. Rev. Implement. Rep. **13**(2), 169–211 (2015)
9. The Canadian Council for Donation and Transplantation. Kidney Allocation in Canada: A Canadian Forum. Report and recommendations (2006). https://professionaleducation.blood.ca/sites/default/files/Kidney_Allocation_FINAL.pdf. Accessed 18 Mar 2022
10. Rao, P.S., et al.: A comprehensive risk quantification score for deceased donor kidneys: the kidney donor risk index. Transplantation **88**(2), 231–236 (2009)
11. Transplant Québec. Procédure d'opération normalisée-Attribution rénale, 14 September 2020. https://www.transplantquebec.ca/sites/default/files/att-pon-104_v7.pdf. Accessed 28 Jan 2022

12. U.S. Department of Health & Human Services. A guide to calculating and inter-preting the kidney donor profile index (KDPI). https://optn.transplant.hrsa.gov/media/1512/guide_to_calculating_interpreting_kdpi.pdf. Accessed 28 Jan 2022
13. Pinsky, M., Karlin, S.: An Introduction to Stochastic Modeling, 4th edn. Academic Press (2011)
14. Schwarz, G.E.: Estimating the dimension of a model. Ann. Stat. **6**(2), 461–464 (1978)

Wrist Ultrasound Segmentation by Deep Learning

Yuyue Zhou, Abhilash Rakkunedeth, Christopher Keen, Jessica Knight, and Jacob L. Jaremko(✉) ⓘD

University of Alberta, Edmonton, Canada
jjaremko@ualberta.ca

Abstract. Ultrasound (US) is an increasingly popular medical imaging modality in clinical practice due to its low cost, portability, and real-time dynamic display. It is ideally suited for wrist and elbow fracture detection in children as it does not involve any ionizing radiation. Automatic assessment of wrist images requires delineation of relevant bony structures seen in the image including the radial epiphysis, radial metaphysis and carpal bones. With the advent of artificial intelligence, researchers are using deep learning models for segmentation in US scans including these to help with automatic diagnosis and disease progression. However, certain specific characteristics of US such as poor signal to noise ratio, presence of imaging artifacts and blurred boundaries around anatomical structures make segmentation challenging. In this research, we applied deep learning models including UNet and Generative Adversarial Network (GAN) to segment bony structures from a wrist US scan. Our ensemble models were trained on wrist 3D US datasets containing 10,500 images in 47 patients acquired from the University of Alberta Hospital (UAH) pediatric emergency department using a Philips iU22 ultrasound scanner. In general, although UNet gave the highest DICE score, precision and Jaccard Index, GAN achieved the highest recall. Our study shows the feasibility of using deep learning techniques for automatically segmenting bony regions from a wrist US image which could lead to automatic detection of fractures in pediatric emergencies. Github.

Keywords: Wrist ultrasound · Image segmentation · Deep learning · UNet · GAN · Pix2pix

1 Introduction

1.1 Ultrasound Segmentation

Ultrasound (US), compared to other medical imaging methods such as CT or X-ray, has the advantages of low cost and high portability. Since it does not involve radiation [1], US as a method for wrist and elbow fracture detection in children is potentially a safe alternative tool to X-ray [2,3], but has not, in most practices, actually replaced X-rays, due in part to lack of user confidence in results. Automatic wrist US segmentation has potential to aid in accurate

M. Michalowski et al. (Eds.): AIME 2022, LNAI 13263, pp. 230–237, 2022.
https://doi.org/10.1007/978-3-031-09342-5_22

fracture detection and evaluation of fracture severity. Automatic assessment of wrist US images requires delineation of relevant bony structures in each image including the epiphysis, metaphysis and carpal bones (as shown in Fig. 1), however, there are many unique challenges with low resolution, speckles, poor signal to noise ratio and blurred boundaries [4]. Finding a method to quickly and accurately segment bony structures on wrist US would reduce variability in interpretation and decrease time required for manual annotation.

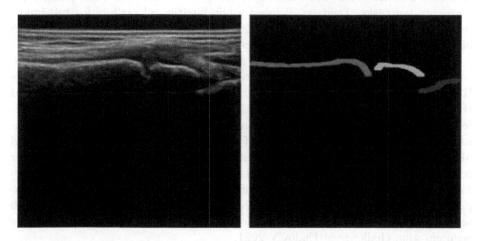

Fig. 1. 3D wrist ultrasound and ground truth mask. Red = metaphysis, green = epiphysis, Blue = carpal bone. (Color figure online)

1.2 Deep Learning and Image Segmentation

With the advent of artificial intelligence, researchers are applying deep learning based models for image segmentation. Convolutional Neural Network (CNN) is a powerful deep learning network for image related tasks as it can learn and extract features from images accurately. There are many CNN models for image segmentation. UNet, a CNN based model, was built for biomedical image segmentation in 2015 [5]. It has a unique U shape symmetric architecture. The first downsampling part uses CNN architecture to extract feature maps from original images. In the second upsampling part, feature maps from the downsampling layers are connected with the corresponding upsampling layers to increase the output resolution and get precise localization. It has had a huge impact on biomedical imaging. As one example, Jin et al. applied multiple U-net models to segment US for patients with ovarian cancer, with high Jaccard similarity and DICE scores demonstrating high segmentation accuracy [6]. However, by its architecture the middle layers of a U-Net emphasize coarse image features and may miss fine detail that can be crucial in tasks such as detecting subtle fractures.

Generative Adversarial Network (GAN) is a framework originally developed by Goodfellow et al. in 2014 [7], which may be helpful in this regard. GAN consists of 2 models trained simultaneously: a generator model capturing the data distribution and a discriminator model estimating the probability that a given sample came from the real training data [7]. The training purpose is to maximize the probability that the discriminator makes a mistake, to make synthesized samples be able to fool the discriminator. Pix2pix is an architecture for paired images based on GAN [8]. It is widely used in image translation as it can accurately synthesize corresponding images based on given images [9], or image augmentation [10]. Nowadays, some researchers are using pix2pix for segmentation tasks. Tsuda et al. used a combination of pix2pix for cell image segmentation [11]. Popescu trained pix2pix model for blood vessel segmentation of retinal images and achieved high accuracy [12].

In the recent years, researchers are using model ensemble for medical image segmentation. Nanni et al. applied CNN model ensembles for bioimage datasets [13]. They trained DeepLab models with different ResNet backbone and applied stochastic activation selection to generate models with same structure but different activation function. They found model ensemble and loss function combination could improve segmentation performance. Dolz et al. combined multipled 3D CNNs for infant brain MRI segmentation using majority voting [14]. Their results showed that ensemble learning is competitive and achieved a better performance than single CNN. Thambawita et al. proposed model TriUNet composed of three UNet and combine TriUNet with other segmentation models such as DeepLap [15]. Their model ensembles make them winners of medical image segmentation challenge at EndoCV 2021.

In this research, we applied UNet, pix2pix GAN, and a model ensemble combining UNet and GAN for wrist US bone segmentation. Instead of combining outputs of different models into the final prediction directly, we used a different model ensemble method: the output of UNet was used as the input of GAN model, while GAN is responsible for generating the final segmentation prediction. We would like to see the potential of using image translation model and our model ensemble approach for medical image segmentation. We sought to determine how accurately wrist US could be segmented by CNN, and whether GAN could improve upon U-Net for wrist US segmentation tasks, either as GAN alone or by combining UNet and GAN layers.

2   Method

2.1   Dataset

Our 3D US dataset was acquired prospectively from the University of Alberta Hospital (UAH) pediatric emergency using a Philips iU22 ultrasound scanner with institutional ethics approval and informed consent. The dataset consists of 12,264 image slices in 113 sweep videos of 57 patients with the corresponding ground truth masks segmented by a pediatric musculoskeletal radiologist with 18 years experience and/or a sonographer with 7 years experience trained by that radiologist. Different bony regions including radial metaphysis, radial epiphysis, carpal bones and fractures were marked on the masks. We split the dataset into training and test sets based on patient ID to avoid overlap. We used 10,500 images in 47 patients as a training set and 1,764 images in 10 patients as a test set. Details of dataset can be found in Table 1 below.

Table 1. Dataset information

Dataset	Train	Test
Patient number	47	10
Patient with fracture number	19	3
Image number	10,500	1,154
Image with fracture number	1,480	144
Sweep video number	93	20
Sweep video with fracture number	26	5

2.2   Models

We first used UNet from Yakubovskiy [16]. The ResNet34 encoder was pre-trained on ImageNet [17] and no attention was added to the decoder. We set the output channel as 3, corresponding to 3 channels representing different bony structures in the mask. A sigmoid activation function ensured that the output ranged from 0 to 1. We added DICE loss to BCE loss as the loss function. We used the pix2pix model from Isola's work [9]. The generator used ResNet with 9 blocks and the discriminator used vanilla CNN as the default settings in the original pix2pix model. Cross entropy loss was used as the loss function. We also used model ensembles of UNet and GAN. After training UNet model, we applied trained UNet model on the dataset to get mask prediction for each image. Then we used the output mask prediction from UNet and ground truth masks as the input to the GAN. The goal is to generate new mask predictions and see if they are better than original UNet segmentation or GAN only segmentation. The UNet and GAN model architectures and loss functions are the same as the previous ones. All models were built on the PyTorch framework.

2.3   Data Preprocessing and Training Process

Images were normalized before being input into the network. Images and masks were kept as their original sizes (typically 512×512) for UNet and rescaled to 256×256 for pix2pix. All images were normalized with pixel value ranging from 0 to 255.

First, we trained UNet to segment wrist US and it produced predictions from UNet. Then we trained the pix2pix GAN model for segmentation: wrist US and ground truth masks were used as input to generate fake masks. Thirdly, we used output from UNet and ground truth masks to train another pix2pix model to see if GAN could help with UNet segmentation. The three models were trained independently and compared their performances based on several evaluation metrics. The overall training process is shown in Fig. 2.

We performed hyperparameter tuning on optimizer learning rate, regularization, batch size of three models. We used a batch size of 5, SGD optimizer with 0.01 learning rate and 0.99 momentum for UNet training and a batch size of 2, Adam optimizer with 0.0002 for pix2pix training. All models were trained on the training set for 100 epochs on V100 GPUs in the Compute Canada cluster. Models were then evaluated and compared on the test set using evaluation metrics including precision, recall, DICE score and Jaccard index.

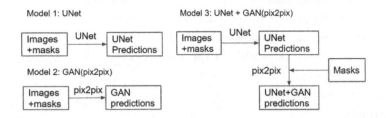

Fig. 2. Overall training process for three models.

3   Results

After training all models for 100 epochs on the training set, we evaluated each model's best performance on the test set. Some image slices at the edge of video sweeps were not optimally centred on bone and contained only a small bony region, so we resized the masks to 256 and excluded image slices with less than a threshold of 750 positive pixels, giving 1154 image slices in total. We then calculated the average evaluation metrics and standard deviation on the test set. Details were shown in Table 2 below.

Table 2. Quantitative results of model performances

Evaluation metrics	UNet	GAN	UNet+GAN
Precision (std)	**0.783** (0.123)	0.644 (0.110)	0.731 (0.121)
Recall (std)	0.642 (0.128)	**0.690** (0.135)	0.625 (0.125)
DICE score (std)	**0.698** (0.118)	0.659 (0.107)	0.665 (0.111)
Jaccard index (std)	**0.548** (0.126)	0.501 (0.110)	0.508 (0.113)

UNet performed the best on wrist US segmentation among all models and model ensembles in most quantitative ways since it achieved the highest precision, DICE score and Jaccard index. However, GAN reached the highest recall. The UNet+GAN model ensemble performed worse than the UNet model. Besides the UNet+GAN model ensemble precision, DICE score and Jaccard index were higher than GAN alone. According to the standard deviation, GAN model tended to generate a more stable prediction than the other two models.

We also performed student's t-test on evaluation metrics to analyze the statistical significance of three models. All model results were very highly significant from each other, with p-value less than 0.001 between two model results, except for the DICE score and Jaccard index between GAN and UNet+GAN model ensemble where p-values are 0.187 and 0.112 respectively. The 0.048 recall increase in GAN compared to UNet is statistically meaningful.

Original wrist US images from the test set, ground truth masks, and predictions of three models are shown in Fig. 3. On the masks and prediction images, the red region represents radial metaphysis structure and fractures, the green region represents radial epiphysis and the blue region represents carpal bones. The top image set in Fig. 2 shows a non-displaced fracture of the distal radial metaphysis and the bottom image set shows a normal wrist. Among all three models and model ensembles, UNet prediction results were closest to ground truth masks. The GAN model generates a smoother radial metaphysis and tends to give more negative predictions, as it failed to segment the small carpal bone region. UNet+GAN predictions are in between the other two models. For the first image with fracture, UNet and UNet+GAN clearly showed the bone discontinuity.

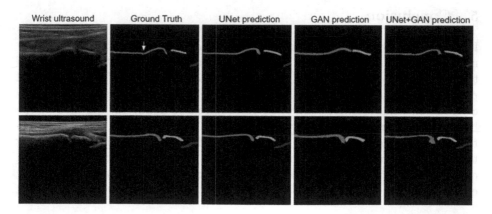

Fig. 3. Prediction results of different models. First row: distal radial fracture (arrow). Second row: no fracture. Red = metaphysis, green = epiphysis, blue = carpal bone. (Color figure online)

4   Discussion

In general, all models were able to model the broad outline of bony regions successfully. The characteristics such as speckles, low signal to noise ratio and low resolution make US segmentation a difficult task, but this was handled well by all architectures tested. The discontinuity predictions could indicate the fractures in wrist bones and have the potential for further bony fracture analysis.

Despite coarsening of features in the middle layers of UNet we found it was still highly successful at capturing even relatively fine image features and achieved the best segmentation in our experiments. GAN acquired the general bone shape through the training process but was less successful at delineating the details of each image. This is likely due to the fact that the generator is trained to fool the discriminator to believe the synthesized images are real. The discriminator is concerned mainly with whether the input could be reasonable or not and it does not concern itself with how precise the input is. Under such a rule, the generator tends to focus more on something that is common in the training set, rather than details or slight differences among training images. This is why GAN usually generates a rather smooth bony structure and the UNet model has better segmentation predictions than GAN. As UNet model predictions are more aggressive with more positive predictions than GAN, it has lower recall compared to GAN. Adding GAN to UNet is a compromise between the two models but in this study was not optimal. Strategies to further optimize fine detail in network segmentation of fractures include use of skip connections in the UNet and/or adjustments to loss functions to emphasize small changes in areas of particular interest such as the commonly fractured portion of distal radius.

5   Conclusion

In this study, we applied UNet and GAN models to segment bony anatomy in wrist ultrasound. We sought a new model ensemble methods for segmentation. All models gave generally visually satisfactory results. The UNet model performed the best based on the evaluation DICE score, precision and Jaccard Index, while GAN showed lower fidelity to fine detail but did achieve the highest recall. An ensemble network combining UNet+GAN did not provide further improvement. Our study demonstrates the feasibility of using deep learning techniques for automatic segmentation of bony anatomy on US images, which could eventually assist in future automatic detection of fractures in pediatric emergencies.

References

1. Reddy, U.M., Filly, R.A., Copel, J.A.: Prenatal imaging: ultrasonography and magnetic resonance imaging. Obstet. Gynecol. **112**(1), 145–157 (2008). https://doi.org/10.1097/01.AOG.0000318871.95090.d9
2. Eckert, K., Ackermann, O., Schweiger, B., Radeloff, E., Liedgens, P.: Sonographic diagnosis of metaphyseal forearm fractures in children: a safe and applicable alternative to standard X-rays. Pediatr. Emerg. Care **28**, 851–854 (2012)
3. Eckert, K., Ackermann, O., Schweiger, B., Radeloff, E., Liedgens, P.: Ultrasound as a viable alternative to standard X-rays for the diagnosis of distal forearm fractures in children. Zeitschrift Orthop. Unfallchirurgie **150**, 409–414 (2012)

4. Slabaugh, G., Unal, G., Wels, M., Fang, T., Rao, B.: Statistical region-based segmentation of ultrasound images. Ultrasound Med. Biol. **35**(5), 781–95 (2009)
5. Ronneberger, O., Fischer, P., Brox, T.: U-net: convolutional networks for biomedical image segmentation. In: Navab, N., Hornegger, J., Wells, W.M., Frangi, A.F. (eds.) MICCAI 2015. LNCS, vol. 9351, pp. 234–241. Springer, Cham (2015). https://doi.org/10.1007/978-3-319-24574-4_28
6. Jin, J., et al.: Multiple U-net-based automatic segmentations and radiomics feature stability on ultrasound images for patients with ovarian cancer. Front. Oncol. **10**, 614201 (2021)
7. Goodfellow, I., et al.: Generative adversarial nets. In: Proceedings of the 27th International Conference on Neural Information Processing Systems, pp. 2672–2680 (2014)
8. Isola, P., Zhu, J., Zhou, T., Efros, A.A.: Image-to-image translation with conditional adversarial networks. In: 2017 IEEE Conference on Computer Vision and Pattern Recognition (CVPR), pp. 5967–5976 (2017)
9. Lewis, A., Mahmoodi, E., Zhou, Y., Coffee, M., Sizikova, E.: Improving tuberculosis (TB) prediction using synthetically generated computed tomography (CT) images. In: ICCV Computer Vision for Automated Medical Diagnosis (CVAMD) Workshop (2021)
10. Abdelmotaal, H., Abdou, A.A., Omar, A.F., El-Sebaity, D.M., Abdelazeem, K.: Pix2pix conditional generative adversarial networks for scheimpflug camera color-coded corneal tomography image generation. Transl. Vis. Sci. Technol. **10**(7), 21 (2021)
11. Tsuda, H., Hotta, K.: Cell image segmentation by integrating pix2pixs for each class. In: 2019 IEEE/CVF Conference on Computer Vision and Pattern Recognition Workshops (CVPRW), pp. 1065–1073 (2019)
12. Popescu, D., Deaconu, M., Ichim, L., Stamatescu, G.: Retinal blood vessel segmentation using pix2pix GAN. In: 2021 29th Mediterranean Conference on Control and Automation (MED), pp. 1173–1178 (2021)
13. Nanni, L., Cuza, D., Lumini, A., Loreggia, A., Brahnam, S: Deep ensembles in bioimage segmentation (2021). arXiv:2112.12955
14. Dolz, J., Desrosiers, C., Wang, L., Yuan, J., Shen, D., Ayed, I.B.: Deep CNN ensembles and suggestive annotations for infant brain MRI segmentation. Comput. Med. Imaging Graph. **79**, 101660 (2020)
15. Thambawita, V.L., Hicks, S., Halvorsen P., Riegler, M., DivergentNets: Medical image segmentation by network ensemble. EndoCV@ISBI (2021)
16. Yakubovskiy, P.: Segmentation models Pytorch. GitHub. GitHub repository. https://github.com/qubvel/segmentation_models.pytorch
17. Deng, J., Dong, W., Socher, R., Li, L.J., Li, K., Li, F.F.: ImageNet: a large-scale hierarchical image database. In: 2009 IEEE Conference on Computer Vision and Pattern Recognition, pp. 248–255 (2009)

Early Detection and Classification of Patient-Ventilator Asynchrony Using Machine Learning

Erdi Gao[1](✉), Goce Ristanoski[1](✉), Uwe Aickelin[1], David Berlowitz[2], and Mark Howard[2]

[1] School of Computing and Information Systems, The University of Melbourne, Melbourne, Australia
egao@student.unimelb.edu.au, gri@unimelb.edu.au
[2] The University of Melbourne and the Institute for Breathing and Sleep, Austin Hospital, Melbourne, Australia

Abstract. During mechanical ventilation, a common problem known as patient-ventilator asynchrony (PVA) occurs when there is a mismatch between the needs of the patient's breathing and the breath cycle delivered by the ventilator. PVA is problematic because it can be associated with adverse effects such as discomfort for the patient, increased work of breathing, longer mechanical ventilation duration and ventilator-induced lung injury. An automated means of early PVA detection and classification could lead to improved health outcomes and help reduce the impact of PVA on hospital resources. This paper presents a machine learning framework to detect PVA events using only the first half second of data after the start of a PVA event. When trained on more than 5000 PVA events sampled from 25 subjects, our logistic classifier achieves a sensitivity (specificity) of 99.81% (99.72%) for detecting PVA events. We then present a system capable of early classification of Ineffective Effort (IE) and Double Trigger (DT) events, which achieves a sensitivity (specificity) of 63.73% (92.88%). By demonstrating the feasibility of early PVA event detection and classification, our findings suggest that more effective intervention processes could be possible, including automated interventions with different response strategies for different PVA event types.

Keywords: Patient-ventilator asynchrony · Classification · Data mining

1 Introduction

Mechanical ventilation is a widely used treatment for patients who need assistance with improving oxygenation and unloading the respiratory muscles [1]. In earlier years, mechanical ventilation was predominantly used in intensive care units. In recent years, technological advancements have seen ventilators used in a wider range of settings, including the transport of critically ill patients, at

M. Michalowski et al. (Eds.): AIME 2022, LNAI 13263, pp. 238–248, 2022.
https://doi.org/10.1007/978-3-031-09342-5_23

home, and even on commercial aircraft [2]. It is also now well understood that ventilators play a critical role during events causing mass respiratory failure such as the 2002 SARS outbreak and the COVID-19 pandemic [3,4].

During mechanical ventilation, a common problem is patient-ventilator asynchrony (PVA) which occurs when there is a mismatch between the needs of the patient's breathing and the breath cycle delivered by the ventilator [5]. PVA is problematic because it is associated with adverse effects such as discomfort for the patient, increased work of breathing, longer mechanical ventilation duration and ventilator-induced lung injury [6].

One approach for reducing PVA begins with identifying individual PVA events; clinicians can then use this data to better adapt the ventilator to the patient by adjusting the ventilator settings [7]. However, the current non-invasive method used to identify the various types of PVA events relies on the manual analysis of waveform data obtained from the mechanical ventilator [8]. As such, the requirements for staff training, skills and time input are significant, and the adjustments to the treatment are periodic instead of one time only.

While there has been significant progress made towards automated detection and classification of PVA events, there have been very few studies focused on the early detection and classification of PVA events. If PVA events could be detected earlier, this would open up the possibility of a ventilator that can automatically adapt itself to the patients needs, which could help reduce the occurrence of PVA and thus improve patient health outcomes. Previous research has relied mostly on features that were developed specifically for the purpose of PVA analysis, but which are generally not suitable for early detection, such as waveform valley depth in the expiratory phase [14].

The waveforms used for PVA detection are time series data, and there is an extensive collection of time series characteristics from other domains - including basic statistics, distribution, correlation and entropy measures - which have been shown to be informative for performing classification across a diverse range of data sets [9]. To the best of the authors knowledge, these time series characteristics have not yet been explored as features for PVA. This paper will investigate whether such time series characteristics are useful for early PVA event detection and classification. The main contributions of this work are:

- To address the gap in current research on automated PVA detection and classification, by proposing a system capable of early detection and classification. In this paper, early detection and classification is said to occur when PVA events are detected and classified in the first 500 ms after the start of a PVA event.
- To explore opportunities for multiple class detection and classification of PVA events. This is desirable as it could allow the ventilator to respond differently based on the type of PVA event.

2   Related Works

Various AI systems have been developed to perform automatic detection and classification of PVA events. Earlier works focused on a rule-based approach whereby a PVA event is detected when predetermined threshold values of waveform derived features are satisfied [10–12]. Since rule-based systems require explicit expressions of decision rules formulated by human experts, such systems can be expensive to build and update, and may be less robust [13]. More recently, studies have investigated the use of machine learning techniques for PVA event detection and classification [14,15]. Provided with data labels and a set of features, a classifier can be trained to automatically learn the relationship between an outcome and the input features, and hence it can learn the subtleties between different types of PVA events and thus make predictions.

An alternative to using hand-crafted features is to use learned features which are obtained by training a neural network. This approach has achieved good results [16], but the black-box nature and lack of interpretability of deep learning models remains an unsolved challenge [17]. Additionally, some researchers have argued that such opaque models fail to elicit trust, and restrict physician-patient dialogue [18]. In contrast, white-box models offer greater interpretability since the way in which features are combined to make a prediction can be clearly explained in the form of a much simpler model.

Most existing machine learning approaches use domain specific features which require the use of data from both the inspiratory and expiratory phase of the breath cycle and thus are not suitable for early PVA detection [14,15,19]. One way to overcome this limitation is to use a data-driven approach which is based on the empirical nature of the data, without relying on domain knowledge or assumptions about the underlying data generation process. A data-driven approach to PVA detection by using similarity and randomness measures has been proposed by [20] . While this approach did not directly address early detection, the findings demonstrate that domain knowledge independent features can provide useful additional information when detecting PVA events.

More broadly, [21] has collected and organised a wide range of techniques which had been developed within other disciplines, to understand the underlying structure and characteristics of time series data. The authors found that when effective feature selection methods were used, these time series features could achieve highly comparable results on a diverse range of data sets including, heart beat intervals, speech signals, and electroencephalogram (EEG) seizure data. Based on these findings, we propose to explore the use of a similar data-driven feature generation approach for early PVA detection and classification.

3   Dataset Description

The data used for this research was initially collected for a randomized control trial approved by the Research Ethics Board of Austin Health (Melbourne, Australia) [22]. The study consisted of a cohort of 58 individuals, mostly with neuromuscular disorders who were supported by noninvasive ventilation (NIV). The aim of the sleep study was to investigate if the use of polysomnographic (PSG) titration of NIV is associated with less PVA and less sleep disruption. This paper assumes that whilst the PSG titration treatment may reduce the number of PVA events experienced by an individual, it would not significantly change the way PVA events are represented in terms of signal waveforms. Thus, no distinction will be made between pre-treatment or post-treatment data. With data available for 58 individuals from the pre-treatment study and 43 individuals from the post-treatment study, we have a total of 101 subject data sets.

In addition to common ventilator readings such as mask pressure and airflow, other measures that were relevant to the sleep study were collected during overnight in-laboratory studies, including thoracic and abdominal movement, eye muscle movement and EMG (refer Appendix for a complete list). Labels indicating the start timestamp, end timestamp and event type for various PVA and sleep disruption events were also provided by a group of respiratory experts based on the signal waveforms.

The PVA index is defined as the number of asynchrony events per hour of sleep. From Fig. 1[a], a high variability of PVA index is observed across the subjects, ranging from 11 to 390. A break down of all labeled events is shown in Fig. 1[b]. Ineffective Effort (IE) comprises about 46% of labeled events, with Double Trigger (DT) at 23% and Autocycle (AC) at 11%. Arousal (AASM), SpO2 artifact and SpO2 desaturation are classed as sleep disruption events, not PVA events and thus will not be considered as part of this paper.

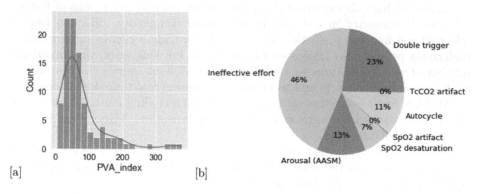

Fig. 1. [a] Histogram showing the distribution of PVA index across all subjects. [b] Pie chart showing the percentage for PVA and sleep disruption events.

4 Methods

4.1 Feature Extraction

In this paper we consider the detection and classification of three PVA event types - Ineffective Effort (IE), Double Trigger (DT) and Autocycle (AC) - which are the most prevalent and clinically significant PVA events [6,23]. In order to obtain a more balanced training set, we used hierarchical clustering - a method which creates nested clusters by successively merging subjects - to select a group of 35 subjects who have a higher percentage of both DT and AC events.

Signals were first re-sampled at a 100 ms interval as many of the signals were originally sampled at different frequencies. The PVA event samples were obtained by taking the first 500 ms of continuous waveform data from the start of a PVA event. Non PVA samples were obtained by taking 500 ms of continuous waveform data that had not been labeled as containing any asynchronies. To reduce the feature extraction computation time, one third of the PVA events for each subject were randomly sampled and a similar number of non PVA events were used. The non PVA samples were taken randomly across the entire over-night sleep study to ensure that they covered a large variety of non PVA breathing cycles.

To avoid reinventing the wheel, the time series properties were calculated from two publicly available python libraries: TSFEL and TSFRESH. Each library provides feature calculation algorithms based on features that have been described in the scientific literature on time-series analysis from a broad range of disciplines, in addition to features commonly used in classical statistics. During implementation, features that were not suitable for the targeted time series for this research were excluded. For example, the ARMA model fit feature was not included because it tends to not work well for a small sample size. The remaining features from each library were then combined together which resulted in 397 features; these features were then calculated for all available signals.

Given the high dimension of the feature space, an effective means of feature selection is necessary in order to reduce model complexity. Effective feature selection can improve prediction accuracy and provide a clearer picture of the underlying process that generated the data [24]. For this work, we limited the number of selected features to 10, which is a reasonable number of features to explain to domain experts and to be deployed during real-time deployment.

Multiple feature selection methods were tested including mutual information (filter method), logistic regression with L1 regularisation, XGboost and Light-GBM (embedded method).

In addition to generating and selecting a set of features from all 20 available signals, we also extracted a set of features using only 4 health expert suggested signals: *Pmask*, *Flow-Tx*, *Abdo* and *Thor*.

4.2   Classification

Since the target labels have been provided by the health experts, supervised machine learning models were developed. We decided to perform two stage classification, so that different sets of features, and different feature selection methods could be used for each learning task.

Binary classification was performed to differentiate PVA events from non-PVA data, followed by multiclass classification to determine if the PVA event is IE or DT.

Both decision tree and logistic regression (with L2 regularisation) were tested for binary classification. In the binary classification setting, logistic regression is a commonly used machine learning algorithm, and is also able to provide insights on the relationship between features and target variables through its interpretable coefficients. Tree representation is popular among medical scientists [25], however preliminary results with this approach were poor and thus it was not pursued further.

Having separated PVA events from non-PVA data, classification was then performed to differentiate IE from DT, without the presence of AC, since IE and DT are the most prevalent forms of PVA events and together make up about 90% of total PVA events (excluding arousal, refer Fig. 1[b]). Multiclass classification on IE, DT and AC was attempted, however performance was poor and thus the results were not included in this paper. Classification was applied to events labelled as IE and DT in the actual dataset, rather than using the predictions. A voting ensemble model that combines predictions from multiple other models including logistic regression, XGBoost and LGBoost was developed and was found to produce a better result than any single one of these models.

4.3 Model Evaluation

Classification metrics were evaluated using the hold out method. 25 subjects were randomly selected for training the model and the remaining unseen 10 subjects were used for testing. Sensitivity and specificity - which measure the proportion of true positives to actual positives, and true negatives to actual negatives respectively - were calculated based on the test data set and were used as the primary metrics. The number of training and testing instances is summarised in Table 1.

Table 1. Number of subjects, PVA events and non PVA events (regular breathing data) for the training and test set

	Subjects	Ineffective effort	Double trigger	Autocycle	Non PVA
Training set	25	1831	2228	1563	5673
Test set	10	568	674	326	2483

5 Results and Discussion

5.1 Binary Classification: PVA Detection

The first classifier performs binary classification to detect PVA, that is, to differentiate between the PVA events (IE, DT and AC) and non-PVA breathing data. We present the results of a logistic classifier with L2 regularisation trained on features selected via logistic regression with L1 regularisation. The performance is found to be superior to other feature selection and classification methods when applied to our data set. The resulting sensitivity and specificity when using domain expert recommended signals and when using all available signals is summarised in Table 2. Using all available signals slightly improves the sensitivity and slightly reduces the specificity, although the differences are found

Table 2. Binary classification (PVA detection) performance statistics (Note: PPV = Positive Predictive Value, NPV = Negative Predictive Value)

	Sensitivity	Specificity	PPV	NPV
Using all available signals	100%	99.40%	99.05%	100%
Using expert recommended signals	99.81%	99.72%	99.55%	99.88%

Table 3. PVA detection - list of the 10 selected features

Using all available signals
PtcCO2: Spectral skew of absolute Fourier transform spectrum, **PtcCO2:** Spectral variance of absolute Fourier transform spectrum, **PtcCO2:** Sample entropy, **Pos:** Coefficients of a Langevin model polynomial, **Thor:** Approximate entropy, **Flow-Tx:** Cumulative sum of samples less than percentile (40%), **E2:** Time series has a large standard deviation (true/false), **E2:** Sample entropy, **F4-M1:** Sample entropy, **O2-M1:** Sample entropy

Using expert recommended signals
Pmask: Augmented Dickey-Fuller test statistic, **Pmask:** Spectral skew of absolute fourier transform spectrum, **Pmask:** Relative index (i) of time series where 40% of time series mass lies left of i, **Pmask:** Count of observed values that are negative, **Pmask:** Variation coefficient, **Thor:** Augmented Dickey-Fuller test statistic, **Abdo:** Augmented Dickey-Fuller test statistic, **Abdo:** Coefficients of a Langevin model polynomial, **Abdo:** Sum of all data points which appear more than once, **Abdo:** Sum of any time series values that appear more than once

to be relatively small. Table 3 lists the 10 features selected when using all available signals and when using the expert recommended signals; we note that these two approaches do not share any features in common, despite achieving similar performance.

5.2   Multiclass Classification: IE and DT Classification

The second classifier performs classification on the detected PVA events, to identify which type of PVA event (IE or DT) occurred. The resulting sensitivity and specificity when using domain expert recommended signals and when using all available signals is summarised in Table 4; we note that the ensemble classifier performance is the same for both cases.

5.3   Clinical Relevance

The above results demonstrate that early detection and classification of PVA is indeed possible. Since our proposed machine learning system was able to identify PVA events during the first 500 ms of a PVA event, a natural next step would be to try shifting the time window earlier to see if the PVA event can be predicted as soon as it begins. This could potentially enable the ventilator to continuously adapt to the changing respiratory dynamics of patients, and thus further reduce the number of PVA events. If this predictive system could

Table 4. Multiclass classification (IE vs DT) performance statistics (Note: PPV = Positive Predictive Value, NPV = Negative Predictive Value. IE is defined as the positive class.)

Algorithm	Sensitivity	Specificity	PPV	NPV	Accuracy
Using all available signals					
Voting ensemble	63.73%	92.88%	88.29%	75.24%	79.55%
Logistic regression	74.12%	66.02%	64.77%	75.17%	69.73%
XGBoost	73.59%	80.42%	76.00%	78.32%	77.29%
LightGBM	33.10%	97.63%	92.16%	63.39%	68.12%
Using expert recommended signals					
Voting ensemble	63.73%	92.88%	88.29%	75.24%	79.55%
Logistic regression	75.18%	65.28%	64.60%	75.73%	69.81%
XGBoost	73.77%	81.16%	76.74%	78.59%	77.78%
LightGBM	37.68%	96.74%	90.68%	64.81%	69.73%

achieve similar classification performance to the system we have proposed - that is, accurate classification of IE and DT - this could enable different response strategies to be implemented, depending on the type of PVA event predicted. As well as improving patient outcomes, since reduced PVA is associated with shorter hospital stays [26], this technology could also help further reduce the impact of PVA on hospital resources.

The proposed machine learning approach could also contribute new insights towards existing medical knowledge. For example, the proposed machine learning system identified some additional signals (E2, F4-M1 and O2-M1) containing valuable information for PVA event detection, which had not been identified by the domain expert. When classifying between IE and DT events, while most of the selected signals were consistent with the domain expert recommended signals, there was one signal that had not been suggested by the expert: *Leak - Tx*, which measures the air leakage from the NIV mask. The results are also interpretable, which could lead to further insights; for example, we found that when comparing PVA events to non-PVA events, the first half second of a PVA event is characterised by a much larger spectral skewness of the absolute Fourier transform of Pmask. These findings could potentially be used to help improve domain experts understanding of PVA and to guide further studies.

In future work, in addition to exploring earlier detection and classification of PVA, we also hope to carry out additional model validation (including cross validation and model validation using a larger number of patients), include AC in the multiclass classification and explore the use of neural networks.

6   Conclusion

A data-driven approach, involving an extensive search through hundreds of time series properties, was used to develop a machine learning system capable of early

PVA event detection and classification. When trained on 5673 non-PVA events
and 5622 PVA events it achieved a sensitivity (specificity) of 99.81% (99.72%) for
detecting PVA events. The results indicate that not only is PVA event detection
possible, but even earlier detection is a promising research direction that could
lead to an automated detection solution ready for clinical testing. Our findings
show that these methods are independent of any patient specific features and can
rely on the breathing data only, making the use of AI for PVA event detection
a promising research field.

Appendix - Description of Signals

Signal name	Description
Oximetry	Blood oxygen levels, displayed as a percentage
PtcCO2	Transcutaneous carbon dioxide
Leak - Tx	Air leakage from NIV mask
Pos	Body position sensor: back-supine, front-prone, sides-left and right
Light	Environmental light sensor (lights "on" or "off")
Pmask	NIV mask pressure signal
Thor	Breathing effort detected by respiratory belt placed over thoracic region
Abdo	Breathing effort detected by respiratory belt placed over abdominal region
Flow - Tx	Airflow through nasal prongs
DB Meter	Decibel meter to detect snoring
ECG+ECG-	Cardiac activity and heart rate
EMGs+- EMGs-	Electromyogram - electrodes placed on both sides of the jaw (bilateral masseter muscles) to detect clenching of the jaw (bruxism) during sleep
E1	Picks up eye muscle movement (E1 and E2). Electrode placed on outer corner of left eye
E2	Electrode placed on outer corner of right eye
F4-M1	Electrode placed on right side of head over the frontal area. Note: M1 refers to reference electrode placed over left mastoid bone area behind the left ear
C4-M1	Electrode placed on right side of the head, centrally
O2-M1	Electrode place on right side of the head, towards the lower back
dEMG+-dEMG-	Electromyogram - electrodes placed over diaphragm area
atEMG/L_T3-atEMG	Electromyogram - electrodes placed on left anterior tibialis muscle on the shin to detect periodic limb movement (PLM) during sleep
atEMG/R_T4-atEMG	Electromyogram-electrodes placed on right anterior tibialis muscle on the shin to detect PLM during sleep
Nasal pressure	Pressure signal derived from nasal prongs

Source: Austin PSG Studies Team

References

1. Murias, G., Lucangelo, U., Blanch, L.: Patient-ventilator asynchrony. Curr. Opin. Crit. Care **22**(1), 53–59 (2016). https://doi.org/10.1097/MCC.0000000000000270
2. Chang, D.W.: Clinical Application of Mechanical Ventilation. Cengage Learning (2013)
3. Daugherty, E.L., Branson, R., Rubinson, L.: Mass casualty respiratory failure. Curr. Opin. Crit. Care **13**(1), 51–56 (2007)
4. Ge, H., et al.: Lung mechanics of mechanically ventilated patients with COVID-19: analytics with high-granularity ventilator waveform data. Front. Med. **7**, 541 (2020)
5. Sassoon, C.S., Foster, G.T.: Patient-ventilator asynchrony. Curr. Opin. Crit. Care **7**(1), 28–33 (2001). https://doi.org/10.1097/00075198-200102000-00005
6. Epstein, S.K.: How often does patient-ventilator asynchrony occur and what are the consequences? Respir. Care **56**(1), 25–38 (2011). https://doi.org/10.4187/respcare.01009
7. Wrigge, H., Girrbach, F., Hempel, G.: Detection of patient-ventilator asynchrony should be improved: and then what? J. Thorac. Dis. **8**(12), E1661–E1664 (2016). https://doi.org/10.21037/jtd.2016.12.101
8. Arellano, D.H.: Identifying patient-ventilator asynchrony using waveform analysis. Palliat. Med. Care: Open Access **4**(4), 1–4 (2017). https://doi.org/10.15226/2374-8362/4/4/00147
9. Fulcher, B.D., Jones, N.S.: Highly comparative feature-based time-series classification. IEEE Trans. Knowl. Data Eng. **26**(12), 3026–3037 (2014). https://doi.org/10.1109/tkde.2014.2316504
10. Mulqueeny, Q., Ceriana, P., Carlucci, A., Fanfulla, F., Delmastro, M., Nava, S.: Automatic detection of ineffective triggering and double triggering during mechanical ventilation. Intensive Care Med. **33**(11), 2014–2018 (2007). https://doi.org/10.1007/s00134-007-0767-z
11. Chen, C.-W., Lin, W.-C., Hsu, C.-H., Cheng, K.-S., Lo, C.-S.: Detecting ineffective triggering in the expiratory phase in mechanically ventilated patients based on airway flow and pressure deflection: Feasibility of using a computer algorithm*. Crit. Care Med. **36**(2), 455–461 (2008). https://doi.org/10.1097/01.ccm.0000299734.34469.d9
12. Cuvelier, A., Achour, L., Rabarimanantsoa, H., Letellier, C., Muir, J.-F., Fauroux, B.: A noninvasive method to identify ineffective triggering in patients with non-invasive pressure support ventilation. Respiration **80**(3), 198–206 (2010). https://doi.org/10.1159/000264606
13. Yu, K.H., Beam, A.L., Kohane, I.S.: Artificial intelligence in healthcare. Nat. Biomed. Eng. **2**(10), 719–731 (2018). https://doi.org/10.1038/s41551-018-0305-z
14. Gholami, B., et al.: Replicating human expertise of mechanical ventilation waveform analysis in detecting patient-ventilator cycling asynchrony using machine learning. Comput. Biol. Med. **97**, 137–144 (2018). https://doi.org/10.1016/j.compbiomed.2018.04.016
15. Rehm, G., et al.: Creation of a robust and generalizable machine learning classifier for patient ventilator asynchrony. Methods Inf. Med. **57**(04), 208–219 (2018). https://doi.org/10.3414/me17-02-0012
16. Zhang, L., et al.: Detection of patient-ventilator asynchrony from mechanical ventilation waveforms using a two-layer long short-term memory neural network. Comput. Biol. Med. **120**, 103721 (2020). https://doi.org/10.1016/j.compbiomed.2020.103721

17. Ching, T., et al.: Opportunities and obstacles for deep learning in biology and medicine: 2019 update (2019)
18. Quinn, T.P., Jacobs, S., Senadeera, M., Le, V., Coghlan, S.: The three ghosts of medical AI: can the black-box present deliver? Artif. Intell. Med. **124**, 102158 (2021). https://doi.org/10.1016/j.artmed.2021.102158
19. Mulqueeny, Q., et al.: Automated detection of asynchrony in patient-ventilator interaction. In: 2009 Annual International Conference of the IEEE Engineering in Medicine and Biology Society, pp. 5324–5327. IEEE, September 2009
20. Wang, C., Aickelin, U., Luo, L., Ristanoski, G.: Patient-ventilator asynchrony detection via similarity search methods. In: ICMHI 2021 Proceeding, vol. 13, no. 1, pp. 15–20. ACM Press (2021). https://doi.org/10.12720/jait.13.1.15-20
21. Fulcher, B.D., Little, M.A., Jones, N.S.: Highly comparative time-series analysis: the empirical structure of time series and their methods. J. R. Soc. Interface **10**(83), 20130048 (2013). https://doi.org/10.1098/rsif.2013.0048
22. Hannan, L.M., et al.: Randomised controlled trial of polysomnographic titration of noninvasive ventilation. Eur. Respiratory J. **53**(5), 1802118 (2019). https://doi.org/10.1183/13993003.02118-2018
23. Thille, A.W., Rodriguez, P., Cabello, B., Lellouche, F., Brochard, L.: Patient-ventilator asynchrony during assisted mechanical ventilation. Intensive Care Med. **32**(10), 1515–1522 (2006). https://doi.org/10.1007/s00134-006-0301-8
24. Guyon, I., Elisseeff, A.: An introduction to variable and feature selection. J. Mach. Learn. Res. **3**, 1157–1182 (2003)
25. Hastie, T., Tibshirani, R., Friedman, J.H.: The Elements of Statistical Learning: Data Mining, Inference, and Prediction, 2nd edn. Springer, New York (2009). https://doi.org/10.1007/978-0-387-84858-7
26. De Wit, M., Miller, K.B., Green, D.A., Ostman, H.E., Gennings, C., Epstein, S.K.: Ineffective triggering predicts increased duration of mechanical ventilation*. Crit. Care Med. **37**(10), 2740–2745 (2009). https://doi.org/10.1097/ccm.0b013e3181a98a05

On Graph Construction for Classification of Clinical Trials Protocols Using Graph Neural Networks

Sohrab Ferdowsi[1,2]([✉]) [ID], Jenny Copara[1,3] [ID], Racha Gouareb[1] [ID], Nikolay Borissov[4] [ID], Fernando Jaume-Santero[1,2] [ID], Poorya Amini[4] [ID], and Douglas Teodoro[1,2,3] [ID]

[1] Department of Radiology and Medical Informatics, University of Geneva, Geneva, Switzerland
{sohrab.ferdowsi,douglas.teodoro}@unige.ch
[2] Business Information Systems, University of Applied Sciences and Arts of Western Switzerland (HES-SO), Geneva, Switzerland
[3] Swiss Institute of Bioinformatics, Lausanne, Switzerland
[4] Risklick AG, Bern, Switzerland

Abstract. A recent trend in health-related machine learning proposes the use of Graph Neural Networks (GNN's) to model biomedical data. This is justified due to the complexity of healthcare data and the modelling power of graph abstractions. Thus, GNN's emerge as the natural choice to learn from increasing amounts of healthcare data. While formulating the problem, however, there are usually multiple design choices and decisions that can affect the final performance. In this work, we focus on Clinical Trial (CT) protocols consisting of hierarchical documents, containing free text as well as medical codes and terms, and design a classifier to predict each CT protocol termination risk as "low" or "high". We show that while using GNN's to solve this classification task is very successful, the way the graph is constructed is also of importance and one can benefit from making a priori useful information more explicit. While a natural choice is to consider each CT protocol as an independent graph and pose the problem as a graph classification, consistent performance improvements can be achieved by considering them as super-nodes in one unified graph and connecting them according to some metadata, like similar medical condition or intervention, and finally approaching the problem as a node classification task rather than graph classification. We validate this hypothesis experimentally on a large-scale manually labeled CT database. This provides useful insights on the flexibility of graph-based modeling for machine learning in the healthcare domain.

Keywords: Graph Neural Networks · Machine learning · Natural language processing · Clinical Trials · Healthcare informatics

1 Introduction

Healthcare-related events and the underlying clinical data sources are typically highly heterogeneous, irregular, consisting of multiple modalities and dealing with various semantic representations [13,24]. The patients records during multiple visits to care

© The Author(s), under exclusive license to Springer Nature Switzerland AG 2022
M. Michalowski et al. (Eds.): AIME 2022, LNAI 13263, pp. 249–259, 2022.
https://doi.org/10.1007/978-3-031-09342-5_24

centers, the large body of medical text generated in hospitals, the multiple imaging modalities required for diagnosis and various other sources like lab reports are potentially all relevant in healthcare practice [22]. A natural choice to model these variations in a unified manner would be the use of graphs, where nodes, edges and features have the flexibility, as well as the capacity to hold these interrelated sources of data, and under many different scenarios [22,23].

While the literature of machine learning and its related fields has evolved primarily to deal with regular grid-like sources of data, recent years have seen significant activities to generalize machine learning concepts to graph-based data. This has given rise to the field of geometric deep learning [1] with high promise and noticeable success using Graph Neural Networks (GNN's) across various disciplines that can benefit from graph-based representations (see e.g., [10] and [21] on the use of GNN's in natural sciences).

The domains of healthcare informatics and machine learning in medicine, therefore, have seen significant activities in this direction and many works have shown promising results in the integration of GNN's to tackle healthcare-related problems. As an example, the work of [3] uses GNN's to supplement Electronic Health Records (EHR) with hierarchical information, showing noticeable improvements in diagnosis prediction compared to Recurrent Neural Networks (RNN's). Similarly, the work of [20] uses GNN's combined with neural language models to better capture the hierarchical structure of medical codes and perform medication recommendation from EHR's. Several prediction tasks again based on EHR's are addressed in the work of [31], where the authors propose a regularization technique to improve the robustness of training.

While the use of GNN's has been shown to be very effective, in this work, we show that the way the graph is constructed and the problem is formulated is also of prime importance. In particular, we build up on our prior work [7], where we encode Clinical Trials (CT) protocols in a hierarchical graph to predict their termination risk, by further linking them with edges according to connections between the CT phases, conditions and interventions. Therefore, rather than considering multiple disconnected graphs and posing the problem as graph classification, we consider a single but very large graph and target a node classification problem to classify CT protocols. Interestingly, while all these newly considered edges between graphs arise directly from the CT protocols and do not contain any extra information that is not already encoded as node features, we show that under all setups, this new formulation, not drastically but very consistently improves the CT classification performance.

2 Background and Related Works

In this section, we showcase the required backgrounds and review some of the relevant methods and efforts in the literature. Section 2.1 discussed data-driven CT risk analysis, which is the main task we target in this paper. Since our proposed methodology is the use of GNN's to tackle this problem, we review some basic concepts of graph-based machine learning in Sect. 2.2. We then very briefly discuss the concept of text featurization in Sect. 2.3.

2.1 Data-Driven Efforts for CT Risk Analyses

The systematic way to assess the safety and efficacy of candidate clinical interventions and medications for the treatment of medical conditions is to carry out randomized studies, a.k.a. Clinical Trials (CT's), on volunteer subjects and during multiple phases. Because of their complexity and extent of the resources needed for these studies, they take around 60–70% of the average 13.8 years long drug development cycle [18] and constitute a major portion of the average estimated 1.3B$ cost for drug development [29]. In spite of the very strict guidelines in place from healthcare authorities and careful planning of trials prior to their execution, unfortunately, no more than only 14% of CT's manage to continue from phase 1 to the market approval [28]. Therefore, in order to minimize these costs and the associated risks, it would be highly beneficial to try to optimize CT protocols prior to their implementation.

Although there are various government registries that provide access to past and current CT records to the public, there has been only few works in the literature reporting data-driven methods to assess the behavior of CT's based on simple risk measures. The works of [9] and [11] use traditional data-mining techniques to classify termination risk of CT's. The more recent work of [5] uses hand-crafted features and feeds them to off-the-shelf classifiers to target "completed" and "terminated" CT status categories. Similar methodologies have been developed in [6] to assess COVID-19 CT's.

To benefit from the power of end-to-end deep learning and to avoid using hand-crafted approaches, our recent work [7] targeted the CT classification problem using GNN's. This was motivated by the highly hierarchical structure of CT's as shown in Fig. 1, where besides their textual content, also the structure of the protocols was shown to be relevant for risk classification, an assumption that was strongly corroborated by the significant performance gains reported. In this work, we revisit this approach by reformulating the graph-based CT classification and show performance improvements. Before presenting our proposed method in Sect. 3, we briefly review some basic concepts from graphs and graph-based machine learning.

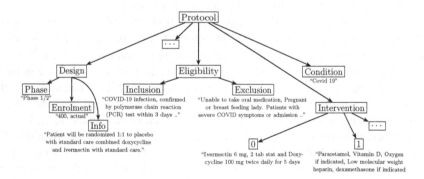

Fig. 1. Simplified schematic view of a CT protocol. Leaf nodes contain free text and medical codes. While the top parent nodes are fixed, children nodes have variable structure across CT examples within the same registry.

2.2   Graph Neural Networks

In its most abstract, yet practically powerful form for many applications, a graph $\mathcal{G} = (\mathcal{V}, \mathcal{E}; \mathcal{X})$ consists of node sets $\mathcal{V} = \{v_1, \cdots, v_{|\mathcal{V}|}\}$, the set of edges $\mathcal{E}$ with pairs of nodes (u_i, v_i), which denote the existence of an edge between the two nodes $u_i, v_i \in \mathcal{V}$, as well as a set of features $\mathcal{X} = \{\mathbf{x}_1, \cdots, \mathbf{x}_{|\mathcal{V}|}\}$ associated to each of the nodes (and/or also to the edges in some applications).

Graph Neural Networks (GNN's) try to generalize the deep learning practice and machine learning concepts to a graph $\mathcal{G}$, or multiple graph objects $\{\mathcal{G}_1, \cdots, \mathcal{G}_N\}$. This, however, is more challenging to deal with than the case of regular grids like images, text, sound or time series data. The difficulty lies primarily in that, unlike grids, there does not usually exist a canonical way to order nodes of a given graph. Hence, all machine learning steps should be agnostic to node orderings[1], both within a graph and also across multiple graphs.

A largely successful approach to tackle this permutation ambiguity is the Message Passing (MP) paradigm of [12], which replaces some of the usual list operation steps of machine learning with set operations that are order-agnostic. Concretely, for a node $u \in \mathcal{V}$ the nodes $v \in \mathcal{N}(u) = \{v \in \mathcal{V} | (v, u) \in \mathcal{E}\}$ in its immediate neighborhood send a "message" using a generic differentiable "aggregation" operation $\mathbb{A}\{\cdots\}$ on their features. This is then used to "update" the features of $\mathbf{u}$, using another generic differentiable operation $\mathbb{U}[\cdot, \cdot]$. These steps can be summarized as:

$$\mathbf{x}_u^{[l+1]} = \mathbb{U}\left[\mathbf{x}_u^{[l]}; \mathbb{A}\left\{\mathbf{x}_v^{[l]}, \forall v \in \mathcal{N}(u)\right\}\right], \tag{1}$$

where super-scripts $1, \cdots, l, \cdots, L$ refer to the fact that this operation is carried out L times, and starting from initial raw features $\mathbf{x}^{[1]} = \mathbf{x} \in \mathcal{X}$. After the L iterations of MP, each $\mathbf{x}_v^{[L]}, v \in \mathcal{V}$ has aggregated features from its L-hop neighbors, so that the content from both the initial raw features, as well as the topology of the graph are captured within the final features. Famous instances of these generic operations are the Graph Convolutional Networks (GCN) from [17], the Graph Attention Network (GAT) from [26], or the GraphSAGE operator of [16], among many others.

Certain machine learning tasks on graphs, e.g., node classification, node regression or link prediction, are performed locally and on the node level, rather than globally on the whole graph. For these tasks, the resultant feature of every node, i.e., $\mathbf{x}_v^{[L]}, v \in \mathcal{V}$, or perhaps a subset of nodes (like those from train, validation or test splits) can further follow processing steps like typical Multi Layer Perceptron (MLP) (i.e., multiple affine layers with non-linearities in between) to be matched against some label information. A common scenario in these cases is that the nodes from all data splits ($\mathcal{V}_{\text{train}}$, $\mathcal{V}_{\text{valid}}$ and $\mathcal{V}_{\text{test}}$) are present at the time of training. However, only the feature information of the test set is used during MP operations and their label information is of course not used during training and loss calculation. This scenario is referred to as the "transductive" case[2], as opposed to the "inductive" case where the test nodes are entirely absent during training.

---

[1] More technically, they should be either "permutation invariant" or "permutation equivariant" to the order of nodes.

[2] which resembles semi-supervised classification in some sense.

On the other hand, other machine learning tasks on graphs, like graph classification, regression or generation, are performed globally and on the whole graph. For these tasks, before continuing from the features $\mathbf{x}_v^{[L]}, v \in \mathcal{V}$ to the target labels, a global "pooling" stage $\mathbb{P}_G\{\cdots\}$ is needed to provide a global representation $\mathbf{z}_{\mathcal{G}_j}$ for the whole graph from individual nodes. While this should again be an order-agnostic set operation, a simple averaging of features is usually sufficient at this stage, since the MP algorithm has already integrated the topological content to the features. For each of the graphs in a given split $\{\mathcal{G}_1, \mathcal{G}_2, \cdots\}$, the pooled representations and their corresponding labels $\{(\mathbf{z}_{\mathcal{G}_1}, y_1), (\mathbf{z}_{\mathcal{G}_1}, y_1), \cdots$ are then treated as typical machine learning feature-target pairs and can be fed to MLP's with standard training recipes.

Note that for both these cases, i.e., the node-level and graph-level scenarios, since the whole pipeline is designed to be differentiable, end-to-end training using stochastic gradient descent is possible, as is the case for other deep learning tasks. However, the concept of mini-batching, while very straightforward in grid-like data, is more intricate for graph-based data and in particular the node-level tasks, since the connectivity of the nodes should somehow be taken into account during random sampling of the nodes. Examples of approaches to tackle this issue are the works of [2] and [30].

2.3 Text Featurization

A crucial step in doing machine learning on text is to perform text featurization to come up with unified-length vectors as representations of textual content. Since vectorial representations are very fundamental for machine learning algorithms, this basic step has been extensively studied within NLP communities and various generations of methods have been proposed. Among the earliest efforts in this direction is the use of Bag-Of-Words (BOW), where the frequency of the appearance of the tokenized items of the collection within a piece of text is considered as its vectorial features. While an important difficulty to do machine learning on such representations is the high dimensionality imposed by the number of the tokens of the collection, one can benefit from their high sparsity to project them to much lower dimensions, as e.g. in [7], where a very practical setup has been implemented suitable for the classification task and with low latencies.

The fundamental shortcoming with BOW-based representations, however, is that they disregard entirely the token context within the text sequence. The state-of-the-art approach to account for this sequential structure is the transformers of [25], where relying on the (self-) attention mechanism, they achieve significant improvements across many tasks, as e.g., in [4]. Due to their very demanding computational complexities, however, instead of always considering a large transformer model within the typical end-to-end machine learning loop, an active line of work (e.g., as in [19]) tries to benefit from them to embed text to vectors, while freezing the transformer weights and obviating the need to always backpropagate the errors through them.

3 Proposed Framework

We now described different elements used in our framework.

3.1 Graph Formation

Individual CT's: A typical biomedical text, notably our example of CT protocols, is usually structured in a hierarchy of different components. This hierarchy can be translated to graphs, most commonly as trees, similar to the example of Fig. 1.

In our case, for every individual CT protocol, pieces of text appear as leaf-nodes, where they are featurized to fixed-length vectors. As a simple baseline, here we use the BOW-based featurization described in Sect. 2.3, which is very fast to execute. To increase performance of featurization, we also use the contextual text embedding approach using transformers which benefits from pre-training on medical text.

These vectorial features will then constitute $\mathbf{x}_v^{[0]} \in \mathcal{V}$, in our terminology of Sect. 2.2, while non-leaf nodes without content will be initialized with all-zero vectors of the same dimension ($d = 768$). This is depicted in Fig. 2 (top), and is performed for all individual CT's of the collection.

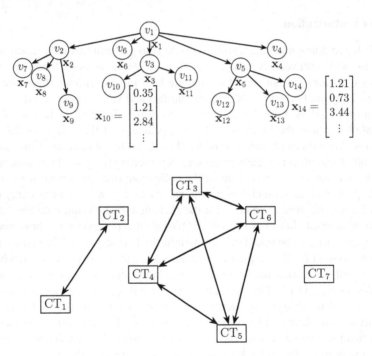

Fig. 2. (top) A sample CT document in the collection forming a graph with nodes consisting of featurized text. (bottom) Connecting graph of the documents in the collection as super-nodes. Each CT document contains a similar sub-graph as in the top figure.

All CT's as One Graph: The above setup considers each protocol independently, so a graph-classification task can be performed to classify them, as in our prior work [7].

As we propose in this work, however, certain criteria can be used to connect these individual CT protocols together so that the MP algorithm of Eq. 1 can benefit from richer and more meaningful connections between the CT's. This implies a single but very large graph containing the individual protocols as super-nodes, keeping all their nodes, edges and features within the large graph. As sketched in Fig. 2 (bottom), similar CT's can send messages between one another during the steps of the MP algorithm.

As for the criteria to connect the CT protocols together, we consider the fields "condition", "intervention", and "phase" of the CT's as important aspects where CT's can be considered as similar. In one model abstraction, we connect every CT, i.e., every super-node of the large graph, if they have at least one condition (among possibly many) and one intervention in common. In the second abstraction, we further require them to have the same trial phase. To benchmark this idea against the case where CT's are considered entirely independently (e.g., as in [7]), we consider these super-nodes as an empty graph, i.e., without any edges between them, while of course considering all the nodes and edges within the super-nodes. Table 1 provides some basic statistics of the connecting graph induced by these 3 cases.

Table 1. Basic statistics of the connecting graphs (considering only super-nodes)

Connecting graph	# nodes	# edges	Avg. degree	# connected components
empty	164326	0	0	164326
cnd.+int.	164326	4766646	$3.53e-04$	95033
cnd.+int.+ph.	164326	1896404	$1.40e-04$	102633

3.2 Classification

Once the large graph corresponding to all CT protocols in the collection is formed, we perform $L = 5$ stages of the MP algorithm of Eq. 1. Note, however that this graph may not entirely fit within a GPU, as e.g., in our case we have more than 15.4 million nodes overall (an average of around 94 nodes per each super-node), as well as more than 24.7 million edges. We therefore need to sample nodes and edges prior to training. In order not to lose the correspondence of nodes and edges, random sampling should be avoided and more meaningful sampling strategies that keep connected nodes within the same bag should be preferred. In our case, we use the cluster-GCN algorithm [2] to sample connected nodes by benefiting from graph clustering techniques.

Finally, once the MP algorithm is run on the sub-graphs and the raw features of all nodes are enriched with connectivity information, all the nodes belonging to the same CT protocol are pooled together to provide a final representation of the CT. This is then followed by an MLP to provide the final class outputs with softmax, where they are matched against the target labels using a class-weighted cross-entropy loss.

4 Experimental Results[3]

Data Preparation: We use the publicly available *ClinicalTrials.gov*[4] with more than 360K CT items Similar to the setting described in [7], we exclude the CT's whose status is not yet settled (e.g., recruiting, not yet recruiting, ..). This leaves us with 164,326 protocols, which we split into train, validation and test sets with ratios of 70%, 15% and 15%, respectively. In order to assign risk-related labels to the CT's, we consider those with "completed" status as low-risk and otherwise consider them as high-risk. Before proceeding with graph formation as described above, we eliminate all label-sensitive content from the protocols (status field, results field, ..).

Classification Results: The results of binary classification on the test set of the CTGov collection described above are presented in Table 2 for the BOW-based featurization approach, and in Table 3 for the transformer-based featurization, where we used the BERT-like language model described in [15], which is pre-trained on a large collection of biomedical text.

Table 2. Binary classification under different connecting graph configurations and graph convolutional layers. Results based on Bag-Of-Words features.

		Precision		Recall		F1-score		AUC	
		Micro	Macro	Micro	Macro	Micro	Macro	ROC	PR
GCN	empty	0.8455	0.8064	0.8455	0.8157	0.8455	0.8108	0.8990	0.8958
	cnd.+int.	0.8502	0.8128	0.8502	0.8179	0.8502	0.8153	0.9006	0.8974
	cnd.+int.+ph.	0.8634	0.8337	0.8634	0.8210	0.8634	0.8270	0.9050	0.9017
GAT	empty	0.8597	0.8283	0.8597	0.8175	0.8597	0.8226	0.9008	0.8989
	cnd.+int.	0.8635	0.8283	0.8635	0.8377	0.8635	0.8327	0.9158	0.9127
	cnd.+int.+ph.	0.8615	0.8297	0.8615	0.8222	0.8615	0.8258	0.9033	0.9011
SAGE	empty	0.8688	0.8395	0.8688	0.8301	0.8688	0.8346	0.9061	0.9048
	cnd.+int.	0.8753	0.8538	0.8753	0.8278	0.8753	0.8392	0.9080	0.9064
	cnd.+int.+ph.	0.8759	0.8537	0.8759	0.8300	0.8759	0.8405	0.9087	0.9076

As it can be seen from the results of Table 2 and 3, for both cases and under all graph convolutional layers, the new edges induced by the introduction of the connecting graphs improves the performance over the baseline "empty" graph. Note that while this improvement is not drastic in this case, because essentially no new source of information has been added, the proposed framework can be highly beneficial when external sources are available that are not straightforward to represent as vectorial features.

As a general conclusion, the use of the super-graph topological features seems to consistently increase the predictive power of the models. This is consistent with works in other domains that show the benefit of topological features in the predictive power of machine learning models based on graph abstractions [14].

---

[3] Source code at https://github.com/sssohrab/ct-classification-graphs.

[4] https://ClinicalTrials.gov/AllAPIJSON.zip.

Table 3. Binary classification under different connecting graph configurations and graph convolutional layers. Results based on pre-trained transformer text featurizers.

		Precision		Recall		F1-score		AUC	
		Micro	Macro	Micro	Macro	Micro	Macro	ROC	PR
GCN	empty	0.8739	0.8476	0.8739	0.8333	0.8739	0.8399	0.9105	0.9095
	cnd.+int.	0.8721	0.8430	0.8721	0.8359	0.8721	0.8393	0.9119	0.9105
	cnd.+int.+ph.	0.8778	0.8542	0.8778	0.8356	0.8778	0.8441	0.9146	0.9129
GAT	empty	0.8647	0.8306	0.8647	0.8357	0.8647	0.8331	0.9118	0.9110
	cnd.+int.	0.8668	0.8324	0.8668	0.8409	0.8668	0.8364	0.9164	0.9148
	cnd.+int.+ph.	0.8641	0.8288	0.8641	0.8395	0.8641	0.8338	0.9155	0.9139
SAGE	empty	0.8666	0.8326	0.8666	0.8388	0.8666	0.8356	0.9147	0.9139
	cnd.+int.	0.8804	0.8520	0.8804	0.8495	0.8804	0.8507	0.9258	0.9238
	cnd.+int.+ph.	0.8736	0.8424	0.8736	0.8439	0.8736	0.8431	0.9202	0.9189

5   Discussions

The literature of CT studies identifies various common reasons behind the very frequent scenario of trial failures (see e.g., [8,27]). While in general, it is useful to know the common reasons behind trial failure on the average, it would perhaps be much more beneficial to be able to predict the outcome of any given trial study, and before its execution. This can be an important step towards optimization of trial design to mitigate the risk factors and eventually to increase the odds of success. Given the central importance of CT's within the whole drug design pipeline, any such risk mitigation can have direct impact on medication prices and their time-to-market.

In this work, relying on large-scale data and machine learning techniques, we proposed one such framework to predict CT behavior from raw protocols. While we showed very high risk classification performance, it should be mentioned, however, that our measure of trial success in this work, i.e., the reported completion vs. non-completion of trials is perhaps rather simplistic. For a more realistic risk quantification and subsequently risk prediction for candidate trials, more detailed criteria like the duration of the study, the attrition rate of patients, or the toxicity reports of drugs should be taken into account. This, however, requires more data resources that are usually not publicly available in large scale.

On another note, our adopted methodology is highly flexible and can benefit from various sources of information while treating them under one common framework, i.e., deep learning using GNN's. This is thanks to the very versatile structure of graphs that can incorporate both vectorial features and topological information. In particular, our main proposition in this work, i.e., to enrich graph classification by using further connectivity information can be very suitable for using external data resources. While we used attributes like trial phase and medical intervention that are already present within the CT protocols, future work can consider external medical onthologies or drug information as better similarity measures to connect CT's.

6 Conclusions

With the increasing popularity of graph-based machine learning approaches within the healthcare domain, this work investigated the role of the problem formulation and the way the graph is constructed on the overall task performance. For our application example of CT protocol classification, we showed that while they can be considered as independent graph objects and hence formulated under a graph classification problem, by connecting the objects to one single large graph using some domain-aware similarity measures and hence formulating the problem as node classification, consistent performance gains can be achieved. This can particularly be useful for cases where some extra metadata is available that cannot be directly encoded as features. Our experiments were performed on the publicly CTGov data, for which we provide the open source codes.

References

1. Bronstein, M.M., Bruna, J., Cohen, T., Veličković, P.: Geometric deep learning: grids, groups, graphs, geodesics, and gauges. arXiv preprint arXiv:2104.13478 (2021)
2. Chiang, W.L., Liu, X., Si, S., Li, Y., Bengio, S., Hsieh, C.J.: Cluster-GCN: an efficient algorithm for training deep and large graph convolutional networks. In: Proceedings of the 25th ACM SIGKDD International Conference on Knowledge Discovery & Data Mining, pp. 257–266 (2019)
3. Choi, E., Bahadori, M.T., Song, L., Stewart, W.F., Sun, J.: GRAM: graph-based attention model for healthcare representation learning. In: Proceedings of the 23rd ACM SIGKDD International Conference on Knowledge Discovery and Data Mining, pp. 787–795 (2017)
4. Devlin, J., Chang, M.W., Lee, K., Toutanova, K.: BERT: pre-training of deep bidirectional transformers for language understanding. arXiv preprint arXiv:1810.04805 (2018)
5. Elkin, M.E., Zhu, X.: Predictive modeling of clinical trial terminations using feature engineering and embedding learning. Sci. Rep. 11(1), 1–12 (2021)
6. Elkin, M.E., Zhu, X.: Understanding and predicting COVID-19 clinical trial completion vs. cessation. Plos one 16(7), e0253789 (2021)
7. Ferdowsi, S., Borissov, N., Knafou, J., Amini, P., Teodoro, D.: Classification of hierarchical text using geometric deep learning: the case of clinical trials corpus. In: Proceedings of the 2021 Conference on Empirical Methods in Natural Language Processing (2021)
8. Fogel, D.B.: Factors associated with clinical trials that fail and opportunities for improving the likelihood of success: a review. Contemp. Clin. Trials Commun. 11, 156–164 (2018)
9. Follett, L., Geletta, S., Laugerman, M.: Quantifying risk associated with clinical trial termination: a text mining approach. Inf. Process. Manage. 56, 516–525 (2019)
10. Gainza, P., et al.: Deciphering interaction fingerprints from protein molecular surfaces using geometric deep learning. Nat. Methods 17(2), 184–192 (2020)
11. Geletta, S., Follett, L., Laugerman, M.: Latent dirichlet allocation in predicting clinical trial failures (2019)
12. Gilmer, J., Schoenholz, S.S., Riley, P.F., Vinyals, O., Dahl, G.E.: Neural message passing for quantum chemistry. In: International Conference on Machine Learning, pp. 1263–1272. PMLR (2017)
13. Glynn, E.F., Hoffman, M.A.: Heterogeneity introduced by EHR system implementation in a de-identified data resource from 100 non-affiliated organizations. JAMIA open 2(4), 554–561 (2019)

14. Gouareb, R., Can, F., Ferdowsi, S., Teodoro, D.: Vessel destination prediction using a graph-based machine learning model. In: Ribeiro, P., Silva, F., Mendes, J.F., Laureano, R. (eds.) NetSci-X 2022. LNCS, vol. 13197, pp. 80–93. Springer, Cham (2022). https://doi.org/10.1007/978-3-030-97240-0_7

15. Gu, Y., et al.: Domain-specific language model pretraining for biomedical natural language processing (2020)

16. Hamilton, W.L., Ying, R., Leskovec, J.: Inductive representation learning on large graphs. In: Proceedings of the 31st International Conference on Neural Information Processing Systems, pp. 1025–1035 (2017)

17. Kipf, T.N., Welling, M.: Semi-supervised classification with graph convolutional networks. arXiv preprint arXiv:1609.02907 (2016)

18. Martin, L., Hutchens, M., Hawkins, C.: Trial watch: clinical trial cycle times continue to increase despite industry efforts. Nat. Rev. Drug Discov. **16**(3), 157–158 (2017)

19. Reimers, N., Gurevych, I.: Sentence-BERT: Sentence embeddings using Siamese BERT-networks. In: Proceedings of the 2019 Conference on Empirical Methods in Natural Language Processing and the 9th International Joint Conference on Natural Language Processing (EMNLP-IJCNLP), pp. 3973–3983 (2019)

20. Shang, J., Ma, T., Xiao, C., Sun, J.: Pre-training of graph augmented transformers for medication recommendation. arXiv preprint arXiv:1906.00346 (2019)

21. Stokes, J.M., et al.: A deep learning approach to antibiotic discovery. Cell **180**(4), 688–702 (2020)

22. Teodoro, D., Pasche, E., Gobeill, J., Emonet, S., Ruch, P., Lovis, C.: Building a transnational biosurveillance network using semantic web technologies: requirements, design, and preliminary evaluation. J. Med. Internet Res. **14**(3), e73 (2012)

23. Teodoro, D., Sundvall, E., João Junior, M., Ruch, P., Miranda Freire, S.: ORBDA: an open EHR benchmark dataset for performance assessment of electronic health record servers. PLoS ONE **13**(1), e0190028 (2018)

24. Teodoro, D.H., et al.: Interoperability driven integration of biomedical data sources. Stud. Health Technol. Inform. **169**, 185–9 (2011)

25. Vaswani, A., et al.: Attention is all you need. arXiv preprint arXiv:1706.03762 (2017)

26. Veličković, P., Cucurull, G., Casanova, A., Romero, A., Lio, P., Bengio, Y.: Graph attention networks. arXiv preprint arXiv:1710.10903 (2017)

27. Williams, R.J., Tse, T., DiPiazza, K., Zarin, D.A.: Terminated trials in the clinicaltrials.gov results database: evaluation of availability of primary outcome data and reasons for termination. PLOS ONE **10**(5), 1–12 (2015). https://doi.org/10.1371/journal.pone.0127242

28. Wong, C.H., Siah, K.W., Lo, A.W.: Estimation of clinical trial success rates and related parameters. Biostatistics **20**(2), 273–286 (2019)

29. Wouters, O., McKee, M., Luyten, J.: Estimated research and development investment needed to bring a new medicine to market, 2009–2018. JAMA **323**, 844–853 (2020)

30. Zeng, H., et al.: Deep graph neural networks with shallow subgraph samplers. arXiv preprint arXiv:2012.01380 (2020)

31. Zhu, W., Razavian, N.: Variationally regularized graph-based representation learning for electronic health records. In: Proceedings of the Conference on Health, Inference, and Learning, CHIL 2021, pp. 1–13. Association for Computing Machinery, New York (2021)

Medical Image Processing

Malignant Mesothelioma Subtyping of Tissue Images via Sampling Driven Multiple Instance Prediction

Mark Eastwood[1]([✉]), Silviu Tudor Marc[2], Xiaohong Gao[2], Heba Sailem[3], Judith Offman[4], Emmanouil Karteris[5], Angeles Montero Fernandez[6], Danny Jonigk[7], William Cookson[8], Miriam Moffatt[8], Sanjay Popat[8], Fayyaz Minhas[1], and Jan Lukas Robertus[8]

[1] TIA Center, University of Warwick, Coventry, UK
Mark.Eastwood@warwick.ac.uk
[2] Department of Computer Science, University of Middlesex, London, UK
[3] Institute of Biomedical Engineering, University of Oxford, Oxford, UK
[4] Kings College London, London, UK
[5] Brunel University, London, UK
[6] Manchester University, Manchester, UK
[7] Medizinische Hochschule Hannover, Hannover, Germany
[8] National Heart and Lung Institute, Imperial College London, London, UK

Abstract. Malignant Mesothelioma is a difficult to diagnose and highly lethal cancer usually associated with asbestos exposure. It can be broadly classified into three subtypes: Epitheliod, Sarcomatoid, and Biphasic. Early diagnosis and identification of the subtype informs treatment and can help improve patient outcome. However, the subtyping of malignant mesothelioma, and specifically the recognition of transitional features from routine histology slides has a high level of inter-observer variablity. In this work, we propose the first end-to-end multiple instance learning (MIL) approach for malignant mesothelioma subtyping. This uses an instance-based sampling scheme for training deep convolutional neural networks on this task that allows learning on a wider range of relevant instances compared to max or top-N based MIL approaches. The proposed MIL approach enables identification of malignant mesothelial subtypes of specific tissue regions. From this a continuous characterization of a sample according to predominance of sarcomatoid vs epithelioid regions is possible, thus avoiding the arbitrary and highly subjective categorisation by currently used subtypes. Instance scoring also enables studying tumor heterogeneity and identifying patterns associated with different subtypes. We have evaluated the proposed method on a dataset of 243 tissue micro-array cores with an AUROC of 0.87 ± 0.04 for this task. The dataset and developed methodology is available for the community at: https://github.com/measty/PINS.

Keywords: Malignant mesothelioma · Multiple instance learning · Computational pathology · Deep learning

F. Minhas and J. Lukas Robertus—Joint last authors.

M. Michalowski et al. (Eds.): AIME 2022, LNAI 13263, pp. 263–272, 2022.
https://doi.org/10.1007/978-3-031-09342-5_25

1   Introduction

Malignant Mesothelioma (MM) is an aggressive cancer of the pleural lining, primarily associated with asbestos exposure [1]. It has a long latency period from initial exposure, to eventual carcinogenesis, and is difficult to diagnose due to its nonspecific clinical manifestations. As a result, diagnosis is usually confirmed in an advanced stage [2], leading to the 5 year survival rate being less than 5% [3]. Hence there is an urgent clinical need to detect MM at its early onset when treatment is more effective. MM is classified into 3 subtypes [4], Epithelioid (EM), Biphasic (BM) and Sarcomatoid (SM) Mesothelioma, with Biphasic characterised by a mix of epithelioid and sarcomatoid components, including Transitional Mesothelioma (TM). Epithelioid mesothelioma are characterised by malignant cells that are cytologically round with varying grading of atypia. Sarcomatoid mesothelioma cells are generally recognised as malignant spindle cells [5] and are associated with worse prognosis in comparison to EM. Recent studies have also shown that the presence of transitional features of TM, which share intermediate cytology between epithelioid and spindle cell also indicate a poorer prognosis [6]. In MM, TM may represent an aspect of Epithelial Mesenchymal Transition (EMT), with cells differentiating between EM and SM, suggesting that MM cases may fall more naturally on a continuum of characterisation according to the relative prevalence of EM, SM and TM components. Part of the motivation for this work is to go beyond the current 2021 WHO 3 basic subtypes and move towards a system whereby we use sub-visual signals on individual cell level, to specify quantitatively where a MM sample lies on the EM-SM continuum.

While distinction of these three histological subtypes of MM is crucial to patient treatment, management and prognosis, it is challenging to differentiate EM, SM and BM through visual analysis as they tend to present similar features to transitional patterns at some stages. A number of deep learning methods for analyzing mesothelioma images have been developed recently. For example, SpindleMesoNET [8] can separate malignant SM from benign spindle cell mesothelial proliferations. To address the challenges of assessing stromal invasion in small biopsies, the most accurate indicator of malignancy, the separation of benign and malignant mesothelial proliferations has been investigated [9], in both epithelial and spindle cell mesothelial processes. However, automated subtyping of mesothelioma from Hemotoxylin and Eosin (H&E) stained tissue sections remains an open problem.

One of the issues associated with development of automated computational pathology approaches for predicting malignant mesothelioma subtypes is that pathologist-assigned ground-truth labels for these images are typically available only at the case level. However, we are often interested in properties of smaller regions of a sample. To address this, tissue images can be tiled into patches for training of deep learning models and the case-level labels used as bag labels. Thus, mesothelioma subtyping can be categorized as a multiple instance learning (MIL) or weak-supervision problem.

A recent approach for survival prediction of MM patients called MesoNet [10] uses an MIL solver originally developed for computer vision applications [11] and classification of lymph node metastases [12]. An attention-inspired pooling method for MIL instance aggregation is proposed in [13]. Another attention-based MIL approach is introduced in [14]. Here, a dual stream approach is used where the final bag score is the mean of max instance pooling and an attention based weighted average of instances attended to by the max instance. This model is applied to Camelyon-16 and TCGA lung cancer datasets. Large datasets on prostate cancer, basal cell carcinoma and breast cancer metastases are assembled in [15] and used to train an MIL model backpropagating only the top K instances per bag. In the IDaRS algorithm proposed in [16], for each slide the training instances used in epoch t are the top k ranked instances by prediction score from the previous epoch $t - 1$, augmented by a number of randomly selected patches from the slide. This approach was used to predict the status of molecular pathways and detect key mutations in colorectal cancer.

In the remainder of the paper, we develop a simple yet effective approach to multiple instance learning for MM subtype prediction with the following major contributions:

1. The introduction of a novel MIL-based method for computational pathology tasks which addresses shortcomings identified in similar methods regarding robustness to initialization and learning on only a small number of the relevant instances in the training data.
2. The collection of a dataset of MM tissue cores labelled by subtype, which we make publicly available for further study by the community.

2   Data and Preprocessing

The dataset used in this work is a collection of H&E stained Tissue Micro-arrays (TMAs) of tumor tissue biopsies collected from St. George's Hospital. It consists of 4 TMA slides each with an average size of $40,000 \times 40,000$ pixels scanned using a Hamamatsu Nanozoomer S360 scanner at 20 $\times$ (0.4415 microns per pixel) with a total of 279 cores covering 102 separate cases (patients). After removal of dropped and severely damaged/incomplete cores, we are left with 243 cores, with 155 EM, 64 BM, and 24 SM cores. We first perform Vahadane stain normalisation [17] to minimise systematic stain variability between slides and cores. We tile each core into patches of 224×224 pixels at 20$\times$ magnification. Only core-level labels are provided, detailed annotations describing how different regions of the core contribute to the core-level label are not available.

3   Problem Formulation

As the biphasic subtype is a mix of epitheliod and sarcomatoid components, and subtype labels are only available at the core level and not for individual image patches within each core, we model the subtype prediction task as a binary Multiple Instance Learning (MIL) problem, with sarcomatoid as the positive class. Under the MIL paradigm [18], an example is represented by a bag of instances, and a bag is considered positive if it contains at least one positive sample. The goal of an MIL predictor is to use training data consisting of bags with bag level labels only to predict both bag and instance level labels in testing. Formally, let $B = \{x_1, ..., x_{n_B}\}$ be a bag corresponding to a single TMA core in our dataset, where x_i are instances (patches) within the bag. The number of instances n_B can vary across bags. Each core, represented by bag B, is associated with a label $Y_B \in \{0,1\}$ in the training dataset. In our formulation, both sarcomatoid and biphasic cores are taken as positive bags $(Y_B = 1)$, as in both cases a noticeable sarcomatoid component is present whereas epitheliod-labelled cores become negative examples $(Y_B = 0)$. Our goal is then to build a machine learning model $F(B; \Phi)$ with trainable parameters Φ that can use a labelled training dataset $D = \{(B_1, Y_1), (B_2, Y_2), ..., (B_M, Y_M)\}$ to generate a predicted label for a test core B. This is done by denoted by aggregating instance level predictions $z_i = f(x_i; \phi)$ to give $Z_B = F(B; \Phi) = Agg(\{z_i = f(x_i; \phi) | x_i \in B\})$ through an appropriate aggregation function $Agg(\cdot)$ such as max or average across top most positive instances.

Modelling the mesothelioma subtyping problem through MIL allows us to use the weakly supervisory signal from core-level labels to learn an instance-level scoring, with which we can identify predominantly EM or SM regions in a core. This enables us to quantify where each tissue component falls in the EM-to-SM continuum according to the proportion of positive (sarcomatoid) instances. This fine-grained and natural characterisation of a tumor can lead to more informed decisions regarding treatment etc. to be made.

4   Sampling-Based MIL Training for CNNs

We propose a simple but powerful approach for solving the MIL problem underlying mesothelioma subtyping based on the fundamental definition of MIL. In the binary case, MIL can be paraphrased as 'only the most positive instance in a bag counts'. Recall from Sect. 3 we label a bag as positive if it contains at least one positive instance. Intuitively, then, during training we wish to make the most positive scoring instances of negative bags less positive, and the positive instances of positive bags more positive. We would also like to avoid forcing negative instances in a positive bag to become positive labelled. Many approaches [10,11], rank instances according to an instance score, and learn only on the max (or top N) of these. However, this has some potential problems:

1. We learn only on very few instances. A significant proportion of the bag may be positive, but only the top few will contribute to learning per bag. This may be fine if we have many example bags to learn from, but can become a big problem if we have relatively few bags.
2. The method can be susceptible to unfortunate initialization. If the initial weights of the model happen to score some unimportant instances highly, a

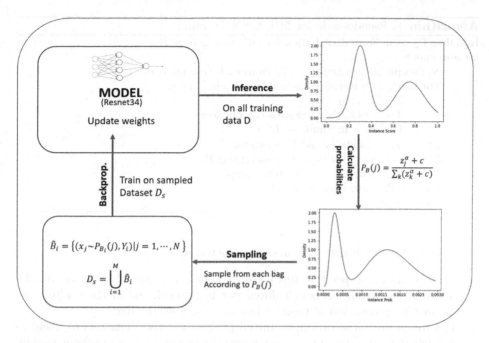

Fig. 1. Overview of proposed method, showing the instance scoring → weight calculation → sampling → training loop.

situation may arise where the model is learning on a small subset of instances which have little to no relation to the bag labels, and may get stuck in an extremely sub-optimal local minimum.

In our approach, we minimise these issues by randomly sampling instances from each bag in proportion to their instance score. Formally, for each bag B we define a probability distribution P_B (initially uniform) over instances in B. Given the prediction scores $z_i = f(x_i, \phi) \in [0, 1]$ for an instance $x_i \in B$, from a CNN f with learnable weights ϕ, we set

$$P_B(i) = \frac{z_i^\alpha + c}{\sum_j (z_j^\alpha + c)}. \tag{1}$$

In Eq. 1, c is a small constant which limits how small $P_B(i)$ can get so that all instances are occasionally sampled, and α controls how heavily we weight for positive instances. For each training epoch, we sample 20% of the patches in each bag according to the distribution in Eq. 1 for training. In the extreme of $\alpha = 0$, all instances are weighted equally and we simply learn on all patches with label inherited from the bag label, disregarding the MIL setting. In the case of $\alpha \to \infty$ (and assuming c is reduced accordingly), we recover something similar to the max-based MIL approach of [12] or [10], where we learn only on the maximal instance of each bag. The pseudo-code for our method can be found in Algorithm 1, and it is illustrated diagramatically in Fig. 1.

Algorithm 1. Pseudo-code for MIL CNN Training

Initialise P_B as uniform distribution for all training bags B
for e in epochs:
     S: Sample 20% instances $\sim P_B$ from each training core
     For batch with instances X and bag labels Y in S:
          $Z = f(X, \phi)$
          $L = \text{CE}(Z, Y)$ #cross-entropy loss
          Update ϕ to minimise L
     Save ϕ_{best} if validation AUC improves
     For instances $x_i \in B$ in each training bag B:
          $z_i = f(x_i, \phi)$ #inference pass
     Update P_B's according to Eq. 1
Return best model $f(\cdot, \phi_{best})$

This approach mitigates the above problems, as

1. We learn from all positive instances in a bag, not just the top N. As the probability distribution is calculated per bag (core), the method adjusts to the varying proportion of positive instances in different bags.
2. It is robust to initialisation, as initial probability distributions are likely to be fairly flat, and (assuming α not large) the sampling does not focus heavily on positive instances until the model has started to become more sure of its predictions (i.e. when its outputs z_i become more polarised).

We use a ResNet34 pre-trained on ImageNet as the backbone in our CNN model [19], due to its consistently strong performance over a wide range of application areas including computational pathology. We train our model using the Adam optimizer [20] with batch size of 64 over a maximum of 200 epochs with early stopping. The learning rate used was 5×10^{-5}, weight decay 10^{-4}, with $\alpha = 2$ and $c = 0.01$ (See Eq. 1). We choose a relatively low learning rate over a larger number of epochs because we update the probabilities used for sampling after each epoch, so we do not want the 'true' distribution to change too quickly over a single epoch. To address class imbalance, losses per class were weighted inversely to their class counts. We use a one-cycle learning rate schedule as introduced in [21]. During inference on cores, we aggregate the instance scores by averaging the top 5 instances. This is more robust than max aggregation, where a single poorly scored instance can completely change the aggregated score. Our model is implemented in PyTorch; code and data is available at https://github.com/measty/PINS.

For performance evaluation we employ a hold-one-out cross-validation strategy over slides, so that for each fold all cores of a single slide are held out as the test set. This is done to avoid any potential bias from systematic differences between slides, and to ensure no mixing of cores from the same patient occurs between the training and testing sets. The cores to be used for training are split 75%–25% into train and validation sets, respectively.

Table 1. Summary of results (mean±stdev). PINS (PL) indicates metric for proposed method after adjustment for labels from expert pathologist.

Metric	AUC-ROC	Avg. precision	Sensitivity	Specificity
max-MIL	0.70 ± 0.04	0.58 ± 0.12	0.54 ± 0.07	0.73 ± 0.09
naive-MIL	0.81 ± 0.04	0.68 ± 0.11	0.72 ± 0.08	0.71 ± 0.1
PINS	0.83 ± 0.04	0.73 ± 0.09	0.77 ± 0.12	0.68 ± 0.11
PINS (PL)	0.87 ± 0.04	0.81 ± 0.07	0.82 ± 0.1	0.71 ± 0.13

5   Results and Discussion

The results of our prediction model (which we name PINS for the Positive INstance Sampling that lies at its core) are reported in Table 1, together with baseline results from max-based MIL, and the model resulting from training on all patches with no regard for the MIL setting during training (naive-MIL in Table 1). Our model achieves an AUROC of 0.83 and average precision (AP) of 0.73. The ROC curve for our method can be found in Fig. 3. As can be seen from Table 1, the max-based MIL strategy performs poorly. This is likely due to the relatively small size of the training dataset. Limiting learning to only one patch per core in each epoch exacerbates this, as the model may rapidly overfit the top patches of positive bags. Our method allows learning from a wider selection of positive instances according to the model estimate of the proportion of positive instances in each bag. Purely patch-based learning, that is simply learning on all patches labelled according to their bag label, performs surprisingly well, scoring quite close to our MIL method. This is likely due to the relatively high proportion of positive instances that are expected to be present in many of the positive bags (for example a sarcomatoid core is expected to comprise of mostly positive instances). This makes the implicit assumption a patch-based model makes, namely that all instances share the label of the bag, less wrong for this dataset compared to other MIL problems.

Labels on histopathology images are often noisy, as the classification into clinical categories is subjective and opinion can vary significantly between pathologists. This is especially true in the context of MM, which is particularly difficult to diagnose. Thus, we sought an independent opinion from an expert pathologist on a small set of examples our method most consistently misclassified, to see to what extent our model could be justified on examples where its predictions differed from the original labelling.

In BM, a TMA core may represent a focal area that is specifically, either epithelioid or sarcomatoid. Of 14 consistently miss-classified cores, the opinion of the expert pathologist was that in 9 cases the model could be justified in its prediction given the representative core that was available for assessment. Further, 3 of the remaining cases contained very few tumor cells or were otherwise very challenging cases. Adjusting for the 9 justified misclassifications improves AUC (see Fig. 3) from 0.83 to 0.87, and AP from 0.73 to 0.81. Heatmaps illustrating the output of our network are discussed in Fig. 2.

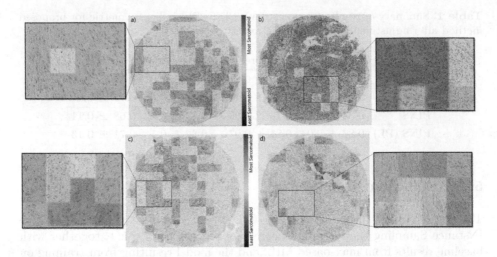

Fig. 2. Representative Heatmaps of model predictions. a) a core labelled Epitheloid, which our model mis-classified as positive (i.e. significant SM component present). This agreed with the second opinion obtained from an expert pathologist, making this an example of a justified mis-classification. From the closeup, spindle-like morphology of cells can be seen. b) A correctly-predicted epithelioid-predominant core. As can be seen in b) and the closeup of c), patches demonstrating the typical rounded cell morphology of the EM subtype appear in bluer shades. c) A correctly-predicted biphasic core with an even mix of EM and SM components. d) A Sarcomatoid core, correctly predicted. In comparison to a) and c), has a much higher proportion of the core identified as SM.

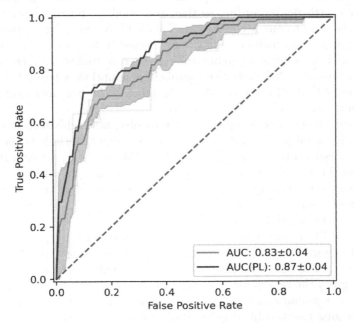

Fig. 3. ROC curves over 4-slide folds. Green plot shows curve after adjustment for labels from expert pathologist (Color figure online)

Quantifying the proportion of a core which is predicted as SM subtype in this way enables a much less subjective characterisation of a tissue sample.

6 Conclusions and Future Work

In this work, we demonstrate for the first time that an MIL framework can successfully predict presence of a sarcomatoid component in local tissue regions, paving the way for a quantitative categorisation of malignant mesothelioma subtypes. We believe our approach opens new opportunities for more objective assessment of Epithelial-Mesenchymal Transformation where intra-tumor heterogeneity represents a gradient that can be difficult to assess by routine examination by histopathology. Therefore, output of the proposed model can be used to create a smoother continuum of disease classification by determining the extent of the different cellular sub-populations at the patch level. Future work will be focused on including contextual information and identifying subtype at the cell level in addition to a detailed comparison with other backbone CNNs and larger-scale multi-centric evaluation on whole slide images.

Acknowledgments. This work was conducted as part of the PRISM project, kindly funded by Cancer Research UK through the CRUK-STFC Early Detection Innovation Award.

References

1. Wagner, J.C., Sleggs, C.A., Marchand, P.: Diffuse pleural mesothelioma and asbestos exposure in the north western cape province. Br. J. Ind. Med. **17**(13782506), 260–271 (1960)
2. Lagniau, S., Lamote, K., van Meerbeeck, J.P., Vermaelen, K.Y.: Biomarkers for early diagnosis of malignant mesothelioma: do we need another moonshot? Oncotarget **8**(28881848), 53751–53762 (2017)
3. Scherpereel, A., Astoul, P., Baas, P., et al.: Guidelines of the European respiratory society and the European society of thoracic surgeons for the management of malignant pleural mesothelioma. Eur. Respir. J. **35**(3), 479–495 (2010)
4. Ai, J., Stevenson, J.P.: Current issues in malignant pleural mesothelioma evaluation and management. Oncologist **19**(25061089), 975–984 (2014)
5. WHO Classification of Tumours Editorial Board, Thoracic Tumours. WHO Classification of Tumours, 5th edn., vol. 5 (2021)
6. Dacic, S.: Pleural mesothelioma classification-update and challenges. Mod. Pathol.: Off. J. U.S. Can. Acad. Pathol. Inc. (2021)
7. Salle, F.G., Stang, N.L., Tirode, F., et al.: Comprehensive molecular and pathologic evaluation of transitional mesothelioma assisted by deep learning approach: a multi-institutional study of the international mesothelioma panel from the mesopath reference center. J. Thoracic Oncol.: Off. Publ. Int. Assoc. Study Lung Cancer **15**, 1037–1053 (2020)
8. Naso, J.R., Levine, A.B., Farahani, H., et al.: Deep-learning based classification distinguishes sarcomatoid malignant mesotheliomas from benign spindle cell mesothelial proliferations. Mod. Pathol. **34**(11), 2028–2035 (2021)

9. Churg, A., Colby, T.V., Cagle, P., et al.: The separation of benign and malignant mesothelial proliferations. Am. J. Surg. Pathol. **24**, 1183–1200 (2000)

10. Courtiol, P., Maussion, C., Moarii, M., et al.: Deep learning-based classification of mesothelioma improves prediction of patient outcome. Nat. Med. **25**, 1519–1525 (2019)

11. Courtiol, P., Tramel, E.W., Sanselme, M., Wainrib, G.: lassification and disease localization in histopathology using only global labels: a weakly-supervised approach. ArXiv, vol. abs/1802.02212 (2018)

12. Durand, T., Thome, N., Cord, M.: Weldon: weakly supervised learning of deep convolutional neural networks. In: 2016 IEEE Conference on Computer Vision and Pattern Recognition (CVPR), pp. 4743–4752 (2016)

13. Ilse, M., Tomczak, J.M., Welling, M.: Attention-based deep multiple instance learning. arXiv preprint arXiv:1802.04712 (2018)

14. Li, B., Li, Y., Eliceiri, K.W.: Dual-stream multiple instance learning network for whole slide image classification with self-supervised contrastive learning. In: Proceedings of the IEEE/CVF Conference on Computer Vision and Pattern Recognition (CVPR), pp. 14318–14328, June 2021

15. Campanella, G., Hanna, M.G., Geneslaw, L., et al.: Clinical-grade computational pathology using weakly supervised deep learning on whole slide images. Nat. Med. **25**, 1–9 (2019)

16. Bilal, M., Raza, S.E.A., Azam, A., et al.: Novel deep learning algorithm predicts the status of molecular pathways and key mutations in colorectal cancer from routine histology images. medRxiv (2021)

17. Vahadane, A., Peng, T., Sethi, A., et al.: Structure-preserving color normalization and sparse stain separation for histological images. IEEE Trans. Med. Imaging **35**, 1962–1971 (2016)

18. Dietterich, T.G., Lathrop, R.H., Lozano-Pérez, T.: Solving the multiple instance problem with axis-parallel rectangles. Artif. Intell. **89**(1), 31–71 (1997)

19. He, K., Zhang, X., Ren, S., Sun, J.: Deep residual learning for image recognition. CoRR, vol. abs/1512.03385 (2015)

20. Kingma, D.P., Ba, J.: Adam: a method for stochastic optimization (2017)

21. Smith, L.N., Topin, N.: Super-convergence: very fast training of residual networks using large learning rates. CoRR, vol. abs/1708.07120 (2017)

Calibrating Histopathology Image Classifiers Using Label Smoothing

Jerry Wei, Lorenzo Torresani, Jason Wei, and Saeed Hassanpour(✉)

Dartmouth College, Hanover, NH 03755, USA
saeed.hassanpour@dartmouth.edu

Abstract. The classification of histopathology images fundamentally differs from traditional image classification tasks because histopathology images naturally exhibit a range of diagnostic features, resulting in a diverse range of annotator agreement levels. However, examples with high annotator disagreement are often either assigned the majority label or discarded entirely when training histopathology image classifiers. This widespread practice often yields classifiers that do not account for example difficulty and exhibit poor model calibration. In this paper, we ask: can we improve model calibration by endowing histopathology image classifiers with inductive biases about example difficulty?

We propose several label smoothing methods that utilize per-image annotator agreement. Though our methods are simple, we find that they substantially improve model calibration, while maintaining (or even improving) accuracy. For colorectal polyp classification, a common yet challenging task in gastrointestinal pathology, we find that our proposed agreement-aware label smoothing methods reduce calibration error by almost 70%. Moreover, we find that using model confidence as a proxy for annotator agreement also improves calibration and accuracy, suggesting that datasets without multiple annotators can still benefit from our proposed label smoothing methods via our proposed confidence-aware label smoothing methods.

Given the importance of calibration (especially in histopathology image analysis), the improvements from our proposed techniques merit further exploration and potential implementation in other histopathology image classification tasks.

Keywords: Label smoothing · Histopathology images · Calibration

1 Introduction

The success of modern deep learning paradigms on computer vision (CV) benchmarks such as ImageNet has led to widespread adoption of neural networks for medical image analysis [1]. Convolutional neural networks, for instance, have been used for tasks such as lung cancer classification [4], colorectal polyp classification [15], and breast cancer detection [22]. The nature of medical image classification tasks, however, differs substantially from standard benchmarks used in computer vision in two major ways.

First, on benchmark classification datasets such as ImageNet, CIFAR-10, and MNIST, most image labels are well-defined and have high annotator agreement (few examples exhibit high annotator disagreement). Labels for medical images, on the

M. Michalowski et al. (Eds.): AIME 2022, LNAI 13263, pp. 273–282, 2022.
https://doi.org/10.1007/978-3-031-09342-5_26

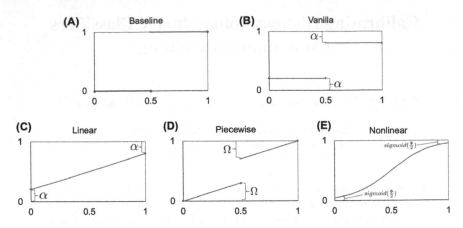

Fig. 1. Proposed label smoothing methods. The x-axis represents annotator agreement level or model confidence, and the y-axis represents the label given to a particular example.

other hand, often have high annotator disagreement, especially for challenging tasks where diagnoses can differ substantially, even among expert clinicians [7,8,23]. This is because the natural progression of diseases inherently creates a range of difficulty that has been observed in many medical image datasets [2,26]. Despite this unique characteristic, existing literature typically uses the classic CV training procedure—using the majority vote of annotators as a one-hot encoded target [3,9,13,14].

The second way that medical image analysis differs from traditional computer vision is how models will be deployed in real-world settings. Whereas traditional CV applications such as facial recognition or self-driving cars are often used as standalone technologies, the initial adoption of medical image analysis models will likely be as artificial intelligence assistants for clinicians. A deep learning system could triage or provide second opinions in an image analysis pipeline, where images predicted to have unclear diagnoses are sent to separate queues for further manual inspection. In these scenarios, the confidence outputs of deep learning classifiers crucially influence clinician decisions, as high-confidence images will receive less attention and low-confidence images will receive more attention. In such settings, calibration is key.

In this paper, we bring attention to applying label smoothing techniques for the classification of histopathology images, digitized images of surgical resection tissue that are typically examined under a microscope. Specifically, we leverage the intuition that many histopathology image datasets have annotations from multiple pathologists [3–6,13–15] and operationalize these annotations into a technique that we call *agreement-aware* label smoothing. The soft targets in agreement-aware label smoothing depend on the annotator agreement for each individual image, providing the model with more information about the contents of the images. We also posit that model confidence can be used as a proxy for example difficulty in lieu of annotator agreement, allowing datasets that do not have annotations from multiple annotators to benefit from our proposed label smoothing methodology. We thus propose an analogous *confidence-aware* label smoothing technique that closely resembles agreement-aware label smoothing but substitutes annotator agreement data with model confidence outputs.

We conduct empirical experiments on colorectal polyp classification—one of the highest volume tasks in clinical pathology. We find that both agreement-aware label smoothing and confidence-aware label smoothing improve calibration more than vanilla label smoothing and hard-target models do, while maintaining or improving accuracy.

2 Label Smoothing

Label smoothing [16] is a paradigm proposing to "smooth" labels by encouraging small logit gaps, addressing the issue of traditional one-hot encoded labels resulting in models being less-calibrated and too overconfident in their predictions. In practice, vanilla label smoothing assigns a smooth label y using a hyperparameter $\alpha \in (0, 1]$, one-hot target y_k, and the total number of classes K, as depicted in Fig. 1B and formalized below.

$$y = (1 - \alpha) * y_k + \frac{\alpha}{K}. \tag{1}$$

2.1 Agreement-Aware Label Smoothing

Because histopathology image classification datasets often contain annotator agreement data that could potentially be used for more-precise label smoothing [3–6, 13–15] , we propose three types of agreement-aware label smoothing paradigms. We first implement a linear agreement-aware label smoothing method (which closely matches vanilla label smoothing) in order to examine the sole effect of including annotator agreement data without changing the format of vanilla label smoothing. This method simply replaces the one-hot label in vanilla label smoothing with n_k—the number of annotators that labeled a given example as class k—divided by the total number of annotators N (Eq. 2). Our linear agreement-aware method continues to use hyperparameter $\alpha \in (0, 1]$. A visual representation of this method is shown in Panel C in Fig. 1.

$$y = (1 - \alpha) * \frac{n_k}{N} + \frac{\alpha}{K}. \tag{2}$$

We also explore whether implementing a variable-sized discontinuity in the vanilla label smoothing equation can improve the precision of smoothed targets. Thus, we implement a piecewise agreement-aware label smoothing method (Eq. 3) which uses a different hyperparameter $\Omega \in (0, 0.5]$. In this system of equations, we define the number of annotators needed for a majority $n_m = \lceil \frac{N}{K} \rceil$. This method can be seen in Panel D in Fig. 1.

$$\begin{cases} y = (1 - \Omega) + \Omega(\frac{n_k - n_m}{n_m - 1}), & \text{if } n_k > n_m \\ y = 0.5, & \text{if } n_k = n_m \\ y = \Omega(\frac{n_k}{n_m - 1}), & \text{if } n_k < n_m \end{cases} \tag{3}$$

Finally, we address whether more-heavily penalizing images with higher disagreement can produce better-calibrated models. In Eq. 4, we define a nonlinear agreement-aware label smoothing method using hyperparameter $\Phi > 0$. For this nonlinear function, we use $f(x) = sigmoid(x)$; the nonlinearity of this function results in the targets of images being more-heavily penalized as annotator disagreement increases. The visual representation of this equation is shown in Panel E in Fig. 1.

$$y = f(\Phi(\frac{n_k}{N} - \frac{1}{2})). \tag{4}$$

We model our agreement-aware label smoothing equations for binary classification tasks, though our equations could be easily adjusted for other scenarios. For example, the nonlinear function can be easily changed to $f(x) = softmax(x)$ if $K > 2$.

2.2   Confidence-Aware Label Smoothing

Many datasets do not have annotation data from multiple annotators, and so a natural question is whether these datasets can still benefit from our proposed label smoothing methods. To answer this question, we use the confidence outputs of a baseline model (which can be obtained regardless of the number of annotators a dataset has) as a proxy for example difficulty. This method thus requires training the model twice—first without label smoothing in order to obtain model confidence scores for each training example, then again with our confidence-aware label smoothing methods.

While prior work has focused mostly on using model confidence as target labels [12,19,24], the novelty of confidence-aware label smoothing lies in its fusion of the idea of using model confidence as target labels with our proposed agreement-aware label smoothing formulas. Thus, for these methods, we replace annotator agreement level $\frac{n_k}{N}$ in our proposed agreement-aware label smoothing equations with the confidence value c_k for a given example to obtain analogous confidence-aware label smoothing equations. This does not change the overall shape of the function, and confidence-aware counterparts for agreement-aware label smoothing methods are still represented by their respective panels in Fig. 1. We first define vanilla confidence-aware label smoothing in this manner, obtaining Eq. 5 from Eq. 1 by substituting model confidence for annotator agreement level.

$$y = (1 - \alpha) * \lfloor c_k \rceil + \frac{\alpha}{K}. \tag{5}$$

Similarly, for linear and nonlinear confidence-aware label smoothing, we simply replace $\frac{n_k}{N}$ with c_k in Eqs. 2 and 4, respectively. Piecewise confidence-aware label smoothing, however, is more complicated and requires additional modifications as a result of the use of n_m, so we show the equation for this separately in Eq. 6.

$$\begin{cases} y = (1 - \Omega) + (\frac{c_k - 0.5}{0.5}) * \Omega, & \text{if } c_k > 0.5 \\ y = 0.5, & \text{if } c_k = 0.5 \ . \\ y = (\frac{c_k}{0.5}) * \Omega, & \text{if } c_k < 0.5 \end{cases} \tag{6}$$

3   Experimental Setup

For our experiments, we use the Minimalist Histopathology Image Analysis Dataset (MHIST) [25], a publicly-available dataset for the classification of colorectal polyps. MHIST focuses on the clinically-important binary classification between hyperplastic polyps (HPs) and sessile serrated adenomas (SSAs), a challenging yet common diagnostic distinction [7,8,26]. MHIST contains a total of 3,152 images (2,175 for training and 977 for evaluation), each annotated with a binary label of either HP or SSA. MHIST includes independently-annotated labels from seven gastrointestinal pathologists—we leverage this annotator agreement data to endow image classifiers with inductive biases about example difficulty.

We also use the ResNet architecture [11], a common choice for classifying histopathology images. We use the same hyperparameters and training/evaluation sets as implemented in the original MHIST paper [25]. We measure model accuracy using the area under the receiver operating characteristic curve (AUC; higher is better) and also measure model calibration using expected calibration error [17] (ECE; lower is better), the weighted average over the difference between accuracy and confidence computed over a given number of bins (for our experiments, we use 15 bins). ECE is best when a model's accuracy and confidence are identical (e.g., the model obtains 90% accuracy on images that it predicts with 90% confidence). For each model, we report the mean and standard deviation of these AUC and ECE values calculated over 10 different seeds.

Table 1. Agreement-aware label smoothing improves performance (higher AUC) and model calibration (lower ECE). Means and standard deviations are reported across 10 seeds.

Model	AUC	ECE
Baseline	84.7 ± 0.8	8.9 ± 1.4
Vanilla label smoothing	85.6 ± 0.6	3.2 ± 0.6
Agreement-aware (linear)	86.1 ± 0.9	5.3 ± 0.7
Agreement-aware (piecewise)	$\mathbf{86.4 \pm 0.4}$	2.9 ± 0.4
Agreement-aware (nonlinear)	86.3 ± 0.7	$\mathbf{2.8 \pm 0.6}$

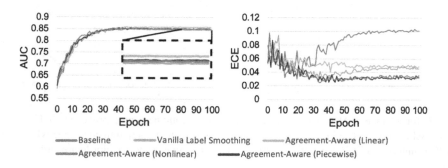

Fig. 2. Whereas the baseline model becomes uncalibrated after training for $\sim$30 epochs (ECE goes up), models trained using agreement-aware label smoothing remained well-calibrated throughout training (ECE stays constant). The models trained using label smoothing achieved similar or better performance (AUC) than the baseline.

4   Label Smoothing: Annotator Agreement

4.1   Improving Accuracy and Calibration

In Table 1, we summarize AUC and ECE values for the best-performing models (which we define as the model with the lowest ECE among models that have a higher AUC than the baseline model) for each label smoothing method. We find that our agreement-aware label smoothing methods decrease mean ECE by up to 6.1% points (a 68.5% decrease) and also improve mean AUC by up to 1.7%, suggesting that our methods can improve calibration without sacrificing accuracy.

We further analyze these models in Fig. 2 by plotting the AUC and ECE of these models on our testing set throughout training. We find that, as expected, the baseline model first experiences a decrease in ECE, then an increase as it begins to overfit to the training set. For models trained with label smoothing, however, the ECE decreases and does not experience a dramatic increase during later epochs. Instead, the ECE holds relatively constantly once it reaches its lowest values. We also found that vanilla label smoothing and linear agreement-aware label smoothing both significantly improved upon the baseline model in terms of ECE. Additionally, piecewise agreement-aware label smoothing and nonlinear agreement-aware label smoothing seem to further improve upon these two methods and achieved the best calibration among models trained using our label smoothing methods.

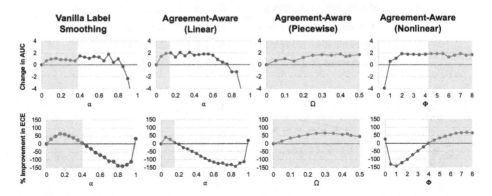

Fig. 3. Top: change in AUC from the baseline model. Bottom: percent improvement in ECE from the baseline model. The highlighted green area indicates the hyperparameter range where both AUC is higher and ECE is lower, compared with the baseline model. (Color figure online)

4.2   Hyperparameter Selection

We conduct extensive ablation studies for each of our label smoothing methods to analyze how robust our models are to different hyperparameter selections and to gain intuition on how different strengths of our agreement-aware label smoothing methods will affect overall performance. In Fig. 3, we show increases/decreases in AUC and ECE on the testing set between the baseline model and models trained using each of the label smoothing methods at many hyperparameter values. We find that all label smoothing methods are able to improve both AUC and ECE for some hyperparameter ranges, and the greatest improvement in calibration (a 68.5% decrease in ECE) occurs when using nonlinear agreement-aware label smoothing with $\Phi = 7.5$. Generally, we find that piecewise agreement-aware label smoothing and nonlinear agreement-aware label smoothing are able to achieve the greatest improvements in model calibration, though vanilla label smoothing and linear agreement-aware label smoothing still yield significant improvements.

5   Label Smoothing: Model Confidence

Because many datasets do not include data from multiple annotators, in this section we conduct experiments on whether our proposed label smoothing methods can still benefit datasets with only one label per example. To do so, we use model confidence in lieu of annotator agreement as a proxy for example difficulty, as proposed in Sect. 2.2. We obtain model confidence data by using each image's confidence output from our baseline model (which was only trained using binary gold standard annotations by majority vote of our seven annotators such as what would be available for a dataset with only one annotator). We then use these confidence outputs to conduct our experiments by using these them to replace the annotator agreement data used in Eqs. 1–4.

Table 2. Confidence-aware label smoothing improves performance (higher AUC) and model calibration (lower ECE). Means and standard deviations are reported across 10 seeds.

Model	AUC	ECE
Baseline	84.7 ± 0.8	8.9 ± 1.4
Confidence-aware (vanilla)	85.2 ± 0.8	3.6 ± 0.5
Confidence-aware (linear)	85.9 ± 0.8	3.5 ± 0.6
Confidence-aware (piecewise)	85.4 ± 0.7	8.4 ± 1.4
Confidence-aware (nonlinear)	$\mathbf{86.2 \pm 1.1}$	$\mathbf{3.2 \pm 0.4}$

5.1   Improving Accuracy and Calibration

We report AUC and ECE values on our testing set for the best-performing models (defined as the model with the lowest ECE among models with a higher AUC than the baseline) for each of our confidence-aware label smoothing methods in Table 2. We find that, although not as effective as agreement-aware label smoothing, confidence-aware label smoothing is still very effective in improving both accuracy and calibration. Confidence-aware label smoothing methods were able to increase AUC by up to 1.5% and decrease ECE by 5.7% points (an improvement of 64.0%). We found, however, that piecewise confidence-aware label smoothing was ineffective, likely because it was overly-complex for already-sophisticated data such as confidence values, resulting in targets that were too convoluted to extract any new information from.

5.2   Hyperparameter Selection

We once again study how robust our confidence-aware label smoothing methods are in terms of choosing a reasonable hyperparameter, and we analyze how different strengths of our confidence-aware label smoothing methods affect model performance. In Fig. 4, we show changes in AUC and improvements in ECE for our confidence-aware label smoothing methods. We find that $0 < \alpha < 0.4$ improves model calibration for vanilla and linear confidence-aware label smoothing, and $3 < \Phi < 8$ improves calibration for nonlinear confidence-aware label smoothing. For piecewise confidence-aware label smoothing, however, model calibration only improves at $\Omega = 0.5$, suggesting that piecewise confidence-aware label smoothing is not robust to hyperparameter selection and offers the least improvement out of all confidence-aware label smoothing methods.

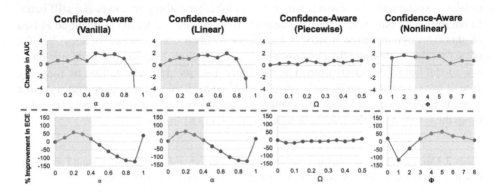

Fig. 4. Top: change in AUC from the baseline model. Bottom: percent improvement in ECE from the baseline model. The highlighted green area indicates the hyperparameter range where both AUC is higher and ECE is lower, compared with the baseline model.

6   Related Work and Discussion

Prior work has found that modern neural networks, though accurate, can be poorly-calibrated [10, 16]. However, calibration is a critical factor to account for when training models (especially for applications such as self-driving cars and health care) and allows for better model interpretability [10]. Label smoothing, originally proposed by Muller et al. [16], seeks to improve calibration and has been found to reduce expected calibration error on computer vision benchmarks such as ImageNet and CIFAR10.

In the domain of medical image analysis, Pham et al. [21] proposed to remap targets to random numbers close to one, finding that this method improved model performance on the CheXpert Dataset [13] by approximately 1.4%. Moreover, Xi et al. [18] addressed uncertainties of correctness using a spatial label smoothing technique to reduce the need for well-annotated data while still achieving satisfactory performance.

Previous research has been largely focused purely on improving calibration and accuracy using label smoothing techniques and primarily uses one-hot encoded labels to do so. However, the existing literature has disregarded the vast amount of information that lies in example difficulty, which could potentially be useful for more-precise label smoothing. Our work thus seeks to expand on existing label smoothing methods by incorporating example difficulty. Perhaps most related to our work, Peterson et al. [20] found that performance on CIFAR10 can be improved by sampling ground truth labels from a distribution of human annotations, which is equivalent to our linear agreement-aware method. Our work proposes a superset of methods operationalized via label smoothing.

Although we intentionally chose the colorectal polyp classification task because it is a common and diagnostically-challenging problem in gastrointestinal pathology—the most-relevant dataset with multiple annotations that we have access to at this time—our study nevertheless is only evaluated on one dataset. As such, we do not consider our encouraging empirical results as validation of our label smoothing methods for all histopathology tasks. Instead, our paper has questioned the traditional practice of assigning hard labels for histopathology image classification and proposed a simple yet effective alternative that invites further research in this direction.

In this paper, we have proposed two well-motivated sets of label smoothing methods for improving the calibration and accuracy of histopathology image classifiers: *agreement-aware* label smoothing, which uses annotator agreement data, and *confidence-aware* label smoothing, which uses model confidence. We apply our method to a colorectal polyp classification task, finding that agreement-aware label smoothing can reduce calibration error by 68.5% while increasing AUC by up to 1.7%, and confidence-aware label smoothing can reduce calibration error by 64.0% while increasing AUC by up to 1.5%. Our paper aims to demonstrate the potential usefulness of including example difficulty when implementing label smoothing, and we hope that our methods can be further implemented across the field of histopathology image classification due to its low computational cost and large potential in improving model calibration and performance.

References

1. Bulten, W., et al.: Automated deep-learning system for Gleason grading of prostate cancer using biopsies: a diagnostic study. Lancet Oncol. **21**(2), 233–241 (2020)
2. Cheplygina, V., Pluim, J.P.W.: Crowd disagreement about medical images is informative. In: Stoyanov, D., et al. (eds.) LABELS/CVII/STENT -2018. LNCS, vol. 11043, pp. 105–111. Springer, Cham (2018). https://doi.org/10.1007/978-3-030-01364-6_12
3. Chilamkurthy, S., et al.: Deep learning algorithms for detection of critical findings in head CT scans: a retrospective study. Lancet **392**, 2388–2396 (2018)
4. Coudray, N., Moreira, A.L., Sakellaropoulos, T., Fenyö, D., Razavian, N., Tsirigos, A.: Classification and mutation prediction from non-small cell lung cancer histopathology images using deep learning. Nat. Med. **24**, 1559–1567 (2017)
5. Ehteshami Bejnordi, B., et al.: Diagnostic assessment of deep learning algorithms for detection of lymph node metastases in women with breast cancer. JAMA **318**(22), 2199–2210 (2017)
6. Esteva, A., et al.: Dermatologist-level classification of skin cancer with deep neural networks. Nature **542**, 115–118 (2017)

7. Farris, A.B., et al.: Sessile serrated adenoma: challenging discrimination from other serrated colonic polyps. Am. J. Surg. Pathol. **32**, 30–35 (2008)
8. Glatz, K., Pritt, B., Glatz, D., Hartmann, A., O'Brien, M.J., Glaszyk, H.: A multinational, internet-based assessment of observer variability in the diagnosis of serrated colorectal polyps. Am. J. Clin. Pathol. **127**, 938–945 (2007)
9. Gulshan, V., et al.: Development and validation of a deep learning algorithm for detection of diabetic retinopathy in retinal fundus photographs. JAMA **316**, 2402–2410 (2016)
10. Guo, C., Pleiss, G., Sun, Y., Weinberger, K.Q.: On calibration of modern neural networks. In: ICML (2017)
11. He, K., Zhang, X., Ren, S., Sun, J.: Deep residual learning for image recognition. In: CVPR (2015)
12. Hinton, G., Vinyals, O., Dean, J.: Distilling the knowledge in a neural network. In: Deep Learning and Representation Learning Workshop at NeurIPS 2014 (2015)
13. Irvin, J., Rajpurkar, P., et al.: CheXpert: a large chest radiograph dataset with uncertainty labels and expert comparison. In: AAAI (2019)
14. Kanavati, F., et al.: Weakly-supervised learning for lung carcinoma classification using deep learning. Nat. Sci. Rep. **10**, 1–11 (2020)
15. Korbar, B., et al.: Deep learning for classification of colorectal polyps on whole-slide images. J. Pathol. Inform. **8**, 30 (2017)
16. Müller, R., Kornblith, S., Hinton, G.: When does label smoothing help? In: NeurIPS (2020)
17. Naeini, M.P., Cooper, G., Hauskrecht, M.: Obtaining well calibrated probabilities using Bayesian binning. In: AAAI (2015)
18. Ouyang, X., et al.: Weakly supervised segmentation framework with uncertainty: a study on pneumothorax segmentation in chest X-ray. In: Shen, D., et al. (eds.) MICCAI 2019. LNCS, vol. 11769, pp. 613–621. Springer, Cham (2019). https://doi.org/10.1007/978-3-030-32226-7_68
19. Papernot, N., McDaniel, P., Wu, X., Jha, S., Swami, A.: Distillation as a defense to adversarial perturbations against deep neural networks. In: 2016 IEEE Symposium on Security and Privacy (SP), pp. 582–597 (2016)
20. Peterson, J., Battleday, R., Griffiths, T., Russakovsky, O.: Human uncertainty makes classification more robust. In: ICCV (2019)
21. Pham, H.H., Le, T.T., Tran, D.Q., Ngo, D.T., Nguyen, H.Q.: Interpreting chest X-rays via CNNs that exploit hierarchical disease dependencies and uncertainty labels. In: MIDL 2020 - Medical Imaging with Deep Learning (2020)
22. Shen, L., Margolies, L.R., Rothstein, J.H., Fluder, E., McBride, R., Sieh, W.: Deep learning to improve breast cancer detection on screening mammography. Nat. Sci. Rep. **9**, 1–12 (2019)
23. Warth, A., et al.: Interobserver variability in the application of the novel IASLC/ATS/ERS classification for pulmonary adenocarcinomas. Eur. Respir. J. **40**(5), 1221–1227 (2012)
24. Wei, J., et al.: Learn like a pathologist: curriculum learning by annotator agreement for histopathology image classification. In: Winter Conference on Applications of Computer Vision (WACV) (2020)
25. Wei, J., et al.: A petri dish for histopathology image analysis. In: Tucker, A., Henriques Abreu, P., Cardoso, J., Pereira Rodrigues, P., Riaño, D. (eds.) AIME 2021. LNCS (LNAI), vol. 12721, pp. 11–24. Springer, Cham (2021). https://doi.org/10.1007/978-3-030-77211-6_2
26. Wong, N., Hunt, L., Novelli, M., Shepherd, N., Warren, B.: Observer agreement in the diagnosis of serrated polyps of the large bowel. Histopathology **55**, 63–66 (2009)

InvUNET: Involuted UNET for Breast Tumor Segmentation from Ultrasound

Trupti Chavan⬤, Kalpesh Prajapati(✉)⬤, and Kameshwar Rao JV

NEXT. ai CoE, HCL Technologies Limited, Noida 201304, India
kalpesh.jp89@gmail.com

Abstract. Breast cancer is one of the fatal health conditions across globe and early detection of such cancerous tumor is life saver. There are various diagnostic ways to detect the tumor, however, ultrasound is more helpful for certain scenarios such as young patient, lactating or pregnant women, radiation sickness and biopsy assistance. This work attempts to detect breast tumors from the ultrasound images using Involuted UNET (InvUNET). It is based on the hybrid combination of deep learning concepts such as UNET and involution layer. UNET has been a popular choice in medical segmentation and the lightweight involution kernels embed the location-specific and channel-agnostic representation learning. The proposed method is validated using Breast Ultrasound Images (BUSI) dataset and jaccard score of 0.7146 is obtained.

Keywords: Breast tumor detection · Convolutional neural networks · InvUNET · Involution · UNET

1 Introduction

According to the survey conducted by World Health Organization (WHO), cancer is the first or second most common reason for the death in more than 100 countries and the majority of the cases suffers from the breast cancer [1]. There are various breast tumor diagnostic methods like mammography, MRI, ultrasound, thermal, histopathological, etc. Although mammogram is highly certified practice for tumor detection, ultrasound has been found more useful for certain scenarios. This includes non-invasive procedure, younger age, lactation state, pregnancy phase, assessment of mammographic abnormalities, clinical breast mass with a negative mammogram, dense or augmented breast, inflammation, and guided biopsy. The use of convolutional neural networks (CNNs) for detection of breast tumors has become very popular and has found to be efficient for automatic diagnostic [2]. The availability of dataset is the key challenge in medical domain, there are very handful datasets available for breast tumor detection from ultrasound. Al-Dhabyani W. et al. [3] have presented the Breast Ultrasound Images (BUSI) dataset and have made publicly available for the research.

A selective kernel UNET (SK-UNET) [4] was introduced to detect breast tumor from ultrasound images; the key idea was to adjust receptive field of network and merge the dilated and conventional convolution feature maps. Irfan R. et al. [5] proposed two

M. Michalowski et al. (Eds.): AIME 2022, LNAI 13263, pp. 283–290, 2022.
https://doi.org/10.1007/978-3-031-09342-5_27

stage convolutional neural network for segmentation and classification tasks. The segmentation network consisted of 24 layers and used transfer learning to extract enriched features. These features are further combined with DenseNet201 features and support vector machine (SVM) was applied to classify the tumor as malignant or benign. To improve segmentation results, authors used erosion morphological operation.

Simple Linear Iterative Clustering (SLIC) was applied to pre-process the ultrasound images and a modified UNET was presented for segmentation of tumors [6]. The authors further used a CNN classifier to distinguish between malignant and benign cases. The pre-trained weights were used to initialize the networks. Xu M. et al. [7] integrated local features and global contextual information in Multi-Scale Self-Attention Network (MSSA-Net) to detect breast tumor from ultrasounds. They also considered self-attention mechanism and multi scales to obtain feature maps.

In this work, an attempt to detect the tumor from ultrasound images is done using Involuted UNET (InvUNET). The proposed architecture is hybrid combination of UNET and involution layer. In medical applications, UNET has become an obvious choice for the segmentation task, while involution layer helps to build lightweight kernels. The results are compared with the state-of-the-art methods for segmentation of medical images.

The rest of the paper is arranged as: Sect. 2 presents the architecture of InvUNET for breast tumor segmentation. In Sect. 3, experimental results are discussed and Sect. 4 reviews the work with concluding remarks.

2 Segmentation of Tumor from Ultrasound Using InvUNET

The automatic segmentation of tumor from ultrasound images using convolutional neural network is presented in this section. The operation of involution layer and the proposed InvUNET architecture is explained.

2.1 Involution Operation

Convolution layer has been very popular in deep learning networks. It has two fundamental properties such as spatial-agnostic and channel-specific; this has led to the phenomenal improvement in performance of CNN models. However, it has limited ability to extract features across different spatial locations due to its locality constraints. Also, the receptive field of convolution operation is an obstacle in capturing the spatial interactions at long range. Along with this, it is seen that, there exists inter-channel redundancy causing to doubt on the channel-specific convolutional kernels. These limitations of convolutional layer motivated Li D. et al. [8] to reassess the fundamental properties of convolutional layer and the authors introduced a reversal operation of convolution called involution. This means involution operation is spatial-specific and channel agnostic in nature i.e. unlike convolution, involution kernels varies spatially but are shared across channels. The challenge of processing varying resolution input features is solved in involution by generating each kernel conditioned on specific spatial locations.

The involution operation is illustrated in Fig. 1 and the output of involution $Y_{i,j,k}$ is given by Eq. 1.

$$Y_{i,j,k} = \sum_{(u,v) \in \Delta K} \mathcal{H}_{i,j,u} + [K/2], v + [K/2], [kG/C]X_{i+u,j+v,k} \tag{1}$$

where, $\mathcal{H}_{i,j,...,g} \varepsilon \mathbb{R}^{K \times K}$ is involution kernel and $g = 1,2,....G$ is designed for pixel $X_{i,j} \varepsilon \mathbb{R}^C$ and denotes the number of groups. The involution kernel which is same for each group is obtained using Eq. 2.

$$\mathcal{H}_{i,j} = \phi(X_{i,j}) = W_1 \sigma(W_0 X_{i,j}) \tag{2}$$

where, ϕ is the kernel generation function and W_0 and W_1 represents the linear transformation functions.

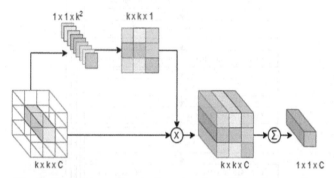

Fig. 1. Illustration of involution operation. (Color figure online)

The summary of involution operation is as below:

1. Consider $1 \times 1 \times C$ feature block (shown in grey color) and convert it into $1 \times 1 \times K^2$ features by using function ϕ which is a convolution layer.
2. These $1 \times 1 \times K^2$ features are reshaped into $K \times K \times 1$ features by using convolution operation.
3. The $K \times K \times 1$ features are treated as filter for performing element-wise multiplication with the input from which it is generated. This helps to broadcast across C channels.
4. The $K \times K$ neighborhood is then summed and $1 \times 1 \times C$ output feature block is obtained.

2.2 Architecture of InvUNET

The architecture of InvUNET is shown in Fig. 2. It is hybrid network of encoder-decoder based segmentation architecture UNET [9] and involution layer [8]. The input size of the InvUNET is 512×512. The backbone network in encoder is similar to VGGNET [11]. It consists of two convolutional layers, involutional layer, maxpool and upsample layer.

The basic block inspired from VGGNET [11] has two convolutional layers with kernel size of 3 × 3 with batch normalization and relu activation function (BR). The involution layer is used after the basic block which has kernel size of 5 × 5. Moreover, we used max-pooling and transposed convolutional layer for down-scale and up-scale the features through UNET architecture respectively. The group channels for involution layer are set

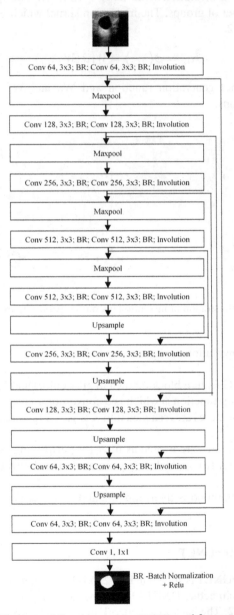

Fig. 2. The architecture of the proposed InvUNET used for tumor segmentation.

to 16 while reduction ratio is 8. The final layer of the InvUNET is convolutional layer of 1 × 1 kernel size and is followed by sigmoid function.

3 Experimental Results

The main objective of the experiments is to segment tumor from breast ultrasound images. The implementation is done in Python (pytorch library). The training is carried out on Nvidia DGX GPU system. To measure the performance, metrics such as jaccard coefficient, dice coefficient, precision, recall and accuracy are used.

The performance of InvUNET is verified on the openly available dataset named as Breast Ultrasound Images (BUSI) [3]. The dataset has been collected by Baheya Hospital for Early Detection and Treatment of Women's Cancer, Egypt and includes breast ultrasound images of 600 women participants in ages between 25 and 75 years old. The dataset consists of 780 images with average size of 500 × 500. There are normal, benign, and malignant categories having 133, 487, and 210 images, respectively. The sample images from the dataset are shown in Fig. 3. Since convolutional neural networks require more data samples, data augmentation techniques such as cropping, rotation, flipping, course dropout, and Gaussian noise are applied to increase the dataset. The dataset is divided into training and testing set containing 517 and 130 samples in each set because of limitation of data.

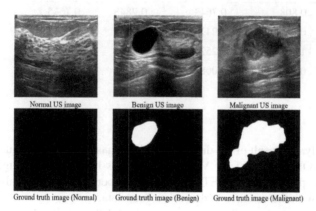

Normal US image   Benign US image   Malignant US image

Ground truth image (Normal)   Ground truth image (Benign)   Ground truth image (Malignant)

Fig. 3. Sample images from BUSI dataset [3]

The InvUNET is trained for 50 epochs using Adam optimization and binary cross entropy (BCE) dice coefficient loss function. The learning rate is kept to 1×10^{-4}, batch size is set to 2.

The details of the comparison among state-of-the-art methods [4, 9, 10] and the proposed method are presented in Table 1. The results are compared with SK-UNET[4], UNET[9] and ColonSegNet [10]. The ColonSegNet [10] has been introduced for polyp segmentation and found to be faster than other existing segmentation networks including

UNET. However, the UNET architecture implemented in this work consists of relatively lesser convolutional layers and hence is found to be faster than the ColonSegNet. We tried the hybrid combination of ColonSegNet and involution layer and named it as InvColonSegNet; the results are found to be improved compared to ColonSegNet, but cannot compete with the InvUNET. From Table 1, it is seen that InvUNET is performing better in terms of performance metrics and the inference time is comparable with most of the methods. InvUNET has achieved better performance at the compromise of little slower prediction time compared to UNET.

Table 1. Comparative results for tumor segmentation from breast ultrasound images

Metric	SK-UNET [4]	ColonSegnet [10]	UNET [9]	Inv-ColonSegNet	Proposed InvUNET
Number of convolutional layers	41	27	19	35	37
Jaccard	NA	0.6271	0.6602	0.6445	0.7146
Dice coefficient	0.709	0.7353	0.7553	0.7491	0.8009
Precision	NA	0.7681	0.8130	0.7958	0.8315
Recall	0.808	0.7643	0.7848	0.7645	0.8277
Accuracy	0.956	0.9478	0.9556	0.9484	0.9609
Mean FPS	16.8350	122.2522	237.8755	100.9807	107.9547
Mean inference Time (s)	0.0594	0.0082	0.0042	0.0099	0.0093

Additionally, the result of the different methods has been validated using statistical test called ANOVA (Analysis of Variance) which is highlighted in Fig. 4. It can be noticed that the proposed InvUNET obtained better performance not only by the mean value but also with the variance of that on various data.

The visual comparison of tumor segmentation of the proposed method with other existing methods are visualized in Fig. 5. It is seen from the figure that the segmentation obtained from InvUNET is better in terms of mitigating false positives and refining segmentation boundaries more accurately.

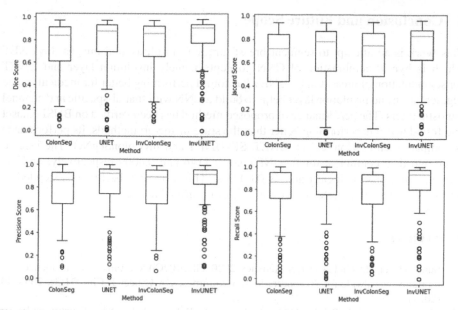

Fig. 4. Statistical analysis by conducting ANOVA test of the proposed method along with other state-of-the-art methods on BUSI data segmentation problem.

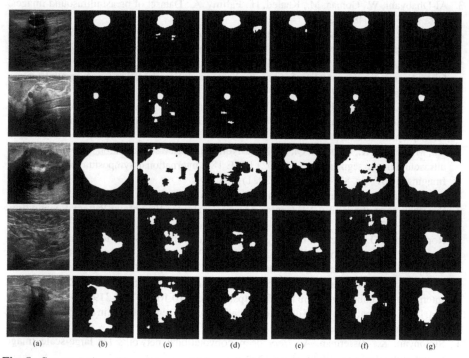

Fig. 5. Segmentation of breast tumor (a) Input image, (b) ground truth, inference results of (c) ColonSegNet [10], (d) UNET [9] (e) SK-UNET [4] (f) InvColonSegNet and (g) InvUNET

4 Conclusion and Future Scope

This work is an attempt to segment breast tumor from ultrasound images. InvUNET which is hybrid combination of CNN concepts namely involution layer and UNET for segmentation of breast tumor. UNET has found performing better for medical image segmentation and involution layer helps to build a CNN with spatial-specific and channel agnostic filters. The performance of proposed method has been verified on BUSI dataset and found that it is performing better than the state-of-the-art methods. Its performance is compared with ColonSegNet, UNET, SK-UNET and InvColonSegNet. The jaccard score and dice coefficient for InvUNET are 0.7146 and 0.8009 respectively; and the inference time for a single frame is 0.0093 s. This work can be further extended to improve the detection performance and is useful during biopsy.

References

1. Sung, H., et al.: Global cancer statistics 2020 GLOBOCAN estimates of incidence and mortality worldwide for 36 cancers in 185 countries. CA Cancer J. Clin. **71**(3), 209–249 (2021)
2. Mahmood, T., Li, J., Pei, Y., Akhtar, F., Imran, A., Rehman, K.U.: A brief survey on breast cancer diagnostic with deep learning schemes using multi-image modalities. IEEE Access **8**, 165779–165809 (2020)
3. Al-Dhabyani, W., Gomaa, M., Khaled, H., Fahmy, A.: Dataset of breast ultrasound images. Data Brief **28**, 104863 (2020)
4. Byra, M., et al.: Breast mass segmentation in ultrasound with selective kernel U-Net convolutional neural network. Biomed. Sign. Process. Control **61**, 102027 (2020)
5. Irfan, R., Almazroi, A.A., Rauf, H.T., Damaševičius, R., Nasr, E.A., Abdelgawad, A.E.: Dilated semantic segmentation for breast ultrasonic lesion detection using parallel feature fusion. Diagnostics **11**(7), 1212 (2021)
6. Inan, M.S.K., Alam, F.I., Hasan, R.: Deep integrated pipeline of segmentation leading to classification for automated detection of breast cancer from breast ultrasound images (2021). arXiv preprint arXiv:2110.14013
7. Xu, M., Huang, K., Chen, Q., Qi, X.: Mssa-Net: multi-scale self-attention network for breast ultrasound image segmentation. In: 2021 IEEE 18th International Symposium on Biomedical Imaging (ISBI), pp. 827–831. IEEE (2021)
8. Li, D., et al.: Involution: inverting the inherence of convolution for visual recognition. In: Proceedings of the IEEE/CVF Conference on Computer Vision and Pattern Recognition, pp. 12321–12330 (2021)
9. Ronneberger, O., Fischer, P., Brox, T.: U-net: convolutional networks for biomedical image segmentation. In: Navab, N., Hornegger, J., Wells, W.M., Frangi, A.F. (eds.) Medical Image Computing and Computer-Assisted Intervention – MICCAI 2015: 18th International Conference, Munich, Germany, October 5-9, 2015, Proceedings, Part III, pp. 234–241. Springer International Publishing, Cham (2015). https://doi.org/10.1007/978-3-319-24574-4_28
10. Jha, D., et al.: Real-time polyp detection, localization and segmentation in colonoscopy using deep learning. IEEE Access **9**, 40496–40510 (2021)
11. Simonyan, K., Zisserman, A.: Very deep convolutional networks for large-scale image recognition (2015). CoRR, abs/1409.1556

MRI Reconstruction with LassoNet and Compressed Sensing

Andrea De Gobbis[1(✉)], Aleksander Sadikov[1,2], and Vida Groznik[1,2,3]

[1] NEUS Diagnostics d.o.o., Ljubljana, Slovenia
a.degobs@gmail.com
[2] Faculty of Computer and Information Science, University of Ljubljana, Ljubljana, Slovenia
[3] Faculty of Mathematics, Natural Sciences and Information Technologies, University of Primorska, Koper, Slovenia

Abstract. One obstacle to Magnetic Resonance Imaging (MRI) is the length of the procedure during which the patient has to stay immobile. Thus, there is a need to reconstruct a MRI scan from a smaller number of measurements and compressed sensing (CS) is a popular method that exploits the sparsity of the image's representation in some domain. In this paper we introduce a way to combine recent deep learning model LassoNet and compressed sensing in the hybrid model CS-LassoNet. Then, we demonstrate how it can be used to rank the importance of frequencies in the k-space and how this allows to design a data driven measurement strategy which focuses on the most important k-values during the acquisition of a MRI scan, resulting in a possible shortening of the procedure without a significant loss in accuracy. We validate our method on the NYU fastMRI datasetwith of knee singlecoil MRI scans and compare the reconstruction results obtained with our strategy (NMSE = 0.0634, SSIM = 0.543) compared to uniform subsampling (NMSE = 0.511, SSIM = 0.183).

Keywords: Magnetic Resonance Imaging · LassoNet · Compressed sensing

1 Introduction

MRI offers an alternative to X-ray scans without using ionizing radiation. Obtaining a MRI scan is a long procedure during which the patient has to stay immobile. In recent years the methods of signal processing and machine learning have been used to reconstruct MR images from a smaller number of measurements with the objective of shortening the acquisition process. Compressed sensing [1] is a mathematically elegant way of reconstructing an image with a number of measurements lower than what is required by the Nyquist criterion, if the image is sparse in some transformed domain. LassoNet [3] is a recently proposed machine learning model that combines the expressive properties of a neural network with the embedded feature selection of Lasso regularization. In this paper

M. Michalowski et al. (Eds.): AIME 2022, LNAI 13263, pp. 291–295, 2022.
https://doi.org/10.1007/978-3-031-09342-5_28

we introduce hybrid model CS-LassoNet that allows to learn the importance of each k-value and at the same time reconstruct the image. We train CS-LassoNet on the NYU fastMRI dataset [2,5], then we demonstrate how a data acquisition strategy based on k-values importance can improve image reconstruction when using compressed sensing, in comparison to uniform subsampling.

2   CS-LassoNet

The method of reconstructing images presented in [4] consists in solving the following optimization problem:

$$y^* = \min_y \quad \frac{1}{2}\|UFy - x\|_2^2 + \mu\|\Psi y\|_{1,1} \tag{1}$$

where $x \in \mathbb{R}^{in}$ are the k-space measurements, $y \in \mathbb{R}^{out}$ is the reconstructed image, F is the Fourier transform, Ψ is the sparsifying transform (in this paper a Haar wavelet transform with 4 levels), U is the undersampling operator, and the norms are defined as

$$\|\mathbf{v}\|_p = \sqrt[p]{\sum_k |\mathbf{v}_k|^p}, \qquad \|A\|_{p,q} = \sqrt[p]{\sum_j \|A_j\|_q^p}$$

with A_j is the j-th column of the matrix. This method is based on the observation that most of the wavelet coefficients of the MR image are close to zero. A LassoNetAE [3] is a feed-forward autoencoder with a skip layer from input to hidden features layer. Our model combines the feature selection of LassoNetAE and the regularization of compressed sensing:

$$\begin{cases} \mathbf{z} = \Theta \cdot \mathbf{x} + \text{Encoder}(\mathbf{x}; W_e, b_e) \\ \hat{\mathbf{y}} = \text{Decoder}(\mathbf{z}; W_d, b_d) \end{cases} \tag{2}$$

where $\mathbf{x} \in \mathbb{R}^{2 \cdot in}$ are the flattened k-values (real and imaginary part), $\mathbf{z} \in \mathbb{R}^k$ are the hidden features, $\hat{\mathbf{y}} \in \mathbb{R}^{out_1 \times out_2}$ the output images, $\Theta \in \mathbb{R}^{(2 \cdot in) \times k}$ is the skip layer weight matrix, Encoder is a fully connected feed forward neural network, Decoder is a convolutional neural network, and $W_{e,d}$, $b_{e,d}$ are the weights and biases. For the network architecture we took inspiration from AUTOMAP [6], which also uses k-space measurements as input; a diagram of the model can be found in Fig. 1. The optimization problem is:

$$\begin{cases} \text{Minimize} & MSE(\mathbf{y}, \hat{\mathbf{y}}) + \mu\|\Psi\hat{\mathbf{y}}\|_{1,1} + \lambda\|\Theta\|_{1,2} \\ \text{Subject to} & \|W_{e,j}^{(1)}\|_\infty \le M\|\Theta_j\|_2 \; \forall j \end{cases} \tag{3}$$

where $W_e^{(1)}$ is the weight matrix of the first layer. We use a dense-to-sparse training strategy denominated λ-path: optimization starts with $\lambda = 0$ for the first 300 epochs and then, starting from $\lambda_0 = 5.0$, λ increases geometrically every 50 epochs. This is repeated until all elements of $\mathbf{x}$ are selected out. Then the *importance* of a feature $\mathcal{I}(\mathbf{x}_j)$ is equal to the λ at which the feature was excluded from the model.

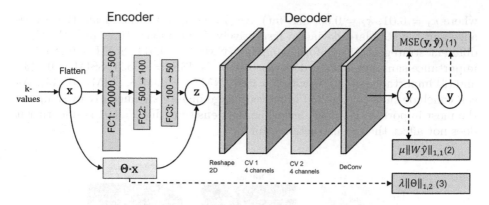

Fig. 1. The architecture of CS-LassoNet: the encoder is a feed forward neural network with three fully connected hidden layers. The decoder is a CNN with two convolutional and one deconvolutional layer. The skipThe loss function is composed of three component: (1) the reconstruction loss, (2) the sparse regularization term, and (3) the skip loss.

3 Methods and Results

We test our model on single coil MRI scans of human knees from the NYU fastMRI dataset [2,5], which consist of a training set of $N_{train} = 973$ patients and a validation set of $N_{val} = 189$ patients. The model input is the raw k-space measurements and the target variable is the RSS-reconstruction. Before training we preprocess the dataset by keeping only the central slice for each patient along the z-axis, cropping the image to dimension 200×200 pixels and cropping the respective k-space array to dimension 100×100 pixels.

This cropping makes the model easier to train, and is motivated by the fact that the highest frequencies in the k-space are located at the center of the image (see Fig. 2). We consider this a preliminary pixel selection. We train CS-LassoNet on a λ-path and computed the importance of each frequency (real and imaginary part separately) in the k-space ($\mathbf{k}_{ij}$), for $\mu = 0.0$ (no sparse regularization) and $\mu = 0.01$. From the *importance values* $[\mathcal{I}(\text{Re}(\mathbf{k}_{ij})), \mathcal{I}(\text{Im}(\mathbf{k}_{ij}))]$ we design a cartesian sampling scheme, called *importance sampling* on the input k-values: $K = 50$ columns are selected without replacement with probability

$$p_j \sim \frac{1}{100} \sum_{i=1}^{100} \log(\sqrt{\mathcal{I}(\text{Re}(\mathbf{k}_{ij}))^2 + \mathcal{I}(\text{Im}(\mathbf{k}_{ij}))^2}),$$

the resulting probability densities are plotted in Fig. 3. The importance values computed by CS-LassoNet appears to be correlated with the module of the k-values (see Fig. 2-A). To validate the result, we assess reconstruction quality obtained with compressed sensing on the validation set and measured by:

$$\text{NMSE}(\mathbf{y}, \hat{\mathbf{y}}) = \frac{\|\mathbf{y} - \hat{\mathbf{y}}\|_2^2}{\|\hat{\mathbf{y}}\|_2^2}, \ \text{SSIM}(\mathbf{y}, \hat{\mathbf{y}}) = \frac{(2m(\hat{\mathbf{y}}) \cdot m(\mathbf{y}) + k_1^2)(cov(\hat{\mathbf{y}}, \mathbf{y}) + k_2^2)}{(m(\hat{\mathbf{y}})^2 + m(\mathbf{y})^2 + k_1^2)(sd(\hat{\mathbf{y}})^2 + sd(\mathbf{y})^2 + k_2^2)},$$

where $k_1 = 0.01$, $k_2 = 0.03$, and $m()$, $cov()$ and $sd()$ are the mean, the covariance and the standard deviation respectively. We compare three over the three different strategies: (1) uniform sampling (NMSE = 0.511, SSIM = 0.183), (2) importance sampling obtained with $\mu = 0.0$ (NMSE = 0.0634, SSIM = 0.543), and (3) importance sampling with $\mu = 0.01$ (NMSE = 0.0648, SSIM = 0.543). We can conclude that our method improved image quality significantly by sampling the most important k-values, but while the density with $\mu = 0.01$ is smoother it does not affect the reconstruction error.

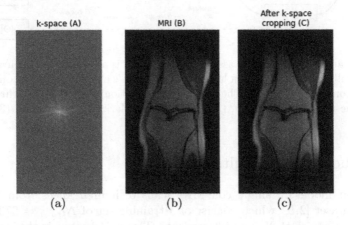

Fig. 2. (A) k-space module in logarithmic scale. It can be noticed that the largest values are found in the center. (B) Original MRI scan. (C) Scan obtained after keeping 25% of the frequencies. The NMSE is 0.035 between normalized images.

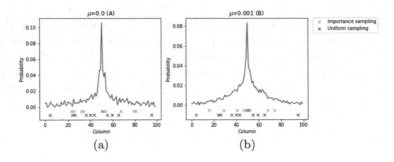

Fig. 3. Sampling strategies based on feature importances computed with CS-LassoNet against a uniform random sampling. With (A) $\mu = 0.0$ and (B) $\mu = 0.01$. Sparse regularization affects the smoothness of the density.

4   Discussion and Conclusions

We presented an introduction of CS-LassoNet and some preliminary results on how it can be used to design sampling strategies based on k-values importance.

We showed how this approach can lead to improved reconstruction compared to uniform random sampling. It is yet unclear how big of an improvement can be obtained with CS-LassoNet compared to simpler subsampling strategies based on k-value magnitudes. The model can be generalized to any sparse signal to design a data-driven sampling strategy optimal for reconstruction, and may allow to reduce the number of measurements when acquisition is costly.

Acknowledgments. This research was partly founded by the Slovenian Research Agency under the Research Program P2-0209 and H20202 MSCA-ITN project PARENT, Grant Agreement N° 956394. Data used in the preparation of this article were obtained from the NYU fastMRI Initiative database (https://fastmri.med.nyu.edu/) [2,5]. As such, NYU fastMRI investigators provided data but did not participate in analysis or writing of this report.

References

1. Donoho, D.: Compressed sensing. IEEE Trans. Inf. Theory **52**(4), 1289–1306 (2006). https://doi.org/10.1109/TIT.2006.871582
2. Knoll, F., et al.: fastMRI: a publicly available raw k-space and DICOM dataset of knee images for accelerated MR image reconstruction using machine learning. Radiol. Artif. Intell. **2**(1), e190007 (2020). https://doi.org/10.1148/ryai.2020190007
3. Lemhadri, I., Ruan, F., Abraham, L., Tibshirani, R.: LassoNet: a neural network with feature sparsity. J. Mach. Learn. Res. **22**(127), 1–29 (2021). http://jmlr.org/papers/v22/20-848.html
4. Lustig, M., Donoho, D., Pauly, J.M.: Sparse MRI: the application of compressed sensing for rapid MR imaging. Magn. Reson. Med. **58**(6), 1182–1195 (2007). https://doi.org/10.1002/mrm.21391
5. Zbontar, J., et al.: fastMRI: an open dataset and benchmarks for accelerated MRI (2019)
6. Zhu, B., Liu, J.Z., Cauley, S.F., Rosen, B.R., Rosen, M.S.: Image reconstruction by domain-transform manifold learning. Nature **555**(7697), 487–492 (2018). https://doi.org/10.1038/nature25988

Predictive Modeling

A 3-Window Framework for the Discovery and Interpretation of Predictive Temporal Functional Dependencies

Beatrice Amico[✉] and Carlo Combi[iD]

Department of Computer Science, University of Verona, Verona, Italy
{beatrice.amico,carlo.combi}@univr.it

Abstract. Clinical databases collect large volume of data. Relationships and patterns within these data could provide new medical knowledge. Temporal data mining has as major scope the discovery of potential hidden knowledge from large amounts of data, offering the possibility to identify different features less visible or hidden to common analysis techniques. In this work, we show how temporal data mining, precisely mining of functional dependencies, can be fruitfully exploited to improve clinical prediction. To develop an early prediction model, a window-based data aggregation approach could be a good starting point, therefore we introduce a new temporal framework based on three temporal windows designed to extract predictive information. In particular, we propose a methodology for deriving a new kind of predictive temporal patterns. We exploit the predictive aspect of the approximate temporal functional dependencies, formally introducing the concept of Predictive Functional Dependency (PFD), a new type of approximate temporal functional dependency. We discuss some first results we obtained by pre-processing and mining ICU data from the MIMIC III database, focusing on functional dependencies predictive of Acute kidney injury (AKI).

Keywords: Temporal data mining · Predictive patterns · Functional dependencies · Temporal windows

1 Introduction

The increasing use and availability of longitudinal electronic data provide the opportunity to discover new knowledge from multivariate, time-oriented data, by using various data mining methods.

Temporal data mining in medicine has been receiving considerable attention since it provides a way of revealing useful information hidden in the clinical data, extracting different temporal patterns. The analysis of such healthcare/medical data collections could greatly help to observe the health conditions of the population and extract useful information that can be exploited in the assessment

---

Student paper submission.

of healthcare/medical processes [2]. For example, together with temporal data mining, clinical data sources enable us to rapidly generate prediction models for thousands of clinical problems, for identifying diagnoses, speed medical processes, risks prevention, prediction of mortality, and risk stratification [11].

Particularly, prediction of medical events, such as clinical procedures, is essential for preventing disease, understanding disease mechanism, and increasing patient quality of care. When we talk about prediction, we associate the well-known machine learning techniques and the already known black box problem. In the last two decades, several supervised learning methods have been introduced [1], but often, it is not possible to understand why machine learning algorithms are proposing specific predictions. On the contrary, temporal patterns represent an explainable way to study the intrinsic data dependencies, to allow physicians to focus on the most interesting and relevant discovered rules.

According to this scenario, the main novelty of this paper is the proposal of an original temporally-oriented data mining technique for the prediction of clinical diseases. Therefore, we propose a new type of functional dependencies, the *approximate predictive functional dependencies* (APFDs). They are evaluated within a new temporal framework based on three temporal windows: observation window, waiting window, prediction window.

The paper is organized as follows. In Sect. 2 we briefly describe some related work, relevant to the topic discussed in this paper. In Sect. 3 we introduce a new temporal framework based on three temporal windows: observation window, waiting window, prediction window. Then, we define the entire framework for the approximate predictive functional dependencies (APFDs), introducing two new error measures. In Sect. 4 we detail the first application of this framework on real clinical data from patients hospitalized in Intensive Care Units, using MIMIC III [6]. In Sect. 5 we draw some conclusions and discuss possible future work.

2   Related Work

In the context of temporal data mining, various techniques are applied to time-oriented data to discover knowledge about relationships among different raw data and abstract concepts, in which the temporal dimension is treated explicitly.

Associations discovery is one of the most common Data Mining (DM) techniques used to extract interesting knowledge from large datasets. Association rules enable the identification of correlations between the elements of a dataset. In literature, we find different methods to mine temporal association rules (TARs) aiming at providing a greater predictive and descriptive potential in different contexts, with a high number of contributions in the context of medicine and healthcare [13].

Mining time intervals data is another interesting research field, especially for the extraction of Time Intervals Related Patterns (TIRPs). In [4], the authors introduce TIRPClo, an efficient algorithm for the discovery of frequent closed TIRPs, a compact subset of all the frequent TIRPs based on which their complete information can be revealed. In addition, it is possible to use patterns as features for classification. For example, in [11], the authors propose a framework for discovering TIRPs only from the cohort of patients having the outcome event. The results showed that representing the TIRPs using the horizontal support outperformed the binary and mean duration representations.

Among temporal abstractions, we also find the trend abstractions that focus on detecting changes in the temporal evolution. In [9], starting from the concept of Trend-Event Pattern [10] and moving through the concept of *prediction*, the authors propose a new kind of predictive temporal patterns, namely Predictive Trend-Event Patterns (PTE-Ps). The framework aims to combine complex temporal features to extract a compact and non-redundant predictive set of patterns composed by such temporal features.

Another type of temporal pattern is functional dependency. In literature there are different extensions, temporal functional dependency (TFD) [3], approximate functional dependency (AFD) [8], and approximate temporal functional dependencies (ATFDs) [2]. Temporal functional dependencies (TFDs) add a temporal dimension to classical functional dependencies (FDs) to deal with temporal data. In [3], Combi et al. propose a new formalism for the representation of TFDs, involving multiple time granularities. They identify four relevant classes of TFDs: Pure temporally grouping, Pure temporally evolving, Temporally mixed, and Temporally hybrid. Moving on, approximate functional dependency (AFD) derives from the concept of plain FD. Given a relation r where an FD holds for most of the tuples in r, we may identify some tuples for which that FD does not hold. In [8], Kivinen and Mannila introduce three measures, known as G_1, G_2 and G_3 considering the number of violating couples of tuples, the number of tuples that violate the functional dependency, and finally the minimum number of tuples in r to be deleted for the FD to hold. In [2], the authors propose the concept of approximate temporal functional dependencies (ATFDs), which are defined and measured either on temporal granules or on sliding windows, considering the psychiatry and pharmacovigilance domains.

3   Predictive Functional Dependencies

In this section, we describe a new temporal framework and detail definitions to mine the approximate predictive functional dependencies (APFDs).

3.1   A 3-Window Framework for the Interpretation of Predictive Temporal Data

As previously said, data mining in medicine has great potential for discovering hidden patterns in data sets from the medical domain. In such conditions, we face the challenge of the extraction of hidden predictive information from large databases. To develop an early prediction model, a window-based data aggregation approach could be a good starting point. As far as we know, the prediction models exploit the use of two-time windows. The first one, called data collection or observation window, concerns the collection of data that allows us to predict the problem of interest, and the second one, the prediction window, in which the key event occurs. Here, we generalize an approach based on three (possibly moving) time windows. So that the prediction becomes effective, it is necessary that clinicians can act before a clinical decline has occurred by: (i) delivering insights on preventable conditions; (ii) offering contextual information to help clinical decision-making; (iii) being generally applicable across a different cohort of patients. The anticipation of a future event is obviously relevant, but the more significant facet is the time needed to anticipate a future event, that is a key aspect, especially in medicine. Acknowledge these prerequisites, in this paper we propose a framework based on three windows: (i) an observation window (OW); (ii) a waiting window (WW); and (iii) a prediction window (PW). The OW is considered as a time interval, where the information is collected, and ends when an event of interest occurs. The WW is held to be the minimum time interval required to act in order to prevent the event in the prediction window. Finally, the PW, the time interval when the predicted event occurs.

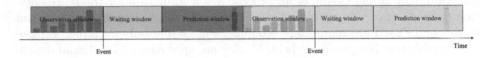

Fig. 1. 3 window-based framework

3.2 Towards the Definition of Predictive Functional Dependencies

A FD is composed of the antecedent (X) and the consequent (Y). Informally, for all the couples of tuples t and t' showing the same value(s) on X, the corresponding value(s) on Y for those tuples are identical. In our specific case, we describe the antecedent as a set of attributes ordered on VT, called *predictive attributes*, and the consequent defined as the *predicted attribute*.

Let us consider a database schema DB as a set of temporal relational schemas $\{R_1, ..., R_n\}$ and a set of corresponding instances $\{r_1, ..., r_n\}$. Any schema R_i has attributes $ZU_i \cup \{VT\}$, where $\forall R_i, R_j$ with $i \neq j$ it holds $U_i \cap U_j = \emptyset$. U_i is a set of attributes representing properties of a patient, which is identified by attributes Z (hereinafter patient identification attributes). VT is the attribute representing the temporal dimension of the tuples.

Given a set of relations $\{r_1, ..., r_m\}$ according to the data schema DB, a **State expression** with schema $ZU \cup \{VT\}$ where $U \equiv U_i U_j ... U_m$ is defined as

$$SE \equiv r | r_i \bowtie r_j \bowtie ... r_m$$

Definition 1 (K-State evolution expression (KSE)). *Given a set of State Expressions* $\{SE_\alpha(ZU_\alpha \cup \{VT\}), ..., SE_\omega(ZU_\omega \cup \{VT\})\}$, *a **K-State evolution expression** with schema* $Z\overline{U}_\alpha^0 \overline{U}_\beta^1 .. \overline{U}_\kappa^k \cup \{\overline{VT}_\alpha^0, \overline{VT}_\beta^1, .., \overline{VT}_\kappa^k\}$ *is defined as:*

$$KSE \equiv \Theta(\overline{SE}^0_\alpha, \overline{SE}^1_\beta, ...\overline{SE}^k_\kappa) \ with \ \overline{VT}^0 < \overline{VT}^1 < .. < \overline{VT}^k$$

$$and \ \overline{SE}^0_\alpha = \rho_{U_\alpha, VT \rightarrow \overline{U}^0_\alpha, \overline{VT}^0} SE_\alpha, \ \ \overline{SE}^1_\beta = \rho_{U_\beta, VT \rightarrow \overline{U}^1_\beta, \overline{VT}^1} SE_\beta, \ ... \tag{1}$$

Function Θ allows different evolutions of the same State Expressions. For example, it can represent suitable join of different State Expressions according to the patient attributes, possibly using the same attribute at different states. It can allow also the join of tuples at distance k (for k = 1, it joins pairs of consecutive corresponding tuples) or allow one to join pairs of successive (concerning the values they take on attribute VT) tuples.

Let us now move to consider the attributes to be considered in the prediction, i.e., boolean attributes representing the presence/absence of a pathological state. We can join such attributes to a KSE to build a K-State Prediction Expression.

Definition 2 (K-State Prediction Expression (KSPE)). *Given a schema $R \in DB$, with attributes $ZU_p \cup \{VT\}$, a K-State Prediction Expression (KSPE) is defined as:*

$$\sigma_{\substack{0 \leq (\overline{VT}^k - \overline{VT}^0) < OW \wedge \\ (\dot{VT} - \overline{VT}^0 \geq OW + WW) \wedge \\ (\dot{VT} - \overline{VT}^0 < OW + WW + PW)}} KSE \bowtie \dot{R} \tag{2}$$

$$and \ \dot{R} = \rho_{U_p, VT \rightarrow \dot{U}_p, \dot{VT}} R$$

Analogously to the previous renaming, $\dot{U}_p$ represents the overall renaming of the attribute set of $\dot{R}$, where $\dot{R}$ is the patient relation.

Definition 3 (Predictive Functional Dependency (PFD)). *Given a K state prediction expression KSPE with schema $Z\overline{U}^0_\alpha \overline{U}^1_\beta .. \overline{U}^k_\kappa \dot{U}_p \cup \{\overline{VT}^0, \overline{VT}^1, .., \overline{VT}^k, \dot{VT}\}$, a Predictive Functional Dependency is a FD, of the following form:*

$$\overline{X}^h \, \overline{S}^i \, ... \overline{W}^j \rightarrow \dot{B} \ with \ 0 \leq h < i... < j \leq k$$

where $\overline{X}^h \subseteq \overline{U}^h, \overline{S}^i \subseteq \overline{U}^i, \overline{W}^j \subseteq \overline{U}^j$ and $\dot{B} \in \dot{U}_p$ is the predicted (Boolean) attribute. $\tag{3}$

Table 1 represents an example of a general KSPE, where the PFD reported below holds.

Table 1. A KSPE where $\overline{Resprate}^0, \overline{SpO_2}^1, \overline{Drug}^2 \to A\dot{K}I$ holds.

Tuple #	Patient	$\overline{RespRate}^0$	VT^0	$\overline{SpO_2}^1$	VT^1	$\overline{Drug}^2$	VT^2	$A\dot{K}I$	$\dot{V}T$
1	Mark Jones	High	1	Low	2	Aspirin	3	F	4
2	Mark Jones	High	3	Medium	4	Indapamide	5	T	6
3	Mark Jones	Medium	5	Medium	6	Metolazone	7	T	8
4	Mark Jones	High	8	Medium	9	Indapamide	10	T	11
5	Viola Thompson	Low	2	High	3	Aspirin	4	F	6
6	Viola Thompson	Low	3	Medium	4	Indapamide	5	F	7
7	Viola Thompson	Low	4	Low	5	Aspirin	2	F	8
8	Paul Walker	Medium	1	High	2	Ibuprofen	3	T	5
9	Paul Walker	Medium	1	High	2	Sulindac	3	T	5
10	Paul Walker	Medium	2	Medium	3	Indapamide	5	T	8

3.3 Discovering Approximate PFDs

The term approximation is about the approximate satisfaction of a normal PFD $\overline{X}^h \overline{S}^i ... \overline{W}^j \to \dot{B}$.

An APFD f requires the PFD to be satisfied by most tuples of temporal relation r. It allows a very small portion of tuples of r to violate the dependency. If it is less than or equal to the satisfaction threshold ε, f is approximately satisfied on r. Several methods have been proposed to calculate the error measure. In the context of PFDs, we reconsider a measure proposed in [8] and we introduce two other error measures, specifically tailored to the predictive purpose of APFDs.

Considering a general KSPE w over a schema $Z\overline{U}_\alpha^0\overline{U}_\beta^1..\overline{U}_\kappa^k\dot{U}_p \cup \{\overline{VT}^0, \overline{VT}^1, .., \overline{VT}^k, \dot{V}T\}$ and any set $s \subseteq w$, where the PFD holds, we define three error measures. We start from G_3 that considers the minimum number of tuples in r to be deleted to obtain a relation where the PFD holds. This measure is defined as follows:

Definition 4 (Error measure G_3). *Given a PFD expressed as in Definition 3, the error measure G3 is expressed as:*

$$G_3 = |w| - max\left\{|s| \mid s \subseteq w \land s \models \overline{X}^h \overline{S}^i ... \overline{W}^j \to \dot{B}\right\} \quad (4)$$

The related *scaled measurement* g_3 is defined as $g_3 = G_3/|w|$.

Secondly, we introduce H_3 that considers the maximality focused on the number of patients that we accept to loose for the sake of the PFD. This maximality permits to delete patients with a very low number of tuples, which could generate noise in our dataset. H_3 can be formalized as follows:

Definition 5 (Error measure H_3). *Given a PFD expressed as in Definition 3, the error measure H3 is expressed as:*

$$H_3 = |\{t[Z] \mid \exists t \in w\}| - \max_s\left\{\left|\{t[Z] \mid \exists t \in s \land s \subseteq w \land s \models \overline{X}^h \overline{S}^i ... \overline{W}^j \to \dot{B}\}\right|\right\} \quad (5)$$

The related *scaled measurement* h_3 is defined as $h_3 = H_3/|\{t[Z] \mid \exists t \in w\}|$.

Finally, we can formalize J_3 that focuses on the number of tuples for each patient we accept to delete in order to satisfy the PFD. This error is very useful to ensure to maintain enough information for each patient, ensuring to be consistent.

Definition 6 (Error measure J_3). *Given a PFD expressed as in Definition 3, the error measure J_3 can be formalized as follows:*

$$J_3 = \max_{(v \in \{t[Z] \mid t \in s\})} \{|\{t[Z] \mid t \in w \wedge t[Z] = v\}| - |\{t[Z] \mid t \in s \wedge t[Z] = v\}|\} \quad (6)$$

The related *scaled measurement* j_3 weights each term of J_3 with respect to the number of tuples in w having value v for $t[Z]$.

After the introduction of these three error measures, we are now ready to define the approximate predictive functional dependency as follows:

Definition 7 (Approximate Predictive Functional Dependency (APFD)). *Let w be a relationship over a K-state prediction expression: let $X, \dot{B} \subseteq R$ be sets of attributes of R. Relation w fulfills the functional dependency $\overline{X}^h \overline{S}^i ... \overline{W}^j \xrightarrow{\varepsilon} \dot{B}$ (written as $w \models \overline{X}^h \overline{S}^i ... \overline{W}^j \xrightarrow{\varepsilon} \dot{B}$) if $G(\overline{X}^h \overline{S}^i ... \overline{W}^j \xrightarrow{\varepsilon} \dot{B}, w) \leq \varepsilon$, where $\varepsilon = < \varepsilon_g, \varepsilon_h, \varepsilon_j >$ and $0 \leq \varepsilon < 1$ is the maximum acceptable error defined by the user. G is the corresponding error of the previously introduced measures.*

Among the several APFDs that can be detected over a relation w, the minimal APFD is particularly interesting. We thus define the minimal APFD as follows:

Definition 8 (Minimal APFD). *An APFD $\overline{X}^h \overline{S}^i ... \overline{W}^j \xrightarrow{\varepsilon} \dot{B}$ is minimal for w, if $w \models \overline{X}^h \overline{S}^i ... \overline{W}^j \xrightarrow{\varepsilon} \dot{B}$ and $\forall \overline{V} \subset \overline{X}^h \overline{S}^i ... \overline{W}^j$ we have that $w \not\models \overline{V} \xrightarrow{\varepsilon} \dot{B}$.*

As an example, according to the data in Table 1, the APFD $\overline{SPO_2}^1, \overline{Drug}^2 \xrightarrow{\varepsilon} A\dot{K}I$ holds with $\varepsilon = 0.1$. Indeed it is enough the delete tuple 6, to have the corresponding PFD satisfied.

4   Deriving APFDs: an Experimental Evaluation

4.1   Dataset and Data Transformation

To illustrate the relevance and the potential meaning of our proposal, we consider a real-world example from the domain of Intensive Care Unit (ICU) with patients suffering from Acute Kidney Injury (AKI). Acute Kidney Injury is a frequent clinical problem, associated with a mortality of 50–80%, characterized by a sudden loss of the ability of the kidneys to excrete wastes, concentrate urine, store electrolytes, and maintain fluid balance [12]. A ground-truth label for the diagnosis of AKI is added using the internationally accepted KDIGO criteria [7]. A patient receives the diagnosis of AKI if one of the following criteria is valid: (i) an increase in serum creatinine by ≥ 0.3 mg/dl ($\geq 26.5\,\mu$mol/l) within 48 h, (ii) an increase in serum creatinine to ≥ 1.5 times baseline within the previous 7 d and (iii) a urine volume ≤ 0.5 ml/kg/h for 6 h.

Our methodology is applied using the MIMIC III (Medical Information Mart for Intensive Care) dataset [6], a freely accessible relational database of de-identified patients, hospitalized in the intensive care units at Beth Israel Deaconess Medical Center between 2001 and 2012.

An ETL (Extract, Transform, Load) process is necessary to transform the MIMIC-III raw data in a form useful for mining the APFDs. To obtain SEs, we use four tables. *Prescriptions* provides information about the administered medications, for a given patient. We mainly consider the following categories: diuretics, Non-steroidal anti-inflammatory drugs (NSAID), radio contrast agents, and angiotensin. *Chartevents* contains information about vital signs measured at the bedside. We mainly consider diastolic blood pressure, glucose, heart rate and temperature. *D_items* is the reference table needed to label every measure related to a patient. *Labevents* was used to extract the information about serum creatinine and urine, useful for the diagnosis of AKI.

Because of the high number of measures, we applied three aggregate functions, minimum, maximum and average every specified time interval. Moreover, *Chartevents* and *Labevents* contain numerical variables, so we categorize the measures into "low, medium, high" according to clinical literature.

To summarize, there is a new table for each considered vital sign, which contains: icustay_id, minimum, maximum, and average of the measure and the valid time expressed by an interval. From these tables, we create different SEs in order to obtain a KSE. PFDs are retrieved from a KSPE, generated joining a KSE and the patient table $\dot{R}$, through an algorithm inspired by TANE [5], a popular approximate functional dependency detection algorithm.

4.2   Results

The final scope of these experiments is to find significant PDFs for the AKI diagnosis. We illustrate the results obtained with the following 3-window framework: an observation window of 48 h, where we collect all the measures related to each patient, a waiting window of 12 h where we do not consider any event, and then a prediction window where there is the onset of the illness according to one of the KDIGO criteria or the discharge from the ward with any criteria satisfied, of 72h hours. Starting from a cohort of 50711 patients, we extract subjects that receive a diagnosis or a discharge from the ICU, at least after 60 h from the admission in ICU, namely the duration of the observation and the waiting windows, thus obtaining 7930 patients. Among these patients, there are 6024 controls and 1906 cases. Starting from the literature [14], we considered six measures: creatinine, glucose, administered drugs, respiratory rate, diastolic pressure, oxygen saturation, and body temperature. We take into consideration the average of each measure every 6 h, a time interval sufficiently long to reduce the number of records, obtaining significant results.

We generate three different KSPEs based on three different Θ expressions:

- a KSE with four states where except for the first state composed of one measure, the other three states involve two measures recorded at the same valid time, temporally ordered, i.e., $\overline{VT}^0 < \overline{VT}^1 < \overline{VT}^2 < \overline{VT}^3$.

– a KSE with four states where, except for the first state composed of one measure, the other three states involve two measures recorded at the same valid time, temporally ordered where $\overline{VT}^k = \overline{VT}^{k-1} + 1$ for $k = 1, .., 3$.
– a KSE with seven states, temporally ordered.

We mine the minimal APFDs, where the approximation is given by G_3. In the three KSPEs, we obtain results using a margin error over 0.2. To achieve functional dependencies with more than one antecedent, we have to consider a margin error between 0.2 and 0.3. Getting closer to 0.3, the temporal states keep dropping until the results of functional dependencies consist of a single antecedent.

In Table 2, we report some functional dependencies regarding the three KSPEs. As we discussed before, it is possible to observe the drop which is inversely proportional to the epsilon value. For each KSPE, we select a PFD to show some value combinations peculiar of the cases, reported in Table 3.

Table 2. A list of PFDs valid on one of the three KPSEs, with a certain epsilon value.

PFD	Epsilon	KSPE
$\overline{Creat}^0, \overline{Drug}^1, \overline{Diastolic}^1, \overline{RespRate}^2, \overline{Glucose}^2, \overline{Temperature}^3, \overline{SpO_2}^3 \to A\dot{K}I$	0,27	KSPE 1
$\overline{Creat}^0, \overline{Drug}^1, \overline{Diastolic}^1, \overline{Glucose}^2, \overline{Temperature}^3, \overline{SpO_2}^3 \to A\dot{K}I$	0,28	KSPE 1
$\overline{Diastolic}^1, \overline{RespRate}^2, \overline{Glucose}^2, \overline{Temperature}^3, \overline{SpO_2}^3 \to A\dot{K}I$	0,29	KSPE 1
$\overline{Creat}^0, \overline{Drug}^1, \overline{RespRate}^2, \overline{Glucose}^2, \overline{Temperature}^3, \overline{SpO_2}^3 \to A\dot{K}I$	0,25	KSPE 2
$\overline{Creat}^0, \overline{RespRate}^2, \overline{Glucose}^2, \overline{Temperature}^3 \to A\dot{K}I$	0,28	KSPE 2
$\overline{RespRate}^2, \overline{Glucose}^2, \overline{Temperature}^3, \overline{SpO_2}^3 \to A\dot{K}I$	0,30	KSPE 2
$\overline{Creat}^0, \overline{Drug}^1, \overline{Diastolic}^2, \overline{RespRate}^3, \overline{Glucose}^4, \overline{Temperature}^5, \overline{SpO_2}^6 \to A\dot{K}I$	0,23	KSPE 3
$\overline{Creat}^0, \overline{Diastolic}^2, \overline{RespRate}^3, \overline{Glucose}^4, \overline{Temperature}^5 \to A\dot{K}I$	0,26	KSPE 3
$\overline{Creat}^0, \overline{Diastolic}^2, \overline{RespRate}^3, \overline{Temperature}^5 \to A\dot{K}I$	0,28	KSPE 3

Table 3. (a) $\overline{Creat}^0, \overline{Drug}^1, \overline{Diastolic}^1, \overline{RespRate}^2, \overline{Glucose}^2, \overline{Temperature}^3, \overline{SpO_2}^3 \to A\dot{K}I$,
(b) $\overline{Creat}^0, \overline{RespRate}^2, \overline{Glucose}^2, \overline{Temperature}^3 \to A\dot{K}I$,
(c) $\overline{Creat}^0, \overline{Diastolic}^2, \overline{RespRate}^3, \overline{Temperature}^5 \to A\dot{K}I$

Num.	Value comb.	F	T
#1	high, diu, low, med, med, low, low	13	39
#2	high, nsaid, low, med, high, low, med	0	23
#3	low, diu, med, high, high, high, med	15	35
#4	high, diu, low, med, high, low, med	30	50
#5	high, diu, med, high, med, low, med	28	47

(a) Value combinations of KSPE 1

Num.	Value comb.	F	T
#1	high, high, med, low	3	7
#2	low, high, med, high	2	7
#3	high, med, high, low	2	4
#4	low, med, high, med	0	4
#5	high, med, low, med	1	3

(b) Value combinations of KSPE 2

Num.	Value comb.	F	T
#1	high, low, high, low	7	20
#2	high, low, med, low	4	14
#3	med, high, high, med	8	13
#4	med, med, low, high	2	7
#5	med, high, high, low	0	6

(c) Value combinations of KSPE 3

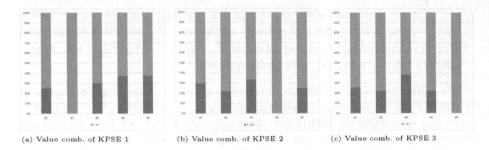

(a) Value comb. of KPSE 1   (b) Value comb. of KPSE 2   (c) Value comb. of KPSE 3

Fig. 2. Graphic representation of value combinations, reported in Table 3

5   Conclusions

In this paper, we introduced and discussed a novel framework for APFDs. The approach fits well into the context of the approximate temporal functional dependencies, adding a new aspect that has never been formalized before. It differs from the previous work because we dealt with the potential predictiveness of the approximate temporal functional dependencies, considering the possibility to exploit data dependencies for the prediction. As future work, we plan to consider the algorithmic aspects taking into account all the proposed error measures.

References

1. Caruana, R., Niculescu-Mizil, A.: An empirical comparison of supervised learning algorithms. In: Proceedings of the 23rd International Conference on Machine Learning, pp. 161–168 (2006)
2. Combi, C., et al.: Mining approximate temporal functional dependencies with pure temporal grouping in clinical databases. Comput. Biol. Med. **62**, 306–324 (2015)
3. Combi, C., Montanari, A., Sala, P.: A uniform framework for temporal functional dependencies with multiple granularities. In: Pfoser, D., Tao, Y., Mouratidis, K., Nascimento, M.A., Mokbel, M., Shekhar, S., Huang, Y. (eds.) SSTD 2011. LNCS, vol. 6849, pp. 404–421. Springer, Heidelberg (2011). https://doi.org/10.1007/978-3-642-22922-0_24
4. Harel, O.D., Moskovitch, R.: Complete closed time intervals-related patterns mining. Proc. AAAI Conf. Artif. Intell. **35**(5), 4098–4105 (2021)
5. Huhtala, Y., Kärkkäinen, J., Porkka, P., Toivonen, H.: TANE: an efficient algorithm for discovering functional and approximate dependencies. Comput. J. **42**(2), 100–111 (1999)
6. Johnson, A.E., et al.: Mimic-iii, a freely accessible critical care database. Sci. Data **3**(1), 1–9 (2016)
7. Khwaja, A.: Kdigo clinical practice guidelines for acute kidney injury. Nephron Clin. Pract. **120**(4), c179–c184 (2012)
8. Kivinen, J., Mannila, H.: Approximate inference of functional dependencies from relations. Theoret. Comput. Sci. **149**(1), 129–149 (1995)
9. Mantovani, M., Amico, B., Combi, C.: Discovering predictive trend-event patterns in temporal clinical data. In: Proceedings of the 36th Annual ACM Symposium on Applied Computing, pp. 570–579 (2021)

10. Mantovani, M., Combi, C., Zeggiotti, M.: Discovering and analyzing trend-event patterns on clinical data. In: 2019 IEEE International Conference on Healthcare Informatics (ICHI), pp. 1–10. IEEE (2019)
11. Moskovitch, R., Polubriaginof, F., Weiss, A., Ryan, P., Tatonetti, N.: Procedure prediction from symbolic electronic health records via time intervals analytics. J. Biomed. Inform. **75**, 70–82 (2017)
12. Schrier, R.W., Wang, W., Poole, B., Mitra, A., et al.: Acute renal failure: definitions, diagnosis, pathogenesis, and therapy. J. Clin. Investig. **114**(1), 5–14 (2004)
13. Segura-Delgado, A., Gacto, M.J., Alcalá, R., Alcalá-Fdez, J.: Temporal association rule mining: an overview considering the time variable as an integral or implied component. Wiley Interdiscip. Rev.: Data Min. Knowl. Discov. **10**(4), e1367 (2020)
14. Xu, Z., et al.: Identifying sub-phenotypes of acute kidney injury using structured and unstructured electronic health record data with memory networks. J. Biomed. Inform. **102**, 103361 (2020)

When Can I Expect the mHealth User to Return? Prediction Meets Time Series with Gaps

Miro Schleicher[1(✉)], Rüdiger Pryss[2], Winfried Schlee[3], and Myra Spiliopoulou[1]

[1] Otto-von-Guericke-University Magdeburg, Magdeburg, Germany
{miro.schleicher,myra}@ovgu.de
[2] University of Würzburg, Würzburg, Germany
[3] University of Regensburg, Regensburg, Germany

Abstract. With mHealth apps, data can be recorded in real life, which makes them useful, for example, as an accompanying tool in treatments. However, such datasets, especially those based on apps with usage on a voluntary basis, are often affected by fluctuating engagement and by high user dropout rates. This makes it difficult to exploit the data using machine learning techniques and raises the question of whether users have stopped using the app. In this paper, we present a method to identify phases with varying dropout rates in a dataset and predict for each. We also present an approach to predict what period of inactivity can be expected for a user in the current state. We use change point detection to identify the phases, show how to deal with uneven misaligned time series and predict the user's phase using time series classification. We evaluated our method on the data of an mHealth app for tinnitus, and show that our approach is appropriate for the study of adherence in datasets with uneven, unaligned time series of different lengths and with missing values.

Keywords: Time series with gaps · Adherence · Law of attrition · Chronic diseases · mHealth · EMA

1 Introduction

The option of recording data in real life is a major advantage of mHealth apps. They are therefore particularly helpful when accompanying treatments. Notwithstanding the potential benefits to all involved, the use of such apps requires the willingness and discipline of the individuals involved to participate consistently. Data coming from such sources are often affected by fluctuating engagement and by high dropout rates. Application of machine learning techniques to such datasets are therefore confronted with these challenges. In concrete terms, a number of problems arise which complicate the handling of the data. First, the high dropout rates that are the subject of the *science of attrition* initiated by Eysenbach [5]. Second, the fluctuating engagement during use. This creates gaps

© The Author(s), under exclusive license to Springer Nature Switzerland AG 2022
M. Michalowski et al. (Eds.): AIME 2022, LNAI 13263, pp. 310–320, 2022.
https://doi.org/10.1007/978-3-031-09342-5_30

in the data of varying size (*missing data*). Third, the sampling of the datasets. There is rarely even spacing between surveys or an equal number of observations. Engagement with the app is beneficial for all parties involved, so it is in the app provider's best interest to assess whether a gap in the data means abandonment or whether the person is likely to return. Therefore, we present a method to identify phases with different dropout rates according to Eysenbach and make a prediction for each phase. We also present an approach to predict what period of inactivity to expect for a user in the current state. We use *Change Point Detection* (CPD) to identify phases, show how to deal with uneven, misaligned time series, and predict the user's phase using time series classification We evaluated our method on data from an mHealth app for tinnitus and show that our approach is suitable for studying adherence in datasets with uneven, unaligned time series of different lengths and with missing values.

The paper is organized as follows: Sect. 2 presents the related works; Sect. 3 encompasses the methods used to solve the problems and Sect. 4 describes the material with which we tested our method and shows the results obtained. Finally, Sect. 5, draws the conclusions and provides directions for future work.

2   Related Work

Related to our approach is research in the *science of attrition*, advances on adherence/compliance modeling and monitoring as well as investigations in dealing with time series with gaps. *Engagement* in the use of self-monitoring apps is often referred to as *adherence* or *compliance*. The WHO has summarized adherence as: "the extent to which a person's behaviour [...] corresponds with agreed recommendations [...]" [15]. They differentiate between adherence and compliance by the agreement of the patient to the recommendations (adherence) [15]. In our study, we investigate 'adherence' in the context of interaction with an mHealth app, and define as 'dropouts' the persons that give up and stop future interactions. Then, we investigate to what extent Eysenbach's *law of attrition* [5] for survey data [7,8] and for longitudinal experimental data [5] can also be applied on our longitudinal, observational data.

Cismondi et al. investigate methods on medical data to deal with the problem and propose alignment methods such as gridding and templating [4]. However, the principle cannot be applied to the data of this paper, since the time series of a user are not collected separately but by the same questionnaire and therefore already have the same time stamp. Since the generation of the time series of the individual users differs substantially in some cases, the principle can only be applied here to a limited extent. We proposed a model of adherence based on such data in our previous work [13], but we did not attempt to predict adherence specifically. Such predictions can be found for specific applications. For example, Williams-Kerver et al. predicted adherence in eating disorder based on data with gaps, but focused on person-level characteristics, such as gender, rather than the data records themselves [14].

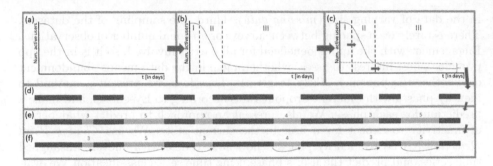

Fig. 1. Big Picture. (a) Attrition curve, (b) Phases of attrition, (c) Predicting the phases, (d) A time series represented as sequences (symbolized example), (e) Sequences with labeled gaps, (f) Predicting the return

3   Materials and Methods

In this section, the dataset for the evaluation is presented at the beginning. Subsequently, the approach is described and its most important steps are addressed in more detail in separate subsections.

3.1   Dataset

The evaluation is performed on a mHealth dataset of the TRACKYOURTINNITUS (TYT) [12] self-monitoring app, dedicated to research on tinnitus and to help users understand their manifestation of the disorder. Tinnitus is a complex chronic disorder that has no uniform way of manifestation and generation [2]. The initial dataset contains 3177 users with a gender distribution of 1028 females, 2097 males and 52 users with no specified gender. The observational period is from 2014-04-10 till 2022-01-17. The mean age is 45.50 years with a standard deviation (STD) of 13.20. The mean age of tinnitus onset is 36.02 years (STD:14.94). When the app randomly sends a request, the users should answer 8 questions if possible. Each of these 8 questions (c.f. [13] Table 1) will form separate time series. How often (or if at all) each individual user adds data points to the time series per day is up to them and cannot be generalized. Also, whether they answer one, several, or all questions in a session. In order to demonstrate our approach, we will focus in this paper the question "How stressful is the tinnitus right now?" ("distress"), but it would be applicable on the other questions as well.

Ethical approval: #15-101-0204. "All users read and approved the informed consent before participating in the study. The study was carried out in accordance with relevant guidelines and regulation." (Ethics Committee of the University Clinic of Regensburg)

3.2   Modelling of the Time Series of the Users

The starting point are the time series generated by the user. A time series consists of the transmitted answers (range $[0, 1]$) to a question. The question can be asked randomly 1:n times per day (by user choice) and can also be refused by the user. In this work we refer to a single question and thus to uni-variate time series.

3.3   Modelling Three Phases in the Time Series of the Users

The first step is to identify the phases with varying dropout rates (c.f. Fig. 1(a)), since according to Eysenbach these represent specific stages of interaction. Eysenbach mainly describes 3 phases [5], namely the *curiosity plateau* (Phase I) as the initial phase where the user are interested in exploring a new technology, followed by the *attrition phase* (Phase II) where the users start to reject the usage and finally, the *stable use phase* (Phase III) where only the 'hardcore users' remain, which will continue to use the application for a long time [5]. All three phases are to be modeled, but we also check if indeed all phases are observable or if one phase has no data. Figure 1(b) symbolizes the phases, which are snapshots and can change over time. Determining them in an automated manner might help to monitor the developments of the dataset. We apply CPD methods to determine the change in dropout rates and use them to determine the phases (c.f. transition Fig. 1(a) to (b)).

Using this information, we can now try to predict whether a user will reach the next phase (from Phase I to II and from I+II to Phase III) as symbolized in Fig. 1(c). A prediction from Phase I to III does not seem reasonable, as the transition from Phase I to Phase II is already characterized by a high dropout rate. Therefore the information in II may be crucial in predicting III.

Individuals in Phase III are considered stable in their continued use, but their usage patterns may fluctuate. Figure 1(d) shows an example of a single user's time series consisting of 7 sequences (blue) with responses and 6 gaps (white). Therefore, the next step is to predict when individuals most likely will return after a break. The basis here is no longer all data before the gap in question, but only the sequence between the last gap and the ones to be predicted. Thus, the approach respects the high variability and the sparsity problem. Each contiguous sequence of data (at least two consecutive days) is assigned the value of the gap until the next entry, providing evidence of the return. The duration of a gap is counted in days. Figure 1(e) symbolizes these gaps between the sequences as orange sections and the numbers above them represent the number of days without data. This cannot apply to a user's last sequence, which hides the information if the user will contribute again. Possible reasons could be a dropout or the database has reached its cut-off date, to name just two. Sequences and gaps will have a high variability in length. To facilitate classification, the gaps, symbolized in Fig. 1(e), can now be grouped together (binning) according to their size in order to form categories. Each category is intended to represent an interval of absence in which similar users have returned. The mean of the interval (in days) corresponds to the expected value of the class and the minimum and maximum values indicate a kind of uncertainty range. Figure 1(f) represents the classification of these target classes by inferring the duration of the gaps from the sequence, represented as arrows from one sequence to the beginning of the next.

3.4   Identifying Phases of Attrition

A potential target for CPD are Eysenbach's [5] proposed *attrition curves*, in which the follow-up rate (in percent) of users still enrolled is plotted over time. But this is under the assumption of a trial, where a dropout is gone forever. In the self-monitoring context a user can return even after a very long time. As a consequence, the true number of enrolled users can be assumed as unknown. Therefore, we created our curve by the number of contributing users over time. Where 'time' is not measured in dates, moreover in subjective days of app usage. The first day (day 1) is the day of the first submitted record. From that day on, the days are counted as usual from 0:00 a.m. on. On each of these days of usage some users might contribute and some might pause in varying combinations. But some users might start at some point to stop their contribution. As a result the number of contributing persons will decrease over the time of aligned days. Based on this data a version of the attrition curve can be plotted and inspected. Depending on the app user's behavior this curve can form the same shapes as described in [5] (c.f. Appendix Fig. 4). Eysenbach presented a sigmoid-shaped attrition curve, which is characterized by its initial plateau of high participation. However, an 'L-shaped' curve has also been mentioned, which is said to be close in appearance to Phase II+III [5]. In order to make this approach applicable to multiple sample of users and applications we decided to search for all 3 phases. Based on the underlying data, it is possible that the initial phase comprises only one day, namely day 1, and the curve thus corresponds more to an L-shaped attrition curve.

We applied 3 change point detection methods: *Linearly penalized segmentation* (PELT) [11], *Dynamic programming* (Dynp) [11] and *Bottom-up segmentation* (BottomUp) [6,10,11] from the python package 'rupture' [11]. To select the best method for the data, the selection must be made initially after visual inspection.

3.5   Predicting Attrition for Each User

For predicting whether a user will contribute in the next phase, the algorithm *XGBoost* from the Python package 'XGBoost' [3] was selected. It iteratively combines different models in the eponymous boosting procedure to reduce the errors of those already implemented. The algorithm was chosen for its broad applicability and excellent performance. Since this is a binary classification, a 10-fold cross-validation (CV) with *Accuracy* (Acc) was chosen to evaluate the results.

3.6   Tuning the Gap Size for Prediction

To create the necessary preconditions for the classification of the sequences, restrictions must be made. User with just a single day and therefore, with just a single day sequence must be excluded. This is also true for users with multiple days but no second sequence, since the return after the gap cannot be verified. If a uni-variate sequence in a multivariate sequence has a missing value on one day, this sequence must be removed (although imputation can be explored) Finally, gaps of a certain length might not worth considering. Depending on the use case of the app, such sequences are not very informative, because the user might try a restart or test a new version of the app after this very long pause. They are sequences with return, but are basically 'hidden dropouts'. We considered three strategies for data binning, namely (a) building equisized intervals, (b) building intervals on frequency and (c) identifying 'natural' groups with the *Fischer-Jenks algorithm* [9] (implementation: *jenkspy* package). Each algorithm delivers a different number of bins of different sizes, which must be categorized manually.

The prediction of the class of a sequence is done using a 1-NN classifier with Dynamic Time Warping (DTW), one of the best performing approaches according to [1]. Since the binning will lead to multiple classes with uneven distribution, a stratified 10-fold CV is selected for evaluation with Acc.

4   Results and Discussion

The following sections describe the results for identifying the attrition phases, followed by the predicitons of the phases for each user, and some details on tuning the gap size parameter. We close with a discussion of the results.

4.1   Identifying Phases of Attrition

Figure 2 presents the adapted attrition curve as described in the methods. On day 1, all 3177 users were active. On day 2, there were 1284 (40.41%), on day 3 1011 (31.82%) and on day 14 only 481 (15.14%) users.

Visual inspection of the graph and the rapid decline in numbers suggest an L-shaped progression rather than the sigmoidal progression shown in [5]. When running the 3 CPD algorithms (PELT, BottomUp, Dynp) on the data shown in Fig. 2, quite different results were obtained. All 3 algorithms were expected to find 2 change points (or 3 phases) in the first 14 days after visual inspection of the curve, but were set to freely find the change points. PELT detected only a single change point on day 2, while BottomUp found 2 points. The first on day 5 and the second on day 14. Dynp detected the first change point on day 2, just like PELT. The second point on day 5, which is the same result as BottomUp. And another one on day 14. In experiments with shorter or longer time series, the algorithms BottomUp and Dynp selected day 14, i.e. the last day, so this last change point should be discarded. Hence, PELT, BottomUp and Dynp, taken together, identified change points at day 2 (two of the three algorithms) and day

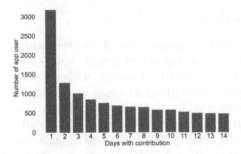

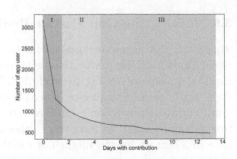

Fig. 2. The figure illustrates the number of users contributing data on Day 1 through Day 14. Day 1 is the first day of use of the app for each individual user. Not every user who submitted data on Day 1 is present in all other days.

Fig. 3. This figure shows the result of the dynamic programming search method for change points (Dynp). The color change symbolizes a different area marked by the calculated change points on day 2 and day 5. Phase I (red) - II (yellow) - III (blue) (Color figure online)

5 (two algorithms). These two changepoints indicate that there are indeed three phases, in agreement with the law of attrition. However, the change from phase II to phase III (at day 5) is not so prominent, as can also be seen on Fig. 3. In that figure, the red area (leftmost) refers to phase I, the yellow area (middle) to phase II and the blue area to phase III.

4.2 Predicting Attrition for Each User

Since Dynp found both changepoints in the time series, we used it to assign labels to users. Anyone who contributed on day 2 or later was assigned a Yes class for Phase II, and everyone else was assigned a No class. A similar procedure was performed with the threshold for Phase III on day 5.

As input for the classifiers, we chose the time series 'distress' because this variable reflects best how the users feel about their tinnitus [2] and because it is likely to be associated to attrition. We excluded 99 users who did not enter distress values on day 1, whereupon we retained 3078 users with an entry in day 1 (i.e. before the change point at day 2). These users we used for prediction. The classes are slightly imbalanced, with n = 1811 (58.84%) for Yes and n = 1267 (41.16%) for No. Since the users have substantial differences in the data contributed on the days and also at very different times, the median per day was chosen to be representative, so that each user has only one value per day. So in this specific case, the algorithm had to try to make a prediction with one value per 3078 users.

One value per day, making the classification task very difficult. We used XGBoost [3] with 10-fold cross-validation and achieved a mean accuracy of 54.52% (SDT:3.68%). The low accuracy reflects the difficulty of the task. For the prediction of phase III, a much higher quality was achieved, namely 76.93% (SDT:1.93%). The class distribution is Yes: 1435 (45.17%) and No: 1742 (54.83%).

Table 1. Gap bins derived by each of the binning strategies on a total of 3749 sequences: strategy of equisized intervals (left column), frequency-based strategy (middle column) and the Fischer-Jenks algorithm that builds natural groups (rightmost column): each entry contains an interval size and the number of intervals of this size, as found by the algorithm. The leftmost column contains the group ID.

GroupID	Equisized intervals		Frequency-based		Fischer-Jenks	
	Interval	Sequences	Interval	Sequences	Interval	Sequences
A: smallest gaps	(1.999–7.6]	3543	(1.9–3.0]	2903	(1.999–3.0]	2903
B: small gaps	(7.6–13.2]	138	(3.0–4.0]	307	(3.0–6.0]	580
C: larger gaps	(13.2–18.8]	40	(4.0–30.0]	539	(6.0–11.0]	61
D: large gaps	(18.8–24.4]	15			(11.0–18.0]	77
E: very large gaps	(24.4–30.0]	13			(18.0–30.0]	28

4.3 Tuning the Gap Size for Prediction

Our dataset contains many sequences with small gaps, but some sequences have gaps of more than 2000 days. We filtered out sequences with a longer gap than one month (30 days). This reduced the dataset size considerably, since only 10 users had gaps of 15 days, and larger gaps were even more rare. Hence, we limited the maximum gap size to 30 and invoked the three binning strategies described in Subsect. 3.6, to build 5 groups of increasing gap size (number of days). The results are on Table 1. There, we sorted the 5 groups by size, with the group of the smallest gaps coming first (c.f. leftmost column). As can be seen in the table, the frequency-based strategy has built only three groups, the 3rd of which contains gaps of very different sizes, from 4 to 30 days. The other two strategies placed in each group sequences of similar gap sizes, whereupon the third (rightmost) strategy achieved a somehow smoother distribution of sequences among groups.

Applying 1-NN algorithm to the sequences in order to predict the gaps (based on Fischer-Jenks binning method) led to a mean accuracy of 61% for stratified 10-fold CV. The minority classes E & D performed worse as well as label C. In each fold, the Precision and Recall values are around 15% for label B and 77% for label A, which corresponds to their class distribution (c.f. Appendix Table 2 for the detailed evaluation metrics). The 1-NN classifier with DTW was chosen because it is the gold standard in performance according to [1].

4.4 Discussion

Only Dynp identified the stages of attrition, according to Eysenbach's [5] description. The L-shape of the curve, is due to the nature of the app. While Eysenbach and Hochheimer et al. [8] work with trial or survey data, the users here are in a voluntary exploration situation. The app is only used over a longer period of time if the relationship fits [5].

The prediction of Phase III from I+II outperforms the prediction of Phase II from I, Since this prediction is close to the class distribution. However, the result is explained by the available input. While the first prediction can only use a single value per user, the second prediction can use 4. The problems of the algorithm, although it can be considered 'state-of-the-art', can be attributed to the large number of users, with subjective manifestations of tinnitus. Moreover, the variable has a very similar value (Mean: 0.357, SDT: 0.27), which further complicates its separation. By changing the setting, e.g. in a clinical study, the results might be better, because the phases might be more sigmoid-shaped.

Learning the gap labels by binning suffers from the skew in the gap size. Nevertheless, the Fischer-Jenks algorithm performed better than the other ones in creating reasonable groups. An adaptation of the number of labels or the time frame of gaps might also influence the result, but were out of scope for this exploratory paper and is future work.

The prediction of the gaps by 1-NN also indicates the aforementioned problems with the complex data. And points in a direction of methods that adjusts not only to the matching of the sequences, but also to the different subgroups of the user in order to achieve better predictive power. The results of the evaluation require justification. This is due to the skewed distribution of the learned classes in the test data on the one hand and to the nature of the data itself on the other hand, since tinnitus is already by definition a very heterogeneous disorder and the patients are very different from each other. Under these conditions, even a different algorithm would perform below expectations.

5   Conclusions

In this paper, we proposed a method to investigate a mHealth dataset for varying phases of attrition according to Eysenbach and predicted if a user might reach the next phase from the current status. We used the fragmentation of the time series to predict users' pauses with the sequences, after determining them by binning.

We have found that the phases of attrition are best detected by the Dynp algorithm using change point detection. We have also shown that they can be predicted by XGBoost for many users, even under challenging data. The Fischer-Jenks algorithm excelled in detecting gap labels. In addition, the results of the predictions indicate that good alignment of the sequences is not sufficient to make good predictions on this data.

Limitation of the approach is the still low predictive power in view of the very heterogeneous users and the high fluctuation of users. The approach should still be tested on a dataset that offers more stable conditions of use of the mHealth app, such as a clinical trial, a survey, or an experiment.

Future studies are the evaluation on datasets with other patterns, in-depth adjustments of the parameters of the individual tools and possibly testing new elements that harmonize better with the properties of the data.

Our approach points in a good direction. Open questions remain, however, regarding the quality of prediction in the domain of self-monitoring mHealth data from volunteers, an issue that warrants further investigation.

Acknowledgements. This project has received funding from the European Union's Horizon 2020 Research and Innovation Programme under grant agreement number 848261. Thanks go to Vishnu Unnikrishnan for his control reading.

Appendix

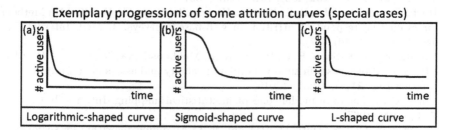

Fig. 4. Three exemplary attrition curves to illustrate the shape of a (a) logarithmic-shaped curve, (b) a sigmoid-shaped curve and (c) a L-shaped curve.

Table 2. This table shows the precision, recall, and f1-score as evaluation metrics for each class and each fold of the 10-fold stratified cross-validation as well as the averages for the 1-NN classifier (Pre–Precision, Rec–Recall, F1–F1-score, Sup–Support, Avg–Average & Acc–Accuracy)

Fold	Class A				Class B				Class C				Class D				Class E				Acc
	Pre	Rec	F1	Sup	Pre	Rec	F1	Sup	Pre	Rec	F1	Sup	Pre	Rec	F1	Sup	Pre	Rec	F1	Sup	
1	0.79	0.80	0.80	291	0.21	0.22	0.22	58	0.08	0.06	0.07	16	0.00	0.00	0.00	7	0.00	0.00	0.00	3	0.66
2	0.78	0.81	0.80	291	0.22	0.19	0.20	58	0.00	0.00	0.00	16	0.00	0.00	0.00	7	0.00	0.00	0.00	3	0.66
3	0.79	0.79	0.79	291	0.16	0.17	0.17	58	0.00	0.00	0.00	16	0.00	0.00	0.00	8	0.00	0.00	0.00	2	0.64
4	0.77	0.73	0.75	290	0.17	0.22	0.19	58	0.00	0.00	0.00	17	0.00	0.00	0.00	8	0.00	0.00	0.00	2	0.60
5	0.77	0.74	0.75	290	0.14	0.17	0.16	58	0.14	0.12	0.13	16	0.00	0.00	0.00	8	0.00	0.00	0.00	3	0.60
6	0.77	0.72	0.75	290	0.13	0.16	0.14	58	0.00	0.00	0.00	16	0.08	0.12	0.10	8	0.00	0.00	0.00	3	0.59
7	0.79	0.73	0.76	290	0.17	0.19	0.18	58	0.00	0.00	0.00	16	0.08	0.12	0.10	8	0.00	0.00	0.00	3	0.60
8	0.78	0.74	0.76	290	0.18	0.21	0.19	58	0.04	0.06	0.05	16	0.08	0.12	0.10	8	0.00	0.00	0.00	3	0.61
9	0.80	0.77	0.79	290	0.20	0.22	0.21	58	0.10	0.12	0.11	16	0.00	0.00	0.00	8	0.00	0.00	0.00	3	0.63
10	0.77	0.71	0.74	290	0.10	0.12	0.11	58	0.00	0.00	0.00	16	0.00	0.00	0.00	7	0.00	0.00	0.00	3	0.57
Avg	0.78	0.75	0.77	290.30	0.17	0.19	0.18	58.00	0.04	0.04	0.04	16.10	0.02	0.04	0.03	7.70	0.00	0.00	0.00	2.80	**0.62**

References

1. Bagnall, A., Lines, J., Bostrom, A., Large, J., Keogh, E.: The great time series classification bake off: a review and experimental evaluation of recent algorithmic advances. Data Min. Knowl. Discov. **31**(3), 606–660 (2016). https://doi.org/10.1007/s10618-016-0483-9
2. Cederroth, C.R., et al.: Towards an understanding of tinnitus heterogeneity. Front. Aging Neurosci. **11**, 53 (2019)

3. Chen, T., Guestrin, C.: XGBoost: a scalable tree boosting system. In: Proceedings of the 22nd ACM SIGKDD International Conference on Knowledge Discovery and Data Mining, KDD 2016, pp. 785–794. ACM (2016)
4. Cismondi, F., Fialho, A.S., Vieira, S.M., Reti, S.R., Sousa, J.M., Finkelstein, S.N.: Missing data in medical databases: impute, delete or classify? Artif. Intell. Med. **58**(1), 63–72 (2013)
5. Eysenbach, G.: The law of attrition. J. Med. Internet Res. **7**(1), e402 (2005)
6. Fryzlewicz, P.: Unbalanced Haar technique for nonparametric function estimation. J. Am. Stat. Assoc. **102**(480), 1318–1327 (2007)
7. Hochheimer, C.J., Sabo, R.T., Krist, A.H., Day, T., Cyrus, J., Woolf, S.H.: Methods for evaluating respondent attrition in web-based surveys. J. Med. Internet Res. **18**(11), e301 (2016)
8. Hochheimer, C.J., Sabo, R.T., Perera, R.A., Mukhopadhyay, N., Krist, A.H.: Identifying attrition phases in survey data: applicability and assessment study. J. Med. Internet Res. **21**(8), e12811 (2019)
9. Jenks, G.F.: The data model concept in statistical mapping. Int. Yearb. Cartogr. **7**, 186–190 (1967)
10. Keogh, E.J., Chu, S., Hart, D., Pazzani, M.J.: An online algorithm for segmenting time series. In: Proceedings of the 2001 IEEE International Conference on Data Mining, pp. 289–296 (2001)
11. Killick, R., Fearnhead, P., Eckley, I.A.: Optimal detection of changepoints with a linear computational cost. J. Am. Stat. Assoc. **107**(500), 1590–1598 (2012)
12. Schlee, W., et al.: Measuring the moment-to-moment variability of tinnitus: the TrackYourTinnitus smart phone app. Front. Aging Neurosci. **8**, 294 (2016)
13. Schleicher, M., et al.: Understanding adherence to the recording of ecological momentary assessments in the example of tinnitus monitoring. Sci. Rep. **10**(1), 1–13 (2020)
14. Williams-Kerver, G.A., et al.: Baseline and momentary predictors of ecological momentary assessment adherence in a sample of adults with binge-eating disorder. Eat. Behav. **41**, 101509 (2021)
15. World Health Organization and Others: Adherence to long-term therapies: evidence for action. World Health Organization (2003)

The Transition Law of Sepsis Patients' Illness States Based on Complex Network

Ruolin Wang[1], Jingming Liu[2], Zheng Chen[2], Minghui Gong[1],
Chunping Li[1(✉)], and Wei Guo[2(✉)]

[1] School of Software, Tsinghua University, Beijing 100084, China
cli@tsinghua.edu.cn
[2] Emergency Department, Beijing Tiantan Hospital, Capital Medical University,
Beijing 100070, China

Abstract. Sepsis is a disease with a high mortality rate of 15%–50%. It is of great significance to study disease development rules of sepsis patients, which can summarize the clinical pattern and provide support for clinicians.

This paper proposes a complex network-based model of sepsis disease progression, which can quantify and study the transition law of sepsis patients. The paper presents that the human body is abstracted into a complex system composed of seven organ systems and the patient's condition state at every moment is expressed as a seven-dimensional vector. The complex network of sepsis disease regression is constructed by using the disease states as nodes and the state changes as connecting edges. The transition law of sepsis patients' illness states is that the complex network of sepsis is scale-free but does not have small-world characteristics. The important state nodes in the network determine the changes of patients' condition, and patients will eventually leave Intensive Care Unit(ICU) or die in ICU. Clinicians should pay attention to intermediate state nodes, especially to patients' respiratory system.

Keywords: Sepsis · Transition law · Complex network

1 Introduction

Sepsis is a deadly organ dysfunction syndrome caused by the host body's maladjustment of the response to infection, and is the common cause of death caused by most infectious diseases. Sepsis has a very high mortality rate, ranging from 15% to 50%. Every year [1].

Early sepsis usually presents with preventable infections, such as respiratory infections, wound and skin infections and so on, so early and timely diagnosis and intervention may allow for reversal of condition [2]. If sepsis patients cannot be identified early and receive effective systematic treatment in time, the difficulty of treatment and the mortality will increase significantly. On the contrary, the

---

First Author and Second Author contribute equally to this work.

© The Author(s), under exclusive license to Springer Nature Switzerland AG 2022
M. Michalowski et al. (Eds.): AIME 2022, LNAI 13263, pp. 321–331, 2022.
https://doi.org/10.1007/978-3-031-09342-5_31

correct treatment taken by clinicians at the critical moment can lead to reversible changes in organ function and even complete recovery in patients with sepsis [3]. Therefore, summarizing the transition law of sepsis condition changes can improve the ability of clinicians to treat sepsis [4].

In recent years, studies on sepsis have emerged one after another. Most studies focus on clinical diagnosis [4], pathogenic mechanism [3], prognostic estimation [5], prediction [6–8], treatment [9,10], outcome [9] and so on. However, there are relatively few studies on the transition law of sepsis. Quantitative research methods such as data science, theoretical modeling have never been used on it.

Complex network is an effective theoretical modeling method, which has been widely used for researches on mental disorders [11], development of vaccination strategies [12], analysis of power systems [13] and other practical issues. At present, no work has been done to apply complex networks to the study of sepsis development, to model sepsis condition changes, and to explore sepsis transition law.

In this paper, we use clinical data of sepsis patients in Intensive Care Unit(ICU) from open dataset. The patient's condition state is represented as a vector of seven dimensions. Then the complex network theory is applied to construct a complex network of sepsis condition transitions (where the condition state is used as nodes and the state change is used as an edge), and its characteristics are analyzed. Finally, the study summarizes the disease development pattern of sepsis. The useful and reusable knowledge is mined and summarized from the massive and complex data of ICU to provide clinical decision basis for clinicians' diagnosis and treatment.

2   Methods

2.1   Concept Definition

Complex Network is a kind of network with self-organization, self-similarity, attractor, small world, scale-free part or all of the properties, which presents a high degree of complexity. In mathematical terms, a complex network is a graph with sufficiently complex topological features. Given a simple, directed, weighted complex network $G = (V, E)$, V denotes to the node collection. E is edge collection. N is node count. L is edge count. The edge weighting function is $w : E \rightarrow R$. The basic parameters of the network include path, degree, degree distribution, average distance and clustering coefficient.

The path $p = v_1 \rightarrow v_2 \rightarrow ... \rightarrow v_k$ is a finite sequence in G. The weight of path p is expressed as:

$$w(p) = w(v_1, v_2) + w(v_2, v_3) + ... + w(v_{k-1}, v_k) \tag{1}$$

The shortest path weights from i to j is defined as $I(i, j) = min\{w(p)\}$, where p is a path from node i to node j. The average shortest path length of the network represents the average of shortest distance between any two points:

$$\bar{d} = \frac{\sum_{i,j} I(i,j)}{N(N-1)/2} \tag{2}$$

The degree of a node in a directed network refers to the number of directly connected edges of nodes, that is the sum of in-degree and out-degree of nodes $k = k^{in} + k^{out}$, The average degree is $k = \frac{2L}{N}$. The average degree of directed network satisfies: $\overline{k^{in}} = \frac{1}{N} \sum_{i=1}^{N} k_i^{in}, \overline{k^{out}} = \frac{1}{N} \sum_{i=1}^{N} k_i^{out}, \overline{k^{in}} = \overline{k^{out}}$

The degree distribution represents the probability that the degree of a randomly selected node in the network is k:

$$P(k) = \frac{N_k}{N} \tag{3}$$

where N_k represents the number of nodes with degree k, N is node count of the network.

The node clustering coefficient represents the density of nodes in the neighborhood of one node, and reflects the proximity degree of adjacent nodes:

$$C_i = \frac{2e_i}{k_i (k_i - 1)} \tag{4}$$

where e_i is the actual number of edges connected to node i, $k_i (k_i - 1)$ is the number of possible edges for the node i.

The average clustering coefficient of the network represents the average clustering coefficient of all nodes in the network:

$$\overline{C} = \frac{1}{N} \sum_{i=1}^{N} C_i \tag{5}$$

Scale-free characteristics and small world phenomenon are the two most typical complex network characteristics. The degree distribution of scale-free networks conforms to the characteristic of power law distribution. If the density function of the random variable X is $p(x) \propto x^{-\alpha}$, then x follows the power law distribution. In general, it is more likely to obey the power law distribution in the range of $x > x_{min}$, called the x tail distribution obeys the power law distribution. Clauset, Shalizi and Newman [14] presented a new method for identifying and measuring power law phenomena: based on the Kolmogorov-Smirnov (KS) statistic [15] and maximum likelihood ratio [16], the maximum likelihood estimation method is combined with the fitting advantage test.

The small-world phenomenon-the principle that people are all linked by short chains of acquaintances-is a fundamental issue in social networks[17]; But there is no precise definition of the small world phenomenon. It is generally believed that if the clustering coefficient of the network is much larger than that of the corresponding Erdős-Rényi(ER) random graph, and the average path length is much smaller than that of the corresponding random network, then the network is said to have small world phenomenon [18]. Because ER Random graph is a kind of network connecting each pair of N nodes with probability P, which satisfies the characteristics of small-world model.

Discovering important nodes in complex networks is a basic problem in complex network research. The commonly used methods are Degree Centrality C_D, Betweeness Centrality C_B, Closeness Centrality C_C and PageRank.

$$C_D(i) = \sum_{j=1}^{N} e_{ij}(i \neq j) \tag{6}$$

$$C_B(i) = \sum_{i,k=1}^{N} sd(j,i,k),(j \neq k) \tag{7}$$

$$C_C(i) = \frac{1}{\sum_{j=1}^{N} d(i,j)} \tag{8}$$

where e_i is the actual number of edges connected to node i, $sd(j,i,k)$ is the shortest path from node j to node k which passes through node i, $d(i,j)$ indicates the distance from node i to node j.

2.2   Research Data

In this study, Medical Information Mart for Intensive Care-IV(MIMIC-IV) v1.0 is used for experiments, which contains real-world data of patients admitted to a tertiary academic medical center in Boston, Massachusetts, USA from 2008 to 2019 (MIMIC-III includes data from 2001 to 2012). We select subjects according to the sepsis 3 criteria [10], as shown in Fig. 1. A total of 17369 subjects are included, including 3175 nonsurvivors and 14194 survivors. Fourteen variables, including demographic data and vital signs are extracted. Then, fourteen variables were extracted from the above 17,369 subjects, including demographic data, vital signs and other indicators.

2.3   Sepsis Complex Network

States and State Space. Sequential Organ Failure Assessment(SOFA) score is a kind of objective method to describe the occurrence and development of sepsis. Lactic acid is a kind of useful prognostic biomarker which associates with an increased risk of adverse outcomes, such as sepsis and shock. So the addition of lactic acid in SOFA and qSOFA scores can better predict the in-hospital mortality [19], improve the ability of qSOFA score to judge patients with suspected sepsis [20]. Therefore, according to clinician's advice, we include lactic acid into the SOFA score. The higher the score, the worse the state of patient's organ system.

As shown in Table 4, seven systems of human body are scored according to the SOFA score, and seven-dimensional vectors of the score are used to represent the patient's state of illness at each moment:

$$S = (x_1, x_2, x_3, x_4, x_5, x_6, x_7) \tag{9}$$

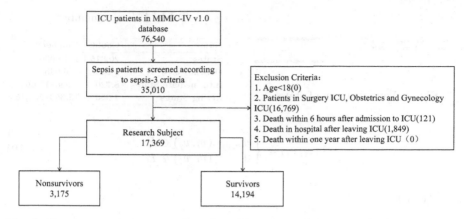

Fig. 1. Data extracting process from MIMIC-IV v1.0. (There are duplicated patients in exclusion criteria.)

where, $x_i \in \{0, 1, 2, 3, 4\}, i = 1, 2, ..., 7$, x_1 respiratory system score, x_2 coagulation system score, x_3 liver score, x_4 cardiovascular system score, x_5 central nervous system score, x_6 renal score, x_7 metabolism score.

According to Table 4, for one patient, we calculate states $S_0, ..., S_t, ...S_T$. In this paper, we need to model sepsis complex network, so the vectors must not be missing. Before and after filling method is used in this paper. If at time t, the score of system J of patient I is missing, the score will be filled as follows:

1. Find the most recent time t_0 before time t of patient I (at time t_0, the score of system J exists) and fill it with the score of system J.
2. If t_0 does not exist, find the last time t_1 after time t(at time t_1, the score of system J exists) and fill it with the score of system J.

As shown in Fig. 2, all states are divided into three types(death states, intermediate states, living states) according to terminal events(death, discharge) of patients. The death states are unique to nonsurvivors who finally died in ICU. The living states are unique to survivors who finally discharge from ICU. The intermediate states are states that both nonsurvivors and survivors have had. Then, the numbers of states are shown in the Table 1.

If $S_{t-1} = S_t$, only S_{t-1} is retained because we only focus on changes of the patient's condition state. The transition of illness states can be represented as (S_t, S_{t+1}) where $S_t \neq S_{t+1}$. We define a collection of all states V as the state space.

Model Construction. Sepsis complex network can be modeled as a directed weighted graph $G = (V, E)$ where, $V = \{v_1, v_2, ..., v_N\}$ is the collection of all kinds of states, N is the count of state collection. $E \subseteq V \times V$ is transition collection, L is count of transition collection, $w : E \to R$ is weighted function. The weight is the number of changes from source state v_i to destination state v_j. The adjacency matrix A of G is a N-order square matrix:

Fig. 2. Venn diagram of states.

Table 1. States number.

Name	Count	Number
States	20,315	1–12,939
Death States	6,945	1–6,945
Intermediate States	8,720	6,946–15,665
Living States	4,650	15,666–20,315

$$A\left(v_i, v_j\right) = \begin{cases} w_{v_i v_j} & \left(v_i, v_j\right) \in E \\ 0 & \left(v_i, v_j\right) \notin E \end{cases} \tag{10}$$

3   Results

3.1   Model Characteristic

The degree distribution of sepsis complex network conforms to a power-law distribution. Figure 3 shows that the degree distributions of sepsis complex network display the feature of heavy tail. Estimation of x_{min} and α are shown in the Table 2.

In Figure 7, four similar power-law distributions are selected: exponential distribution, truncated power law distribution, lognormal distribution, stretched exponential distribution. We use the likelihood ratio R and p-value to test which is more consistent with the data distribution, by verifying if $R > 0, p < 0.1$. Figure 7(a) shows that seven alternative hypothetical distributions are $R < 0$, which indicates that they fit better than the power law distribution does. However, in Fig. 7(b), except exponential distribution and truncated power law, the results are $p > 0.1$, which indicates that the R value is unreliable and the test does not favour any model. Combined with Figure 8, for all degree distributions, the power law distribution fitting error is the smallest. It is shown that the long-tailed part of the sepsis complex network is almost power law distribution, and the network conforms to the scale-free network model. The sepsis complex network is not connected, so the average shortest path length cannot

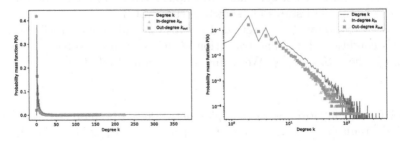

Fig. 3. Degree distribution of sepsis outcome complex network in (a) linear coordinate, (b) logarithmic coordinate

be calculated. However, the network contains a largest strongly connected component (LSCC) with 18490 nodes and a largest weekly connected component with 20296 nodes. We compare largest connected components with the ER random graphs of the same size to determine whether the network conforms to the small-world property. In Table 3, the average clustering coefficients and the average shortest path lengths of sepsis complex networks are greater than that of ER networks. The results does not meet the requirements of the small world network: $\overline{d} < \overline{d}_{small-world}$, $\overline{C} > \overline{C}_{small-world}$. Therefore, sepsis complex networks do not conform to the small world attribute.

Table 2. Maximum likelihood estimation and KS test to estimate power law exponent.

	α	D	x_{min}
$P(k)^a$	1.5022	0.0679	1.0
$P(k_{in})^b$	1.4815	0.0686	4.0
$P(k_{out})^c$	1.4369	0.0703	1.0

Degree distribution of sepsis complex network.
[a] Degree distribution.
[b] In-degree distribution.
[c] Out-degree distribution.

Table 3. Small world characteristics analysis.

Network	N	L	$\overline{k}$	$\overline{d}$	$\overline{C}$
G	20311	90417	4.4516	-	0.0611
LSCC	18490	88518	4.7873	8.2962	0.0676
LWCC	20296	90406	4.4544	7.7368	0.0824
ER^a	-	-	-	4.5451	0.0005
LSCC-ER^b	-	-	-	3.6871	0.0010
LWCC-ER^c	-	-	-	3.6337	0.0010

[a] ER network of the same size with G.
[b] ER network of the same size with LSCC.
[c] ER network of the same size with LWCC.

3.2 Analysis of Important Nodes

Figure 4 shows that the degree centrality, betweeness centrality, closeness centrality and PageRank score of intermediate states are significantly higher, indicating that intermediate states are crucial to the state transition and play an important role as an intermediate bridging node.

We select top 50 nodes from each method to get a intersection. Finally, we get 110 nodes, 109 of which are intermediate states and only 1 living state. We analyze the SOFA scores of three kinds of states. According to traditional common sense: total SOFA score has a positive relationship with the condition of organ failure in patients. However, As shown in Fig. 5, the total SOFA scores shows a normal distribution, and the mean value increase in order, which is inconsistent with traditional clinical common sense, indicating that low total SOFA score dose not mean stable condition.

Figure 6 shows that the system score of living states are generally lower than 1.5. For every systems, the average scores in death states are higher than that of living states except for central nervous system scores, indicating that the condition in the death states is more serious than that in the survival state. In intermediate states, except for respiratory system, the mean scores of systems are lower than that in living states. The average score of respiratory system in the intermediate state is 1.5, so the patient's respiratory system needs extra attention during treatment.

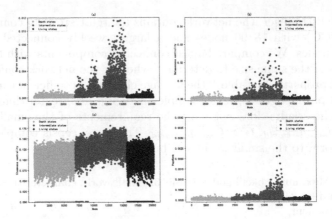

Fig. 4. Scatter plot of centrality of important nodes. (a) Degree centrality, (b) Betweenness centrality, (c) Closeness centrality, (d) PageRank

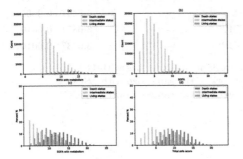

Fig. 5. Bar chart of SOFA scores for three kinds of states.

Fig. 6. Radar chart of SOFA scores for three kinds of states.

4   Conclusion

In this paper, we use improved SOFA scores to model the sepsis progression based on complex network theory and then summarize the transition law of sepsis patients' illness states.

The patient's body is regarded as a complex system composed of seven organs systems (respiratory system, coagulation system and etc.). We use seven-dimensional vector to represent the patient's condition status, and define the changes between the illness states as the state transition, so as to construct a weighted directed network with the states as nodes and the state transitions as edges to describe the process of sepsis condition change.

The transition law of sepsis patients' illness states are as follows:

1. Sepsis complex network has the scale-free property, which means that the degree distribution of the network conforms to a power-law distribution.

There are a few nodes connected to very large number of nodes in the network, while most nodes are connected to a few nodes. Therefore, the key nodes play a crucial role in the treatment.

2. Sepsis complex network does not have small-world characteristics. In a small-world network, most nodes are not adjacent, but any two nodes can be connected by a very short path. The sepsis complex network does not conform to the small-world characteristics. Because it is impossible for patients to stay in the ICU all the time. Patients will eventually leave the ICU or die in the ICU.

3. Intermediate states are critical to the change in condition. Patients in intermediate states are unstable. The disease may get worse or get better.

4. The respiratory system of sepsis patients needs extra attention during treatment. Clinicians should pay attention to each separately, especially the unstable conditions where single system scores are high, and should especially focus on the respiratory system of sepsis patients.

However, there are still shortcomings. Because the patients' development pathway is too mixed to discuss. Patients are likely to develop sepsis due to other diseases, making it difficult to conduct retrospective studies, reproduction and guidance. In our future work, we will use machine learning and deep learning methods to explore individualized diagnostic strategy, which can provide extra auxiliary decision support.

A   Appendix

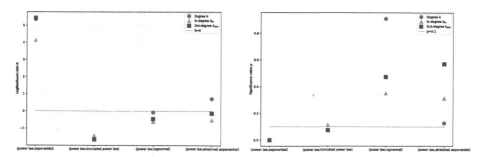

Fig. 7. KS test comparison of alternative hypothetical, (a) Maximum likelihood ratio R, (b) Significance level p

Table 4. State Score Table

System	Test Item	$x = 0$	$x = 1$	$x = 2$	$x = 3$	$x = 4$
Respiratory System	PaO_2/FiO_2 $mmHg(kPa)$	≥400 (53.3)	<400 (53.3)	<300 (40)	<200 (26.7)	<100 (13.3)
	mechanical ventilation (yes/no)				Yes	Yes
Coagulation System	Platelets $\times 10^3/\mu L$	≥150	<150	<100	<50	<20
Liver	Bilirubin $mg/dL\,(\mu mol/L)$	<1.2 (20)	1.2–1.9 (20–32)	2.0–5.9 (33–101)	6.0–11.9 (102–204)	>12.0 (204)
	Mean arterial pressure $(mmHg)$	≥70	<70			
	Dopamine $(\mu g/kg/min)$			≤5 or	>5 or	>15 or
Cardiovascular System	Epinephrine $(\mu g/kg/min)$				≤0.1 or	>0.1 or
	Norepinephrine $(\mu g/kg/min)$				≤0.1	>0.1
	Dobutamine $(\mu g/kg/min)$			>0		
Central Nervous System	Glasgow Coma Scale	15	13–14	10–12	6–9	<6
Renal	Creatinine $mg/dL\,(\mu mol/L)$	<1.2 (110)	1.2–1.9 (110–170)	2.0–3.4 (171–299)	3.5–4.9 (300–440)	>5.0 (440)
	24 h Urine output $(mL/24h)$				<500	<200
Metabolism	Lactic acid $(mmol/L)$	≤1.5	1.5–2.0	2.1–4.0	4.1–10.0	>10

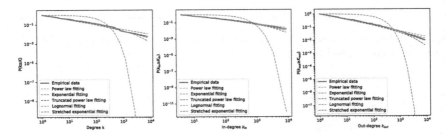

Fig. 8. Comparison of alternative hypothetical fitting (a) degree, (b) in-degree, (c) out-degree

References

1. Fleischmann, C., et al.: Assessment of global incidence and mortality of hospital-treated sepsis. Current estimates and limitations. Am. J. Respir. Crit. Care Med. **193**(3), 259–272 (2016)
2. Alliances, R.S.: Regional sepsis alliances. https://www.global-sepsis-alliance.org/sepsis
3. Lelubre, C., Vincent, J.L.: Mechanisms and treatment of organ failure in sepsis. Nat. Rev. Nephrol. **14**(7), 417–427 (2018)
4. Harley, A., Johnston, A., Denny, K., Keijzers, G., Crilly, J., Massey, D.: Emergency nurses' knowledge and understanding of their role in recognising and responding to patients with sepsis: a qualitative study. Int. Emerg. Nurs. **43**, 106–112 (2019)
5. Mannhardt, F., Blinde, D.: Analyzing the trajectories of patients with sepsis using process mining. In: RADAR+ EMISA@ CAiSE, pp. 72–80 (2017)
6. Nemati, S., Holder, A., Razmi, F., Stanley, M.D., Clifford, G.D., Buchman, T.G.: An interpretable machine learning model for accurate prediction of sepsis in the ICU. Crit. Care Med. **46**(4), 547 (2018)
7. Fleuren, L.M., et al.: Machine learning for the prediction of sepsis: a systematic review and meta-analysis of diagnostic test accuracy. Intensive Care Med. **46**(3), 383–400 (2020). https://doi.org/10.1007/s00134-019-05872-y
8. Goh, K.H., Wang, L., Yeow, A.Y.K., Poh, H., Li, K., Yeow, J.J.L., Tan, G.Y.H.: Artificial intelligence in sepsis early prediction and diagnosis using unstructured data in healthcare. Nat. Commun. **12**(1), 1–10 (2021)
9. Tsoukalas, A., Albertson, T., Tagkopoulos, I.: From data to optimal decision making: a data-driven, probabilistic machine learning approach to decision support for patients with sepsis. JMIR Med. Inform. **3**(1), e3445 (2015)
10. Komorowski, M., Celi, L.A., Badawi, O., Gordon, A.C., Faisal, A.A.: The artificial intelligence clinician learns optimal treatment strategies for sepsis in intensive care. Nat. Med. **24**(11), 1716–1720 (2018)
11. Hofmann, S.G., Curtiss, J.: A complex network approach to clinical science. Eur. J. Clin. Inv. **48**(8), e12986 (2018)
12. Liu, Y., Sanhedrai, H., Dong, G., Shekhtman, L.M., Wang, F., Buldyrev, S.V., Havlin, S.: Efficient network immunization under limited knowledge. Natl. Sci. Rev. **8**(1), nwaa229 (2021)
13. Pagani, G.A., Aiello, M.: The power grid as a complex network: a survey. Physica A: Stat. Mech. Appl. **392**(11), 2688–2700 (2013)
14. Clauset, A., Shalizi, C.R., Newman, M.E.: Power-law distributions in empirical data. SIAM Rev. **51**(4), 661–703 (2009)
15. Alstott, J., Bullmore, E., Plenz, D.: Powerlaw: a python package for analysis of heavy-tailed distributions. PLoS One **9**(1), e85777 (2014)
16. Vuong, Q.H.: Likelihood ratio tests for model selection and non-nested hypotheses. Econometrica: J. Econometric Soc. **57**(2), 307–333 (1989)
17. Kleinberg, J.M.: Navigation in a small world. Nature **406**(6798), 845–845 (2000)
18. Watts, D.J., Strogatz, S.H.: Collective dynamics of 'small-world'networks. Nature **393**(6684), 440–442 (1998)
19. Aksu, Arif, Gulen, Muge, Avci, Akkan, Satar, Salim: Adding lactate to SOFA and qSOFA scores predicts in-hospital mortality better in older patients in critical care. Eur. Geriatr. Med. **10**(3), 445–453 (2019). https://doi.org/10.1007/s41999-019-00179-z
20. Shetty, A., et al.: Lactate≥ 2 mmol/l plus qsofa improves utility over qSOFA alone in emergency department patients presenting with suspected sepsis. Emerg. Med. Australasia **29**(6), 626–634 (2017)

Learning a Battery of COVID-19 Mortality Prediction Models by Multi-objective Optimization

Mario Martínez-García[1]([✉]) [iD], Susana García-Gutierrez[2] [iD],
Rubén Armañanzas[1] [iD], Adrián Díaz[1] [iD], Iñaki Inza[3] [iD], and Jose A. Lozano[1,3] [iD]

[1] Basque Center for Applied Mathematics, BCAM, Bilbao, Spain
{mmartinez,rarmananzas,adiaz,jlozano}@bcamath.org
[2] Galdakao Hospital, Osakidetza, Basque Country, Spain
susana.garciagutierrez@osakidetza.eus
[3] Computer Science Faculty, University of the Basque Country UPV/EHU,
San Sebastián, Spain
inaki.inza@ehu.es

Abstract. The COVID-19 pandemic is continuously evolving with drastically changing epidemiological situations which are approached with different decisions: from the reduction of fatalities to even the selection of patients with the highest probability of survival in critical clinical situations. Motivated by this, a battery of mortality prediction models with different performances has been developed to assist physicians and hospital managers. Logistic regression, one of the most popular classifiers within the clinical field, has been chosen as the basis for the generation of our models. Whilst a standard logistic regression only learns a single model focusing on improving accuracy, we propose to extend the possibilities of logistic regression by focusing on sensitivity and specificity. Hence, the log-likelihood function, used to calculate the coefficients in the logistic model, is split into two objective functions: one representing the survivors and the other for the deceased class. A multi-objective optimization process is undertaken on both functions in order to find the Pareto set, composed of models not improved by another model in both objective functions simultaneously. The individual optimization of either sensitivity (deceased patients) or specificity (survivors) criteria may be conflicting objectives because the improvement of one can imply the worsening of the other. Nonetheless, this conflict guarantees the output of a battery of diverse prediction models. Furthermore, a specific methodology for the evaluation of the Pareto models is proposed. As a result, a battery of COVID-19 mortality prediction models is obtained to assist physicians in decision-making for specific epidemiological situations.

Keywords: COVID-19 · Mortality prediction · Multi-objective optimization · Classification evaluation

© The Author(s), under exclusive license to Springer Nature Switzerland AG 2022
M. Michalowski et al. (Eds.): AIME 2022, LNAI 13263, pp. 332–342, 2022.
https://doi.org/10.1007/978-3-031-09342-5_32

1   Introduction

The entire world has been paralyzed due to a virus, COVID-19, with unusually high levels of mortality and transmission. As of 10 January 2022, the numbers are still rising, with around 290 million infections and 5.5 million deaths since the beginning of the pandemic [1]. The fear and bewilderment experienced during the first months motivated researchers from all over the world to provide valuable information in the fight against COVID-19. The need to anticipate and correctly identify an early prognosis became an urgent challenge. Artificial intelligence through machine learning (ML) was the perfect tool to address this problem.

From the multitude of papers published, Wynants et al. [9] developed a review and critical appraisal of prediction models for diagnosis and prognosis of COVID-19. Out of the hundreds of models collected, only the contributions of Yann et al. [10] and Knight et al. [7] were identified as clinically relevant. Yann et al. [10] proposed a mortality model trained and tested on patient data obtained just one day before discharge, using XGBoost as a classifier. Knight et al. [7] compute from a logistic regression an index between 0 and 21 that establishes a prognosis of the patient's risk mortality. Subsequently, Gupta et al. [5], from the same research group as the previous work, propose a deterioration model based on a logistic regression model.

All these models provide information of interest to healthcare professionals when making final decisions. However, the continual changes in the epidemiological situation mean that having only a single model is limited, and non-useful for physicians. At some pandemic stages physicians seek to reduce the number of deceased by improving the sensitivity of the model i.e., focusing on decreasing the number of patients predicted as surviving who subsequently decease. Nonetheless, when the resources are limited or health centres are overcrowded, focusing on improving the specificity of the model i.e., reducing the number of patients detected as deceased who subsequently survive, is a realistic option for physicians. In line with this trend, we propose not only a single model based on a single metric, but a battery of models with a diverse spectrum of performances in both areas of interest. Hence, depending on the pandemic stage, physicians will have the possibility of selecting the most suitable model.

For this purpose, a set of logistic regression models is trained in a specific way. The common log-likelihood function used to learn the logistic regression coefficients is divided into two different objective functions: one focused on deceased and the other on survivors. A multi-objective optimization is applied to both objective functions to obtain a set of models, known as Pareto or non-dominated set which can not be improved by another model in both objective functions simultaneously. Furthermore, a specific methodology for the evaluation of the Pareto models is proposed. Consequently, a battery of non-dominated COVID-19 mortality prediction models is obtained.

The paper is organized as follows. Section 2 covers data collection and preprocessing. Section 3, the design and development aspects: an in-depth explanation of the multi-objective optimization problem, the method for the evaluation of the Pareto models and the validation of the models. Section 4 presents the final results and Sect. 5 a brief conclusion.

2   Clinical Dataset

2.1   Data Collection and Characteristics

Osakidetza, the Basque Country public health service in Spain, made a prospective cohort study recruiting patients infected by severe acute respiratory syndrome coronavirus 2 (SARS-CoV-2) confirmed by naso- and/or oropharyngeal swab polymerase chain reaction (PCR). Collected data contains blood tests, demographic and clinical data from the emergency department or up to 24 h after hospital admission. The target, mortality, indicates infected deceased and hospital discharges labeled as survivors. Furthermore, all patients in the study are from Basque Country hospitals and pertain to the first (from February to April 2020) and second wave (from July to November 2020).

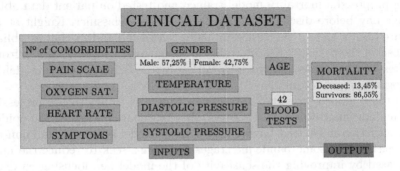

Fig. 1. Structure of the clinical dataset composed of demographic, clinical features and 42 different blood tests as inputs. Mortality represents the output of our model. (see Appendix)

2.2   Data Pre-processing

In order to pre-process the data, we start by analyzing the distribution of values. Those features with unexpected distributions are studied in detail, contrasting information about their range and establishing valid ranges for collected data. All those features with a coherent distribution did not undergo any range modification. Apart from this modification, two filters are applied to treat missing values, one filter on the features and another on the patients [2].

- Feature filter. Blood tests, demographic and clinical features with more than 30% of missing values are removed from the study.
- Patient filter. Patients with three or more missing values in the features (blood tests, demographic or clinical data) are removed for further analysis.

Remaining missing values are afterwards imputed by unsupervised similarity [8]. Specifically, a five nearest-neighbours method with Euclidean distance is used to impute the data.

2.3   Final Dataset

Finally, a total of 2215 patients and 53 features are retained (see Fig. 1). The final cohort is unbalanced with many more survivors than deceased (86.55% vs. 13.45%), and the sex distribution is balanced between male and female (57.25% vs. 42.75%). All features used in the modelling process are compiled in the Appendix. Moreover, features are normalized before starting with the development of the models.

3   Design and Development Aspects

Standard logistic regression returns a single model with specific evaluation scores that is not useful in changing epidemiological situations. However, having a battery of mortality models with different performances allows physicians and hospital managers to select the right model for a specific pandemic scenario. With this objective in mind, logistic regression coefficients are obtained by focusing on both sensitivity and specificity scores [6]. Instead of using the log-likelihood function (see Eq. 1), new functions are obtained from this one.

$$J(\theta) = -\sum_{i=1}^{N} y_i \cdot log(P_i(\theta)) + (1 - y_i) \cdot log(1 - P_i(\theta)) \tag{1}$$

The log-likelihood function is composed of the class (y_i), a summation on the N instances and the sigmoidal function (P_i) in terms of the coefficients (θ). As we address a binary mortality problem, the log likelihood function could be split into two objective functions: one for survivors (class 0) and the other for deceased patients (class 1) (see Eqs. 2 and 3 respectively).

$$J_0(\theta) = -\sum_{i=1}^{G} (1 - y_i) \cdot log(1 - P_i(\theta)) \tag{2}$$

$$J_1(\theta) = -\sum_{i=1}^{K} y_i \cdot log(P_i(\theta)) \tag{3}$$

The instances $(N = G + K)$ of the problem are divided into G and K survivors and deceased patients, respectively. The two new objective functions allow us to focus on key metrics for physicians when choosing a model: specificity (recall 0) and sensitivity (recall 1). Instead of performing a complex optimization of sensitivity and specificity scores, we have opted for a straightforward process: the optimization of J_0 and J_1 functions equivalent to these scores.

However, it is not feasible to compute the coefficients by gradient descent with two objective functions. Therefore, we rely on multi-objective optimization to address this issue. It is worth noting that the individual optimization of J_0, whose minimization optimizes the specificity, or J_1, whose minimization optimizes sensitivity, may be conflicting objectives. The improvement of one of them may surely imply the worsening of the other. By means of the multi-objective optimization paradigm we try to find a set of diverse models: some with balanced performances, others focused on specificity, and others on sensitivity.

3.1 Multi-objective Optimization

Multi-objective optimization provides the ability to address the problem in the exposed way:

- Computation of **logistic regression coefficients**. The paradigm seeks model coefficients that optimize both objective functions in order to maximize the performance of the model.
- Obtaining a **battery of models**, known as a Pareto set, with different performance scores. The Pareto set is composed of models not improved by another model in both objective functions simultaneously.
- **Resolution of the imbalance problem**. Separation of the log-likelihood into two class-dependent functions causes both classes to have the same relevance when applying the multi-objective optimization procedure.

Multi-objective Optimization Development. The multi-objective optimization is undertaken by one of the most popular implementations called non-dominated sorting genetic algorithm II (NSGA-II) [3,4].

NSGA-II procedure (see Fig. 2) is adopted taking as the individuals of the population the coefficients of a logistic regression. Note that any unspecified steps are matched to the generic one of the algorithm. The process begins with a parent population P_0 composed of M different models, where coefficients are randomly selected by means of Latin hypercube sampling. A non-domination sorting, divided into different fronts, is carried out over the pair of objective functions. After that, an individual selection, a simulated binary crossover and a polynomial mutation are used to create an offspring population Q_0, of size M. Thus, the first generation is obtained.

The procedure is different for the next generations. For the $t-th$ generation of the genetic algorithm, a combined population $R_t = P_t \cup Q_t$ of size $2M$ is initially formed. Then, population R_t is sorted according to non-domination and the best M models are selected. In order to choose exactly M models, the models of the last non-dominated front are sorted by crowding distance sorting. Consecutively, a new population P_{t+1} is obtained and used for subsequent individual selection, simulated binary crossover and polynomial mutation in order to create a new offspring population Q_{t+1}. This procedure is repeated for a number of generations established. As a result, a Pareto set of solutions with their associated objective functions values and models coefficients is obtained.

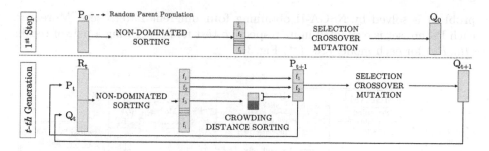

Fig. 2. NSGA-II procedure.

In our implementation the initial population is fixed to 500 random models, the number of generations is 200 and a constraint on the objective functions values ($J_0 + J_1 < 1.5$) is applied to mitigate bias.

3.2 Validation of the Models

In order to maximize the representativeness of Pareto set models, our aim is to implement NSGA-II on the entire data cohort. Nonetheless, the validation of the models from the obtained Pareto set is not trivial. Performing a cross-validation is not possible because the models obtained in the Pareto set of each fold are different and no relationship between them can be established. Therefore, we propose a novel Method for the Evaluation of PAreto Models (MEPAM). The feasibility of the method is studied by comparing MEPAM's performance internally estimated in a train partition with the performance estimated in an external test set. Once MEPAM is accepted as feasible, the process is applied to the full cohort in order to validate the final models that will be deployed. Note that both used scores, sensitivity (recall 1) and specificity (recall 0), are called recalls.

Method for the Evaluation of Pareto Models (MEPAM). We propose a method (see Fig. 3) for the evaluation of the models located in the Pareto set obtained with a entire data cohort. Specifically, the evaluation of the models consists of assigning to each model a recall value for each of the classes. It is needed to note that the method is described for a generic dataset. The following sections show how MEPAM is implemented on our dataset.

First of all, the multi-objective optimization framework is implemented on the **entire dataset** and a Pareto set is obtained (See (*) Fig. 3). All of the models obtained in this Pareto set are the ones we want to validate. For this purpose, and as the core of the method, the dataset is also split into **four stratified folds**: four training sets with their respective test sets. The objective of the four stratified folds is to obtain a representative set of validated models in order to be able to infer a realistic evaluation of the models from the Pareto set of the entire dataset. Thus, for each of the train subsets, the multi-objective optimization problem is solved by NSGA-II obtaining four different Pareto sets. Moreover, each Pareto set is evaluated in its respective test fold generating a pair of recalls (R_0, R_1) for each model (See (**) Fig. 3).

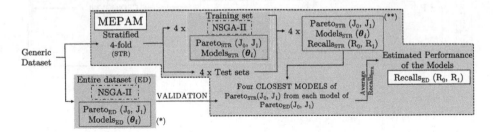

Fig. 3. Workflow for the validation of Pareto set models from a generic dataset. Method for the Evaluation of Pareto Models (MEPAM) is described within the yellow shading.

Accordingly, we proceed to validate the models from the Pareto set of the entire dataset by a recall estimation. For the validation of a single model from the Pareto set of the entire dataset, we focus on its objective functions (J_0, J_1) and collect the models with the four closest existing objective function pairs in the four Pareto sets of the stratified folds. Euclidean distance is used to collect these models for which recalls (R_0, R_1) are known. The mean of the R_0 recall of these models is considered as the estimated recall R_0 for the model to validate. The same procedure is followed for the generation of the estimated recall R_1. By repeating the process for each of the models included in the Pareto set of the entire dataset, an evaluation of the Pareto models is achieved.

MEPAM Feasibility. After the explanation of the method, its feasibility (see Fig. 4) is studied on our data cohort, which is divided into train (80%) and test (20%) sets.

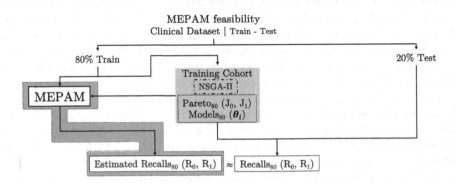

Fig. 4. Workflow to determine MEPAM feasibility.

MEPAM is applied to the training cohort for its validation by deriving an internal estimation of models recalls. Models obtained in the training cohort are externally evaluated by using the test set. Therefore, if test set recalls and those estimated internally in the train partition exhibit a low difference between their respective models, MEPAM method is assumed as feasible to be implemented in the full data cohort to evaluate the final models.

Validation of the Final Models. At this stage no test set is extracted and the models are computed from all available data. MEPAM is implemented to the full data cohort in order to estimate the recalls of the final models.

4   Results

MEPAM Feasibility. After the execution of NSGA-II algorithm on the training cohort, a Pareto set with 500 models is obtained. On the left graph of Fig. 5, the external recall evaluation on the test set and the internally estimated recalls by MEPAM in the train partition are displayed.

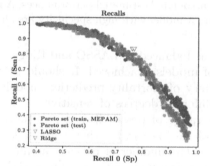

Range	No. Mod.	%	Cum. %
[0, 0.025)	89	17.8%	17.8%
[0.025, 0.05)	204	40.8%	58.6%
[0.05, 0.075)	114	22.8%	81.4%
[0.075, 0.1)	58	11.6%	93%
[0.1, 0.15)	35	7%	100%

Fig. 5. *Left graph.* R_1 (Sensitivity) vs. R_0 (Specificity). Blue dots represent the recall of the Pareto set models internally estimated by MEPAM. Red dots represent recalls externally computed on the test set. LASSO and Ridge recalls are plotted. *Right table*: Euclidean distance from estimated recalls to externally evaluated recalls on the test set.

Furthermore, LASSO and Ridge logistic regression recall values are shown as a comparative reference for the models. These models are trained with 80% of the data and tested with the remaining 20%. Although for high specificity and low sensitivity values slightly overestimated recalls are obtained, we can appreciate a solid behaviour of MEPAM.

In addition, Euclidean distance from the recalls estimated by MEPAM to those computed externally on the test set is always lower than 0.15, and 58.6% of models show a difference below 0.05 (see right Table in Fig. 5). Consequently, MEPAM is considered as a accurate performance estimation method.

Validation of the Final Models. NSGA-II is implemented on the full data cohort obtaining 500 different mortality prediction models in the Pareto set. The left graph of Fig. 6 highlights the difference between estimated recalls by MEPAM and those by LASSO and Ridge (trained with the 80% of the data and tested on the remaining 20%).

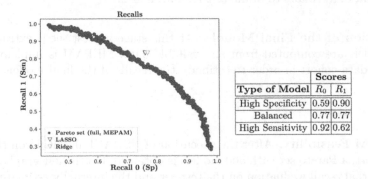

	Scores	
Type of Model	R_0	R_1
High Specificity	0.59	0.90
Balanced	0.77	0.77
High Sensitivity	0.92	0.62

Fig. 6. *Left graph.* R_1 (Sensitivity) vs. R_0 (Specificity). Blue dots represent estimated recalls by MEPAM on the full data cohort. LASSO and Ridge recalls are plotted. *Right table*: Examples of three models with their associated estimated performances. A model with high sensitivity, a balanced model and a model with high specificity are shown.

Although we do not obtain models as balanced as LASSO and Ridge regressions, a wide and competitive range of models is achieved. It should be noted that our objective is to provide a battery of mortality prediction models with different performances. Models with different degrees of sensitivity and specificity allow physicians to broaden the range of possibilities depending on the epidemiological situation (see right Table in Fig. 6) . In other words, depending on the availability of hospital resources, the number of patients admitted and other clinical aspects, physicians and hospital managers can choose the model that best suits a particular situation.

5   Conclusion

From a cohort of first and second wave data of the Basque Country, Spain, a battery of models with different performances is obtained. The multi-objective optimization framework allows us to focus on two key metrics: sensitivity and specificity. Although the optimization of both scores may be conflicting, it can also be beneficial for the learning of models with different performances. A new procedure known as MEPAM for an honest validation of the Pareto set models is also proposed.

The strength of the battery of mortality models resides not in outstanding performances but in the provision of models with varied performances for immediate use. Although having this large set of models can be overwhelming, a reduce set of different models (e.g. 3, 5) can be chosen to obtain a less aggressive and more comprehensible and explainable set of models.

A wave and its strength are not possible to predict. However, physicians have external help for any situation. From low intensity waves, where a sensitive model may be of interest to avoid fatalities, to waves of exceptional strength that collapse hospitals and deplete resources where specific models may be considered. Furthermore, the variety of models obtained in the Pareto set allows our health system to fight against any unexpected outbreak. Definitively, this battery of COVID-19 mortality prediction models is a powerful tool to support physicians and hospital managers in different epidemiological situations.

Acknowledgements. This research is supported by the Basque Government (IT1504-22, Elkartek) through the BERC 2022–2025 program and BMTF project, and by the Ministry of Science, Innovation and Universities: BCAM Severo Ochoa accreditation SEV-2017-0718 and PID2019-104966GB-I00. Furthermore, the work is also supported by the AXA Research Fund project "Early prognosis of COVID-19 infections via machine learning".

A   Appendix

A detailed explanation of the variables used in the model is shown in Table 1.

Table 1. Blood tests, demographic, clinical and mortality outcome information collected from medical records. Depending on the feature, mean (μ), standard deviation (σ), median or interquartile range ($Q1$-$Q3$) are displayed.

Feature	Overall	Feature	Overall
Mortality, n(%)		PT, median (Q1-Q3)(%)	91(78, 100)
Deceased	298 (13.45%)	HCB, median (Q1-Q3)(x10^6/μL)	4.63(4.22, 5.04)
Survivors	1917 (86.55%)	MCV, median (Q1-Q3)(fL)	91.20(87.6, 94.8)
Gender, n(%)		PLT, median (Q1-Q3)(x10^3/μL)	181(143, 236)
Male	1268 (57.25%)	CL, median (Q1-Q3)(mEq/L)	101.0(98.6, 103.6)
Female	947 (42.75%)	ALT, median (Q1-Q3)(U/L)	26(17, 41)
Age, $\mu(\sigma)(years)$	67.12 (17.55)	MCH, median (Q1-Q3)(pg)	29.9(28.6, 31.1)
Oxygen Sat., $\mu(\sigma)(\%)$	95.14(3.04)	INR, median (Q1-Q3)	1.06(1.00, 1.17)
Heart rate, $\mu(\sigma)(bpm)$	79.84(14.73)	CREA, median (Q1-Q3)(mg/dL)	0.92(0.76, 1.13)
No. of comorbi., $\mu(\sigma, range)$	0.39(0.66, [0,1])	CRP, median (Q1-Q3)(mg/L)	56.42(22.11, 110.64)
Symptoms, $\mu(\sigma, range)$	0.3(0.67, [0,3])	BR, median (Q1-Q3)(mg/dL)	0.48(0.36, 0.67)
Pain Scale, $mu(\sigma, range)$	0.21(0.55, [0,4])	MPV, median (Q1-Q3)(fL)	10.10(8.46, 11.10)
Temperature (oC), $\mu(\sigma)$	36.78(0.82)	APTT, median (Q1-Q3)(sg)	32.54(29.60, 36.35)
DBP, $\mu(\sigma)(mmHg)$	74.78(11.63)	NA, median (Q1-Q3)(mEq/L)	138(136, 140)
SBP, $\mu(\sigma)(mmHg)$	128.42(20.89)	HB, median (Q1-Q3)(g/dL)	13.9(12.5, 15.0)
Lipemia, median (Q1-Q3)	8.9 (4.0, 13.0)	K, median (Q1-Q3)(mEq/L)	4.1(3.8, 4.4)
Leukocytes, median (Q1-Q3)(x10^3/μL)	6.17 (4.76, 8.21)	UREA, median (Q1-Q3)(mg/dL)	36(27, 50)
Neutrophils, median (Q1-Q3)(%)	73.20(65.10, 80.90)	Haemolysis, median (Q1-Q3)	6.0(2.0, 18.0)
Neutrophils, median (Q1-Q3)(x10^3/μL)	4.44(3.17, 6.28)	RDW, median (Q1-Q3)(%)	13.10(12.30, 14.05)
Monocytes, median (Q1-Q3)(%)	7.60(5.50, 10.0)	HCT, median (Q1-Q3)(%)	42.20(38.50, 45.60)
Monocytes, median (Q1-Q3)(x10^3/μL)	0.46(0.33, 0.65)	Jaundice, median (Q1-Q3)	1.0(0.7, 10)
Lymphocytes, median (Q1-Q3)(%)	17.40(11.40, 24.25)	D-Dimer, median (Q1-Q3)(ng/ml)	750(460, 1400)
Lymphocytes, median (Q1-Q3)(x10^3/μL)	1.03(0.73, 1.38)	MCHC, median (Q1-Q3)(ng/ml)	32.7(31.9, 33.4)
Basophils, median (Q1-Q3)(%)	0.20(0.11, 0.40)	GLU, median (Q1-Q3)(mg/dL)	110.3(98, 132.5)
Basophils, median (Q1-Q3)(x10^3/μL)	0.012(0.01, 0.02)	PCT, median (Q1-Q3)(ng/ml)	0.09(0.05, 0.17)
Eosinophils, median (Q1-Q3)(%)	0.2(0, 0.55)	LDH, median (Q1-Q3)(U/L)	272(223, 343)
Eosinophils, median (Q1-Q3)(x10^3/μL)	0.01(0, 0.03)		

References

1. World health organization (2022). https://www.who.int/emergencies/diseases/novel-coronavirus-2019/situation-reports
2. Armañanzas, R., Díaz, A., Martínez-García, M., Mazuelas, S.: Derivation of a cost-sensitive COVID-19 mortality risk indicator using a multistart framework. In: IEEE International Conference on Bioinformatics and Biomedicine (BIBM), pp. 2179–2186 (2021). https://doi.org/10.1109/BIBM52615.2021.9669288
3. Blank, J., Deb, K.: Pymoo: multi-objective optimization in python. IEEE Access **8**, 89497–89509 (2020). https://doi.org/10.1109/ACCESS.2020.2990567
4. Deb, K., Pratap, A., Agarwal, S., Meyarivan, T.: A fast and elitist multiobjective genetic algorithm: NSGA-ii. IEEE Trans. Evol. Comput. **6**(2), 182–197 (2002). https://doi.org/10.1109/4235.996017
5. Gupta, R.K., Harrison, E.M., Ho, A., Docherty, A.B., Knight, S.R.: Development and validation of the ISARIC 4C deterioration model for adults hospitalised with COVID-19: a prospective cohort study. Lancet Respir. Med. **9**(4), 349–359 (2021). https://doi.org/10.1016/S2213-2600(20)30559-2
6. Ircio, J., Lojo, A., Mori, U., Lozano, J.A.: A multivariate time series streaming classifier for predicting hard drive failures. IEEE Comput. Intell. Mag. **17**(1), 102–114 (2022). https://doi.org/10.1109/MCI.2021.3129962
7. Knight, S.R., Ho, A., Pius, R., Buchan, I.: Risk stratification of patients admitted to hospital with COVID-19 using the ISARIC who clinical characterisation protocol: development and validation of the 4C mortality score, **370** (2020). https://doi.org/10.1136/bmj.m3339
8. Troyanskaya, O., Cantor, M., Sherlock, G., Brown, P.: Missing value estimation methods for DNA microarrays. Bioinformatics **17**(6), 520–525 (2001). https://doi.org/10.1093/bioinformatics/17.6.520
9. Wynants, L., Van Calster, B., Collins, G.S., Riley, R.D.: Prediction models for diagnosis and prognosis of COVID-19: systematic review and critical appraisal, **369** (2020). https://doi.org/10.1136/bmj.m1328
10. Yan, L., Zhang, H.T., Goncalves, J., Xiao, Y.: An interpretable mortality prediction model for COVID-19 patients. Nat. Mach. Intell. **2**(5), 283–288 (2020). https://doi.org/10.1038/s42256-020-0180-7

Oblique Dipolar Tree for Survival Data with Time-Varying Covariates

Malgorzata Kretowska[✉] [iD]

Faculty of Computer Science, Bialystok University of Technology,
Wiejska 45a, 15-351 Bialystok, Poland
m.kretowska@pb.edu.pl

Abstract. The majority of models for survival data analysis were designed to work with right-censored observations with time-invariant covariates. Since the survival data is often collected during a long period of time, despite a baseline feature vector, each subject can be described by a number of covariates that vary over time. Statistical analysis often requires many assumptions which are difficult to fulfill, hence some alternative, assumption-free approaches are proposed, among which we can distinguish survival trees. In the paper, the extension of an oblique dipolar survival tree was proposed to cope with left-truncated right-censored survival data with time-varying covariates. The tree was designed to analyze discrete survival data, where the failure time was divided into a number of time intervals. The proposed modification enables a straightforward adaptation of the tree to time-varying covariates and gives results being a conditional probability of failure. Oblique splits are obtained through the minimization of a convex, piece-wise linear criterion function and next pruned with the use of a cost-complexity technique. The method was evaluated on the basis of Mayo Clinic primary biliary cirrhosis data.

Keywords: Survival analysis · Dipolar criterion function · Oblique tree · Time-varying covariates

1 Introduction

The main idea of survival data analysis is the prediction of failure occurrence. In its basic form, survival data contain information about objects (e.g. patients) observed from any starting event (e.g., surgery, disease diagnosis) and the failure time - usually time to death or disease relapse.

Analyzing survival data one should face many issues which do not exist in regression or classification tasks. One of the most common problems is censoring. For right-censored observations the exact failure time is unknown, the only information they provide is their follow-up time, while left-truncated data exists when objects are not observed from the starting event but are included in the trial later. Another issue is related to variables, which can be both time-invariant or change over time.

Supported by grant W/WI-IIT/3/2020 from Bialystok University of Technology.

The majority of tree-based models proposed for survival analysis are developed to cope with right-censored survival data with time-invariant covariates [1–3]. The prediction of survival time is here based on the patient's condition at the beginning of the observation and does not take into account feature changes across the follow-up time. Such techniques may help us understand the influence of time-invariant variables (e.g., gender or type of treatment) but the impact of time-varying covariates cannot be assessed. Hence, the improvement of prediction may be obtained by including time-varying covariates in the learning process. The first tree extended to handle time-varying covariates was proposed by Bacchetti and Segal [4]. The method based on creating several pseudo-subjects for each observation, each representing a nonoverlapping time interval and using log-rank test adjusted to accommodate left-truncated data as a splitting criterion. In [5], the tree built around a discrete-time proportional odds model with a splitting rule based on maximum likelihood was developed. The algorithm proposed in [6] partitioned the data based on time-varying Cox models with time-varying indicators as regression variables. In [7], Fu and Simonoff proposed modifications of already existed tree models designed for right-censored data by transforming subjects with the time-varying covariates into pseudo-subjects. Several subject transformations were also proposed in [8] to analyse survival data with time-varying covariates with the use of random forests.

The already-presented tree-based models are narrowed to univariate trees, where every split tests the value of only one variable. In the paper, I propose an extension of oblique dipolar tree originally designed for right-censored discrete-time survival data [9]. Discrete-time models are less common and are reasonable when the medical examinations are conducted every certain period of time (e.g., monthly, quarterly or yearly). One of advantages of methods designed for discrete event times is a more intuitive interpretation of hazards as conditional probabilities [10]. A new model is able to analyse left-truncated right-censored data with time-varying covariates by appropriate data modifications resulting from treating the time as a discrete variable. Mayo Clinic primary biliary cirrhosis data [11] was used to assess capabilities of the proposed model.

This paper consists of four section. In Sect. 2, a definition of discrete-time survival data is presented. Section 3 contains a description of the dipolar criterion function and the induction of the dipolar tree, while Sect. 4 shows preliminary results of the experiments. Section 5 concludes the results.

2   Survival Data with Time-Varying Covariates

The survival time, in discrete-survival data, is divided into K distinct time intervals $I_1, I_2, \ldots, I_K$ where $I_1 = (0, t_1], I_2 = (t_1, t_2], \ldots, I_K = (t_{K-1}, \infty)$ and $0 < t_1 < t_2 < \ldots < t_{K-1} < \infty$. The learning set, LS, is defined as $LS = (\mathbf{x}_i, k_i, \delta_i)$, $i = 1, 2, \ldots, M$, where $\mathbf{x}_i = [x_{i1}, x_{i2}, \ldots, x_{iN}]^T$ is N-dimensional time-invariant covariate vector, $k_i \in \{1, 2, \ldots K\}$ is an index of the time interval (I_{k_i}) in which the failure occurred or the observation was lost to follow-up, and $\delta_i \in \{0, 1\}$ is a failure indicator that is equal to 1 for uncensored cases and to 0 otherwise. In case of left-truncated time-varying covariates, the representation of the ith subject in the kth time interval takes the form: $\mathbf{x}_i^k = [x_{i1}^k, x_{i2}^k, \ldots, x_{iN}^k]^T$, where $k \in \{b_i, \ldots, k_i\}$, b_i is the first time interval in which the ith subject was observed. We assume constant value of $\mathbf{x}_i^k$ in the whole kth time interval.

The distribution of the random variable T representing the survival time may be described by the discrete-time hazard, defined as the conditional failure probability

$$\lambda_k = \lambda(k) = P(T \in I_k | T \geq t_{k-1}), \tag{1}$$

the survival function

$$S_k = S(k) = P(T > t_k) = \prod_{i=1}^{k}(1 - \lambda_i), \tag{2}$$

where $S_0 = 1$, and the probability function

$$f_k = f(k) = P(T \in I_k) = S_{k-1} - S_k = \lambda_k \prod_{i=1}^{k-1}(1 - \lambda_i). \tag{3}$$

The likelihood function calculated for survival data is as follows:

$$L = \prod_{i=1}^{M} f_{ik_i}^{\delta_i} S_{ik_i}^{(1-\delta_i)}, \tag{4}$$

where k_i denotes the last time interval in which the ith subject was observed. For uncensored observations, for which the failure occurred in the interval I_{k_i}, the contribution to the likelihood function is $f_{ik_i} = f(k_i | \mathbf{x}_i)$; the contribution of censored observations is $S_{ik_i} = S(k_i | \mathbf{x}_i)$, since the failure time is unknown for them.

Suppose, that we replicate the information about each patient ($i = 1, \ldots, M$) for each time interval in which he/she was observed ($k = b_i, \ldots, k_i$) in such a way that a given vector $\mathbf{x}_i^k$ is replicated for time intervals greater than k but less then the successive time-interval available for the ith observation. Additionally for each newly-created observation we add a failure indicator d_{ik} equal to 1 for the last time interval I_{k_i} for uncensored patients and 0 otherwise. The likelihood function takes the following form

$$L = \prod_{i=1}^{M} \prod_{k=b_i}^{k_i} \lambda_{ik}^{d_{ik}} (1 - \lambda_{ik})^{1-d_{ik}} \tag{5}$$

where λ_{ik} is a hazard function in the kth time interval for the patient i. The maximum-likelihood estimator of the hazard function λ_{ik} is $\hat{\lambda}_{ik} = d_{ik}$. Assuming a homogeneous population, Eq. (5) may be presented in the binomial form [12] for which the maximum-likelihood estimator of the hazard function in the kth time interval, λ_k, is calculated as $h_k = \hat{\lambda}_k = \frac{m_{k1}}{m_k}$ where m_k and m_{k1} are a number of subjects at risk and a number of events in the kth time interval, respectively.

3 Oblique Dipolar Tree

An oblique dipolar tree (ODT) is a binary tree that divides the feature space into areas represented by terminal nodes. Each internal node contains a split in the form of any hyperplane $H(\mathbf{w}, \theta) = \{\mathbf{x} : \mathbf{w}^T \mathbf{x} = \theta\}$, obtained through the minimisation of a convex piece-wise linear criterion function - a dipolar criterion [3].

3.1 Dipolar Criterion Function

One of the basic stages of a tree induction algorithm is to decide how to divide the feature space in order to receive the best outcome from the point of view of the criterion used. Applied here, the dipolar criterion function is based on dipoles. They are pairs of feature vectors – $(\mathbf{z}_i, \mathbf{z}_{i'})$, $i \neq i'$, $i = 1, 2, \ldots, M$ and $i' = 1, 2, \ldots, M$ – which can be either mixed or pure. If two vectors are different from the point of view of a given problem, they should be separated. For this purpose, we create a mixed dipole between them. Pure dipoles are formed between similar observations that should not be separated. If we cannot decide whether two vectors are similar or not, we do not create any dipole between them. Having a set of mixed and pure dipoles, we are interested in obtaining such a hyperplane that divides as many mixed dipoles as possible and avoids splitting the pure ones.

For this purpose, for any augmented, feature vector $\mathbf{z}_i = [1, x_{i1}, x_{i2}, \ldots, x_{iN}]^T$, $i = 1, 2, \ldots, M$ from the learning set LS, we define two types of convex, piece-wise linear (CPL) penalty functions:

$$\varphi_i^+(\mathbf{v}) = \begin{cases} \gamma_i - \mathbf{v}^T \mathbf{z}_i & \text{if } \mathbf{v}^T \mathbf{z}_i \leq \gamma_i \\ 0 & \text{if } \mathbf{v}^T \mathbf{z}_i > \gamma_i \end{cases} \tag{6}$$

and

$$\varphi_i^-(\mathbf{v}) = \begin{cases} \gamma_i + \mathbf{v}^T \mathbf{z}_i & \text{if } \mathbf{v}^T \mathbf{z}_i \geq -\gamma_i \\ 0 & \text{if } \mathbf{v}^T \mathbf{z}_i < -\gamma_i \end{cases} \tag{7}$$

where $\mathbf{v} = [-\theta, w_1, w_2, \ldots, w_N]^T$ is an augmented weight vector, and $\gamma_i \geq 0$ is a margin usually equal to 1.

With each mixed dipole, we associate the sum of two different penalty functions, denoted by $\varphi_{ii'}^m$ ($\varphi_{ii'}^m(\mathbf{v}) = \varphi_i^+(\mathbf{v}) + \varphi_{i'}^-(\mathbf{v})$ or $\varphi_{ii'}^m(\mathbf{v}) = \varphi_i^-(\mathbf{v}) + \varphi_{i'}^+(\mathbf{v})$). Its minimization causes the feature vectors $\mathbf{z}_i$ and $\mathbf{z}_{i'}$ to be separated by the hyperplane $H(\mathbf{v})$. On the other hand, the sum of two penalty functions of the same type associated with the pure dipoles denoted by $\varphi_{ii'}^p$ ($\varphi_{ii'}^p(\mathbf{v}) = \varphi_i^+(\mathbf{v}) + \varphi_{i'}^+(\mathbf{v})$ or $\varphi_{ii'}^p(\mathbf{v}) = \varphi_i^-(\mathbf{v}) + \varphi_{i'}^-(\mathbf{v})$) prevents them from being divided. The dipolar criterion function is the sum of penalty functions over the whole set of dipoles and takes the following simplified form:

$$\Psi_d(\mathbf{v}) = \sum_{(i,i') \in I^p} \alpha_{ii'} \varphi_{ii'}^p(\mathbf{v}) + \sum_{(i,i') \in I^m} \alpha_{ii'} \varphi_{ii'}^m(\mathbf{v}) \tag{8}$$

where $\alpha_{ii'}$ is a price (importance) of the dipole $(\mathbf{z}_i, \mathbf{z}_{i'})$, p and m stand for pure and mixed dipoles, respectively, and I^p and I^m are sets of pure and mixed dipoles. The dipolar criterion is calculated for each internal node on the basis of the data that reach the node and minimized with the use of basis exchange algorithm [14]. As a result, we obtain the parameters of the splitting hyperplane $H(\mathbf{v})$. A node becomes a leaf when it contains no more than a determined number of observations or when we cannot create any mixed dipoles for it. A more detailed description of the dipolar criterion function is given in [3].

3.2 Construction of Oblique Dipolar Tree

Our goal is to divide observations from the learning set into areas with similar values of the hazard function. As it was shown in paragraph 2 (Eq. 5), the maximum-likelihood estimator of the hazard function for subject i in the kth time interval is equal to d_{ik} - the patient's status in the kth time interval. Hence, our aim can be reached by separating observations with different values of d_{ik} what is a binary classification task [9].

Since d_{ik} values are not included in the original data, induction of the oblique dipolar tree requires an additional initial phase of data preparation. Each observation, i, from the learning set, LS, should be replicated for each time interval, I_k, $k = b_i, \ldots, k_i$, in which he/she was observed. Time-invariant covariates are constant in all time intervals. The values of time-varying covariates change over time intervals. They can be available only for a part of intervals. If there is no new covariate value in a given time interval, k', the value from the nearest time interval $k < k'$ is replicated. Hence, we receive a new augmented learning set $LS_{aug} = (\mathbf{u}_{ik}, d_{ik})$, where $i = 1, \ldots, M$, $k = b_i, \ldots, k_i$, $d_{ik} \in \{0, 1\}$ is a failure indicator that is equal to 1 only for the observed last time interval of uncensored subjects and to 0 otherwise, and $\mathbf{u}_{ik} = [x_{i1}^k, x_{i2}^k, \ldots, x_{iN}^k, k]^T$.

The dipolar classification tree is inducted by the minimization of the dipolar criterion function calculated on the basis of dipoles formed according to the following rules:

1. a pair of input vectors $(\mathbf{u}_{ik}, \mathbf{u}_{jk'})$ forms the pure dipole, if $d_{ik} = d_{jk'}$.
2. a pair of input vectors $(\mathbf{u}_{ik}, \mathbf{u}_{jk'})$ forms the mixed dipole, if $d_{ik} \neq d_{jk'}$.

Although the target is a binary variable, terminal nodes can be characterised by the hazard rate, h_k, calculated as the ratio of the number of failures ($d_{ik} = 1$) and the number of all observations that reach the node. The stopping criteria cover two conditions. The node becomes a leaf when 1) we cannot form any mixed dipole for it or 2) it contains no more than 10 observations.

To calculate the conditional probabilities of failure for a new patient $\mathbf{x}_{new}$, for a given time interval, k, we should create an input vector $[\mathbf{x}_{new}^T, k]^T$. Dropping the vectors down the tree, we obtain the hazards for corresponding time intervals.

The obtained dipolar trees are usually deep and have poor generalization. Additional pruning of irrelevant tree branches improves the results. I used a cost-complexity method [15] as a pruning technique.

4 Preliminary Experimental Results

The experiments were conducted with the use of Mayo Clinic primary biliary cirrhosis data (PBCseq) - extension of basic PBC data [11]. The data is available in the R package `survival` and contains information about 312 patients with primary biliary cirrhosis taking part in clinical trial conducted between 1974 and 1984 (and then extended to 1988) to evaluate the use of D-penicillamine for treating PBC. It consist of 1945 patient visits. An analysis based on the data can be found in Murtagh *et al.* [13]. The PBCseq dataset contains the following covariates: trt - treatment, age - age at registration, sex, ascites - presence of ascites, hepato - presence of hepatomegaly, spiders - presence of spiders, edema - presence of edema, bili - serum bilirubin, chol - serum cholesterol, albumin - serum albumin, alk.phos - alkaline phosphatase, ast - aspartate aminotransferase, platelet - platelets per cubic, protime - prothrombin time, and stage - histologic stage of disease). Failure indicator takes three values: 0 - censored observation, 1 - transplantation, 2 - death.

The PBCseq data was prepared according to the rules presented in Sect. 3.2. Each time-varying covariate of o given subject, i, from the learning set, LS, was repeated for the consecutive time intervals until a new value of the covariate was available. Since for several subjects there were some missing baseline covariate values (at the beginning of the follow-up time), they could not be filled in. Hence, these subjects were represented by the feature vectors in successive time intervals, what makes the observations left-truncated. Taking into account half-year time intervals, the augmented learning set consists of 4333 observations with 16 variables, including time interval. The experiments were focused on the prediction of the conditional probability of death, treating subjects with the failure indicator equal to 1 (transplantation) as right-censored.

To estimate the performance measure, the mean absolute error (MAE), a bootstrap cross-validation procedure [16] was applied. In this approach, in each of B runs of the procedure, the training set L_{tr}^b, $b = 1, 2, \ldots, B$ is drawn with replacement from the original learning set. The test set L_{ts}^b contains those feature vectors that are not sampled in L_{tr}^b. The performance measure estimate is calculated as a mean value over B iterations:

$$MAE = \frac{1}{B} \sum_{b=1}^{B} \frac{1}{M_b} \sum_{ik \in In(L_{ts}^b)} |d_{ik} - h_{ik}| \tag{9}$$

where M_b is the number of observations in the bth test set and $In(L_{ts}^b)$ is a set of indexes of observations belonging to L_{ts}^b.

In the paper, I did not investigate the impact of dipole prices. They were set constant: 1 for pure dipoles and 100 for the mixed [9].

The data set obtained as a result of the preliminary phase of data preparation is similar to classification problems in which the model output is interpreted as the conditional probability of failure, therefore the results were compared with those obtained by the tree proposed by Schmidt *et al.* [17] with BIC-based cardinality pruning (*SchTree*), CART [15] with nodes representing the hazard values, a random forest algorithm with Hellinger distance decision trees [18] (RFH) and Gini impurity measure (RFG). R package rpart was used to generate $SchTree$ and CART; R package ranger to generate RFH and RFG with 200 trees.

Table 1 shows the results obtained for the analysed models. Additionally, the MAE was calculated separately for observations with the target values $d_{ik} = 0$ and $d_{ik} = 1$. As we can see, the MAE and MAE_0 calculated for ODT are better than the results obtained for CART, RFH, and RFG. The median number of nodes obtained for ODT was 14, for CART - 15 and for $SchTree$ - 25. As we can see, the mean absolute errors calculated for $SchTree$ are better than for ODT, which, however, consists of a much smaller number of nodes.

Table 1. Mean absolute errors obtained for PBCseq data. MAE_0 means the MAE calculated for the observations with the target value $d_{ik} = 0$; MAE_1 means the MAE calculated for the observations with the target value $d_{ik} = 1$. The results are presented as mean (standard deviation) values calculated over 100 runs of the experiment.

	MAE	MAE_0	MAE_1
ODT	0.049 (0.005)	0.025 (0.003)	0.8 (0.076)
$SchTree$	0.046 (0.04)	0.023 (0.003)	0.79 (0.042)
CART	0.052 (0.005)	0.029 (0.005)	0.775 (0.05)
RFH	0.056 (0.09)	0.032 (0.09)	0.818 (0.062)
RFG	0.057 (0.09)	0.034 (0.09)	0.79 (0.062)

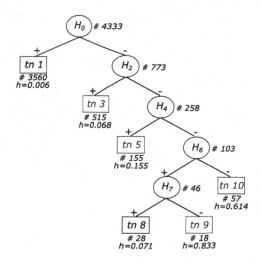

Fig. 1. Dipolar classification tree for PBCseq data set; # means the number of cases, h - the hazard value.

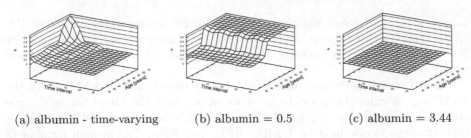

(a) albumin - time-varying   (b) albumin = 0.5   (c) albumin = 3.44

Fig. 2. The influence of age on the hazard function across time intervals with different values of albumin; the other covariates were constant: trt=1, sex=1, ascites=0, hepato=0, spiders=0, edema=0, bili=1.4, chol=280, alk.phos=1072, ast=107, platelet=228, protime=10.8, stage=3.

In Fig. 1, we can see the tree obtained for PBCseq data. It consists of 11 nodes including 7 terminal nodes. Each terminal node is described by the hazard function, h, and the number of cases that reached the node. For internal nodes, the number of cases is only given. Since the pruning technique is based on the 10-fold cross-validation technique, the result trees can differ. During the experiments, I obtained also smaller trees in which the 6th internal node became a leaf with the hazard function, $h = 0.505$.

4.1   Clinical Relevance

The oblique dipolar tree may be a good tool for investigating the influence of analysed time-dependent variables on the risk of failure, especially for data which do not fulfill the assumptions required by statistical analysis. For given values of variables and specified time interval we can predict the probability of failure, additionally, we can present and evaluate the existing dependencies between variables and the hazard function in graphs.

In Fig. 2, we can see three graphs representing the influence of age on the hazard function across time intervals. Additionally, the influence of albumin was evaluated. The other covariates were set constant. Continuous variables took their median values. In Fig. 2a, albumin values were changed with time - I defined here an increasing linear relationship between albumin and time interval. We can see that the smaller values of albumin in first time intervals caused a higher risk of death for older people than for people below 50. Starting from the 12th time interval the risk of death is very low and does not depend on age. In Figs. 2b and 2c, the albumin was constant and equal to 0.05 and 3.44, respectively. As we can see, the albumin equal to 3.44 does not influence the hazard function, for all time intervals and the entire age range, its values are very low. For a lower value of albumin, 0.5, we observe a significant difference between the hazard values obtained for men below 50 compared with those over 50 years old. The risk of death increases from about 0.15 to 0.6 for older men.

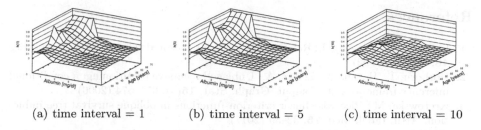

(a) time interval = 1   (b) time interval = 5   (c) time interval = 10

Fig. 3. The influence of age and albumin for the hazard function in three time intervals; the other covariates were constant: trt=1, sex=1, ascites=0, hepato=0, spiders=0, edema=0, bili=1.4, chol=280, alk.phos=1072, ast=107, platelet=228, protime=10.8, stage=3.

In Fig. 3, we can see the risk of death for men with primary biliary cirrhosis calculated for separate time intervals, taking into account the influence of albumin and age. Three time intervals were taken into account. As we can see, the shape of the hazard function does not differ between the first and the fifth time interval (Fig. 3a and 3b, respectively), but the conditional probabilities of death in the 10th time interval (Fig. 3c) are significantly lower, especially for smaller values of albumin.

5 Conclusions

In the paper, the tree-based method intended for left-truncated right-censored survival data with time-varying covariates as an extension of discrete-time dipolar tree was proposed. The approach uses a procedure of data preparation, which enables using time-varying covariates in a natural way, together with the time interval as a covariate. The preliminary experimental results based on Mayo Clinic primary biliary cirrhosis data showed that the proposed method gives good results and can be used to investigate the influence of time-varying covariates on the risk of failure (hazard), which in a discrete-time approach can be interpreted as the conditional probability of failure. The already existing survival trees, which allow to analyse time-varying covariates, are narrowed to univariate trees. Proposed here, oblique trees with splits of a form of any hyperplane can model more complex relationships between covariates and the predicted value.

The future work will concern modification of the dipolar criterion function in order to perform a feature selection in each internal node of the tree. Additionally, the obtained training data is highly unbalanced. The number of positive $(d_{ik} = 1)$ cases is very low compared to the number of negative ones. It may be useful to consider some additional changes in dipolar criterion function (e.g., higher mixed dipole prices) or data preparation procedure to improve the model performance.

References

1. LeBlanc, M., Crowley, J.: Relative risk trees for censored survival data. Biometrics **48**, 411–25 (1992)
2. Hothorn, T., Hornik, K., Zeileis, A.: Unbiased recursive partitioning: a conditional inference framework. J. Comput. Graph. Stat. **15**(3), 651–674 (2006)
3. Kretowska, M.: Piecewise-linear criterion functions in oblique survival tree induction. Artif. Intell. Med. **75**, 32–39 (2017)
4. Bacchetti, P., Segal, M.R.: Survival trees with time-dependent covariates: application to estimating changes in the incubation period of aids. Lifetime Data Anal. **1**, 35–47 (1995). https://doi.org/10.1007/BF00985256
5. Bou-Hamad, I., Larocque, D., Ben-Ameur, H.: Discrete-time survival trees and forests with time-varying covariates: application to bankruptcy data. Stat. Modell. **11**(5), 429–446 (2011)
6. Bertolet, M., Brooks, M.M., Bitter, V.: Tree-based identification of subgroups for time-varying covariate survival data. Stat. Methods Med. Res. **25**, 488–501 (2016)
7. Fu, W., Simonoff, J.S.: Survival trees for left-truncated and right-censored data, with application to time-varying covariate data. Biostatistics **18**(2), 352–369 (2017)
8. Moradian, H., Yao, W., Larocque, D., Simonoff, J.S., Frydman, H.: Dynamic estimation with random forests for discrete-time survival data. Can. J. Stat. (2021). https://doi.org/10.1002/cjs.11639
9. Kretowska, M.: Oblique survival trees in discrete event time analysis. IEEE J. Biomed. Health Inf. **24**(1), 247–258 (2020)
10. Tutz, G., Schmid, M.: Modeling Discrete Time-to-Event Data. SSS, Springer, Cham (2016). https://doi.org/10.1007/978-3-319-28158-2
11. Fleming, T.R., Harrington, D.P.: Counting Processes and Survival Analysis. John Wiley and Sons, New York (1991)
12. Biganzoli, E., Boracchi, P., Mariani, L., Marubini, E.: Feed forward neural networks for the analysis of censored survival data: a partial logistic regression approach. Stat. Med. **17**(10), 1169–1186 (1998)
13. Murtaugh, P.A., et al.: Primary biliary cirrhosis: prediction of short-term survival based on repeated patient visits. Hepatology **20**(1.1), 126–34 (1994)
14. Bobrowski, L., Niemiro, W.: A method of synthesis of linear discriminant function in the case of nonseparability. Pattern Recogn. **17**, 205–210 (1984)
15. Breiman, L., Friedman, J., Olshen, R., Stone, C.: Classification and Regression Trees. Wadsworth, Belmont, CA (1984)
16. Mogensen, U., Ishwaran, H., Gerds, T.: Evaluating random forests for survival analysis using prediction error curves. J. Stat. Softw. **50**(11), 1–23 (2012). https://doi.org/10.18637/jss.v050.i11
17. Schmid, M., Kuchenhoff, H., Hoerauf, A., Tutz, G.: A survival tree method for the analysis of discrete event times in clinical and epidemiological studies. Stat. Medincine **35**(5), 734–751 (2016)
18. Schmid, M., Welchowski, T., Wright, M.N., Berger, M.: Discrete-time survival forests with Hellinger distance decision trees. Data Min. Knowl. Disc. **34**(3), 812–832 (2020). https://doi.org/10.1007/s10618-020-00682-z

An Anytime Querying Algorithm for Predicting Cardiac Arrest in Children: Work-in-Progress

Michael A. Skinner[1,2(✉)], Priscilla Yu[2], Lakshmi Raman[2],
and Sriraam Natarajan[1]

[1] University of Texas at Dallas, Dallas, TX 75080, USA
[2] University of Texas Southwestern Medical Center, Dallas, TX 75390, USA
mas140130@utdallas.edu

Abstract. Cardiac arrest (CA) is a devastating complication for children in the cardiac intensive care unit (CICU). We developed an "anytime" algorithm to predict CA, using the first few hours of EHR data for initial approximation, and then using information from subsequent time periods to augment the predictive model, improving performance at each iteration. Our initial empirical evaluation on EHR CICU data shows that the model achieves significantly higher performance than learning with all the available data at each iteration when predicting CA inside CICU.

Keywords: Gradient boosting · Anytime algorithms · Cardiac arrest

1 Introduction

Congenital heart disease is a significant cause of death and morbidity in neonates and children. A devastating complication in children with heart disease is cardiac arrest (CA). If the condition is not quickly reversed, there will be significant damage to other organ systems and possibly death [4]. An important challenge is to develop machine learning algorithms using the electronic health record (EHR) to predict which critically ill children in the cardiac intensive care unit (CICU) are at increased risk of cardiac arrest [7]. A desirable property for these algorithms is the ability to generate a reasonable approximation of the desired result with few data, and then to refine the prediction with time as more data accumulate. Such *anytime algorithms* [8] exhibit improved accuracy with time, allowing for reasoning continuously as more data arrive.

We devised an anytime algorithm to compute the probability of CA in children with congenital heart disease in the CICU. Using the Functional Gradient Boosting paradigm [2], we create a set of regression trees whose cardinality grows as more clinical data accumulate in the EHR. The data are collected in increments of several hours, and at each increment, new trees are concatenated to the previous model in a stacking fashion, improving predictive ability with time.

S. Natarajan—Supported in part by NICHD grant 1R01HD101246 and The Precision Health Initiative of Indiana University.

2   Methods

2.1   Patients and EHR Data

We obtained an exemption from the UTSW IRB as the data are deidentified. Hemodynamic, laboratory, demographic, medication data were collected from EHR in patients managed in the pediatric CICU at Children's Medical Center of Dallas. Records were obtained for 160 patients (age ≤ 21) who experienced CA over a 10 year period; EHR data were collected from the 48 h prior to CA. We also collected the first 48 h of data from 711 control (non-CA) patients selected at random from CICU patients managed during the same time period.

The ages in each group ranged from 1 day to 20 years (average age in arrest is 2.88 while in control is 3.45). *Our goal is to predict the probability of CA progressively from 13 h before the arrest to the hour of arrest.*

We extracted 11 EHR features, listed in Table 1. Each of the features was discretized into three "bins", using scikit-learn [6] "kmeans" strategy. To address the challenge of working with pediatric patients whose normal vital signs vary with age, and to account for the CICU patients where "normal" values may be quite abnormal compared to healthy patients, many of the features were normalized to reference values obtained by computing average parameter values over the first four hours of the 48 h trajectory. These features were selected by a pediatric ICU physician, and are marked with "*" in Table 1.

Table 1. Clinical features and measurement units used in predictive models. Those marked with * are standardized for each patient (explained in text).

Feature	units
Pulse rate	*
Diastolic blood pressure	*
Oxygen saturation	%
Urine output	*
Base excess	*
Anion gap	mEq/L
Fraction inspired O2 (fiO2)	*
Vasoactive inotropic score (VIS)	(None)
End tidal pCO2	mmHG
Near infrared spectroscopy rso 1	*
Near infrared spectroscopy rso 2	*

We discretized the time into one-hour increments; when multiple feature values were present during the hour, the mean of the values was used. Finally, to devise models that operate using symbols rather than simple features, and to avoid the imputation of missing results, we converted the data into predicate logic format. For example, the predicate "pulse(subj1001, LE 0.9, 16)" indicates that subject 1001 at 16 h prior to cardiac arrest exhibited a pulse rate less than or equal to 0.9 times his/her reference pulse rate.

2.2   Boosted Predictive Regression Trees

After transforming EHR data into a relational predicate format, we exploit the tools of Statistical Relational Learning (SRL) [3] to create models predicting cardiac arrest. In particular, we employed the SRLBoost framework described by Natarajan *et al.* [5] to create boosted sets of weakly-effective regression trees trained to generate the probability of our target concept, cardiac arrest.

Algorithm 1. Pseudocode to construct anytime predictive model

---

Input: positive and negative example trajectories with time-indexed predicate
facts, k hours per model stage, T hours in trajectories, l number of trees
per stage
Output: Boosted predictive model
Initialize: model M = {}
1 $hourLast = 0$ // Last hour for current model stage.
2 **while** $T - hourLast < k$ **do**
3 | (We add stages until trajectory ends.)
4 | $hourLast = hourLast + k$
5 | $currentFacts = \{facts | fact.time \leq hourLast\}$
6 | $m = SRLboost(M, l, currentFacts)$
7 | $M = M + m$
8 **end while**
9 **return** M

Briefly, regression trees are constructed in a top-down manner [1] so that each decision node represents an EHR finding at a particular time prior to arrest (in the positive example learning set). At each iteration, the goal is to identify the predicate that maximizes the weighted variance. Leaf nodes contain regression values which can be converted a probability value. The algorithm employs single path semantics – i.e., each instance only satisfies one path in each tree – and thus returns one regression value from each tree. They are then added across the trees and converted to a probability by applying the sigmoid function. The depth of the trees was limited to 4.

In Algorithm 1, the model M is initially empty. Then, l trees are constructed using the observations annotated with times from the first k hours of the trajectory. Then, the next stage of the model is created by training an additional l trees using the initial data augmented by data from observations from the next k hours, and so on until there are fewer than k hours remaining in the trajectories, and the predictive model M is returned.

3   Results

We trained the models using 75% of the patient examples, and tested them with 25% of the examples. Example down sampling was employed to deal with the significant class imbalance.

For training and prediction, we used EHR data from 16 h prior to cardiac arrest (in those who arrested) and the final 16 h of data (of the 48 h of data collected) in the control patients. The model was initialized using the first 4 h of data (16-13 h before arrest), creating a set of 5 boosted regression trees. For each subsequent 4 h period, another 5 trees were learned using the data from all of the hours seen so far; the new trees are concatenated to the model obtained thus far. So, after the data over the entire 16 h trajectory are evaluated, the final model consists of 20 trees.

The results are seen in Fig. 1. The models include our concatenated model (solid red line), a model derived without concatenating previous models but with increasing number of model trees learned from scratch (dashed blue line), and a baseline model where 20 trees are learned for each time point (dotted green line).

Presented are the mean, standard deviation of 5 models. The model created as a concatenation of models created over previous time periods exhibits the best predictive performance.

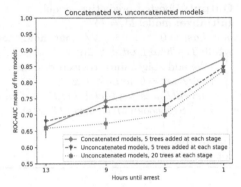

We conclude that a boosted model using EHR data converted to a time-indexed predicate format exhibits improved predictive performance when the model is constructed by iteratively adding new stages to the existing model as new, more recent results become available.

Fig. 1. ROC-AUC for the models predicting CA.

4   Discussion

It is interesting to consider why the concatenation of models by adding regression trees to a previously constructed model provides better predictive performance than simply starting from scratch at each time point, using all of the earlier data to construct a new set of regression trees. We speculate that physiologic data from later time points, which are closer to the time of cardiac arrest in the training set, are more useful in prediction. Thus, whenever a new model is created, the greedy nature of the construction selects later data to create the trees, ignoring earlier data that may be less helpful. However, when we create a model using only clinical facts from a limited period of time, as in the concatenation scheme, the model is forced to do what it can with those data to improve prediction, using data that might be ignored in a full-on greedy algorithm. This finding may have implications for other greedy predictive algorithms.

One advantage of our approach is the fact that we produce fairly robust predictive models from a relatively small number of subjects. In particular, we create the models using 75% of positive examples, or about 120 subjects. This contrasts with deep neural network models, which often require thousands of examples for model training. Moreover, in this non-parametric model, there are only a very few hyper-parameters to select, avoiding the necessity for extensive model tuning. Finally, the conversion of clinical results into a predicate format discharges the need to impute missing data elements; the models depend only on the findings actually present in the medical record by applying a closed world assumption.

It is the hope that any medical predictive model will extract causal factors responsible for the outcome of interest; then, those managing the patient might be able to intervene on the identified cause to improve outcome. Such usefulness in turn is dependant on model interpretability so that model findings can be understood, which is a challenge in many machine learning algorithms. For example, deep neural network models (DNNs) are notoriously difficult to understand. Although we are not yet able to meaningfully understand how the boosted trees in our model can be used to guide medical treatment, the recognizable predicates represent meaningful medical concepts. There exist methods that reweigh samples based on the learned boosted model to learn a single, more interpretable, tree. These techniques are similar to knowledge distillation in DNNs, but do not generally create a tree that is logically equivalent to the boosted model, and are therefore unsatisfactory for this predictive task. Explainability is a topic for future research. Moreover, we aim to more formally evaluate whether there are advantages to the predicate representation of data as against the more commonly used vector representation.

Clinical significance: Even as the medical and surgical management of children with cardiac disease has improved outcomes, CA in the CICU remains a significant challenge. In this preliminary work, we have devised an anytime algorithm to predict this devastating complication; the model holds promise that children at risk of CA can be identified early, allowing intervention and possibly CA prevention.

References

1. Dietterich, T.G., Ashenfelter, A., Bulatov, Y.: Training conditional random fields via gradient tree boosting. In: Proceedings of the Twenty-First International Conference on Machine Learning, p. 28 (2004)
2. Friedman, J.H.: Greedy function approximation: a gradient boosting machine. Ann. Stat. **29**, 1189–1232 (2001)
3. Getoor, L., Taskar, B.: Statistical Relational Learning (2007)
4. Meyer, L., et al.: Incidence, causes, and survival trends from cardiovascular-related sudden cardiac arrest in children and young adults 0 to 35 years of age: a 30-year review. Circulation **126**(11), 1363–1372 (2012)
5. Natarajan, S., Khot, T., Kersting, K., Gutmann, B., Shavlik, J.: Gradient-based boosting for statistical relational learning: the relational dependency network case. Mach. Learn. **86**(1), 25–56 (2012). https://doi.org/10.1007/s10994-011-5244-9
6. Pedregosa, F., et al.: Scikit-learn: machine learning in Python. J. Mach. Learn. Res. **12**, 2825–2830 (2011)
7. Ruiz, V.M., et al.: Early prediction of clinical deterioration using data-driven machine learning modeling of electronic health records. J. Thorac. Cardiovasc. Surg. **164**(1), 211–222 (2021)
8. Zilberstein, S.: Operational rationality through compilation of anytime algorithms. AI Mag. **16**(2), 79–79 (1995)

A Novel Survival Analysis Approach to Predict the Need for Intubation in Intensive Care Units

Michela Venturini[1,2]($\boxtimes$) (iD), Ingrid Van Keilegom[3] (iD), Wouter De Corte[4] (iD),
and Celine Vens[1,2]($\boxtimes$) (iD)

[1] Department of Public Health and Primary Care, KU Leuven, Campus KULAK, Etienne Sabbelaan 53, 8500 Kortrijk, Belgium
{michela.venturini,celine.vens}@kuleuven.be
[2] ITEC - imec and KU Leuven, Etienne Sabbelaan 51, 8500 Kortrijk, Belgium
[3] Research Centre for Operations Research and Statistics, KU Leuven, Naamsestraat 69, 3000 Leuven, Belgium
[4] Department of Anesthesiology and Intensive Care Medicine, AZ Groeninge Hospital, President Kennedylaan 4, 8500 Kortrijk, Belgium

Abstract. Intubation for mechanical ventilation (MV) is a common procedure performed in Intensive Care Units (ICUs). Early prediction of the need for intubation may have a positive impact by providing timely alerts to clinicians and consequently avoiding high risk late intubations. In this work, we propose a new machine learning method to predict intubation for MV, based on the concept of cure survival models. We tested our approach and compared it to other predictive models on a dataset collected from a secondary care hospital (AZ Groeninge, Kortrijk, Belgium). The results corroborate that our approach can improve the prediction of the need for intubation for MV in critically ill patients by using routinely collected data within the first hours of admission in the ICU. Early warning of need for intubation may be used to help clinicians predicting the risk of intubation and ranking patients according to their expected time to intubation.

Keywords: Cure survival models · Machine learning · Intensive care unit · Intubation prediction

1 Introduction

Intubation for mechanical ventilation (MV) is one of the highest risk procedures performed in ICU. Patients intubated in operating rooms are usually physiologically stable and the primary objective of the procedure is the induction of anesthesia. In contrast, ICU patients are often instable and in case of emergent intubation the timing is crucial to avoid risks related to late intubation [1, 2].

ICUs provide close monitoring of patients, by collecting and storing a large amount of heterogeneous data. In this context, Machine Learning (ML) can handle such high dimensional data to provide decision-support systems to help clinicians for timely diagnosis and treatments. Previous ML studies on predicting the need for intubation in ICU

M. Michalowski et al. (Eds.): AIME 2022, LNAI 13263, pp. 358–364, 2022.
https://doi.org/10.1007/978-3-031-09342-5_35

population focus on predicting the risk for intubation, disregarding the time information, or only considering a fixed time window [3, 4].

In this paper, we proposed a new machine learning approach, based on the concept of cure survival models, to predict the need for intubation for MV in ICU setting, that integrated time-to-event information in the model. We used both binary classifiers and survival analysis approaches as benchmarks. We collected data from several ICU sources (comorbidities, vital signs, laboratory measurements, and medications) and we focused on data recorded during the first hours after ICU admission. The contribution of this research is a new ML approach to predict the need for intubation for MV, that provides clinicians with information regarding patient's risk and timing of intubation during ICU stay.

2 Materials and Methods

2.1 Machine Learning Model

In this work we focused on ML models, able to handle complex and nonlinear relationships among variables. Specifically, we chose tree-based models that hand over a level of interpretation, since we wanted to provide clinicians with useful information about the prediction. We used random forest (RF) as the basic technique to develop our model and we adapted it to the concept of cure survival model, to incorporate the time-to-event information. High dimensionality and sparsity were also considered since they are common characteristics of clinical datasets.

A fundamental assumption of standard survival methodologies is that all patients in the dataset are at risk for the considered event [5]. However, in many clinical datasets, patients that experience the events are largely outnumbered by patients who will never experience the event of interest (called cured patients). Survival models that take this feature into account are called cure models. Mixture cure models are a family of cure regression models and rewrite the survival function

$$S(t \mid x, z) = P(T > t \mid X = x, Z = z) \tag{1}$$

as:

$$S(t \mid x, z) = 1 - P(y = 1 \mid x) + P(y = 1 \mid x) \times S_u(t \mid z), \tag{2}$$

where $P(y = 1 \mid x)$ is the probability of being susceptible to the event (called incidence), and S_u is the conditional survival function of the susceptible population (called latency) [5]. Here x and z are the set of predictors (joint or disjoint sets) that determine incidence and latency, and y is the event indicator ($y = 1$ in case the patient experiences the event, 0 otherwise). Usually, incidence and latency are obtained by using logistic regression and Cox regression, respectively. However, in case of high dimensionality of data and complex nonlinear relationship between covariates, ML models can offer a suitable alternative.

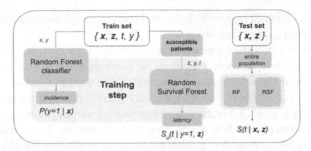

Fig. 1. ML framework.

We proposed a new ML framework to deal with the cured fraction and overcome the assumption of standard survival ML models. Unlike typical cure models applications, in our case the cure fraction was known and no censoring was present, given that we collected the full length of stay in ICU for the patients. We estimated the incidence part by using a RF trained on the entire population, while we obtained the latency by using a random survival forest [6] trained only with the susceptible fraction of patients (those who are eventually intubated). Figure 1 shows a graphical representation of the framework explained.

2.2 Dataset

To train and evaluate the models, we used a single-center, retrospective study, by gathering routinely collected structured data available from the ICU in AZ Groeninge Hospital (Kortrijk, Belgium). Specifically, data consisted of comorbidities, vital signs, laboratory measurements, medications, date and time of admission and intubation. Our cohort comprised patients admitted to the ICU from 2015 to 2021. We excluded patients already intubated at ICU admission, aged below 18 and over 90, patients with therapy restriction with level ≥ 2 (we checked the entire ICU stay), and patients affected by covid-19. We extracted validated measurements up to 6 h upon admission in addition to demographics and comorbidities and consequently we excluded patients intubated within this time interval. This procedure resulted in a total of 4130 patients (59% male, median (IQR) age of 66 years (55–76)), of which 8.3% received intubation for MV during their ICU stay (see *Appendix* for further details).

2.3 Data Preprocessing

To address sparsity and high dimensionality of data (for example, some medications are only administered to few patients in the study population) we employed the FIDDLE framework [7]. We excluded rarely collected variables through custom thresholds, selected taking into account imbalance in the dataset (see *Appendix* for further details). Moreover we handled multiple measurements for the same patients by extracting mean, maximum, and minimum of time-dependent variables, within the six-hours window.

3   Experiments

We evaluated our method and compared it both with binary classification and survival analysis models. More precisely, we evaluated the discriminative capabilities of the adjusted survival curve produced by our model at several time points (12, 24, 48, 72, 96 h after ICU admission). For the comparison with binary classification models, we discarded the time information and trained RF models for the same time points, predicting whether or not intubation had occurred. For the survival analysis models, we trained a RSF (on the complete training set), and we considered the survival function at the mentioned time points. We evaluated the probability of death at each time point as: $1 - S(t)$, where t was the time of interest. To test the models' performance, we used three-fold cross validation, stratified according to the number of events. At each step we collected predictions on the test set to calculate area under the ROC curve, average precision (AP) score and Harrel's c-index. We repeated the evaluation for each aforementioned time point. All experiments were performed in Python, version 3.8. All models were fitted using the scikit-learn and scikit-survival Python packages with default parameters.

4   Results and Discussion

Table 1 shows the results of our methodology (denoted as cure-ML) compared to the benchmark models. According to all the considered metrics, our model outperformed the considered benchmarks. Regarding ranking capability, we obtained a better C-index in comparison to the standard survival model (RSF). As far as regards discriminative performance, we observed an improvement both according to ROC-AUC score and AP score. Although AP score seemed low, one needs to consider that the dataset was highly unbalanced, and the total number of intubations was ~8%, therefore the AP score of a random classifier would correspond to 0.08. Our model reached a score above such value for each time point, meaning that there was a gain in discriminative capabilities.

Table 1. Performance evaluated with 3-fold cross validation. Reported values indicate mean (standard deviation), with the best values for each time point in bold.

Model	t	C-index (SD)	ROC-AUC (SD)	AP score (SD)
RF	12	–	0.77 (0.06)	0.05 (0.02)
	24		0.77 (0.01)	0.08 (0.02)
	48		0.76 (0.03)	0.14 (0.04)
	72		0.78 (0.02)	0.15 (0.02)
	96		0.77 (0.01)	0.17 (0.03)
RSF	12	0.74 (0.02)	0.75 (0.03)	**0.11 (0.07)**
	24		0.81 (0.00)	0.11 (0.05)
	48		0.78 (0.02)	0.15 (0.04)
	72		0.77 (0.02)	0.17 (0.04)
	96		0.76 (0.01)	0.18 (0.02)
cure-ML	12	**0.76 (0.02)**	**0.84 (0.02)**	0.09 (0.06)
	24		**0.83 (0.01)**	**0.12 (0.04)**
	48		**0.82 (0.02)**	**0.18 (0.04)**
	72		**0.81 (0.03)**	0.17 (0.06)
	96		**0.80 (0.02)**	**0.19 (0.04)**

5 Conclusion

We introduced a novel ML survival methodology to predict time to intubation for MV in a general ICU population by using routinely collected information within the first hours upon admission. This model was meant to be a first screening and prioritization tool. As future work, we intend to extend our study to allow the model to handle multiple time windows for each patient to predict an updated risk score across their ICU stay. Interpretability will also be taken into account by extracting feature importance from the models.

Acknowledgements. This research was funded by the Research Fund Flanders (project G0A2120N). The authors also acknowledge the Flemish Government (AI Research Program).

Appendix

(See Fig. 2 and Tables 2 and 3).

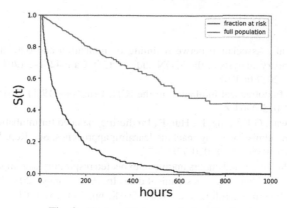

Fig. 2. Kaplan-Meier survival estimate.

Table 2. Cohort characteristics. RF patients with respiratory failure, COPD patients with chronic obstructive pulmonary disease, HR heart rate, RR respiratory rate, SBP systolic blood pressure, DBP diastolic blood pressure. Values are expressed in median and interquartile range, unless differently specified.

	All patients (N = 4130)	Non-intubated (N = 3788)	Intubated (N = 342)
Male (%)	2428 (58.8%)	2219 (58.6%)	209 (61.1%)
Age	66.0 [55.0;76.0]	66.0 [54.8;76.0]	65.0 [56.0;74.0]
Medical (%)	2065 (50.0%)	1820 (48.0%)	245 (71.6%)
Surgical (%)	1569 (38.0%)	1500 (39.6%)	69 (20.2%)
Trauma (%)	347 (8.4%)	322 (8.50%)	25 (7.31%)
RF (%)	282 (6.8%)	240 (6.34%)	42 (12.3%)
COPD (%)	761 (18.4%)	680 (18.0%)	81 (23.7%)
Saturation (%)	97.4 [96.3;98.7]	97.4 [96.1;98.7]	97.1 [96.6;98.9]
PO$_2$ (mmHg)	105.2 [82.9;130.5]	104 [82.2;130]	113 [91.2;141]
PH	7.41 [7.38;7.45]	7.41 [7.38;7.45]	7.41 [7.37;7.44]
HR (bpm)	81.0 [69.0;95.0]	81.0 [70.0;95.0]	77.0 [68.0;90.0]
RR (breaths/min)	18.0 [15.0;22.0]	18.0 [15.0;22.0]	17.0 [15.0;20.0]
DBP (mmHg)	61.1 [53.5;68.2]	61.1 [53.2;68.0]	61.1 [55.5;68.4]
Lactate (mmol/L)	1.50 [0.90;2.05]	1.50 [0.90;2.07]	1.91 [1.10;1.91]

Table 3. FIDDLE custom parameters. T size of the time window, dt granularity of the window, Theta 1 threshold for the pre-filter step, Theta 2 threshold for the post filter step, Theta freq average number of measurements per time window at which a variable is considered frequent "frequent".

Parameter	T	Dt	Theta 1	Theta 2	Theta freq	Binarize
Value	6	6	0.001	0.001	1	No

References

1. Bauer, P.R., et al.: Association between timing of intubation and outcome in critically ill patients: a secondary analysis of the ICON audit. J. Crit. Care **42**, 1–5 (2017). https://doi.org/10.1016/J.JCRC.2017.06.010
2. Lapinsky, S.E.: Endotracheal intubation in the ICU. Crit. Care **19**(1) (2015). https://doi.org/10.1186/s13054-015-0964-z
3. Siu, B.M.K., Kwak, G.H., Ling, L., Hui, P.: Predicting the need for intubation in the first 24 h after critical care admission using machine learning approaches. Sci. Rep. **10**(1), 1–8 (2020). https://doi.org/10.1038/s41598-020-77893-3
4. Ren, O., et al.: Predicting and understanding unexpected respiratory decompensation in critical care using sparse and heterogeneous clinical data. In: Proceedings - 2018 IEEE International Conference on Healthcare Informatics, ICHI 2018, pp. 144–151 (2018). https://doi.org/10.1109/ICHI.2018.00024
5. Amico, M., Van Keilegom, I.: Cure models in survival analysis. **5**, 311–342 (2018). https://doi.org/10.1146/ANNUREV-STATISTICS-031017-100101
6. Ishwaran, H., Kogalur, U.B., Blackstone, E.H., Lauer, M.S.: Random survival forests. Ann. Appl. Stat. **2**(3), 841–860 (2008). https://doi.org/10.1214/08-AOAS169
7. Tang, S., Davarmanesh, P., Song, Y., Koutra, D., Sjoding, M.W., Wiens, J.: Democratizing EHR analyses with FIDDLE: a flexible data-driven preprocessing pipeline for structured clinical data. J. Am. Med. Inform. Assoc. **27**(12), 1921–1934 (2020). https://doi.org/10.1093/JAMIA/OCAA139

Awareness of Being Tested and Its Effect on Reading Behaviour

Marta Malavolta[1]([☒]) [ID], Emiliano Trimarco[2], Vida Groznik[1,3,4],
and Aleksander Sadikov[1,3]

[1] Faculty of Computer and Information Science, University of Ljubljana,
Ljubljana, Slovenia
`{marta.malavolta,vida.groznik,aleksander.sadikov}@fri.uni-lj.si`
[2] Instituto de Investigación e Innovación Biomédica de Cádiz, INiBICA,
Hospital Universitario Puerta del Mar, Cádiz, Spain
`emiliano.trimarco@inibica.es`
[3] NEUS Diagnostics, d.o.o., Ljubljana, Slovenia
[4] Faculty of Mathematics, Natural Sciences and Information Technologies,
University of Primorska, Koper, Slovenia

Abstract. The Hawthorne effect, a behaviour change in response to
the awareness of being tested, during the execution of an eye-tracking
battery for the detection of mild cognitive impairments (MCI) has not
yet been considered. The present work has a twofold aim: (*i*) to search
for the potential differences between eye-tracking signals recorded during
the reading in two different experimental conditions, when subjects are
aware of being tested or not and (*ii*) to determine which of the two signals
best predicts cognitive impairments (CI). The reading behaviour from 94
subjects was collected, comprised of 53 healthy controls (HE) and 43 CI
subjects. For each subject, we recorded their reading behaviour during
three different tasks and machine learning algorithms were used to distinguish between the eye-tracking signal in case people are aware/are not
aware of being tested. The results suggested that only the HE subjects
are affected by the Hawthorne effect (with an AUC of 80%), so the best
way to distinguish between HE and CI participants is when the subjects
are not aware of being tested.

Keywords: Behavioural analysis · Reading behaviour · Mild cognitive
impairment · Eye-tracking · Machine learning

1 Introduction

Eye-tracking is becoming a popular tool, particularly for the detection of cognitive disorders. Eye-tracking data obtained during reading has been suggested
to be a powerful biomarker to detect mild cognitive impairment (MCI) [2]. This
disease is characterized by deterioration of memory, attention, and cognitive
function beyond expected based on age and educational level [4]. The MCI subjects could also be impaired in social cognition and social functioning [1].

M. Michalowski et al. (Eds.): AIME 2022, LNAI 13263, pp. 365–370, 2022.
https://doi.org/10.1007/978-3-031-09342-5_36

In this field, less is known about the role of Hawthorne effect due to awareness of being tested (in this case during a reading task) or participating in research potentially leading to a change in their behaviour [5]. A recent study demonstrated relatively successful MCI detection from gaze behaviour during reading a short text without the awareness of being tested [3].

The goal of the present work is to explore the occurrence of the Hawthorne effect as a consequence of the subjects' awareness of being actively tested during the different stages of the neuropsychological test battery. Hence, to understand which eye-tracking signal is better for the classification between MCI patients and healthy controls.

2   Methods

2.1   Dataset

We used a cohort of 94 participants that were split into two groups: 53 healthy (HE) and 41 cognitively impaired (CI) subjects, i.e. the ones who were diagnosed with a cognitive decline through a neurological and psychological examination. The latter include participants diagnosed with either mild cognitive impairment (MCI) or dementia.

The participants' gaze behaviour was recorded using 90 Hz Tobii 4C eye-tracker and a dedicated software produced by NEUS Diagnostics, d.o.o. The subjects sat approximately 70 cm from a display (23.6″ display with a 1920 × 1080 px resolution) where the visual stimuli were presented using the NEUS software. Participants were able to perform the test battery with their eyes only, as they had no direct contact with the equipment. We recorded their eye movements for each subject while reading three different texts displayed on the screen. In the first case, the *initial instructions* (II) were presented after the initial 5-point eye-tracker calibration and before employing the digitalised neuropsychological test battery. During that phase the subjects were not aware of being tested. The other two texts, the *story about a cycling trip* (SC) and the *story with a curious girl* (SG), were part of the neuropsychological test battery, meaning the participants were aware of being tested.

We pre-processed the data by removing the first 5% and the last 10% of each recording and all the points where the eyes were not detected by the eye-tracker. We computed fixations (the retention of the gaze on a single point) and saccades (the rapid eye movement between two fixations) from the remaining signals. The latter could be either backward (left) or forward (right). To understand which is the reading behaviour of the participants, we defined 11 reading features from fixations and saccedes. The backward saccade distance (*bdist*), computed as the median distance of all backward saccedes, and its standard deviation (*bdist.stdev*). This feature is associated with re-reading of a previous text or with starting a new line, and also related to the backward and forward saccade speed (*bspeed* and *fspeed*), calculated as the median speed of all detected saccades, as well as the forward saccade distance (*fdist*). We also calculated the number of detected fixations per second and its minimum and maximum value (*fxt.min* and *fxt.max*), and the duration of fixations (*fdur*), i.e. the median duration of all detected fixations, and its standard deviation (*fdur.std*), that may be linked to the readers' irregular or confused behavior. Lastly, we computed the ratio between the number of detected forward saccades and the number of detected backward saccades (*fsVbs.min* and *fsVbs.max*)

2.2   Machine Learning Algorithms

We assessed (*i*) the effect of the awareness of being tested during reading in two different experimental conditions, as well as (*ii*) the ability to detect cognitive impairments based on reading behavior in the two cohort groups using (a) a statistical analysis on the 11 features and (b) four different machine learning classifiers, logistic regression (LR), Naive Bayes (NB), stochastic gradient boosting (XGB) and random forests (RF).

3   Results

We performed a statistical analysis on the 11 features described above by computing an independent t-test with Bonferroni correction in the two cohorts (HE and CI) between the three different tasks. The feature that mainly exhibited significant difference was the *bdist* in the HE subject and, in particular, between the reading behaviour in the two stories during the neuropsychological test battery and the II reading, as shown in Fig. 1.

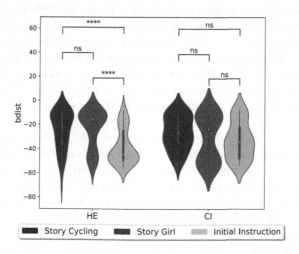

Fig. 1. Distribution of the *bdist* attribute in the two cohorts (HE and CI) during the reading of the II and the reading of the two different stories. P-value annotation legend: *ns*: p ≥ 5.00e−02; ****: p ≤ 1.00e−04

Figure 2a. shows the distribution of *bdist* between the reading tasks and highlights that the study participants had different behaviour in the case of reading the II (orange line) with respect to the reading of the two other stories. We divided the subjects into HE and CI groups and Fig. 2b shows the multimodal distribution of HE subjects with an average smaller *bdist* attribute values in the II reading, i.e. subjects re-read some parts of the text more than once or started reading a new line of text. The same behaviour was not found in the CI subject and the distributions on the three datasets seemed to have no significant differences (p-values = 0.99), as shown in Fig. 2c.

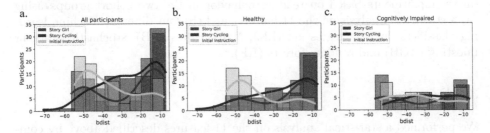

Fig. 2. Distribution of the *bdist* attribute during the reading of the II (orange line) and during the reading of two different stories during the neuropsychological test battery (SC green line and SG yellow line) for a) all participants, b) HE control, and c) CI subjects.

Using ML models we investigated whether it was possible to detect potential differences between the eye-tracking signals recorded during the reading of a text when subjects are aware of being tested or not. All the results shown were obtained using a 10-times repeated 10-fold cross-validation. At first, we classified the reading behaviour of all the participants during reading the II and the two stories (SC and SG) in the neuropsychological test battery. The results show that the ML algorithms cannot distinguish reading behaviour between the three reading tasks.

Therefore we decided to divide the participants into HE controls and CI subjects. Looking at the HE subjects we can see that the ML algorithms were able (*i*) to distinguish between the reading of the initial instruction and the girl story, as shown in Fig. 3. In particular, the LR model is the one that achieves the best results (AUC of 80%, std 16%) for the classification between the reading tasks. Moreover, all the models cannot find a significant division between the reading behaviour in the SC and SG (AUC of 68%, std 14%), despite they are both part of the neuropsychological test battery. The same results were not achieved in the CI population, in fact, the models used cannot distinguish any of the reading tasks.

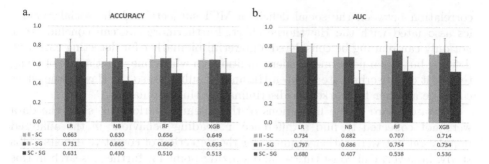

Fig. 3. The picture shows the results of 10-times-repeated 10-fold cross validation for the four ML models used for the classification between reading II and SC (pink bars), between reading II and SG (blue bars) and between reading SC and SG (green bars) in the HE population. **a.** Average accuracy. **b.** Average AUC.

Finally, we tried (*ii*) to determine which signal best predicts CI patients and HE controls. Figure 4 shows that the best way to classify between the two groups in the three reading tasks is the reading behaviour during the reading of the II, i.e. the subjects are not aware of being tested. Moreover, the ML model that better performs is the RF with an AUC of 76% (std 17%).

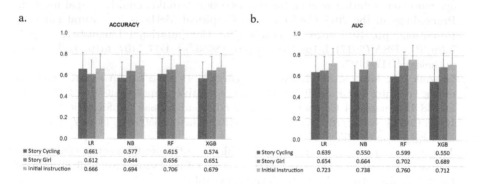

Fig. 4. The picture shows the results for the four ML models used for the classification between HE controls and CI patients during reading the SC (green bars), the SG (yellow bars), and the II (orange bars). **a.** Average accuracy. **b.** Average AUC.

4   Discussion and Conclusions

In this work, we investigated how awareness of being tested during an eye-tracking study can influence the individual behaviour. We observed that HE controls are more sensitive to the Hawthorne effect than CI subjects. In fact, the models used are better able to detect the difference in reading behaviour during the two experimental conditions. This result may be due to the strong correlation between the social deficit of MCI subjects and the social dynamics associated with the Hawthorne effect. Furthermore, we can conclude that not only can reading be considered a powerful biomarker for detecting cognitive deficits, but when performed under conditions in which one is not aware of being tested, it can discriminate between HE and CI subjects, so the Hawthorne effect could be another biomarker for discriminating this population.

We are aware of the limitations of the research performed, since the data were not collected to find a difference in reading behaviour in the analyzed population but were rather acquired for the detection of cognitive deficits. This study, however, can constitute a valid starting point for further research in this field due to the potential of the used technology.

Acknowledgements. This research was funded by the EU H2020 MSCA-ITN project PARENT (grant no. 956394) and the Slovenian Research Agency under the research programme Artificial Intelligence and Intelligent Systems (grant no. P2-0209).

References

1. Bora, E., Yener, G.G.: Meta-analysis of social cognition in mild cognitive impairment. J. Geriatr. Psychiatry Neurol. **30**(4), 206–213 (2017). https://doi.org/10.1177/0891988717710337
2. Fraser, K.C., Lundholm Fors, K., Kokkinakis, D., Nordlund, A.: An analysis of eye-movements during reading for the detection of mild cognitive impairment. In: Proceedings of the 2017 Conference on Empirical Methods in Natural Language Processing, pp. 1016–1026. Association for Computational Linguistics, Stroudsburg, PA, USA (2017). https://doi.org/10.18653/v1/D17-1107, http://aclweb.org/anthology/D17-1107
3. Groznik, V., Mozina, M., Lazar, T., Georgiev, D., Sadikov, A.: Gaze behaviour during reading as a predictor of mild cognitive impairment. In: 2021 IEEE EMBS International Conference on Biomedical and Health Informatics, pp. 1–4. IEEE (2021). https://doi.org/10.1109/BHI50953.2021.9508586, https://ieeexplore.ieee.org/document/9508586/
4. Jongsiriyanyong, S., Limpawattana, P.: Mild cognitive impairment in clinical practice: a review article. Am. J. Alzheimer's Dis. Other Dementias® **33**(8), 500–507 (2018). https://doi.org/10.1177/1533317518791401
5. McCambridge, J., Witton, J., Elbourne, D.R.: Systematic review of the hawthorne effect: new concepts are needed to study research participation effects. J. Clin. Epidemiol. **67**(3), 267–277 (2014). https://doi.org/10.1016/j.jclinepi.2013.08.015

Natural Language Processing

Generating Extremely Short Summaries from the Scientific Literature to Support Decisions in Primary Healthcare: A Human Evaluation Study

Primoz Kocbek[1,2]([✉]) [iD], Lucija Gosak[1] [iD], Kasandra Musović[1] [iD], and Gregor Stiglic[1,3] [iD]

[1] Faculty of Health Sciences, University of Maribor, Maribor, Slovenia
{primoz.kocbek,lucija.gosak2,kasandra.musovic1,
gregor.stiglic}@um.si
[2] Faculty of Medicine, University of Ljubljana, Ljubljana, Slovenia
[3] Usher Institute, University of Edinburgh, Edinburgh, UK

Abstract. Recent advancements in Natural Language Processing (NLP) using large pre-trained neural language models were recently used in various downstream tasks, such as text generation. In primary healthcare, such systems can generate very short summaries of research papers to save healthcare experts' time when browsing through the literature search results, especially in scenarios where the communication with a patient can be supported by the latest scientific literature immediately at the point of care.

A use case scenario was explored using recent abstracts and short summaries from the Sematic Scholar platform (baseline TLDR model - an acronym for "too long; didn't read"). Four state-of-the-art models (OpenAI Davinci, OpenAI Curie, Pegasus-XSum, and BART-SAMSum) were used to generate short summaries. Ten healthcare experts evaluated five short summaries generated for each of the 20 included scientific paper abstracts.

Results showed that Informativeness, Naturalness, and Quality were the highest in the baseline TLDR model with an average score of 4.87 (SD = 1.48), 4.94 (SD = 1.36), and 4.81 (SD = 1.5), respectively. No statistically significant differences between the baseline TLDR and OpenAI Curie/Davinci models were detected. The other two models, i.e., Pegasus-XSum and BART-SAMSum scored significantly lower in Informativeness and Quality.

Our study demonstrated that we could effectively summarize scientific literature abstracts even with general AI-based text generation models such as OpenAI Curie and Davinci models. However, it should be noted that a higher variance was observed in the general models. Therefore, fine-tuning of the model is still recommended for practical use in the clinical environment.

Keywords: Natural language processing · Human evaluation · Healthcare

M. Michalowski et al. (Eds.): AIME 2022, LNAI 13263, pp. 373–382, 2022.
https://doi.org/10.1007/978-3-031-09342-5_37

1   Introduction

The recent advent of general artificial intelligence supported natural language processing (NLP) research has greatly advanced over the past several years. One of the most prominent breakthroughs in the field was the development of large pre-trained neural language models which are sometimes referred to as Foundation Models, such as Bidirectional Encoder Representations from Transformers (BERT) [1] and Generative Pre-trained Transformer (GPT) [2]. Both BERT and GPT based solutions were used in a variety of downstream tasks including text generation, question answering, text summarization.

The BERT and GPT models are massive deep learning language models that are pretrained using an enormous amount of unannotated data to provide a general-purpose deep learning model. By fine-tuning these pretrained models, downstream users can create task-specific models with smaller annotated training datasets (a technique called transfer learning). These models represent a breakthrough in NLP: now state-of-the-art (SOTA) results can be achieved with significantly smaller training datasets compared to solutions from a few years ago [3].

For an illustration of the potential, we can look at the OpenAI's API, which uses GPT-3 in the background and can for example perform very specific code related tasks such as explain code, calculate time complexity of a function, summarize code to natural language and many others [4].

Great potential use of the NLP can be seen in healthcare. Recently, interest in the use of NLP in healthcare has grown. NLP is currently the most commonly used analytical technique in healthcare. However, the complexity and ambiguity of medical language [5], alongside patient privacy [6], is challenging its application in healthcare. Nevertheless, the NLP has been used in identifying disease risk factors, evaluation of care and costs efficiency, extracting the information from clinical narratives within electronic health records (EHRs) [5], identification of biomedical concepts from radiology reports, nursing documentation, and discharge papers [7]. Adopting NLP in healthcare could help decision support systems or workflows and automatically extract clinically meaningful information that could delay or prevent disease onset [7]. However, the pre-training of large language models on medical texts is a complex task and therefore the adoption of such systems in healthcare is lagging behind other fields of application [8].

One such problem is extracting very short and concise summaries of research paper content to save healthcare experts' time when browsing through the search results, especially in scenarios when the advice to the patient should be supported by the latest scientific literature immediately at the point of care. Recently proposed TLDR (an acronym that stands for "too long; didn't read") extraction learning strategies developed by the Allen Institute for AI [9] can solve this problem. This field of research is commonly known as Natural Language Generation (NLG), a subfield of NLP. Their front-end solution, Semantic Scholar, which included a corpus of over 190 million research papers from thousands of academic journals and conferences by the end of 2020, covers all scientific fields and has started a mission to help scholars avoid information overload by offering quick access to the most relevant information from the world's scientific literature [10]. In this study the Semantic Scholar TLDR solution for text summarization was used as a baseline and compared to multiple SOTA text summarization models using GPT-3 [4], Pegasus [11] and BART [12].

For the development of NLG models, such as text summarization, human evaluation is crucial and is still an understudied aspect, which lacks a common evaluation. A good evaluation aims to assess the quality of a system, its properties and to demonstrate the progress of the task [13]. The typical human evaluation method is a scaled survey, and the most evaluated parameters are meaning, syntactic correctness, novelty, relevance, and emotional value [14]. There are automatic evaluations with some positive aspects such as being cheap, quick, repeatable, and can be used for error analysis and system development, but are criticized for being uninterpretable, unsuitable for assessing linguistic properties, unable to correlate with human evaluations [13] and are under informative. Therefore, human evaluation remains the gold standard for addressing the system's usefulness in real-world NLG applications [15]. Human evaluation is currently trending, which has led to the development of several evaluation frameworks [14]. In this paper we follow van der Lee et al. [15] best practice guidelines.

The main contributions of the paper are summarized as follows:

- Finding a solution for a potential real-world problem, providing a short and concise summary of a research paper to a healthcare expert, which can be seen as support by the latest scientific literature immediately at the point of care;
- Comparing a fine-tuned model for scientific literature and comparing it with multiple general SOTA models in text summarization;
- Using best practice human evaluation guidelines for text summarization and presenting interesting AI-generated results in the form of color-coded short summary analysis.

2 Materials and Methods

2.1 Data

The initial dataset from Semantic Scholar API [16] consisted of 26 scientific paper abstracts and their TLDR summaries that were derived using search terms "hypertension", "bmi", "diabetes" and "behavior change", using year of publication 2020, 2021 and scientific field of Medicine. Since our focus was on research papers, we additionally excluded two commentaries, one editorial, one research and one study protocol together with one book excerpt. That limited the final set of results to 20 scientific paper abstracts with a mean of 394.5 (SD = 184.7) words. The readability of these abstracts was classified as an average college level text corresponding to a Flesch Reading Ease (FRE) [17] score of 35.2 (SD = 13.8).

Baseline Semantic Scholar TLDR summaries were generated using the CATTS (Controlled Abstraction for TLDRs with Title Scaffolding) model, where initial training was performed on the multi-target SCITLDR dataset [9]. Next, we generated short summaries with five current off-the-shelf general SOTA NLG models. More specifically, we used two OpenAI GPT-3 based models [18], Curie and Davinci, where the task was TL;DR summarization [18]. OpenAI defines the 2 models as engines, where Davinci is the most capable OpenAI engine and is intended for applications requiring a lot of understanding of the content, such as summarization for a specific audience, whereas Currie is less complex, but still considered powerful in multiple tasks which include summarization [19].

The task TL;DR summarization trained a model to optimize for human preference, i.e. it used a large, high-quality dataset of human comparisons between summaries, trained a model to predict the human-preferred summary, and used that model as a reward function to fine-tune a summarization policy using reinforcement learning [18]. Next, we used two Hugging Face API [20] models. The first one being PEGASUS (Pre-training with Extracted Gap-sentences for Abstractive Summarization) [11] which is a pre-training large Transformer-based encoder-decoder model that performs a specific self-supervised objective and was fine-tuned on the XSum [21] dataset consisting of 226,711 BBC news articles from 2010 to 2017 accompanied with a one-sentence summary. The last model used was BART, a denoising autoencoder for pretraining sequence-to-sequence models [12] that was fine-tuned on the SAMSum [22] dataset consisting of around 16,000 messenger-like conversations with corresponding summaries.

To recap, the evaluation was performed on 20 abstracts with 5 short summaries each created by the aforementioned models. In order to minimize human evaluation bias, the order of the 5 short summaries was randomized for each abstract as well as the order of the 20 abstracts.

The short summary model names were abbreviated as follows, Semantic Scholars TLDR summaries were abbreviated to *SS_TLDR_Baseline*, Curie and Davinci TL;DR summarization was abbreviated to *OpenAI_TLDR_Curie* and *OpenAI_TLDR_Davinci*, PEGASUS on XSum was abbreviated to *PEGASUS-XSum* and BART tuned on the SAMSum dataset was abbreviated to *BART-SAMSum*.

2.2 Human Evaluation

We used an online survey platform called 1KA Arnes [23]. Participants with a healthcare background were invited via email to take part in the study. The participants provided their profession or field of work and started to read the abstracts and evaluate the five summaries for informativeness, naturalness and quality. A total of 13 participants (8 experts from the Nursing profession, 2 Teaching Assistants in Nursing and 2 Health Informatics/Computer Science experts, and one non-response) started the assignment with 10 completing (77% completion rate).

Our evaluation study followed the relevant best practice guidelines for human evaluations published by van der Lee et al. [15]. The *SS_TLDR_Baseline* was used to compare performance, intrinsic evaluation was used to evaluate properties of the models' output, i.e. a questionnaire was used. Constructs of interest were defined for each summary and three measures were evaluated: informativeness ("Does the summary provide all the useful information from the abstract?"), naturalness ("Does the summary sound like it was written by a native speaker?") and quality ("Is the summary grammatically correct and fluent?"). A 7-point Likert scale (1 - very poor to 7 - excellent) was used as there is some consensus in the literature that it maximizes reliability, validity, and discriminative power [24–27].

Analysis was performed using the R programming language (version 4.1.0). Paired samples t-test was used to assess statistical significance when comparing average scores of SOTA models to the *SS_TLDR_Baseline*. Additionally, a qualitative analysis of the best rated abstract in terms of Informativeness was performed.

3   Results and Discussion

The online study was conducted between 28.12.2021 and 9.01.2022. A total of 13 participants started with 10 of them also completing the study. The average time spent on the evaluation of all abstract summaries was 112 min. Eight participants identified Nursing as their profession, 2 as Teaching Assistant in Nursing, 2 as Computer Science and 1 did not give a response.

3.1   Comparison of Generated Summaries with Fined-Tuned Baseline

Table 1. Evaluation of the short summaries of a case study comparing a fine-tuned baseline with four SOTA models.

Model	Informativness	Naturalness	Quality
SS_TLDR_Baseline*	4.87 (SD = 1.48)	4.94 (SD = 1.36)	4.81 (SD = 1.5)
OpenAI_TLDR_Davinci	4.59 (SD = 1.87) $p = 0.116$	4.71 (SD = 1.54) $p = 0.134$	4.56 (SD = 1.68) $p = 0.143$
OpenAI_TLDR_Curie	**4.74** (SD = 1.72) $p = 0.436$	**4.83** (SD = 1.36) $p = 0.445$	**4.76** (SD = 1.58) $p = 0.787$
PEGASUS-XSum	4.22 (SD = 1.77) $p < 0.001$	**4.83** (SD = 1.52) $p = 0.472$	4.43 (SD = 1.73) $p = 0.028$
BART-SAMSum	3.98 (SD = 1.75) $p < 0.001$	4.5 (SD = 1.63) $p = 0.005$	4.25 (SD = 1.65) $p < 0.001$

*p-values compared and calculated to baseline model

Results showed that Informativeness, Naturalness, and Quality were the highest in the *SS_TLDR_Baseline* with an average score of 4.87 (SD = 1.48), 4.94 (SD = 1.36), and 4.81 (SD = 1.5), respectively (Table 1). No statistically significant differences between the *SS_TLDR_Baseline* and *OpenAI_TLDR_Curie/Davinci* models were detected. *PEGASUS-XSum* averages were significantly lower in Informativeness and Quality, *BART-SAMSum* averages were both significantly lower in Informativeness, Quality and Naturalness.

3.2   Qualitative Analysis of a Use Case

For the use case we selected the abstract with the highest Informativeness score in the *SS_TLDR_Baseline* as it was evaluated slightly better than other models, for example Fig. 1 shows the evaluation results for Abstract12 which we evaluated in more details.

It can be observed that Abstract 12 was ranked as 12th out of 20 documents in the Semantic Scholar results using the keywords from our use case scenario. It contains 248 words, 41 sentences and 444 syllables (Fig. 2) giving it an FRE score of 49.23 or borderline college-level readability. The abstract was also structured, i.e. it contains Background, Objective, Methods, Results and Conclusions sections. The *SS_TLDR_Baseline*

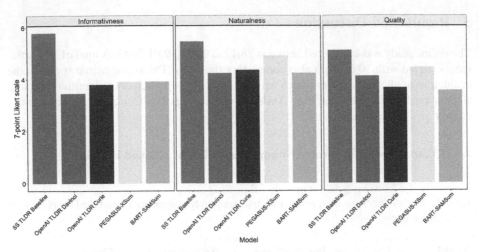

Fig. 1. Evaluation scores of Informativeness, Naturalness and Quality for Abstract 12.

received the highest rating in all aspects of Informativeness, Naturalness, and Quality and includes high coverage of summary phrases. The *OpenAI_TLDR_Davinci* model generated a short summary by extracting a part of the results of the abstract (*"Paternal BMI status and hypertension were inversely associated with the level of nutrition literacy of their children by b = −0.043 (95%CI: (−0.082, −0.003; p = 0.036) and by b = −0.600 (95%CI: −1.181, −0.019; p = 0.043), respectively."*). Also, the *BART-SAMSum* model extracted only a part of the results, but it was shorter than in the previously mentioned model as it did not contain numerical results (*"Paternal BMI and hypertension are inversely associated with the level of nutrition literacy of their children."*). Although the summary using this method provided less information compared to the *OpenAI_TLDR_Davinci* summary, the Informativeness was rated higher (3.89 vs. 3.44). Both received the lowest Naturalness score (4.22). It was also interesting to note that the *OpenAI_TLDR_Curie* model provided both a summarization and an opinion (*"I'll be honest, I'm not sure what to make of this study"*).

4 Discussion and Conclusion

Systematic reviews usually take weeks or months to be prepared and are not suitable to support clinical practice in many cases, mainly due to emerging costs and the availability of expertise [28]. The text summary allows users to find and understand relevant texts faster and easier [29]. However, the authors conducting the evaluation studies of automated or semi-automated review systems cite perceived limitations, such as the elimination of essential sentences, low coverage, poor sentence coherence, and redundancy [30]. The recent advances in general AI-supported natural language processing research allowed significant progress in the field of computer-generated text. One of the most prominent breakthroughs in the field was the development of large pre-trained neural language models that could be used in streamlining the "real-time" automated

Abstract 12 (Internal ID)	FRE=49.2

BACKGROUND: Children's dietary behaviors seem tract into adulthood and as a result preventing strategies to establish healthy behaviors from early stages of life are needed. Nutrition knowledge is essential for behavioral change.
OBJECTIVE: To examine whether the status of parental health related to their children's nutrition literacy level through their perceptions mainly of healthy eating attitudes
METHODS: A cross-sectional survey was conducted in Greece among 1,728 schoolchildren aged 10-12 years old. The sample was collected in the school setting during the school years of 2014-2016. Children completed anonymously a self-administered questionnaire about their knowledge and perceptions of a healthy diet while their parents completed another suitable questionnaire about family health status.
RESULTS: Paternal BMI status and hypertension were inversely associated with the level of nutrition literacy of their children by b = -0.043 (95%CI: (-0.082, -0.003; p = 0.036) and by b = -0.600 (95%CI: -1.181, -0.019; p = 0.043), respectively. Parental health status, specifically, paternal diabetes and maternal dyslipidemia were associated with children's higher level of nutrition literacy by b = 0.729 (95%CI: 0.002, 1.456; p = 0.049) and by b = 0.730 (95%CI: 0.086, 1.374; p = 0.026), respectively.
CONCLUSIONS: Parental health status partially affects, either negatively or positively the level of nutrition literacy of their children. This impact depends on whether parents follow nutritional recommendations to improve their health.

SS_tldr_baseline
I: 5.78 (SD=1.09), **N: 5.44** (SD=1.33), **Q: 5.11** (SD=1.54)   **FRE=22.1**
Examination of parental health related to their children's nutrition literacy level through their perceptions mainly of healthy eating attitudes in Greece found that parental health status partially affects the level of nutrition literacy of their children.

OpenAI_tldr_Davinci
I: 3.44 (SD=2.01), **N: 4.22** (SD=1.64), **Q: 4.11** (SD=1.45)   **FRE= 3.3**
Paternal BMI status and hypertension were inversely associated with the level of nutrition literacy of their children by b = -0.043 (95%CI: (-0.082, -0.003; p = 0.036) and by b = -0.600 (95%CI: -1.181, -0.019; p = 0.043), respectively.

OpenAI_tldr_Curie
I: 3.78 (SD=1.92), **N: 4.33** (SD=1.5), **Q: 3.67** (SD=1.73)   **FRE= 13.4**
Children's dietary behaviors seem to be influenced by their parents' health status. The impact of parental health status on children's nutrition literacy seems to depend on whether parents follow nutritional recommendations to improve their health. The impact of parental health status on children's nutrition literacy seems to depend on whether children have a healthy diet. I'll be honest, I'm not sure what to make of this study.

PEGASUS-xsum
I: 3.89 (SD=2.09), **N: 4.89** (SD=1.9), **Q: 4.44** (SD=2.01)   **FRE=11.1**
The aim of this study was to assess the impact of parental health status on the level of nutrition literacy among schoolchildren in Greece

BART-samsum
I: 3.89 (SD=1.62), **N: 4.22** (SD=1.64), **Q: 3.56** (SD=1.59)   **FRE=16.5**
Paternal BMI and hypertension are inversely associated with the level of nutrition literacy of their children.

I - Informativness, N - Naturalness, Q - Quality, FRE - Flesch Reading Ease

Fig. 2. Evaluation scores of Informativeness, Naturalness and Quality for Abstract 12. (*Similar word or words are colored with same colors if a specific color is not present in abstract the word or words are generated only in summary*).

systematic review of the literature. We are still a few steps away from this goal, but the progress in many fields needed to achieve such a goal is evident.

This study demonstrated the capabilities of some very advanced extreme text summarization models and evaluated them against each other. In all three observed metrics (Informativeness, Naturalness, and Quality) the model that was fine tuned for the task of scientific literature summarization performed the best on average. This was expected, although the results also showed that the largest and currently most advanced general language models (OpenAI models) performed as good as the specialized model as there were no significant differences between them in any of the observed metrics.

Our study demonstrated that we could effectively summarize scientific literature abstracts even with general AI-based text generation models such as OpenAI Curie and Davinci. However, it should be noted that a higher variance was observed in the general models. Therefore, fine-tuning of the model is still recommended for practical use in the clinical environment. In the future, more fine-tuning of the models in the evaluation process as well as introduction of different limits in the maximal length of the extreme summaries should be explored. However, to evaluate many different settings for each model, the manual evaluation soon reaches some limits in terms of time needed for human evaluators to assess the summaries. Therefore, a creation of curated database of abstracts and short summaries in the field of healthcare should represent a goal for the NLP community. This would open new possibilities in the automated evaluation of the novel language generation models.

Acknowledgements. The work described in this article was supported by the Slovenian Research Agency (ARRS Grants P2-0057 and N2-0101).

References

1. Devlin, J., Chang, M.W., Lee, K., Toutanova, K.: BERT: pre-training of deep bidirectional transformers for language understanding. In: NAACL HLT 2019 - 2019 *Conference* of the *North* American *Chapter* of the *Association* for *Computational Linguistics*: Human Language *Technologies* - Proceedings Conference, vol. 1, pp. 4171–4186 (2018)
2. Korngiebel, D.M., Mooney, S.D.: Considering the possibilities and pitfalls of generative pre-trained transformer 3 (GPT-3) in healthcare delivery. NPJ Digit. Med. **4**, 1–3 (2021). https://doi.org/10.1038/s41746-021-00464-x
3. Ajayi, D.: How BERT and GPT models change the game for NLP - Watson Blog
4. OpenAI. https://openai.com/. Accessed 20 Feb 2022
5. Koleck, T.A., Dreisbach, C., Bourne, P.E., Bakken, S.: Natural language processing of symptoms documented in free-text narratives of electronic health records: a systematic review. J. Am. Med. Inform. Assoc. **26**, 364–379 (2019). https://doi.org/10.1093/jamia/ocy173
6. Spasic, I., Nenadic, G.: Clinical text data in machine learning: systematic review. JMIR Med. Inform. **8** (2020). https://doi.org/10.2196/17984
7. Sheikhalishahi, S., Miotto, R., Dudley, J.T., Lavelli, A., Rinaldi, F., Osmani, V.: Natural language processing of clinical notes on chronic diseases: systematic review. JMIR Med. Inform. **7** (2019). https://doi.org/10.2196/12239
8. Davenport, T., Kalakota, R.: The potential for artificial intelligence in healthcare. Futur. Healthc. J. **6**, 94 (2019). https://doi.org/10.7861/FUTUREHOSP.6-2-94

9. Cachola, I., Lo, K., Cohan, A., Weld, D.S.: TLDR: extreme summarization of scientific documents. In: Findings of the Association for Computational Linguistics Findings of ACL: EMNLP 2020, pp. 4766–4777. Association for Computational Linguistics (ACL) (2020). https://doi.org/10.18653/V1/2020.FINDINGS-EMNLP.428

10. Dunn, A.: Semantic Scholar Adds 25 Million Scientific Papers in 2020 Through New Publisher Partnerships (2020)

11. Zhang, J., Zhao, Y., Saleh, M., Liu, P.: {PEGASUS}: pre-training with extracted gap-sentences for abstractive summarization. In: III, H.D., Singh, A. (eds.) Proceedings of the 37th International Conference on Machine Learning, pp. 11328–11339. PMLR (2020)

12. Lewis, M., et al.: BART: denoising sequence-to-sequence pre-training for natural language generation, translation, and comprehension. In: Proceedings of the 58th Annual Meeting of the Association for Computational Linguistics, pp. 7871–7880. Association for Computational Linguistics (ACL) (2020). https://doi.org/10.18653/V1/2020.ACL-MAIN.703

13. van der Lee, C., Gatt, A., van Miltenburg, E., Wubben, S., Krahmer, E.: Best practices for the human evaluation of automatically generated text. In: INLG 2019 – Proceedings of 12th *International Conference* on Natural Language Generation, pp. 355–368 (2019). https://doi.org/10.18653/V1/W19-8643

14. Hämäläinen, M., Alnajjar, K.: Human evaluation of creative NLG systems: an interdisciplinary survey on recent papers, pp. 84–95 (2021). https://doi.org/10.18653/V1/2021.GEM-1.9

15. van der Lee, C., Gatt, A., van Miltenburg, E., Krahmer, E.: Human evaluation of automatically generated text: current trends and best practice guidelines. Comput. Speech Lang. **67** (2021). https://doi.org/10.1016/j.csl.2020.101151

16. Semantic Scholar|AI-Powered Research Tool. https://www.semanticscholar.org/

17. Flesch, R.: How to write plain English

18. Wu, J., et al.: Recursively summarizing books with human feedback (2021). https://arxiv.org/abs/2109.10862v2

19. OpenAI engines. https://beta.openai.com/docs/engines. Accessed 18 Dec 2021

20. Hugging face: hugging face – the AI community building the future

21. Narayan, S., Cohen, S.B., Lapata, M.: Don't give me the details, just the summary! Topic-aware convolutional neural networks for extreme summarization (2018). https://doi.org/10.18653/v1/d18-1206

22. Gliwa, B., Mochol, I., Biesek, M., Wawer, A.: SAMSum corpus: a human-annotated dialogue dataset for abstractive summarization. In: Proceedings of the 2nd Workshop on New Frontiers in Summarization, pp. 70–79. Association for Computational Linguistics (ACL) (2019). https://doi.org/10.18653/V1/D19-5409

23. 1KA Arnes English homepage. https://1ka.arnes.si/index.php?lang_id=2. Accessed 12 Jan 2022

24. Miller, G.A.: The magical number seven, plus or minus two: some limits on our capacity for processing information. Psychol. Rev. **63**, 81–97 (1956). https://doi.org/10.1037/H0043158

25. Green, P.E., Rao, V.R.: Rating scales and information recovery—how many scales and response categories to use? J. Mark. **34**, 33–39 (2018). https://doi.org/10.1177/002224297003400307

26. Cicchetti, D.V., Shoinralter, D., Tyrer, P.J.: The effect of number of rating scale categories on levels of interrater reliability : A Monte Carlo investigation. J. Appl. Psychol. **9**, 31–36 (1985). https://doi.org/10.1177/014662168500900103

27. Preston, C.C., Colman, A.M.: Optimal number of response categories in rating scales: reliability, validity, discriminating power, and respondent preferences. Acta Psychol. (Amst) **104**, 1–15 (2000). https://doi.org/10.1016/S0001-6918(99)00050-5

28. Tsafnat, G., Glasziou, P., Choong, M.K., Dunn, A., Galgani, F., Coiera, E.: Systematic review automation technologies. Syst. Rev. **3**, 74 (2014). https://doi.org/10.1186/2046-4053-3-74

29. Mishra, R., et al.: Text summarization in the biomedical domain: a systematic review of recent research. J. Biomed. Inform. 457 (2014). https://doi.org/10.1016/J.JBI.2014.06.009
30. Ramanujam, N., Kaliappan, M.: An automatic multidocument text summarization approach based on Naïve Bayesian classifier using timestamp strategy. Sci. World J. **2016** (2016). https://doi.org/10.1155/2016/1784827

RuMedBench: A Russian Medical Language Understanding Benchmark

Pavel Blinov[✉], Arina Reshetnikova, Aleksandr Nesterov, Galina Zubkova, and Vladimir Kokh

Sber Artificial Intelligence Laboratory, Moscow, Russia
{Blinov.P.D,AAnReshetnikova,AINesterov,GVZubkova,Kokh.V.N}@sberbank.ru

Abstract. The paper describes the open Russian medical language understanding benchmark covering several task types (classification, question answering, natural language inference, named entity recognition) on a number of novel text sets. Given the sensitive nature of the data in healthcare, such a benchmark partially closes the problem of Russian medical dataset absence. We prepare the unified format labeling, data split, and evaluation metrics for new tasks. The remaining tasks are from existing datasets with a few modifications. A single-number metric expresses a model's ability to cope with the benchmark. Moreover, we implement several baseline models, from simple ones to neural networks with transformer architecture, and release the code. Expectedly, the more advanced models yield better performance, but even a simple model is enough for a decent result in some tasks. Furthermore, for all tasks, we provide a human evaluation. Interestingly the models outperform humans in the large-scale classification tasks. However, the advantage of natural intelligence remains in the tasks requiring more knowledge and reasoning.

Keywords: Natural Language Processing · Benchmark · Russian medical data · EHR · BERT

1 Introduction

In recent years deep neural network models have shown their effectiveness in solving multiple general Natural Language Processing (NLP) tasks. The progress in language model development actively extends to more narrow specific domains like medicine and healthcare. This trend intensified by the ongoing process of health industry digital transformation producing large volumes of data and posing challenging tasks requiring intelligent methods for processing. The primary source of text data in the medical domain is Electronic Health Records (EHRs). A series of models with novel BERT [8] architecture, e.g., ClinicalBERT [1], BioBERT [14], BlueBERT [16], successfully applied to a range of healthcare and biomedical domain tasks.

In Artificial Intelligence (AI) research field, similar tasks often are grouped to a special benchmark containing a set of formalized Machine Learning (ML)

M. Michalowski et al. (Eds.): AIME 2022, LNAI 13263, pp. 383–392, 2022.
https://doi.org/10.1007/978-3-031-09342-5_38

problems with defined input data and performance metrics. For example, ImageNet [7] benchmark for image classification or General Language Understanding Evaluation (GLUE) benchmark [25]. The comparison of human and ML-model performances allows measuring the progress in a particular field. Thus, a domain benchmark is vital for AI research standardization and prerequisites for model development and evaluation.

Language dependency is a serious obstacle for NLP models development. An overwhelming majority of NLP research conducts on English datasets. It induces inequality in resources and benchmarks available for other languages as Russian. Although recently the general benchmark for Russian language understanding evaluation RussianSuperGLUE [20] was proposed, there is still no similar test for the medical domain. This work tries to close such a problem and propose the Russian medical language understanding benchmark. Two issues complicate the creation of such a benchmark. The first one is the private nature of textual medical data. For example, EHRs contain notes about patient identity, disease and treatment details, etc. Therefore, it is hard to automate the anonymization process, and it requires a thorough manual look-through. The second issue is the lack of annotations for a target task, which often involves the tedious hand labeling of samples.

In this paper, we make the following contributions:

- Introduce *RuMedBench*, the first comprehensive open *R*ussian *Med*ical language understanding *Bench*mark. The RuMedBench contains five tasks based on four medical text types. The overall score allows to rank models on their ability to cope with medical specific tasks;
- Propose three new datasets and tasks: *RuMedTop3* for diagnosis prediction, *RuMedSymptomRec* for symptoms recommendation, *RuMedDaNet* for medical Question Answering (QA). Present *RuMedNLI*, the translated version of the medical Natural Language Inference (NLI) task. Include Named Entity Recognition (NER) task on an existing dataset for broader ML task types coverage;
- Perform a thorough comparison of several baselines from essential NLP approaches and estimate human performance for all proposed tasks.

The *RuMedBench* data and baseline models source code available in this repository: https://github.com/sberbank-ai-lab/RuMedBench.

2   Related Work

The most known representatives of NLP benchmarks are GLUE [25] and SuperGLUE [24]. The latter is the successor of the former, proposed with more challenging tasks to keep up with pacing progress in the NLP area. Both of them are designed for English general language understanding evaluation. For the Russian language, the analog of this benchmark is RussianSuperGLUE [20]. All those benchmarks include only single- or pair-centric text tasks. In this work, we also mostly use such task types but include a tokens-level problem. Because a typical medical text is full of specific terms, we want the benchmark to check models' ability to extract such terms and entities.

As already mentioned, medical privacy is one of the main difficulties for new datasets and relevant tasks creation. The publication in 2016 of the Medical Information Mart for Intensive Care (MIMIC-III) database [11] led to active researches and a plethora of tasks appearance. In 2017, Purushotham et al. [17] proposed a benchmark of three tasks: forecasting length of stay, mortality, and ICD-9 code group prediction. Only the last task overlaps with our ones as we focus on text data. The authors use 20 diagnosis groups to classify an intensive care unit admission. In our similar task, we use the newer 10th version of the International Classification of Diseases (ICD) [26], the target set of predicted codes is five times larger, and input texts are from outpatient notes.

Next, Peng et al. [16] introduced the Biomedical Language Understanding Evaluation (BLUE) benchmark on ten datasets. Also, substantial work has been done in [15], where the authors present a large-scale study across 18 biomedical and clinical NLP tasks. Our work is similar to these papers by the scope of task types. Although our test is inferior in the number of used datasets and tasks but differs positively by the broader range of medical text types. Moreover, our work has one intersection with [16] and [15], a natural language inference task on the MedNLI [18] dataset. For this, we translated original data (see Sect. 3.4). That allows to test models in a similar task and also produced counterpart medical corpus.

All the above-discussed works refer to tasks in English. Recently similar works appeared for other languages, for example, a Chinese Biomedical Language Understanding Evaluation (CBLUE) benchmark [27]. However, that cannot be said for Russian, where only a few separate datasets exist. We can note an interesting work of Tutubalina et al. [23] on the NER task. Due to data availability, we incorporate this task in our benchmark. Another paper [21] on information extraction from EHRs contains only 112 fully annotated texts. The data and labels are under user agreement license. In comparison to [21], EHR-related data in our work are open and by one order of magnitude larger in size (see Sect. 3.1). Therefore our work is the first to introduce several new open Russian medical datasets and tasks: two for large-scale classification on outpatient notes, one for question answering, and one for natural language inference.

3 Tasks and Data

Medicine probably is one of the oldest areas of human knowledge containing a broad range of disciplines. It is a priori impossible to cover whole aspects of this area in a single benchmark. For this work, we omit other than text modalities of medical tasks.

All datasets in this study are prepared in compliance with fundamental principles of privacy and ethics. Table 1 lists the *RuMedBench* sub-tasks along with some data characteristics and metrics. *Accuracy* is the mandatory metric for all tasks, with additional metrics in exceptional cases. To estimate models' abilities in Russian medical language understanding, we propose to infer an overall score as mean over task metric values (with prior averaging in the case of two metrics).

Table 1. The *RuMedBench* tasks.

Name	Type	Metrics	Train	Dev	Test	# of tokens / sents. Avg tokens per input	Text type
Top3	Classif.	Acc Hit@3	4,690	848	822	164,244 / 13,701 25	Outpatient notes
SymptomRec			2,470	415	415	89,944 / 7,036 27	
DaNet	QA	Acc	1,052	256	256	102,708 / 7,307 65	Misc. medical
NLI	Infer.		11,232	1,395	1,422	263,029 / 29,352 18	Clinical notes
NER	NER	Acc F1	3,440	676	693	68,041 / 4,809 14	User reviews

3.1   RuMedTop3

In a medical code assignment task [6], a set of codes is supposed to be assigned to a raw medical report for analytical, insurance, or billing purposes. In other words, the task concept is multiple answers, multiple predictions. In our task formulation, the concept is a single answer, multiple predictions. A sample implies the only ground truth disease code, but we expect the three most probable ICD-10 codes. Therefore based only on raw text from a patient, the model should produce a ranked list of 3 codes. The model that decently solves this task has multiple practical applications, for example, the second opinion component in a clinical decision support system or part of an automatic patient triage system.

Both *RuMedTop3* and *RuMedSymptomRec* tasks are based on *RuMedPrime* data [22]. The dataset contains 7,625 anonymized visit records from an outpatient unit of Siberian State Medical University hospital. Each record is represented with several columns. We are interested in the text field *symptoms* and *ICD10*. We use only the second level of the ICD-10 classification code hierarchy to prepare the target and drop the records with rare codes (under threshold 10). Thus only 6,360 visits have left with 105 target codes. Formally the task is defined as multi-class classification. Table 2 gives examples of input data and labeling for this and the following tasks.

For the evaluation, we propose to use *Hit@1* (the same as *Accuracy*) and *Hit@3* metrics [19]. The general formula is:

$$Hit@k = \frac{1}{N} \sum_{i=1}^{N} hit(\hat{y}_i, top_i^k), \qquad (1)$$

where N is the number of samples; $hit(\hat{y}, top^k)$ is 1 if ground truth ICD code $\hat{y}$ is on a ranked list of k predicted codes top^k and 0 otherwise.

The *Hit@3* metric allows lessening the evaluation criterion as a decision about the diagnosis code has to be made in case of incomplete and limited information.

3.2 RuMedSymptomRec

This task is designed to check models' ability to recommend a relevant symptom based on a given text premise. The task is beneficial in symptom checker applications where user interactions start with incomplete medical facts. Then, additional refining questions about possible user symptoms enable a more accurate diagnosis.

Table 2. Task examples from *Dev* sets (in English for readability purpose (For the original examples in Russian, please look at https://github.com/sberbank-ai-lab/ RuMedBench/blob/main/data/README.md)). Fragments in **bold** are the labels, `monospaced` text represents field names, unformatted text is an input.

Top3	`symptoms`: Palpitations, sleep disturbances, feeling short of breath. Pain and crunch in the neck, headaches for 3 days in a row. `code`: **M54**	
SymptomRec	`symptoms`: The patient at the reception with relatives. According to relatives - complaints of poor sleep, a feeling of fear, obsessive thoughts that 'someone is beating her' `code`: **fluctuations in blood pressure**	
RuMed* DaNet	`context`: Epilepsy is a chronic polyetiological disease of the brain, the dominant manifestation of which is recurrent epileptic seizures resulting from an increased hypersynchronous discharge of brain neurons. `question`: Is epilepsy a disease of the human brain? `answer`: **yes**	
NLI	`ru_sentence1`: During hospitalization, patient became progressively more dyspnic requiring BiPAP and then a NRB. `ru_sentence2`: The patient is on room air. `gold_label`: **contradiction**	
NER	`tokens`: Viferon has an antiviral effect · `ner_tags`: **B−Drugname** *O* *O* **B−Drugclass** *O* *O*	

We define a *symptom* as an explicit substring indicating a symptom-concept in the Unified Medical Language System (UMLS) metathesaurus [4]. Preliminary, we use the same *symptoms*-field and our internal tool for symptoms extraction. Further, we select a random symptom as the target for each record and strip it from the initial text. After that, the task again transpires to multi-class classification with 141 symptom-codes. Finally, the same as *RuMedTop3* metrics (1) are exploited for evaluation.

3.3 RuMedDaNet

Our firm belief is that a genuinely medical AI model should have knowledge and "understanding" of different health-related domains. Partially this skill can be verified by checking the model's ability to answer context-specific yes/no questions. We designed the current task inspired by *BoolQ* [5] and *DaNetQA* from [20].

A task sample consists of *(context, question, answer)* triple. The context is an excerpt (up to 300 words long) from a medical-related text. We tried to collect the contexts from diverse fields: therapeutic medicine, human physiology and anatomy, pharmacology, biochemistry. In similar tasks, the questions are gathered from aggregated search engine queries. One disadvantage of such an approach is an explicit template-like question structure which produces unwanted lexical effects (like repeated patterns) and may shift the final assessment. We tried to avoid this issue and involved assessors for the questions generation from scratch.

First, the context passages are mined from open sources. Then given a context, an assessor was asked to generate a clarifying *question* that can be definitely answered with either *yes* or *no*, thus completing triplet creation. All contexts are unique and paired with only one question. During the generation process, the balance between positive and negative questions is kept so that the *Accuracy* metric is well suited for this task results' evaluation.

3.4 RuMedNLI

The objective of the original NLI task is to compare a *premise* and *hypothesis* text and inference their relation as either *entailment*, *contradiction*, or *neutral*. The paper [18] proposed the medical formulation of the task called *MedNLI*. The premises are extracted from the *Past Medical History* section of MIMIC-III records; hypotheses are generated and labeled by clinicians. In the absence of similar data and labeling, we translated *MedNLI* to Russian.

First, each text is independently processed by two automatic translation services. However, purely automatic results are poor because of domain-specific language and terminology; therefore, each sample needs a thorough second look by a human corrector to compile the final translation. Examples of such corrections include abbreviations and drug names adaptation, measurements conversion to the metric system units (Fahrenheit to Celsius, feet to meters, blood groups from ABO system to numeric, etc.), cultural and language phenomena replacement. The final counterpart *RuMedNLI* dataset [3] is available through the MIMIC-III derived data repository. Along with data, we keep the original data split and evaluation metric – *Accuracy*.

3.5 RuMedNER

As mentioned in Sect. 2, we included the NER task from [23] in our benchmark. The data are user reviews about drug products. Each review is split into sentences and annotated with six types of named entities: drug name, class and form, adverse drug reactions, drug indications and symptoms of a disease, and "finding" (a miscellaneous type). The dataset with 4,566 entities is stored in IOB format (see Table 2 for the example). Formally this is a multi-class per token classification task with *Accuracy* and macro *F1-score* [19] evaluation metrics.

4 Experiments

4.1 Baselines

The most naive baseline method does not require modeling and is based solely on label statistics memorization. We estimate distributions in a *Train* and select the most common labels as answers accordingly.

As more advanced baseline NLP methods, we selected the following ones.

Feature-based Methods. Statistical models are still decent first-choice options, especially with limited training data. In the case of the *RuMedNER* task, we apply the Conditional Random Fields (CRF) model [13] with token-level features. In all other tasks for feature extraction, we use *tf-idf* weighting scheme [19] with analysis of char N-grams ($N = 3..8$). Then apply the logistic regression model [10] with the one-versus-all strategy for the final decision.

Recurrent Neural Networks (RNNs). From the family of RNNs, we pick the Bidirectional Long Short-Term Memory (BiLSTM) architecture [9]. In all tasks, we use a two-layer model with 300-dimensional word embeddings. We tried pre-trained word vectors as starting weights but, during experiments, found that random initialization yields better results.

Bidirectional Encoder Representations from Transformers (BERT). We selected general domain RuBERT (12 layers, 12 self-attention heads, and 768 hidden layer size) [12] as the base model for evaluation with the transformer models and RuPoolBERT [2] as its extended version. Both models fine-tuned for each task with the fixed set of hyperparameters, e.g., an input *sequence length* is 256 tokens, 25 training *epochs* with a *learning rate* of 3×10^{-5}. The only task-specific parameter is the *batch size*. After the training, the best checkpoint was selected (regarding *Dev* metrics) for the final prediction on the *Test* set.

Human Baseline. To get an idea about human performance, we ask assessors to solve the tasks. A non-medical assessor solves the *RuMedDaNet* and *RuMedNER* task as they imply more common health-related knowledge and answers can be inferred from a context. Independent clinicians addressed the rest three tasks.

4.2 Results and Discussion

Table 3 shows the performance results of tested baselines.

The naive method gains some performance in the tasks with unbalanced labels, e.g., $Acc = 10.58$ in the *RuMedTop3* task means that more than 10% of test samples belong to a most common ICD code. Nevertheless, the method is like a random guess for tasks with balanced label distribution (*RuMedDaNet*, *RuMedNLI*).

Generally, the transformer models outperform recurrent and feature-based ones. However, it is interesting to note the strong result of the linear model in the *RuMedTop3* task. We attribute this to the simplicity of the task, e.g., from the statistical point of view, mapping between char N-grams and a set of target codes is quite trivial. The method advantage diminishes with task complexity growth. For example, in the *RuMedDaNet*, simple methods are close to naive ones. In contrast, BERT-like models fare above them because the task involves more knowledge and a deeper "understanding" of nuances between context and question. The BERT model with an advanced pooling strategy works better in classification and QA tasks but slightly worse in NER and NLI.

Table 3. Baseline performance metrics (%) on the *RuMedBench* test sets. The best models' results for each task are shown in **bold**.

| | RuMed* | | | | | |
Model	$Acc/Hit@3$ Top3	$Acc/Hit@3$ SymptomRec	Acc DaNet	Acc NLI	$Acc/F1$ NER	Overall
Naive	10.58/22.02	1.93/5.30	50.00	33.33	93.66/51.96	35.21
Feature-based	**49.76/72.75**	32.05/49.40	51.95	59.70	94.40/62.89	58.46
BiLSTM	40.88/63.50	20.24/31.33	52.34	60.06	94.74/63.26	53.87
RuBERT	39.54/62.29	18.55/34.22	67.19	**77.64**	**96.63/73.53**	61.44
RuPoolBERT	47.45/70.44	**34.94/52.05**	**71.48**	77.29	96.47/73.15	**67.20**
Human	25.06/48.54	7.23/12.53	93.36	83.26	96.09/76.18	61.89

Further, it is worth noting that models performances in the first two tasks are much better than clinicians. To clarify this finding, we discussed the result with the assessor-clinicians. During labeling, their main concern was insufficient and noisy information provided in the *Symptom* field. Thus gender, age, physical examination results, and patient anamnesis are essential in medical diagnostic tasks; their exclusion leads to a substantial downgrade in human performance. Without such details, a model is a better conditional estimator of statistical distribution over many target classes.

Finally, human assessors hold the lead with substantial margins in the last three tasks. The *RuMedDaNet* is the most challenging one of the proposed tasks, with the gap between the human level and the best model of more than 20%. We hope the lag will be reduced after more advanced and specialized Russian medical models appear. Regarding the *MedNLI* dataset, to the best of our knowledge, this is the first human performance assessment on the task, and the current model state-of-the-art result on its English edition is 86.57%.

4.3   Clinical Relevance

We believe our experience outlined in this paper will provide a good reference for the research community developing AI methods in medicine. Specifically, the paper is notable either as an academic user case of non-English medical benchmark creation or starting point for Russian practitioners looking for open datasets and novel tasks. Overall, the proposed benchmark allows one to test Russian language models in the medical context and make better decisions before deployment.

5   Conclusions

In the study, we introduce the comprehensive open Russian medical language understanding benchmark, combining classification, QA, NLI, and NER tasks, four of them presented for the first time on newly created datasets. For comparison, we evaluate essential types of NLP methods and single-human performance. As expected, BERT-like models show the most promising results. However, even linear models can perform well for restricted, straightforward tasks. Moreover, in the current setup of medical diagnostic tasks, the models perform even better than humans. Therefore, future reformulations of such tasks should encompass more patient-related information, not only symptoms.

We hope our work will provide a sound basis for data practitioners and spur the research of text medical tasks in Russian. We release the source code and data in a unified format to start with the proposed benchmark quickly. Our further plan is the extension of *RuMedBench* with more advanced tasks and the creation of a full-fledged evaluation platform with private tests.

References

1. Alsentzer, E., et al.: Publicly available clinical BERT embeddings. In: Proceedings of the 2nd Clinical Natural Language Processing Workshop, pp. 72–78. Association for Computational Linguistics, Minneapolis, Minnesota, USA (2019)
2. Blinov, P., Avetisian, M., Kokh, V., Umerenkov, D., Tuzhilin, A.: Predicting clinical diagnosis from patients electronic health records using BERT-based neural networks. In: Michalowski, M., Moskovitch, R. (eds.) AIME 2020. LNCS (LNAI), vol. 12299, pp. 111–121. Springer, Cham (2020). https://doi.org/10.1007/978-3-030-59137-3_11
3. Blinov, P., Nesterov, A., Zubkova, G., Reshetnikova, A., Kokh, V., Shivade, C.: RuMedNLI: a russian natural language inference dataset for the clinical domain. PhysioNet (2022). https://doi.org/10.13026/gxzd-cf80
4. Bodenreider, O.: The unified medical language system (UMLS): integrating biomedical terminology. Nucleic Acids Res. **32**(suppl-1), D267–D270 (2004)
5. Clark, C., Lee, K., Chang, M.W., Kwiatkowski, T., Collins, M., Toutanova, K.: Boolq: exploring the surprising difficulty of natural yes/no questions. arXiv preprint. arXiv:1905.10044 (2019)
6. Crammer, K., Dredze, M., Ganchev, K., Talukdar, P., Carroll, S.: Automatic code assignment to medical text. In: Biological, translational, and clinical language processing, pp. 129–136 (2007)
7. Deng, J., Dong, W., Socher, R., Li, L.J., Li, K., Fei-Fei, L.: Imagenet: a large-scale hierarchical image database. In: 2009 IEEE conference on computer vision and pattern recognition, pp. 248–255. IEEE (2009)
8. Devlin, J., Chang, M.W., Lee, K., Toutanova, K.: Bert: Pre-training of deep bidirectional transformers for language understanding. arXiv preprint. arXiv:1810.04805 (2018)

9. Gers, F., Schmidhuber, E.: LSTM recurrent networks learn simple context-free and context-sensitive languages. IEEE Trans. Neural Netw. **12**(6), 1333–1340 (2001)
10. Hastie, T., Tibshirani, R., Friedman, J.: The elements of statistical learning: data mining, inference and prediction, 2 edn. Springer (2009). https://doi.org/10.1007/978-0-387-21606-5
11. Johnson, A.E., et al.: MIMIC-III, a freely accessible critical care database. Sci. Data **3**(1), 1–9 (2016)
12. Kuratov, Y., Arkhipov, M.: Adaptation of deep bidirectional multilingual transformers for russian language. arXiv preprint. arXiv:1905.07213 (2019)
13. Lafferty, J.D., McCallum, A., Pereira, F.C.N.: Conditional random fields: probabilistic models for segmenting and labeling sequence data. In: Brodley, C.E., Danyluk, A.P. (eds.) Proceedings of the Eighteenth International Conference on Machine Learning (ICML 2001), Williams College, Williamstown, MA, USA, 28 June - 1 July 2001, pp. 282–289. Morgan Kaufmann (2001)
14. Lee, J., et al.: BioBERT: a pre-trained biomedical language representation model for biomedical text mining. Bioinformatics **36**(4), 1234–1240 (2020)
15. Lewis, P., Ott, M., Du, J., Stoyanov, V.: Pretrained language models for biomedical and clinical tasks: understanding and extending the state-of-the-art. In: Proceedings of the 3rd Clinical Natural Language Processing Workshop, pp. 146–157 (2020)
16. Peng, Y., Yan, S., Lu, Z.: Transfer learning in biomedical natural language processing: an evaluation of bert and ELMO on ten benchmarking datasets. arXiv preprint. arXiv:1906.05474 (2019)
17. Purushotham, S., Meng, C., Che, Z., Liu, Y.: Benchmark of deep learning models on large healthcare mimic datasets. arXiv preprint. arXiv:1710.08531 (2017)
18. Romanov, A., Shivade, C.: Lessons from natural language inference in the clinical domain. arXiv preprint. arXiv:1808.06752 (2018)
19. Schütze, H., Manning, C.D., Raghavan, P.: Introduction to Information Retrieval, vol. 39. Cambridge University Press, Cambridge (2008)
20. Shavrina, T., et al.: RussianSuperGLUE: a Russian language understanding evaluation benchmark. In: Proceedings of the 2020 Conference on Empirical Methods in Natural Language Processing (EMNLP), pp. 4717–4726. Association for Computational Linguistics (2020)
21. Shelmanov, A., Smirnov, I., Vishneva, E.: Information extraction from clinical texts in Russian. In: Computational Linguistics and Intellectual Technologies, pp. 560–572 (2015)
22. Starovoytova, E.A., et al.: Rumedprimedata (2021). https://doi.org/10.5281/zenodo.5765873
23. Tutubalina, E., et al.: The Russian drug reaction corpus and neural models for drug reactions and effectiveness detection in user reviews. Bioinformatics **37**(2), 243–249 (2020)
24. Wang, A., et al.: Superglue: a stickier benchmark for general-purpose language understanding systems. arXiv preprint. arXiv:1905.00537 (2019)
25. Wang, A., Singh, A., Michael, J., Hill, F., Levy, O., Bowman, S.R.: Glue: a multitask benchmark and analysis platform for natural language understanding. arXiv preprint. arXiv:1804.07461 (2018)
26. WHO: International statistical classification of diseases and related health problems. World Health Organization, 10th revision, fifth edition, 2016 edn. (2015)
27. Zhang, N., et al.: Cblue: a chinese biomedical language understanding evaluation benchmark. arXiv preprint. arXiv:2106.08087 (2021)

Biomedical Semantic Textual Similarity: Evaluation of Sentence Representations Enhanced with Principal Component Reduction and Word Frequency Weighting

Student Paper Submission

Klaudia Kantor[1,2] and Mikołaj Morzy[2]

[1] Roche Poland, Warsaw, Poland
[2] Poznan University of Technology, Poznan, Poland
klaudia.kantor@doctorate.put.poznan.pl, mikolaj.morzy@put.poznan.pl

Abstract. Biomedical texts encode semantics in domain vocabulary, extensive use of acronyms, proper nouns, named entities, and numerical values with implied meaning. This information is absent from the surface text form, making semantic textual similarity challenging for models trained on the general English language. This paper evaluates different techniques of sentence embedding in semantic textual similarity search in the biomedical domain. We compare static embeddings, transformer-based representations (focusing on models fine-tuned to the biomedical domain), and sentence transformers. We also introduce two auxiliary techniques: principal component reduction and word frequency embedding weighting. To gain better insights into the latent properties of sentence embeddings, we perform directional expectation tests. We conduct our experiments on two benchmark datasets: the BIOSSES and the Clinical Outcomes. We find that sentence transformers are surprisingly effective, outperforming fine-tuned transformer-based models. Initial experiments also suggest the efficacy of principal component reduction and embedding weighting by word frequency.

1 Introduction

The objective of semantic textual similarity (STS) is to determine the similarity score between two texts, where the similarity is defined based on the likeness of meaning (semantics) rather than on lexical features of compared texts. To compute STS, one has to select an appropriate text representation. Prior to the advent of neural networks, most popular text representations included various bag-of-word models, such as TF-IDF, combined with lexical features

The research was conducted as part of the Polish Ministry of Education and Science's Industrial Doctorate Program implemented from 2020 to 2024 (Contract No. DWD/4/24/2020).

(part-of-speech tags, dependency tags, named entities, dictionary-based taggers). Recently, dense vector representations (embeddings) have gained popularity. The results of STS are useful in many downstream tasks, such as information retrieval, recommendation, filtering, or document clustering. STS assessment is also an intrinsic method of text embedding quality evaluation.

STS is heavily domain-dependent. In particular, the biomedical domain poses a significant challenge due to the excessive use of hermetic language, rare words, acronyms, numerical values with implied semantics, and distinct classes of named entities. State-of-the-art language models trained on general English corpora are capable of solving general semantic similarity tasks for biomedical texts, but they struggle when high precision is required (e.g., when processing eligibility criteria for clinical trials). Corpus annotation for supervised training of domain-adapted models is very expensive. The annotation task cannot be crowd-sourced, and medical experts do not have enough time to annotate corpora large enough to train language models. Consequently, the only viable solution is training models on the general English language corpus and unsupervised fine-tuning of models.

This paper examines the effectiveness of different unsupervised text representations in biomedical STS tasks. We evaluate popular text pre-processing methods and text representations: static embeddings, general language models, language models fine-tuned to the biomedical domain, and sentence transformers. We introduce two auxiliary techniques: principal component reduction and word frequency weighting. When applied to embeddings, these techniques consistently improve the STS task results for most models. We conduct our experiments on two benchmark datasets for biomedical STS. Finally, we show how directional expectation tests can provide deeper insights into the characteristics of sentence representations for biomedical STS.

2   Data

In the evaluation of sentence representations for biomedical STS, we use two public benchmark datasets:

- **BIOSSES** dataset consists of 100 sentence pairs extracted from the biomedical literature [23]. The pairs have been manually annotated by five medical experts with the similarity score ranging from 0.0 (unrelated) to 4.0 (semantically equivalent).
- **Clinical Outcomes (CO)** dataset consists of pairs of texts extracted from 3938 randomized controlled trials published in the PMC [11]. Each pair includes one phrase from the primary outcomes and one phrase from the reported outcomes of the same trial. Medical experts manually annotated pairs with a binary label indicating whether both outcomes refer to the same medical concept. The train set consists of 2108 pairs of unrelated texts and 616 pairs of similar texts. The test set consists of 226 pairs of unrelated texts and 78 pairs of similar texts.

One of the main differences between the datasets is the text length. The BIOSSES dataset consists of complete sentences, whereas CO includes single words or phrases extracted from sentences. Therefore, we expect the contextualized models to work better on the BIOSSES dataset, where the model can process the context. In the CO dataset, we require that the model understands the abbreviations or synonyms, since the context is often missing.

3   Models

We select GloVe pre-trained vectors [17] with cosine distance as the baseline for comparison. We examine 50-dimension and 300-dimension GloVe models built on Wikipedia corpus and 300-dimension models trained on the Common Crawl. We choose the BERT model [7] trained on BookCorpus and English Wikipedia for neural-based sentence representations. Recently, many new transformer models trained on biomedical texts were introduced. In our experiments we compare six such domain-adapted models: BioBERT [13], SciBERT [4], PubMedBERT [8], BlueBERT [16], ClinicalBERT [2], and CODER [27].

The training objective of BERT combines two related NLP tasks: predicting the masked word and predicting the next sentence. This model is not designed to provide accurate sentence representations, because it works on token-level embeddings. Sentence vectors are usually created by averaging token vectors or extracting [CLS] token embedding but such representations were proven to be less accurate than averaged GloVe embeddings. Sentence-BERT (SBERT) [20] is a new model explicitly trained to deliver semantically rich sentence representations. SBERT uses Siamese and triplet networks to produce meaningful sentence representations for downstream regression and classification tasks. In this paper we examine the performance of four sentence transformers, SMiniLM (all-MiniLM-L6-v2), SRoBERTa (all-distilroberta-v1), SMPNet (all-mpnet-base-v2) and SBERT (multi-qa-distilbert-cos-v1), which use different base models: distilled RoBERTa [22], MiniLM [25], MPNet [24] and distilled BERT [22], respectively. They have all been trained on general English corpora. Currently, no sentence transformers fine-tuned to the biomedical domain are available.

4   Experiments

Our experiments evaluate the performance of different text pre-processing techniques combined with varying sentence representations on the biomedical STS task. The list of text pre-processing techniques includes lower-casing, lemmatization, splitting words on punctuation marks, stop-word removal, filtering of punctuation and numbers. We use spaCy and NLTK Python libraries to perform these transformations. Text representations are generated from language models by [CLS] token embedding, extracting the last layer, extracting the second to the last layer, and extracting the first layer. Sentence representations are computed by either averaging or max-pooling of token embeddings.

4.1 Weighting Embeddings by Word Frequency

We introduce two techniques that can be easily applied to any embedding extracted from a language model. The first technique, inspired by Smooth Inverse Frequency [3], weights individual token embeddings by the relative frequency of the token in general English[1]. We consider three modes of weighting embeddings:

- *simple weighting*: we add token frequency as a weight when calculating the average sentence embedding,
- *concatenation*: we split tokens into rare and frequent tokens based on a frequency threshold, then we compute the average or max-pooled embedding of these two sets of tokens and we concatenate the resulting vectors,
- *rare words*: we filter out frequent tokens before vectorization using a predefined frequency threshold.

The rationale behind using word-frequency weighting of embeddings is to lower the impact of common English words on the final sentence embedding, thus increasing the weight of in-domain rare words. Common English words may introduce false similarity in the biomedical domain when describing similar processes in semantically unrelated topics. Consider two sentences: *"AST and ALT ≤ 2.5 x ULN with the following exception"* and *"Serum bilirubin ≤ 1.5 x ULN with the following exception"*. *"ULN"* is a common abbreviation for *"upper limit of normal"* and the two sentences describe unrelated medical concepts of AST/ALT and bilirubin.

4.2 Principal Component Reduction

The second technique for embedding fine-tuning is removing of the first principal component of the embedding matrix. It has been observed [14,19] that static embeddings have a large mean vector and after subtracting the mean, the remaining mass of the embedding is concentrated in just a few dimensions. All vectors share the mean and these dominating dimensions, it is hypothesized that the information content of these dimensions encodes the general grammatical structure of the language (e.g., part-of-speech sequence, idiomatic expressions, syntactic rules of phrase composition). We subtract the first principal component from all token embeddings. As a result, the remaining vectors carry more semantic information and less syntactic information.

4.3 Evaluation Metrics

The evaluation of STS techniques on the BIOSSES dataset consists in training a regression model. We choose Pearson's r (Pearson correlation coefficient), Spearman's ρ (Spearman's rank correlation coefficient), and the mean squared error (MSE) as evaluation metrics. These metrics are commonly used to evaluate the quality of unsupervised STS tasks in the literature.

---

[1] We use use the wordfreq Python library which calculates token frequencies based on Google Books, Leeds Internet Corpus, Wikipedia and Para Crawl.

Table 1. Evaluation on the BIOSSES dataset.

Model	Embedding	Freq. weight	PCA	r	ρ	MSE
BERT base	First layer mean	Concat	✓	0.777	0.783	0.153
BioBERT	First layer max	-	✓	0.795	0.799	0.166
SciBERT	First layer max	Rare words	✓	0.813	0.808	0.143
PubMedBERT	First layer max	Rare words	✓	0.803	0.803	0.139
BlueBERT	Last layer max	Rare words	✓	0.809	0.789	0.129
ClinicalBERT	Last layer mean	Rare words	✓	0.800	0.785	0.098
CODER	last layer max	rare words	✓	**0.849**	**0.834**	**0.096**
SMiniLM	-	-	-	0.842	0.813	0.029
SRoBERTa	-	-	-	**0.878**	**0.843**	**0.023**
SBERT	-	-	-	0.820	0.821	0.033
SMPNet	-	-	-	0.845	0.804	0.032
GloVe$_{wiki50}$	Maximum	-	✓	0.624	0.639	0.161
GloVe$_{wiki300}$	Maximum	-	✓	**0.775**	**0.775**	0.154
GloVe$_{crawl300}$	maximum	-	✓	0.757	0.742	**0.138**
Jaccard distance	-	-	N/A	**0.776**	**0.807**	**0.222**

The task in the CO dataset is the binary classification, so we have to binarize the continuous semantic similarity score returned by the distance function (either cosine or Jaccard). We set the threshold to mean similarity scores between the first quartile of distances for similar pairs and the third quartile of cosine distances for unrelated pairs of sentences from the test set. This threshold is used to classify a given pair of sentences as either similar or unrelated. We evaluate the quality of STS for the CO dataset using precision, recall, and the F1-score.

We run all the models with different combinations of sentence embedding and text pre-processing methods, which results in 74 048 experiments (64 for the Jaccard distance, 768 for GloVe, 8 064 for base transformers, 64 512 for base transformers with wordfreq, and 640 for sentence transformers). We repeat all experiments for BIOSSES and CO datasets, giving 148 096 experiments in total.

4.4 Directional Expectation Tests

To evaluate the robustness of the models, we create three directional expectation tests (DETs) [21] related to the following medical concepts: hemoglobin level, neutrophil count, and age. The idea of DETs is straightforward: given a test instance with a known expected outcome, one perturbs the test instance in such a way that there is an expectation of the direction and scale of change of the test result. In the case of biomedical STS, we select one similar (or almost identical) sentence pair for each DET, and we create additional pairs by introducing minor changes in the second sentence. For example, we replace the word *hemoglobin* with its abbreviation *Hb* or a different word *bilirubin*. In the first case, we expect that the similarity score does not change significantly or, in the best scenario, it remains the same. In the second case, we expect the semantic similarity score to drop.

5   Results

Table 1 shows the evaluation results on the BIOSSES. The baseline is GloVe$_{wiki300}$ vectors. Interestingly, the baseline is outperformed even by a simple Jaccard distance computed on the sets of unique tokens appearing in compared sentences. All transformers outperform the baseline, with the models fine-tuned on the biomedical domain achieving better results than the vanilla BERT model. The CODER model wins among the transformers with Pearson's r of 0.849. Sentence transformers perform even better, despite the fact that these models are trained on general English corpora and have not been fine-tuned to the biomedical domain. The highest Pearson's r of 0.878 is achieved by SRoBERTa.

Table 2. Evaluation on the Clinical Outcomes dataset.

Model	Embedding	Freq. weight	PCA	F1	Precision	Recall
BERT base	First layer max	-	✓	0.756	0.667	0.872
BioBERT	First layer max	-	✓	0.746	0.667	0.846
SciBERT	First layer max	-	✓	0.737	0.653	0.846
PubMedBERT	First layer max	-	✓	0.725	0.635	0.846
BlueBERT	First layer max	-	✓	0.739	0.663	0.833
ClinicalBERT	First layer max	-	✓	0.754	0.680	0.846
CODER	Last layer max	-	✓	**0.798**	**0.710**	**0.910**
SMiniLM	-	-	-	0.719	0.640	0.821
SRoBERTa	-	-	-	0.705	0.598	**0.859**
SBERT	-	-	-	**0.729**	**0.641**	0.846
SMPNet	-	-	-	0.663	0.583	0.769
GloVe$_{wiki50}$	Mean	-	✓	0.640	0.525	**0.821**
GloVe$_{wiki300}$	Mean	-	✓	0.674	0.592	0.782
GloVe$_{crawl300}$	Maximum	-	✓	**0.696**	**0.612**	0.808
Jaccard distance	-	-	N/A	**0.757**	**0.677**	**0.859**

We also evaluate the impact of the sentence embedding method on the biomedical STS performance. The best performing strategy for GloVe embeddings is max-pooling of token vectors and removing the first principal component. In general, principal component reduction significantly boosts the performance of GloVe representations. For instance, we observe a 0.220 increase in Pearson's r for the GloVe$_{wiki300}$ model. Principal component reduction and embedding weighting by word frequency (mostly selecting rare words only) improve the results of almost all BERT-based models, except for the BioBERT (where only principal component reduction is successful). We see at least a 0.1 increase of Pearson's r after applying principal component reduction for other models. However, we do not see the benefit of this technique for embeddings extracted from sentence transformers, since sentence transformers produce a semantically rich representation with less syntactic information.

As shown in Table 2, CODER enhanced with the principal component reduction outperforms other models on the CO dataset binary classification with an F1-score of 0.798. Again, GloVe embeddings are the baseline for the evaluation. Surprisingly, the second-best result is achieved by a simple Jaccard distance with a threshold. Fine-tuned transformers do not perform better than the vanilla BERT trained on the general English corpus. Sentence transformers perform on par with traditional transformers. The best representations are created by average-pooling of embeddings from the first layer of the model. We do not observe consistent improvement from embedding weighting by word frequency. At the same time, principal component reduction improves the performance of all examined models, with the most significant improvement of the F1 by 0.129 noted for GloVe$_{crawl300}$ model. The results on the CO dataset differ significantly from the results observed for the BIOSSES dataset. However, we need to stress an additional step in the pipeline after the STS calculation. The similarity score must be converted into a binary label based on a dynamically selected threshold for the CO dataset. This conversion may be responsible for the loss of information and different behavior of models. Also, the vocabulary, syntax, and sentence length vary between the datasets, impacting the evaluation results.

We perform the directional expectation test on two best-performing models: SRoBERTa and CODER. As shown in Table 3, the overall performance of both models is satisfying because, in most cases, STS scores change accordingly to the expectations. There are examples where the embeddings do not preserve the semantic differences, which results in incorrect STS scores. For example, the cosine similarity score between the embeddings from the SRoBERTa model is higher for this pair of sentences: (*Age $\geq$ 18 years at the time of signing Informed Consent Form, Signed Informed Consent Form*) than for the following pair: (*Age $\geq$18 years at the time of signing Informed Consent Form, Age $\geq$ 18 years*). The algorithm pays more attention to the second part of the sentence *signing Informed Consent Form* than to the age limit. Similar behavior can be observed in the sentence *No history of other diseases at the age $\geq$ 18 years* where CODER focuses on the age limit, resulting in a very similar embedding to the base sentence. Another interesting finding is that CODER created more similar embedding for *Adult* than for *Age $<$ 60 years*, this indicates that the model "understands" the semantics of the clause *Age $\geq$ 18*. There are also differences in STS scores between *Age $\geq$ 18 years* and *Age $<$ 60 years*. On the one hand, it might suggest that CODER has the basic ability to perform numerical inference and numerical comparisons. On the other hand, terms *age* and *18* may be common in training corpora as the age of majority, and this may result in the false perception of CODER's inference abilities.

Table 3. Results of directional expectation tests for three example sentences

	CODER	SRoBERTa
Hemoglobin $\geq$ 9 g/dL		
Hemoglobin $\geq$ 10 g/dL	1.00	0.95
Hemoglobin greater than or equal to 9 g/dL	0.95	0.98
Hb $\geq$ 9 g/dL	0.98	0.70
Hemgolobin $\geq$ 9 g/dL	0.89	0.78
Bilirubin $\geq$ 9 g/dL	0.83	0.54
ECOG performance status $\geq$ 1	0.83	0.26
Absolute neutrophil count $\geq$ 1500/μL without granulocyte colony-stimulating factor		
Absolute neutrophil count $\geq$ 1500/μL	0.94	0.83
ANC $\geq$ 1.5 $\times$ 109/L (1500/μL) without granulocyte colony-stimulating factor support	0.92	0.69
Lymphocyte count $\geq$ 0.5 $\times$ 109/L (500/μL)	0.83	0.59
WBC count >= 2.5 $\times$ 109/L (2500/μL)	0.79	0.34
Neutrophil count normal	0.82	0.66
Age $\geq$ 18 years at the time of signing Informed Consent Form		
Age $\geq$ 18 years	0.89	0.58
Adult	0.76	0.34
Age $\geq$ 18	0.88	0.55
Signed Informed Consent Form	0.79	0.67
Age >= 18	0.87	0.57
Age < 60 years	0.72	0.45
No history of other diseases at the age >=18 years	0.77	0.34
Age <= 15 years	0.73	0.51

We also notice that CODER handles medical abbreviations better. The similarity score slightly changes when we replace *Hemoglobin* with its abbreviation *Hb*, or substitute *Absolute Neutrophil Count* with *ANC*. However, we note that the differences between all the STS scores of CODER vectors are minimal. SRoBERTa is better at distinguishing between sentences. DET scores vary from 0.26 to 0.98 for SRoBERTa, whereas for CODER, the same scores range from 0.72 to 1.0. We observe that the scores for SRoBERTA representation of *Bilirubin $\geq$ 9 g/dL* and *ECOG Performance Status $\geq$ 1* drop significantly, which is the correct behavior as these terms are not related to hemoglobin. The neutrophils test also proves that both models can correctly encode the meaning of medical terms such as *neutrophil*, *WBC*, and *lymphocyte*.

6   Related Work

Blagec *et al.* [5] evaluated several sentence embedding models for biomedical semantic text similarity: fastText [6], sent2vec [15], Skip-Thought [10] and Paragraph Vector [12]. The authors conclude that the Paragraph Vector model produces the best representations (0.819 Pearson correlation), but sent2vec, a much cheaper model, attains a competitive Pearson correlation of 0.798. They also report a significant difference between the skip-gram and CBOW models (0.766 vs. 0.253 Pearson correlation), suggesting that rare domain-specific words pose a challenge to CBOW.

Ranasinghe *et al.* [18] explore contextualized word representations in the biomedical STS task. The analysis compares ELMo [9], BioBERT [13], Flair [1], and a stacked ELMo+BioBERT model. The authors use word2vec embeddings as the baseline. The metrics used in the evaluation include the cosine similarity of averaged word vectors, the Word Mover's Distance, and the cosine similarity with Smooth Inverse Frequency (SIF) [3]. Surprisingly, only the stacked ELMO+BioBERT model surpasses the baseline when using the cosine similarity with SIF, and other models do not outperform the baseline.

Koroleva *et al.* [11] investigate the similarity of clinical trial outcome descriptions formulated as a binary classification task. The models decide if two descriptions relate to the same medical concept or not. The analysis includes BERT [7], BioBERT [13], and SciBERT [4]. BioBERT achieves the best F1-score without having to refer to external knowledge sources such as UMLS or WordNet. However, the error analysis shows that some sentences require additional domain knowledge to judge the similarity correctly.

7   Conclusions

In this paper we experiment with different sentence embeddings to find the best representation for the biomedical STS. We assess biomedical BERT models and several sentence transformers trained on general English language corpus. We introduce two pre-processing techniques which improve the expressiveness of embeddings. The first technique applies word frequency weights to word embeddings. We hypothesize that separating rare and frequent words helps to reduce the impact of more generic language on the final sentence embedding. The second technique removes the first principal component from embeddings, effectively shifting the informational content of embeddings from encoding the grammatical syntax of the sentence to the semantics of the sentence. Principal component reduction improves all BERT models and static GloVe embeddings.

We evaluate the algorithms on two use cases: the similarity score estimation and the binary label prediction. Sentence transformers outperform other models. CODER comes in second, beating biomedical BERT models and achieving the highest F1-score in the binary label prediction task. Our research points to sentence transformers as the most versatile and best performing models for biomedical STS. The representations extracted from SRoBERTa are more polarised and have larger expressiveness even for potentially similar biomedical sentences. This result is somewhat surprising because sentence transformers used in our experiments are trained on the general English corpora, in contrast to domain fine-tuned BERT models. To further strengthen the conclusions of our research we plan to incorporate more datasets to our evaluation, in particular, we want to test the models on the ClinicalSTS datasets [26].

References

1. Akbik, A., et al.: Flair: an easy-to-use framework for state-of-the-art nlp. In: NAACL-HLT (Demonstrations) (2019)
2. Alsentzer, E., et al.: Publicly available clinical bert embeddings. arXiv preprint arXiv:1904.03323 (2019)
3. Arora, S., et al.: A simple but tough-to-beat baseline for sentence embeddings. In: International Conference on Learning Representations (2017)
4. Beltagy, I., et al.: Scibert: A pretrained language model for scientific text. arXiv preprint arXiv:1903.10676 (2019)
5. Blagec, K., et al.: Neural sentence embedding models for semantic similarity estimation in the biomedical domain. BMC Bioinform. **20**(1), 1–10 (2019). https://doi.org/10.1186/s12859-019-2789-2
6. Bojanowski, P., et al.: Enriching word vectors with subword information. arXiv preprint arXiv:1607.04606 (2016)
7. Devlin, J., et al.: Bert: pre-training of deep bidirectional transformers for language understanding. arXiv preprint arXiv:1810.04805 (2018)
8. Gu, Y., et al.: Domain-specific language model pretraining for biomedical natural language processing. ACM Trans. Comput. Healthc. **3**(1), 1–23 (2021)
9. Jin, Q., et al.: Probing biomedical embeddings from language models. arXiv preprint arXiv:1904.02181 (2019)
10. Kiros, R., et al.: Skip-thought vectors (2015)
11. Koroleva, A., et al.: Measuring semantic similarity of clinical trial outcomes using deep pre-trained language representations. J. Biomed. Inf. **100**, 100058 (2019)
12. Le, Q.V., et al.: Distributed representations of sentences and documents (2014)
13. Lee, J., et al.: Biobert: a pre-trained biomedical language representation model for biomedical text mining. Bioinformatics **36**(4), 1234–1240 (2020)
14. Mu, J., Bhat, S., Viswanath, P.: All-but-the-top: simple and effective postprocessing for word representations. arXiv preprint arXiv:1702.01417 (2017)
15. Pagliardini, M., et al.: Unsupervised learning of sentence embeddings using compositional n-gram features. arXiv preprint arXiv:1703.02507 (2017)
16. Peng, Y., et al.: Transfer learning in biomedical natural language processing. arXiv preprint arXiv:1906.05474 (2019)
17. Pennington, J., et al.: Glove: global vectors for word representation. In: Proceeding of the 2014 EMNLP, pp. 1532–1543 (2014)
18. Ranashinghe, T., et al.: Enhancing unsupervised sentence similarity methods with deep contextualised word representations. RANLP (2019)
19. Raunak, V., et al.: Effective dimensionality reduction for word embeddings. In: Proceeding of the RepL4NLP, pp. 235–243 (2019)
20. Reimers, N., Gurevych, I.: Sentence-bert: sentence embeddings using siamese bert-networks. arXiv preprint arXiv:1908.10084 (2019)

21. Ribeiro, M.T., et al.: Beyond accuracy: Behavioral testing of nlp models with checklist. arXiv preprint arXiv:2005.04118 (2020)
22. Sanh, V., et al.: Distilbert, a distilled version of bert: smaller, faster, cheaper and lighter. arXiv preprint arXiv:1910.01108 (2019)
23. Soğancıoğlu, G., et al.: Biosses: a semantic sentence similarity estimation system for the biomedical domain. Bioinformatics **33**(14), i49–i58 (2017)
24. Song, K., et al.: Mpnet: masked and permuted pre-training for language understanding (2020)
25. Wang, W., et al.: Minilm: deep self-attention distillation for task-agnostic compression of pre-trained transformers (2020)
26. Wang, Y., et al.: The 2019 n2c2/ohnlp track on clinical semantic textual similarity: overview. JMIR Med. Inf. **8**(11), e23375 (2020)
27. Yuan, Z., et al.: Coder: knowledge-infused cross-lingual medical term embedding for term normalization. J. Biomed. Inf. **126**, 103983 (2022)

Demonstration Papers

Blockchain and IoT Enhanced Clinical Workflow

Manan Shukla, Jianjing Lin, and Oshani Seneviratne[✉]

Rensselaer Polytechnic Institute, Troy, NY 12180, USA
{shuklm,linj17,senevo}@rpi.edu

Abstract. Continuous health monitoring for complex healthcare conditions such as chronic comorbid diseases and post-operative care after complex surgical procedures can be implemented using Internet of Medical Things (IoMT) devices that collect sensor data from various devices for efficient health diagnosis and monitoring and treatment. However, given the complex data schemes, disparate devices, and multiple stakeholders involved, collecting and utilizing such IoMT data streams in clinical practice is not a straightforward process. We have developed a blockchain and IoMT integrated system called *BlockIoT* that simplifies various aspects of such complex healthcare management processes by providing a trustworthy and reliable method for aggregating IoMT device data and smart contracts that automatically provide relevant alerts to the healthcare providers. The use of blockchain technology to transfer previously inaccessible data from IoMT devices to healthcare providers enables these healthcare providers with relevant insights into their patients' situations, which provides better outcomes for patients in general. We evaluated the utility of *BlockIoT* using a participatory design study that provided further insights as to how such a system can simplify healthcare providers' complex workflows.

1 Introduction

Electronic Health Records (EHR) can be used for learning insights that could inform the treatment of acute and complex medical conditions. However, their utility for learning insights for informing preventive care and managing chronic conditions has remained limited due to the unavailability of longitudinal data related to some patients' complicated medical situations. As healthcare delivery is becoming increasingly personalized, a patient's condition would be understood through biological markers, patient-reported symptoms, and sustained behavior change that could be ascertained through their wearable IoMT device data. Healthcare providers would be in a better position to treat their patients if such information is available to them in addition to the patients' usual EHRs. For this reason, the addition of Observations of Daily Living (ODL) to the EHR has been proposed [1]. The combination of medical, social, behavioral, and lifestyle information about the patient is essential for allowing medical events to be understood in the context of one's life. For example, a diabetic individual

M. Michalowski et al. (Eds.): AIME 2022, LNAI 13263, pp. 407–411, 2022.
https://doi.org/10.1007/978-3-031-09342-5_40

requires changes in their lifestyle with proper diet and exercise in addition to their medication. Conversely, allowing lifestyle choices to be considered jointly with one's medical context requires an ecosystem with complex healthcare needs and processes that the current EHR systems cannot yet fulfill satisfactorily.

As studies have found that a significant portion of office visits are for preventative care [2], in complex care ecosystems, ODL data captured in a trustworthy and secure manner plays a significant role in healthcare delivery, which would lead to better patient outcomes as well as lower healthcare costs. However, collecting and managing these additional data streams is extraordinarily complex and susceptible to data misuse, given the different stakeholders and disparate systems involved. Therefore, there is a need to build trustworthy, secure, privacy-preserving technologies that leverage data across different levels and facets of this complex healthcare ecosystem.

2   Blockchain and Internet of Medical Things Integration

Unlike centralized mechanisms, blockchain uses a decentralized ledger mechanism to record data transactions on multiple devices, which can help prevent data losses, breaches, and other types of cyberattacks plaguing healthcare systems [8]. Furthermore, smart contracts deployed on blockchain enable capturing logic that implements clinical decision support systems in decentralized environments [5]. Similarly, advances in IoMT have enabled capturing and monitoring of movement and physiological data using wearable sensors [3]. The decentralized and distributed feature reduces the risk of a potential cyber-attack, which has plagued many centralized patient data management systems currently on the market.

Specifically for healthcare scenarios that involve chronic at-home care that needs to integrate with EHR systems managed by healthcare providers, we have developed a blockchain and IoMT integrated system called BlockIoT [6]. We have addressed several challenges in using smart contracts in decentralized health applications due to several inherent problems in blockchain-based systems in the BlockIoT Read Execute Transact Erase Loop (BlockIoT-RETEL) implementation [7] (Fig. 1).

Using this BlockIoT architecture, healthcare providers can monitor a patient's real-time health and even initiate timely interventions in abnormal situations with the help of the smart contract factory. For example, data collected through wearable sensors such as heart-rate monitors and blood pressure cuffs can be used to manage comorbid disease conditions as well as post-surgical care outside of hospital environments,

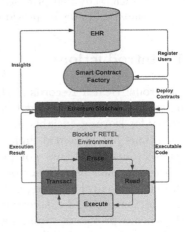

Fig. 1. BlockIoT architecture

smart pill bottles can be used to notify healthcare providers of drug dosage errors, and observations of daily living collected from wearable fitness trackers can streamline diagnosis and treatment processes for chronic diseases such as diabetes and hypertension. All of these can be done remotely via telemonitoring and telemedicine, and thus, patients who have difficulty with physical visits can still receive quality care and avoid expensive future treatments. Through BlockIoT, it is possible to reduce the number of preventative visits by allowing healthcare providers to monitor the patient's physiological data from the patient's personal health devices and schedule office visits only when data seems to be outside of normal limits.

Figure 2 shows a screenshot from a user interface of BlockIoT that presents real-time data captured by a smart pill bottle.

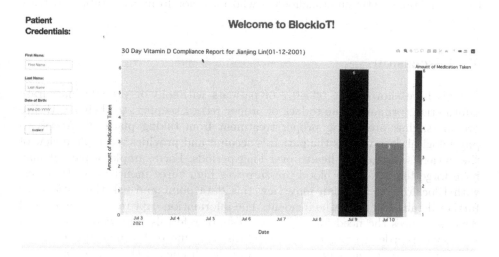

Fig. 2. BlockIoT user-interface that allows real-time access to IoMT data

3   Participatory Design Study

We conducted a participatory design evaluation of BlockIoT to assess the system as a means to supplement healthcare providers' clinical practice and increase their efficiency [6]. The evaluation consisted of 13 healthcare providers from several different healthcare specialties, including cardiology, pulmonology, endocrinology, and primary care. Many of these healthcare providers agreed on the need to have such a system in place to manage their patients' increasingly complex healthcare situations, whereas currently, the information captured by IoMT devices can only be accessed via additional laborious efforts outside the clinical setting, such as establishing an extra data transmission mechanism that could be reliable to transfer data between the IoMT device servers and the provider's EHRs.

All of the providers found the proposed system useful, with 87% of providers reporting that they would be willing to use the summary views as well as the patient/physician interventions throughout the patient care (the other providers were more inclined to just use the summary views of the medical device data). The healthcare providers we interviewed appreciated that BlockIoT allows access to accurate and objective data on a patient's health through smart contracts that can pull in data from various IoMT devices. The continuous flow of the patient's physiological data provides a complete view of the patients' day-to-day health over long periods, thus bridging the gap of lack of ODL data in traditional EHR systems. Accessibility to these data allows providers to better determine the patient's health status, which is particularly important in time-sensitive and/or complicated healthcare situations. BlockIoT also facilitates more transparent communication between healthcare providers and patients and enables trustworthy interactions between stakeholders who have not formally established trust relationships.

4 Discussion

Studies have shown that 60–80% of patients withhold or provide inaccurate information (primarily due to lack of proper record keeping) to their healthcare providers, thus preventing proper treatment from taking place [4]. Access to physiological data verifies the patient's account and provides a complete view of the patient's day-to-day health over long periods. For example, a patient may have forgotten when the blood pressure was high three months ago. However, with BlockIoT, a physician may view this data point and ask the patient for further details regarding the incident. The information captured by the medical devices reduces the need for additional tests or referrals that would have been necessary in order to rule out potential diseases due to the incomplete understanding of the patient's health status and the absence of the device data.

Moreover, information captured by BlockIoT can be further incorporated into specific learning algorithms to assist in clinical decision-making via smart contracts. Consider a patient, who had been wearing a device (or even a typical smartphone-based sensor) monitoring the patient for possible heart arrhythmias, and complained of shortness of breath and heart palpitations. BlockIoT can incorporate and analyze those data through a smart contract that implements a clinical decision support algorithm and potentially rule out atrial fibrillation. As a result, one can potentially avoid an expensive cardiologist visit and an electrocardiogram (EKG) test. We have so far implemented smart contracts to alert healthcare providers of several adverse situations, and we are working towards implementing other algorithms available in clinical practice guidelines for chronic diseases such as diabetes, hypertension, asthma, and chronic obstructive pulmonary disease.

5   Conclusion

We have introduced a blockchain and IoT integrated system called BlockIoT, which connects personal IoMT devices to EHRs using blockchain technology, to improve clinical decision making and enable more efficient delivery of health care for better patient outcomes. BlockIoT receives data from a patient's IoMT devices and analyzes and relays insights to the healthcare provider, who can, as a result, better understand the patient's health holistically, and directly address the patient's complex healthcare needs, and provide better care for patients.

A video demonstration of the BlockIoT system is available at https://www.youtube.com/watch?v=VotFGWCX2x0.
More information about the system is available at https://idea.rpi.edu/research/projects/blockiot.

Acknowledgements. This work is partially supported by IBM Research AI through the AI Horizons Network and the Flash Grant from the School of Humanities, Arts, and Social Sciences (HASS) at Rensselaer Polytechnic Institute.

References

1. Backonja, U., Kim, K., Casper, G.R., Patton, T., Ramly, E., Brennan, P.F.: Observations of daily living: putting the "personal" in personal health records. Am. Med. Inf. Assoc. **2012** (2012)
2. Hing, E., Cherry, D.K., Woodwell, D.A.: National ambulatory medical care survey: 2004 summary. Adv. Data **374**, 1–33 (2006)
3. Joyia, G.J., Liaqat, R.M., Farooq, A., Rehman, S.: Internet of medical things (iomt): applications, benefits and future challenges in healthcare domain. J. Commun. **12**(4), 240–247 (2017)
4. Lyu, H., et al.: Overtreatment in the united states. PLoS One **12**(9), e0181970 (2017)
5. Pham, H.L., Tran, T.H., Nakashima, Y.: A secure remote healthcare system for hospital using blockchain smart contract. In: 2018 IEEE Globecom Workshops (GC Wkshps), pp. 1–6. IEEE (2018)
6. Shukla, M., Lin, J., Seneviratne, O.: BlockIoT: Blockchain-based health data integration using IoT devices. American Medical Informatics Association (2021)
7. Shukla, M., Lin, J., Seneviratne, O.: Blockiot-retel: Blockchain and iot based read-execute-transact-erase-loop environment for integrating personal health data. In: 2021 IEEE International Conference on Blockchain (Blockchain), pp. 237–243. IEEE (2021)
8. Spanakis, E.G., et al.: Cyber-attacks and threats for healthcare-a multi-layer thread analysis. In: 2020 42nd Annual International Conference of the IEEE Engineering in Medicine & Biology Society (EMBC), pp. 5705–5708. IEEE (2020)

The PERISCOPE Data Atlas:
A Demonstration of Release v1.2

Enea Parimbelli[1]($\boxtimes$) (iD), Cristiana Larizza[1], Vladimir Urosevic[2],
Andrea Pogliaghi[3], Manuel Ottaviano[4], Cindy Cheng[5], Vincent Benoit[6],
Daniele Pala[1], Vittorio Casella[1], Riccardo Bellazzi[1], and Paolo Giudici[1]

[1] University of Pavia, Pavia, Italy
enea.parimbelli@unipv.it
[2] Belit doo, Belgrade, Serbia
[3] GeneGIS GI, Milan, Italy
[4] Universidad Politecnica de Madrid, UPM, Madrid, Spain
[5] Technical University of Munich, Munich, Germany
[6] Assistance Publique Hospitaux de Parix, APHP, Paris, France

Abstract. The Data Atlas is the centerpiece of the PERISCOPE
project's data-driven research. The Atlas constitutes a centralized access
point for the exploration, visualization and analysis of the original data
produced by PERISCOPE partners, integrated with the most relevant
information about the COVID-19 pandemic and its effects on health,
economics, policy-making, and society at large. The Atlas interfaces and
tools make such data readily available to the research community, decision makers and the general public, providing the means to amplify its
reach and impact. The present demo, showcases the features of v1.2
release of the Atlas, 18 months from the project kick-off, and some of the
planned enhancements to be delivered until project month 24.

Keywords: COVID-19 · Data warehouse · Data integration · GIS ·
Pandemic · Policy · Impact · Ontology

1 Introduction

With its 32 partners and 15 work packages, the PERISCOPE project[1] is due to
last three years, from November 2020 until the end of October 2023. It aims to
develop data-driven tools to learn and respond to the impacts of the COVID-
19 pandemic. These tools include a COVID Data Atlas, which offers access to
time-space referenced data as well as to qualitative research; and a comprehensive interactive platform (PERSEUS-COVE), offering access to data on global
governance. In this context, the Data Atlas is the technological centerpiece of the
project's research. It constitutes the main access point for the exploration, visualization and analysis of the original data produced by PERISCOPE partners,
integrated with the most relevant information about the COVID-19 pandemic

---

[1] See www.periscopeproject.eu for further details.

M. Michalowski et al. (Eds.): AIME 2022, LNAI 13263, pp. 412–415, 2022.
https://doi.org/10.1007/978-3-031-09342-5_41

and its effects on health, economics, policy-making, and society at large. Data from several sources has been effectively collected in an integrated data repository, enabling the development of rich interfaces to explore and visualize data about policies in response of the COVID-19 pandemic, and their impact on health, economics and policy-making dimensions of society.

2   Description of the Demo

2.1   Technical and Research Novelty

The logical architecture and software components of the Data Atlas, represented in Fig. 1, are described in the following paragraphs.

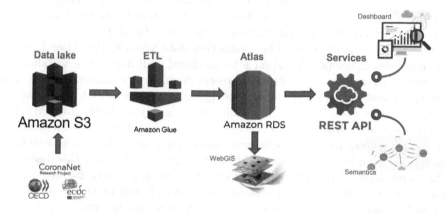

Fig. 1. The Periscope Data Atlas components and logical architecture.

Data sources - The Data Atlas integrates several sources, which can be categorized in three groups: health, economic and socio-political data sources. Health data sources concern monitoring of cases, hospitalizations and deaths, incidence rates, number and results of screening tests etc. The main source of health data is the European Centre for Disease Control (ECDC), with some data from local, more fine-grained sources also available. Economic data comes from the Organization for Economic Cooperation and Development (OECD), which provides information about GDPs, import-export, employment and similar key figures of the EU27 countries and beyond. The socio-political data integrated in the Data Atlas mainly regards governments' COVID-19 response policies, which is provided by the CoronaNet Research Project, an international research collaboration which documents data on COVID-19 policies for countries all over the world at both the national and subnational levels [1]. The Atlas integrates CoronaNet data from the 27 EU countries in both its original event data form as well as in the form of summary indicators, a.k.a. policy intensity scores. The original event data includes not only contains detailed information on discrete COVID-19 policies, e.g. school closures, travel bans, it also contains important contextual information such as the policy timing, initiators, as well as geographic and demographic targets of each policy. The taxonomy for the event dataset closely follows the original CoronaNet taxonomy[2] with some PERISCOPE-specific adaptations.

WebGIS - A WebGIS module has been developed in order to provide the visualization of georeferenced data within an interactive map. This component allows users and researchers to explore, query and analyze the data spatially, leveraging the concept of spatial-enablement (i.e. the addition of a spatial description to a dataset and/or an analysis procedure). It offers a double-map visualization and a temporal navigation tool that allows it to compare various phenomena that have occurred in different places and times, making it possible to detect patterns or correlations in the data that otherwise would be difficult to spot. The WebGIS uses standard protocols and data structure, is fully configurable and is able to display data originating from different sources, comprising both vector and raster data. Finally, the WebGIS is integrated with the Visualization dashboard, which provides complementary access to the data.

Visualization dashboard - The interactive data visualization User Interface (UI) has been developed based on a hierarchical drill-down-type workflow co-designed with relevant stakeholders (researchers, policymakers...), from top-level (previously mentioned) interactive geomap on the initial page down to the increasingly complex advanced multivariate analytic dashboards. We have designed a rich UI dashboard to visualise data in a way that has been optimally tailored for presenting clear, uncluttered spatio-temporal data with several interactive drill-down levels. We have additionally taken care to make this dashboard both as intuitive as possible and in a way that we hope is as familiar as possible to the targeted user. For instance, we have chosen to visualise the data in a radar/spider diagram, which is commonly used and intuitively understood in social sciences, mental health research and related disciplines. It is moreover suitable for exploring as many as 10 variables simultaneously.

API services for data population (ETL) and data provision - The Atlas is fed by periodical ETL processes developed using cloud-native technologies (i.e. Amazon Glue) pulling pre-processed data, after appropriate data cleaning and curation, from a specially built, scalable data lake built on Amazon S3 service. The data lake is accessible, through appropriate access control, by all the partners of PERISCOPE, enabling them to develop procedures for data curation and loading on the atlas data lake.

Data for the visualizations are fetched and served by underlying RESTful API services and jOOQ ORM layer over the data warehouse (DW), modular and generally decoupled/agnostic as much as possible from the specific visualization types/diagrams consuming the data on the front-end, enabling their re-use for provision to future improved versions of the dashboard UI or additional front-end tools and components to be developed.

Semantics - The Data Atlas integrates a semantic engine that is based on an ontology that is used as a knowledge model and as an interoperability resource

---

[2] See https://bit.ly/3vzXZ3H.

for data dictionary, data mapping to harmonize the heterogeneous data sets of this research. The ontology has been designed together with different stakeholders involved in the societal study of the pandemic impact including experts in policy-making, social science researchers, economists, medical team, data science researchers and experts in computer science. These inputs have also been harmonized according to the specific data requirement of the Data Atlas. The core model in particular will: 1) provide a mapping of the data and provide unique definitions inside the Data Atlas data warehouse 2) provide semantics on the API layer, by extending the API response with a reference context using the JSON-LD format 3) create an open data set semantically enriched with the reference to the PERISCOPE ontology. The ontology is currently available for download at: http://ontology.periscopeproject.eu.

2.2 What Will be Showcased

The demo will feature a guided overview of the various user-interfacing components of the Periscope Data Atlas. The demonstration will be performed live, using the publicly accessible version of the tool (i.e. engaged participants can follow the demo as a hands-on session), currently at its v1.2 release available at https://atlas.periscopeproject.eu. A preview of the demo, in form of a 10-minute screencast is also accessible at the same webpage. Also, a series of 9 videos presenting specific functionalities of the Atlas have been posted on the Project's Linkedin page. Depending on attendees specific interests, late-breaking functionalities may be also previewed, including: a web-based statistical modeling sandbox, advanced timeline visualization for timeseries data, and preliminary results of analyses investigating impact of COVID-related policies on mental healthcare utilization data in selected EU countries.

3 Conclusion and Future Work

Having released v1.0 in Nov 2021, and recently updated the Data Atlas to v1.2, attendees will have the opportunity to see an organic overview of its publicly available tools. Further improvements are planned until the feature-complete release of v2.0 in Nov 2022. This work has been funded by European Union's Horizon 2020 program GA No. 101016233 (PERISCOPE).

References

1. Cheng, C., Barceló, J., Hartnett, A.S., et al.: COVID-19 government response event dataset (CoronaNet v.1.0). Nat. Hum. Behav. 4(7), 756–768 (2020)
2. Hale, T., Angrist, N., Goldszmidt, R., et al.: A global panel database of pandemic policies (Oxford COVID-19 Government Response Tracker). Nat. Hum. Behav. 5(4), 529–538 (2021)
3. Kubinec, R., Barceló, J., Goldszmidt, R., at al., Statistically validated indices for COVID-19 public health policies. Statistically validated indices for COVID-19 public health policies. SocArXiv. (2021)

Cordelia: An Application for Automatic ECG Diagnostics

Lubomir Antoni[2], Erik Bruoth[2], Peter Bugata[1], Peter Bugata Jr.[1],
Dávid Gajdoš[1], Šimon Horvát[2], Dávid Hudák[1], Vladimíra Kmečová[1(⊠)],
Richard Staňa[2], Monika Staňková[1], Alexander Szabari[2],
and Gabriela Vozáriková[2]

[1] Data Science Laboratory, VSL Software, a.s., Lomená 8, 040 01 Košice, Slovakia
{cordelia,kmecova}@vsl.sk
[2] Institute of Computer Science, Faculty of Science, Pavol Jozef Šafárik University
in Košice, Jesenná 5, 040 01 Košice, Slovakia
http://www.vsl.sk/en/, https://www.upjs.sk/en/faculty-of-science/

Abstract. The authors present a prototype of an application named
Cordelia, which enables the prediction of selected cardiac findings on
standard 12-lead ECG recordings. The application is based on an ensemble model consisting of ten deep residual convolutional neural networks.
In order to eliminate the different scope of the assessed labels, as well as
the different approach in assessing the presence (or absence) of certain
labels in different datasets, the model was trained using 3-valued logic.
Cordelia allows not only to determine the probability value of each of
the assessed labels, but also to draw an ECG recording and evaluate the
technical conditions of the record, which can have negative impact on the
prediction outcomes (e.g., significant baseline shift, signal outages, etc.)
The application can be beneficial especially for primary care physicians
less experienced in the evaluation of ECG recordings. As a part of the
telemedicine platform, it could enable very fast consultation of practitioners with specialists without the need for a physical visit of patient.
The basis of the developed solution can also be used to create models
for evaluating the presence of arrhythmia in long-term ECG recordings
(Holter monitoring) with reference to the location and duration of the
episode(s).

Keywords: ECG diagnostics · Artificial intelligence · Online tool

1 Introduction

The ever-increasing demand for health care, caused by the growing proportion
of the elderly and more sick population, has been a challenge in recent years.
Telemedicine responds to it as one of the possibilities of effective triage of the
need for physical contact of the patient with the specialists. Since cardiovascular diseases occupy one of the leading positions in the morbidity of the world's
population [1], it is not surprising that a large number of telemedicine solutions

M. Michalowski et al. (Eds.): AIME 2022, LNAI 13263, pp. 416–420, 2022.
https://doi.org/10.1007/978-3-031-09342-5_42

address this issue. The prestigious PhysioNet Challenge also deals with the topic of automatic ECG diagnostics, most recently in 2020 [2] and 2021 [3]. The VSL Software, a.s. in cooperation with Pavel Jozef Šafárik University in Košice, Slovakia, participated in the PhysioNet 2021 Challenge (team CeZIS) with the best solution in the follow-up phase [4] and subsequently developed a prototype application for the automatic evaluation of digital ECG recordings presented in this manuscript.

2   Brief Description

Cordelia[1,2] is a publicly available web application, and a web browser is sufficient to use it without the need to install additional components locally.

The application is used for automatic detection of 21 different labels/findings on the heart (heart rhythm disorders, conduction blocks, P/T wave anomalies, extrasystoles, etc.) on 12-lead ECG recordings of adults. A current list of all predicted labels can be found in Table 1. Cordelia evaluates the probability of the presence of each label and at the same time evaluates the technical condition of the recording with a possible warning of poor quality, which may affect the predictive and diagnostic value. The application includes rendering all 12 leads of both raw and preprocessed signal (with baseline compensation and noise removal) [5]. In addition to the ability to evaluate ambulatory made ECG recording, the application has also a demo section, which can be used, for example, for educational purposes.

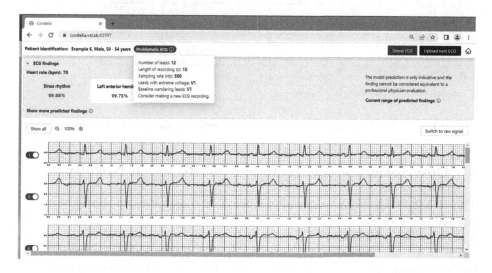

Fig. 1. Notification of a problematic technical status of the recording

---

[1] https://cordelia.vsl.sk.

[2] Demo video: https://www.youtube.com/watch?v=2s8qDlNUxkM.

3   Screenshots

On the application's home page, you can select a demo or upload your own ECG recording. There are a lot of examples with descriptive ECG recordings available in the demo section, which are organized in a tree structure according to the types of anomalies.

After uploading the ECG, the technical condition of the recording is evaluated and its basic properties and identified problems are displayed (Fig. 1). Subsequently, R-peaks are found, the heart rate is calculated and the regularity of the rhythm is evaluated. The signal is then processed by the neural network and the positive predicted labels (with predicted probabilities greater than 50%) are displayed. The application also allows the user to view the probabilities of other labels (Fig. 2).

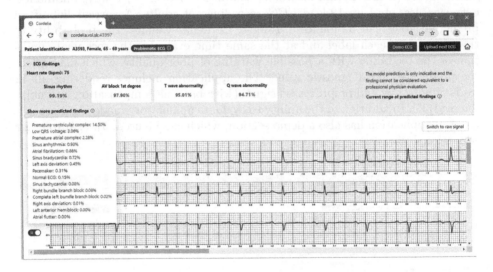

Fig. 2. Predicted labels on the ECG recording with their probabilities

4   Description of the Technical or Research Novelty

The classifier is based on ensemble model than consists of ten neural networks, trained on more than 120,000 ECG recordings from six publicly available ECG databases [3,6]. Models are based on a deep residual convolutional neural network, based on 1D modification of the popular ResNet50 architecture [7]. The obtained latent factors are placed on the unit sphere using ℓ_2 normalization and a simple linear layer with 21 neurons corresponding to anomalies is added (multilabel prediction). A more detailed description of the neural network architecture can be found in [4]. Several augmentation data techniques, including Flow-Mixup [8], were used. Each training ECG recording was evaluated in terms of the presence of the predicted label in the original data by three-valued logic:

1, 0, NA. The NA value was used if the presence of the label was not evaluated in the original data or the label was inconsistent with others. This solution largely eliminated the differences in the clinical assessment of the labels in the databases, and at the same time responded to the different scope of the labels marked in the individual datasets. The weights of the positive and negative classes were set separately for each label to compensate for differences in the number of their positive occurrences. The F2 metric was used in the selection of the optimal model, as we consider a false-negative finding to be more serious from a clinical point of view than a false-positive one. Table 1 shows the results of a 10-fold cross-validation on the training set[3].

Table 1. F2 score for individual labels obtained using 10-fold cross validation.

Label	F2 score	Label	F2 score
Sinus bradycardia	99.39	Right axis deviation	82.90
Sinus tachycardia	98.68	Sinus arrhythmia	80.78
Normal ECG	98.18	AV block 1st degree	80.72
Sinus rhythm	97.12	Premature atrial complex	78.45
Atrial fibrillation	94.72	Atrial flutter	77.98
Pacemaker	93.66	T wave abnormality	77.72
Complete right BBB	91.96	Left anterior hemiblock	76.10
Right BBB	90.30	Low QRS voltage	69.84
Complete left BBB	89.63	Incomplete right BBB	67.74
Premature ventricular complex	86.05	Q wave abnormality	64.84
Left axis deviation	84.83		

5   Potential Applications for Solving Biomedical Problems

The application can be helpful especially to primary care physicians who do not have so much skills in the evaluation of ECG recordings comparing with specialists-cardiologists. When the ECG recording is processed online, the model can evaluate it and provide the physician with the feedback in a few seconds, thus enabling the patient to be sent for a specialized examination in case of uncertainty or detection of a new pathology. The basis of the developed solution can also be used to create ML models for evaluating the presence of arrhythmia in long-term ECG recordings (Holter monitoring) with reference to the location and duration of the episode(s).

Acknowledgements. This work was supported by ERDF EU grant and by the Ministry of Economy of the Slovak Republic under contract No. ITMS313012S703 and by the Scientific Grant Agency of the Ministry of Education, Science, Research and Sport of the Slovak Republic under contract VEGA 1/0177/21 Descriptive and computational complexity of automata and algorithms.

---

[3] BBB abbreviation is used for bundle branch block.

References

1. World Health Organization: WHO cardiovascular diseases (CVDs). https://www. who.int/news-room/fact-sheets/detail/cardiovascular-diseases-(cvds). Accessed 01 Apr 2022
2. Perez Alday, E.A., et al.: Classification of 12-lead ECGs: the physionet/computing in cardiology challenge 2020. Physiol. Measur. **41**(12), 124003 (2021). https://doi. org/10.1088/1361-6579/abc960
3. Reyna, M.A., et al.: Will two do? varying dimensions in electrocardiography: the physionet/computing in cardiology challenge 2021. Comput. Cardiol. **2021**(48), 1–4 (2021)
4. Antoni, L., et al.: Automatic ECG classification and label quality in training data. Physiol. Measur. (2022). https://doi.org/10.1088/1361-6579/ac69a8
5. Zhang, D.: Wavelet approach for ECG baseline wander correction and noise reduction. In: IEEE Engineering in Medicine and Biology 27th Annual Conference, pp. 1212–1215 (2005). https://doi.org/10.1109/IEMBS.2005.1616642
6. Hefei Hi-tech Cup ECG Intelligent Competition. https://tianchi.aliyun.com/ competition/entrance/231754/introduction. Accessed 15 Aug 2021
7. He, K., Zhang, X., Ren, S., Sun, J.: Deep residual learning for image recognition. In: 2016 IEEE Conference on Computer Vision and Pattern Recognition (CVPR), pp. 770–778 (2016). https://doi.org/10.1109/CVPR.2016.90
8. Chen, J., Yu, H., Feng, R., Chen, D.Z., Wu, J.: Flow-mixup: classifying multi-labeled medical images with corrupted labels. In: 2020 IEEE International Conference on Bioinformatics and Biomedicine (BIBM), pp. 534–541. IEEE Computer Society, Los Alamitos, CA, USA (2020). https://doi.org/10.1109/BIBM49941.2020.9313408

Clinical Guidelines as Executable and Interactive Workflows with FHIR-Compliant Health Data Input Using GLEAN

William Van Woensel[1(✉)] ⓘ, Samina Abidi[1] ⓘ, Karthik Tennankore[2,3] ⓘ,
George Worthen[2] ⓘ, and Syed Sibte Raza Abidi[1] ⓘ

[1] Dalhousie University, Halifax, NS B3H 4R2, Canada
`william.van.woensel@dal.ca`
[2] Nova Scotia Health, Dalhousie University, Halifax, NS, Canada
[3] Kidney Research Institute Nova Scotia (KRINS), Halifax, NS, Canada

Abstract. By computerizing paper-based clinical guidelines on diagnosing and treating illnesses, knowledge-driven Clinical Decision Support (CDS) can issue salient and timely recommendations in line with the latest evidence. To access up-to-date patient health data, such CDS require interoperability with Electronic Health Records (EHR). The GLEAN model supports knowledge-based CDS by (a) encoding the guideline decision logic using Task Network Models (TNM) based on an extensible Finite State Machine (FSM); and (b) associating clinical tasks with HL7 FHIR resources that offer interoperability with FHIR-compliant EHR. In this demo, we show an online visualization tool that explains GLEAN CIG as visual and interactive workflows. Clinicians can dynamically submit HL7 FHIR patient data using the tool to drive the traversal of the workflow.

Keywords: Clinical decision support · Workflow visualization · Notation3

1 Introduction

Task Network Models (TNM) [1] allows the computerization of clinical guidelines as workflow-oriented Computer Interpretable Guidelines (CIG). These CIG can be loaded into Clinical Decision Support (CDS) to execute the guidelines as workflows driven by health data. The execution semantics of existing TNM-based CDS, such as PROforma [2] and GLIF3 [3], are typically described in terms of a Finite State Machine (FSM); a task is assigned one of a finite number of states (e.g., active, completed), with transitions between states depending on decisional criteria, among others. However, these FSM are often rather informally described, making existing work difficult to reproduce and extend. The GuideLine Execution and Abstraction in N3 (GLEAN) model is a resource for building CDS that is based on state-of-the-art TNM systems. GLEAN encodes explicit and formal execution semantics in terms of a core FSM, which can be easily extended with semantics for new or customized TNM constructs. Moreover,

M. Michalowski et al. (Eds.): AIME 2022, LNAI 13263, pp. 421–425, 2022.
https://doi.org/10.1007/978-3-031-09342-5_43

GLEAN supports integration with Electronic Health Records (EHR) through the HL7 FHIR [4] (Fast Healthcare Interoperability Resources) standard; tasks can be associated with *PlanDefinition* resources that define taxonomy concepts (e.g., SNOMED) and data constraints (e.g., ranges) for the task's health data input, if any. Prior work showed that UI forms can be generated from these FHIR resources [5], which validate the input health data and submit a self-contained EHR record annotated with taxonomy codes.

The GLEAN OWL ontology captures the core concepts for encoding TNM workflows and integrating with HL7 FHIR [4]. GLEAN FSM, which include a finite set of states and transition rules between them, are implemented using the Notation3 (N3) Semantic Web language [6]. As a result, GLEAN FSM can be defined in an expressive way using a range of N3 builtins, and can be executed on any standards-compliant N3 reasoner (eye [7] and jen3 [8]). The GLEAN model can be found online [9] and is detailed by a full paper at AIME 2022 [10]. This demo paper will demonstrate the CIG visualization tool and discuss the overall GLEAN architecture (which was not covered by the full paper). In our demo (preview: https://youtu.be/U2AFwk57bww), we utilize GLEAN to visualize lipid management guidelines for chronic kidney disease.

2   GLEAN System Architecture

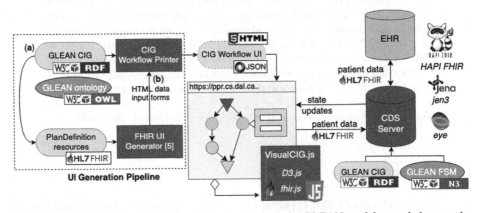

Fig. 1. Overall GLEAN architecture. (ellipses constitute the GLEAN model; rounded rectangles represent input data artifacts; deep blue rectangles and cylinders constitute software components.)

The GLEAN architecture consists of 3 major components:

(1) *UI Generation Pipeline*, where the *FHIR UI Generator*, based on HL7 FHIR Plan-Definition resources, generates a series of HTML forms for manual input of health data [5]. Based on (a) the original GLEAN CIG, written in RDF based on the GLEAN OWL ontology, together with (b) generated HTML data input forms, the *CIG Workflow Printer* will construct a CIG Workflow UI encoded using JSON and HTML5.

(2) *VisualCIG.js* library, which visualizes the CIG Workflow UI in the browser as an interactive workflow using *D3.js* [11]. This library packages manually inputted patient data as a FHIR EHR record, using *N3.js* [12] and *rdfa.js* [13]; sending the record to the *CDS Server* using *fhir.js* [14], and updating the visual workflow based on the response.

(3) *CDS Server*, which accepts data input from the client and will return relevant state transitions, if any. To that end, the server loads the GLEAN CIG (clinical guideline) and GLEAN FSM (execution semantics) into an N3 reasoner (e.g., eye [7] or jen3 [8]). The *CDS Server* relies on HAPI FHIR [15] as a Java HL7 FHIR library, and utilizes jen3 [8], a fork of Apache Jena [16], to work with RDF and serve as N3 reasoner.

(4) *EHR Server*, which exchanges FHIR-compliant patient data with the CDS Server.

3 Interactive and Visual Lipid Management CIG

We fully computerized the KDIGO guidelines for lipid management in chronic kidney disease (CKD) [17] using only the core TNM constructs from the GLEAN ontology; including modular sub-guidelines, such as evaluate lipid profile, dyslipidemia treatment, and follow-up lipid profile. Following the UI generation pipeline (Fig. 1), we generated a *CIG Workflow UI* that was visualized by *VisualCIG.js* as shown in Fig. 2:

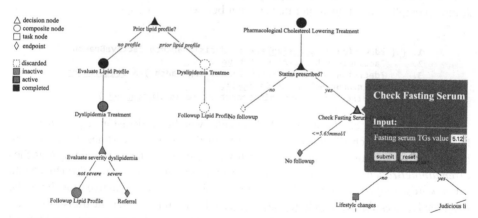

Fig. 2. Lipid management for CKD: (A) Main guideline; (B) Dyslipidemia treatment.

At the top left, Fig. 2A shows a legend that associates node shapes with TMN constructs (e.g., decision node) and node colors with task states (e.g., discarded). In the Fig. 2A workflow, the *Prior lipid profile?* decision task will branch the workflow; either proceeding to the *Dyslipidemia Treatment* (right branch) or *Evaluate Lipid Profile* (left branch) sub-guidelines, respectively. Since no prior lipid profile was available, the right-hand branch was discarded; in the left branch, *Evaluate Lipid Profile* was manually completed by the clinician, meaning that *Dyslipidemia Treatment* is *active*, i.e., next in line for execution; the remaining tasks are currently still *inactive*. Double-clicking a composite task (i.e., sub-guideline) will open a new window (Fig. 2B); clicking a task that requires health data input opens an HTML input form.

All task states are determined by the GLEAN FSM. State transition rules will fire depending on whether decisional criteria are met based on patient data, states of related tasks, and other criteria. We offer a high-level formalism based on N3 for writing state transition rules. In a nutshell, N3 encodes information in terms of subject-predicate-object (s/p/o) statements that form a graph; curly braces indicate a quoted graph, which can be used as an s/p/o term; and a "?" indicates a variable. For more details on N3, see the W3C Community Group report [6]. We show an example transition rule below:

```
1. { { ?entity :conditional true .
2.       ?entity :precondition ?cond . ?cond cond:conditionMet true } a state:Guard .
3.    ?entity state:in :Ready
4. } state:transit { ?entity state:in :Active } .
```

A state-transition condition is met if (a) all guard conditions, i.e., within the quoted graph with type *state:Guard* (lines 1–2) are met, and (b) the TNM construct is within the indicated state (line 3); if so, the TNM construct will be moved to the new state (line 4). In this case, the guard condition checks whether a TNM construct (*?entity*; line 1) is conditional and has a precondition that was met (*cond:conditionMet*; line 2). If so, the construct (*?entity*) will be moved from the *ready* state (line 3) to the *active* state (line 4). In other words, this rule will activate any TNM construct with a satisfied pre-condition. A more complex state transition rule is shown below:

```
1. { { ?decision a :DecisionTask ; :decisionBranch ?activeBranch .
2.       ?activeBranch state:in :Active .
3.       ?decision :decisionBranch ?remainingBranch } a state:Guard .
4.    ?remainingBranch state:in :Ready .
5. } state:transit { ?remainingBranch state:in :Discarded } .
```

Here, the guard condition (line 1–3) checks whether a decision task (*?decision*) has a decision branch (*?activeBranch*) that is in the *active* state (lines 1–2); i.e., the branch's pre-condition was met (see prior rule). If so, any of the task's remaining branches (*?remainingBranch*) (line 3) will be moved from *ready* (line 4) to *discarded* (line 5). In other words, all the remaining branches of a decision task with an active branch will be discarded; this is illustrated in Fig. 2A (right branch). To implement state transition rules, N3 code performs introspection on the rules and generates Linear Logic implications [18] in N3. We refer to our online code repository [9] for details.

4   Conclusions and Future Work

We demonstrated a visualization tool for CIG workflows encoded using GLEAN; providing background on the GLEAN architecture, UI generation process, and state transition rules. In future work, we aim to support different types of CIG visualizations. The current tool, which shows a process/activity diagram, served as (a) debugging tool; helping clinicians with fixing the workflow logic; and (b) educational tool; helping GPs learn about effective lipid management for CKD patients. We plan to build a complementary wizard-style UI that focuses more on facilitating patient data input.

References

1. Peleg, M.: Computer-interpretable clinical guidelines: a methodological review. J. Biomed. Inform. **46**, 744–763 (2013)
2. Sutton, D.R., Fox, J.: The syntax and semantics of the PROforma guideline modeling language. J. Am. Med. Inform. Assoc. **10**, 433–443 (2003). https://doi.org/10.1197/jamia. M1264
3. Boxwala, A.A., Peleg, M., Tu, S., Ogunyemi, O., Zeng, Q., Wang, D.: GLIF3: a representation format for sharable computer-interpretable clinical practice guidelines. J. Biomed. Inform. **37**, 147–161 (2004)
4. HL7 International: HL7 Fast Health Interop Resources (FHIR). https://www.hl7.org/ind ex.cfm
5. Van Woensel, W., Abidi, S.R., Abidi, S.S.R.: Towards model-driven semantic interfaces for electronic health records on multiple platforms using notation3. In: 4th International Workshop on Semantic Web Meets Health Data Management (SWH 2021), New York, NY, USA (2021)
6. Arndt, D., Van Woensel, W., Tomaszuk, D.: Notation3: draft community group report. https:// w3c.github.io/N3/spec/. Accessed 08 Jan 2022
7. De Roo, J.: Euler yet another proof engine - EYE. https://josd.github.io/eye/
8. Van Woensel, W.: jen3. https://github.com/william-vw/jen3
9. Van Woensel, W.: GLEAN. https://github.com/william-vw/glean
10. Van Woensel, W., Abidi, S., Tennankore, K., Worthen, G., Abidi, S.S.R.: Explainable decision support using task network models in notation3: computerizing lipid management clinical guidelines as interactive task networks. In: 20th International Conference on Artificial Intelligence in Medicine (AIME 2022). Springer, Halifax (2022). (to appear)
11. D3: data-driven documents. https://d3js.org/. Accessed 11 Dec 2021
12. Lightning fast, asynchronous, streaming RDF for JavaScript, https://github.com/rdfjs/N3.js/. Accessed 04 Apr 2022
13. RDFa Streaming Parser
14. fhir.js. https://github.com/FHIR/fhir.js/. Accessed 31 Mar 2022
15. HAPI FHIR. https://hapifhir.io/. Accessed 31 Mar 2022
16. Apache: Apache Jena. https://jena.apache.org/
17. KDIGO: clinical practice guideline for lipid management in chronic kidney disease. https:// kdigo.org/wp-content/uploads/2017/02/KDIGO-2013-Lipids-Guideline-English.pdf
18. Girard, J.-Y.: Linear logic: its syntax and semantics. In: Girard, J.-Y., Lafont, Y., Regnier, L. (eds.) Advances in Linear Logic, pp. 1–42 (1995)

A Goal-Oriented Methodology for Treatment of Patients with Multimorbidity - Goal Comorbidities (GoCom) Proof-of-Concept Demonstration

Alexandra Kogan[1]([✉]) [iD], Mor Peleg[1] [iD], Samson W. Tu[2] [iD], Raviv Allon[3] [iD], Natanel Khaitov[3] [iD], and Irit Hochberg[3,4] [iD]

[1] Department of Information Systems, University of Haifa, 3498838 Haifa, Israel
[2] Center for BioMedical Informatics Research, Stanford University, Stanford, CA 94305, USA
[3] Bruce Rappaport Faculty of Medicine, Technion - Israel Institute of Technology, Haifa, Israel
[4] Institute of Endocrinology, Diabetes and Metabolism, Rambam Medical Center, Haifa, Israel

Abstract. Advancement in medicine has increased the average population age, however, physicians are still burdened with the complexity of treatment of multimorbidity patients due to many potential interactions among the patient's medications, and diseases. We developed a goal-oriented methodology for management of multimorbidity patients called GoCom (for Goal Comorbidities). GoCom's aim is to help manage the patient's changing health state that may prompt new goals to arise. GoCom utilizes computer-interpretable clinical guidelines formalized using the PROforma representation. The guidelines are modeled according to a previously published guide on modeling goal-oriented, metaproperty enriched tasks in PROforma. The tasks are retrieved by the main algorithm of the system named the "Controller" that creates a hierarchical goal-oriented tree structure that is personalized for the patient according to their specific data. Tree structures are created for all of the patient's problems and are formed as a patient forest. The Controller behavioral patterns reason over the patient data and create clinically-valid solutions that are presented to the physician with generated explanations. We evaluated GoCom for correctness and completeness with complex multimorbidity case studies. The first evaluation was a pilot study with ten 6th year medical students and the second evaluation was with 27 6th year medical students and interns. Use of GoCom increased completeness and correctness and the explanations and visualization were viewed as useful by the participants.

Keywords: Multimorbidity · Comorbidity · Decision-support · Computer-interpretable guidelines

1 Introduction

Multimorbidity has become more common with the increase of the average age of patients. Physicians have many skills and tools to rely on, but the complexity of treatment for multimorbidity patients remains a burden. Physicians may use Clinical Practice Guidelines (CPGs) and Computer Interpretable Guidelines (CIGs) to support their

M. Michalowski et al. (Eds.): AIME 2022, LNAI 13263, pp. 426–430, 2022.
https://doi.org/10.1007/978-3-031-09342-5_44

decision making [1], however CPGs and CIGs focus largely on single morbidities that do not account for interactions among the patient's diseases and medications that may occur when recommending treatments from multiple guidelines [2]. Goals are especially important for clinical decision support as they aid in analyzing the patient's treatment regimen [3], detecting problems [4] and suggesting solutions [5].

In this research we developed a goal-oriented methodology for treatment of multimorbidity patients called GoCom (for Goal Comorbidities) [6]. The methodology presents the process of creating and adjusting the patient's treatment regimen as a combination of goals acquired by the patient as their health state changes. This approach helps detect and mitigate inconsistent recommendations that can result in adverse events. Additionally, explanations are generated for each proposed non-conflicting management plan and the goals that are addressed in that plan. The methodology is designed using existing health standards (HL7 FHIR [7]), terminologies and vocabularies (NDF-RT [8], SNOMED [9], MedDRA [10]), which are combined with the goal-oriented modeling of guidelines represented using the PROforma formalism [11] that are enriched with metaproperties in order to represent clinical goals such as diagnosis goals, treatment or prevention goals, action-enactment goals and state achievement goals (e.g., for expressing physiological effects such as decreased platelet aggregation) [12]. This representation facilitates the creation of a flexible range of solutions, with different levels of abstraction of reasoning.

2 Methods

GoCom's architecture is based on the Model-View-Controller pattern [13]. The "Model" is used to store the CIG knowledge base and patient specific data in a Fhirbase database. The "View" is implemented as the interface (Fig. 2) and a demo of the system can be found online [14]. The "Controller" is extended to contain the main algorithm of the system. The Controller utilizes the PROforma CIGs and standards to create a patient-specific goal-forest structure that contains a hierarchical goal-tree for each of the patient's problems. The Controller then searches the goal-forest for inconsistencies [6], while considering the different levels of abstraction of medications and groups of medications in the NDF-RT (e.g., Omeprazole is-a Proton Pump Inhibitor).

2.1 Mitigation

An example case study that one may consider for explaining GoCom's mitigation process, involves a 78-y-old female patient. The patient is taking Aspirin for secondary prevention of cardiovascular disease and Omeprazole for her duodenal ulcer that she was diagnosed with after she started taking the Aspirin. Currently, the patient is diagnosed with osteoporosis. Since Proton-pump Inhibitors are a risk-contributing factor in osteoporosis, the guideline recommends to stop them. Thus an inconsistency occurs between the duodenal ulcer guideline that recommends Omeprazole and the osteoporosis guideline that recommends to stop Proton-pump Inhibitors – a medication group that subsumes Omeprazole.

428   A. Kogan et al.

When the Controller finds an inconsistency between a pair of goals (e.g., Start Omeprazole – goal_1, stop Proton Pump Inhibitor-goal_2), a duplicate alternative patient-forest is created for each goal in the inconsistency and mitigation is attempted. The Controller activates the guideline that recommended the goal and searches for an alternative sibling that could be recommended by the guideline instead of the active goal. If such a sibling is not found, the Controller removes the inconsistent goal (goal_1) from the alternative forest and proceeds to apply the same reasoning to the other side of the inconsistency (goal_2). This creates a total of two alternative patient forests for each inconsistency. Additional patient forests may be created if one of the inconsistent goals (goal_1 or goal_2) has a dependency that associates it with another goal (e.g., Omeprazole was prescribed to counteract the effects of Aspirin). The dependency is indicated as part of the goal metaproperties in the CIG (Fig. 1). When the Controller identifies such a dependency, it is mitigated in the same way as an inconsistency. The Controller tries to find a replacement sibling for the goal that has the dependency (e.g., start Omeprazole to counteract Aspirin) as well as for the dependent goal (e.g., start Aspirin) and removes the goal in the respective alternative forest. Finally, each alternative forest is checked for inconsistencies and inconsistent or duplicate alternative forests are removed from the solution range. We refer to a non-conflicting alternative forest as an "Option-set". The controller generates an explanation for each Option-set as well as for each recommended goal in the Option-set, based on the goal's life cycle status (e.g., accept, reject, cancel, complete) and the Option-sets with explanations are displayed to the user. Additional descriptions of the algorithm and patterns can be found in Kogan et al. [15].

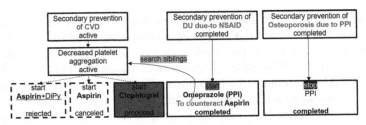

Fig. 1. The third option-set that is created when the Controller identifies the dependency "start Omeprazole to counteract Aspirin".

2.2   Presentation

The interface (Fig. 2) displays to the physician-user information and functionalities that aid the decision-making process: (a) Patient demographic details, (b) Patient visits, (c) Patient investigations (including extended tables and images), (d) Patient problems and their associated goals and treatments, (e) The Controller window where the system suggests solutions to inconsistencies and also displays non-conflicted goals.

The user can search for a patient, as well as create a new patient and add a new diagnosis or a visit to the patient record.

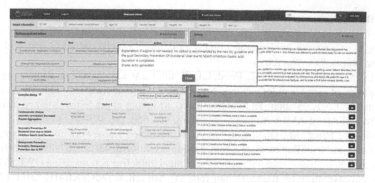

Fig. 2. A screenshot showing an example of the user interface produced by GoCom for a patient with three morbidities. The insert shows an explanation for the goal Inhibition Gastric Acid Secretion for one of the option sets (Option 3).

3   Results

GoCom was evaluated for functionality and usefulness with six complex multimorbidity case studies. The evaluation was done according to the guideline-based gold standard that was defined and confirmed by three physicians. The first evaluation was a pilot study with ten 6th year medical students and two cases. The second evaluation had 27 6th year medical students and interns and 6 cases. GoCom was shown to increase completeness significantly: 0.44 without the system, 0.71 with the system (P-value of 0.0005) in the first evaluation, and in the second evaluation: 0.31 without the system, 0.78 with the system (P-value < 0.0001). In the first evaluation correctness was high and did not increase significantly: 0.91 without the system, 0.98 with the system (P-value $\geq$ 0.17). In the second evaluation the correctness did increase significantly: 0.68 without the system, 0.83 with the system, (P-value of 0.001).

4   Conclusion

GoCom is a goal-based methodology that combines hierarchical goal modeling, standard ontologies and terminologies and evidence-based recommendations in order to produce aggregated Option-sets with explanations that would provide a flexible range of solutions that can help guide the patient to a better treatment plan. GoCom was implemented as a proof-of-concept [14] and has limitations as elaborated in [15], such as integration into real-world setting and absence of temporal reasoning. Nevertheless, it seems feasible that GoCom can help physicians to be more complete and correct in diagnosis and management. Our planned future work includes detection of adverse events, implementation of temporal reasoning, addressing goal prioritization and patient preferences.

References

1. Peleg, M.: Computer-interpretable clinical guidelines: a methodological review. J. Biomed. Inform. **46**(4), 744–763 (2013)
2. Boyd, C.M., Darer, J., Boult, C., Fried, L.P., Boult, L., Wu, A.W.: Clinical practice guidelines and quality of care for older patients. New Engl. J. Med. **294**(6), 716–724 (2005)
3. Advani, A., Lo, K., Shahar, Y.: Intention-based critiquing of guideline-oriented medical care. In: Proceedings of AMIA Annual Symposium, vol. 650, pp. 483–487 (1998)
4. Grando, A., Peleg, M., Glasspool, D.: A goal-oriented framework for specifying clinical guidelines and handling medical errors. J. Biomed. Inform. **43**(2), 287–299 (2010)
5. Peleg, M., et al.: Reasoning with effects of clinical guideline actions using OWL: AL amyloidosis as a case study. In: Riaño, D., ten Teije, A., Miksch, S. (eds.) KR4HC 2011. LNCS, vol. 6924, pp. 65–79. Springer, Heidelberg (2011). https://doi.org/10.1007/978-3-642-27697-2_5
6. Kogan, A., Tu, S.W., Peleg, M.: Goal-driven management of interacting clinical guidelines for multimorbidity patients. In: AMIA Annual Symposium Proceedings 2018, pp. 690–699 (2018)
7. HL7: Fast Healthcare Interoperability Resources Release 3 Specification (2017). https://www.hl7.org/fhir/documentation.html
8. U.S. Department of Veterans Affairs and US Dept. of Veterans Affairs: National Drug File – Reference Terminology (NDF- RT TM) Documentation U.S. Department of Veterans Affairs (2015)
9. Stearns, M.Q., Price, C., Spackman, K.A., Wang, A.Y.: SNOMED clinical terms: overview of the development process and project status. In: Proceeding AMIA Symposium, p. 662 (2001)
10. Brown, E.G., Wood, L., Wood, S.: The medical dictionary for regulatory activities (MedDRA). Drug Saf. **20**(2), 109–117 (1999)
11. Button, D.R., Fox, J.: The syntax and semantics of the PRO forma guideline modeling language. J. Am. Med. Inform. Assoc. **10**(5), 433–443 (2003)
12. Peleg, M., Kogan, A., Tu, S.: A methodology for goal-oriented guideline modeling in PROforma and its preliminary evaluation. In: Marcos, M., et al. (eds.) KR4HC TEAAM 2019. LNCS, vol. 11979, pp. 17–28. Springer, Cham (2019). https://doi.org/10.1007/978-3-030-37446-4_2
13. Krasner, G.E., Pope, S.T.: A description of the model-view-controller user interface paradigm in the smalltalk-80 system. J. Object Oriented Program. **1**(3), 26–49 (1988)
14. GoCom AIME2022 demo – YouTube (2022). https://www.youtube.com/watch?v=Jwx7ZfYmfZ8
15. Kogan, A., Peleg, M., Tu, S.W., Allon, R., Khaitov, N., Hochberg, I.: Towards a goal-oriented methodology for clinical-guideline-based management recommendations for patients with multimorbidity: GoCom and its preliminary evaluation. J. Biomed. Inform. **1**(112), 103587 (2020)

Development of AI-Enabled Apps by Patients and Domain Experts Using the Punya Platform: A Case Study for Diabetes

Evan Patton[1], William Van Woensel[2]([✉]), Oshani Seneviratne[3],
Giuseppe Loseto[4], Floriano Scioscia[5], and Lalana Kagal[1]

[1] Massachusetts Institute of Technology, Cambridge, MA 02139, USA
{ewpatton,lkagal}@mit.edu
[2] Dalhousie University, Halifax, NS B3H 4R2, Canada
william.van.woensel@dal.ca
[3] Rensselaer Polytechnic Institute, Troy, NY 12180, USA
senevo@rpi.edu
[4] LUM University "Giuseppe Degennaro", 70010 Casamassima, BA, Italy
loseto@lum.it
[5] Polytechnic University of Bari, 70125 Bari, BA, Italy
floriano.scioscia@poliba.it

Abstract. It is challenging for programmers to build a mobile health app that is rich in AI features, and near impossible for non-technical users such as domain experts and patients. However, it is exactly these users that possess the domain knowledge and experience on how to best manage health conditions, and how AI features can help achieve that goal. End-user development environments, such as MIT Punya, can help lay users to better collaborate on mobile health apps; and even open the door for these users, given some training, to prototype their own mobile health apps. As a subfield of AI, Semantic Web technology can help with integrating online data sources with patient health data, and reasoning over the integrated data to issue smart health recommendations.

Keywords: Patient apps · Diabetes management · Semantic web

1 Introduction

The Punya platform [9] provides a visual programming environment for non-technical end-users to build AI-enabled Android apps—i.e., apps enhanced with Artificial Intelligence (AI) features[1]. Punya natively supports Semantic Web and Linked Data concepts, such as querying and manipulating Knowledge Graphs (KGs), rule-based reasoning, and integrating data from Internet of Things (IoT) devices as part of the Semantic Web of Things (SWoT). Additionally, Punya includes extensions that can embed Machine Learning (ML) models within

---

[1] https://punya.mit.edu/;http://punya.appinventor.mit.edu/.

M. Michalowski et al. (Eds.): AIME 2022, LNAI 13263, pp. 431–435, 2022.
https://doi.org/10.1007/978-3-031-09342-5_45

mobile apps. The Punya platform is currently used by 400 active users per year and is built on the more widely known MIT App Inventor, which is used by roughly 1 million users per year and offers a rich community[2].

2   App Description

We will demonstrate the usage of the Punya platform in developing an AI-enabled health app for the self-management of diabetes. This demo paper, together with our online video, will illustrate that Punya allows non-technical stakeholders, such as patients and clinical experts, to be actively involved in the app's development. The app includes multiple AI features, such as KG and ML models and rule-based reasoning, as well as integration with IoT devices.

Part 1. Building the User Interface. Figure 1 shows a low-fidelity prototype UI to report food intake, developed using an intuitive drag-and-drop environment within Punya. By associating the UI elements with ontology terms (e.g., Food Ontology [5]), the form can generate a KG that semantically annotates the user's food intake data, as shown in Fig. 1. Moreover, by integrating with online KG, such as the FoodKG [6], the user-produced personal KG can be enriched with additional knowledge (e.g., food type). Aside from manual entry, form data can come from a variety of sources, such as images processed from the phone's camera, or from sensors such as Bluetooth-enabled food scales.

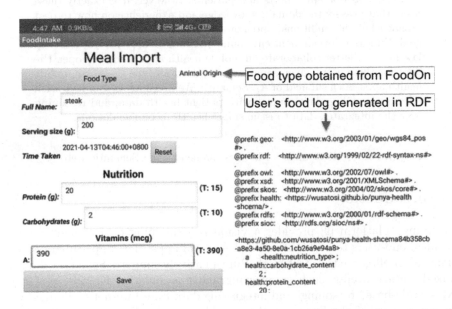

Fig. 1. Overview of the meal import screen and the corresponding KG in RDF.

---

[2] https://community.appinventor.mit.edu/.

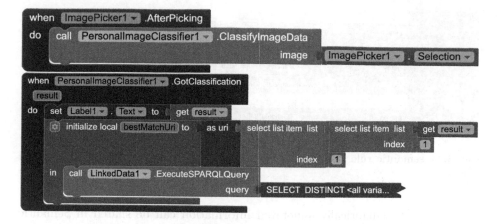

Fig. 2. Blocks used to classify and respond to the neural network.

By producing a KG that is structured using domain ontologies (Food Ontology) and integrated with the FoodKG, other applications familiar with these concepts may consume the KG produced by this app. Likewise, this app can consume data from others apps using the same terminologies.

Part 2. Machine Recognition of Foods. The Punya platform includes the *PersonalImageClassifier* [14] component, which enables one to easily deploy domain-specific computer vision models on the device, which were pre-trained on MobileNet [10]. For this demonstration app, we manually trained a neural network on a handful of different foods. The application "code" needed to implement computer vision is shown in Fig. 2. As seen in the figure, Punya uses a "puzzle-piece" paradigm to program application logic. After the user picked an image, the *PersonalImageClassifier1* component is called to classify the selection. After classification (*GotClassification*), the *result* is a list of tuples constituting classification results, sorted by confidence. Then, the UI (*Label1*) is updated with the label of the first result (first element of the nested list). Moreover, the unique ID of the result is utilized to issue a query (not shown) to an online KG to retrieve additional data, which allows auto-populating parts of the form in Fig. 1.

Part 3. Retrieving Physical Measurements and Reporting to the Diabetologist. Punya supports Bluetooth Low Energy (BLE) for retrieving physical measurements related to health by means of the MIT App Inventor *BluetoothLE* extension [8]. For many popular device categories, specific *application profiles* have been standardized by the Bluetooth Special Interest Group (SIG) [4]. The diabetes management demo app can communicate with glucometers and with glucose monitors via the *Glucose Profile* [2] and *Continuous Glucose Monitoring Profile* [1], respectively. Similarly, data from scales for measuring food or body weight can be retrieved via the *Weight Scale Profile* [3].

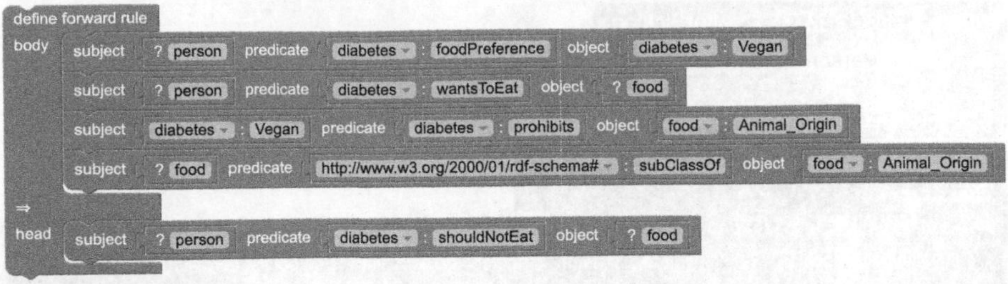

Fig. 3. A semantic rule that determines if a given food item is suitable for a vegan individual

In general, semantically annotated information can be shared in Semantic Web of Things scenarios, using Punya's client and server components for the Linked Data Platform over Constrained Application Protocol (LDP-CoAP) [7]. The LDP World Wide Web Consortium (W3C) standard [13] allows organizing collections of RDF and non-RDF resources hierarchically and expose them to clients through a RESTful HTTP-based interface. LDP-CoAP adapts the LDP to CoAP protocol, an HTTP-like protocol for machine-to-machine (M2M) communications in resource-constrained environments [12]. Using all the aforementioned features, the diabetes patient's app can construct a personal health KG [11] to be shared using the *LdpCoapServer* component as a report for the physician; who may access it through a counterpart application exploiting the *LdpCoapClient* Punya component or another compatible implementation.

Part 4: Applying Rules & Knowledge Graphs. The built-in rules engine in Punya allows developers to author expert medical knowledge in terms of intuitive *if-then* rules, which can issue health-related recommendations by referring to the patient's Personal Health KG as well as other online KG. For example, Fig. 3 shows a rule that checks whether the patient's food preference is vegan; if so, and in case the patient's food, as recognized by the image classifier, includes any ingredients of animal origin, the rule will issue a warning.

3   Summary

Addressing disparities in healthcare access will require reaching more people using the technology they are most accustomed to—mobile apps and smartphones. The MIT Punya platform works to address this by making AI-enabled health apps, tailored to particular chronic illnesses, cognitive abilities, and personal needs, easier to develop and/or customize by non-technical stakeholders including patients and health experts. To support this claim, we aim to perform user evaluations with these stakeholders to gauge their ability and comfort in utilizing the Punya platform; with tasks ranging from customizing existing AI-enabled health apps, to prototyping simple apps from scratch, given some initial training. The diabetes app illustrated in this demo is available online https://punya.mit.edu/#diabetes-usecase along with a video demonstration; it will also be available for AIME attendees to try out and customize in real-time during the demo session[3].

References

1. Bluetooth SIG: glucose profile 1.0 specification. https://www.bluetooth.com/specifications/specs/glucose-profile-1-0/ (2012). Accessed 28 Mar 2022
2. Bluetooth SIG: continuous glucose monitoring profile 1.0.1 specification (2015). https://www.bluetooth.com/specifications/specs/continuous-glucose-monitoring-profile-1-0-1/. Accessed 28 Mar 2022
3. Bluetooth SIG: weight scale profile 1.0 specification. https://www.bluetooth.com/specifications/specs/weight-scale-profile/. Accessed 28 Mar 2022
4. Bluetooth SIG: Bluetooth core specification 5.3 (2021). https://www.bluetooth.com/specifications/specs/core-specification-5-3/. Accessed 28 Mar 2022
5. Dooley, D.M., et al.: Foodon: a harmonized food ontology to increase global food traceability, quality control and data integration. NPJ Sci. Food **2**(1), 1–10 (2018)
6. Haussmann, S., et al.: FoodKG: a semantics-driven knowledge graph for food recommendation. In: Ghidini, C. (ed.) ISWC 2019. LNCS, vol. 11779, pp. 146–162. Springer, Cham (2019). https://doi.org/10.1007/978-3-030-30796-7_10
7. Loseto, G., et al.: Linked data (in low-resource) platforms: a mapping for constrained application protocol. In: Groth, P. (ed.) ISWC 2016. LNCS, vol. 9982, pp. 131–139. Springer, Cham (2016). https://doi.org/10.1007/978-3-319-46547-0_14
8. Patton, E.W.: MIT app inventor BluetoothLE extension (2020). https://iot.appinventor.mit.edu/#/bluetoothle/bluetoothleintro. Accessed 29 Mar 2022
9. Patton, E.W., Van Woensel, W., Seneviratne, O., Loseto, G., Scioscia, F., Kagal, L.: The punya platform: building mobile research apps with linked data and semantic features. In: Hotho, A. (ed.) ISWC 2021. LNCS, vol. 12922, pp. 563–579. Springer, Cham (2021). https://doi.org/10.1007/978-3-030-88361-4_33
10. Sandler, M., Howard, A., Zhu, M., Zhmoginov, A., Chen, L.C.: Mobilenetv 2: inverted residuals and linear bottlenecks. In: Proceedings of the 2018 IEEE/CVF Conference on Computer Vision and Pattern Recognition (2018)
11. Seneviratne, O., Harris, J., Chen, C.H., McGuinness, D.L.: Personal health knowledge graph for clinically relevant diet recommendations. arXiv preprint arXiv:2110.10131 (2021)
12. Shelby, Z., Hartke, K., Bormann, C.: The Constrained Application Protocol (CoAP)(2014). http://www.ietf.org/rfc/rfc7252.txt. Accessed 28 Mar 2022
13. Speicher, S., Arwe, J., Malhotra, A.: Linked data platform 1.0 (2015). http://www.w3.org/TR/ldp/. Accessed 28 Mar 2022
14. Tang, D.: Empowering novices to understand and use machine learning with personalized image classification models, intuitive analysis tools, and MIT App Inventor. Master's thesis, Massachusetts Institute of Technology (2019)

---

[3] A video of a portion of the demo is available at https://www.youtube.com/watch?v=fFv-sPmd_G4.

Using Visual Analytics to Optimize Blood Product Inventory at a Hospital's Blood Transfusion Service

Jaber Rad[1]($\boxtimes$), Jason Quinn[2], Calvino Cheng[2], Samina Raza Abidi[3], Robert Liwski[2], and Syed Sibte Raza Abidi[1]

[1] NICHE Research Group, Faculty of Computer Science, Dalhousie University, Halifax, Canada
jaber.rad@dal.ca
[2] Department of Pathology and Laboratory Medicine, Dalhousie University, Halifax, Canada
[3] Department of Community Health and Epidemiology, Dalhousie University, Halifax, Canada

Abstract. A Blood Transfusion Service (BTS) must manage its inventory to meet clinical demand for blood products, whilst ensuring that there is minimal wastage. Reducing wastage due to discards is challenging as a discard is due to the stochastic lifecycle of the blood unit, as opposed to outdates which are related to the expiry date. In this paper, we present an interactive Blood Inventory Management Dashboard (BIMD) using advanced visual analytics methods to monitor three blood products—i.e., red blood cells, platelets, and plasma—and provide BTS staff information about (a) current inventory with alerts for blood units that are potentially heading for a discard, and (b) retrospective lifecycle patterns of all blood units to probe the underlying causes for discards.

Keywords: Blood inventory management · Visual analytics · Dashboard

1 Introduction

Blood transfusion is a lifesaving treatment that supports many therapeutic interventions, such as surgeries and chemotherapy. Aside from blood donations (supply) and clinical use (demand), a key factor that affects the efficiency of blood inventory management is *wastage* [1]. Notwithstanding the effectiveness of *outdates* reduction strategies (e.g. [2]), reducing blood product wastage due to *discards*—i.e. disposal due to a variety of reasons, including, but not limited to improper storage temperature, handling, or unsafe transportation—is still a challenging problem since a discard is not related to the blood product's shelf life, rather to its *lifecycle* [3]. Given the rapid transactions taking place in a Blood Transfusion Service (BTS), an up-to-date account of blood products within their inventory is needed to (a) ensure there is an adequate supply of different types of blood products to meet demand; (b) minimize blood unit's wastage due to expiry; (c) find matching blood units in response to specialized transfusion criteria as per the demand from medical units; and (d) audit the retrospective blood transaction data to identify the causes leading to discards. The complexity of the BTS data makes it difficult to manage inventory using just analytical methods. On the other hand, examination of the current dashboard solutions for blood inventory management (e.g. [4]) shows that the existing dashboards are cumbersome with limited interactivity and filtering criteria, whilst lacking the ability to audit retrospective transfusion logs to identify operational inefficiencies that lead to discards. We argue that Visual Analytics (VA) methods can be employed to visualize, monitor, select, and audit blood products across the hospital network in real-time to improve BTS inventory management.

This demo paper presents an interactive *Blood Inventory Management Dashboard (BIMD)* using advanced VA methods. BIMD consists of two interfaces; *BIMD-Live* and *BIMD-Audit*. Explanations of the interfaces are provided in Sect. 3 with full demos accessible from [5] for BIMD-Live and [6] for BIMD-Audit.

2   BIMD Design and Implementation

BIMD consists of two data visualization interfaces: (a) BIMD-Live for real-time inventory visualization for three blood products—i.e., Red Blood Cell (RBC), Platelets and Plasma—to both inform inventory levels and select blood units as per the transfusion request; (b) BIMD-Audit to visualize historical blood unit transitions to help visualize underlying transaction patterns to audit BTS efficiency and to identify the patterns that lead to wastage. BIMD-Live also incorporates a machine learning-based discard prediction model based on Markovian sequence prediction methods [7] that flags in real-time blood units that are heading for a potential discard after n transition steps. The blood product inventory is refreshed every 30 min (the update rate can be adjusted based on the transaction frequency in the blood product supply chain) by collecting data from the laboratory information system. Figure 1 shows the overall architecture of BIMD.

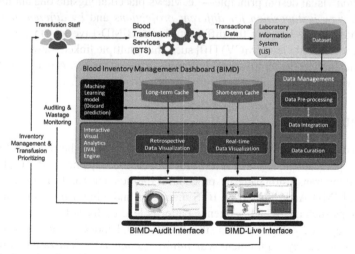

Fig. 1. The functional architecture of the Blood Inventory Management Dashboard (BIMD)

The BIMD's backend is developed incorporating Java Spring framework to have a RESTful web service. The frontend is a combination of React and D3.js, JavaScript-based libraries optimized for fast interactive multidimensional visualizations. BIMD is designed as a VA system [8] using a range of VA methods [9] specific to the functionalities needed by the BTS staff. We employed an agile and extreme programming methodology to develop BIMD, where the end-users—i.e., blood transfusion experts and BTS staff—provided us the BTS inventory management workflow, blood unit selection criterion, dashboard functionality specification and its usage scenarios and at each design iteration, tested and approved the interface design and functionality; Adobe XD was used to capture the users' feedback. BIMD is specially designed and implemented for the Central Zone-BTS (CZ-BTS) servicing Halifax (Canada) hospitals.

3   BIMD Interface Design and Functionality

3.1   BIMD-Live

BIMD-Live interface (Fig. 2) visualizes the current blood product inventory at BTS, with the added functionality where BTS staff can pose specialized queries to find units matching specific characteristics—i.e., time to expiry, blood type, product attributes, inventory location. As pointed out by BTS staff, for swift and convenient exploration of the inventory, the two key requirements are (i) *projection* of the units' attributes to multiple views so that the inventory can be explored from different *angles* and (ii) allowing data *filtering* based on a combination of attributes whilst getting an instant inventory response with each selected criterion. These requirements of BTS staff were formulated into two visualization strategies: (i) 'Scan Sequentially': the staff examine characteristics of blood units serially, and (ii) 'Select Subset': The staff examine a subset that is created by selection and filtering. To meet these requirements, we adopted the *juxtaposition* visual design principle—i.e. views placed alongside one another—and in particular, *view juxtaposition for different projections* and *by different data* [10]. To achieve interactivity between the different views, BIMD-Live interface is inspired by multiple coordinated views (MCV) [10] such that multiple linked views are provided to explore and analyze the multivariate data from different angles. A demo of BIMD-Live interface with multiple application scenarios is provided in [5].

3.2   BIMD-Audit

BIMD-Audit interface (Fig. 3) allows the BTS staff to audit the retrospective transactional data, presented in terms of blood unit transaction sequence patterns [11], to identify underlying transfusion patterns, procedural inefficiencies and causes for discards. In operation, BIMD-Audit is used by BTS managers and administrators to answer auditing questions such as "Which sequence patterns lead to discard more frequently?". As pointed out by BTS staff, for auditing the inventory and understanding underlying operational processes, a key requirement is an intuitive *summary* visualization of blood units' lifecycle. For BIMD-Audit, we decided to use space-filling visualization techniques [12] that use adjacency diagrams, particularly a *Lifecycle Pattern Sunburst (LPS)* diagram to visualize the progressive sequence of a blood unit's transaction states whilst highlighting the frequency of different transition patterns; the rings starting from the centre represent the progression of the transition steps, and the sweep angle of each segment

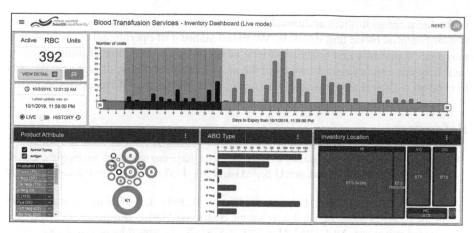

Fig. 2. A screenshot of the BIMD-Live interface (demo in [5] for more details)

shows the frequency of occurrence of the corresponding state, whereby in each level of the hierarchy the states are sorted in descending order clockwise based on the transaction state's frequency. A demo of BIMD-Audit interface with multiple application scenarios is provided in [6].

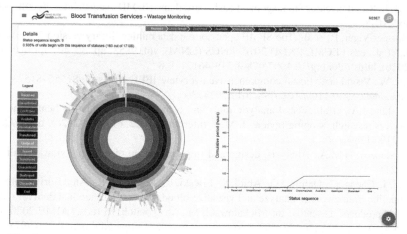

Fig. 3. A screenshot of the BIMD-Audit interface (demo in [6] for more details)

4   Conclusions and Future Work

We demonstrated BIMD to support BTS staff visualize the current inventory of all fresh blood products and select blood units in response to transfusion requests. BIMD represents considerable progress over existing inventory management dashboards described in the literature as it offers additional features such as machine learning-driven prediction of potential blood unit discards, VA-based auditing of operational procedures that may lead to discards and analytics-driven suggestions for selection of units based on their lifecycle characteristics instead of the more traditional metric of unit age. We plan to conduct a clinical assessment of the impact of BIMD on the efficiency of CZ-BTS.

References

1. Guan, L., et al.: Big data modeling to predict platelet usage and minimize wastage in a tertiary care system. Proc. Natl. Acad. Sci. U. S. A. **114**, 11368–11373 (2017). https://doi.org/10.1073/pnas.1714097114
2. Soares, H.L.F., Arruda, E.F., Bahiense, L., Gartner, D., Filho, L.A.: Optimisation and control of the supply of blood bags in hemotherapic centres via Markov decision process with discounted arrival rate. Artif. Intell. Med. **104**, 101791 (2020). https://doi.org/10.1016/j.artmed.2020.101791
3. Cheng, C.K., Trethewey, D., Sadek, I.: Comprehensive survey of red blood cell unit life cycle at a large teaching institution in eastern Canada. Transf. (Paris) **50**, 160–165 (2010)
4. Woo, J.S., et al.: Development and implementation of real-time web-based dashboards in a multisite transfusion service. J. Pathol. Inform. **10**, 3 (2019). https://doi.org/10.4103/jpi.jpi_36_18
5. Rad, J.: Blood inventory management dashboard demo (BIMD-Live). https://youtu.be/1iAy6H2KPjA
6. Rad, J.: Blood inventory management dashboard demo (BIMD-Audit). https://youtu.be/G1A5exRMJP0
7. Fournier-Viger, P., et al.: The SPMF open-source data mining library version 2. In: Berendt, B., et al. (eds.) ECML PKDD 2016. LNCS (LNAI), vol. 9853, pp. 36–40. Springer, Cham (2016). https://doi.org/10.1007/978-3-319-46131-1_8
8. Cui, W.: Visual analytics: a comprehensive overview. IEEE Access **7**, 81555–81573 (2019). https://doi.org/10.1109/ACCESS.2019.2923736
9. Chishtie, J.A., et al.: Visual analytic tools and techniques in population health and health services research: scoping review. J. Med. Internet Res. **22**, e17892 (2020). https://doi.org/10.2196/17892
10. Al-Maneea, H.M.A.: Analysis, design and implementation of multiple view visualisations (2021)
11. Rad, J., Cheng, C., Quinn, J.G., Abidi, S., Liwski, R., Abidi, S.S.R.: An AI-driven predictive modelling framework to analyze and visualize blood product transactional data for reducing blood products' Discards. In: Michalowski, M., Moskovitch, R. (eds.) AIME 2020. LNCS (LNAI), vol. 12299, pp. 192–202. Springer, Cham (2020). https://doi.org/10.1007/978-3-030-59137-3_18
12. Guo, Y., Guo, S., Jin, Z., Kaul, S., Gotz, D., Cao, N.: A survey on visual analysis of event sequence data. IEEE Trans. Vis.Comput. Graph. 1 (2021). https://doi.org/10.1109/TVCG.2021.3100413

Tutorials

Using Machine Learning on mHealth-based Data Sources

Rüdiger Pryss[1]([✉]), Marc Schickler[2], Johannes Schobel[3], Winfried Schlee[4], Myra Spiliopoulou[5], Thomas Probst[6], and Felix Beierle[1]

[1] Institute of Clinical Epidemiology and Biometry, University of Würzburg, 97080 Würzburg, Germany
{ruediger.pryss,felix.beierle}@uni-wuerzburg.de

[2] Institute of Databases and Information Systems, Ulm University, 89081 Ulm, Germany
marc.schickler@uni-ulm.de

[3] Institute DigiHealth, Neu-Ulm University of Applied Sciences, 89231 Neu-Ulm, Germany
johannes.schobel@hnu.de

[4] Department of Psychiatry and Psychotherapy, University of Regensburg, 93053 Regensburg, Germany
winfried.schlee@gmail.com

[5] Knowledge Management and Discovery Lab, Otto-von-Guericke University, 39106 Magdeburg, Germany
myra@ovgu.de

[6] Department for Psychotherapy and Biopsychosocial Health, Danube University Krems, Krems an der Donau, Austria
thomas.probst@donau-uni.ac.at

Abstract. The application of machine learning algorithms has become important for the medical domain. However, the concrete application of these type of algorithms strongly depends on how a corresponding data source was created. Most importantly, domain knowledge must be linked with data science knowledge. Data collected using smartphones or smart mobile devices (e.g., smart watches) is commonly referred to as mHealth data. The possibilities and strategies for collecting data in this area now appear to be as diverse as the machine learning algorithms that have emerged. This tutorial will therefore discuss how mHealth data is structured and which aspects need to be taken into account when evaluating it with machine learning algorithms, using concrete examples.

Keywords: mHealth · Machine learning · Data collection strategies

1 Background Information and Tutorial Content

The use of smartphones - and, by extension, smart mobile devices - for clinical trials is no longer a niche phenomenon. Above all, it has been recognized that smartphones can measure data in-situ in order to achieve a high transferability of

© The Author(s), under exclusive license to Springer Nature Switzerland AG 2022
M. Michalowski et al. (Eds.): AIME 2022, LNAI 13263, pp. 443–445, 2022.
https://doi.org/10.1007/978-3-031-09342-5

the results to reality; also known as high ecological validity of the data. Of note, only a few standards have been established in this area so far, so that this domain is still characterized by many utilized data collection strategies and also new developments [1]. Another circumstance complicates the situation, the utilized or developed concepts that are currently used come from different scientific domains and therefore often make little use of each other's achievements. To get a better impression, Fig. 1 shows the predominant concepts and which scientific domain they originate from.

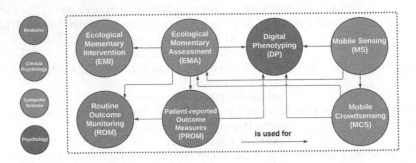

Fig. 1. mHealth Research and Data Collection Concepts

As can be seen in Fig. 1, currently seven major flavors can be distinguished to collect mHealth data. Some of these are combined, and some have additional sub-flavors. The implementation of these strategies for clinical studies mainly leads to two consequences. First, comparing study data is often very difficult, as it is rarely specified exactly which paradigm was used. Second, the strategies lead to the fact that if a study design is not strictly clinically supervised, which is not wanted in the mHealth context most of the time (i.e., ecological validity can only be achieved when data is gathered in the wild), then participants fill in data in very different frequencies, intervals and quantities [2]. These different distributions ultimately lead to the fact that evaluations by means of machine learning should take very many bias types into account in order to achieve meaningful results. For the reasons mentioned above, it is then very often argued that there is simply too little data available to be able to make meaningful statements. From our project experience, this view is not proper in many respects.

To summarize, many aspects play a role that currently need to be considered when machine learning is applied to mHealth data. Moreover, there are many types of software development flavors (e.g., native vs. cross-development) that also play a role in the sketched data collection settings. Considering all of the mentioned aspects, we want to discuss in this tutorial along existing evaluations on mHealth data, which possibilities of addressing them exist and how a suitable interpretation of the data using machine learning can look like.

References

1. Kraft, R., et al.: Combining mobile crowdsensing and ecological momentary assessments in the healthcare domain. Front. Neurosci. **14**, 164 (2020). https://doi.org/10.3389/fnins.2020.00164
2. Schleicher, M., et al.: Understanding adherence to the recording of ecological momentary assessments in the example of tinnitus monitoring. Sci. Rep. **10**, 22459 (2020). https://doi.org/10.1038/s41598-020-79527-0

Mobile, AI-based and IoT-enabled Clinical Apps by End-Users Using Punya

Evan W. Patton[1(✉)], Floriano Scioscia[2], William Van Woensel[3],
Giuseppe Loseto[4], and Oshani Seneviratne[5]

[1] Massachusetts Institute of Technology, Cambridge, MA 02139, USA
ewpatton@mit.edu
[2] Polytechnic University of Bari, Bari BA I-70125, Italy
floriano.scioscia@poliba.it
[3] Dalhousie University, Halifax, NS B3H 4R2, Canada
william.van.woensel@dal.ca
[4] LUM University "Giuseppe Degennaro", Casamassima BA I-70010, Italy
loseto@lum.it
[5] Rensselaer Polytechnic Institute, Troy, NY 12180, USA
senevo@rpi.edu

Long-term chronic patients are increasingly being encouraged to self-manage their illness in a home setting, to improve their quality of life and reduce avoidable healthcare costs. To that end, personal patient diaries on mobile devices can help with daily vital and symptom recording, medication adherence, and positive health behavior change. This paints a picture of *exploratory app development*, where evolving and new insights will require the prototyping and evaluation of new or updated apps. Unfortunately, this can be problematic in research-oriented settings: mobile app development requires specialized skills and thus tends to incur high development costs, whereas researchers often rely on one-shot grant funding. We aim to demonstrate how healthcare and medical informatics researchers can benefit from using the Punya platform [1], a fork of MIT App Inventor, to overcome these issues. Punya aims to empower people with a non-technical background to develop their own mobile apps. The platform provides an intuitive, visual environment with drag-and-drop features and a puzzle-piece metaphor, all within a user-friendly Web tool. This tutorial focuses on using Punya for prototyping mobile health apps, such as patient diaries for chronic illness self-management, exploiting advanced features including: (1) Semantic Web technologies to query online data sources and reason over health data to provide smart health recommendations, (2) lightweight machine learning techniques to support image classification and train patient-specific models, and (3) integration of health peripheral devices using IoT technologies. Punya enables participatory design and prototyping workflows, where clinicians, patients, and developers work together to create mobile health apps with direct input from all stakeholders.

Reference

1. Patton, E.W., Van Woensel, W., Seneviratne, O., Loseto, G., Scioscia, F., Kagal, L.: The Punya platform: building mobile research apps with linked data and semantic features. In: Proceedings of the 20th International Semantic Web Conference (2021)

© The Author(s), under exclusive license to Springer Nature Switzerland AG 2022
M. Michalowski et al. (Eds.): AIME 2022, LNAI 13263, p. 446, 2022.
https://doi.org/10.1007/978-3-031-09342-5

Machine Learning for Complex Medical Temporal Sequences – Tutorial

Panagiotis Papapetrou[1]([⊠])[iD] and Myra Spiliopoulou[2][iD]

[1] Data Science Group, Stockholm University, Stockholm, Sweden
`panagiotis@dsv.su.se`
[2] Knowledge Management & Discovery Lab, Otto-von-Guericke-Univ Magdeburg,
Magdeburg, Germany

Abstract. Advances in machine learning and their application to medical data receive increasing attention and demonstrate immense benefits for patients and practitioners. The adoption of Electronic Health Records (EHRs) in combination with the penetration of smart technologies and the Internet of Things give a further boost to initiatives for patient self-management and empowerment, with new forms of health-relevant data becoming available and requiring new data acquisition and analytics' workflows. In this tutorial, we elaborate on what temporal sequences of healthcare-related data look like, and we focus on two particular challenges: how to learn on medical sequences with gaps and how to deliver reasoning about what the model has learned.

Keywords: Time series · Counterfactuals · Missingness · Medical data

1 Introduction

The proliferation of applications for medical data has increased the need for extracting useful knowledge that can be effectively used by healthcare experts. This tutorial elaborates on the complexity of temporal medical data. We focus on sequential forms of health-related data, including ,event sequences such as sequences of EHR events, and mHealth data. We elaborate on why such sequences are short and contain gaps, and we discuss methods for filling the gaps, learning despite the gaps and learning from the gaps. Then, we turn to the demand for interpretable and explainable models that can inspire trust and facilitate informed decision making. Towards this goal we elaborate on actionable models and counterfactual explanations for sequential medical data.

2 Dealing with Gaps in Medical Sequences

A medical temporal sequence for a patient x has the form $v_{x,t_1}, \ldots, v_{x,t_{n_x}}$, where $t_i, i = 1, \ldots, n$ are time points, and each v_{x,t_i} is a vector over a feature space F

M. Michalowski et al. (Eds.): AIME 2022, LNAI 13263, pp. 447–449, 2022.
https://doi.org/10.1007/978-3-031-09342-5

that may contain both categorical and numerical features. The number and locations of the time points in the horizon of observation are also patient-dependent.

In the realm of randomized clinical trials (RCT), missing data would translate into gaps or into sequences that end before the RCT is over. Jakobsen et al. provide guidelines on how to interpret the absence of data and to deal with missingness in an RCT [2]. In an RCT and in many clinical studies, the time horizon is predefined, so it is possible to span a grid of time points and align the individual sequences to it [1]. Missingness can be 'informative' though [4], so it is essential to recognize when it is permissible to align/impute and when not [1].

When analysing mHealth data to predict and/or interpret the mHealth users' behaviour, the time horizon is not fixed and alignment is impractical: one sequence may contain 10 observations and another may contain 1000. However, neighbourhood-based solutions can be exploited [8] and may even lead to better predictions than methods that ignore the observation-patient link [7].

3   Counterfactuals in Medical Sequences

While there exist inherently explainable models allowing practitioners to directly interpret their results 'black-box' models focus primarily on predictive performance and are hence characterized by high-opacity [10]. In practical high-stake scenarios such as diagnoses, optimizing model explainability is highest priority. One way to convey such knowledge to medical practitioners is to define a counterfactual explanation for a given test instance. In short, a counterfactual is a new variable configuration of a given instance so that an underlying opaque classifier changes its prediction for that instance. In a medical scenario, a counterfactual will suggest transforming patient features by, e.g., prescribing drugs, or performing a treatment procedure. Counterfactuals may be obtained through different algorithms which optimize diverse metrics, such as proximity, sparsity, feasibility, and faithfulness [5, 6]. Nonetheless, there is currently no clear consensus on the best metric to be optimized for improving the quality of explanations.

In this tutorial we focus on counterfactuals for medical data, due to their sequential nature the main emphasis has been given to sequence-based counterfactuals, such as shapelet-based classifiers for time series data [3]. A 1-Nearest Neighbor approach was recently introduced as a baseline solution for medical time series couterfactuals alongside a text style-transfer solution, adapted for dealing with medical event sequences as input and complying with the objectives of the problem of generating medical counterfactual explanations [9].

4   Outlook

This tutorial addresses two challenges in learning from medical sequences. Further challenges include drift and the interplay between data sparsity and model reliability. We envisage the establishment of an agenda with open issues and first solutions for the whole broad domain of learning on medical temporal data.

References

1. Cismondi, F.C., Fialho, A., Vieira, S., Reti, S., Sousa, J., Finkelstein, S.: Missing data in medical databases: impute, delete or classify? Artif. Intell. Med. **58**(1), 63–72 (2013)
2. Jakobsen, J.C., Gluud, C., Wetterslev, J., Winkel, P.: When and how should multiple imputation be used for handling missing data in randomised clinical trials - a practical guide with flowcharts. BMC Medical Research Methodology (2017)
3. Karlsson, I., Rebane, J., Papapetrou, P., Gionis, A.: Explainable time series tweaking via irreversible and reversible temporal transformations. In: 2018 IEEE International Conference on Data Mining (ICDM) (2018)
4. Mikalsen, K.Ø., Soguero-Ruiz, C., Jenssen, R.: A kernel to exploit informative missingness in multivariate time series from EHRs. In: Shaban-Nejad, A., Michalowski, M., Buckeridge, D.L. (eds.) Explainable AI in Healthcare and Medicine. SCI, vol. 914, pp. 23–36. Springer, Cham (2021). https://doi.org/10.1007/978-3-030-53352-6_3
5. Molnar, C.: Interpretable machine learning: a guide for making black-box model explainable (2021). https://christophm.github.io/interpretable-ml-book/limo.html
6. Rudin, C.: Stop explaining black box machine learning models for high stakes decisions and use interpretable models instead. Nat. Mach. Intell. **1**(5), 206–215 (2019)
7. Shahania, S., et al.: Predicting ecological momentary assessments in an app for tinnitus by learning from each user's stream with a contextual multi-armed bandit. Front. Neurosci. 16 (2022)
8. Unnikrishnan, V., et al.: Love thy neighbours: a framework for error-driven discovery of useful neighbourhoods for one-step forecasts on ema data. In: 2021 IEEE 34th International Symposium on Computer-Based Medical Systems (CBMS), pp. 295–300. IEEE (2021)
9. Wang, Z., Samsten, I., Papapetrou, P.: Counterfactual explanations for survival prediction of cardiovascular ICU patients. In: Tucker, A., Henriques Abreu, P., Cardoso, J., Pereira Rodrigues, P., Riaño, D. (eds.) AIME 2021. LNCS (LNAI), vol. 12721, pp. 338–348. Springer, Cham (2021). https://doi.org/10.1007/978-3-030-77211-6_38
10. Zhou, B., Bau, D., Oliva, A., Torralba, A.: Interpreting deep visual representations via network dissection. IEEE Trans. Pattern Anal. Mach. Intell. **41**(9), 2131–2145 (2019)

Data Science for Starters: How to Train and Be Trained

Blaž Zupan[✉]

Faculty of Computer and Information Science, University of Ljubljana,
Večna pot 113, Ljubljana, Slovenia
blaz.zupan@fri.uni-lj.si

Abstract. Given the right tool, it may take only a few hours to familiarize outsiders with data science. Data science, machine learning, and artificial intelligence are drivers of change in all fields of science, including biomedicine. The computational approaches that can sip through vast collections of data, extract interesting patterns, and devise predictive models are becoming omnipresent. But only a few professionals understand the essential concepts behind data science, and even fewer engage in building models using their data. We here report on the contents of the tutorial at AIME-2022, where we aim to explain how anybody who can spare a few hours can learn the essential mechanics behind data science and machine learning. With the training we have designed, the professionals can gain enough intuition about data science to recognize opportunities that this field can offer and actively engage in data science projects. Besides good mentors and an encouraging working environment, the right tool is critical for such training. We advocate the workflow-based construction of analytical pipelines with interactive visualizations and show that they can be the key to the simplicity of the interface and flexibility to adopt analytics to any data type and problem domain.

Keywords: Data science · Machine learning · Hands-on training

1 Introduction

Machine learning and data science are vital tools in the biomedical sciences, and there is a high demand for these skills. Despite a widely acknowledged need for data science literacy in the biomedical sciences, there is a gap between researchers' skills and current level of expertise [5]. Thus, there is a great demand for opportunities to develop data science skills within graduate coursework and continued training for those already in the field [4].

Data science courses and courses that introduce machine learning abound. For instance, on popular MOOCs, like edX or Coursera, about 20% of all the courses target these topics. Yet, they mainly involve learning data science by scripting in R or Python. Classes requiring programming knowledge impose constraints on trainees who are either not skilled in computer science or trainees who would instead focus on concepts rather than implementations.

© The Author(s), under exclusive license to Springer Nature Switzerland AG 2022
M. Michalowski et al. (Eds.): AIME 2022, LNAI 13263, pp. 450–454, 2022.
https://doi.org/10.1007/978-3-031-09342-5

Scripting in R or Python for machine learning and data science is excellent due to the availability of many libraries for data visualization, statistics, and machine learning. Programming in these languages offers flexibility in data management, modeling, and development of any solution the data owners require. However, reliance on a scripting environment may burden data science training. This is especially true if we would like to focus on data science concepts. In classes where programming skills do not abound, explaining data science through scripting often evolves into copying scripting lines from the instructor or refocusing the lecture to cover the topics from computer programming.

2   Methods and Approach

Since the early 2000 s, our group at the University of Ljubljana has developed an innovative data mining software called Orange Data Mining[1] [1, 2]. Orange uniquely implements visual analytics by combining visual programming for workflow design and interactive visualizations for exploratory data analysis. Since its beginnings, its focus has been on explanation and storytelling. Its target audience was both novice users that would benefit from Orange's gentle learning curve and data science experts that would enjoy its support for the fast construction of potentially complex workflows and interactivity in data exploration. In terms of data analysis pipelines, Orange resembles other workflow-based systems like KNIME and RapidMiner. Its essential difference is in workflow components, which - by design - tend to be few and rather in hundreds than thousands and, wherever possible, implement interactive visualizations. Orange features on-the-fly computation, where any change in the settings or in the selection of the visualization elements instantaneously propagates through the network, in this way supporting essential features of visual analytics.

We designed Orange in the academic environment. When crafting its user interface, it was always on our mind that we should be able to use Orange to explain the workings of every component we include in the software. Intended explanations were conceptual, where we would present the utility of the component, its effect on exemplary data, and even some of its inner workings, though not necessary at the level of the algorithms. Later, in about 2015, it only occurred to us that these features are helpful, if not essential, for any training. We started with experiments to use Orange in short, few-hours long hands-on workshops at about that time. We aimed to provide hands-on tutoring in data science. The audience would not necessarily have any prior training in the field and would have expertise in biomedicine, molecular genetics, economics, spectroscopy, anthropology, engineering, and alike. The workshops would start with the data, and we would Orange to explain distance estimation, clustering, data projection and embedding, classification, regression, and other elements of machine learning. To our surprise, we covered a wide range of techniques in a short time. Since 2015, we have carried out over a hundred workshops around the globe and, recently, online. They were mainly carried out within a day or two, but we have also

---

[1] http://orangedatamining.com.

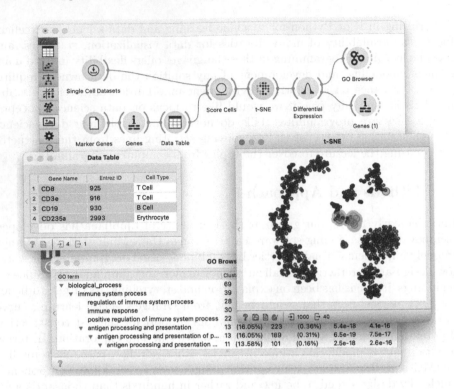

Fig. 1. Orange features workflows and blends interactive visualizations and machine learning. The figure shows the workflow to analyze the landscape of single cells using their expression data and supports the highlighting of selected gene markers and gene marker discovery. The user can select a gene in the Data Table in the presented workflow. The cells are scored according to selected genes' expression and highlighted in the t-SNE visualization. Here, the user chose the marker for the B cells, used t-SNE to select a group of cells that expressed the CD19 marker, and found other actual and potential markers through differential gene expression analysis. Note that any change in the selection, whether in the set of markers or the cells, triggers changes in the workflow's downstream components and updates their visualizations accordingly.

turned Orange into a vehicle for courses that last longer and span several weeks (see Fig. 1).

We usually accompany workshops with written notes, where most of our written material is available freely on the GitHub[2]. Our YouTube videos, which collectively gathered over two million views, also offer a glimpse into our training style. Orange is today used for teaching in over five hundred universities around the globe[3].

---

[2] https://github.com/biolab/orange-lecture-notes.
[3] https://orangedatamining.com/blog/2022/2022-01-14-universities.

3   Tutorial at AIME-2022

For the presentation at AIME-2022, we have designed the tutorial aimed at the prospective or actual teachers and professors of machine learning and data science to show how to: organize a short introductory or advanced course in data science that can take only a few hours but cover a substantial number of topics from machine learning and data visualization,

- train intuitive concepts of data science, rather than dive into details of mathematics and statistics,
- use the workflows-based environment to soften the learning curve and train data science without invoking any computer programming,
- use interactive visualizations and visual analytics to engage in data exploration and additionally motivate the trainees and make training lessons exciting and engaging,
- design a practical training course that immediately dives into the data and helps trainees understand data science on practical use cases,
- design a course that uses case-based studies and avoids using any powerpoints.

Our aim was also to provide a tutorial for anyone interested in learning about data science, or those who would like to enjoy a fast-paced walk through the machine learning landscape can join the tutorial. Our intention was to cover the following topics:

- clustering, including hierarchical clustering, k-means, visualization of clustering results and explanation of clusters,
- dimensionality reduction approaches and design of data maps with methods like MDS and t-SNE,
- predictive modeling using essential supervised machine learning techniques (logistic regression, random forests, neural networks) and several tools that can explain the structure of the models, like nomograms,
- overfitting, how to cheat with it and how to avoid it,
- evaluation of prediction models, including cross-validation and assessment of accuracy.

The listed topics conceptually cover a substantial part of the machine learning landscape. The workshop aimed to demonstrate that using the right tools and pedagogical approaches, these can be covered, in an intuitive way, in only a few hours.

4   Conclusion

The growing need for access to quality data science education, the need for guided, hands-on experiences with data mining, and the absence of approaches that tie training with workflow-based data mining software all encourage the developments in these fields. We wish to fulfill this gap with Orange and methods and material for hands-on training. While we have yet to improve our systematic efforts to support the community of teachers, interested readers are welcome to overview our reported techniques for training in single-cell gene expression analytics [7], training to recognize and avoid overfitting in machine learning [3], and approaches to democratize image analytics [6].

Acknowledgements. Development of Orange and Orange-based educational material has been supported by the Slovenian Research Agency (P2-0209), Google.org and Chan Zuckerberg Initiative.

References

1. Curk, T., et al.: Microarray data mining with visual programming. Bioinformatics **21**(3), 396–398 (2005)
2. Demšar, J., et al.: Orange: data mining toolbox in Python. J. Mach. Learn. Res. **14**, 2349–2353 (2013)
3. Demšar, J., Zupan, B.: Hands-on training about overfitting. PLOS Comput. Biol. **17**(3), e1008671 (2021)
4. Dunn, M.C., Bourne, P.E.: Building the biomedical data science workforce. PLOS Biol. **15**(7), e2003082 (2017)
5. Federer, L.M., Lu, Y.L., Joubert, D.J.: Data literacy training needs of biomedical researchers. J. Med. Library Assoc. **104**(1), 52 (2016)
6. Godec, P., et al.: Democratized image analytics by visual programming through integration of deep models and small-scale machine learning. Nat. Commun. **10**(1), 4551 (2019)
7. Stražar, M., et al.: scOrange—a tool for hands-on training of concepts from single-cell data analytics. Bioinformatics **35**(14), i4–i12 (2019)

Author Index

Printed in the United States
by Baker & Taylor Publisher Services